19th International Conference on Cognition and Exploratory Learning in Digital Age (CELDA 2022)

Lisbon, Portugal
8-10 November 2022

Editors:

Demetrios G. Sampson
Dirk Ifenthaler
Pedro Isaías
Luís Rodrigues

ISBN: 978-1-7138-6378-6

Printed from e-media with permission by:

Curran Associates, Inc.
57 Morehouse Lane
Red Hook, NY 12571

Some format issues inherent in the e-media version may also appear in this print version.

Printed with permission by Curran Associates, Inc. (2023)

For permission requests, please contact International Association for Development of the Information Society (IADIS) at the address below.

International Association for Development of the Information Society (IADIS)
Rua Sao Sebastiao Da Pedreira
No. 100, 30, 1050-209
Lisbon, Portugal

Phone: 351 21 3151373
Fax: 351 21 3151244

secretariat@iadis.org

Additional copies of this publication are available from:

Curran Associates, Inc.
57 Morehouse Lane
Red Hook, NY 12571 USA
Phone: 845-758-0400
Fax: 845-758-2633
Email: curran@proceedings.com
Web: www.proceedings.com

19th INTERNATIONAL CONFERENCE
on

COGNITION
AND EXPLORATORY
LEARNING IN THE DIGITAL
AGE
(CELDA 2022)

19th International Conference on
Cognition and Exploratory Learning in Digital Age

CELDA 2022

8 - 10 November
Lisbon, Portugal

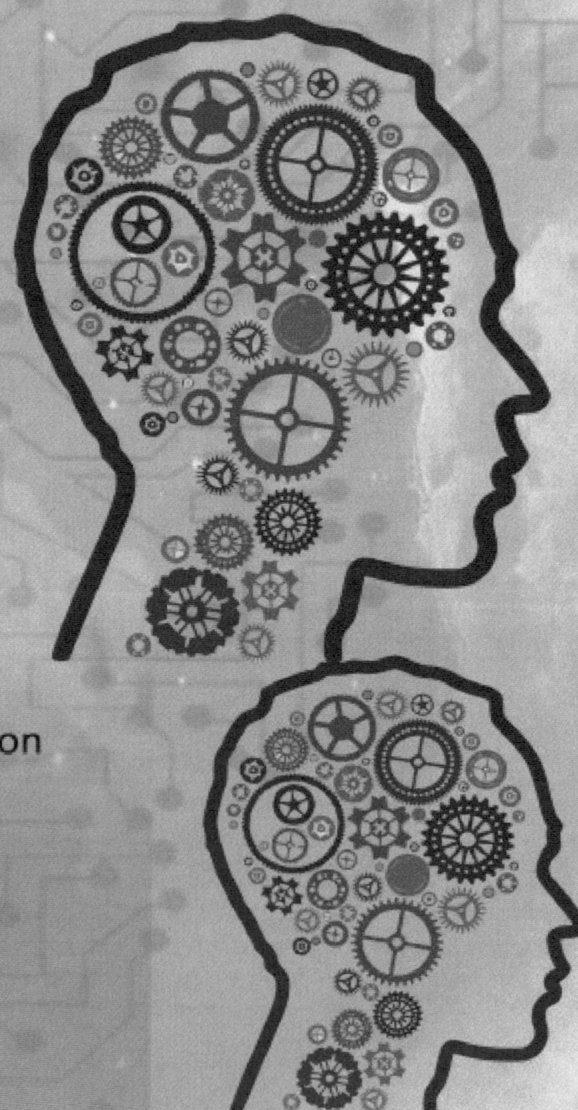

PROCEEDINGS

Edited by
Demetrios G. Sampson
Dirk Ifenthaler
Pedro Isaías

iadis
international association for development of the information society

PROCEEDINGS OF THE
19th INTERNATIONAL CONFERENCE
on

COGNITION AND EXPLORATORY LEARNING IN THE DIGITAL AGE (CELDA 2022)

NOVEMBER 8 - 10, 2022

Organised by

iadis

international association for development of the information society

As a member of Crossref (a non-profit membership organization for scholarly publishing working with the purpose to make content easy to find, link, cite and assess) each published paper in this book of proceedings will be allocated a DOI (Digital Object Identifier) number for its fast and easy citation and indexation.

Edited by Demetrios G. Sampson, Dirk Ifenthaler and Pedro Isaías

Associate Editor: Luís Rodrigues

TABLE OF CONTENTS

SHORT PAPERS

REFLECTION PAPERS

FOREWORD

These proceedings contain the papers of the 19th International Conference on Cognition and Exploratory Learning in the Digital Age (CELDA 2022), held in Lisbon, Portugal, from 8 to 10 November 2022 and organized by the International Association for Development of the Information Society (IADIS).

The CELDA conference aims to address the main issues concerned with evolving learning processes and supporting pedagogies and applications in the digital age. There have been advances in both cognitive psychology and computing that have affected the educational arena. The convergence of these two disciplines is increasing at a fast pace and affecting academia and professional practice in many ways.

Paradigms such as just-in-time learning, constructivism, student-centered learning and collaborative approaches have emerged and are being supported by technological advancements such as simulations, virtual reality and multi-agent systems. These developments have created both opportunities and areas of serious concerns. This conference aims to cover both technological as well as pedagogical issues related to these developments. Main tracks have been identified. However innovative contributions that do not easily fit into these areas will also be considered as long as they are directly related to the overall theme of the conference – cognition and exploratory learning in the digital age.

The following areas are represented in the submissions for CELDA 2022:

- Acquisition of Expertise
- Assessing Progress of Learning in Complex Domains
- Assessment of Exploratory Learning Approaches
- Assessment of Exploratory Technologies
- Cognition in Education
- Collaborative Learning
- Educational Psychology
- Exploratory Technologies (Simulations, VR, i-TV, etc.)
- Just-in-Time and Learning-on-Demand
- Learner Communities and Peer-Support
- Learning Communities & Web Service Technologies Pedagogical issues related with Learning Objects
- Learning Paradigms in Academia
- Learning Paradigms in the Corporate Sector
- Life-long Learning
- Student-centered Learning
- Technology and Mental Models
- Technology
- Learning and Expertise
- Virtual University

The CELDA 2022 Conference received 63 submissions from more than 25 countries. Each submission was reviewed in a double-blind review process by at least two independent reviewers to ensure quality and maintain high standards. Out of the papers submitted, 35 were accepted as full papers for an acceptance rate of 56%; 17 were accepted as short papers and 3 were accepted as reflection papers. Authors of the best published papers in the CELDA 2022 proceedings will be invited to publish extended versions of their papers in a book from Springer.

In addition to the presentation of full, short and reflection papers, the conference also includes one keynote presentation from an internationally distinguished researcher. We would therefore like to express our gratitude to this year keynote speaker: Professor Laura Hirsto, University of Eastern Finland.

A successful conference requires the effort of many individuals. We would like to thank the members of the Program Committee for their hard work in reviewing and selecting the papers that appear in this book. We are especially grateful to the authors who submitted their papers to this conference and to the presenters who provided the substance of this meeting. We wish to thank all members of our organizing committee.

Last but not least, we hope that everybody enjoyed the presentations and we invite all participants for next year's edition of the International Conference on Cognition and Exploratory Learning in the Digital Age.

Pedro Isaías, Information Systems & Technology Management School,
The University of New South Wales, Australia
Conference Chair

Demetrios G. Sampson, University of Piraeus, Greece & Curtin University, Australia
Dirk Ifenthaler, University of Mannheim, Germany & Curtin University, Australia
Program Co-Chairs

November 2022

PROGRAM COMMITTEE

CONFERENCE CHAIR

Pedro Isaías, Information Systems & Technology Management School, The University of New South Wales, Australia

PROGRAM CO-CHAIRS

Demetrios G Sampson, University of Piraeus, Greece & Curtin University, Australia
Dirk Ifenthaler, University of Mannheim, Germany & Curtin University, Australia

COMMITTEE MEMBERS

Ah-Choo Koo, Multimedia Univerisity, Malaysia
Anthony Y. H. Liao, Asia University, Taiwan
Carol H.C Chu, Soochow University, Taiwan
ChanMin Kim, Penn State University, USA
Charalampos Karagiannidis, University of Thessaly, Greece
Chien Sing Lee, Sunway University, Malaysia
Chung Hsien Lan, Nanya Institute of Technology, Taiwan
Chun-Wang Wei, Kaohsiung Medical University, Taiwan
Daniel Otto, Carl von Ossietzky University Oldenburg, Germany
Farshad Badie, Aalborg University, Denmark
Flavio Manganello, National Research Council, Italy
Georgios Zacharis, Aristotle University of Thessaloniki, Greece
Giuliana Guazzaroni, MI, Italy
I-fang Liu, National Central University, Taiwan
Jon Dron, Athabasca University, Canada
Julie-Ann Sime, Lancaster University, United Kingdom
Katherine Sinitsa, International Research and Training Center for Information Technologies and Systems, Ukraine
Kuo-Liang Ou, National Tsing Hua University, Taiwan
Kyparisia Papanikolaou, School of Pedagogical and Technological Education, Greece
Lence Miloseva, Goce Delcev University, Macedonia
Luis Anido, University of Vigo, Spain
Maiga Chang, Athabasca University, Canada
Michael Kerres, University of Duisburg-Essen, Germany
Michail Kalogiannakis, University of Crete, Greece
Mike Joy, University of Warwick, United Kingdom
Ming-Chi Liu, Feng Chia University, Taiwan
Minjeong Kim, Dankook University, Republic of Korea
Monica Divitini, Norwegian University of Science and Technology, Norway
Muhittin Sahin, University of Mannheim, Germany
Patrick Blumschein, University of Education Freiburg, Germany
Patrick Jost, Vorarlberg University of Applied Sciences, Austria
Radu Vasiu, Politehnica University of Timisoara, Romania
Richard Huntrods, Athabasca University, Canada
Stamatios Papadakis, University of Crete, Greece

KEYNOTE LECTURE

LEARNING ANALYTICS IN SUPPORTING TEACHING AND LEARNING – PEDAGOGICAL PERSPECTIVES

Professor Laura Hirsto
University of Eastern Finland,
Finland

Abstract

Viewpoints to learning analytics and self-regulated learning has attracted increasing attention in the educational technology research field, however, pedagogical perspectives have not been equally considered. The aim of this keynote is to present key issues and findings of a research and development project, which aimed to draw together and better understand the possibilities to support higher education and primary education students' self-regulated learning through the pedagogical use of Learning Analytics (LA). In the project we set out to develop and investigate learning environments that would intensively support the development of students' learning through an integrative learning environment, pedagogical design and solutions, and learning analytics and its visualizations. Various perspectives of general logdata, students' questionnaire responses and interviews, and teachers' interviews and classroom observations have been used to acquire a multifaceted perspective to the learning environments integrating LA. Our research project examines the development of learners' skills, the learning process, learning outcomes and the key elements in the pathway in multiple learning contexts through multiple case-studies, utilizing the same learning analytics tools.

FULL PAPERS

SYNCHRONOUS AND ASYNCHRONOUS ONLINE LEARNING IN ENGLISH LANGUAGE CLASSROOMS IN INDONESIA: A LITERATURE REVIEW

Akhyar Rido, Heri Kuswoyo and Berlinda Mandasari
Faculty of Arts and Education, Universitas Teknokrat Indonesia
Zainal Abidin Pagaralam Street 9-11 Bandar Lampung, Lampung, Indonesia

ABSTRACT

As the whole learning ecosystem is changing because of covid-19 pandemic outbreak, education institutions and teachers are demanded to cope with technology for online learning and give the best learning experience to their students. The aim of this research is to identify synchronous and asynchronous online learning in English language classrooms in Indonesian schools and universities during covid-19 pandemic, focusing on technological applications used and challenges faced by both teachers and students. By implementing Systematic Literature Review (SLR) approach from Indonesian Science and Technology Index known as SINTA and SCOPUS database, 31 research papers published between 2020-2022 in the Indonesian context are selected. This research creates a table of synchronous and asynchronous online learning applications used in English language classrooms as well as activities done and challenges faced by both teachers and students during covid-19 pandemic in the Indonesian context. The results of this research can be used by relevant stakeholders to help incorporate a balanced synchronous and asynchronous online learning in their English language classrooms as well as anticipate and prepare for future learning in their respective schools and universities, especially after covid-19 pandemic.

KEYWORDS

Synchronous, Asynchronous, Online Learning, English Language Classrooms, Indonesia

1. INTRODUCTION

In early 2020, ministry of education in all counties required all levels of education to apply online learning as the main learning mode in all courses because of covid-19 pandemic outbreak. This caused tens of thousands of educational institutions close most of their classes. As a result, 1.5 billion students and 63 million teachers have transformed face-to-face learning into online learning mode using technology (UNESCO, 2020; World Bank, 2020). All counties required all levels of education to apply online learning as the main learning mode in all courses, including in English language classrooms in Indonesia (Ministry of Education Republic of Indonesia, 2020; Kompas, 2020).

English is important in Indonesia, a developing country in Southeast Asia with a population totaling around 260 million individuals, the fourth largest in the world. The growing importance of English in Indonesia have created new purposes and needs for learning English mainly by young Indonesians who have previously learned English as a foreign language (EFL) for communication and academic purposes. Nowadays, learning English is always associated with globalization where the nation needs to perform on the global stage for the sake of economy. (Rido, 2020a; Di Grapello, 2013).

During covid-19 pandemic, English language learning becomes more challenging (Ministry of Education Republic of Indonesia, 2020; Kompas, 2020). Teachers have difficulty to adapt with the situation, especially learning using technology for online learning as well as incorporate a balanced and effective online learning, determining the most appropriate applications, interesting and relevant learning media which make students engaged in learning and more productive, and learning resources that can be easily accessed. Meanwhile, students also face challenges in terms of coping with the latest technology and demotivation in learning (Kusumawati, 2020; Mandasari, 2020; Valverde-Berrocoso et al, 2020).

This research is initiated in line with those concerns and an effort to understand the situation of online learning in English language classrooms, looking at the common practice of synchronous and asynchronous online learning during covid-19 pandemic by reviewing the existing literatures in the Indonesian school and university context. It further tries to reveal the technological applications used as well as the activities and done and the challenges faced by English language teachers and students. At the end, this research will provide relevant stakeholders with tables of alternatives of synchronous and asynchronous online learning applications for school and university English language classrooms, including activities in their online classrooms and some potential challenges that can be anticipated to improve the quality of teaching, promote engagement, and make learning more productive in the future, particularly after covid-19 pandemic.

2. ONLINE LEARNING

Online learning has its own characteristics, including student-centered; built in a structured and organized manner; involving massive participants and participation; integrated, timely and authentic. Because of these characteristics, online learning is carried out in two platforms namely synchronous and asynchronous (Wilkins, 2018; Dron & Anderson, 2016; Salmon, 2013). In general, teachers and students incorporate both platforms for online teaching and learning process.

Synchronous learning is principally a type of real-time learning; interaction between teacher and student as well as between student and student are carried out simultaneously like regular face-to-face meetings, facilitated by a system, usually video-conferencing (O'Rourke & Strickler, 2017; Ziegler, 2016). Meanwhile, asynchronous online learning is not time bound and students can carry out electronic activities in their own way, independently according to their own time availability. Normally, students only interact with learning resource or material such as reading materials, learning videos that are related to the topic of discussion while teachers only supervise or check (Rido, 2021; Rido, et al, 2020).

3. METHODOLOGY

This research is conducted in three research steps. First, a protocol review based PICOC formula (Population, Intervention, Comparison, Results, Context) is done. Second, the research questions and criteria for the selection process, namely inclusion and exclusion which cover data extraction and data synthesis are formulated. Inclusion and exclusion criteria for this study means that the articles contain keywords 'synchronous and asynchronous online learning' and 'English language classrooms in Indonesia' and are indexed in Indonesian Science and Technology Index known as SINTA and SCOPUS database, published between 2020-2022 (during covid-19 pandemic outbreak), and written in English. The search process is conducted manually by going through specific journal papers in the database. At this stage, there are 198 articles found. Then, 64 papers are chosen due to excluding papers that do not directly discuss synchronous and asynchronous online learning in the Indonesian context with its challenges based on the titles and abstracts. Finally, 31 articles are selected for this research after conducting the quality assessment.

4. RESULTS AND DISCUSSION

The results of this research show that much study has been done focusing on the use of digital technology for synchronous and asynchronous online learning in English language classrooms both in schools and universities in Indonesia during Covid-19 pandemic. In this part, synchronous online learning will be firstly presented and discussed, followed by asynchronous online learning.

4.1 Synchronous Online Learning in English Language Classrooms in Indonesia

There are twelve papers on synchronous online learning during covid-19 pandemic in the Indonesian context that have been documented and reviewed. For synchronous online learning, the findings indicate a number of video conferencing applications used by both teachers and students, including the activities that they do and challenges that they experience. It can be seen in table 1 below.

Table 1. Synchronous Online Learning in English Language Classrooms in Indonesia

Synchronous Online Learning Applications	Activities	Challenges
▪ *Zoom* ▪ *Google Meet* ▪ *Skype* ▪ *Cisco WebEx* ▪ *Discord* ▪ *Microsoft Team*	▪ Teachers display the materials on screen, mainly in reading, writing, and listening comprehension classes ▪ Teachers explain materials and related topics relevant with students' presentations ▪ Students give respond to teachers and to other friends verbally, mainly in writing and speaking classes ▪ Students respond in the form of text in chat-box in writing and speaking classes ▪ Students present their papers in speaking class	▪ Teachers and students experience poor internet connection ▪ Teachers and students spend a lot of money to pay big internet data ▪ Teachers and students have incompatible technological devices ▪ Teachers lack of technology literacy ▪ Teachers need more time to explain the materials ▪ Students cannot focus because of other domestic tasks from parents ▪ Students are afraid to speak

From Table 1 above, it can be seen that video conferencing applications like *Zoom, Google Meet, Skype, Cisco WebEx*, *Discord*, and *Microsoft Team* are used for synchronous online learning in English language classrooms in Indonesian schools and universities. Principally, those video conferencing applications have similar function, facilitating a two-way communication between teachers and their students, in the same time, engaging students with their classmates in a real-time basis (Atmojo & Nugroho, 2020; Kusuma, et al, 2021; Lie & Prijambodo, 2021; Putri & Sari, 2022). *Zoom, Google Meet, Skype, Cisco WebEx*, *Discord*, and *Microsoft Team* applications provide teachers with various supporting features such as *screen sharing* where teachers could display the materials on the screen to aid understanding, *mics* feature where teacher and students can talk as well as respond to each other, *chat box* where students can respond in a form of writing text and upload files. Therefore, this promotes listening and speaking skills of the students (Rahayu, 2020; Fitria, 2021; Prasetya, 2021).

However, the use of those video conferencing applications for English language learning has several challenges for both teachers and students. First, they experience poor internet connection, especially those who live in rural areas. As a result, the voice of teachers become unclear so that they need to repeat the explanation many times. Besides, those applications cost big internet data which become a serious matter for both teachers and students. In addition, there are some other issues such as incompatible devices—smartphones with middle-low specification, limited number of laptops, and lack of technology literacy, and technical problems make it more difficult to operate and use the applications. Because of low quality of personal devices, they frequently install and re-install the applications. Teachers also mention that they have limited time to explain all the materials because of time reduction of teaching hours during covid-19 pandemic and some technical issues (Hermansyah & Aridah, 2021). Meanwhile, from students' side, they become reluctant to speak during the class (Hamid, 2020; Mannong, 2020; Handayani, et al, 2021; Fitria, 2021; Hermansyah & Aridah, 2021; Septianingsih & Erliza, 2021). In addition, in many cases, students cannot focus because while attending the class via video conference, they are also helping their parents at home (Lie & Prijambodo, 2021).

4.2 Asynchronous Online Learning in English Language Classrooms in Indonesia

There are nineteen research articles on asynchronous online learning during covid-19 pandemic that have been identified and reviewed. For asynchronous online learning, the results show that some technological applications used and activities done by both teachers and students during teaching and learning process, including for students' assessment. The findings also identify some challenges faced by them in their asynchronous online learning. Please refer Table 2.

Table 2. Asynchronous Online Learning in English Language Classrooms in Indonesia

Asynchronous Online Learning Applications	Activities	Challenges
▪ *WhatsApp*	▪ Teachers share learning materials ▪ Teachers check students' attendance ▪ Teachers initiate discussion mainly in speaking and writing classes ▪ Teachers give assignments ▪ Students submit assignments	▪ Teachers get difficulties to monitor students' engagement and contribution as they cannot see them in person ▪ Students need to scroll up to find the correct shared information or materials from their teachers because of overlapping talk ▪ Students do not get detailed explanation ▪ Students do not understand the tasks
▪ *Screencast-O-Matic*	▪ Teachers record their own teaching and set the learning materials (ppt slides) as the background ▪ Teachers share the recorded video to students ▪ Students listen/watch the video recording	▪ Students become passive learners as it is only one way interaction
▪ *Google Classroom*	▪ Teachers provide forum for discussion ▪ Teachers give assignments ▪ Students share their thoughts on a particular topic ▪ Students respond to their teacher' and classmates' statements	▪ Students do not get direct feedback from their teachers
▪ *SPADA and Moodle*	▪ Teachers check attendance ▪ Teachers share learning materials ▪ Teachers provide discussion forum, especially in writing and speaking classes ▪ Teachers give assignments online examination in reading and writing classes ▪ Students access materials	▪ Teachers face difficulties to prepare all activities and materials as it is time consuming ▪ Students experience poor internet connection ▪ Students face many compulsory tasks

	▪ Students give comments in speaking and writing classes ▪ Students submit assignments and sit for online examinations in reading and writing classes	▪ Students are demotivated for participation
▪ *Facebook, Instagram, YouTube*	▪ Teachers give instructions and tasks ▪ Teachers share learning materials ▪ Teachers upload their own teaching videos or other relevant videos ▪ Students post pictures with English captions ▪ Students give comments on their classmates' posts ▪ Students watch videos ▪ Students give respond in comment box	▪ Students use a lot of data ▪ Students experience unstable internet connection
▪ *Google Form, Kahoot, Quizzes*	▪ Teachers create interactive and fun based-game assessment in many forms ▪ Students do the test and get the score directly on screen	▪ Teachers spend a lot of time to prepare the assessment ▪ Teachers get difficulty to check the originality of students' answers or works

Table 2 above shows that in order to facilitate asynchronous online learning in English language classrooms, some applications are used such as *WhatsApp, Screencast-O-Matic, Google Classroom, SPADA*, *Moodle*, and *Google Form*. Teachers also use social media such as *Facebook, Instagram and YouTube*, including online assessment platform such as *Kahoot* and *Quizziz* for learning.

WhatsApp is used by English language teachers to share learning materials, check students' attendance, start discussion, as well as give and submit assignments (Lie at al., 2020; Prasetio & Priyana, 2021). Even though *WhatsApp* is internet-friendly, some students still face difficulties such as overlapping chat as they always need to scroll up to find the correct shared information or materials from their teachers. In *WhatsApp*, teachers also do not give detailed explanations; they just simply share the materials, then ask students to do assignments even though students still do not fully understand the task. As for teachers, it is difficult to monitor students' engagement and contribution because they cannot see them in person (Hariadi & Simanjuntak, 2020; Ariyanti, 2020; Rabbianty, et al, 2021; Putri, 2021).

In delivering materials through asynchronous platform, some teachers also use *Screencast-O-Matic* where they can record their own teaching and set the learning materials (power point slides) as the background, then, share the recorded video to their students. Students can watch the recording at home. However, it tends to be one way, only for material delivery and student only become passive recipient of knowledge (Basri, et al, 2021).

Besides, teachers utilize *Google Classroom*. Some studies focusing on the use *Google Classroom* in English language classrooms indicate that teachers and students express their positive responses due to its flexibility. *Google Classroom* provides many features like *discussion forums* where students can share their thoughts about the topics and respond to their teacher' and classmates' statements. In addition, teachers can easily share and students also can download the learning materials. *Google Classroom* also has a *reminder* feature when it comes to assignment or project deadlines, but it has no direct interaction feature as students need immediate feedback on their shared thoughts and responses (Hariadi & Simanjuntak, 2020; Rinekso, et al, 2021; Prasetya, 2021; Prasetio & Priyana, 2021).

Moreover, it is also revealed that many university English language classrooms in Indonesia are also mediated by an official learning management systems provided by the government namely SPADA, using Moodle as its platform, which provides various features in order to facilitate both administrative and learning activities such as attendance, learning materials, chat box, discussion forum, assignment submission, and online examination which help improve the students' reading and writing skills (Maulana & Lintangsari, 2021; Sari, 2020; Sari & Oktaviani, 2021). However, in the implementation, students argue that poor internet connection and too many compulsory tasks demotivate students' participation (Sari, 2020). Meanwhile, teachers mention time management, admitting that it takes a huge amount of time and dedication to design and upload all materials in the system and prepare all devices before teaching and learning process (Lie at al., 2021; Suherman, et al, 2021).

This research also finds that teachers use social media such as such as *Facebook* and *Instagram* as well as streaming application like *YouTube* in their English language classrooms. In using *Facebook*, teachers create *Facebook* group, invite all students, post instructions, share learning materials, and let students discuss in the comment box. Meanwhile, in using *Instagram*, teachers ask students to post a picture with English captions and their classmates respond in the comment box (Nugroho & Mutiaraningrum, 2020). As for *YouTube*, teachers normally upload their teaching videos and students are asked to watch them, then, respond in comment box (Ariyanti, 2020; Hariadi & Simanjuntak, 2020; Lie at al., 2020; Meliala et al, 2021; Rinekso, et al, 2021). Teachers claim that the use of social media enhance students' writing skills and improve both their grammar and vocabulary. However, students mention that these social media use a lot of data and while internet connection is unstable, learning becomes slower (Nugroho & Mutiaraningrum, 2020; Rabbianty, et al, 2021; Basri, et al, 2021).

Meanwhile, in assessing students' knowledge, teachers use *Google Form*, *Kahoot* and *Quizziz*. *Google Form* is used by teachers develop questions for quizzes or examinations in order to assess students' knowledge (Putri, 2021; Rinekso, et al, 2021). Furthermore, allow teachers to create interactive and fun based-game examination in form of multiple choice, essay, and true-and-false questions. Students can get the results directly on scoreboard right after completing the test which is efficient and transparent. However, it takes time and energy to prepare those assessments, including marking students' essays (Lie at al., 2020; Nugroho & Mutiaraningrum, 2020; Nugroho, et al, 2021; Atmojo & Nugroho, 2020). What lack is that these applications only have 'one function'—for assessment, besides, it is difficult for teachers to check the originality of their students' answers or works. (Basri, et al, 2021).

5. CONCLUSION

This research aims at revealing synchronous and asynchronous online learning in English language classrooms in Indonesian schools and universities by reviewing the existing literatures. The results indicate that Indonesian teachers employ synchronous and asynchronous online learning in their online classrooms. For synchronous online learning, video conferencing applications like *Zoom, Google Meet, Skype, Microsoft Team* as well as social media such as *Discord* are utilized. These applications are principally used to facilitate a-two-way communication between students and teachers and among students in classes which promote listening and speaking skills. Meanwhile, for asynchronous online learning, applications such as *WhatsApp, Google Classroom, Google Form, Screencast-O-Matic, SPADA* and *Moodle* as well social media such as *Facebook, Instagram and YouTube*, including online assessment platform such as *Kahoot* and *Quizziz* are used. These applications are mostly used for self-directed learning in classes which emphasize listening, reading, and writing skills.

However, some challenges are also identified. From teachers' side, both synchronous and asynchronous online learning platforms consume their times to arrange both schedules and materials and big internet data. Teachers also experience poor internet connection and difficulties to monitor students' engagement. In the same vein, students face some issues such as poor internet connection, incompatible computer and smartphone, lack of technological literacy, lack of interpersonal connection with their teachers, failure in understanding the materials, demotivation, overload tasks, and lack of participation. In short, technical and personal issues are the most dominant challenges experienced by both teachers and students.

Interestingly, this research also finds a number benefits of online learning. Teachers and students have more flexibility in their teaching and learning activities and become more creative as there are more spaces and platforms for improvisation and sharing ideas. As there are so many materials to study, tasks to do, assignments to complete, and examinations to pass, the use of these applications also help improve speaking, listening, reading, and writing skills of students, especially during covid-19 pandemic. The implication of this research will give contributions to policy makers and teachers in terms of providing alternatives and options for synchronous and asynchronous online learning during covid-19 pandemic and in the future learning.

This research has some limitations. The data gained from the existing literatures are contextual case studies with limited number of participants and do not cover all provinces in Indonesia. Thus, the results of this research cannot be generalized. This research must be follow-up with field research which includes direct observation, interview, and survey to get a holistic picture. This will significantly help relevant stakeholders to prepare for future learning in English language classrooms in Indonesian and neighboring countries, especially after covid-19 outbreak.

ACKNOWLEDGEMENT

We would like extend our highest appreciation to Directorate General of Research, Technology, and Community Services Ministry of Education, Culture, Research and Technology Republic of Indonesia for granting this research [Grant number 1421/LL2/PG/2022; 050/UTI/LPPM/E.1.1/VI/2022] and Universitas Teknokrat Indonesia for supporting this research.

REFERENCES

Ariyanti., 2020. EFL Students' Challenges towards Home Learning Policy during Covid-19 Outbreak. *In Indonesian Journal of English Language Teaching and Applied Linguistics, Vol.* 5, No. 1, pp. 167-175.

Atmojo, A. E. P. and Nugroho, A., 2020. EFL Classes Must Go Online! Teaching Activities and Challenges during COVID-19 Pandemic in Indonesia. *In Register Journal*, Vol. 13, No. 1, pp. 49-76.

Basri, M. et al, 2021. University Students' Perceptions in Implementing Asynchronous Learning during Covid-19 Era. In *Metathesis: Journal of English Language, Literature, and Teaching*, Vol. 4, No. 3, pp. 263-276.

Di Grapello., E., 2013. Role of Education and Training Sector in Addressing Skill Mismatch in Indonesia. *In Education in Indonesia*. Institute of Southeast Asian Studies, Singapore pp. 236-266.

Dron, J and Anderson, T., 2016. The Future of E-Learning. *In The Sage Handbook of E-Learning Research.* Sage, Haythornwaite, C.A, pp 537-556.

Fitria, T. N., 2021. Students' Perception toward the Implementation of Synchronous Learning during COVID-19 Pandemic in English Language Teaching (ELT). *In E-Structural*, Vol. 4, No. 1, pp. 1-16.

Hamid, S. M., 2020. Online Digital Platforms During Covid-19 in EFL Classes: Visual Impairment Student' Perception. *In English, Teaching, Learning, and Research Journal*, Vol. 6, No. 2, pp. 328-339.

Handayani, S. T. D. et al, 2021. Synchronous Computer-Mediated Interactions in English: A Case of Indonesian Learners-English Non-native Speakers Communication. *Proceedings of the Thirteenth Conference on Applied Linguistics. Bandung, Indonesia*, pp. 546-555.

Hariadi, I. G. and Simanjuntak, D. C., 2020. Exploring the Experience of EFL Students Engaged in Asynchronous E-Learning. *In Academic Journal Perspective: Education, Language, and Literature,* Vol. 8, No. 2, pp. 72-86.

Hermansyah, H. and Aridah, A., 2021. Teachers' Perception toward the Challenges in Online English Teaching during Covid-19 Pandemic. *In Indonesian Journal of EFL and Linguistics, 6(1)*: 63-77.

Kompas, 2020. Menteri Nadiem Wacanakan Belajar Jarak Jauh Permanen setelah Pandemi Covid-19, Mungkinkah?. Tersedia online: https://www.kompas.com/tren/read/2020/07/03/155830065/menteri-nadiem-wacanakan-belajar-jarak-jauh-permanen-setelah-pandemi-covid?page=all.

Kusuma, P. C. et al, 2021. EFL teachers' perception towards online classroom interaction during covid-19 pandemic. *In ETERNAL: English Teaching Journal*, Vol. 12, No. 2, pp. 68-79.

Kusumawati, A. J., 2020. Redesigning Face-to-Face into Online Learning for Speaking Competence during Covid-19: ESP for Higher Education in Indonesia. *In International Journal of Language Education*, Vol. 4, No. 2, pp. 276-288.

Lie, A. and Prijambodo, C., K., 2021. Senior High School Students' Readiness and Motivation to Learn English Using Synchronous Video Conferences. *In Journal of Information Technology Education: Research*, Vol. 20, pp. 429-457.

Lie, A. et al, 2020. Secondary School Language Teachers' Online Learning Engagement during the Covid-19 Pandemic in Indonesia. *In Journal of Information Technology Education: Research*, Vol. 19, pp. 803-832.

Mandasari, B., 2020. The Impact of Online Learning toward Students' Academic Performance on Business Correspondence Course. *In Journal of Education and Technology*, Vol. 4, No. 1, pp. 98-110.

Mannong, A. B. M., 2020. The Students' Eyesight: The Effectiveness of Learning-Based Applications on ELT in Pandemic Era. *In Eternal: English, Teaching, Learning, and Research Journal*. Vol. 6, No. 2, pp. 394-407.

Maulana, N. R. and Lintangsari, A. P., 2021. The Use of Moodle in English Language Learning During the Pandemic: The Students' Voice. *In The Journal of English Literacy Education,* Vol. 8, No. 1, pp. 27-41.

Meliala, E. P. et al, 2021. An Analysis of English Teachers' Creativity in Media-Based Learning at the Tenth-Grade Students. *In Journal of Languages and Language Teaching*, Vol. 9, No. 1, pp. 105-110.

Ministry of Education Republic of Indonesia, 2020. Mendikbud Terbitkan SE tentang Pelaksanaan Pendidikan dalam Masa Darurat Covid-19. Tersedia online: https://www.kemdikbud.go.id/main/blog/2020/03/mendikbud-terbitkan-se-tentang-pelaksanaan-pendidikan-dalam-masa-darurat-covid19.

Nugroho, A. et al, 2021. Emergency Remote Teaching Amidst Global Pandemic: Voices of Indonesian EFL Teachers. *In VELES: Voice of English Language Education Society,* Vol. 5, No. 1, pp. 66-80.

Nugroho, A., and Mutiaraningrum, I., 2020. EFL Teachers' Beliefs and Practices about Digital Learning of English. *In EduLite: Journal of English Education, Literature, and Culture*, Vol. 5, No. 2, pp. 304-321.

O'Rourke, B and Strickler, U., 2017. Synchronous Communication Technologies for Language Learning: Promise and Challenges in Research and Pedagogy. *In CercleS*, Vol. 7, No.1, pp. 1–20.

Prasetio, E. and Priyana, J., 2021. Tourism Vocational High School Students' Online EFL Learning Experience during Covid-19 Pandemic. *In Jurnal Pendidikan dan Pengajaran*, Vol. 54, No. 3, pp. 596-610.

Prasetya, R. E., 2021. Engagement Strategies in Electronic Tools English Online Learning: Higher Education Context. *In Indonesian Journal of English Education,* Vol. 8, No. 2, pp. 309-326.

Putri, E. R., 2021. EFL Teachers' Challenges for Online Learning in Rural Areas. *In Proceedings UNNES-TEFLIN National Seminar*, Semarang, Indonesia, pp. 402-409.

Putri, N. R. and Sari, F. M., 2021. Investigating English Teaching Strategies to Reduce Online Teaching Obstacles in The Secondary School. *In Journal of English Language Teaching and Learning*, Vol. 2, No. 1, pp. 23-31.

Rabbianty, E. V. et al, 2021. Maximizing The Use of WhatsApp in English Remote Learning to Promote Students' Engagement at Madura. *In LET: Linguistics, Literature and English Teaching Journal*, Vol. 11, No. 1, 42-60.

Rahayu, D., 2020. Students' E-Learning Experience through a Synchronous Zoom Web Conference System. *In Journal of ELT Research: The Academic Journal of Studies in English Language Teaching and Learning*, Vol. 5, No. 1, pp. 68-79.

Rido, A., 2020a. English for University Graduate Employability: Students and Employers' Voices. *In Advances in Social Science, Education and Humanities Research*, Vol. 430, pp 6–10.

Rido, A. et al, 2020. *Interaction and Pedagogy of Indonesian Vocational English Language Master Teachers*. Universiti Kebangsaan Malaysia Press, Kuala Lumpur.

Rinekso, A. B. and Muslim, A. B., 2020. Synchronous Online Discussion: Teaching English in Higher Education amidst the Covid-19 Pandemic. *In Journal of English Educators Society*, Vol. 5, No. 2, pp. 155-162.

Rinekso, A. B. et al, 2021. Teaching Online in Pandemic Time: The Experience of Indonesian EFL Teachers. *In ETERNAL: English Teaching Learning and Research Journal*), Vol. 7, No. 1, pp. 117-133.

Salmon, G., 2013. *E-tivities: The Key to Achieve Online Learning*. Routledge, London.

Sari, F. M., 2020. Exploring English Learners' Engagement and Their Roles in the Online Language Course. *In Journal of English Language Teaching and Linguistics*, Vol. 5, No. 3, pp. 349-361.

Sari, F. M. and Oktaviani, L., 2021. Undergraduate Students' Views on the Use of Online Learning Platform during COVID-19 Pandemic. *In TEKNOSASTIK: Jurnal Bahasa dan Sastra*, Vol. 9, No. 1, pp. 41-47.

Sari, M. I. and Putri, A. A., 2022. Exploring Online Learning Tools Used by EFL Teachers during the Covid-19 Pandemic. *In Journal of Foreign Language Teaching and Learning*, Vol. 7 No.1, pp. 61-76.

Septianingsih, P. A. and Erliza, S., 2021. Urban and Rural Area Graduate Students' Perceptions toward Synchronous English Learning amidst Covid-19 Pandemic. *In Journal of English Language Teaching and Linguistics,* Vol. 6, No. 3, pp. 643-658.

Suherman, R. et al, 2021. Learning English Utilising Online Platform During Covid-19 in Tertiary Level: Indonesian EFL Learners' Retrospective Perception. *In ENGLISH REVIEW: Journal of English Education*, Vol. 10, No. 1, pp. 277-286

UNESCO, 2020. COVID-19 Educational Disruption and Response. Tersedia online: https://en.unesco.org/covid19/educationresponse.

Valverde-Berrocoso, J. et al, 2020. Trends in Educational Research about E-Learning: a Systematic Literature Review (2009-2018). *In Sustainability*, Vol. 12. No. 5153, pp. 1-23.

Wilkins, B., 2018. Asynchronous collaboration integrating online learning in foreign language classoroom. *In The Journal of Language and Teaching*, Vol. 8, No. 2, pp. 101-108.

World Bank., 2020. Individuals Using the Internet (% of population) | Data. Available Online: https://data.worldbank.org/indicator/IT.NET.USER.ZS?name_desc=false.

Ziegler, N., 2016. Synchronous Computer-Mediated Communication and Interaction. *In Studies in Second Language Acquisition*, Vol. 38, No. 3, pp. 553–586.

DIDACTIC ACTIVITIES ON ARTIFICIAL INTELLIGENCE: THE PERSPECTIVE OF STEM TEACHERS

Cecilia Fissore[1], Francesco Floris[2], Marina Marchisio[2] and Matteo Sacchet[2]
[1]*Dipartimento di Lingue e Letterature Straniere e Culture Moderne , Via Giuseppe Verdi Fronte 41, 10124 Torino TO, Italy*
[2]*Dipartimento di Biotecnologie Molecolari e Scienze per la Salute , Via Nizza 52 - 10126 Torino TO, Italy*

ABSTRACT

The concept of Artificial Intelligence (AI) might seem something very distant from the world of schools: a theme that is far from today's reality, especially when the education and training system is committed to tackling the problems associated with the pandemic situation. However, the impact that AI is producing in various areas of our life also requires reflection on the world of education and training. Research and education policies are therefore required to direct education to prepare students for technological challenges, enabling schools and teachers to guide innovation. It is necessary to train teachers not only on the theoretical contents inherent to these themes, but also and above all on the planning of didactic activities to adopt innovative educational approaches. The context of this research is the immersive 3-hour workshop on the theme "Mathematics and AI" which involved 52 teachers from all over Italy from primary to secondary school. The research questions are: What is the current teaching practice in schools in Italy in terms of AI? Which characteristics should be emphasized, and which aspects should be favored in the planning of didactic activities by school teachers? To answer the research questions, we analyzed teachers' responses to the initial questionnaire before the workshop and to the final questionnaire at the end of the workshop. Key findings show that teachers do not treat AI-related topics too much with their classes while being aware of the importance of recognizing and understanding AI.

KEYWORDS

Artificial Intelligence, Didactic Activities, Mathematics, Primary School, Secondary School, Teachers

1. INTRODUCTION

When we talk about Artificial Intelligence (AI), we often think of futuristic technologies, robots that behave like human beings making decisions and taking actions and a world in which machines and humans coexist. The world of cinema has also found inspiration for films and TV series on the theme of AI, fueling curiosity but also concerns on the subject. However, AI and its use are much more real than believed and are now used in various aspects of daily life and recently also in the education area at all levels.

In (Digital Education Action Plan 2021-2027), a renewed European Union policy initiative that sets out a common vision of high-quality, inclusive and accessible digital education in Europe, introduces the theme of AI and the importance of updating digital skills curricula to include it. The theme of AI appears in two actions: "Ethical guidelines on the use of AI and data in teaching and learning for educators" (Action 6); and "Updating the European Digital Competence Framework to include AI and data-related skills" (Action 8). The document "The Future of Education and Skills: Education 2030 – OECD" (OECD, 2018) says: "There is a growing demand for schools to prepare students for faster economic and social changes, for jobs that are not created, technologies that have not yet been invented and solving social problems that did not exist in the past". Research and education policies are therefore required to direct education to prepare students for technological challenges, enabling schools and teachers to guide innovation. In the document "Proposals for an Italian Strategy for Artificial Intelligence" (Ministry for Economic Development, 2020) the expert group of the Ministry of Economic Development argues that "The strategy is strongly focused on issues related to education, skills and lifelong learning. One of the fundamental requirements to face this transformation concerns the ability to train figures with digital skills, among which AI plays a leading role. [...] It is necessary to focus not only on improving the skills of the teaching staff already inserted in schools, but also on a structural updating of school curricula".

On the one hand, in fact, students will increasingly need to acquire skills on AI and awareness of the implications of its use. On the other hand, this issue could open new scenarios for teaching practices. To achieve these objectives, it is necessary to understand what is meant by “Artificial Intelligence”, from a theoretical and technical point of view. By doing so, it is possible to understand the opportunities and the limits too, as well as the most immediate and effective areas of application. It is therefore necessary to train teachers not only on the theoretical contents inherent to these themes but also and above all on the planning of didactic activities to adopt innovative educational approaches.

The DELTA Research Group of the University of Turin has developed and implemented two open online courses as an online repository to host curated AI-related training resources. The courses were implemented in collaboration with the Liceo Peano Pellico of Cuneo within their online platform for MOOCs (Liceo Classico e Scientifico Statale "Pellico-Peano" Cuneo - Piattaforma Moodle). The titles of the courses are "Data protection and digital identity awareness" and "STEAM and equal opportunities". The online courses, for teachers and students, contain mathematical didactic activities from primary school to upper secondary school. The courses are part of the Action entitled #FUTURA IA AND DIGITAL CITIZENSHIP, within the National Networks on Innovative Teaching Methods promoted by the Italian Ministry of Education (Basteris et al., 2021). The main objective of the project is to include the issues of AI and digital citizenship within the curricula of the Italian school, being aware that an approach to these issues from a simply technological point of view is not enough, but that it is essential to promote a critical reflection on the social, ethical, and relational aspects that these issues will raise in the future in the short, medium, and long term. As a result of this collaboration involving also the National Ministerial Project Problem Posing and Solving (Fissore et al., 2020), the DELTA Research Group organized a training workshop for teachers on the theme "Mathematics and AI". The context of this research is the immersive 3-hour workshop which involved 52 teachers from all over Italy from primary to secondary school, with a desire to learn and innovate their teaching practices. The workshop took place face-to-face, and it was structured as follows:

- filling in an initial questionnaire;
- theoretical introduction on the topic with group discussion and interactions by teachers;
- illustration of several examples of educational activities of different levels on these topics;
- group planning of a didactic activity through the compilation of a guided form;
- filling in a final questionnaire.

One main reference for the activity of the workshop is the DigCompEdu (Punie et al., 2017), which was mentioned to highlight the educational digital competencies that teachers should consider and develop for effective teaching.

In this paper we analyze the results arising from the answers of teachers about the connection between Ai and education. The research questions are the following:

(RQ1) What is the current teaching practice in schools in Italy in terms of AI?

(RQ2) Which characteristics should be emphasized, and which aspects should be favored in the planning of didactic activities by school teachers?

The paper is structured as follows: in Section 2 the Theoretical background is outlined, in Section 3 research Methodology is presented together with workshop modalities and type of data collected, in Section 4 the Results are illustrated while in the final Section results are discussed and Conclusions are drawn.

2. THEORETICAL BACKGROUND

AI has been introduced as a branch of science that tries to simulate the methods that humans use to solve their problems. The term intelligence is defined as the competence or ability to solve a problem, and artificial means any systematic human method that may accomplish problem-solving goals (Kouveliotis and Mansuri, 2022). AI experts try to teach the machine to act like a human. Thus, intelligence in the expression "Artificial Intelligence" means essentially that implemented models enable a machine to solve problems, in the sense that solutions of these problems have not been a priori encoded, but that they are constructed originally by the machine (Balacheff, 1993). Research in AI has focused chiefly on the following components of intelligence: learning, reasoning, problem solving, perception, and using language (Pedro et al., 2019). AI applications affect the most varied areas of daily life, with important social implications. For this reason, all citizens must be able to understand AI, recognize AI techniques and know the potential and limits of AI. On the one hand, this implies that the systems must be transparent and explainable even to the user who does not have advanced scientific and technological knowledge; on the other hand, it calls for particular attention to skills, intended both as a necessary tool to develop competitiveness and empowerment and as a tool for protecting the citizen facing the complexities of modern technologies.

In education, AI began producing new teaching and learning solutions that are now undergoing testing in different contexts. However, AI research in the field of education dates back to several years ago. The first significant projects of AI in the field of educational technology for mathematics education appeared in the early seventies (Balacheff, 1993), according to whom the main contribution of AI to mathematics education is to provide concepts, methods, and tools for the design of flexible and relevant computer-based systems for teaching and learning purposes. The connection between AI and education involves three areas: learning with AI (e.g. the use of AI-powered tools in classrooms), learning about AI (its technologies and techniques) and preparing for AI (e.g. enabling all citizens to better understand the potential impact of AI on human lives). To prepare teachers for an AI-powered education while preparing AI to understand education is a two-way road: teachers must learn new digital skills to use AI in a pedagogical and meaningful way and AI developers must learn how teachers work and create solutions that are sustainable in real-life environments.

Schools that are expected to adapt to the digital age and embed 21st century skills in their main agendas are some of the main institutions that could be most affected by the development of AI (Gocen & Aydemir, 2020). Karsenti (2019) points out that new forms of technology will fill in our lives and captivate our youth, and this may leave schools with no choice but to make room for them. The online document of UNESCO (Pedro et al., 2019) gathers examples of the introduction of AI in education worldwide, particularly in developing countries, discussions in the context of the 2019 Mobile Learning Week and beyond, as part of the multiple ways to accomplish Sustainable Development Goal 4, which strives for equitable, quality education for all. In particular, the paper explores the different means by which governments and educational institutions are rethinking and reworking educational programs to prepare learners for the increasing presence of AI.

With the increase in studies about AI in the educational field, many scholars in the field want to study how the role of teachers, school and leaders in education will change, and what benefits there may be (see for example Gocen & Aydemir, 2020). In light of the existing initiatives and technologies to come, different studies have recently contributed to the ways in which AI can help improve learning opportunities for students and management systems (Luckin et al., 2016; Pedro et al., 2019). It is certainly important to study what kind of implications it can reveal for the future of schools. However, it is important to introduce the topic in schools, training students and teachers and investigating their perceptions towards AI. Most research in mathematics education aims at the creation of AI milieus to work on mathematics, to the AI-supported learning of mathematics and to the coordination of "usual" paper/pencil techniques and "new" AI-aided educational working spaces (Richard et al., 2022)

Possible topics related to AI and that can be used to introduce the topic and to design educational activities are: Artificial intelligence in everyday life; Machine Learning (the ability to learn without being explicitly programmed); Deep learning (a specific subfield of machine learning); neural networks (from the biological to the computer model); Fuzzy logic (extension of the Boolean logic to manage ambiguity and vagueness, since AI wants to imitate human behavior); Big Data (any collection of data sets so large or complex that it becomes difficult to process them using traditional data management techniques); Data Mining (the process of discovering interesting patterns and knowledge from large amounts of Data); GDPR (General Data Protection Regulation); and personal data protection (education systems must clearly delimit how learners' data are used and be expressly based on learners' consent to their data being used). Also, if AI is to mimic human behavior but algorithms are annotated by humans, they must be bias-free as much as possible. For this reason, AI techniques in educational processes require further study on the issues of the "digital divide" and social inclusion, on the risks associated with these innovations but also on the opportunities that technologies offer to manage these issues with new approaches. Certainly, the topic of AI offers many ideas for the design of interdisciplinary educational activities. The topic of AI is closely related to the concept of 'Learning Analytics' in the literature. Learning analytics is defined as the collection, measurement, analysis, and reporting of information about learners and their context to understand and improve learning and its environments (Long & Siemens, 2011). The spread of AI technologies in education is important for the formation of a flexible, editable curriculum and Learning Analytics can also contribute to the provision of individualized learning content. The function of learning analytics holds a prominent place as an important function of AI applications (Floris et al., 2020; Marchisio et al., 2019).

3. METHODOLOGY

The teachers worked in groups on the guided planning of the didactic activity by filling in a specific form. The form was divided into two parts. The first part "Information on the activity" required title, disciplines involved, class, school, duration, topic, objectives. The second part concerned the description of the activity (type of activity, brief description, supporting digital tools, evaluation).

To answer the research questions, we analyzed the responses of the teachers to the initial questionnaire before the workshop and to the final questionnaire at the end of the workshop. The initial questionnaire was structured in two parts: first part about teachers' data (age, level of education, school, discipline, etc.) and second reflective part. Using Likert scale questions (from 1 = Completely disagree, or Never or Not at all to 5 = Completely agree, or Very often, or A lot) we asked teachers their experience about AI and data protection in the school. In the final questionnaire the teachers reflected on the characteristics of the activity they designed and on how this favors the understanding of different aspects. Furthermore, teachers expressed their appreciation for the workshop in various aspects and for the methodologies of the workshop, for instance adaptive teaching, and formative practices.

Likert scale questions are analyzed through descriptive statistics: median and IQR (Inter Quartile Range).

To answer the research questions, the activities planned by the teachers were also analyzed, some explanatory examples of which will be shown.

The sample of respondents to the questionnaire is composed by 52 teachers for the initial questionnaire. As it can be seen in Figure 1, most respondents are female (69%) in the range 46 – 55 years old (47%) with more than 16 years of teaching experience (58%). Teachers from all grades participated: from primary schools (4%), passing through Lower secondary schools (29%) up to Upper secondary schools (65%). Most participants are teachers in Mathematics (45%), but even other STEM disciplines are represented: Physics (11%), Computer Science (11%), Natural Science (9%). 42 teachers responded to the final questionnaire. Even if some teachers responded only to the initial questionnaire (10 teachers), we consider all their responses as expression of their pre-workshop perspectives on Didactics and AI.

4. RESULTS

The first question of the initial questionnaire (I1) asked the agreement on different sentences about education and AI: the importance of teaching students and teachers to recognize and understand AI, where it intervenes in daily life and the ethics linked to AI, AI education to promote critical thinking and problem solving, the usefulness of understanding AI for students who will not deepen computer science, the awareness about shared data, the importance of managing data and the role of mathematics in conveying issues related to data protection. There is a general strong agreement on these sentences (median 5 over a 5-point Likert scale) with very low dispersion (IQR 0 or 1). Little less agreement on two sentences about the introduction to AI at any school level and mathematics as a vehicle for AI themes (median 4 over a 5-point Likert scale, IQR 1), even though teachers of all grades participated to the workshops.

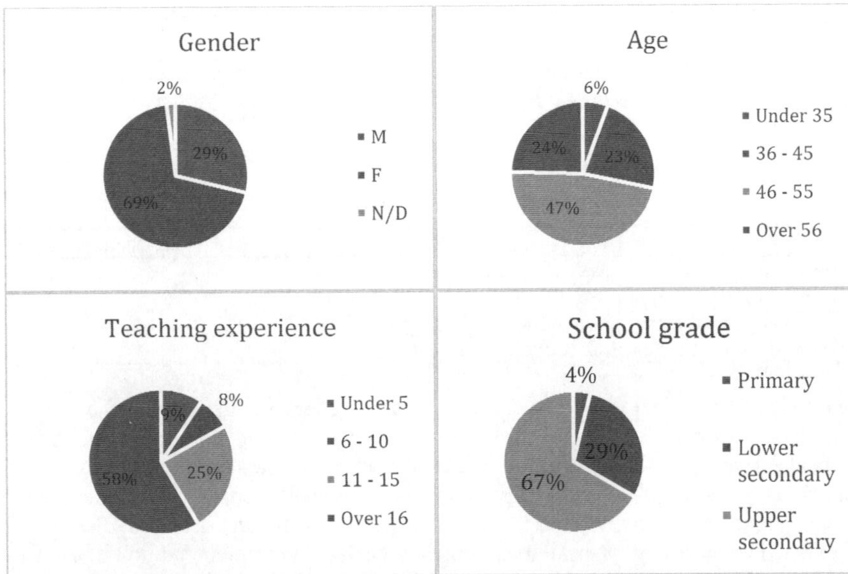

Figure 1. Distribution of Gender, Age, years of Teaching experience, and School grade of respondents

Then, teachers had to respond about how much they treat the topics in Table 1 with the students (I2).

Table 1. Median and IQR related to I2 "How often have you addressed the following topics with your classes?"

Topic	Median	IQR	Topic	Median	IQR
Big Data	2	2	GDPR	2	2
Cryptography	2	2	Digital identity	3	3
Cybersecurity	3	2	AI	2	2
Data ethics	3	1	Machine learning	2	2

It emerges that teachers do not treat AI-related topics a lot with their classes, with cybersecurity being the one that is discussed more than the others. This is probably due to the urgent need of digital literacy for every citizen in Europe and in the world, in order to protect personal and sensitive data, with a focus that is geared more towards practical aspects (how to set up a strong password, how to protect one's own communications, etc.) rather than legal aspects. In fact, the item about GDPR shows rare appearance within classes: anyway, teachers have to deal with the European regulation not in didactics but in other aspects of their job.

The last question of the initial questionnaire (I3) asked teachers their agreement about the use of technologies at school, as it can be seen in Table 2.

Table 2. Median and IQR related to I3 "How much do you agree with the following statements relating to teaching and the use of technologies?"

Topic	Median	IQR
It is recommended to use technologies very often during teaching	4	2
Teachers would need more resources for technology-mediated teaching	4	1
Teachers would need more training for technology-mediated teaching	4	1
Preparing lessons using technologies takes more time	4	2
The use of smartphones within schools must be allowed	4	2
The use of smartphones within schools must be regulated	5	1
The use of smartphones within schools must be prohibited	2	2

The results show that technologies are widely accepted and adopted in daily teaching activities and teachers would like to have more resources and more training to better use technology-enhanced methodologies (median 4 over a 5-point Likert scale). Provocative items investigated the attitude of teachers towards the use of smartphones in education. It is agreed that there must be some regulation to monitor their usage (median 5 over a 5-point Likert scale), but most teachers even favor it (median 4 over a 5-point Likert scale) and do not agree with prohibitions (median 2 over a 5-point Likert scale).

From the final questionnaire, after one or two hours working on activities related to AI, we asked teachers to mark items on the importance they have given to specific didactical aspects in connection with AI (F1). Results are shown in Table 3.

Table 3. Median and IQR related to F1 "To what extent do you believe that the planned activity favors the following aspects?"

Topic	Median	IQR
Understanding how AI intervenes in daily life	4	2
Understanding the importance of AI	4	2
Understanding the importance of personal data protection	4	2
Understanding the close link between math and AI	4	2

Other questions of the final questionnaire concerned teachers' judgement on the whole workshop. The following aspects are evaluated in (F2): congruence of the training contents with respect to the stated objectives, speakers' mastery of the contents, speakers' communication skills, adequacy of topics to didactical practices, interaction between speakers and participants (median 4 over a 5-point Likert scale). Last question of the final questionnaire (F3) investigates the teachers' point of view on the methodologies to be adopted with students, Table 4. The workshop presented examples of design and implementation of didactical activities on AI-related topics to favor teachers' reflection on the possible applications in the class.

Table 4. Median and IQR related to F3, agreement about the methodologies

Topic	Median	IQR
The proposed methodologies are interesting	5	1
The proposed methodologies are clear	4	1
The proposed methodologies support innovative teaching	5	1
The proposed methodologies support collaborative learning	5	1
The proposed methodologies help students' learning	4	1
The proposed methodologies help students develop skills	5	1
I intend to use the methodologies proposed in the classroom	4	1
I intend to deepen the proposed methodologies	5	1

Beyond a general agreement with the methodologies, teachers aim at emphasizing the following aspects with their activities: Adaptability to different types of students, Peer collaboration, Interactivity, Micro learning, Possibility of alternating different tools and contents in a non-linear way, Use and integration of different techniques and instruments (median 4 over a 5-point Likert scale).

4.1 Examples of Teaching Activities Designed by Teachers

The first example of activity designed by teachers is for a third grade of primary school. The activity is titled "Sensitive Data" and aims to make pupils think about the data that identify people. The disciplines involved are mathematics, history, and civic education. The pupils work as a team on the collection and classification of personal data that identify them. The goal is to create a facsimile of an identity card. The activity can be implemented for the lower secondary school by adding a part on the encryption of personal data and on the sharing of personal data on social networks.

The second example is titled "Applications of Machine Learning to Electron Microscopy". The activity is intended for grade 12 students and the disciplines involved are chemistry and computer science. The goal of the activity is to develop an AI algorithm to recognize from images of microscopic sections of plastics if they are recyclable. The activity consists of 4 parts: classification of plastics on microscopic surfaces; management and cataloguing of images; use of the "Google Colab" environment for the recognition of images of plastic materials; design of the classification algorithm in Python.

The third example is titled "Digital Signals". The activity is intended for grade 11 students and the disciplines involved are electronics, telecommunications, and information technology. The objectives of the activity are to recognize and verify the tolerance band of logic families and to model the real digital signal. The activity consists of a first part of theoretical introduction on the definition of an ideal and real digital signal, on the 74xx and fuzzy logic families. After an individual asynchronous comparison on the data sheet of the two logic families, a laboratory activity is planned on the assembly of devices of the two logic families. The activity ends with an analysis of the output signals as the input data gradually changes.

The fourth example is titled "AI and biodata to assess the impact of climate change on the ecosystem". The activity is intended for grade 13 students and the disciplines involved are civics, science, mathematics, biology, English. The purpose of the activity is to use new technologies to collect data, structure and analyze them. The objective of the activity is to make students reflect on the phenomenon of climate change through reality assignments.

The activity consists of three parts: photogrammetry for the collection of biodata through the use of the school drone; data structuring using existing python libraries; integration of the dataset with data taken from the network. The digital tools used are Desmos, "Google Colab", drone, digital camera.

5. CONCLUSION

This paper presents the results of a workshop on Mathematics and AI which involved 52 Italian teachers of different levels. The results highlight the current teaching practice in Italian schools about AI-related topics (RQ1). Teachers do not usually treat these kinds of topics in their daily didactics, and the reasons can be multiple: lack of time for topics partly outside their own discipline, (presumed) lack of experience in things related to AI, fear of exploring something beyond their own knowledge. On the other side, teachers perceive the importance of treating AI within classes, since it is a widespread field in computer science and it has numerous applications. When working on activities connecting education and AI, teachers know different characteristics to emphasize (RQ2):

- adaptability, which aims at including from low to high performing students;
- peer collaboration, since AI involves many expertise, group work and collaboration help the development of skills;
- interactivity, in order to let students experiment and put into practice the theoretical aspects;
- micro learning, to distribute and divide learning into atomic elements (learning objects);
- exploring tools and contents in a non-linear way, for example in a learning-by-doing or learning on demand practice;
- use and integration of different techniques and instruments, following multimedia learning principles.

As an overall conclusion from this research, it emerges the greater importance that needs to be given to the issues of artificial intelligence in schools. AI technologies are an exciting area for humankind. Strictly related to this is the need of training teachers on these issues and on the planning of educational activities to propose them to students. AI lends itself very well to interdisciplinary activities (mathematics, computer science, philosophy, history, civics, etc.) and to the design of educational activities for all levels of education. The legal, ethical, pedagogical, psychological, and sociological harms and benefits are to be considered. Subsequently, students' development of digital skills to understand and recognize artificial intelligence, being aware of both the risks and benefits. AI for education includes excitement and promising developments for schools. New developments, contexts and effects can be carefully managed and discussed in classes.

REFERENCES

Balacheff, N. (1993). Artificial intelligence and mathematics education: Expectations and questions. In 14th Biennal of the Australian Association of Mathematics Teachers (pp. 1-24). Curtin University.

Basteris, L., Daperno, M. C., Rosso, G., Ribero, A. (2021). #FUTURA IA AND DIGITAL CITIZENSHIP, Metodologie Didattiche Innovative in School Kit per sperimentare le tematiche dell'IA nei vari ordini di scuola, In Atti del Convegno Didamatica 2021 (pp. 76-83). AICA.

Digital Education Action Plan (2021-2027) | European Education Area, retrieved from https://education.ec.europa.eu/it/focus-topics/digital-education/action-plan, last accessed July 25th, 2022.

Fissore, C., Marchisio, M., & Rabellino, S. (2020, June). Secondary school teacher support and training for online teaching during the covid-19 pandemic. In EDEN Conference Proceedings (No. 1, pp. 311-320).

Floris, F., Marchisio, M., Rabellino, S., & Sacchet, M. (2020). Learning analytics to evaluate the effectiveness of higher education student failure prevention. In Proceedings of the 17th International Conference on Cognition and Exploratory Learning in the Digital Age (CELDA 2020) (pp. 265-272).

Gocen, A., & Aydemir, F. (2020). Artificial Intelligence in Education and Schools. Research on Education and Media, 12(1), pp. 13-21.

Karsenti, T. (2019). Artificial intelligence in education: the urgent need to prepare teachers for tomorrow's schools. Formation et profession, 27(1), pp. 112–116. Doi:10.18162/fp.2019.a166.

Kouveliotis, K. & Mansuri, M. (2022), "How artificial intelligence has changed E-learning education in the meta era", Proceedings of the International Conference E-Learning 2022, IADIS, pp. 195-198.

Liceo Classico e Scientifico Statale "Pellico-Peano" Cuneo - Piattaforma Moodle, retrieved from https://mooc.liceocuneo.it/corsi/, last accessed July 25th, 2022.

Long, P., & Siemens, G. (2011). Penetrating the fog: Analytics in learning and education. EDUCAUSE Review, 46(5), pp. 31–40.

Luckin, R., Holmes, W., Griffiths, M., & Forcier, L. B. (2016). Intelligence Unleashed: An argument for AI in Education. Pearson Education, London.

Marchisio, M., Rabellino, S., Roman, F., Sacchet, M., & Salusso, D. (2019). Boosting up data collection and analysis to learning analytics in open online contexts: an assessment methodology. Journal of e-Learning and Knowledge Society, n°3, pp. 49-59, Sie-l.

Ministry for Economic Development (2020), Proposte per una Strategia italiana per l'intelligenza artificiale, Elaborata dal Gruppo di Esperti MISE sull'intelligenza artificiale. Retrieved from https://www.mise.gov.it/images/stories/documenti/Proposte_per_una_Strategia_italiana_AI.pdf, last accessed July 25th, 2022.

Organisation for Economic Co-operation and Development (OECD). (2018). The future of education and skills: Education 2030. OECD Education Working Papers.

Pedro, F., Subosa, M., Rivas, A., & Valverde, P. (2019). Artificial intelligence in education: Challenges and opportunities for sustainable development, Education 2030, UNESCO (https://unesdoc.unesco.org/ark:/48223/pf0000366994)

Punie, Y., & Redecker, C. (2017). European Framework for the Digital Competence of Educators: DigCompEdu, EUR 28775 EN, Publications Office of the European Union, Luxembourg, ISBN 978-92-79-73718-3 (print), 978-92-79-73494-6 (pdf), doi:10.2760/178382 (print),10.2760/159770 (online), JRC107466

Richard, P. R., Vélez, M. P., & Van Vaerenbergh, S. (2022). Mathematics education in the age of artificial intelligence. How artificial intelligence can serve the mathematical human learning, Springer Cham

A SYSTEMATIC REVIEW OF RESEARCH ON EFL ONLINE LEARNING: EFFECTIVENESS, CHALLENGES, LEARNING TOOLS, AND SUGGESTIONS

Heri Kuswoyo, Akhyar Rido and Berlinda Mandasari
Faculty of Arts and Education, Universitas Teknokrat Indonesia
Pagar Alam Street No 9-11, Kedaton, Bandarlampung, Lampung, 35142, Indonesia

ABSTRACT

Due to COVID-19 pandemic, educational departments such schools, colleges, and universities have been experiencing significant disruptions. All teaching and learning activities of face-to-face learning have switched to online learning. This study provides a systemic review of the literature with the aim to investigate the effectiveness, challenges, learning tools, and suggestions in EFL online learning based on an analysis of 40 published article journal from 2019 to 2022. This study has not yet been reviewed in the literature as part of a systematic review of studies. This study is based on Kitchenman's (2009) systemic literature review (SLR) approach, which allows it to gather data from a variety of sources. The dataset has been collected from SCOPUS databases. These data were analysed using Creswell's (2012) content analysis. The research findings revealed that all e-learning tools (e.g., *Voki*, *LMS 'TES Blended Space'*, *Pigai*, *Zoom meeting* etc) used by universities teachers were very effective and beneficials for learners. However, some challenges were also identified during learning activities such as students lack of learning climate, poor internet connections, financial problems, technical problems, students' demotivation etc. Thus, the research findings suggested three aspects should be considered, namely a) having extensive and high-quality online resource access, b) using online resources on a regular basis, and (c) not only students but also teachers are being trained to use ICTs-in. In addition, teachers need to keep working on reinforcing the connection between digital technology and education meanwhile students need to made aware that it is acceptable to use digital media even it the most formal of educational settings. To summarize, this study suggests that once the Covid-19 pandemic is ended, the use of technology integration on online learning in EFL classrooms can be extended for equitable quality education for students.

KEYWORDS

EFL Online Learning, Effectiveness, Challenges, Learning Tools, Suggestions, Systematic Literature Review (SLR)

1. INTRODUCTION

The pandemic Covid-19 has changed the entire educational sector and forced all academics and students to switch to digital mode of teaching and learning process suddenly (Huang et al., 2021). All in-person face-to-face learning was instantly replaced with entirely online learning (Buhari, Suganya, & Rajaram, 2022; Purwati, Suryawati, & Eliwarti, 2022; Chandra & Palvia, 2021; Al-khresheh, 2022). Online learning models carry their significant advantages, in their increased accessibility and adaptability and in their students' autonomy and independence (Mihai et al., 2022). It can be seen from the use of e-learning platforms rapidly such as Google classroom and Zoom meeting in their learning (Szopinski & Bachnik, 2022; Perveen, 2016). Online learning has the ability to improve teaching and learning by revamping traditional classroom instructional methodologies and improving the quality of learning experiences (Basar et al., 2021). However, even online teaching has many advantages, the traditional offline teaching can completely be replaced (Song et al, 2021). As online education becomes more popular in the future, colleges should make greater efforts to improve it (Song et al., 2021). It can be seen that most teachers nowadays are still striving to elevate the quality of online learning engagement (Lie et al., 2020; Adnan & Anwar, 2020) in Thongmak & Ruangwani (2021). In their study, Huang et al. (2021) reported that in online teaching, it is extremely time-consuming and exhausting. Thus, Teachers must improve their technology skills in order to teach online (Thongmak & Ruangwanit, 2021; Chandra & Palvia, 2021). In respond to these issues, most of the ministry of education in all countries suggested to all universities to apply online learning in all courses, including EFL online learning classroom. According to Rahimi and Hasheminasab (2020), EFL language learning and teaching have undergone considerable changes as a result of immediate technological advancements and new pedagogical opportunities. It causes EFL teachers have 'various challenges in their endeavour to practice effective online learning and teaching (Zou et al., 2021). It is in line with William and Burden (1997). They argue that learning a foreign language is not simply learning the skills, rules or grammar, it involves self-image, cultural behaviour and way of being that impact on the social nature of the learner. It is also because as the passive recipients of a range of stimuli, learners need to achieve a desire outcome, which is ultimately language knowledge, predominantly from environment (Mihai et al, 2022). Then, from brain's cognitive process, learners also need a tool for language learning process to actively think about, participate with and make sense of the language learning process. At the end, learners need a community designed for fostering problem solving skills where social experiences, collaborations, and reflection lead to practical and interactive learning (Mihai et al., 2022).

Many researchers investigated EFL online learning during COVID-19, which give educational benefits, including online reading (Park, Yang, & Hsieh, 2014); English teaching (Al-khresheh, 2022; Hedman & Mannish, 2022; Purwati, Suryawati, & Eliwarti, 2022); oral presentation (Atifnigar et al., 2022); Debriefing in online English classroom (Kandasamy, Hua, & Sultan, 2022); and listening comprehension (Jiang et al, 2021). Al-khresheh (2022) reported that using blackboard technology improved EFL classes. As a result, technical obstacles persist in efficiently integrating this technology into modern classrooms. Then, Hedman and Mannish's (2022) work provided fresh perspectives on collaborative agency in English online distance learning from the setting of Sweden. Another study conducted by Kandasamy, Hua, and Sultan (2022), who explored the the debriefing 's effects in online ESL classroom. According to the research, debriefing can help students in teamwork, critical thinking, reflective thinking, and easy understanding. Purwati, Suryawati, and Eliwarti (2022) indicated that students' evaluations of video lectures were high, and this was consistent with how they positively regarded video lectures in the flipped classroom. Then, Atifnigar et al. (2022), from Afghanistan context, revealed that class-size related factor is the first influential factor in affecting oral participation among students. The final study, conducted by Park, Yang, and Hsieh (2014), investigated the information-seeking strategies and decision-making processes of L2 readers while reading online. The results show that L2 readers use prior knowledge of the structure of both offline and online resources to help them with their online reading.

The time has come to assess the effectiveness of these efforts after several months, nearly three years of operation in this new highly virtual mode (Szopinski & Bachnik, 2022). Moreover, it is also very essential to discuss the challenges, learning tools, and the suggestions during the post-COVID 19 pandemic. According to Szopinski and Bachnik (2022), it is critical to ask questions about the quality of online teaching and student satisfaction because any unresolved issues may have long-term implications for the structure of the higher education sector and the future format of the programs designed and offered. In addition, the perspective of students, as well as universities and faculty members, is critical to the future design and delivery of online education (Szopinski & Bachnik, 2022). As a result, the current study conducts a systematic assessment of the most recent literature on EFL online learning classroom to analyse the effectiveness, problems, and suggestions in responding to the influence of the post-Covid-19 epidemic on education, as well as the key learning instruments. Consequently, this research aims to investigate (1) what were the effectiveness, challenges, and suggestions involved in the research on EFL online learning classroom? (2) What were the main learning tools involved in the research on online learning in EFL classroom?

2. METHOD

The method used in this study is systemic literature review (SLR) pioneered by Kitchenham et al. (2009). This strategy provides insights into a research problem and allows a study to collect information from a variety of sources (Al-Araibi, Mahrin, & Mohd, 2016). The techniques employed have also been adapted for use in the EFL online learning classroom. Adapting from Hisyam et al. (2021), the review process consists of three steps. They are planning stage, implementation stage, and final stage. In details, it can be seen in the following figure 1.

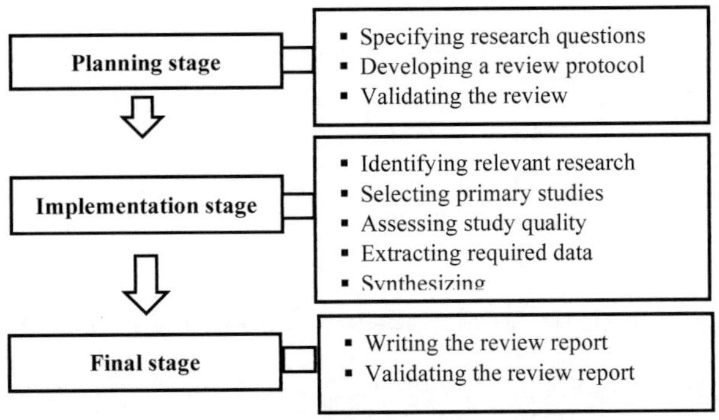

Figure 1. Steps in the review process (adopted from Hisyam et al, 2021)

First, in the planning stage, the present writers formulated two research questions, (1) what were the effectiveness, challenges, and suggestions involved in the research in EFL online learning? and (2) what were the main learning tools involved in EFL online learning? Then, in the next stage, the present writers selected a scientific publication database, from Scopus. Following that, the primary review process is required to aid in classification using the PICOC approach (population, intervention, comparison, outcomes, context). Following that, the identification process determined that the population is "online learning" in the context of "effectiveness, challenges, learning tools, and suggestions." The intervention section was carried out to obtain information on focuses, such as a publication on a year 2019 and 2022. In the selection process, the Scopus database (www.scopus.com) was used for the primary research using the Boolean operator (Search documents= ("online learning" OR "e-learning" OR "electronic learning") AND Search document=(EFL)). The literature type was set as 'article' and 'conference paper'. The research generated 55 articles published from 2019 to 2022. The reason for this limitation is to narrow the updated papers discussing online learning during COVID-19 pandemic. The present writers selected the articles based on the following criteria: (1) investigating EFL online learning; (2) concerning the effectiveness, challenges, learning tools, and suggestion in EFL online learning; (3) published article; (4) article in English; and (5) open access article. The present writers then checked the articles independently, and 15 articles were excluded. They were excluded as they were not about EFL online learning. Thus, a total for the review in this present study is 40 article journals. The data were retrieved and synthesized from the paper and analyse them using a content analysis (Creswell, 2012), a technique extensively used in humanities and the social sciences.

3. RESULTS

This study provides a systemic review of research with the aim to investigate the effectiveness, challenges, learning tools, and suggestions in EFL online learning based on an analysis of 40 published article from 2019 to 2022 from SCOPUS databases (see Table 1).

Table 1. Publication years and journals (scopus.com)

Year	Journal Names	Studies
2022	*Journal of Language Teaching and Research, World Journal of English Language; Journal of language teaching and research, SiSAL Journal, Studies in English Language and Education, Theory and Practice in Language Studies, Asia Pacific Journal of Second and Foreign Language Education, Cogen Arts and Humanities, SAGE Open, World Journal of English Language*	Mudra et al, (2022); Anggoro & Khasanah (2022); Zhang., Gao, & Chen, (2022); Mohamed (2022); Fischer & Yang (2022); Jeong (2022); Kristianto & Gandajaya (2022); De Gracia et al. (2022); Muharom., Nugroho., & Putra., (2022); Maretha & Anggoro (2022); Phanphech (2022); Reflianto (2022); Tang & Quan (2022); Wangdi & Shimray (2022); Dai (2022)
2021	*Revista de Lingustica y Lenguas Aplicadas, Journal of language and education, 3L: Language, Linguistics, Literature, Ilha do Desterro, Corpus Pragmatics, Indonesian Journal of applied linguistics, SAGE Open, International Journal of Language Education, Journal of language and Education*	Hanh & Huong (2021); Damayanti & Rachmah (2020); Di Zou et al (2020); Farros (2020); Heng & Sol (2020); Rahaman (2021); Sulha., Famela., Harahap, (2021); Warman & Gusti (2021)

2020	*RELC Journal, ReCALL, Theory and Practice in Language studies, Rupkatha Journal on Interdisciplinary studies in Humanities*	Zaghlool (2020); Gao (2020); Hou (2020); Akhter (2020); Regmi & Jones (2020).
2019	*Journal of Language and Literary Studies, Indonesian Journal of applied linguistics, Humanities & Social Sciences Reviews*	Marjanović (2019); Farhan & Yusoff (2019); Pouromid (2019); Tamine (2019)

3.1 Effectiveness, Challenges, Learning Tools, and Suggestions in EFL Online Learning

EFL online teaching and learning has been largely conducted during the COVID-19 period all over the world. Based on the review, online learning can create new learning as perceived by students (Suharsih & Wijayanti, 2020), and has been found beneficial to learners' EFL learning (Zhang & Wu, 2022; Mohamed, 2022). However, the effectiveness, challenges, learning tools, and suggestions of EFL online teaching and learning is a need to be investigated (Zou et al., 2021). Table 2 shows the review of effectiveness, challenges, learning tools, and suggestions in EFL online learning conducted by 41 studies.

Table 2. Review of Effectiveness, challenges, learning tools, and suggestions in EFL online learning

Effectiveness	Challenges	Learning tools	Suggestions	Relevant References
Students are enthusiastic about using ICTs to improve their English pronunciation	Some students continue to prefer traditional teaching methods, Slow video uploading, be afraid of making mistake	Voki, Open Educational Resource (OER), Flipgrid-based portfolio	Access to a wide range of high-quality online resources, regular use of online resources, and training not only students but also teachers	Datt & Singh (2021); Hanh & Huong (2021)
The use of LMS TES Blend Space had positive influences in learning EFL	Instructor should develop activities in the LMS	LMS 'TES Blend Space'	LMS TEST BlendSpace has promoted students' self-directed learning skills and improved learning performance	Jiang et al, (2021); Zhao, Zhang, & Chen, (2022)
COIL-based curricula can provide valuable opportunities for learners to engage in intercultural interaction without the expense of traveling abroad	Learner's English proficiency	Collaborative Online International Learning (COIL) program	To fully utilize the potentials of computer technology and the internet, innovative curricula for foreign language pedagogy are required	Pouromid (2019); Huang, et al, (2021); Kandasamy, et al, (2022)
EFL university students were enthusiastic about using CALL online writing activities and Pigai in the teaching and learning of writing	Students lack of learning climate	CALL online writing activities, Automated essay scoring (AES)'s Pigai	University professors should incorporate CALL online writing activities into their writing classes on an ongoing basis. Students can use Pigai for self-directed learning	Hou (2020); Zaghlool (2020)
The DMC process increased students' knowledge of the importance of empathy when participating in online activities.	Students have lower English language proficiency or low student participation	Digital Multimodal Composing (DMC)	Students with lower English language proficiency need to trained differently by mixing English with their first language	Tour & Barnes (2022); Jiang et al (2021);
All applications used by teachers were beneficial and effective to be used	Limited resources, poor connectivity, technical issues, inability to operate program like Ms Word, ppt, and financial problem, more time and energy are demanded to prepare for lesson	Zoom, Google classroom, & LMS applications, QQ, Tencent meeting, Blackboard, Moodle, Facebook Closed Group (CMC)	Give students access to tools like the free messaging app in the online learning framework. Teachers may modify the techniques they learned	Santoso (2021); Al-khresheh (2022); Hisyam et al (2021); Farhan & Yusofi, (2019); Mudra et al, (2022)

From Table 2 above, it can be seen that students and teachers have positive feedbacks towards the use of EFL online teaching and learning during COVID-19. Datt & Singh (2021) study reported that students have a positive attitude towards ICTs and Open Educational Resources (OERs) for learning pronunciation using Voki. Voki is an online tool like the 'text-to-speech' option for developing students pronunciation performance. Consequently, despite the potential benefits of OERs like Voki, some students still favor receiving education via traditional instructional approaches. Thus, Datt & Singh (2021) suggested that in the future, universities and teachers must have three aspects to be considered. They are as follows: a) having broad and high-quality access to online resources, b) regularly using online resources, and c) teaching not only students but also teachers to use ICTs. Similar studies, Hanh & Huong (2021) claimed that an online platform, flipgrid-based portfolio also significantly can be used to improve learners' speaking performances in terms of pronunciation and fluency. In terms of online applications, Online Social Network (OSN), such as Zoom, Google classroom, & LMS applications, Blackboard, Moodle etc were dominantly used by university teachers to teach online. They were beneficial and effective to be used in EFL online learning (Farhan & Yusofi, 2019; Mudra et al, 2022; Zhao, Zhang, & Chen, 2022; O'Doherty, 2018). However, based on the reviews, implementing such applications in the classroom has been challenging such as poor connectivity, technical issues, inability to operate program like Ms Word and power point, financial problem, more time and energy to prepare lesson, and students lack of learning climate.

Table 2 also reveals that a wider range of e-tools were employed in online learning activities. Not only OSN but also other online learning platforms such as video-making tools, video watching tools, online discussion tools, reading tools, and writing tools were also applied by university teachers. The video-making tools included Digital Multimodal Composing (DMC) video production. Jiang (2020) claimed in his study that the usage of DMC such as video creation, podcasting, and webpage designing as a viable and productive English language learning activity is extensively documented in the field of English language education. The DMC process raised students' understanding of the importance of having more empathy when participating in online activities. Beside DMC could enhance students' awareness, students could also learn how to use digital technologies for resolving important social issues and then became more active and responsible participants online. However, the reviews suggested that students have lower English language proficiency or low student participation need to trained differently by mixing English with their first language. Meanwhile, in terms of writing, the writing tools included the Automated essay scoring (AES)'s Pigai (Hou, 2020) and CALL online writing activities (Zaghlool, 2020). AES (automated essay scoring) system, such as Pigai, is a computer technology that evaluates written texts using artificial intelligence, computational linguistics, and cognitive science foundations. Pigai, the most extensively used of them, is intended to assist Chinese EFL learners in evaluating their own works by offering ratings and feedback based on the target text. In the future, Pigai can be used students as self regulated learning. Meanwhile, Zaghlool's (2020) study stated that the incorporation of computer-assisted language learning (CALL) into EFL programs has recently become an integral aspect of the teaching and learning process. According to the findings of the study, EFL university students had positive opinions regarding using CALL online writing activities in teaching and learning writing. Newly added online learning platforms included tools for learners to experience intercultural interaction without having to bear the burden of traveling overseas. The tool is called as COIL (Collaborative Online International Learning). COIL is a type of online learning that involves classes from two or more countries in order to raise learners' understanding of intercultural competency (Pouromid, 2019).

For online discussion tools, *Facebook messenger* and *Facebook Closed Group (CMC)*, were mainly used by university lecturers (Farhan & Yusoff, 2019). Computer-Mediated Communication or CMC is defined as the direct use of computers in text-based communication processes. According to Santoso (2021), CMC can occur synchronously or in real-time, as well as asynchronously, when people interact in a delayed fashion. Along with the advancement of CMC tools, computer interactions now include not just reading and writing but also speaking. Based on the findings, the learners had good attitudes toward the integration in online discussion forums, and their perceptions of the effects of online discussion forums on new learning were disclosed. However, one important issue that impedes the quality of engagement is the lack of an internet connection.

4. CONCLUSION

Based on an analysis of 40 published articles from 2019 to 2022, this study aims to investigate the effectiveness, obstacles, learning tools, and suggestions in EFL online learning. The results of the present review indicate that the varied and integrated e-tools for teaching and learning in EFL online classroom (e.g.,Voki, LMS 'TES BlendedSpace', Facebook messenger, CMC, Pigai, Zoom, Google classroom, & LMS applications, Blackboard, Moodle, and Flipgrid-based portfolio used by university teachers were effective and beneficials. Both teachers and learners get more insights in gaining online teaching and learning. They also have more flexibility in teaching learning time because they can teach from anywhere. Further, the use of these various learning tools is able to overcome teaching and learning during COVID-19 pandemic. According to present review, some challenges also identified in the pre- teaching, during teaching, and post-teaching. In terms of teachers, more time and energy are demanded to prepare for lesson and use big internet data. Teachers also sometimes got some problems such as limited resources, poor connectivity, technical issues etc. In similar challenges, learners also face some problems such as some students still prefer traditional instruction models, network problem, demotivation, internet data, technical issues, inability to operate program like Ms Word and power point, financial problem and many others.

Besides, this study also gets some suggestion related to the use of e-leaning tools in EFL online teaching and learning. In general, teacher or university needs to consider three aspects namely a) having broad and high-quality access to online resources, b) making use of online resources on a regular basis, and (c) training not only students but also teachers to use ICTs-in. Then, teachers also need to keep working on reinforcing the connection between digital technology and education meanwhile students need to made aware that it is acceptable to use digital media even it the most formal of educational settings. The implication of this research findings could give contributions to policy makers, stakeholders, and teachers in terms of providing for the effectiveness, challenges, learning tools, and suggestions in EFL online learning during covid-19 pandemic and in the future learning. The current study has numerous limitations because it only analysed 40 articles on online learning published in SCOPUS journal databases between 2019 and 2022. A broader range of published sources, such as SSCI, IEEE, and SINTA journals, may be considered in future research. To that end, the present writers feel the review demonstrated that online learning could increase the capabilities of both teachers and learners.

ACKNOWLEDGEMENT

The present writers would like to thank Directorate General of Research, Technology, and Community Services Ministry of Education, Culture, Research and Technology Republic of Indonesia for the research funding [No. 049/UTI/LPPM/E.1.1/VI/2022] and Universitas Teknokrat Indonesia for the administrative support.

REFERENCES

Adnan, M., & Anwar, K, 2020. Online learning amid the COVID-19 pandemic: Students' perspectives. *Journal of Pedagogical Sociology and Psychology,* 2(1), 2–8.

Al-Araibi, A.A.M et al, 2016. A systemic literature review of technological factors for e-learning readiness in higher education. *Journal of Theoretical and Applied Information Technology,* 93 (2), 500-521.

Al-khresheh, M.H, 2022. Revisiting the effectiveness of blackboard learning management system in teaching English in the era of COVID-19. *World Journal of English Language,* 12 (1), 1-14. https://doi.org/10.5430/wjel.v12n1p1

Atifnigar, H., et al, 2022. Oral participant practices in classroom among university students in Afghanistan. *International Journal of Evaluation and Research in Education,* 11(1), 409-420.

Basar, Z.M., et al, 2021. Effectiveness and challenges of online learning for secondary school students – A Case Study. *Asian Journal of University Education (AJUE),* 17 (3), 119-129.

Buhari, S.M., et al, 2022. Students' performance through online and offline in core information technology courses: A comparison. *Journal of Engineering Education Transformations,* 35, 243-248.

Chandra, S & Palvia, S, 2021. Online education next wave: peer to peer learning. *Journal of Information Technology Case and Application Research,* 23 (3), 157-172, https://doi.org/10.1080/15228053.2021.1980848

Creswell, J. W, 2012. *Educational research: Planning, conducting, and evaluating quantitative and qualitative research* (4th ed). Upper Saddle River, NJ: Pearson Education.

Dai, Y, 2022, Online English teaching quality assessment based on K-Means and improved SSD algorithm. *Advances in Multimedia*, 1-9. https://doi.org/10.1155/2022/8213637

Damayanti, F.L., & Rachmah, N, 2020. Effectiveness of online vs offline class for EFL classroom: A study case in a higher education. *Journal of English Teaching Applied Linguistics and Literatures*, 3 (1), 19-26.

Datt, G., & Singh, G, 2021. Acceptance and Barriers of Open Educational Resources in the context of Indian Higher Education. *Canadian Journal of Learning and Technology*, 47 (3), 1-15.

De Gracia et al, 2022. An Analysis of the perception of students and teachers towards the Home-Based online learning modality and the students' academic achievement of a private school in the National Capital Region (NCR) of the Philippines. In 2022 13th International Conference on E-Education, E-Business, E-Management, and E-Learning (IC4E 2022), January 14–17, 2022, Tokyo, Japan. ACM, New York, NY, USA, 8 pages.

Di Zou et al, 2020. A systematic review of research on flipped language classrooms: theoretical foundations, learning activities, tools, research topics and findings. *Computer Assisted Language Learning*, https://doi.org/10.1080/09588221.2020.1839502

Farros, J.N, 2020. The effect of synchronous discussion sessions in an asynchronous course. *Journal of Behavioural Education*, https://doi.org/10.1007/s10864-020-09421-2

Farhan, R.N & Yusoff, Z.S, 2019. Integration of Facebook messenger in the English literature classroom: learners' attitudes and perceptions. *Humanities and social sciences review,* 7 (6), 988-999.

Fischer, I.D., & Yang, J.C, 2022. Flipping the flipped class: using online collaboration to enhance EFL students' oral learning skills. *International Journal of Educational Technology in Higher Education,* 19 (15), 1-24.

Heng, K., & Sol, K, (2020, December 08). Online learning during COVID-19: Key challenges and suggestions to enhance effectiveness. *Cambodian Education Forum.* https://cambodianeducationforum.wordpress.com/2020/12/08/online-learning-during-covid-19-key-challenges-and-suggestions-to-enhance-effectiveness/.

Hedman, C., & Mannish, S, 2022. Student agency in relation to space and educational discourse. The case of English online mother tongue instruction, *English in Education,* 56 (2), 160-173, https://doi.org/10.1080/04250494.2021.1955618

Hisyam et al, 2021. Moodle implementation for E-learning: A Systematic Review. 6th International Conference on Sustainable Information Engineering and Technology 2021. *Association for Computing Machinery*, New York, NY, USA,

Huang, R. et al, 2021. Emergence of the Online-Merge-Offline (OMO) learning wave in the Post-COVID-19 era: A Pilot Study. *Sustainability,* 13, 3512. https://doi.org/10.3390/su13063512

Jeong, K.-O, 2022. Facilitating sustainable self-directed learning experience with the use of mobile-assisted language learning. *Sustainability,* 14, 2894. https://doi.org/10.3390/su14052894

Jiang Y, et al, 2021. The Effect of the online and offline blended teaching mode on English as a foreign language learners' listening performance in a Chinese context. *Front. Psychol.* 12:742742.

Jiang, L. et al. 2021, Teacher engagement with digital multimodal composing in a Chinese tertiary EFL curriculum. *Language Teaching Research*, 25 (4), 613-632.

Kandasamy, S. et al, 2022. The impact of a debriefing strategy in online ESL classroom. *International Journal of Learning, Teaching and Educational Research, 21* (3), 247-262. https://doi.org/10.26803/ijlter.21.3.13

Kitchenham, B. et al, 2009. Systematic literature reviews in software engineering– A systematic Literature Review. *Information and software technology,* 51(1), 7-15.

Kristianto, H. & , 2022. "Offline vs online problem-based learning: a case study of student engagement and learning outcomes", *Interactive Technology and Smart Education*. https://doi.org/10.1108/ITSE-09-2021-0166

Lie, A., et al, 2020. Secondary school language teachers' online learning engagement during the Covid-19 pandemic in Indonesia. *Journal of Information Technology Education: Research,* 19, 803- 832, https://doi.org/10.28945/4626

Maretha, A.L., & Anggoro, K.J, 2022. App Review TikTok: Benefits, drawbacks, and implications for the ELT field. *MEXTESOL Journal,* 46 (2), 1-5

Mihai, M. et al, 2022. "Emotional and social engagement in the English language classroom for higher education students in the COVID-19 online context" *Sustainability* 14, no. 8: 4527. https://doi.org/10.3390/su14084527

Mudra, H. et al, 2022. EFL learners' pedagogical views on the online social networks in EFL classroom. *Journal of Language Teaching and Research,* 13 (1), 110-118, https://doi.org/10.17507/jltr.1301.13

Muharom, F. et al, 2022. Self-directed use of digital devices for out-of-class English learning. *International Journal of Education in Mathematics, Science, and Technology*, 10(1), 257-271. https://doi.org/10.46328/ijemst.2245

O'Doherty, D., et al, 2018. Barriers and solutions to online learning in medical education – an integrative review. *BMC Medical Education,* 18 (130), 1-11. https://doi.org/10.1186/s12909-018-1240-0

Park, J., et al, 2014. University level second language readers' online reading and comprehension strategies. *Language Learning & Technology,* 18(3), 148–172. Retrieved from http://llt.msu.edu/issues/october2014/parkyanghsieh.pdf

Perveen, A, 2016. Synchronous and asynchronous E-language learning: A Case study of virtual university of Pakistan. *Open Praxis,* 8 (1), 21-39. http://dx.doi.org/10.5944/openpraxis.8.1.212

Phanphech, P. et al, 2022. An Analysis of student anxiety affecting on online learning on conceptual applications in physics: Synchronous vs. asynchronous learning. *Educ. Sci.,* 12, 278. https://doi.org/10.3390/educsci12040278

Pouromid, S, 2019. Towards multimodal interactions in multilingual EFL classroom: Lesson from a COIL experience. *Indonesian Journal of Applied Linguistics*, 8, 627-637. Doi: 10.17509/ijal.v8i3.15262.

Purwati, I.T., Suryawati, E., & Eliwarti, 2022. Video lectures in online EFL flipped-classroom: Effectiveness, students' evaluation and experiences. *European Journal of Educational Research,* 11(2), 885-898. https://doi.org/10.12973/eu-jer.11.2.885

Rahaman, I. H. et al, 2021. Online Learning in Bangladesh during COVID-19: Perceived effectiveness, Challenges, and Suggestions, 1 (3). https://doi.org/10.52631/jemds.v1i3.51

Rahimi, A., & Hasheminasab, M, 2020. The Effect of Online vs. Offline Flipped Instruction on EFL Learners' Writing Ability. *Beyond words,* 8 (2), 111-123

Reflianto. et al, 2022. English teachers' competency in flipped learning: question level and questioning strategy in reading comprehension. *International Journal of Instruction,* 15(1), 965-984. https://doi.org/10.29333/iji.2022.15155a

Regmi, K., & Jones, L, 2020. A systematic review of the factors – enablers and barriers – affecting e-learning in health sciences education. *BMC Medical Education,* 20 (91), https://doi.org/10.1186/s12909-020-02007-6

Santoso, M. N, 2021. Utilizing a Facebook closed group for EFL e-learning environment: Students' views. *Studies in English Language and Education,* 8(3), 1026-1044

Suharsih, S., & Wijayanti, M.A. 2020. Online learning for EFL learners: perceptions, challenges, and expectation. *Journal of English Language Studies,* 6 (2)

Sulha, A.H., et al, 2021. The implementation of synchronous and asynchronous learning in English as foreign language setting. *Indonesian Journal of Research and Educational Review,* 1 (1), 17-27. https://doi.org/10.51574/ijrer.v1i1.50

Song, Y. et al, 2021. Online education at the medical school of Tongji University during COVID1-19 pandemic: a cross-sectional study. *BMC Medical Education,* 21, 1-6. https://doi.org/10.1186/s12909-021-02951-x

Szopinski, T., & Bachnik, K, 2022. Student evaluation of online learning during the COVID-19 pandemic. *Technological forecasting & Social Change,* 174, 1-8. https://doi.org/10.1016/j.techfore.2021.121203

Tamine, L., et al, 2019. Offline versus Online Representation Learning of Documents Using External Knowledge. *ACM Trans. Inf. Syst.* 37 (4), https://doi.org/10.1145/3349527

Tang, Y., & Quan, Z, 2022. College classroom English teaching methods and practice based on big data technology. *Wireless Communications and Mobile Computing, 2022*, 1-8. https://doi.org/10.1155/2022/1797726

Thongmak, M. & Ruangwanit, N, 2021. Online Learning vs. Offline learning in an MIS course: Learning outcomes, readiness, and suggestions for the post-COVID-19 world. In Proceedings of The International Conference on Electronic Business, Volume 21 (pp. 312-332). ICEB'21, Nanjing, China

Tour, E., & Barnes, M, 2021. Engaging English language learners in digital multimodal composing: pre-service teachers' perspectives and experiences, *Language and Education*, http://dx.doi.org/10.1080/09500782.2021.1912083.

Wangdi, T., & Shimray, R, 2022. Thai EFL school students' perceptions of using L1 in English Language classrooms. *The Journal of Asia TEFL,* 19 (1), 257-264. http://dx.doi.org/10.18823/asiatefl.2022.19.1.17.257

Warman, J.S. & Gusti, U.A, 2021. Offline versus Online Learning: Biology Department Students' Perceptions during COVID-19 Pandemic. *Bioeducation Journal.* 5 (2), 129-136.

Zaghlool, Z.D, 2020. The impact of using CALL online writing activities on EFL University students' writing achievement. *Theory and Parctice in Language Studies,* 10 (2), 141-148, http://dx.doi.org/10.17507/tpls.1002.01

Zhang, Z., et al, 2022. Evaluating English language teaching quality in classrooms using OLAP and SVM algorithms. *Mobile information systems, 2022*, 1-11. https://doi.org/10.1155/2022/9327669

Zhao, S., et al, 2022. Exploring the Online EFL Classroom Ecology of Middle Schools During the COVID-19 Lockdown. *Theory and Practice in Language Studies,* 12 (1), 65-74. https://doi.org/10.17507/tpls.1201.08

Zou, B., Huang, L., Ma, W., & Qiu, Y. 2021. Evaluation of the effectiveness of EFL online teaching during the COVID-19 pandemic. SAGE Open, 1-17. https://doi.org/10. 1177/21582440211054491.

CLUSTERING TECHNIQUES TO INVESTIGATE ENGAGEMENT AND PERFORMANCE IN ONLINE MATHEMATICS COURSES

Francesco Floris[1], Marina Marchisio[1], Fabio Roman[1], Matteo Sacchet[1] and Sergio Rabellino[2]
[1]*Department of Molecular Biotechnology and Health Sciences, Via Nizza 52 - 10126 Turin, Italy*
[2]*Department of Computer Science, Corso Svizzera 185 - 10149 Turin, Italy*

ABSTRACT

Among the various kinds of learning analytics emerging especially in the latest decade, clicking patterns cover a prominent role, fostered by their success in analyzing several types of data concerning activity on the web. They can be defined as sets of clicks performed by users, in which every set is treated as the basic unit. Few research has been performed on clicking patterns in educational contexts. In this paper, we perform analysis regarding clicks to an online course in Mathematics, aimed at allowing students to follow courses at a distance, both before and after enrolling at University. We used clustering techniques on students learning behavior, which have been defined for this research as visualizations of activities and resources of the course, to detect differences on students' grade according to their online learning behavior. Our results show that students tend to proceed on the course in both activities and resources. There is no correlation between participation and course grades, even if the most active students show higher scores. Moreover, patterns differ significantly according to the degree program of each student, showing the importance of tailored path.

KEYWORDS

Clicking Patterns, Clustering, Digital Education, Learning Analytics, Mathematics Teaching, Open Educational Resources, Open Online Courses

1. INTRODUCTION

The role of learning analytics (Siemens, 2012) has been widely established in studying students' behavior inside online courses. Since big data are extensively used as tools to perform analyses in a plethora of contexts, it is natural to consider their use in educational settings. Indeed, they allow optimizing courses under various aspects, such as structurally and strategically (Marchisio et al., 2019a; Barana et al., 2019). The importance of similar approaches has further increased in the latest few years due to the changes the COVID-19 pandemic required, when modalities such as blended (Ossiannilsson, 2017; Marchisio et al., 2020) and hybrid (Raes et al., 2020; Marchisio et al., 2022) became of common use, with the concrete perspective to retain them also after the definitive end of the emergency.

An analytic that is gaining interest over the years, also because it has already been experimented in other fields, are the click patterns. We can define them as the results of capturing the relationship between clicks, by treating the set of those a user performs as a single unit. Before their consideration in education, they have been widely used for instance as part of web analytics, since they allow a rich representation of mixtures of multiple navigational and informational intents (Duan et al., 2012). The main concept motivating their use is that each click, being it to a web result in a search engine output, or to educational resources and activities in the context of didactics, does not represent in general one unique intent. On the contrary, the intent of the user is often to explore many elements, so it is not possible to assume the presence of a one-to-one relation between clicks and intentions. Therefore, it could be important to aggregate actions to detect the actual presence of these complex mixtures of intents, and to give them, after being identified, a characterization with a meaning in the field of interest, in our case education.

In this paper, we apply click patterns to an online course in Mathematics simply called *Matematica in e-Learning*. This course falls within the *Start@UniTo* project (Marchisio et al., 2019b), started in 2017 and allowing students to follow online courses even before entering University, while they are still high school students. This enables brilliant students to take one or more exams in advance with respect to the first session traditionally available to first year students, thus starting their career in a comfortable way. The courses, which are opened also to university students that wish to study independently, cover disciplines from basically all the usual areas of knowledge: sciences (exact, life, social), humanities, languages, law studies, and so on. Some of them are taught entirely in English, for the sake of internationalization.

The course of *Matematica in e-Learning* is composed of twelve modules, each one corresponding to a topic of Mathematics generally taught during the first years of university in most scientific tracks: they include sets and numbers (01), linear algebra (02), univariate calculus (03-05), differential equations (06), bivariate calculus (07), probability and statistics (08-10), vector-valued functions (11), and numerical analysis (12).

It is usually addressed to students following a path in sciences, but not in the *hardest* STEM disciplines, since a student in Mathematics, Physics or Computer Science requires a more specific mathematical knowledge than what this course can grant. On the other hand, this course can be of interest for students following nonscientific paths since the importance of Mathematics extends also in everyday life and in forming conscious citizens. In this regard, it must be noted that the course is modular: it is not mandatory to require the students to study all the modules, but rather just some of them can be selected for specific paths. Indeed, several paths agreed with the university to consider *Matematica in e-Learning* as a course which is part of their curricula, often as an alternative to the course in Mathematics already present.

This research aims at investigating the differences in students' performance compared to their path in viewing activities and resources. Activities are interactive contents, those who require students to insert some inputs and receive outputs, usually a grade. Resources on the other side are transmissive contents (videos, books, pages, documents). The online course *Matematica in e-Learning* contains 58 activities and 193 resources. Students do not have to view and complete all these contents, the total number for each student depend on their program. The paper is structured as follows: Section 2 deals with some theoretical framework, while Section 3 presents the research questions and describes the methodology used. Section 4 reports all the results and discusses them; finally, some concluding remarks constitute Section 5.

2. THEORETICAL FRAMEWORK

In the last decade, several studies considered click patterns as a tool to analyze and predict students' behavior in the framework of an online course. (Sinha et al., 2014) studied clicks on videos, by considering interactions such as pressing "play" and "pause" or seeking and scrolling forward and backward. They were used to try devising predictions about how long students' interactions within the video lectures were, how much they felt engaged, and which patterns could be profiled as leading to in-video dropouts or stopping to view subsequent videos. (Crossley et al., 2016) combined such an approach with a natural language processing (NLP) analysis; this highlights the feasibility of studying clicks through different disciplines, and in conjunction with other automatic tools giving more points of view. (Tellakat et al., 2019) correlated clicks with psychological and psychometric aspects, but also suggested a wider perspective, by considering peculiarities like stability of clicks during time, temporal significance relative to when they click and study, how the way they click and study influences their final grade. (Rizvi et al., 2020) considered also how students relate with features allowing them to track their progresses via manual intervention designed to require awareness of the learning path. They were divided into three groups, based on how much they marked their activities as completed (all of them, only a part, none of them), and clicks were studied by taking account of this subdivision.

These studies fit into the challenges regarding the use of artificial intelligence (AI) in education (UNESCO, 2019). Two of them are of prominent interest here: the development of quality and inclusive data systems and, in turn, to make research on AI in education significant. Indeed, to possess reliable and timely data is necessary to have algorithms generate correct outputs, since predictions can be complete and accurate only if also the data on which they based are. Therefore, it is important to devote efforts in improving the techniques of analysis themselves too, because an attentive automatization implies the ability to retrieve more and better data in less time. This would allow students to learn better, more, and differently: personalization can be enhanced, better outcomes can result from their learning, and some learning goals unattainable without the use of technology can be obtained, an aspect which some models such as the SAMR (Hamilton et al., 2016) already highlighted.

As for other groundbreaking fields, it is still difficult to devise a theory in the strict sense of the term, since various research groups are developing the matter in different directions, thus requiring yet more time to identify that organic unity which allows for a precise formalization of all the aspects. This does not exclude these researchers from blazing a trail on which to base the search for evidence. In the case of our study, the relations between clicks, time, and grades, are of inspiration, as for some of the authors previously cited, but jointly with methods that we experimented in the context of other research projects. For example, we consider how the digital learning environment we use allows for the insertion of interactive worksheets designed with the Advanced Computing Environment (ACE) *Maple*, which fosters more interactivity and problem-solving skills in students (Fissore et al., 2021). This suggests considering how much students considered worksheets with respect to the overall resources and activities explored, as one of the characteristics useful to draw profiles of the students themselves.

3. RESEARCH QUESTION AND METHODOLOGY

Our research has the goal to find answers to the following questions:

- (RQ1) Which trend exhibits the clicking activity of students? Is it substantially uniform, or on the contrary there is some significance in identifying lower or higher online activity?
- (RQ2) If students use different patterns to learn, are there implications on their performances?
- (RQ3) Which specific patterns characterize the learning behavior of students from different degree programs?

This investigation is divided in two parts. At a first glance, we collected macro data on the students' attendance to the course, to provide an overview of the way students navigate the various type of contents. We considered a subset of students for answering, since we need their final grades for measuring performance, and a certain quota of course accesses and completion to look for statistically significant relations. These students are those who obtained a grade higher than 24/30. We compared on the one hand the final grades, and on the other hand the ratios between how many times students' opened *Maple* worksheets inside the course and the course completion percentages. The idea to construct such an indicator was fostered by observing that these worksheets, being based on an ACE, are more interactive than most of the other materials in the course, thus suggesting looking for a correlation between grades and proportion of study on resources with which students are well able to interact. In the second part, we considered the activity of students who completed the course, which means those who have a grade on the final test, a much smaller number of students compared to the total amount of subscribers, due to the open nature of the course. We decide to limit our analysis on this subset since students who completed the course should have a defined and complete learning pattern, which we defined by two numbers. The first is the percentage between the resources viewed by the user over the total number of resources that each student has to study. The second is the percentage between the activities viewed by the user over the total number of activities that each student has to study. Activities, in this setting, means interactive contents that require students to explore or insert some input. We then performed a clustering on the sample of students using the aggregative k-means algorithm. For the analysis, we used KNIME Analytics Platform 4.6.0. Data were collected from different databases and different systems, since the Digital Learning Environment that hosts the online course makes use of integrated tools. Data were cleaned, even for excluding resources and activities that should not be considered, such as information pages, evaluation questionnaires, activities for the issue of the certificate. Moreover, from the point of view of grades, the highest scores were considered, since students can attempt tests more than one time, even just for studying and reviewing.

4. RESULTS AND DISCUSSION

The overall sample of students who self-subscribed to the course is huge: 4,869 students entered the course at least once, with a slight majority of students from University of Turin (2,665). Globally, as can be seen in Figure 1, there is a similar trend regarding readings (darker line) and interventions (lighter line), with a different order of magnitude. The peaks mainly appear during winter exam sessions (mainly, from December to February), but not during the summer exam sessions. Furthermore, the longest period in which values remained high was the winter part of the academic year 2020-21, when a long wave of the COVID-19 pandemic forced institutions to provide minimal didactics in presence, and so online courses had one more reason to be useful. As a matter of fact, there is no uniformity, even just substantial: the periods of higher activity can be identified in a significant way.

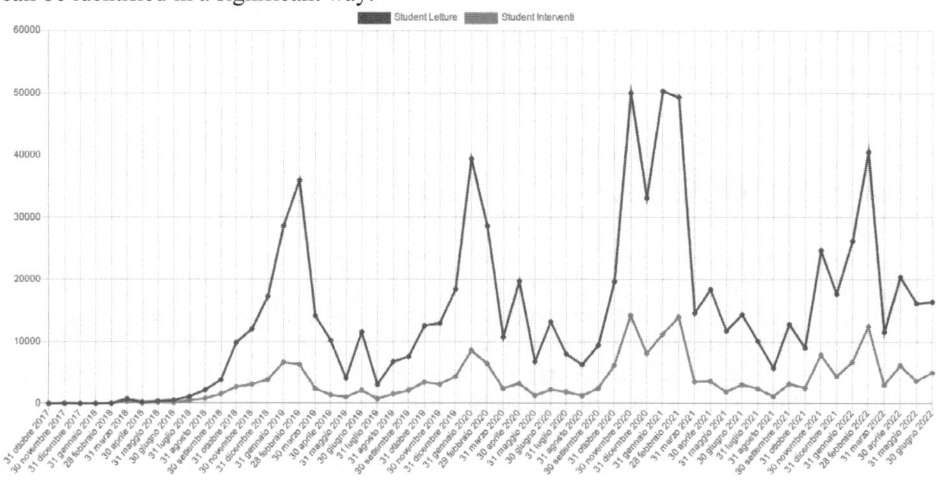

Figure 1. Click activity: Readings and interventions during time

Moreover, Figure 2 shows the scatterplot of ratios of openings of Maple worksheets versus grades. We see that the regression line, depicted as dashed in the plot, does not fit very well with the data: indeed, the Pearson correlation coefficient (PCC) is just about 0.09, highlighting a weak positive relation between the two variables. Another remark regards the quadrants in which the scatterplot is divided: the vertical and the horizontal line performing the division are respectively the median of the ratio and the median of the grades. Under the hypothesis of independence between the two variables, every quadrant should contain 25% of the data. The lower-right quadrant, referring to students obtaining grades below the median despite having a ratio above the median, contains in fact a 20% of the data, a lower value. Albeit not strong, this can be seen as evidence of the fact that accessing the ACE worksheets to a greater relative extent with respect to all the resources and the activities accessed helps to achieve a better performance.

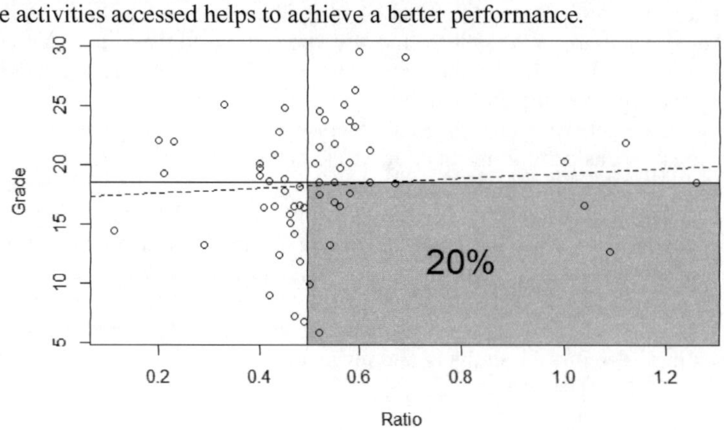

Figure 2. Ratios between ACE worksheet openings and completion percentages, versus final grades

Another statistic considers ordering grades decreasingly and counting how many ratios lie above the median for a certain number of the top grades: under the hypothesis of independence, they should be the half, so for example five in the top 10 and ten in the top 20. Table 1 shows the situation in our case: as depicted, for all the top 10, 20, and 30, the actual ratios above the median are more than half, thus establishing a high-high trend (which in turn implies a low-low trend), rather than exhibiting an independent behavior. Analogously, we can order ratios decreasingly, and count how many grades lie above the median for a certain number of the top ratios: again, Table 1 depicts how for all the top 10, 20, and 30, the actual grades above the median are more than half, so the previous considerations still hold.

Table 1. Number of ratios above median among best grades and number of grades above median among best ratios

Best grades	Expected ratios above median	Actual ratios above median	Best ratios	Expected grades above median	Actual grades above median
Top 10	5	8	Top 10	5	6
Top 20	10	14	Top 20	10	14
Top 30	15	18	Top 30	15	18

Table 1 confirm the presence of a positive relation between preferring ACE worksheets and obtaining better grades at the exam, which is not powerful, but it is also not negligible. Different learning patterns imply changes in how students perform, even if not extremely marked.

For the second part of the analysis, we collected the data of 237 students who completed the course (they submitted the final test). Figure 3 shows the scatterplot of users according to usage of resources and activities (scaled with respect to the different program that each student must follow) and the clustering output (the color of the points). Indeed, to grant a substantial equivalence between the *Matematica in e-learning* course and its in-person equivalent course (and thus avoiding students to select the simpler one, rather than basing the selection on the preferred modalities), the topics to be declared part of the exam had to be tuned on each path. For example, in the paths where probability and statistics were already part of the program, the relative modules were present at the exam, while in the paths lacking the (compulsory) study of probability and statistics, these modules were not included in the exam. Of course, students have in all cases access to every module, allowing them to explore and study at their will, regardless of what is mandatory (and part of the exam) for their track.

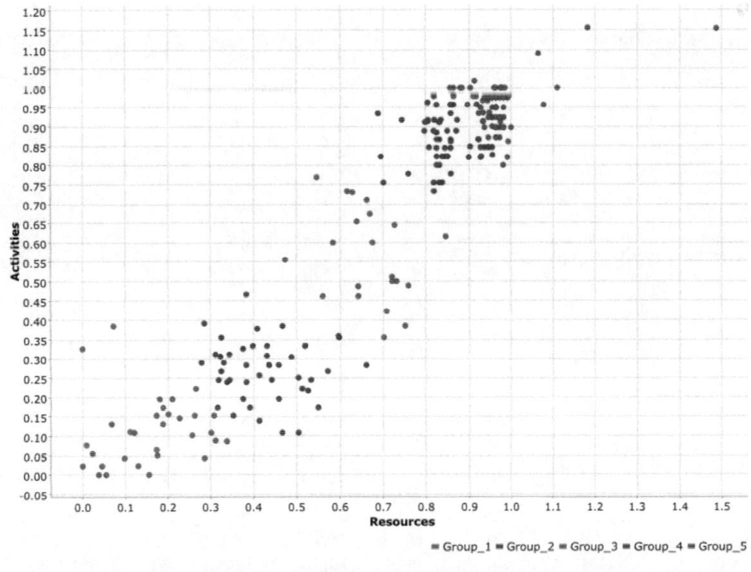

Figure 3. Scatterplot of students with respect to resources and activities viewed divided into 5 groups

Most of the students lies on the diagonal, meaning that they tend to perform in the same way activities and resources, the PCC is 0.8, a strong correlation. It must be noted that, even if the values of the grids are in percentages, there are some points which lie above 1 in both directions: this is due to the fact that the online course is completely open, so even if students choose the degree program in the online course and the system shows them just the related contents, they can anytime modify their choice and attend more than expected. The analysis considered just the last degree program choice of the user. Clustering algorithm divided the sample of students into 5 groups which differ in general for the number of online contents they viewed. After checking the goodness of the algorithm for different number of partitions, we opted for 5 clusters since it is a good turning point for the Sum of Squared Error (SSE), with more than 5 partitions the reduction of the SSE is not significant.

Moreover, as it can be seen from the boxplot in Figure 4, going from the group with less active students to the group with most active students there is a general tendence of increasing scores, in the boxplot the displayed scores are the median score and the quartiles. Students in Group 1 have larger dispersion since excellent students who do not need too much study belong together with less active and performing ones. Dispersion has a general tendence of decreasing, too. Every group contains low and high performing students, the difference is in the numerosity.

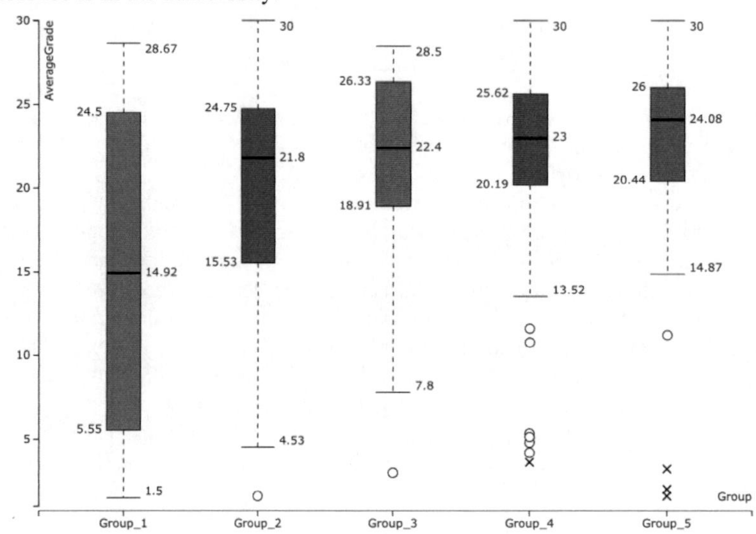

Figure 4. Conditional boxplot showing the distribution of grades with respect to the 5 clusters

Table 2. Number of ratios above median among best grades and number of grades above median among best ratios

Degree programs	Group 1		Group 2		Group 3		Group 4		Group 5	
	Count	Average	Count	Average	Count	Average	Count	Average	Count	Average
Biotechnology	0	0.0	2	26.4	1	24.4	2	24.6	0	0.0
Chemistry and Chemical Technologies	18	17.8	18	16.7	2	15.1	3	21.7	8	17.8
Pharmaceutical Chemistry and Technology	1	3.8	4	16.1	0	0.0	9	18.0	3	24.3
Pharmacy	1	27.8	0	0.0	5	23.1	2	29.0	2	24.4
Materials Science and Technology	2	3.7	0	0.0	0	0.0	0	0.0	1	20.6
Biological sciences	0	0.0	0	0.0	0	0.0	1	21.0	3	21.4
Agricultural Sciences and Technology	1	28.0	3	23.8	4	20.6	6	25.2	24	21.6
Forestry and Environmental Sciences	2	4.8	0	0.0	0	0.0	0	0.0	8	23.6
Natural Sciences	5	12.8	15	21.2	9	21.6	34	21.3	16	25.1
Strategic Sciences	0	0.0	0	0.0	0	0.0	0	0.0	1	25.2
Food Technology	1	6.8	2	24.3	0	0.0	1	19.1	11	24.3
Viticulture and Enology	0	0.0	1	26.0	0	0.0	1	28.0	4	24.2
Total / Average	**31**	**15.08**	**45**	**19.62**	**21**	**21.27**	**59**	**21.67**	**81**	**22.80**

Since students from different degree programs can attend the online course, we checked the number of students in the clusters for each degree program, as it can be seen in Table 2.

There is a large difference in the behavior of students according to their program. Students in Agricultural programs (Agricultural Sciences and Technology, Forestry and Environmental Sciences, Food Technology, Viticulture and Enology) who have the same study materials tend to view and complete most resources and activities since most of them are in Group 5. This is tendentially also true for students in Natural Sciences, where most of them are in Group 4, with Group 5 following as the second greatest one. Moreover, Group 5 in Natural Sciences has the greatest average grade among programs with more than three students. Students in the pharmaceutical sector concentrate on Groups 3, 4 and 5, thus they are quite active in online course attendance. On the other side, students in Chemistry and Chemical Technologies belong more to Groups 1 and 2. Some courses do not present enough students, they will be considered in the future when more data will be collected. It can also be noted that the online course *Matematica in e-learning* is not used in the same way by students of different program, and this suggests an implementation of online contents that are more suited to the training needs of students.

5. CONCLUSION

We can see that different students behaved differently. Of course, every student has his or her favorite ways to study and learn, and so we cannot exclude the personal component from these considerations. Moreover, they can explore different kinds of objects, either during a single session or in diverse sessions. The investigation of clicking patterns allowed us to determine some information about students' engagement and how they perform during the course, consequently resulting in certain grades at the exam. The answer to RQ1, relating students' patterns to the discriminant values that we choose of resources and activities, shows a quite uniform trend: students tend to complete both activities and resources in the same relative amount. Moreover, as it was seen from the first part of the analysis, the uniformity does not hold with respect to time: there is higher students' activity in the cold months, while winter exams are in program, thus in future elaborations even the time of access could be considered. We answered RQ2 by considering the average grade for each of the group that were created by the clustering algorithm, containing students with similar patterns. As a general remark, students with more visualization of resources and activities tend to have higher scores in the final test, thus it is clear that online attendance is important for the preparation of students, even though it was not supervised due to the open modality of teaching. Other specific indexes considered the interactivity of the resources and activities students explored. We detected how the more they use ACE worksheets, the more they are prone to perform well, by obtaining good grades. Finally, to answer RQ3 we analyzed the presence on each group of students from the different degree programs: there is a tendency even in this case, students from the same degree program seems to belong to the same clusters.

As future work, we would like to extend our inquiry to include a more systematic analysis of those patterns with automatized tools. The main challenge lies in dealing with massive databases, to be queried with detailed requests not so simple to connect, giving results that can require much work for their interpretation. It is also possible to consider a larger number of students (not just those who complete the final test) and study and predict their behavior, according to these indicators and to other ones that can be extracted from the data, with more than two parameters. It will help gaining further evidence regarding how students click on online platforms, their engagement and performance.

Another analysis we would like to conduct is related to the relationship between course content. The goal will be to understand how students move from one resource to another (also from a time perspective) and try to find common paths. In this way, on the one hand, we can find possible marginal content (which is perceived as disconnected from others within the course), and on the other hand, identify paths of content enjoyment that can then be proposed to other students who are in similar situations.

REFERENCES

Barana, A. et al., 2019. Learning analytics to improve formative assessment strategies. *Journal of E-Learning and Knowledge Society*, Vol. 15, No. 3, pp. 75-88.

Crossley, S. et al., 2016. Combining click-stream data with NLP tools to better understand MOOC completion. *Proceedings of the 6th International Conference on Learning Analytics and Knowledge (LAK)*, Edinburgh, UK, pp. 6-14.

Duan, H. et al., 2012. Click patterns: An empirical representation of complex query intents. *Proceedings of the 21st International Conference on Information and Knowledge Management (CIKM)*, ACM, Maui, USA, pp. 1035-1044.

Fissore, C. et al. 2021. Development of Problem Solving Skills with Maple in Higher Education. In: Corless R.M., Gerhard J., Kotsireas I.S. (eds.) Maple in Mathematics Education and Research. MC 2020. Communications in Computer and Information Science, Vol. 1414. Springer, Cham.

Hamilton, E.R. et al., 2016. The Substitution Augmentation Modification Redefinition (SAMR) Model: a Critical Review and Suggestions for its USE. *TechTrends*, Vol. 60, pp. 433-441.

Marchisio, M. et al., 2019a. Boosting up data collection and analysis to learning analytics in open online contexts: An assessment methodology. *Journal of E-Learning and Knowledge Society*, Vol. 15, No. 3, pp. 49-59.

Marchisio, M. et al., 2019b. Start@unito: Open Online Courses for Improving Access and for Enhancing Success in Higher Education. *Proceedings of the 11th International Conference on Computer Supported Education (CSEDU)*, Heraklion, Greece, Vol. 1, pp. 639-646.

Marchisio, M. et al., 2020. Teaching Mathematics in Scientific Bachelor Degrees Using a Blended Approach. *Proceedings of IEEE 44th Annual Computer Software and Applications Conference (COMPSAC)*, IEEE, virtual, pp. 190-195.

Marchisio, M. et al., 2022. Valuable features of hybrid teaching in a higher education context. *Proceedings of European Distance and E-Learning Network Conference*, EDEN, Tallinn, Estonia, in press.

Ossiannilsson, E., 2017. Blended Learning State of the Nation. *International Council for Open and Distance Education (ICDE).*

Raes, A. et al, 2020. A systematic literature review on synchronous hybrid learning: gaps identified. *Learning Environments Research*, Vol. 23, pp. 269-290.

Rizvi, S. et al., 2020. Investigating variation in learning processes in a FutureLearn MOOC. *Journal of Computing in Higher Education*, Vol. 32, pp. 162-181.

Siemens, G., 2012. Learning analytics: envisioning a research discipline and a domain of practice. *2nd International Conference on Learning Analytics and Knowledge (ACM)*, Vancouver, Canada, pp. 4-8.

Sinha, T. et al., 2014. Your click decides your fate: Inferring Information Processing and Attrition Behavior from MOOC Video Clickstream Interactions. *Proceedings of the 2014 Conference on Empirical Methods in Natural Language Processing (EMNLP)*, ACL, Doha, Qatar, pp. 3-14.

Tellakat, M. et al., 2019. How do online learners study? The psychometrics of students' clicking patterns in online courses. *PloS ONE*, Vol. 14, No. 3, pp. 1-17.

UNESCO, 2019. Artificial Intelligence in Education: Challenges and Opportunities for Sustainable Development. *Working Papers on Education Policy*, 07.

MIDDLE SCHOOL STUDENTS' INFORMATION AND COMMUNICATION LITERACY DEFICITS STUDY

Svetlana Avdeeva[1] and Alexander Uvarov[2]
[1]*Institute of Education at National Research University Higher School of Economics, Moscow, Russia. National Training Foundation. Moscow, Russia*
[2]*The Federal Research Centre "Computer Science and Control" of the Russian Academy of Sciences. Institute of Education, National Research University Higher School of Economics, Moscow, Russia*

ABSTRACT

Some results of the basic school (14 years old) students' information and communication competence (ICC) in the digital environment study are discussed. About 30,000 students (14 years old) took part in the study. Information and Communication Literacy is considered as the ability to use digital technologies to search, manage, integrate, evaluate and create information. It is one of the key competencies that all of basic school graduates should obtain. As the availability of digital technologies grows, the gap in the ability of students to use them productively becomes more and more noticeable. The study identifies the actual students' information and communication competencies deficits at the stage of middle school completion. Performance-based online Information and Communication Literacy test (ICL-test) was the main research tool of the study. An attempt was made to determine to what extent the level of students' ICC is related to the work of the school, and to what extent it depends on the extracurricular environment. The results of the study indicate a strong connection between the ICC of ninth graders and their out-of-school environment and a weak connection with the work of the school. The reasons for the insufficient level of the ICC in a significant part of the graduates of the basic school are discussed and recommendations for its increase are proposed. It was found that ICL-test is a reliable online instrument to measure students' information and communication competence.

KEYWORDS

ICT-Based Assessment, Information-Communication Literacy, Testing, Middle School Graduates

1. INTRODUCTION

As the availability of digital technologies grows, the gap in the ability of students to use them productively becomes more and more noticeable. A new digital divide is growing, driven by inequality between those who are able to use digital transformation for productive work and those who can only use it at the substitution level (Warschauer, 2012). The growth of a new digital divide leads to an increase in the number of "digital outsiders" who are vulnerable to manipulation and attacks in Internet services, hindering their participation in the digital economy. It exacerbates the educational inequality of students belonging to different social groups. The ability of each graduate of the basic school to act productively in the digital information environment (information and communication competence) is a key condition for overcoming the new digital divide. The OECD recommends by law all member countries regularly assess the digital literacy of schoolchildren (OECD, 2021). According to the state educational standard, information and communication competence (ICC) is one of the main meta-subject competencies that the main school's graduates should possess. The formation of this competence is considered as one of the tasks of preparing students for life in the information society. However, until recently, there was no reliable valid tool for conducting a mass ICC assessment of the main school graduates (the ninth grade students). Assessment of information and communication competence of students is the task of assessing educational achievements in a complex subject area and requires the use of ICT tools. To carry it out in a public school, it is necessary not only to develop a new measuring tool but also to create conditions in schools for such an assessment. There are such conditions in public schools today.

According to the national educational standard, ICC of students is one of the main meta-subject competence that graduates of the basic school should have. The full formation of this competence is considered an important task in preparing students for life in the information society. ICC is necessary for young people to increase their readiness for life in a digital economy, and the daily use of cyberspace resources to continue education throughout life. However, until recently, there was no reliable and valid tool for conducting a mass assessment of the ICC among students in the 9th grade (graduates of the basic school). Such a tool was recently developed and proved to be valid (Avdeeva et al. 2017). The task of assessing the information and communication competence of students belongs to the class "Evaluation of learning progress in complex subject areas." To run such an assessment, it is necessary not only to develop a new measuring tool but also to create conditions for such an assessment in schools. Today, most schools have such conditions.

The information and Communication Literacy test (ICL-test) (Avdeeva et al. 2017) was the main tool of our research. ICL-test is a modern intelligent online-based instrument. It uses performance-based assessment and consists of scenario-based items, which simulate the main features of students' real-life situations. The innovativeitems were developed according to an evidence-centered Design methodology (Mislevy et al. 2012). All scenario-based items simulate features of students' real-life situations. ICL-test uses Bayesian networks to process the test results (Mislevy, 2018). The ICC assessment in our study was a low-stakes one. It just informs test-takers, and their teachers about students' actual information and communication literacy levels and gaps in their development found.

The purpose of our study was to assess the extent to which the mainstream school solves the problem of forming the ICC in ninth-grade students. At the same time, it was necessary to check to what extent the achieved level of ICC of schoolchildren is related to the development of the digital educational environment in school, and to what extent it is related to the students' out-of-school environment. In the course of the study, along with the assessment of the ICL of ninth-graders, an Internet survey of teachers and school leaders was conducted on the use of ICT in the learning process. The study also needed to test the extent to which the new online tool is suitable for assessing the student ICC in a public school.

2. METHODOLOGY

The study was conducted in 2020 and covered graduates of the basic school in 21 regions of the country. All ninth-grade students in the selected regions were considered as the general population of the sample. Classes were randomly added to the formed sample (classes less than 6 or more than 30 students were discarded). The selection of classes was carried out separately among urban and rural schools in proportion to the total sample size and their representation in the general population. More than 30,000 ninth-graders took part in the study. Simultaneously with the students' ICC assessment, a survey was conducted of teachers who taught in the classes where the testing was carried out, as well as school leaders.

The students' information and communication competence were considered as the ability to use digital technologies to search, manage, integrate, evaluate and create information (ETS, 2002). The used ICC framework includes seven components:

- Correctly describe the problem for purposeful search and processing of information;
- Search and find information from various sources in different digital environments;
- Organize and classify information according to various criteria;
- Interpret and reconstruct information, highlight the main thing, compare data from different sources,
- Evaluate the quality, relevance, and usefulness of the information and its sources;
- Process, create/adapt information taking into account the problem being solved and give arguments confirming the correctness of the result obtained;
- Communicate information tailored to specific audiences.

The ICL-test developers analyzed the extent to which the results of the ICC assessment make it possible to judge the readiness of ninth graders for life in the modern digital world, including their readiness for education and work (Milsom, Curry, 2017; Kyllonen, 2012; Soule, Warrick, 2015; Tannenbaum et al., 2019). On this basis, the level of ICC was determined, which is necessary for a graduate of a basic school to work with information for further self-development and self-education, continue studies or work in an ICT-rich environment without additional training. A representative group of international experts has prepared a readiness standard that linked the required "readiness" to the five levels of the ICC for ninth-graders (Table 1).

Table 1. Abilities Corresponding to Different ICL Levels of Ninth Grade Students

ICL level	Abilities
Advanced	The student performs the tasks at a high level, related to abilities to: ▪ Formulate the problem correctly; ▪ Find information from different sources; ▪ Organize information according to certain criteria; ▪ Assess the quality of information and the reliability of its sources; ▪ Compare and synthesize information from different sources; ▪ Draw the right conclusions from existing information; ▪ Present information to other people.
Above basic	The student performs the tasks at a high level, related to abilities to: ▪ Formulate the problem correctly; ▪ Find information from different sources; ▪ Organize information according to certain criteria; ▪ Draw the right conclusions from existing information; ▪ Share information with other people. The student performs the tasks at a satisfactory level, related to abilities to: ▪ Assess the quality of information and the reliability of its sources; ▪ Compare and synthesize information from different sources..
Basic	The student performs the tasks at a satisfactory level, related to abilities to: ▪ Formulate the problem correctly; ▪ Find information from different sources; ▪ Organize information according to certain criteria; ▪ Assess the quality of information and the reliability of its sources; ▪ compare and synthesize information from different sources; ▪ Draw the right conclusions from existing information; ▪ Share information with other people.
Below basic	The student performs the tasks at a satisfactory level, related to abilities to: ▪ Formulate the problem correctly; ▪ Find information from different sources; ▪ Organize information according to certain criteria; ▪ Assess the quality of information and the reliability of its sources; ▪ Compare and synthesize information from different sources; ▪ Draw the right conclusions from existing information; ▪ Share information with other people.
Developing	The student fails to perform the tasks related to abilities to: ▪ Formulate the problem correctly; ▪ Find information from different sources; ▪ Organize information according to certain criteria; ▪ Draw the right conclusions from existing information; ▪ Share information with other people.

During the use of the ICL-test, students are immersed in the digital environment of the tool. The ICL-test computer environment uses a common user interface (browser, text editor, e-mail, etc.) that is similar to, but not the same as, the interface of widely used software tools. This made it possible to level the experience of using various specific applications by the testers. The experiments show that ninth-graders successfully operate in the environment with models of general user applications at a basic level.

The ICL-test automatically processes the results during testing, informs the student about the level of his/her ICC, and offers recommendations for its development immediately after the test is completed. Thus, the ICL test can be used both for the resulting (monitoring studies) and for the formative (during the educational process) assessment of the ICC level.

The developed tool became the subject of a patent for an invention (Patent…, 2018). It has gained international recognition: the University of Helsinki is localizing it for use in Finland, while the Inter-American Development Bank is adapting it for Latin American countries.

3. RESULTS

The research show (Figure 1) that about one-third of students (29.6%) have a basic level of ICC. 12.4% are at the level above the basic level, and 3.4% are at the advanced level. Thus, less than half of ninth-graders (45.4%) are fully prepared for life in the digital economy. More than a third of all students are below the basic level (35.3%). There is a need to correct their ICC in order to reach the baseline (and above) level. For those who are at the developing level (19.3%), additional classes are not enough: here systematic work is required for the specially organized development of their ICC.More than a quarter of rural school students (25.6%) turned out to be at the developing level. At the advanced level, they are almost half as many as in urban schools (1.9% versus 4.1%). Unlike a city, in a rural area, a school is practically the only institution to provide all students with the conditions to work with digital equipment, software, and digital resources (individual learning tasks, joint projects, online courses, etc.) to develop of their ICC (search and find information, organize, interpret, evaluate and process it with the help of digital transformation).

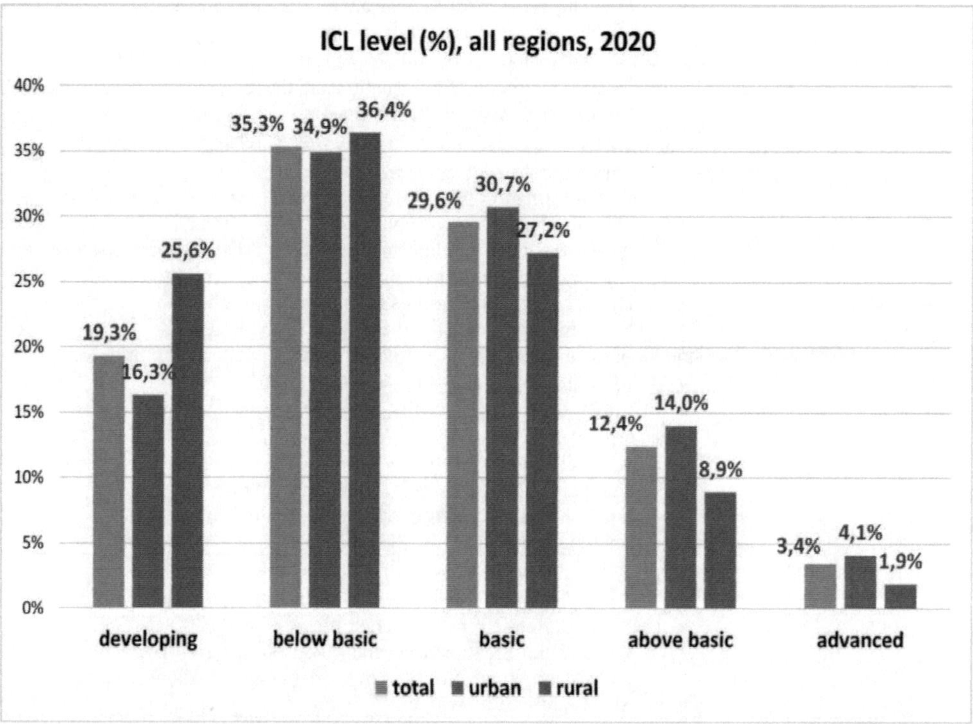

Figure 1. The ICC level of ninth graders in 2020

The study indicates a significant gap between the ICC of graduates from urban and rural schools. Although the type of distribution (left-skewed) of test results for both is the same, the number of graduates of rural schools at the "developing level" turned out to be one and a half times more (25.6% versus 16.3%). At the "above basic" level, graduates from rural schools turned out to be one and a half times less than urban ones (8.9% versus 14%), and at the advanced level, two times less (1.9% versus 4.1%). At the same time, the gap in the share of urban and rural school graduates who are at the "below basic" and "basic" levels is not so large. This gives grounds to assume the presence of a systemic problem that impedes the formation of ICC in the conditions of a mass school.

The ICL test was developed with the method of evidence-based argumentation. Therefore, the analysis of the behavioral characteristics of the test-takers, which is embedded in the patterns of test tasks, makes it possible to indicate the students' abilities they demonstrate freely from those that are difficult to demonstrate.

Many ninth graders were unable to compare and generalize information from different sources, evaluate its quality, and organize it according to specified criteria. Completing the task of preparing an information product (small article) in accordance with the task and using the available material, the majority of those tested (61.2%), despite the detailed instructions (which were an integral part of the task), could not organize the available material in accordance with standard structure (title, introduction, body, etc.). The majority of those tested (85.3%) could not select relevant information for their text (the content of the article they prepared did not correspond to the task).

When completing the slide preparation task (give an informative answer to a question on a given topic), 58.1% of students were unable to formulate a relevant title and insert the missing captions on the graph. 65.7% of students could not select relevant information from the available data array, and 67.6% could not correctly correlate the material they chose with the title. When preparing a presentation on a given topic, the majority of ninth-graders (76.2%) were unable to build a coherent story using the materials available to them (drawings, graphs, texts, and tables). The majority (83.3%) did not cope with the task of linking the materials at their disposal into a coherent information product (sequence of slides in a presentation), which contains complete information that meets the task.

When completing the task of their profile design on a social network (a life situation close to them), 75.1% of ninth-graders were unable to select information in accordance with its purpose and submit it with confidentiality requirements. Not all ninth-graders coped with the tasks of classifying and organizing information. 71.6% of students were unable to sort information objects according to their purpose (organize emails into folders), and more than 85.5% were unable to delete spam (letters containing advertising). More than half of the students (56%) were able to formulate a specific search query to solve their task.

A significant part (about 60%) of the graduates of the middle school turned out to be unable to assess the quality of information and the reliability of its sources, compare and generalize information from different sources, draw correct conclusions based on existing information, integrate information according to specified rules, and interpret the results obtained. The performance of the relevant operations during the ICL test caused significant difficulties for more than half of the students

At the same time, the majority of those tested demonstrated the ability to transfer information to other people, create search queries, and use various digital services. About 80% are able (by chatting) to ask clarifying questions that help solve the problem under discussion. Many ninth-graders can visualize information: 46.6% are aware of the expediency of visualization, and 54.2% used visualization in their information product as arguments.

Students generally demonstrate good technical skills. The majority (91.8%) are able to choose the right tools when working on social networks. Many ninth-graders are able to choose the appropriate tools (in the application interface) to solve the problem they are facing (79.5%). More than half (66.4%) are well versed in digital services. The majority (68.3%) successfully work in the interfaces of e-books, as well as digital learning instruments (68.3%).

The collected data shows, that more than 90% of graduates of the basic school actively use modern digital devices. 93% of students believe that they can freely use the Internet for their own purposes, and the time they spend on the Internet for educational purposes does not exceed 15%.

It can be stated that the technological digital divide is decreasing. At the same time, data on ICT use patterns by ninth graders show that the time they spend watching videos, listening to music, or using various services is weakly related to their level of ICC. The use of ICT to perform routine operations (telephony, video viewing, text exchange, etc.) does not reduce the new digital divide - the inequality between those who are able to use ICT for productive work with information, and those who use them at the substitution level (SAMR). This is also evidenced by the revealed relationship between the ICC level of ninth-graders and their work in office applications and viewing content on specialized sites. The results of the study show a strong relationship between the ICC of ninth graders and their out-of-school environment and a weak relationship with the work of the school.

4. CONCLUSION

1. The study showed that less than half of the graduates of the basic school (45.4%) demonstrate a level of competence that corresponds to readiness for life in the digital economy. Most students were unable to demonstrate:
   - the ability to critically evaluate the reliability and value of information,
   - the ability to make responsible decisions about what information should be published in the public domain and what should not,
   - the ability to make your information products as informative and effective as possible.

2. A weak relationship has been found between the level of the students' ICC and the school's digital educational environment development. This confirms the notion that increasing the availability of digital devices (reducing the technological digital divide) does not lead by itself to bridging the second digital divide. The school focuses mainly on reproductive learning today. Teachers use ICT mainly at the level of substitution and/or improvement level according to SAMR (presentations in frontal learning work). Although over 90% of school administrators declare the importance of the ICT to improve educational outcomes and 78% of teachers say that they have access to ICT at school, more than a third of all respondents (39%) answered that using ICT is not among their priorities.
3. The results show that the ICC level of ninth-graders is strongly related to their out-of-school environment (mother's education, plans to continue education, possession of a smartphone, and number of books at home). At the same time, the connection between the ICC of ninth-graders and the opportunity to work in the digital environment of the school is weak.
4. The study showed that the ICL-test makes it possible to carry out an automated assessment of the ICC of schoolchildren quite simply and reliably. The development of a digital educational environment and the connection of schools to the Internet create favorable conditions for the widespread use of such a tool and its derivatives in a public school. Further research and development are needed, which will allow in real-time give individualized (targeted) recommendations for increasing the level of ICC for each student, his parents, and teachers. The use of AI and big data will automate the preparation of analytical reports for school leaders, heads of education, and methodologists to improve the work of the school and bring continuous formative assessment of students' ICC into the everyday work of the public school.

ACKNOWLEDGEMENT

The article was prepared in the framework of a research grant funded by the Ministry of Science and Higher Education of the Russian Federation (grant ID: 075-15-2022-325).

REFERENCES

Avdeeva S., et al, 2017. Assessing Information and Communication Technology Competence of Students: Approaches, Tools, Validity and Reliability of Results. *Educational Studies Moscow*. No. 4, pp. 104—132. (in Russian)

ETS, 2002. Digital Transformation for ICT Literacy: A Report of the International ICT Literacy Panel, ETS, 2002. https://www.ets.org/research/policy_research_reports/publications/report/2002/cjik

Kyllonen P.C., 2012. Measurement of 21st Century Skills within the Common Core State Standards. *Paper presented at the Invitational Research Symposium on Technology Enhanced Assessments*. May 7–8, 2012. https://www.ets.org/research/policy_research_reports/publications/paper/2012/jvhx

Milsom A., Curry J.R., 2017. Career and College Readiness Counseling in P-12 Schools. https://www.semanticscholar.org/paper/Career-and-College-Readiness-Counseling-in-P-12-Milsom-Curry/c85fe56fad9b5c906360107cc8221ef4ab9e102a

Mislevy R. J., et al, 2012. Design and discovery in educational assessment: Evidence-centered design, psychometrics, and educational data mining. *Journal of Educational Data Mining*, 4(1), 11-48.

Mislevy R.J., 2018. *Sociocognitive Foundations of Educational Measurement*. N.-Y.: Routledge.

OECD, 2021. Recommendation of the Council on Children in the Digital Environment. OECD / LEGAL / 0389. Amended on: 30/05/2021. https://legalinstruments.oecd.org/en/instruments/OECD-LEGAL-0389%20

Patent for invention №2656699. ICL-test - an instrument for measuring information and communication literacy in digital environment. Authors: Avdeeva et al. Date of state registration in the State Register of Inventions of the Russian Federation on June 6, 2018.

Soulé H., Warrick T., 2015. Defining 21st Century Readiness for All Students: What We Know and How to Get There./ *Psychology of Aesthetics, Creativity, and the Arts.* Vol. 9(2). P. 178–186. http://doi: 10.1037/aca0000017

Tannenbaum R., et al., 2019. Skills for a New Economy: What the Workforce of Tomorrow Needs Today ETS report. https://www.ets.org/s/sne/pdf/skills-for-a-new-economy-report.pdf

Warschauer M., 2012. The digital divide and social inclusion // *Americas Quarterly*. Vol. 6 (2). P. 131-135.

DETERMINING LEARNERS' BEHAVIORAL PATTERNS IN A TECHNOLOGY AND ANALYTICS ENHANCED ASSESSMENT ENVIRONMENT

Muhittin Şahin[1] and Dirk Ifenthaler[1,2]
[1]*University of Mannheim, Mannheim, Germany*
[2]*Curtin University, Australia*

ABSTRACT

Within digitally-supported learning environments, learners need to observe themselves so that they can reflect on their strengths and weaknesses and take a step toward autonomous learning. Within the scope of this research, a technology and analytics enhanced assessment environment in which students can assess themselves was implemented and tested. In order to determine $N = 108$ students' ability to use the assessment environment, behavioral patterns were determined based on their individual characteristics, system interactions, lesson performances, achievement motivation, confidence, and study interest. Findings indicate different system usage and behavioral engagement with the assessment system. The outcomes of this design-based research project indicate hints on how such assessment systems can be made more effective in future implementation stages.

KEYWORDS

Computer Classification Testing, Learner Behavioral Pattern, Behavioral Engagement, Optimal Scaling

1. INTRODUCTION

Assessment is a basic component of effective learning (Bransford, Brown, & Cocking, 2000). Learning and teaching processes should be assessment-centered to develop learning (Gikandi, Morrow, & Davis, 2011). At this point, web-based assessment systems provide important opportunities (Pachler et al., 2010). These systems are named in different ways such as Computer Based Assessment, Computerized Testing, and Computer-Administered Testing, and the goal of these systems carry out assessment activities via technology (Redecker, 2013). In such assessment environments, immediate feedback can be provided to learners and scoring can be done instantly. Nowadays, it is seen that especially Computer Adaptive Testing (CAT) and Computerized Classification Testing (CCT) applications are developed and presented frequently as a technology and analytics enhanced assessment system. Technology and analytics-enhanced assessment systems are required to include flexible, adaptable, automated reports for the management of large amounts of data, analysis of unstructured data, immediate feedback to both instructors and learners, and educational decision-making (Ifenthaler, 2022).

On the other hand, learners need to observe themselves (Boud, 2000), so that learners can realize their strengths and weaknesses (Gikandi, Morris, & Davis, 2011) to self-assess and take a step toward autonomous learning. Self-assessment plays a key role in formative assessment (Andrade & Valtcheva, 2009). Educational tests are used to develop students' understanding (Bull & McKenna, 2004). Educational testing is used to make judgments about the individuals' progress, status, or accomplishments to make decisions about learning, instruction, and educational policy (AERA, 2014). It is seen that the tests contribute to the monitoring of the students' development (Rudman, 1989).

In the scope of this research, CCT was used as a technology and analytics enhanced assessment system. The CCT aims to classify the students into two or more categories rather than determine their ability estimate (Lin & Spray, 2000). Besides this, the item pools of the classification tests need not be as large as the adaptive tests (Parshall et al., 2002). Since there are limited items and the students are classified according to their achievements, the CCT environment was presented to the students within the scope of this research. CCT has various goals in the learning process such as; a) making a judgment about the students, b) assessing the learning process, c) assessing the students and school groups, and d) making a judgment about the quality of the education (van Groen, 2012).

Interactions of learners in assessment systems constitute their assessment experiences. These experiences differ according to the individual characteristics of the learners. The motivation of learners is important for their assessment experience (Vaessen et al, 2017). On the other hand, study interest is related to the perceived support of motivation, autonomy, and competence (Müller & Louw, 2004). In addition to the above-mentioned, acceptance structures are known to affect the use of e-assessment systems (Deutsch, et al., 2012). In this context, study interest, achievement motivation, and acceptance structures (perceived usefulness and intended use) were considered as individual learner characteristics in this study.

In this context, a CCT environment was implemented in which students can assess themselves and determine whether they are masters or non-masters in a subject. To determine the students' ability to use these environments more effectively and efficiently, behavioral patterns were determined based on their individual characteristics. Learners' CCT system interactions, lesson performances, achievement motivation, confidence, study interest, and acceptance structure were examined.

2. METHOD

2.1 Participants

Participants of this design-based research study included $N = 108$ students from an European university in the area of economic and business education. Two-thirds (67%; $N_F = 72$) of the participants are female and 33% ($N_M = 36$) are male students. Participants' average age was 23.42 years ($SD = 2.69$) while they studied for an average of 5.8 semesters ($SD = 1.50$). Students interacted with the assessment system where they could assess themselves throughout the semester (12 weeks). Ethics consent was obtained for this research.

2.2 Computer Classification Testing Environment

The aim of Computer Classification Testing (CCT) is to group learners into two or more categories (Weiss, 1982; van Groen, 2012). Two categories (Spray & Reckase, 1994; Huebner, 2012; van Groen, Eggen, & Veldkamp, 2016) and three and more categories (Eggen & Straetmans, 2000; Nydick, Nozawa, & Zhu, 2012) CCT Classification tests are frequently used for classification and licensing (Parshall et al., 2002). CCT is an effective test method that aims to classify students into groups with the least number of items by reducing classification errors (Thompson, 2007). For this purpose, in this study CCT environment was presented to the learners that classify the learners based on the Sequential Probability Ratio Test (SPRT) algorithm. SPRT was put forward by Wald (1947) and it tries to decide which of the two simple hypotheses is more correct. If the aim of a test is to classify individuals into two or more categories instead of predicting the ability or skill levels of individuals, SPRT which selects and applies the most appropriate items based on statistical hypothesis testing can be applied as a CCT procedure (Spray & Reckase, 1996). The primary focus of CCT applications with SPRT is to determine individuals' competency levels according to a standard (Parshall et al., 2002). The SPRT algorithm is less complex, more practical, and needs less time for rendering by computers (Frick, 1990). Frick (1992) found that the SPRT algorithm can classify a student as master or non-master in an average of ten items. Since there are not too many items in the item pool, SPRT which can give the most effective result with fewer items were used in this study.

A CCT environment was provided to students, where they were able to test themselves on a specific subject whenever and wherever they wanted. Learners are classified into two categories as master and non-master by the system. The CCT environment provided tests to the learners on five subjects: a) research process, b) research design, c) statistical correlation, d) statistical differences, and e) research quality criteria. However, there were limited items available for the corresponding lecture. Accordingly, the SPRT algorithm, which can work effectively with a limited number of items, was used as the classification algorithm. In addition, random item selection was used as an item selection algorithm. After students are classified by the system, their performances based on the items are automatically presented via a dashboard chart (see Figure 1).

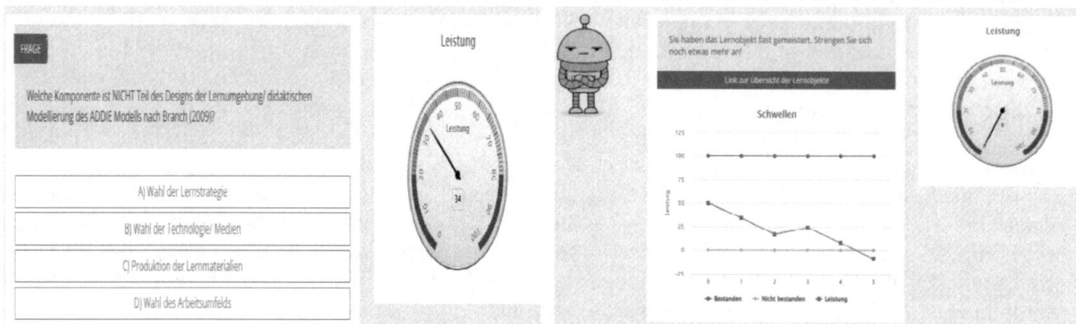

Figure 1. Screen-shot of the CCT system

2.3 Data Collection and Data Analysis

Both log data and self-report data were collected as a data collection tool. Log data consists of interaction data of learners in the CCT environment such as number of responses, number of test attempts, number of correct answers, number of incorrect answers, number of master subjects, and number of non-master subjects. On the other hand, information about learners' achievement motivation, confidence, study interest were collected as self-report data. In addition to these, end-of-term performances from the final exam were also included in the analysis.

Optimal scaling was conducted as a data analysis method. Optimal scaling is an analysis in which canonical correlation can be examined between categorical variables. The most important advantage is that more than two categorical variables can be analyzed and the results can be presented in a two-dimensional centroid graph. As the correlation among the variables increases, the points on the graph that represent them become closer, as the correlation decreases the points become distant.

3. FINDINGS

Optimal scaling analysis was employed in order to reveal the relationship between the behavior patterns of the students in the CCT environment and their psycho-educational structures. In order to perform this analysis, firstly, continuous data were converted to discrete form. For this purpose, the mean values for each structure were taken as a reference and the data were made discrete. Information on the discrete variables is presented in Table 1.

Table 1. Descriptive information about the discrete variables

Variable	Category	Frequency	Code	Measure
Achievement	Low	54 (50%)	1	Nominal
Motivation	High	54 (50%)	2	
Behavioral	Low	73 (68%)	1	Nominal
Engagement	High	35 (32%)	2	
Confidence	Low	62 (57%)	1	Nominal
	High	46 (43%)	2	
Performance	Low	48 (44%)	1	Nominal
	High	60 (56%)	2	
Study Interest	Low	58 (54%)	1	Nominal
	High	50 (46%)	2	
Use	Low	43 (40%)	1	Nominal
	High	65 (60%)	2	

As seen in Table 1, individuals above the mean were coded as High and those below the mean as Low. The interactions of the students in the CCT environment were considered behavioral engagement. In order to produce this variable, the log data of the students in the system were used. Log data consists of the number of logins, number of correct answers, number of incorrect answers, number of master subjects, number of non-master subjects, and number of attempts. With these data, principal component analysis was used and the behavioral engagement score was obtained. Other variables consist of self-report data collected from students with scales. In the second stage, it was determined which data set the variables would be included in the analysis. Variables and analysis sets are presented in Table 2.

Table 2. Datasets and variables

Set	Variables
Set 1	Achievement Motivation
	Confidence
	Study Interest
	Acceptance Structures
Set 2	Performance
Set 3	Behavioral Engagement

As can be seen in Table 2, as set 1, achievement motivation, confidence, study interest, and use; course performances of the students as set 2, and behavioral engagement as set 3 were included in the analysis. The analysis results obtained are presented in Figure 2.

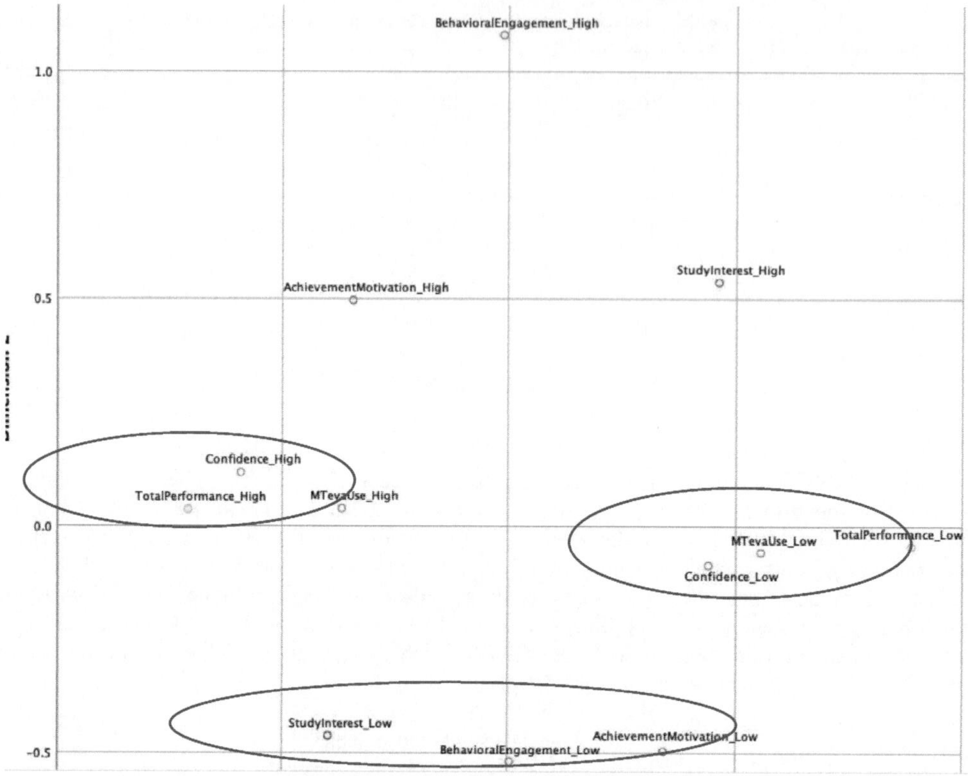

Figure 2. Results of the optimal scaling analysis

As seen in Figure 2, there are 3 basic clusters. It is possible to interpret the obtained findings as follows.

- Learners who have high-level confidence have high performance and high-level AMT perceived usefulness and intended use
- Learners who have low-level confidence have low performance and low-level AMT perceived usefulness and intended use
- Learners who have low-level achievement motivation have low-level behavioral engagement and study interest. Learners' behavioral engagement in the system is negatively affected by their achievement motivation and study interest structures.

4. DISCUSSION AND CONCLUSION

Student-centered assessments aim at supporting learning and development, or increasing motivation (Andrade, Huff, & Brooke, 2012). Within the scope of this research, a technology and analytics enhanced assessment environment in which students can assess themselves was presented. The behaviors of the students in this environment and the structures associated with these behaviors were determined. For this purpose, optimal scaling analysis was employed. The findings show that learners who have low-level study interest and achievement motivation have low-level system usage or behavioral engagement. Holmes (2015) supports this finding because it revealed that there is a positive relationship between learner engagement and motivation. In this case, interventions, feedback, or recommendations are needed to increase students' motivation and study interest in order to increase their use of the system. On the other hand, it is seen that the end-of-term performance of the students who have low confidence and low system use is also low.

On the other hand, it was found that the learners who have high performance have high system use and confidence levels. It can be said that students' self-confidence affects their performance positively. In addition, students with a high level of perceived usefulness also have a high intention to use the system (Yurdugül & Bayrak, 2014). Therefore, it was expected that students with high use of behavioral engagement levels would also be high. However, within the scope of this research, no findings were reached regarding this assumption.

In the current study, the system behaviors of the learners were revealed based on psycho-educational structures. On the other hand, dispositions such as cognitive strategies, sources of motivation, and learning strategies that may affect students' system usage behaviors should also be tested. If the structures that affect the students' CCT behaviors can be determined, it is thought that important clues will be obtained on how the systems can be made more effective. In this way, behavior patterns will be revealed first and necessary improvements can be made in CCT systems.

Student-centered assessments are important for self-directed and self-regulated learning (Andrade, Huff, & Brooke, 2012). Self-assessment is given when students assess themselves and decide about the next step (Boud, 2013). In the system presented in this context, learners are presented with master or non-master status for a subject. The presentation of information on students' interactions with the system and their performance also positively affects their judgment and decision-making processes in the assessment environment. For this purpose, it is planned to integrate dashboards into the assessment system in the next stage. In this way, it is thought that students' self-assessment processes will be supported.

REFERENCES

American Educational Research Association. (2014). *Standards for educational and psychological testing.* American Educational Research Association American Psychological Association National Council on Measurement in Education.

Andrade, H., & Valtcheva, A. (2009). Promoting learning and achievement through selfassessment. *Theory into Practice, 48*(1), 12-19.

Andrade, H., Huff, K., & Brooke, G. (2012). Assessing learning. *Education Digest, 78*(3), 46-53.

Boud, D. (2000). Sustainable assessment: rethinking assessment for the learning society. *Studies in Continuing Education, 22*(2), 151-167.

Boud, D. (2013). Enhancing learning through self-assessment. Routledge.

Bransford, J. D., Brown, A. L., & Cocking, R. R. (2000). "How People Learn: Brain, Mind, Experience, and School", Expanded Edition, Washington, DC: National Academy Press.

Bull, J., & McKenna, C. (2004). *Blueprint for computer-assisted assessment.* London, RoutledgeFalmer.

Deutsch, T., Hermann, K., Frese, T., & Sandholzer, H. (2012). Implementing computer-based assessment – A web-based mock examination changes attitudes. *Computers & Education, 58*, 1068-1075.

Eggen, T. J. H. M., & Straetmans, G. J. J. M. (2000). Computerized adaptive testing for classifying examinees into three categories. *Educational and Psychological Measurement, 60*(5), 713-734.

Frick, T. W. (1990). A comparison of three decision models for adapting the length of computer-based mastery tests. *Journal of Educational Computing Research, 6*(4), 479-513.

Frick, T. W. (1992). Computerized adaptive mastery tests as expert systems. *Journal of Educational Computing Research, 8*(2), 187-213.

Gikandi, J. W., Morrow, D., & Davis, N. E. (2011). Online formative assessment in higher education: A review of the literature. *Computers & Education, 57*(4), 2333-2351.

Holmes, N. (2015). Student perceptions of their learning and engagement in response to the use of a continuous e-assessment in an undergraduate module. *Assessment & Evaluation in Higher Education, 40*(1), 1-14.

Huebner, A. (2012). Item overexposure in computerized classification tests using sequential item selection. *Practical Assessment, Research, and Evaluation, 17*(1), 12.

Ifenthaler, D. (2022). Automated Essay Scoring Systems. In *Handbook of Open, Distance and Digital Education* (pp. 1-15). Singapore: Springer Nature Singapore.

Lin, C. J., & Spray, J. (2000). *Effects of Item-Selection Criteria on Classification Testing with the Sequential Probability Ratio Test.* ACT Research Report Series.

Müller, F. H., & Louw, J. (2004). Learning environment, motivation and interest: Perspectives on self-determination theory. *South African Journal of Psychology, 34*(2), 169-190.

Nydick, S. W., Nozawa, Y., & Zhu, R. (2012, April). Accuracy and efficiency in classifying examinees using computerized adaptive tests: an application to a large scale test. In *annual meeting of the National Council on Measurement in Education, Vancouver, Canada.*

Pachler, N., Daly, C., Mor, Y., & Mellar, H. (2010). Formative e-assessment: Practitioner cases. *Computers & Education, 54*, 715–721.

Parshall, C. G., Spray, J. A., Kalohn, J., & Davey, T. (2002). *Practical considerations in computer-based testing.* Springer Science & Business Media.

Redecker, C. (2013). The use of ICT for the assessment of key competences. *Joint Research Centre of the European Commission Scientific and Policy Report.*

Rudman, H. C. (1989). *Integrating testing with teaching.* ERIC Clearinghouse.

Spray, J. A., & Reckase, M. D. (1994). The Selection of Test Items for Decision Making with a Computer Adaptive Test. *Paper presented at the Annual Meeting of the National Council on Measurement in Education, New Orleans, LA, April 5-7, 1994.*

Spray, J. A., & Reckase, M. D. (1996). Comparison of SPRT and sequential Bayes procedures for classifying examinees into two categories using a computerized test. *Journal of Educational and Behavioral Statistics, 21*(4), 405-414.

Thompson, N. A. (2007). A practitioner's guide for variable-length computerized classification testing. *Practical Assessment, Research, and Evaluation, 12*(1), 1.

Vaessen, B. E., van den Beemt, A., van de Watering, G., van Meeuwen, L. W., Lemmens, L., & den Brok, P. (2017). Students' perception of frequent assessments and its relation to motivation and grades in a statistics course: a pilot study. *Assessment & Evaluation in Higher Education, 42*(6), 872-886.

van Groen, M. M. (2012). Computerized Classification Testing and Its Relationship to the Testing Goal. *Psychometrics in Practice at RCEC*, 125.

Wald, A. (1947). Sequential analysis. New York: John Wiley.

Weiss, D. J. (1982). Improving measurement quality and efficiency with adaptive testing.

Yurdugül, H., & Bayrak, F. (2014). The acceptance of web based formative assessment system for primary school students. *Journal of Educational Sciences & Practices, 13*(26), 167-186.

TOWARD BETTER DRIVING WITH GAZE AWARENESS ENVIRONMENT SUPPORTED BY AREA SEGMENTATION

Taketo Yamada[1], Kenji Matsuura[1], Hironori Takeuchi[1], Akihiro Kashihara[2], Kenichi Yamasaki[3] and Genta Kurita[3]
[1]Tokushima University, Japan
[2]The University of Electro-Communications, Japan
[3]Mitsubishi Precision Co., Ltd., Japan

ABSTRACT

It is important to make car-drivers improve their way of looking for recognizing key objects or areas precisely. This study designs a system following such a motivation that distinguishes several areas in a display with weights of importance. A present proposing function for successful area detection offers drivers an opportunity to compare their gaze with experts. Concrete method for this implementation includes U-Net that is one of major techniques of machine learning combined with grid segmentation.

KEYWORDS

Driving Simulator, U-Net, Grid Segmentation, Eye Tracker

1. INTRODUCTION

It is important for car-drivers to keep both safety way of driving and mature their cognitive ability. More than 40,000 people die and more than one million are injured in traffic accidents each year in European Union member countries. Road fatalities account for only a small number of deaths but are the leading cause of death in developed countries for people under the age of 40 (Plainis et al., 2006). Most automobile accidents are caused by drivers' violation of their duty of safety. In road traffic accidents, 57% are directly caused by human factors and 90% revolved human factors (Green & Senders, 1999). Among other things, findings from the 100-car naturalistic study showed that almost 80% of traffic accidents could be attributed to inattention (Klauer et al., 2006). In fact, it has been argued that young drivers have higher accident rates because of their immature cognitive abilities (Deery, 1999). These facts indicate that drivers may lack the ability to recognize danger objects, routes, places or areas and the awareness of danger avoidance. Thus, it is necessary to approach the internal processing of humans such as cognition and judgment, in order to reduce the number of accidents caused by these factors.

However, it is difficult for learners to judge whether they appropriately recognize and understand the conditions of traffic compared with internal vital state and sensed result of the environment. Even though a driver sees something, sometimes s/he might not consciously recognize it. Therefore, the function that enables a system to determine whether a learner as a driver is aware of the place to be focused and to make an objective judgment to identify a better way for her/his recognition.

Driving a car or a motorbike is available to apply the traditional knowledge in motor skill learning, in which the following processes can be transferred: recognition of external and environmental aspects, correct judgment based on proper recognition (selection of driving behavior), and implement the actual behavior based on prior judgment (operation of a car or a motorcycle). The result of the action is recognized again both externally and intrinsically and reflected succeeding actions during driving.

In the present study, the project is conducted using a driving simulator (DS) with Virtual Reality (VR), rather than learning on the premise of actual car driving. The DS used can change the course with deliberate events according to the driving scenario applied. Our study presents the images of accidents and the driving conditions leading up to them play an important role as human visual input (Yamada et al. 2022).

This study designs an environment to support driving skill improvement using both machine learning and eye tracking technologies. It is assumed that tracked data of eye movements presents high quality of appropriate eye tracking measures. Then, the study analyzes the data using machine learning technique for classifying areas of same semantics and provides a learning support information following the context. However, for the sake of simplicity, the present study starts using only gaze information related to the perception of the outside world, without direct manipulation of the driving object such as accelerating, braking, or steering wheel operation. For example, it is possible to capture how the viewpoint differs from that of skilled drivers and how the viewpoint changes when behavioral change is observed.

2. ANALYSIS BY SCREEN AREA SEGMENTATION

2.1 Analysis of Gaze Coordinates

There are a lot of tools that treat time-series data of eye movements based on (x, y) screen-coordinates. Eye tracking is often performed with either fixed camera or a specific devise of wearing glass during driving. Our environment adopts a DS, in which we can select a fixed camera in front of the screen because the scenery of the outside world can be reflected on it. Actual analysis method for such time-series data evaluates the similarity between two different series, for example, with DTW (Dynamic Time Warping) (e.g. Stana and Philip 2007, Naito et al. 2020) which is available to apply under certain conditions. The advantage of applying DTW is that the analyst only needs to focus on the series data, regardless of object-meanings such as a walker and a car displayed in the background. However, the general viewing angle (e.g., 40 degrees for both left and right side respectively) may not be sufficiently considered from physiological perspective.

In an actual situation for tracking, however, it is necessary to take into account that mixed elements may influence errors with visual processing by humans as well as the processing conditions of the computer, including observation errors. Specifically, humans do not always accurately perceive the smallest unit of (x, y) coordinates corresponding to the screen resolution. It may be, if anything, more natural to perceive the target area or the object as part of a plane. Therefore, we propose a method to divide the entire screen into partial areas.

2.2 Analysis of Gaze Coordinates in a Predefined Area

Gaze information is one of the major keys for solving the traffic accidents (Vicente, F. et al. 2015). A lot of studies introduce machine learning techniques to this domain from technical perspectives (Yoon, H.S. et al. 2019). However, they are still focusing on the technical innovation of precise detection of eyes and therefore we need the applied approach for learning a way of gaze. When drivers learn the better way of looking at several important objects or areas according to the condition of actual road, the driving way including cognition and operation is refined.

In this study, we aim to provide a learning support system that improves the driver's ability to recognize hazardous areas by guiding the driver's gaze through comparison with other gaze data which is obtained from skilled drivers in advance and regarded as a referential model. In this case, it is necessary to develop a system that estimates the degree of hazard discrimination from the gaze data and prompts the driver to pay attention to the hazardous area.

By dividing the entire screen into partial areas of homogeneity based on a latticed pattern, it is possible to determine which area the driver is looking at if the driver's gaze coordinates are available for tracking. However, it is necessary to determine the scale of the unit area occupied and the location of the area that can be considered to correspond to the gaze. Since the DS used in this study introduces VR technology, it is possible to calculate the two-dimensional coordinates of the objects drawn on the DS screen based on the relationship between the position of the object itself and the camera from which it is drawn. However, our system is different from the original DS and the proposed function is independently developed from the DS itself considering its future extension to the real view in real driving.

3. METHODS INTEGRATION AND GAZE EVALUATION

3.1 U-Net

Segmentation is the process of dividing an image into subregions with similar features and meanings. In recent image processing fields, the regions of the target object and background in an image are often segmented and recognized pixel by pixel, and the image cells are classified to simultaneously recognize the region and class of the object in the image. In 2012, a method using feature maps obtained by CNN, which is an abbreviation of convolutional neural network, was proposed (Farabet, C. et al, 2012.), and since then, deep learning has become the mainstream method for image segmentation.

U-Net has a CNN architecture for image segmentation developed by Oraf et al. (2015). The network consists of a contraction path and an expansion path. It is called U-Net because of its U-shaped architecture. In the contracting path, features are mapped by convolution. In U-Net, the same hierarchy of contraction and expansion paths are connected by a mechanism called skip connection, which ensures that the positional relationship of each pixel in the input image is not lost.

As for our actual implementation of U-Net, an original image is converted into 160 × 160 square size at first in terms of a contraction phase. We configured batch size as 4 and 40 epochs. We used *Keras* and *Tensorflow* for the default library of U-Net and we set *Adam* as an optimizer.

This study uses the GTA5 dataset created by Stephan R. et al. (2016). These images are rendered using the open-world video game Grand Theft Auto 5, and are all from the perspective of a car on the streets of a virtual city. The dataset consists of 2,500 original images of 1,914 × 1,052 pixels and 2,500 segmented images, 30% of which are used as test data for comparison and evaluation. Actual number of the test data we used was 750 and the rest was used for train data. The training was performed with a batch size of 4 and an epoch count of 40, and predictions were made for each frame of the DS video.

3.2 Grid Segmentation

In this study, the model gaze data of a skilled driver and the gaze data of a learner are compared for each frame of the DS video using U-Net based area segmentation, and identification ability for danger areas/objects is evaluated by the degree of agreement between the areas segmented with both techniques. However, even if the gaze coordinate in an area of a skilled driver and that of a learner are the same, they may be looking at locations that are quite far apart in terms of coordinates of the same area by U-Net segmentation. In this case, for example, a road spans a wide area from the left end to the right end, and unified area segmentation using simple U-Net would result in a problem where gaze on the extreme left or right are regarded identically. Therefore, in addition to area segmentation by U-Net, the entire image is independently divided into an N × N grid (3 × 3 in this experiment) to subdivide the viewing direction. This process suppresses the problematic patterns and enables highly accurate evaluation.

3.3 Gaze Evaluation

When evaluating gaze using the combination of U-Net and lattice domain segmentation described in the previous sections, we focus on the vertical and horizontal distance traveled to the opponent's gaze based on the position of a learner's or an expert's gaze and add the evaluation points (EP) as shown in Table 1. where N is the number of grid segmentations, and L is the cost of reaching the line of sight from the referential point. For example, if the cell in upper left corner of Figure 1 is the reference and the lower right corner is the same area in U-Net, the EP sets 0, but for adjacent cells, the EP sets 0.5.

Table 1. Evaluation weight points at the time of gaze detection

Grid Segmentation	Segmentation by U-Net	Evaluation Point
Match	Match	1
Match	Not match	0.75
Not match	Match	1-(L/(N-1))
Not match	Not match	0

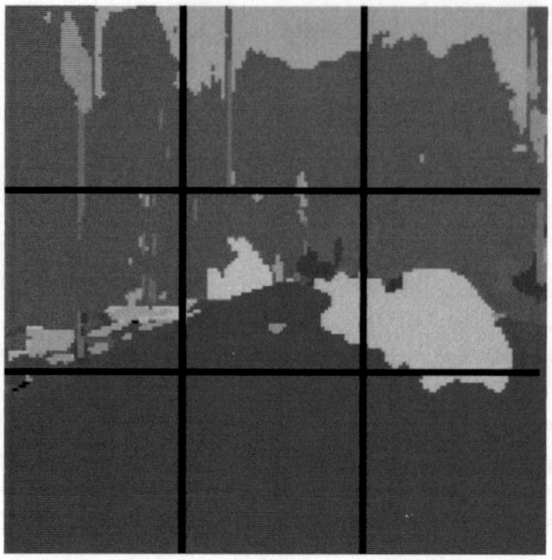

Figure 1. Combined method of area segmentation using U-Net and grid

3.4 Feedback to Learners

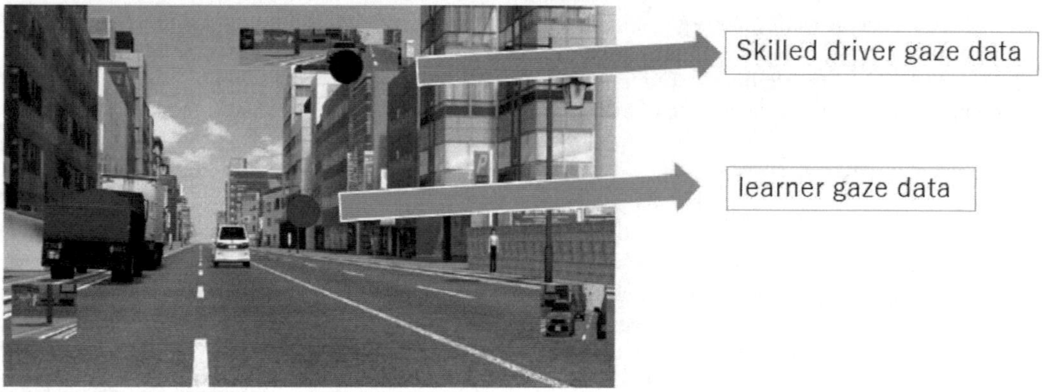

Figure 2. Screen dump; feedback circles on the screen of driving simulator

In this study, after acquiring the gaze information of the learner, the gaze coordinates of the learner and those of the skilled driver acquired beforehand are simultaneously displayed on the screen as a circular area together with the DS video of a background layer, as shown in Figure 2, to support learning how to set the viewpoint on the screen at each frame. In this process, a gradation of colors is applied to the drawing according to the evaluation points in the previous section to make it easier to understand visually which points are different each other. The fundamental idea for gaze improvement is that they can identify how and where the instructor or the expert looks on in case learners are aware of the model view. They can get such information with two circles with independent colors. The color is set based on the previous discussion based on the analysis shown in Figure 1. At that time, the gaze coordinate data of the skilled driver is always drawn in blue. On the other hand, the gaze data of the learner is also drawn in blue, the same color as the gaze coordinate data of the skilled driver when the evaluation score is 1. The color is set as green when the score is 0.75, and yellow when the score is 0.5. When the score is 0, the color is set as red. The difference indicates the gap between them and therefore the learner should learn where and how s/he should look on with such colored circles as feedback.

4. EXPERIMENTAL USE AND THE RESULTS

4.1 Experimental Use

The project conducted an experimental use of this system. The purpose of this experiment was to evaluate the effectiveness of the proposed method for supporting gaze learning and its implemented system. First, five people who drive at least once every two days tried the system as skilled drivers, and their gaze data were obtained through the system. Though we have to provide a model data for reference to subjects, there are several ways for this purpose. Among several options, the model data to be used in the experiment was determined by voting within the skilled drivers at this time. Then 15 men and women ranged in their 20s to 50s whose driving frequency were less than once every two days joined voluntarily as learners and randomly divided into Group A, Group B, and Group C. Group A was the group that used the system (proposed system) in which both the learner's and the skilled person's gaze coordinates were displayed together in different colors according to the evaluation points, and Group B was the group that used the system that displays only the gaze coordinates of the proficient driver. Group C was the group that used the system that displayed only the gaze coordinates of the learner.

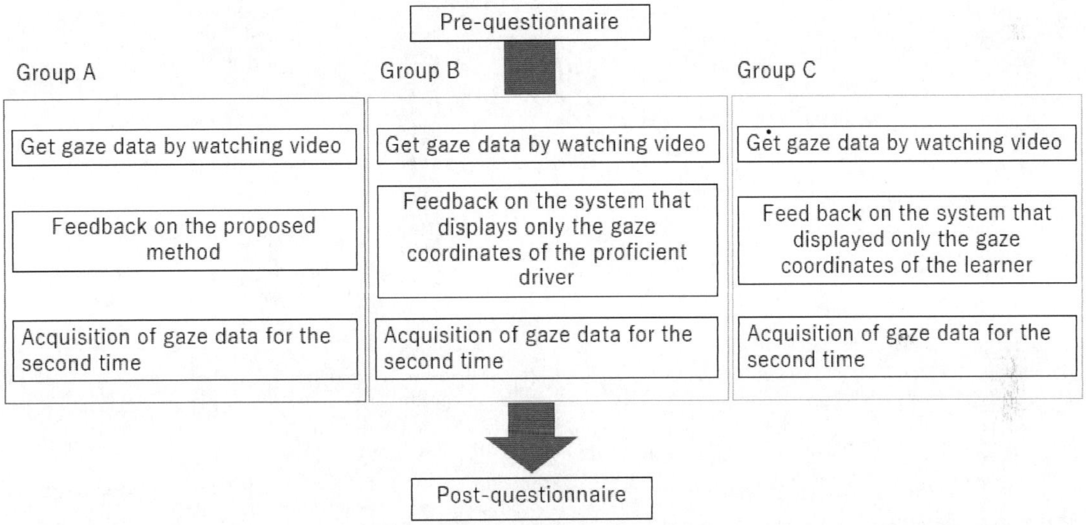

Figure 3. Flow of the experiment

Experiments on learners were conducted according to the flow shown in Figure 3. First of all, all the learners were asked to answer the questionnaire for the preliminary survey. The contents of the preliminary questionnaire asked about the mileage in the last year, accident history, violation history and so forth. Then, they watched the image of each group in drive simulator and we acquired gaze data. After that, the system gave feedback according to each group property. After the feedback, each group members watched the same video again and acquired the gaze data. The difference in cumulative evaluation scores between the groups was then investigated. In order to investigate changes in learners' behaviors, each group was given a questionnaire with a 4-point scale after the feedback given at each trial on how much they contributed to the learning of their viewpoints.

Table 2 and Figure 3 show the mean difference between the pre- and post-feedback scores of weighted gaze agreement for each group of learners in the experiment, and the box plots with medians and quartiles, respectively. The higher scores indicate the improvement which is the influence of the system contribution. Figure 4 shows the results of a questionnaire in which participants rated on a 4-point scale the extent to which the feedback provided in each trial contributed to the learning of the learner's point of view after each feedback session. The results of the questionnaire after the feedback showed that about 67% of the responses was "Contributed" and about 27% was "Contributed a little" in group A. In group B, 20% of the responses was "contributed" and 67% was "contributed a little". As for the same question, in Group C, about 33% of the responses was "contributed" and about 53% was "contributed a little". It means that positive effects were found dominantly at Group A, Group B and Group C just in order.

Table 2. Mean difference in gaze scores before and after feedback

learners	Group A	learners	Group B	learners	Group C
A1	0.0787	B1	-0.0113	C1	0.0961
A2	0.0471	B2	0.0106	C2	-0.0239
A3	0.1312	B3	0.1869	C3	- 0.0445
A4	0.1587	B4	0.1558	C4	0.0188
A5	0.0625	B5	0.0047	C5	-0.0107
average	0.0956	average	0.0693	average	0.0072

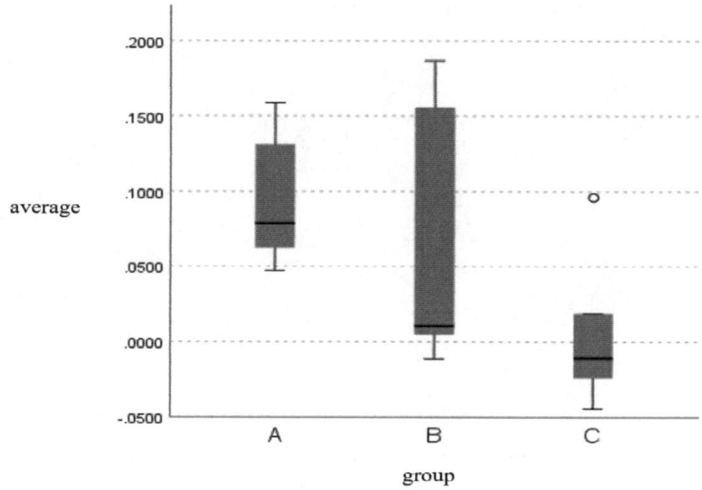

Figure 4. Resulting graph in a box-plot format

4.2 Discussion

The results of the experiment showed that Group A had the highest improvement scores on the average though the highest improvement among all subjects appears in Group B (see Table 2). The median values in cumulative evaluation score were different between the groups, which was seen in Figure 4. The box plot also indicates that the degree of data distribution. Interesting discussion could arise between Group A of comparative middle variation and B of large variation. Our belief is that subjects with our system were influenced by a sound comparison including their own gaze tracking data to some extent while the improvements on subjects using model trajectory without their own gaze had diverse influence. In particular, one of subjects in group B indicated that the behavioral change had been worse through the feedback. In addition, improvements by two subjects, B2 and B5, were almost zero which means no actual improvements found while the other two indicated highly improved.

Next, as the number of subjects were small but when we compare group A with group C, we can find large difference between them in several viewpoints. Therefore, we think the feedback through the gaze-detection with area-segmentation brings positive effects.

If a way of driving operation conforms to the model, the learner gets good feedback but otherwise not. In addition, the results of the questionnaire requested after the feedback showed that Group A had the highest ratio about "contributed" with 67% of the learners. It means that they got positive impression from subjective viewpoint.

5. CONCLUSION

In this study, we designed a support environment that captures and analyzes the driver's gaze during driving using a driving simulator in order to make the driver aware of the areas s/he should pay attention to, and to provide visual feedback. The current proposal focuses just on the simple and solid style on detecting gaze and analysis thereof. In addition, we assume the technical proposal is based on the VR environment. However, we can apply it to the real driving with further improvement on machine learning techniqeus.

Future issues to be addressed implied as follows.

- The environment needs to draw on a larger screen because the current screen size used (12 inches) is small and the entire image can be seen, which is because of the limitation of the eye tracking device, including parts of the image that are not normally visible unless the driver gazes at them when driving.
- We need to improve the accuracy of region segmentation by U-Net. The model data is created from the actual drive simulator videos for training U-Net but we should provide more precise one.
- We have to consider the flexibility in viewpoint evaluation based on congruency. With the current system, grid area is congruent, and the U-Net area is incongruent, the agreement points are not uniformly set to a constant score of 0.75, but are variable based on the area ratio and other factors.
- We can arrange the focus not only on viewpoint information, but also on auditory and other non-visual perceptions.

ACKNOWLEDGEMENT

We would like to thank all members joined at project meetings for their fruitful discussions and Mitsubishi Precision Co., Ltd. for its support.

REFERENCES

Deery, H.A., 1999. Hazard and risk perception among young novice drivers. *Journal of Safety Research*, Vol.30, No. 4, pp. 225-236.

Farabet, C., Couprie, C., Najman, L., & LeCun, Y. (2013). Learning hierarchical features for scene labeling. *IEEE transactions on pattern analysis and machine intelligence*, Vol. 35, No. 8, pp. 1915—1929.

Green, M., & Senders, J. (1999). Human error in road accidents. http://www.visualexpert.com/Resources/roadaccidents.html. (accessed 2022 May 19)

Klauer, S.G., Dingus, T.A., Neale, V.L., Sudweeks, J.D., & Ramsey, D.J. (2006). The Impact of Driver Inattention on Near-Crash/Crash Risk: An Analysis Using the 100-Car Naturalistic Driving Study Data. *National Highway Traffic Safety Administration*, DOT HS 810 594, Washington DC.

Naito, H., Matsuura, K., & Yano, S. (2020). Learning Support for Tactics Identification Skills in Team Sports by Gaze Awarenesss. *Proceedings of IIAI-AAI2020*, Taiwan, pp. 209-212.

Plainis, S., Murray, I.J., & Pallikaris, I.G. (2006). Road traffic casualties: understanding the night-time death toll. *Injury Prevention*, Vol. 12, No.2, pp. 125—138.

Richter, S.R., Vineet, V., Roth, S., & Koltun, V. (2016). Playing for Data: Ground Truth from Computer, *Games* , LNCS 9906, pp.102—118.

Ronneberger, O., Fischer. P., & Brox. T. (2015). U-Net: Convolutional Networks for Biomedical Image Segmentation. avab. N. et al. (Eds.) *MICCAI Part III*, LNCS 9351, pp.234—241.

Stana, S., & Philip, C. (2007). Toward accurate dynamic time warping in linear time and space. *Intelligent Data Analysis*, Vol. 11, No. 5, pp. 561-580.

Vicente, F., Huang, Z., Xiong, X., De la Torre, F., Zhang, W. & Levi, D. (2015). Driver Gaze Tracking and Eyes Off the Road Detection System, *IEEE Trans. On Intelligent Transportation Systems*, Vol.16, No.4, pp.2014-2027, 2015.

Yamada, T., Matsuura, K., Takeuchi, H., Kashihara, A., Yamasaki, K., & Kurita, G. (2022). Learning driving with improving gaze through area division methods, *2021 Shikoku student workshop proceedings of JSiSE*, Japan, pp. 215—216. (In Japanese).

Yoon, H.S., Baek, N.R., Truong, N.Q. & Park, K.R. (2019). Driver Gaze Detection Based on Deep Residual Networks Using the Combined Single Image of Dual Near-Infrared Cameras, *IEEE Access*, Vol.7, pp. 93448-93461, 2019.

LINKING GAMIFICATION, LUDOLOGY AND PEDAGOGY: PRINCIPLES TO DESIGN A SERIOUS GAME

Joshua Esterhuizen, Günther Drevin, Dirk Snyman and Lynette Drevin
School of Computer Science and Information Systems, North-West University, Potchefstroom, South Africa

ABSTRACT

Education is shifting towards a more technology focused mode of delivery, or at least combining technology use with standard methods. A potential effect of this could be the introduction and use of games in classrooms. This study looks at the possibility of adapting various domains of knowledge into digital games referred to as serious games. The implementation of serious games within teaching may help keep certain students engaged with the content being presented and create further interest in the topic. However, before reaching this stage the means to transform these knowledge domains into serious games must be studied. This is done by focusing on three fields: gamification, ludology, and pedagogy. Through the use of a literature analysis, both a literature review and a focus on previous implementations, several key principles for the design of a serious game were identified, namely reflection, feedback, a story-based environment, and thorough structuring of content. These principles stem from the design choices of the previous implementations and pedagogical theories - Merrill's First Principles and the ARCS model. The aim of the study is to investigate the possibility of using digital games as a means to encourage learning in teaching environments.

KEYWORDS

Education, Gamification, Ludology, Pedagogy, Serious Games

1. INTRODUCTION

In the years leading up to the new century there was a shift into the "information age". This age is characterised by the fact that information is being transmitted and generated at an ever-increasing rate due to further technological developments (Gibson *et al.*, 2006; Reigeluth, 1996). The most notable changes from the previous "industrial age" are that the previous focused on conformity and compliance while initiative and diversity – where greater value is placed on each individual's strengths and contribution to a project or organisation – is the focus of the information age (Reigeluth, 1996).

Due to these aforementioned paradigm shifts between the ages, and in what requirements are desired by most organisations in the information age, a shift in instructional theory is also taking place. With the recent developments in technology and the fact that technology in general is becoming more accessible, many institutions have adopted some forms of digital learning or supplemented traditional teaching with digital assistance such as having virtual sessions of a class and having courses entirely online (Tîrziu & Vrabie, 2015).

Deshpande and Huang (2011) state that the current generation of students is the first to grow up with abundant access to technology. On average, these students spend almost double the time playing video games that they do reading (Deshpande & Huang, 2011). Virvou, Katsionis and Manos (2005) echo the point that computer games are popular among individuals who are in schools and as such could provide a means to deliver content in an interesting and engaging manner. The movement for the inclusion of digital games to be used in teaching and training environments first started in 2003, two years after the field of *ludology*, the study of games, began to gain traction in academic literature (Annetta, 2008). This initiative is what started the concept of a serious game as one that can be used in an academic sense to relay information. Furthermore, gamification has recently garnered focus from a technology specific view and due to the use of game elements, it can have an impact on how a serious game is designed albeit the result of a digital gamified environment differs to a serious game (Kalogiannakis *et al.*, 2021).

As such, the motivation behind this study is to further investigate the possibility of using digital serious games as a means to encourage learning in teaching environments due to the aforementioned interest and uptake of digital technologies in education as well as the potential improvements they can bring (Zourmpakis *et al.*, 2022). This study aims to present a set of design principles for serious games through answering the question *what qualities are required for a serious game to be effectively used in an educational environment on several topics*. This will be accomplished through a literature analysis focusing on the fields of ludology, gamification, and pedagogy with a focus on Merrill's First Principles and the ARCS Model resulting in the synthesis of design principles.

2. RESEARCH METHODOLOGY

This research study primarily made use of a literature analysis to answer the aforementioned primary question. This was done is two major phases. The first is that of a literature review on the fields of ludology, gamification, and pedagogy while the second focused on previous implementations of serious games. Firstly, the three key fields were studied, and notable definitions and theories were selected. These were used to provide an informed background on what design principles to look for. Following this, the design principles of the previous implementations were noted down and then compared with each other and the major ones identified and then, with the information from the literature review, expanded upon.

3. LITERATURE REVIEW

3.1 Serious Games and Ludology

Ludology is the formal and academic study of games and has roots in studying games through a cultural and social lens by discussing how each interacts with the so-called "spirit of play" (Huizinga & Hull, 1949). The field also encompasses the study of digital computer-based games and has a focus on discussing and understanding the individual elements of games as well as creating models to explain the various mechanics and rules of games (Frasca, 2013). As such, this study will use the definition that, *"Ludology can be defined as a discipline that studies games in general, and video games in particular"* (Frasca, 2013, p. 222). Serious games were introduced as a concept in 2002 with the intention of them to be used as a means of training certain tasks and skills which was typically done through simulation type games (De Gloria *et al.*, 2014).

Simulations attempt to model reality in a consistent manner usually through modelling physical or social systems through another system which in this case would be a computer and the digital video game (Squire, 2003). There are two main types of simulations – high fidelity and low fidelity. High fidelity simulations attempt to model every interaction in a given system, phenomena, or environment as accurately as possible (Squire, 2003). In contrast, a low fidelity simulation will make use of a fair bit of abstraction as it aims to only demonstrate a few key characteristics of the phenomena or environment (Squire, 2003). Games as simulations would comprise of both of these types depending on the content that it attempts to simulate.

The endeavour to create serious games has yet to reach schools due to certain criticisms about games in general that hinders this (Virvou *et al.*, 2005). While this was previously due to the fact that discussions around games by educators focused on the social consequences of playing games (Squire, 2003) it may now be due to the resources required for a serious game to be developed (Helms *et al.*,2015). Thus, the study of serious games became more theoretical and discussion-based at lower levels and more applied with actual use at higher levels. This can be seen by implementations in several fields including medical rehabilitation, ecological studies, learning languages, and business studies (Burke *et al.*, 2009; Costanza *et al.*, 2014; Ranalli, 2008; Tao *et al.*, 2009). These types of games have already had an impact on the military, medical, and higher education sectors early in their conception and this trend continues to this day with serious games being used within the medical fields specifically (Annetta, 2008; De Gloria *et al.*, 2014).

3.2 A Pedagogical Understanding

Pedagogy is the field that deals with the transferral of knowledge in an educational environment through several lenses such as social, political, and cultural (Li, 2012). As such it encompasses the themes and discussions of instructional design and theory as well as any learning theories.

Learning by doing functions on the principle that skills can be improved through practice and self-perfection on a particular topic or knowledge base (Fisch *et al.*, 2009). This means of instruction has become increasingly popular amongst companies where they are able to make use of "on the job" training as it allows for a person to be productive immediately as well as become more proficient at tasks gradually (Fisch *et al.*, 2009). The learning by teaching method works under the assumption that learners are able to increase their understanding of a certain topic by teaching it to other learners (Fisch *et al.*, 2009). This method of learning garners more usage in environments with too few teachers and increases the overall learning process (Fisch *et al.*, 2009). Learning methods that place the learner in control are very flexible and as such can be incorporated when attempting to teach various and different fields or subjects (Ackoff, 1991).

Gibson *et al.* (2006) list several learning and instructional design theories that have the potential to be applied to a game used for learning. This study will, however, only look at Merrill's *First Principles of Instruction* as it is the most recent (Gibson *et al.*, 2006). Before discussing the principles that the name refers to in this theory, Merrill (2002) provides a few definitions for the terms that are used. A *Principle* in this context is a relationship that is always true regardless of the environment it is applied within. A *Practice* is any instructional activity. A *Program* is a means of instruction that makes use of several practices (Merrill, 2002). These first principles described are able to be implemented in any instructional system or environment as they are "design-oriented" and as such relate more to creating learning environments rather than describing the means of knowledge transfer. Each of the following principles is also accompanied by three "corollaries" each of which Merrill (2002) likewise explains:

The first principle is that the learning is problem centred. This principle describes three corollaries, the first of which being "Show Task" which states that learners should be shown the types of problems they will be able to solve with the knowledge that they attain. The next is the "Task Level" which explains that the problems presented should keep learners engaged due to the complexity and not just the action of solving it. The last corollary, "Problem Progression" describes that the problems presented should have some form of increasing complexity while still being comparable to the previous iteration of the type of problem (Merrill, 2002).

The second principle is "Activation" which means that learning happens whenever previous experiences are used. The first corollary, "Previous Experience", states that the learning process is enhanced when a learner is able to draw upon relevant past experiences and apply the associate knowledge as a foundation for new knowledge. "New Knowledge" is the second and explains that learners should be provided with a relevant experience as an additional foundation to add to their knowledge base. The last corollary is "Structure" and details that learners should be encouraged to organise new knowledge according to some relevant structure (Merrill, 2002).

The third principle, Demonstration, proposes that learning takes place when the activities that are undertaken impart the knowledge instead of stating the information. "Demonstration Consistency" explains that any examples or visualisation should be kept in line with the original learning goals. The next is "Learner Guidance" and states that learners should be shown where the relevant information for problems can be found be it in the form of comparative examples or various representations of one source. "Relevant Media" explains that when media is used as a means of demonstration, distinct types can be used provided that they do not fight for a learner's attention (Merrill, 2002).

The fourth principle is Application which states that learning takes place when learners actively solve problems with the new knowledge they have acquired. "Practice Consistency" is similar to Demonstration consistency but with a focus on the application of knowledge. "Diminishing Coaching" is where the learners are provided with relevant feedback, but it is slowly lessened over time. It is also important that the problems provided to learners for practice have a good variety, defined under "Varied Problems" (Merrill, 2002).

The fifth, and final, *principle* is Integration which is when the knowledge a learner has acquired is used by them in their everyday life. The first corollary, "Watch Me", explains that learners are provided to showcase the new knowledge or skill they have acquired. "Reflection" deals with giving learners time to be able to debate with others on the topic involved. Lastly, "Creation" states that learners should be able to make use of their new knowledge or skill in some personal capacity (Merrill, 2002).

The principles and corollaries provided by Merrill (2002) provide an expansive and detailed structure to be used when developing any learning opportunity making it an exceptional choice to adapt specifically for a digital game learning environment. It does, however, lack a comprehensive discussion on how to keep learners engaged with the content and, as such, this will be discussed with some theories pertaining to the role of motivation in learning.

One model for motivating learners is the **ARCS** Model which was developed by John Keller (1987) which is frequently referenced in the aforementioned field of instructional design (Kapp, 2012a). It comprises four main elements with each focusing on designing instruction in a different way (Kapp, 2012a; Keller, 1987).

The first of these is Attention and it is an element that is concerned with gaining and then keeping the learners' interest. There are three main methods to accomplish this: gaining **A**ttention through the use of examples, create curiosity within the learners through means such as role-playing or hands-on examples, and variability which means periodically changing the method of delivery (Kapp, 2012a; Keller, 1987).

Relevance refers to having the content be relevant to the learner (Keller, 1987). Kapp (2012a) mentions that this can be done through orienting the environment around achieving goals, creating a link between the motives of learners and that of the instruction means, displaying that the content is familiar to the learners and finally developing a model of the results of learning the presented knowledge (Keller, 1987).

Another element of this model, **C**onfidence, is the expectations of success set by the learner and as such when they meet these expectations, they are confident in their ability to do the work (Kapp, 2012a; Keller, 1987). This can be aided by providing learners with clear expectations and requirements upfront about the required skill or knowledge. It is also helpful to provide smaller opportunities to succeed as with each success the learners will become more confident (Kapp, 2012a; Keller, 1987).

The last element in the ARCS model is **S**atisfaction and is concerned with giving learners a sense of accomplishment and that the effort in the learning process has some value and weight to it (Kapp, 2012a; Keller, 1987). This can be accomplished by allowing learners to see how their new-found knowledge can be used, either through the use of a real-world demonstration or via some form of simulation (Kapp, 2012a; Keller, 1987).

3.3 Gamification and the Knowledge Domains

Gamification can be defined as making use of game-like mechanics, aesthetics, and thinking to create motivation, solve problems and produce a more suitable learning environment (Kapp, 2012a). Kapp (2012b) states that while gamification makes use of game elements, it only makes use of a few of them as in a gamified system. In a gamification context, learners are not constantly engaged in playing the game as there are sections of respite from this, such as video explanations. While elements such as points and achievements are found in most games, gamification strives to add more than just these to a classroom. The absence of other elements contributes to a resulting system that is dull (Kapp, 2012b).

Gamification is often not implemented within a classroom but is rather presented to learners through some external means (Kapp, 2012b). It should be noted, while a digital gamified environment is the result of gamification and differ from serious games (Kapp, 2012a), the use of game elements within one such environment results in this field being one of interest when discussing serious games as the understanding of these systems from a gamification standpoint may prove beneficial to the design of a serious game such as with the ability gamification provides to create problems relative to a students' skill level (Zourmpakis *et al.*, 2022). The main difference between these two systems is that learning is more direct in a serious game as the content causes learning while in gamification learning is done indirectly (Kalogiannakis *et al.*, 2021).

Kapp (2012a) describes various types of knowledge and how to begin developing a gamified system to effectively teach each of them. This provides the groundwork for answering the question this study poses and as such allows for a more in-depth discussion on how to implement serious games. Table 1 describes the knowledge domains.

One important aspect to note about these knowledge domains is that they are not mutually exclusive as one particular topic can be placed in several of them as the components of that topic may require multiple domains to be properly contained under them. Kapp (2012a) also provides some ways that each domain can be taught to best relay that particular type of knowledge. While these recommendations are derived under a gamification perspective (Kapp, 2012a), they can also be applied for a digital game as shown in Table 1.

Table 1. Knowledge Domain Recommendations (Kapp, 2012a)

Knowledge Domain	Description	Recommendation
Declarative Knowledge	Facts and jargon within a topic	Sorting games
Conceptual Knowledge	Grouping of related information with an underlying common descriptor	Demonstrations and sorting type games
Rules-Based Knowledge	Strict statements linking concepts	Demonstration of failure when not complying with the rules
Procedural Knowledge	Progression-based path to reach an outcome	Working through the procedure
Soft Skills	General strategies for dealing with various social interactions	Repeated application of a skill within various scenarios
Affective Knowledge	Subjective phenomena	Immersing the learner within a phenomenon
Psychomotor Domain	Making use of cognitive knowledge through physical skills	Observation

4. ANALYSIS OF PREVIOUS IMPLEMENTATIONS

In addition to looking at the aforementioned academic fields, it is also vital to look at how previous serious games were designed, and which principles are most commonly used. Several studies (Allers *et al.*, 2021; Dincelli & Chengalur-Smith, 2020; Sheng *et al.*, 2007) were examined in which some form of a gamified system or serious game was developed in addition to the author(s) detailing what design principles were followed during the development process.

The first of these is titled, "*Choose your own training adventure: designing a gamified SETA artefact for improving information security and privacy through interactive storytelling*" and focused on developing a gamified system to teach employees about security issues with a focus on social media and social engineering (Dincelli & Chengalur-Smith, 2020). For the development of the artefact, Dincelli and Chengalur-Smith (2020) made use of literature from instructional theory and gamification and, as a result, made use of a few key design principles. The first design principle followed is that the gamified system should make use of a story-based agent (Dincelli & Chengalur-Smith, 2020). This means that a game should include some figure or character to guide users through the content as well as making use of storytelling in some capacity which is found to create curiosity within users (Dincelli & Chengalur-Smith, 2020; Kapp, 2012a). The second design principle used was that of reflection which states that users should be given a moment of respite to comprehend on what has been presented to them (Dincelli & Chengalur-Smith, 2020; Sheng *et al.*, 2007). Feedback on various metrics of a user's performance is also a design principle which allows for users to perform self-evaluation (Dincelli & Chengalur-Smith, 2020).

The findings of this case study were that making use of a gamified system that used either visual stimuli or text were better at relaying information than traditional means. Visual stimuli were better than text in terms of recognition, recollection and ease of learning and they performed similarly in terms of recall, satisfaction, and usability (Dincelli & Chengalur-Smith, 2020).

The next case study is titled "*Anti-phishing Phil: the design and evaluation of a game that teaches people not to fall for phish*" and focused on teaching people about phishing and how to avoid becoming a victim to these attacks (Sheng *et al.*, 2007). Sheng *et al.* (2007) made use of learning science theories in the development of the game and to refine the various iterations throughout the development process. The first two design principles discussed are reflection and story-based agent environment. These have already been mentioned in the previous case study. Additionally, feedback is also discussed in this study but specifically how it was implemented. Anti-phishing Phil makes use of feedback both during, though displaying a short message for each choice made, and after a round of the game, through a score sheet and brief explanation of the links used. The next design principle followed is the procedural-conceptual principle. This principle states that these two knowledge domains, conceptual and procedural, hold a mutually supportive influence over the other. In practice, and thus the development of a serious game, this means that learners should be given context to the processes they are being taught as without the context they may incorrectly apply them (Sheng *et al.*, 2007).

The findings of Anti-phishing Phil showed that the serious game approach made users more knowledgeable on the topic and how to go about dealing with phishing. While the game was a success it falls behind in the aspect that some users may become more susceptible to phishing as the game provided a fixed number of indicators to be aware of (Sheng *et al.*, 2007).

The final case study used is titled "*Children's Awareness of Digital Wellness: A Serious Games Approach*" and was targeted towards teaching children, particularly pre-schoolers, about digital wellbeing and fostering cyber security awareness through a mobile-based serious game, which will be referred to as *Digital Wellnests* (Allers *et al.*, 2021). This case study focused on the design and research needed for such a serious game and stated that future work could include the development and deployment of the game (Allers *et al.*, 2021).

While this case study (Allers *et al.*, 2021) made use of instructional theory targeted towards preschool children (Callaghan & Reich, 2018; Matthews *et al.*, 2007) some of the frameworks and learning theory used can also be applied to all serious games. The first design principle followed was simplicity as it allows a user to follow the content adequately and as such learn effectively (Allers *et al.*, 2021). The study goes on to cite Matthews *et al.* (2007) on the ways children tend to learn which includes Observation, Listening Exploring, Experimentation and Asking questions. Learning through play, such as a serious game, is an effective way to implement all of these methods (Allers *et al.*, 2021) and as such provides an additional framework targeted specifically at younger children as opposed to the previous studies (Dincelli & Chengalur-Smith, 2020; Sheng *et al.*, 2007) which were focused on adults. While this does not provide direct principles to follow during the design process, including ways for these methods of learning to be present in a serious game should be taken into consideration. In addition to the above, the study also made use of several elements identified by Callaghan and Reich (2018) which are based on how young children learn. The first of these is clear and simple goals which is concerned with presenting a user with concise outcomes to work towards (Callaghan & Reich, 2018). Similarly with Anti-phishing Phil (Sheng *et al.*, 2007), is the element of quality of feedback and rewards which deals with how feedback is presented to a user - for example, pre-schoolers may not yet be able to read and as such, the feedback must be structured accordingly (Allers *et al.*, 2021). The next element is structure of the challenge consisting of setting the difficulty of tasks and changing the difficulty depending on how the user is performing (Callaghan & Reich, 2018). This element can also be described using some of the corollaries from Merrill's First Principles (Merrill, 2002) - which will be discussed in the following section. The last element Callaghan and Reich (2018) is that of Motion based learning which describes the physical interaction a user will have with applications which in this case would be designing larger touch controls to account for a preschool child's current level of motor functions. This particular aspect is certainly vital when dealing with any knowledge from the psychomotor domain.

As previously mentioned, this case study has not yet developed the serious game and as such cannot be evaluated by users. However, an expert review was conducted on the design of this serious game of which the outcomes were positive as the reviewers "found the implementation of each element was satisfactory, but there is still room for improvement" (Allers *et al.*, 2021).

The following table visualizes the major design principles of each case study.

Table 2. Design Principles Defined by Case Study (Allers *et al.*, 2021; Dincelli & Chengalur-Smith, 2020; Sheng *et al.*, 2007)

SETA Artifact	Anti-Phishing Phil	Digital Wellnests
Story-based	Story-based	Simplicity
Reflection	Reflection	Clear and simple goals
Feedback	Feedback	Quality of feedback
	Conceptual-Procedural	Structure of the challenge
		Motion-based interaction

5. SYNTHESIS FROM RESEARCH

From the literature and case studies examined, there are several key qualities that are common either under the same descriptor or with similar descriptions with different names. It is these qualities that will form the basis to answer the research question of this study.

The first quality, reflection, is shared amongst Merrill's First Principles (Merrill, 2002) and two of the case studies (Dincelli & Chengalur-Smith, 2020; Sheng *et al.*, 2007) and is vital to a serious game if intended to be used in an educational environment. Reflection is described as giving a user time after being presented with new knowledge or a task to garner a better understanding through internalisation.

The second quality a serious game should make use of is that of feedback. All of the case studies (Allers *et al.*, 2021; Dincelli & Chengalur-Smith, 2020; Sheng *et al.*, 2007) and Merrill (2002) refers to it under the diminishing coaching corollary. A user should be presented with feedback on how they are progressing on a given set of tasks within the game. As they progress, the amount of feedback should be slowly diminished. The feedback amount should also be tied to the performance of the user - increasing if they begin to struggle and decreasing if not. Since feedback can take on many different forms, the type of feedback, as well as the method of delivery, is dependent on the topic being taught. As part of this quality, a serious game should also be designed to create an environment in which users are able to complete smaller tasks and are rewarded for these smaller successes as per the ARCS model (Keller, 1987).

Another quality that should be implemented is that the serious game should showcase and teach topics through the use of storytelling. The case studies (Allers *et al.*, 2021; Dincelli & Chengalur-Smith, 2020; Sheng *et al.*, 2007) all mention the use thereof. The ARCS model (Keller, 1987), specifically under the attention element, also states that this is a proponent of keeping users engaged. A game should then allow for a story to take place during the teaching of a topic which can also be done in several ways - such as contextually with *Anti-phishing Phil* (Sheng *et al.*, 2007) or as the main focus of the topic as with the SETA artefact (Dincelli & Chengalur-Smith, 2020) and *Digital Wellnests* (Allers *et al.*, 2021). Another means to accomplish this is to make use of an agent that guides the user through the game which can be used in accordance with the "Learner Guidance" corollary from Merrill's First Principles (Merrill, 2002).

The last major quality a serious game should possess is that of structuring. This quality refers to the content the game will deal with in terms of the instructions given as well as how the difficulty of problems could progress. It is derived from both Merrill's First Principles (Merrill, 2002), the ARCS model (Keller, 1987), and the framework by Callaghan and Reich (2018). From the ARCS model (Keller, 1987), specifically Confidence, and Callaghan and Reich's (2018) framework it is clear that a serious game should be structured with simple goals and clear expectations for the user and by structuring a game's instructions in this manner the user will be motivated to continue playing and therefore learning. The problems and tasks within the game should be increasing in difficulty as a user gets them correct and lowering the difficulty when they are struggling to keep engagement once again with the game at a high level. Merrill's First Principles (Merrill, 2002) discusses this quality in several principles and their subsequent corollaries with some referring to the difficulty scaling mentioned above. As such, a serious game's structure should be centred around the problems themselves or the knowledge being taught when dealing with affective knowledge and soft skills. The tasks given to a user should be both varied to keep the users' attention as well as be consistent in the ways the user interacts with them. This approach should keep users motivated to use the game according to the ARCS model (Keller, 1987) as it makes use of both the Attention and Relevance elements.

While the remaining aspects of the pedagogical theories and design principles from the case studies are also useful in the implementation of a serious game, they are specific to the content being taught and as such should be considered in greater detail if a similar game to those were to be developed. Kapp's (2012a) recommendations are a helpful starting point on how to effectively teach content relating to the knowledge domains. Referring back to Squire's (2003) descriptions of games as simulations - both high fidelity and low fidelity - these types of serious games are certainly the most useful for teaching content found in the affective, soft skills, and psychomotor domains since the best means to teach these is through immersing the user in the phenomena, repeated application of skills and observation respectively (Kapp, 2012a). Simulation-type serious games can also be used in the other domains (teaching physics as described by Deshpande and Huang (2011)). These types of games are also the most effective means for the psychomotor domain as shown by various studies (Burke *et al.*, 2009; Costanza *et al.*, 2014; Ranalli, 2008; Tao *et al.*, 2009).

The remaining knowledge domains tend to have some heavy overlap depending on the topic being covered. Sheng *et al.* (2007) discussed the Conceptual-Procedural principle in their game's development. To reiterate, it simply states that a topic cannot be fully understood from only the procedures or context - both are needed for a deeper understanding. As such, if the recommendations for one domain do not translate well into a digital game, the recommendations for another may.

Earlier works attempting to accomplish something similar have also identified some of the above principles. Helms *et al.* (2015) provide a "Educational Game Element Database" which includes mentions of a storyline, challenge, and feedback where challenge can refer to the structuring principle mentioned above. Additionally, Quinn (2005) discusses many approaches to designing e-learning game simulations and mention the importance of a storyline, adjusting the challenge, feedback, and reflection all of which are above.

6. LIMITATIONS AND FUTURE WORK

This study made use of various fields of academia as well as studies of serious games and their design in order to answer the research question. The current limitations on answering this question centre around the amount of literature sourced. The fields (pedagogy, ludology, and gamification) discussed seem to be sufficient in terms of what literature can be used and as such it is the specific literature used that imposes limitations. There are many more instructional theories that could be considered and as such future research could delve into more theories and expand the supporting knowledge base. Another limitation comes from the case studies used. All of the main case studies discussed in this article had a focus on computer security to varying degrees. Due to this, future research could include case studies on the design, implementation, or development of serious games in other fields as the findings may not generalise to certain topics or domains. These design principles provide the possible foundation for a further framework that could be devised and used for serious game design in general as opposed to specifically for one type of game. The principles presented account for major sections of serious game design but lack specifics on the more intricate aspects.

In terms of future research, a more practical approach could include the development of a serious game on a topic based on one of the knowledge domains mentioned. This could include the development of an artefact for user testing, similarly to *Anti-phishing Phil* (Sheng *et al.*, 2007), based on the findings of this study or the designing of such an artefact more in line with the *Digital Wellnests* game (Allers *et al.*, 2021). Future research could also include looking at several types of games and how they could teach content in the different knowledge domains to build upon Kapp's (2012a) recommendations.

7. CONCLUSION

This study discussed the shift educational institutions are making towards including more technology in the teaching process. As such, research into how serious games can be used in an educational environment was conducted with a specific focus on the fields of pedagogy, ludology, and gamification in order to answer the question, what qualities are required for a serious game to be effectively used in an educational environment on assorted topics. Furthermore, several research papers were used as case studies to discover what design principles are typically followed in the development of serious games. This information was then used to identify what are the major qualities which a serious game should have in order to be effective in an educational environment as well as provide specific recommendations for various knowledge domains. The qualities identified were allowing for reflection, providing feedback, making use of story elements and a well thought out structuring of the game.

REFERENCES

Ackoff, R. L. (1991). Teaching versus learning. *Systems practice*, 4(3), 179–180.

Allers, J., Drevin, G., Snyman, D., Kruger, H., & Drevin, L. (2021). Children's awareness of digital wellness: A serious games approach. *IFIP World Conference on Information Security Education,* 95–110.

Annetta, L. A. (2008). Video games in education: Why they should be used and how they are being used. *Theory into practice*, 47(3), 229–239.

Burke, J. W., McNeill, M., Charles, D., Morrow, P., Crosbie, J., & McDonough, S. (2009). Serious games for upper limb rehabilitation following stroke. *2009 Conference in Games and Virtual Worlds for Serious Applications*, Washington DC, United States, 103–110.

Callaghan, M. N., & Reich, S. M. (2018). Are educational preschool apps designed to teach? an analysis of the app market. *Learning, Media and Technology*, 43(3), 280–293.

Costanza, R., Chichakly, K., Dale, V., Farber, S., Finnigan, D., Grigg, K., Heckbert, S., Kubiszewski, I., Lee, H., & Liu, S. (2014). Simulation games that integrate research, entertainment, and learning around ecosystem services. *Ecosystem Services*, 10, 195–201.

De Gloria, A., Bellotti, F., & Berta, R. (2014). Serious games for education and training. *International Journal of Serious Games*, 1(1).

Deshpande, A. A., & Huang, S. H. (2011). Simulation games in engineering education: A state-of-the-art review. *Computer applications in engineering education*, 19(3), 399–410.

Dincelli, E., & Chengalur-Smith, I. (2020). Choose your own training adventure: Designing a gamified seta artefact for improving information security and privacy through interactive storytelling. *European Journal of Information Systems*, 29(6), 669–687.

Fisch, D., Janicke, M., Kalkowski, E., & Sick, B. (2009). Learning by teaching versus learning by doing: Knowledge exchange in organic agent systems. *2009 IEEE Symposium on Intelligent Agents*, Nashville, TN, USA, 31–38.

Frasca, G. (2013). Simulation versus narrative: Introduction to ludology. *In The video game theory reader*, pp. 221-235.

Gibson, D., Aldrich, C., & Prensky, M. (2006). *Games and simulations in online learning: Research and development frameworks*. IGI Global.

Helms, R. W., Barneveld, R., & Dalpiaz, F. (2015). A Method for the Design of Gamified Trainings. In 2015 Proceedings of the Pacific Asia Conference on Information Systems, Singapore, 59.

Huizinga, J., & Hull, R. F. C. (1949). *Homo ludens: a study of the play-element in culture*. [translated by rfc hull]

Kalogiannakis, M., Papadakis, S., & Zourmpakis, A. I. (2021). Gamification in science education. A systematic review of the literature. Education Sciences, 11(1), 22.

Kapp, K. M. (2012a). *The gamification of learning and instruction: Game-based methods and strategies for training and education*. John Wiley & Sons

Kapp, K. M. (2012b). What is gamification. *The gamification of learning and instruction: gamebased methods and strategies for training and education*, 1–23.

Keller, J. M. (1987). Development and use of the arcs model of instructional design. *Journal of instructional development*, 10(3), 2–10.

Li, G. (2012). *Culturally contested pedagogy: Battles of literacy and schooling between mainstream teachers and asian immigrant parents*. Suny Press.

Matthews, D., Lieven, E., & Tomasello, M. (2007). How toddlers and preschoolers learn to uniquely identify referents for others: A training study. *Child development*, 78(6), 1744–1759.

Merrill, M. D. (2002). First principles of instruction. *Educational technology research and development*, 50(3), 43–59.

Quinn, Clark. (2005). Engaging Learning: Designing e-Learning Simulation Games. John Wiley & Sons.

Ranalli, J. (2008). Learning english with the sims: Exploiting authentic computer simulation games for l2 learning. *Computer Assisted Language Learning*, 21(5), 441–455.

Reigeluth, C. M. (1996). A new paradigm of isd? *Educational technology*, 36(3), 13–20.

Sheng, S., Magnien, B., Kumaraguru, P., Acquisti, A., Cranor, L. F., Hong, J., & Nunge, E. (2007). Anti-phishing phil: The design and evaluation of a game that teaches people not to fall for phish. *Proceedings of the 3rd symposium on Usable privacy and security*, Pittsburgh, Pennsylvania, USA, 88–99.

Squire, K. (2003). Video games in education. *Int. J. Intell. Games & Simulation*, 2(1), 49–62.

Tao, Y.-H., Cheng, C.-J., & Sun, S.-Y. (2009). What influences college students to continue using business simulation games? the taiwan experience. *Computers & Education*, 53(3), 929–939.

Tîrziu, A.-M., & Vrabie, C. (2015). Education 2.0: E-Learning Methods. *Procedia - Social and Behavioral Sciences*, 186, 376–380.

Virvou, M., Katsionis, G., & Manos, K. (2005). Combining software games with education: Evaluation of its educational effectiveness. *Journal of Educational Technology & Society*, 8(2), 54–65.

Zourmpakis, A. I., Papadakis, S., & Kalogiannakis, M. (2022). Education of preschool and elementary teachers on the use of adaptive gamification in science education. International Journal of Technology Enhanced Learning, 14(1), 1-16.

DEVELOPING AN ONTOLOGY OF MULTIPLE PROGRAMMING LANGUAGES FROM THE PERSPECTIVE OF COMPUTATIONAL THINKING EDUCATION

Lalita Na Nongkhai[1], Jingyun Wang[2] and Takahiko Mendori[1]
[1]*Graduate School of Engineering, Kochi University of Technology, Japan*
[2]*Department of Computer Science, Durham University, UK*

ABSTRACT

This paper proposes the design of an ontology of multiple programming languages and give three examples to show the methodology. Our ontology aims to summarize the core of computational thinking logic by elaborating the concepts of three object-oriented programming languages in the industry: Python, Java, and C#. Therefore, the construction of the ontology lies not only on these three programming languages but also on their common concepts. This kind of ontology design facilitates the ontology extension and merging when concepts of other programming languages are added in the future. This ontology could be used to not only provide a guideline for any research work focusing on computational thinking education but also describe the common concept of visual programming tools and existing programming languages. Based on this ontology, an adaptive tutoring system intended to provide learners with personalized programming exercises, is under development.

KEYWORDS

Computational Thinking, Ontology, Programming Education

1. INTRODUCTION

Computational Thinking (CT) is a fundamental skill of a problem-solving approach in various skills such as English, Science, Mathematics, etc. (Jeannette, 2006). There are many approaches to teach computational thinking model. Learning with visual programming (VP) tools is suggested to be one of suitable method for children between 8 and 12 years old (or primary and secondary students) (Mercier et al, 2021). The existing VPs normally use gamification and animation elements to make the learning environment more engaging (Rose, Simon P. et al., 2017). Furthermore, in order to support CT skills learning, the basic programming concepts (such as variables, repetition, and conditional statements), to some extension, are abstracted by VP languages with the more advanced concepts (such as recursion, traversal, or indexing). However, few evidence supports that programming language can help those students learn CT skill easier. Also, those VP tools do not cover the same concepts. For example, Springin (2016) enables learners to make their drawing as a character and define the character ability, and relations, etc., by tapping the icons. VISCUIT (Watanabe et al., 2018), defines a glasses-shape item; after adding drawings in both glasses, users can create sequences and conditions to activate image in left turning to the one in right. Both of those two tools focus on a sequential logic in order to support learners easily understand conditional and repetition. Another popular type is the block-based VP tool, such as Scratch (Maloney et al., 2010), Blocky (Fraser et al., 2012) and MOONBlock (Mukai and mLAB, 2016), which enable learners to make programs by blocking-code. Some of them (such as Blocky) have a feature to convert from blocking-code to programming languages (Javascript, Python, etc). This feature not only supports learners to compare VP with PL, but also makes those tools involve more programming concepts (variables, conditions, repetitions, function) than other types of VP tools.

In higher education, explaining problem solving examples while teaching a specific programming language (PL) is another methodology for computational thinking logic education. Obviously, a PL covers more content than any existing VP and its education is more complicated. The trend of PL has changed quickly, as new VP tools are continually developing. This makes it more difficult for teachers to find a suitable teaching strategy. Because VP and PL have many programming concepts and not all concepts are included in every VP tool or PL. To address this issue, the summary of the common concept of any programming course, whatever it is VP, or any existing PL, can help any programming teacher find a strategy to design material or exercise. Also, it can help researchers/developers to design new programs or expand existing e-learning platforms or tools to support CT education.

Ontology can be used to represent any domain knowledge concept and relationship in any interested fields. In the education field, the e-learning systems adopting ontology as a semantic network to enhance their functions have been proven with the ability to support learners and instructors to search the information quickly and accurately (Wang, J. et al, 2014; Wang, J. et al, 2020). The object properties of ontology can be used to describe the relationship between knowledge concepts and its data properties can be used to elaborate information and examples of knowledge concepts. Furthermore, these ontologies can be easily reused in other research or systems.

In this work, we propose a COmputatioNal ThinkIng oNtology mUltiple prOgramming langUageS (CONTINUOUS, can be accessed by https://github.com/lalita-nk/CONTINUOUS.git) to describe common concepts of any programming course (no matter VP or PL). Our research questions are: can CONTINUOUS benefit (1) novice learners in understanding and determining their learning orders, (2) programming lectures in making teaching plan and preparing materials/exercises, and (3) the researcher working on the designs new VP/PL or the development of the existing VP/PL? For the education of programming languages, most of the previous systems incorporate only one ontology of an existing programming language. The ontology designed in our research involves the domain knowledge of three programming languages: Python, Java, and C# (C sharp), which are the most popular programming languages for beginner learners. CONTINUOUS is intended be the foundation of any intelligent tutoring systems which need to record the metadata of programming knowledge.

2. LITERATURE REVIEW

Most previous ontologies implemented in programming language fields focus on the procedural programming language C or object-oriented programming language Java. Sosnovsky and Gavrilova (2006) proposed a step-designing approach to create an educational ontology for C programming to explain knowledge concepts and their relationship in C. The top-level class of this ontology is "C programming", following with the second-level classes "SYNTAX", "PROGRAMMING TECHNIQUES", and "PLATFORMS". They claimed that this ontology shows the important concept of C programming from the researchers' vision. However, their ontology only includes "has part" relation to show the hierarchical structure. Ming-Che Lee et al. (2005) proposed the ontology of a Java programming language, one of the object-oriented programming languages. The objective of this research is to guide instructors to design learning strategies for teaching. The relationship between concepts can help instructors to build more suitable material. This research also proposed a methodology to build this ontology so that any researchers interested in the Java programming language can refer to this ontology in their research.

Pierrakeas et al. (2012) proposed to organize Learning Object (LOs) based on two ontologies of two programming languages: C and Java. Their ontologies included the basic concept of two languages as metadata of the corresponding Learning Objects (LO) to help instructors make clearly the domain concepts. The instructors can follow the information in the ontology for the creation of learning material and teaching strategies. However, their ontology only describes the content of C and Java separately, no common content is summarized.

Our research proposed and implemented an ontology (called "CONTINUOUS") which combines the concepts of three programming languages. We designed a top-level class "common concepts" which summarizes the basic concepts shared by all the three programming languages and designed the concepts in each language in a separate class. "CONTINUOUS" may benefit instructors, learners, and others to apply this basic programming language concept in their work or research.

3. THE DESIGN OF A COMPUTATIONAL THINKING ONTOLOGY BASED ON MULTIPLE PROGRAMMING LANGUAGES (CONTINUOUS)

3.1 The Design of Top-level & Second-level Classes

The construction of the programming language ontology in this research covering the concepts of Python, Java, and C#, is consistent with the knowledge emerging in our Question Bank (include 20 basic concepts) (Na Nongkhai et al., 2021), which are design based on opinion of instructors who have several years of programming teaching experience, and existing programming tutorials. CONTINUOUS was built by Protégé (Musen and Protégé Team, 2015), a popular and open-source ontology editor.

According to CONTINUOUS design which includes more than one programming language. The top-level concepts consist of 4 classes: common concepts, C sharp, Java, and Python, as shown in Figure 1. For the top-level, our design first focuses on the "common concepts" which covers all basic concepts of the three programming languages such as built-in function, data structure, conditionals (if, if-else, etc.), repetition (for-loop, etc.), method, etc. CONTINUOUS defines the basic programming concepts as a "class" (Top-level and Second-level as shown in Figure 1) and the syntax of a specific programming language is located on the leaf as an "instance".

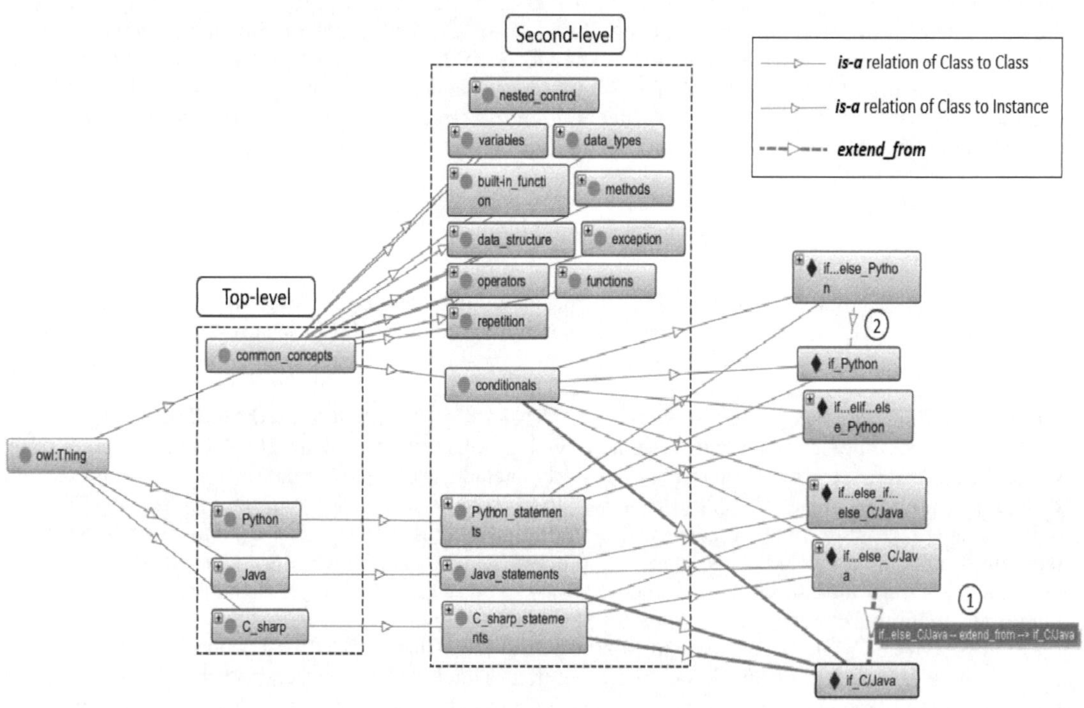

Figure 1. An example of instance in class "conditionals"

For example, "if_C/Java" is designed as one instance of "conditionals" because the "if statement" has the same programming syntax in both C# and Java while "if_Python" as another instance due to its different syntax. On the other hand, "if_C/Java" is also an instance of the second-level concept "Java_statements" and "C_sharp_statements" while "if_Python" is also an instance of "Python_statements". We also designed a relation named "extend from" between "if…else_C/Java" and "if_C/Java" (① in Figure 1) because "if-else statement" is the syntax that extends from the "if statement", this relation (② in Figure 1) also exists between "if_Python" and "if…else_Python" for the same reason. In summary, the design of the instances and their relations is based on the similarity and the difference of syntax of the three programming languages. Therefore, as shown in Figure 2, the object property of "if…else_C/Java" in CONTINUOUS includes "extend from" connecting to "if_C/Java", which corresponds to ① in Figure 1. And the data property is designed to include "definition" (③ in Figure 2), "example" (② in Figure 2, which shows a code snippet), and "grammar specification" (① in Figure.2, which describes the syntax) to explain the usage of "if-else statement".

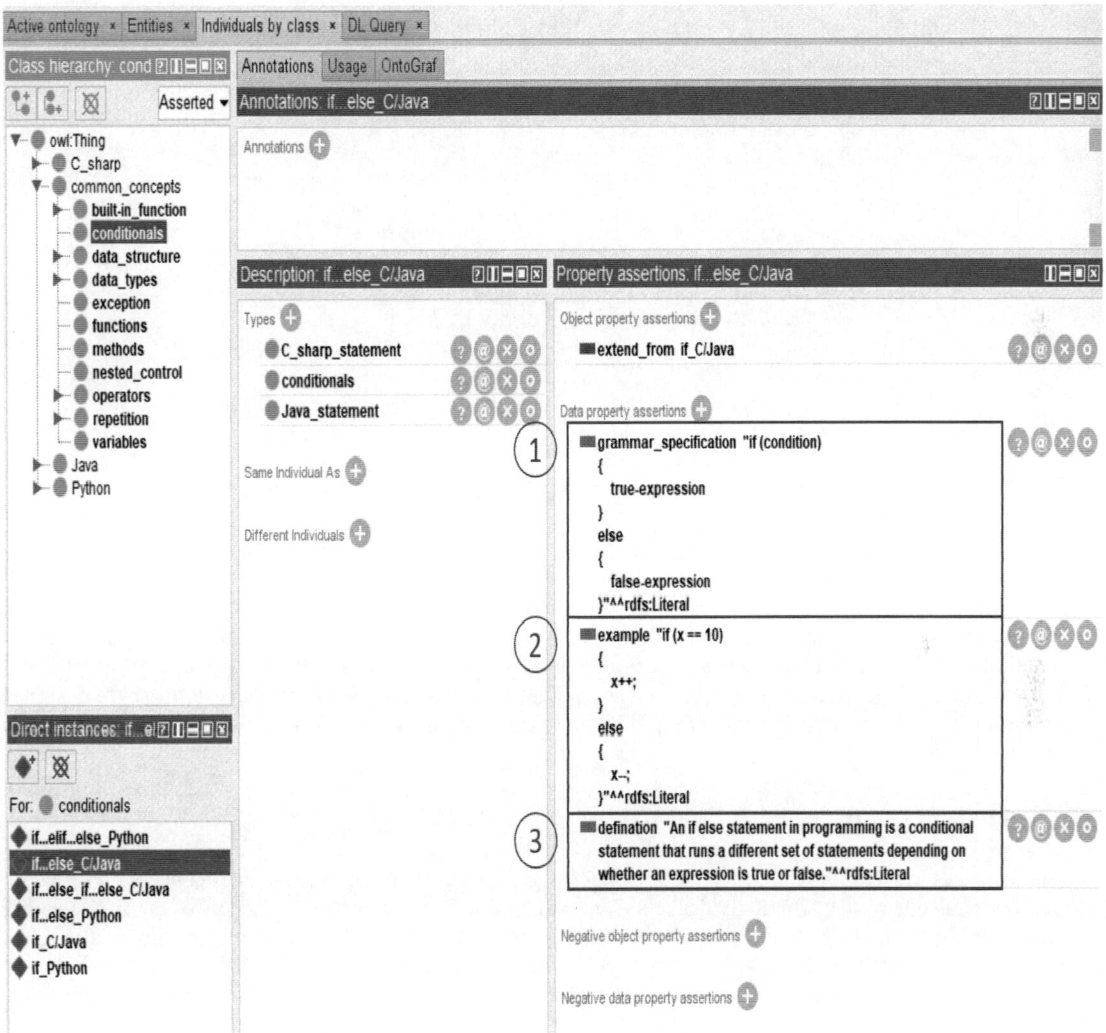

Figure 2. An example of all properties in "if…else_C/Java"

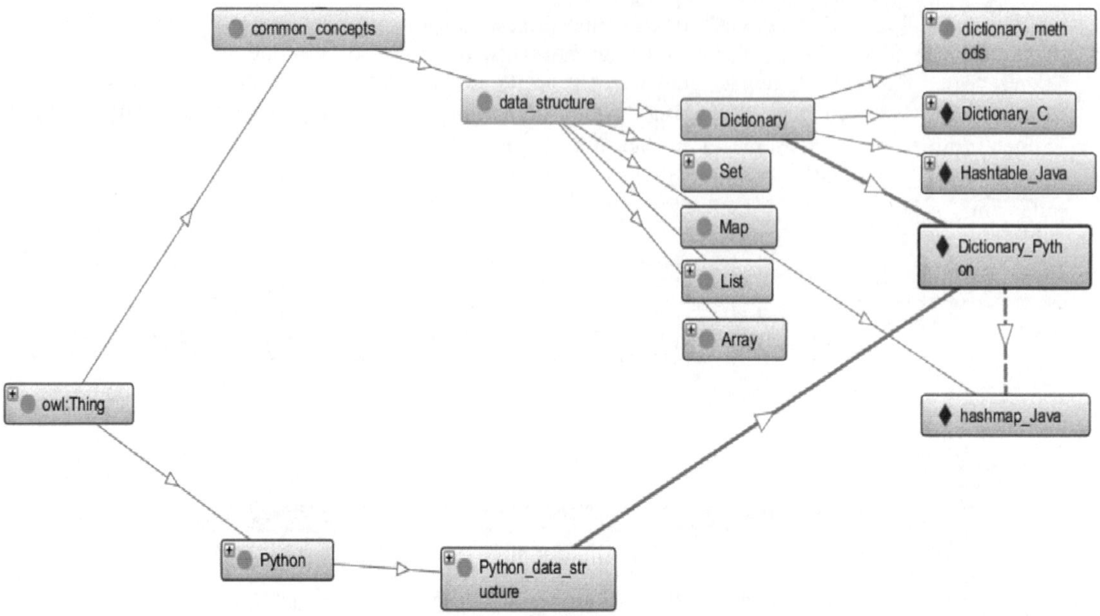

Figure 3. An example of "common concepts" and "Python"

3.2 The Design of "Data_Structure" in "Common_Concepts"

Another design focus of "common_concepts" is on "data_structure", which are the most essential in any PL (Wegner, 1971) but rarely appears in VP. As shown in Figure 3, there are 5 common Data structures: Dictionary, Set, Map, List and Array. Some of the structures (such as "List") are shared by the three languages, but some (such as "Dictionary") only appear in two of the languages: Python and C#. "Dictionary" is a data structure that shared by C# and Python, but its grammar in Python is different from the grammar in C#. Therefore, to describe the specific usage in Python, the "Dictionary_Python" is designed as an instance of the second-level concept "Python_data_structures" which is the subclass of the top-level concept "Python".

3.3 Abstract Concepts in "Common_Concepts"

The instances in CONTINUOUS could be either programming statements or abstract concepts. For example, "methods" as one of the "common_concepts", is designed to include abstract concepts of the functionality of each specific method (such as "add_an_element"), and "list_methods" consists of the methods in List (an abstract data type) We design "has_an_instance" (which has a reverse relation called "is_an_instance_of") to link the abstract concept (such as "sort_the_elements") to its corresponding method in each specific programming language (such as "sort()_Python", an instance of "Python_built-in_function"). These abstract concepts provide the summary of the common concepts needed in computational thinking logic while each programming language has their own syntax. This kind of design not only provide the perspective from one specific programming language but also from general similarity of all programming languages.

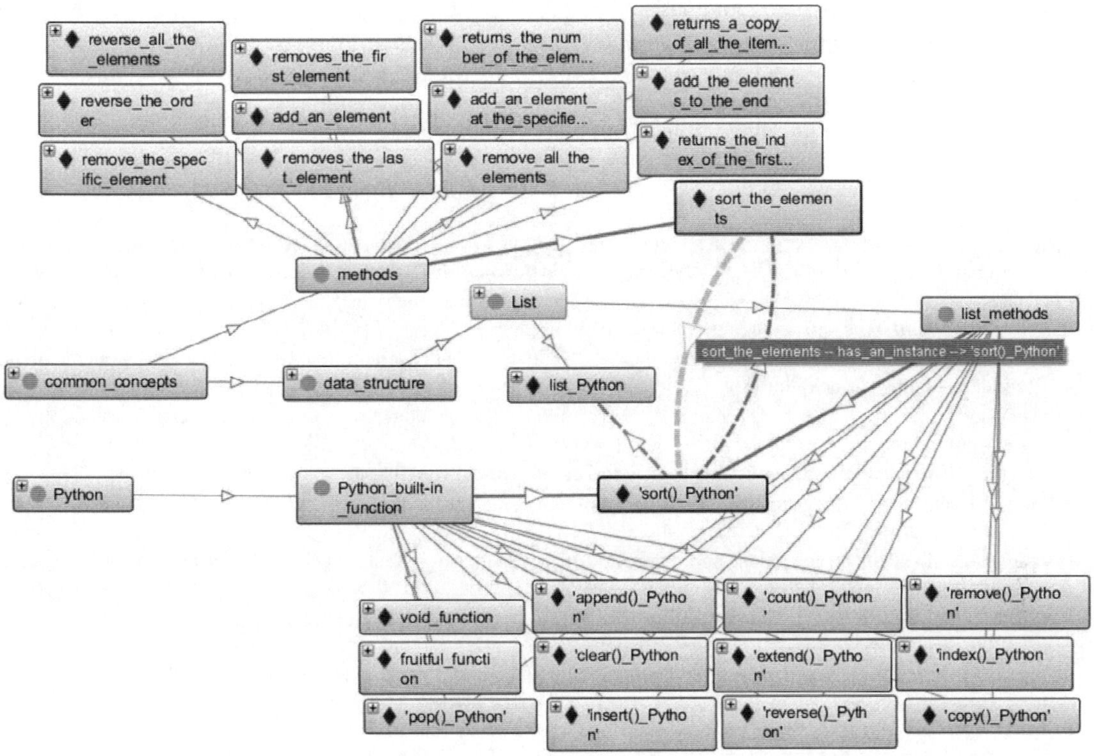

Figure 4. An example of direct instinct and object property of "sort_the_elements"

4. CONCLUSION AND FUTURE WORK

This paper describes some examples of CONTINUOUS to show how we identify the core concept of CT education by merging the concepts of existing programming languages. We intend to support CT education no matter what kind of programming language is used as a tool for the implementation. The common concepts designed in CONTINUOUS may benefits novice learners in determining learning orders, instructors in making strategies of pedagogies, and researchers in expanding CONTINUOUS or applying CONTINUOUS as metadata in any intelligent tutoring systems.

In the future, CONTINUOUS can be easily extended to include more programming language by simply adding more top-level concepts named with the names of programming languages and modifying the content inside the "common concepts". In other words, the feasibility and reusability of ontology facilitate the expansion of its contents. Based on CONTINUOUS, we are implementing a system (Na Nongkhai et al., 2021) to help instructors to design exercises that can be used to provide personalized support for learners. This system will allow instructors to add exercises based on the knowledge defined in CONTINUOUS and enable learners to check their personal progress with visualization support.

REFERENCES

Fraser, N. et al, 2012. *Blockly. Google Developers*. Retrieved from https://developers.google.com/blockly

Jeannette M. Wing. 2006. Computational thinking. Communication of the ACM. ACM 49, 3 (March 2006), 33–35.

Maloney, J. et al, 2010. The scratch programming language and environment. *ACM Transactions on Computing Education (TOCE)*, Vol. 10 No. 4, pp. 1-15.

Mercier, C. et al, 2021. Formalizing Problem Solving in Computational Thinking: An Ontology approach. *2021 IEEE International Conference on Development and Learning (ICDL)*. Beijing, China, pp. 1-8.

Ming-Che Lee et al, 2005. Java learning object ontology. *Fifth IEEE International Conference on Advanced Learning Technologies (ICALT'05)*. Kaohsiung, Taiwan, pp. 538-542.

Mukai, N. and mLAB, 2016. Game programming with MOONBlock.Retrieved from https://mukai-lab.info/pages/tech/enchant_js/moonblock/

Musen, M. A., and Protégé Team, 2015. The Protégé Project: A Look Back and a Look Forward. *AI matters*, Vol. 1, No. 4, pp. 4–12.

Na Nongkhai, L. et al, 2021. A Framework of Exercise Recommendation for Novice Learners in Computer Programming. *ICCE 2021: The 29th International Conference on Computers in Education Online*. pp. 746-749.

Pierrakeas, C. et al, 2012. An Ontology-Based Approach in Learning Programming Languages. *16th Panhellenic Conference on Informatics*. Piraeus, Greece, pp. 393-398.

Rose, Simon P. et al, 2017. An exploration of the role of visual programming tools in the development of young children's computational thinking. *Electronic Journal of e-Learning*, Vol. 15, pp. 297-309.

Sosnovsky, S.A., and Gavrilova, T., 2006. Development Of Educational Ontology for C-Programming. *International Journal "Information Theories & Applications"*, Vol. 13, No. 4, pp. 303-307.

Springin, 2016. *Springin' – Creative Programming Tool*. Retrieved from https://www.springin.org/en/

Wang, J. et al, 2014. A language learning support system using course-centered ontology and its evaluation. *Computers & Education*, Vol. 78, pp. 278-293.

Wang, J. et al, 2020. Development and evaluation of a visualization system to support meaningful e-book learning. *Interactive Learning Environments*, pp. 1-18.

Watanabe, T. et al, 2018. Programming Lessons for Kindergarten Children in Japan. *Constructionism2018*. Vilnius, Lithuania, pp. 741-744.

Wegner, P., 1971. Data structure models for programming languages. *ACM SIGPLAN Notices*, Vol. 6 No. 2, pp. 1-54.

STUDENT PERCEPTIONS OF AI-POWERED WRITING TOOLS: TOWARDS INDIVIDUALIZED TEACHING STRATEGIES

Michael Burkhard
Institute for Educational Management and Technologies
St.Jakob-Strasse 21, University of St.Gallen, Switzerland

ABSTRACT

Due to the advances of artificial intelligence (AI) and natural language processing, new kinds of Internet-based writing tools have emerged. Among other things, these AI-powered writing tools can be used by students for text translation, to improve spelling or for rewriting and summarizing texts. On the one hand, they can provide detailed recommendations for the adaptation of text elements within seconds. On the other hand, they also produce inconsistencies and errors, that students might not be aware of. How to deal with these tools in an educational context is a difficult question. Since writing tools are usually used unsupervised and without further instructions, students may need guidance from the teacher in interacting with those tools, to prevent the risk of misapplication. To better understand this underlying issue, the paper at hand uses survey data of 365 freshmen students to describe and analyze student perceptions of AI-powered writing tools. Regarding AI-powered writing tools, different student types were identified by using the k-means clustering method. The results suggest that students have different attitudes towards AI-powered writing tools. Some students may use them in an unreflective, non-sceptical way, which can lead to (un)voluntary plagiarism. Other students may not use writing tools at all, partly because they are sceptic, but also because they may lack meaningful learning strategies in general (course repeaters). Depending on the different student types, individualized teaching strategies might be helpful to promote or urge caution in the use of these tools.

KEYWORDS

Artificial Intelligence in Education, Writing Tools, Writing Competencies, Language Learning, Student-Centered Learning, K-Means Clustering

1. INTRODUCTION

The digital age is changing the way we learn and brings with it new tools that can support us in many ways. In the field of academic writing and language learning, students' writing habits are changing due to the rise of new technologies and the Internet (Moore et al., 2016; Peters & Cadieux, 2019). Advances in artificial intelligence (AI) and natural language processing lead to language and writing tools, that become increasingly powerful (Geitgey, 2018; Brown et al., 2020; Heaven, 2020). New kind of AI-powered writing tools have emerged (see e.g., Rogerson & McCarthy, 2017; Prentice & Kinden, 2018) that are often freely available on the Internet.

Among other things, these *AI-powered writing tools* can be used for *text translation* (e.g., www.deepl.com, https://translate.google.com), to *improve spelling* (e.g., https://mentor.duden.de), for *text analysis* (e.g., https://hemingwayapp.com), for *rewriting and summarizing texts* (e.g., https://quillbot.com) or for *plagiarism checks* (e.g., https://www.grammarly.com/plagiarism-checker). These tools can provide detailed suggestions and recommendations for the adaptation of text elements within seconds. However, they also produce inconsistencies and errors, that may not be obvious to all students (Rogerson & McCarthy, 2017).

People are raising their voices to warn about the dangers of these digital writing tools and their potential misuse, which could lead, among other things, to new types of plagiarism (see e.g., Rogerson & McCarthy, 2017; Prentice & Kinden, 2018). Since text content can be quickly and easily changed and reused, there is a danger that students will un-sceptically follow the recommendations of digital writing tools without critically questioning them. An important function of *writing* is to construct one's own identity (e.g., Ivanic, 1998), but also to develop meaningful arguments and points of view (e.g., Van Eemeren & Grootendorst, 2016). Is there a risk of losing these competences, when we increasingly rely on AI-powered writing tools, who support us in our writing?

How to deal with these tools in an educational context is still largely an unexplored field. Given the fact that these tools are freely available on the Internet, a straight ban for these tools inside the classroom may not be effective, as students might use them anyway at home. Since AI-powered writing tools are usually used unsupervised and without further instructions (no possibility to ask questions), students may need guidance and support from the teacher in interacting with those tools. Otherwise, there is a risk of misapplication such as intentional, or unintentional plagiarism as well as the unreflective adoption of recommendations (see e.g., Rogerson & McCarthy, 2017; Prentice & Kinden, 2018). Kranzberg (1986, p. 545) said, that "technology is neither good nor bad; nor is it neutral". Depending on the circumstances and the context, a given technology may lead to different results (Kranzberg, 1986, pp. 545-548). Therefore, the goal should be to better understand student perceptions of AI-powered writing tools, to better grasp the circumstances in which the use of such tools may be appropriate, and to develop teaching methods that are more individually adapted to specific student needs. In light of the identified research desideratum, the following research question should be addressed:

What attitudes do freshmen students have towards AI-powered writing tools?

The objectives of the paper at hand are therefore twofold:

- describing and analyzing student perceptions of AI-powered writing tools, to obtain a nuanced picture and evaluate underlying assumptions;
- identifying different student stereotypes regarding AI-powered writing tools, to reflect on meaningful, individualized teaching strategies for these tools.

For this purpose, survey data from 365 freshmen students at the University of St.Gallen in Switzerland are analyzed. The survey data was collected in September 2021 during the first-semester course "Introduction to Academic Writing" via the survey tool Unipark (https://www.unipark.com/en). To identify meaningful student types, the k-means cluster analysis was used.

From a theoretical point of view, the paper at hand can serve as a starting point for future research as it categorizes student perceptions in a systematic way and highlights important variables related to AI-powered writing tools. From a practical standpoint, the paper at hand may be valuable for (language) teachers, who are interested in the implications of AI-powered writing tools and look for ways, how to address and deal with them. The identified student clusters may help to better understand the individual student standpoints, when teaching with or about AI-powered writing tools.

To this end, section 2 further elaborates on the method used in this paper and describes the survey and the setting in which it was conducted. Section 3 shows the survey results. While section 3.1 describes and analyzes the stated student perceptions of AI-powered writing tools, section 3.2 uses the k-means clustering method to identify different student types. Section 4 wraps up the previous findings and discusses them critically. Section 5 concludes with some final remarks.

2. METHOD

The survey was conducted in fall term 2021 in the first-semester course "Introduction to academic writing" (IAW), which is mandatory for all 1615 freshmen at the University of St.Gallen. The course has an English track (510 students) and a German one (1105 students). In the course, students learn necessary skills for writing their own scientific paper (e.g., finding and narrowing down a topic, conducting literature research). During the on-site kick-off lecture, students were introduced to different projects in the field of artificial intelligence (e.g., IBM Project Debater). In addition, several videos gave an overview of different writing tools that can be used amongst other things for text translation, spelling, text analysis, summarizing or plagiarism checks (one of the videos shown was: https://www.youtube.com/watch?v=4I-F-mj20l4).

After the initial kick-off lecture, students were asked to complete the voluntary 20 minutes online survey. In total, 370 of 1615 students participated (23%). 5 entries had to be removed because of missing values but for 365 participants all necessary information could be gathered. Table 1 gives an overview over the student participants.

Table 1. Participant Description: Summary of Features

Feature	Mean	St. Dev.	Min	Max	Scale
Age (number of years)	19.68	1.489	17	27	Integer (0-99)
Gender (1=female)	0.375	-	0	1	Binary (0 / 1)
Language track (1= English)	0.362	-	0	1	Binary (0 / 1)
Course attendance (1= first try)	0.901	-	0	1	Binary (0 / 1)
Socioeconomic status	0.833	0.237	0	1	Decimal (0-1)
Attitude towards writing	2.749	0.847	1	5	5-point Likert scale (1-5)
Self-efficacy in relation to studying	3.756	0.719	1.33	5	5-point Likert scale (1-5)
Big-5-Openness	3.433	0.768	1	5	5-point Likert scale (1-5)
Big-5-Conscientiousness	3.474	0.820	1	5	5-point Likert scale (1-5)

Number of observations = 365.

On average student participants were 19.68 years old. 37.5% of the participants were female (62.5% male), and 36.2% of the participants were enlisted in the English track (63.8% in the German track). Most of the participants attended the course for the first time (90.1%), as only 9.9% of the participants had to repeat the course. An instrument for the *socioeconomic status* was created by using the *numbers of books in the parents' household* as well as the *highest educational level of either mother or father*. Four questions related to writing (e.g., writing is a hobby of mine) were used to build the instrument *attitude towards writing,* which was measured on a 5-point Likert scale (Disagree strongly, Disagree a little, Neutral, Agree a little, Agree strongly). Six questions related to self-efficacy (e.g., I am confident that I can use the time available for exam preparation productively for learning) were used to build the instrument *self-efficacy in relation to studying*. In addition, the big five inventory (BFI-10) was used to capture personality traits (see Rammstedt et al., 2014).

3. RESULTS

3.1 Student Perceptions of AI-Powered Writing Tools

The 365 participants were asked on a 5-point scale (ranging from *Completely useless*, *Somewhat useless*, *Neutral*, *Somewhat useful*, *Very Useful*), how useful they find AI-powered writing tools with regard to *text translation* (e.g., DeepL, Google Translate), *spelling* (e.g., Duden-Mentor), *text analysis* (e.g., Hemmingwayapp), *summarizing* (e.g., Quillbot) and *plagiarism checking* (e.g., Grammarly). For each category, an example of a writing tool was given that the students had learned about in the kick-off lecture. Table 2 gives an overview over the stated student perceptions.

Table 2. Variables related to AI-powered writing tools

Feature	Mean	Median	St. Dev.	Min	Max
Perceived usefulness text translation	4.573	5	0.762	1	5
Perceived usefulness spelling	4.162	4	0.895	1	5
Perceived usefulness text analysis	3.879	4	0.915	1	5
Perceived usefulness summarizing	3.748	4	0.942	1	5
Perceived usefulness plagiarism check	4.359	5	0.858	1	5

Number of observations = 365. 5-point scale used.

The overall perception of students regarding the usefulness of writing tools is positive. *Text translation tools* are rated the most useful, followed by tools for *plagiarism checking* and tools to *improve spelling*. Writing tools for *text analysis* or tools for *summarizing texts* are considered comparatively less useful.

In addition, all participants were asked the following three open-ended questions:

1) "In your opinion, what are the advantages of AI-powered writing tools?"
2) "In your opinion, what are the disadvantages of AI-powered writing tools?"
3) "What ethical concerns do you have regarding the use of AI-powered writing tools?"

268 of 365 students (73.4%) answered these voluntary questions and Table 3 shows examples of different student responses. Based on the information provided in the open-ended questions, each student was assigned into one of five attitude levels towards AI-powered writing tools (*positive*, *rather positive*, *differentiated/nuanced*, *rather negative*, *negative*). 76 participants (28.4%) had a clearly *positive* attitude towards AI-powered writing tools, as they mentioned only advantages but no disadvantages or ethical concerns with regard to these tools (see Table 3). 59 participants (22%) had a *rather positive* attitude as they mentioned advantages together with only few minor concerns. 108 participants (40.3%) had a *differentiated/nuanced* attitude towards AI-powered writing tools, as they mentioned advantages as well as disadvantages and ethical concerns in a differentiated way. 21 participants (7.8%) had a *rather negative* attitude towards AI-powered writing tools, as they explicitly stated disadvantages or ethical concerns combined with only minor perceived advantages (e.g., fast, second view). 4 participants (1.5%) had a *negative* attitude towards these tools, as they stated only disadvantages or ethical concerns.

Overall, 135 participants (50.4%) had a *positive* or *rather positive* attitude, 108 participants (40.3%) a *differentiated/nuanced* attitude and only 25 participants (9.3%) a *rather negative* or *negative* attitude towards AI-powered writing tools.

Table 3. Student perceptions of AI-powered writing tools: examples of student responses

Assigned attitude level		Perceived advantages	Perceived disadvantages	Ethical concerns	(#n)	(%)
5 =	Positive	*"No spelling mistakes."*	*"Can't think of any."*	*"None."*	76	28.4
4 =	Rather positive	*"Fast, cheap and available 24/7."*	*"Not always as accurate as specialists."*	*"I do not know yet."*	59	22
3 =	Differentiated/ Nuanced	*"Assisting: Spelling, Translation etc."*	*"Can be misleading, if one does not know the exact meaning or context of certain words, e.g., synonyms can have different meaning and context."*	*"Makes certain jobs redundant."*	108	40.3
2 =	Rather negative	*"Fast, second view."*	*"You shouldn't just let the AI write your text."*	-	21	7.8
1 =	Negative	-	*"I really don't like so therefore no advantages for me."*	-	4	1.5

Number of observations = 268.

Different advantages were mentioned by the students with regard to AI-powered writing tools. Most students mentioned just one advantage (n=184) of using AI-powered writing tools, but some also stated two (n=59) or three (n=11). The mentioned advantages were grouped into four broad categories, which are depicted in Table 4. Most students mentioned either *quality* (47.8%) or *efficiency* (43.7%) as an advantage of using AI-powered writing tools (see Table 4). The aspect that these tools are always *available* on the Internet and can provide "quick support anytime and anywhere" was mentioned by 25.7% of the participants. Roughly 9% of the participants also stated advantages that relate to the complementary skill set between humans and smart machines (*human augmentation*). For example, AI-powered writing tools might be helpful for "finding things humans might overlook", because they provide a "chance to double-check" or because they may serve as a "back-up and self-control".

Table 4. Perceived advantages with regard to AI-powered writing tools

Advantage	Example 1	Example 2	(#n)	(%)
Quality	*"Precise and correct"*	*"Improve writing skills"*	128	47.8
Efficiency	*"fast & efficient"*	*"efficient feedback"*	117	43.7
Availability	*"Quick support anytime and anywhere"*	*"Easy to use and always available"*	69	25.7
Human augmentation	*"Finding things humans might overlook"*	*"Chance to double-check"*	23	8.6
No advantages mentioned	-	-	2	0.7

Number of observations = 268. Students have sometimes expressed zero or more than just one concern. Therefore, the sum of the partial percentages is higher than 100 percent.

Different disadvantages and concerns were mentioned by the students with regard to AI-powered writing tools. Most students mentioned just one disadvantage or concern (n=154) of using AI-powered writing tools, but some also stated two (n=65), three (n=3) or five (n=1). The mentioned disadvantages and concerns were grouped into six categories, which are depicted in Table 5.

Table 5. Perceived disadvantages and concerns with regard to AI-powered writing tools

Concern	Example 1	Example 2	(#n)	(%)
Accuracy	*"Not always as accurate as specialists."*	*"Sometimes wrong translation/words: not fully developed sometimes."*	139	51.9
Influence on own writing	*"Humans getting lazy and loosing basic writing skills."*	*"My big question is: is it really still your text or the text of the tool?"*	62	23.1
Human replacement	*"Take away human jobs."*	*"Lecturers could be made redundant."*	49	18.3
Data abuse	*"How data is processed and stored, and who might have access to and what might be done with it."*	*"Misuse of the data."*	35	13.1
Plagiarism	*"Will it start fostering plagiarism?"*	*"Sometimes it is like cheating".*	12	4.4
Fairness	*"it's rather unfair, no access -> disadvantage."*	*"Easier to get good grades."*	5	1.9
No Concerns at all	*"None."*	-	43	16

Number of observations = 268. Students have sometimes expressed zero or more than just one concern. Therefore, the sum of the partial percentages is higher than 100 percent.

The limited *accuracy* is seen by most students (51.9%) as a major disadvantage and concern of today's AI-powered writing tools. 23.1% of the students stated, that using AI-powered writing tools have *influence on their own writing*. For example, students said that these tools make them lazy, that they hinder their learning of how to write good texts, that they take away the individual writing style or that they become dependent from these tools. 18.3% of the students stated reasons addressing *human replacement*, such as the loss of jobs or the replacement of teachers, lecturers and translators due to these writing tools. 13.1% of the students mentioned concerns in relation to *data abuse*, such as data leaks, privacy breaches or espionage. 4.4% of the students stated *plagiarism* concerns as these tools can support the act of writing in so many aspects. 1.9% of the participants also argued, that such tools raise *fairness* considerations, as it may be easier to get good grades using such tools. In addition, not all the tools are available for free which may be unfair for the students who cannot afford paid subscription plans.

3.2 Cluster Analysis: On the Lookout for Different Student Types

The previous section described overall student perceptions of AI-powered writing tools. However, students' perceptions of AI-powered writing tools may be quite heterogeneous. They may range from students who like the tools very much and at the same time critically reflect them, to students who do not like them and possibly do not use them at all. If we could identify specific types of students, students could be trained more individually and appropriately in dealing with AI-powered writing tools. Clustering could be used to identify homogenous groups of students with similar features and interests (Elia et al., 2019). Based on the clusters, teaching methods could be individualized and adapted.

To descriptively analyze and cluster student perceptions of AI-powered writing tools, the k-means clustering method was used (see Lantz, 2019, pp. 287-312). The k-means clustering method is well suited for interval-based (numerical) data, but not for the analysis of responses to open-ended questions (such as unstructured textual data in string format). Therefore, the responses to the open-ended questions were only used indirectly by generating two further numerical instruments from the students' comments (the *overall attitude level* as well as the *sum of concerns* mentioned by each student).

For all calculations the statistical software *R* (version 4.1.3) was used. To simplify the interpretation of our clusters, first a z-score standardized data frame was created. This new data frame with a mean of zero for each variable, included all five variables related to the *perceived usefulness of AI-powered writing tools* (text translation, spelling, text analysis, summarizing, plagiarism check), the *overall attitude level* of the three comments made as well as the *sum of concerns* an individual participant stated with regard to AI-powered writing tools.

As an initial value for k, sometimes the square root of (n/2) is suggested (Lantz, 2019, p. 296). However in our case, this would be k = sqrt(266/2) ≈ 12, which is too high, as we hope to achieve a k<7 in order to have a dimensionality reduction. Applying the elbow method (Lantz, 2019, p. 297), k=2 was taken as an initial value and then k was increased step by step until the additional cluster did not add anymore much additional value in separating students into meaningful groups. Through this approach, four meaningful clusters could be identified, whose cluster centers are shown in Table 6. Because a z-score standardized data frame is used with a mean of zero for each variable, positive numbers indicate values higher than the average, negative numbers indicate values below average.

Table 6. Cluster centers using a z-score standardized distribution

Cluster	Sceptical limited user (Cluster 1)	Not sceptical limited user (Cluster 2)	Not sceptical general user (Cluster 3)	Sceptical non-user (Cluster 4)
Size	76	72	89	29
Perceived usefulness text translation	0.252	0.012	0.405	-1.936
Perceived usefulness spelling	-0.252	-0.249	0.724	-0.942
Perceived usefulness text analysis	-0.197	-0.586	0.986	-1.053
Perceived usefulness summarizing	-0.312	-0.577	0.880	-0.448
Perceived usefulness plagiarism check	0.086	-0.048	0.449	-1.485
Overall attitude level of comment	-0.833	0.813	0.252	-0.609
Sum of concerns	0.686	-0.485	-0.393	0.610

Cluster 1 consists of *sceptical limited users* as the cluster is characterized by students who perceive only certain specific tools as useful (text translation and plagiarism checking) combined with a sceptical attitude and a lot of concerns when using these tools. Cluster 2 (*not sceptical limited user*) is characterized by students who think that only translation tools are useful and at the same time have a very positive attitude towards these tools and only few concerns. Cluster 3 (*not sceptical general user*) finds all kind of writing tools useful, has a positive attitude and only few concerns towards AI-powered writing tools. Cluster 4 consists of *sceptical non-users*. Within this group, the usefulness of writing tools in general is perceived relatively low, combined with an overall negative attitude and a lot of concerns when using these tools. Figure 1 summarizes the four derived clusters with regard to the attitude (*sceptical* vs. *not sceptical*) as well as the user type (*non-user*, *limited user*, *general user*).

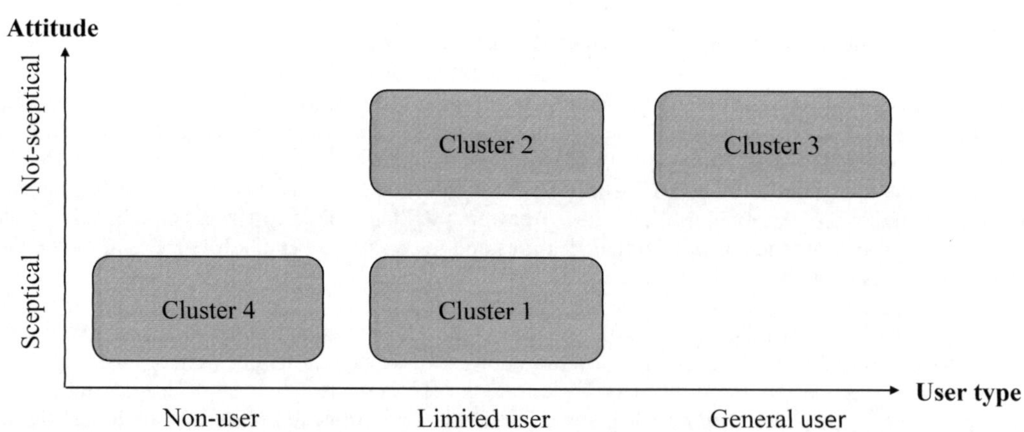

Figure 1. Overview over the derived student clusters

To describe and distinguish the different clusters, Table 7 gives an overview of important summary statistics. Note, that cluster 0 (*not answered*) was added, which consists of the 99 students, who did not answer the three voluntary open-ended questions. For these students, the *overall attitude* of the comments as well as the *sum of stated concerns* could not be calculated, which is why they had to be excluded from the cluster analysis in the first place. Nevertheless, they may serve as an interesting baseline in comparison to the other clusters.

Table 7. Summary of k-means cluster analysis: mean values for each cluster

Cluster	Not answered (Cluster 0)	Sceptical limited user (Cluster 1)	Not sceptical limited user (Cluster 2)	Not sceptical general user (Cluster 3)	Sceptical non-user (Cluster 4)
Size	99	76	72	89	29
Overall attitude of comment	-	2.84	4.51	3.94	3.07
Sum of concerns	-	1.61	0.78	0.84	1.55
Age (number of years)	19.79	19.74	19.58	19.45	20.1
Gender (1=female)	0.32	0.39	0.35	0.42	0.45
Language track (1= English)	0.29	0.51	0.24	0.46	0.21
Course attendance (1= first try)	0.90	0.89	0.93	0.93	0.75
Socioeconomic status	0.73	0.86	0.85	0.83	0.79
Attitude towards writing	2.68	2.80	2.67	2.81	2.87
Self-efficacy in relation to studying	3.58	3.76	3.79	3.95	3.66
Big-5-Openness	3.38	3.41	3.43	3.60	3.19
Big-5-Conscientiousness	3.31	3.48	3.49	3.65	3.45

Number of observations = 365.

As can be observed in Table 7, the student clusters are quite homogenous regarding certain criteria (e.g., age, socioeconomic status). However, regarding other criteria, the cluster also differ. Especially cluster 4 (*sceptical non-user*) separates itself from the other clusters. While in all other clusters the fraction of course repeaters (course attendance) lie between 7 and 11%, this number is much higher in cluster 4. 25% of the students in cluster 4 have failed their first year at the university and undertake a second attempt. As a result, the average age in cluster 4 is higher than in the other clusters. Compared to the other clusters, the typical *sceptical non-user* (cluster 4) has relatively low self-efficacy in relation to studying, low conscientiousness and a low openness to try out new things. In contrast, the typical *not sceptical general user* (cluster 3) has, compared to the other clusters, the highest self-efficacy in relation to studying, the highest conscientiousness and the highest openness.

Regarding the language track (English vs. German), the clusters also differ. 51% of the *sceptical limited users* (cluster 1) are enlisted in the English track. *Not sceptical limited users* (cluster 2) are mainly students from the German track (76%). *Not sceptical general users* (cluster 3) have again many students in the English track (46%) and *sceptical non-users* (cluster 4) consist mainly of students from the German track (79%).

4. DISCUSSION

The analysis in the previous section suggests, that there might exist different student types with regard to AI-powered writing tools. The *sceptical limited users* (cluster 1) are characterized by many students who are enlisted in the English-track (51%). In contrast, most of the *not sceptical limited users* (cluster 2) are students from the German track (76%). In academia but also in many other contexts, English has become the common language, the *lingua franca*, to communicate with each other (Ozdemir, 2014, Stephens, 2021). Therefore, many translation tools will be used to translate from or into the English language. Could it be that students of the English-language track are generally more aware of the limitations and weaknesses of translation tools due to their better proficiency in English?

Regarding learning with AI-driven writing tools in the digital age, a certain scepticism when using these tools is probably desirable. On the one hand, if students see only advantages but no disadvantages in using digital writing tools, there is a risk of using these tools carelessly, which can quickly lead to plagiarism. On the other hand, not using writing tools at all also entails certain risks, as they can support and improve the writing, as long as they are used in a responsible and appropriate way. Coping with difficult situations in life is part of the human experience (Straud et al., 2015). In education, the use of effective learning strategies is considered important for improving educational outcomes (e.g., learning success) and many students struggle in developing and implementing them (Hui et al., 2021). Higher performing students may have more effective learning strategies (Geller et al., 2018). Using digital writing tools under certain conditions might be part of an effective learning strategy.

This described field of tension is well reflected in clusters 3 and cluster 4. *Not sceptical general users* (cluster 3) are characterized by only few course repeaters (7%), a high self-efficacy in relation to studying, high conscientiousness and a high openness. On the contrast, *sceptical non-users* (cluster 4) have a high course repeater rate (25%), as well as a low self-efficacy in relation to studying, low conscientiousness and low openness. Students of cluster 4 may lack effective learning strategies.

The teacher could address the different student types with individualized teaching strategies. To the students of cluster 3, the teacher could point out potential disadvantages of digital writing tools in order to raise a healthy scepticism. To the students of cluster 4, the teacher could encourage them to try out writing tools together with him. Together with all students, a discussion could take place about the conditions under which writing tools can be used appropriately. In this way, teaching methods could be more individually adapted to specific student needs.

5. CONCLUSION

In this paper, based on survey data of 365 freshmen students, student perceptions of *AI-powered writing tools* were described and analyzed. Different student types with regard to AI-powered writing tools were identified by using the k-means clustering method. The results suggest that students have different attitudes towards AI-powered writing tools and that *individualized* teaching strategies might be helpful to promote (cluster 1 and 4) or urge caution (cluster 2 and 3) in the use of these tools. From the teacher's point of view, the aim should be to empower students to use writing tools in a meaningful way. Depending on the student type, some students may need to be encouraged by the teacher to use writing tools at all to enhance their learning strategies. For other students, it might be important to point out the limitations of writing tools in order to promote a healthy scepticism towards such tools and to counteract a possible unreflective use.

This study underlies several limitations. The data in our study represents only a snapshot at the beginning of the course. Student preferences may change over time, depending on personal characteristics and increased experience at the university. Furthermore, as the cluster differences regarding the language track (English vs. German) suggest, perceptions might be different for students with different language backgrounds (e.g., native vs. non-native English speakers).

From a theoretical point of view, the paper at hand can serve as a starting point for future research as it categorizes student perceptions in a systematic way and highlights important variables related to AI-powered writing tools. From a practical standpoint, the paper at hand may be valuable for (language) teachers, who are interested in the implications of AI-powered writing tools and look for ways, how to address and deal with them. The identified student clusters may help to better understand the individual student standpoints, when teaching with or about AI-powered writing tools.

In the future, the ability to write effectively will remain an important skill (Purcell et al., 2013, p. 21). However, to what extent and in which way this activity should or should not be supported by AI-powered writing tools is still an open question. Since these tools are freely available on the Internet and may be used by students even if it was forbidden, new approaches might be needed, that incorporate AI-powered writing tools in a meaningful way into the curriculum. Ideally, in this way, the disadvantages of these tools may be mostly avoided, and the advantages become even more apparent.

REFERENCES

Brown, T.B., Mann, B., Ryder, N., Subbiah, M., Kaplan, J., Dhariwal, P., Neelakantan, A., Shyam, P., Sastry, G., Askell, A., Agarwal, S., Herbert-Voss, A., Krueger, G., Henighan, T., Child, R., Ramesh, A., Ziegler, D. M., Wu, J., Winter, C., ... Amodei, D. (2020). *Language models are few-shot learners*. arXiv preprint. https://arxiv.org/abs/2005.14165

Elia, G., Solazzo, G., Lorenzo, G., & Passiante, G. (2019). Assessing learners' satisfaction in collaborative online courses through a big data approach. *Computers in Human Behavior, 92*, 589-599. https://doi.org/10.1016/j.chb.2018.04.033

Geitgey, A. (2018, July 18). *Natural Language Processing is Fun! How computers understand Human Language*. Medium. https://medium.com/@ageitgey/natural-language-processing-is-fun-9a0bff37854e

Geller, J., Toftness, A. R., Armstrong, P. I., Carpenter, S. K., Manz, C. L., Coffman, C. R., & Lamm, M. H. (2018). Study strategies and beliefs about learning as a function of academic achievement and achievement goals. *Memory, 26*(5), 683-690. https://doi.org/10.1080/09658211.2017.1397175

Heaven, W. D. (2020, July 20). OpenAI's new language generator GPT-3 is shockingly good and completely mindless. *MIT Technology Review.* https://www.technologyreview.com/2020/07/20/1005454/openai-machine-learning-language-generator-gpt-3-nlp/

Hui, L., de Bruin, A. B., Donkers, J., & van Merriënboer, J. J. (2021). Stimulating the intention to change learning strategies: The role of narratives. *International Journal of Educational Research, 107*, 101753. https://doi.org/10.1016/j.ijer.2021.101753

Ivanic, R. (1998). *Writing and Identity: the discoursal construction of identity in academic texts*. John Benjamins e-Platform. https://doi.org/10.1075/swll.5

Kranzberg, M. (1986). Technology and History:"Kranzberg's Laws". *Technology and culture, 27*(3), 544-560. https://doi.org/10.2307/3105385

Lantz, B. (2019). *Machine learning with R: expert techniques for predictive modeling* (3rd digital ed.). Packt Publishing Ltd.

Moore, J. L., Rosinski, P., Peeples, T., Pigg, S., Rife, M. C., Brunk-Chavez, B., Lackey, D., Kesler Rumsey, S., Tasaka, R., Curran, P., & Grabill, J. T. (2016). Revisualizing composition: How first-year writers use composing technologies. *Computers and Composition, 39*, 1-13. https://doi.org/10.1016/j.compcom.2015.11.001

Ozdemir, N. O. (2014). The role of English as a lingua franca in academia: The case of Turkish postgraduate students in an Anglophone-centre context. *Procedia-Social and Behavioral Sciences, 141*, 74-78. https://doi.org/10.1016/j.sbspro.2014.05.014

Peters, M., & Cadieux, A. (2019). Are Canadian professors teaching the skills and knowledge students need to prevent plagiarism?. *International Journal for Educational Integrity, 15*(1), 1-16. https://doi.org/10.1007/s40979-019-0047-z

Prentice, F. M., & Kinden, C. E. (2018). Paraphrasing tools, language translation tools and plagiarism: an exploratory study. *International Journal for Educational Integrity, 14*(1), 1-16. https://doi.org/10.1007/s40979-018-0036-7

Purcell, K., Buchanan, J., & Friedrich, L. (2013). *The impact of digital tools on student writing and how writing is taught in schools*. National Writing Project, Pew Research Center.

Rammstedt, B., Kemper, C. J., Klein, M. C., Beierlein, C., & Kovaleva, A. (2014). Big Five Inventory (BFI-10). *Zusammenstellung sozialwissenschaftlicher Items und Skalen (ZIS)*. https://doi.org/10.6102/zis76

Rogerson, A. M., & McCarthy, G. (2017). Using Internet based paraphrasing tools: Original work, patchwriting or facilitated plagiarism?. *International Journal for Educational Integrity, 13*(1), 2. https://doi.org/10.1007/s40979-016-0013-y

Stephens, T. (2021). *English as a common language in Switzerland: a positive or a problem?* Swissinfo (SWI). https://www.swissinfo.ch/eng/english-as-a-common-language-in-switzerland--a-positive-or-a-problem-/46494332

Straud, C., McNaughton-Cassill, M., & Fuhrman, R. (2015). The role of the Five Factor Model of personality with proactive coping and preventative coping among college students. *Personality and Individual Differences, 83*, 60-64. https://doi.org/10.1016/j.paid.2015.03.055

Van Eemeren, F. H., & Grootendorst, R. (2016). *Argumentation, communication, and fallacies: A pragma-dialectical perspective*. Routledge.

PHYSICAL COMPUTING SYSTEMS – A SYSTEMATIC APPROACH

Eric Schätz and Alke Martens[1]
University of Rostock, Germany
[1]Prof. Dr.

ABSTRACT

As we talked with school teachers about the use of physical computing systems in class, one major drawback of these systems became obvious: almost nobody – next to enthusiastic autodidacts – has been able to tell us on an abstract basis for which educational purposes a certain physical computing system can be used, i.e. in a goal-oriented way. This insight lead to the approach to structure the field of physical computing systems with the overall goal to make it easier for teachers to improve their lectures due integrating physical computing systems into computer science education. The aim of this paper is to structure the field, to find categories and to show how existing devices can be integrated into the founded structure.

KEYWORDS

Physical Computing, Computer Science Education, Categories

1. INTRODUCTION

In the field of computer science education, teachers are confronted with a quite diverse situation. On the one hand, they find pupils which are still completely new to computer science and think themselves naive in this context. On the other hand, they find kids, which call themselves nerds and think that they are hackers yet. Thus, a classroom-oriented education, where this plethora of individuals can be found, can be a really demanding task. Being researchers in the field of computer science education at school (in Germany this is called Informatics Didactics, in some language regions better sketched as Instructional Design for Informatics), we have observed different reactions to these difficult situations: some teachers reduce computer science education to programming, some teachers really focus on the theoretical aspects of computer science and completely neglect the practical parts in computer science education, just to sketch some extremes. Coming from the mindset, that *constructivist learning* is an important approach about learning, we have tried to offer workshops about physical computing systems, as we have learned in working with school kids that almost all kids from the scale of naive users up to ones who are really interested in computer science have fun and a really good and continuous high level of motivation while working with these systems. Being aware of the plethora of physical computing systems available on the market, we will make clear that we are only focusing on physical computing system which can be used for educational purposes (cf. (Hodges, Sentance, Finney & Ball 2020)).

In contrast to our observation with school kids, we have to admit, that there is a gap between the oral feedback we get from teachers right after a workshop and the one we get some weeks later about the teachers' intentions to use physical computing systems in their lectures. This is also reflected by other researchers in the field, e.g. (Schmalfeldt, Thomas & Przybylla, Mareen 2021), and (Mareen Przybylla, Ralf Romeike 2017). Thus, we interviewed several teachers to find out what might be the hindrance of integrating physical computing systems as one part of their educational spiral. In the result, we got the insight, that there is a certain barrier in using these tools: there are so many of them, it is not clear how they can be used in a goal-oriented way, they are inherently complex and not that easy to handle from the computer science perspective. Plus, the really "freaky" ones cost a lot of money. Even if the last point could be handled by using cheaper and more flexible devices, like the BBC Micro:Bit (Microbit Foundation 2020), the problem there is that teachers feel that there is a lot of work required before they are able to use them in class.

Thus, our approach is to firstly investigate existing systems, secondly to develop a way to organize them, i.e. categories for systems, which in the best cases can also be used for future systems, and thirdly, to connect the pedagogical planning process (which is the process of planning a lesson) with the developed categories.

In this paper we are going to focus on the first two steps. In the following we are going to show how we have structured the field, which aspects we have found most important for our target group and how we have realized them. The remainder of the paper is organized as follows: in the next section, we will show some background of concepts of physical computing systems, then we will demonstrate the categories and the attribute system and sketch its relation to the pedagogical planning process. We will give some examples, how devices fit into the attribute system. The paper closes with a discussion and an outlook.

2. STATE OF THE ART

Physical Computing Systems (PhCS) are a field which developed really fast over the last years – comparably all the new technologies available have been developed in the last ten years, even if the field can look back on a comparably long tradition (O'Sullivan & Igoe 2004). Thus, it can by all rights be called a comparably young field of research. Only few approaches exist, which help to structure the field (e.g. (Mareen Przybylla, Ralf Romeike 2017), and (Przybylla & Grillenberger 2021).

But which gap are physical computing systems closing, when they are embedded in the educational processes at schools and why should this be done?

This question is answerable on two levels: first of all, PhCS are surprising, non-conventional, not obviously found everywhere and they are no smartphones or the strange boxlike things the adults work with every day. Most of them are way less complex as high-level computer systems like laptops or smartphones are and they contain less black-boxes, a term we are going to discuss in an upcoming paper. Thus, school kids tend to be surprised when working with PhCS in educational school setting, as they in most cases have not done this before and somehow these things are what kids call "interesting", as they come with the feeling of a playful approach. PhCS can come in the shape of a controller board like the BBC Micro:Bit (Halfacree 2017) or a Calliope Mini (Calliope gGmbH 2022), or in the shape of a small robot, like for example the Anki Cozmo (Wilhelm 2021). On the other level, these systems are in most cases no complex computer systems, like a "real" computer or a laptop, but more like "computing systems" (Assaf 2018), which means that you have to do more to get the system running, but you find less overload, less unimportant things, and in the end kids have the chance to put their fingers directly onto the point where programming, algorithmic thinking have to take place, where input and output are clearly connected and are not processed somewhere mystical (O'Sullivan & Igoe 2004) (Hüwe & Hüwe 2019). Additionally, for the named examples but also for almost all the systems we have investigated, it can be said that multilevel programming interfaces are available, with a range from very simple and intuitive block like languages (like Scratch, (Scratch Foundation 2022)), more complex ones, and finally "real" programming languages like Python or Java for example.

Naturally, with these systems, teachers have to be really aware of which aspect they want to mediate – i.e. do they want to teach algorithmic thinking and shift to a PhCS after doing this in an unplugged way, or do they want to teach connections of items in a digital world. Related to the goal of the educational setting, different physical computing systems are best suited to this approach. For example, the BBC Micro:Bit comes in the shape of a tiny controller board, which has to be connected to something, e.g. a computer or at least a battery package. When connected to sensors, the program has to be loaded on the BBC Micro:Bit to be available. But how can this take place? So instead of teaching aspects of computer boards on a theoretical basis, like processing unit, storage, input and output, an educational question might be: how can the information be brought to this tiny mini-computer? What is required? Later the kids learn that at the core, all the "big computers" work in a comparable way. Another example might be to actually teach programming: kids, and admittedly also students in their first semesters, as we found out, really loved to get a Cozmo or a Lego Mindstorms robot (LEGO Group 2022) running and doing its tasks, instead of having a console program doing something with code and numbers. This observation is valid for all genders and has been part of gender related research (e.g. (Katterfeldt, Dittert, Ghose, Bernin & Daeglau 2019)).

However, the gap between the assumed advantages of PhCS in educational settings and the amount of systems found at schools and used in educational settings are divergent. Thus, in our project we tried to put the finger on the reasons for it and, surprisingly, it is not (only) the technical barrier and the lack of time (or money) but also that teachers in some cases do not know about the full educational potential of a certain system. Following these insights, gathered by interviewing teachers in federal state Mecklenburg Western Pomerania, Germany, we put the focus on the PhCS, and developed a systematic overview, based on categories and attributes.

3. CATEGORIES AND ATTRIBUTES

In the planning process of a lecture (e.g. in (Meyer 2015), (Heckmann & Padberg 2012) page 114), the teacher goes through these phases:

- content analysis (theoretical/ scientific background of the content of the lesson),
- organizational analysis (how is the situation in the classroom regarding school kids and technical stuff alike),
- educational analysis (which parts of the topic are important, which can be reduced) and finally the
- methodological analysis (how the teaching takes place, how shall the kids work, etc.).

Here, the content analysis is also our starting point, where the first categories and attributes of the PhCS are needed. Thus, with the background knowledge of the pedagogical planning process in mind, we started to look deeper at the PhCS. We investigated a number of 7 PhCS, and came to the following result: We found 11 categories, under which we can focus certain aspects of a PhCS, and related attributes for each of the category. The attributes are sometimes used like a range or a scale where the named attributes denote the upper and lower boundary of the range.

1. Hardware focusing – attributes: usability with periphery, without periphery
2. Form of the representation of supported programming languages – attributes that describe the supported programming languages, for example graphical or textual language
3. Processing degree of the actuating components – range between technical and physical borders of the hardware, range between levels of quality borders
4. Processing degree of sensor components – range of sensor quality, attributes denoting technical and physical borders of hardware components
5. Supported programming paradigm – attributes: imperative, state oriented, logical, object oriented (mixed attributes are usable)
6. Robustness against wrong handling – attributes with related ranges: ranges for connectors and ports, ranges for software robustness, ranges for robustness of the case (of the device) e.g. against dropping
7. Openness of the ecosystem – attributes: to other manufacturers, open source, etc. (there might still be other items to be found, which we have not located yet)
8. Extensibility – range in software extensibility and range in hardware extensibility
9. Administrational aspects – range of inventory administration effort of hardware, range of providing of software modules, range in effort for putting into service
10. Price – attribute absolute price, range, attribute or matrix: price compared to other opportunities
11. Availability of supporting systems – range of documentation from the manufacturer, range for community, attributes availability (and potentially also quality) of lecture material

As readable in the list, our categories start from all the well-known places. We came from the hardware, went over to the software and then focused on other aspects as well. As the system has been developed of an analysis of numerous available PhCS in our lab, we claim that upcoming PhCS can be described with attributes from the developed categories. As an example, we show in the following picture (figure 1) how the category "Robustness" with an exemplary range applied to the complete system can be displayed in a computer-based system helping the teachers to find their best suited PhCS. The PhCS investigated here is the BBC Micro:Bit (cf. (Microbit Foundation 2020)). In the blue box, the overall robustness of the device is shown – the Micro:Bit is one of the most robust PhCS in our collection. However, regarding the range, we can make a more detailed description regarding the overall robustness of the Micro:Bit with periphery and the Micro:Bit without periphery. Pictures of the devices are added to the figure: on the left side the Micro:Bit without periphery is shown, on the right side, there is the Micro:Bit with periphery (just as an example). The range makes visible, that the Micro:Bit itself is very robust (orange scale in figure 1), but the more peripherical add-ons are used, the less robust the system becomes (grey scale in figure 1).

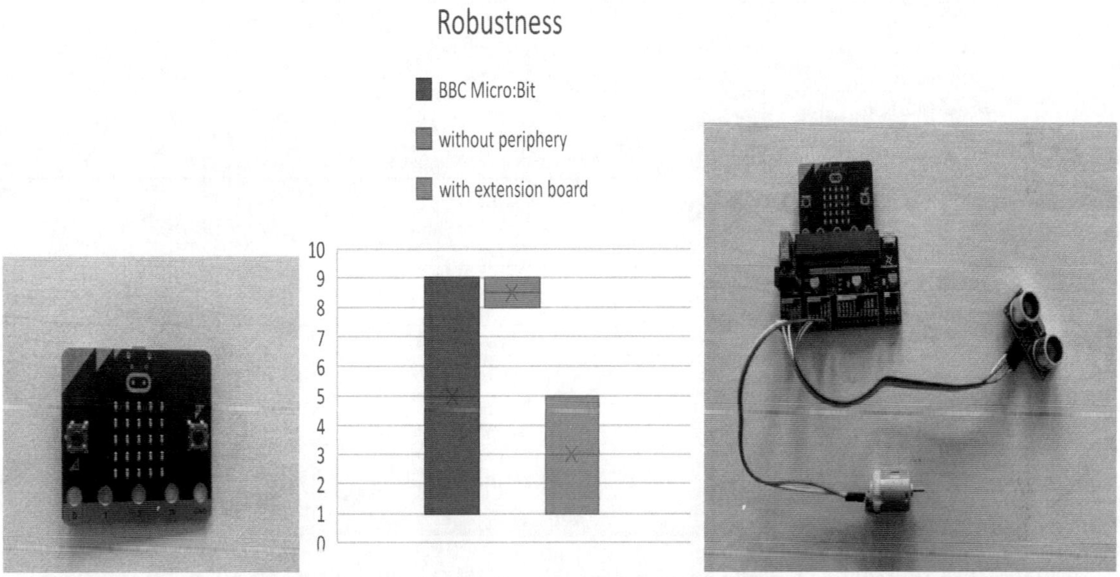

Figure 1. Microbit and the category "Robustness"

As a next step, we made an approach to integrate the categories and their relevance in each of the steps in the above-mentioned planning process. The result is shown in table 1. In this table, the entries +, o, and – show, how important the according category is for the related step in the planning process, meaning + = important, o = semi, and - = not important. The table can be read as follows (again with the robustness example and the Micro:Bit): Regarding Robustness, those attributes are not important for the content analysis but really important for the organizational analysis. In case of the BBC Micro:Bit, which is really robust without periphery and can be rather fragile while using an extension board, it should used in a way, the behavior of the students in the analyzed class allow. So if there is a big number of students which tend to ignore instructions, the Micro:Bit can only be used without external periphery.

Table 1. Relation between Attributes and Pedagogical Planning Process (Schätz & Martens 2022)

	Content analysis	Organizational analysis	Educational analysis	Methodical analysis
Hardware focusing	0	+	+	0
Form of the representation of supported programming languages	+	0	+	0
Processing degree of the actuating components	+	-	+	-
Processing degree of sensor components	+	-	+	-
Supported programming paradigms	0	0	+	0
Robustness against wrong handling	-	+	-	+
Openness of the ecosystem	-	+	-	0
Extensibility	-	+	0	0
Administrational aspects	-	+	-	+
Price	0	+	-	-
Availability of supporting systems	+	0	-	0

Based on this table, an overall hint towards usability of PhCS can be derived.

The categories, attributes and the investigated system shall as a next step be transformed to a digital version, which can be used in the pedagogical planning process by the teachers. Also, we are going to investigate more concrete PhCS. As a result, teachers can decide which PhCS have the potential to increase the quality of a specific lesson based on the shown table and the results we get from our investigation (which we are going to provide to teachers as well) during their lecture planning process.

4. DISCUSSION AND OUTLOOK

Computer Science education is not state of the art in all parts of Germany. Due to federalism, the content of the school education system is slightly different in all German federal states. In Mecklenburg-Western Pomerania for example, the government is proud to say that their country has the longest tradition of school education with computer science as a full-fledged topic, starting at the fifth grade (kids are around 11 years old), and with the possibility to have this topic till the end of school time (e.g. baccalaureate) (Schwarz, Richard, Hellmig, Lutz & Friedrich, Steffen 2021). Thus, there is a number of really motivated teachers, which are comparably good supported by their schools. As a result, bringing the idea of physical computing systems to the school falls on a fruitful ground in this federal state. However, we were surprised that even over the years, all the offerings, e.g. workshops and other forms of vocational training, have not led to a raised level of teachers using PhCSs in computer science classes in more situations that really needed.

Based on the combination of the attribute system with the planning process, we hope that we might fill the gap. Admittedly, integrating a PhCS into a school setting is still a demanding task for a teacher and requires a lot of basic knowledge, which the teachers have to take care of in their free time. It is, thus, part of the lesson planning process, but, like all the computer science stuff, PhCSs are susceptible for failure (let it be hard- or software), require a stable internet connection and shall best not be thrown off the table too often. In addition to the integration into the planning process, we advise our computer science teachers to be, that they best always have a plan B in their pockets when it comes to using any device in computer science lectures. This is valid for full-fledged computers, but even more for PhCS.

Regarding the attribute system and the categories, we are optimistic that this will help the teachers to at least think about using the PhCSs in their lectures, as they can see that these systems can be integrated smoothly. First tests have shown promising results, which are as the next step now put into an empirical evaluation, which has been started and will run for the next two years. Looking at our teacher students, the system has proved its viability, yet.

Another quite important aspect of this system of categories might be the idea, that so many new PhCSs have been developed over the last years, not all of which have a clear purpose, but many of which come with the promise, that programming can be learned. The system of categories with the focus on educational settings allow for companies, to check their newly developed system-to-be regarding the fitness for educational settings and hopefully, sooner or later, PhCSs especially for educational purposes will be developed which are really supportive, enjoyable and useful for school settings.

REFERENCES

Assaf, D., 2018, viewed 18 July 2022, from https://mia.phsz.ch/pub/Informatikdidaktik/PhysicalComputing/PhysicalComputing_PHSZ_DA_V2.0.pdf.

Calliope gGmbH, 2022, 'Calliope', in *Calliope*, viewed 18 July 2022, from https://calliope.cc/.

Halfacree, G., 2017, *The Official BBC micro:bit® User Guide*, John Wiley & Sons, Inc., Indianapolis, Indiana, doi.org/10.1002/9781119413752.

Heckmann, K. & Padberg, F., 2012, *Unterrichtsentwürfe Mathematik Sekundarstufe I*, Spektrum Akademischer Verlag, Heidelberg, doi.org/10.1007/978-3-8274-2934-6.

Hodges, S., Sentance, S., Finney, J. & Ball, T., 2020, 'Physical Computing: A Key Element of Modern Computer Science Education', *Computer*, 53(4), 20–30, doi.org/10.1109/MC.2019.2935058.

Hüwe, P. & Hüwe, S., 2019, *IoT at Home: Smart Gadgets mit Arduino, Raspberry Pi, ESP8266 und Calliope entwickeln*, (#makers do it), Hanser, München.

Katterfeldt, E.-S., Dittert, N., Ghose, S., Bernin, A. & Daeglau, M., 2019, 'Effects of Physical Computing Workshops on Girls' Attitudes towards Computer Science', in *Proceedings of the FabLearn Europe 2019 Conference*, ACM, Oulu Finland, pp. 1–3, doi.org/10.1145/3335055.3335066.

LEGO Group, 2022, 'MINDSTORMS EV3 | MINT ab der neunten Klasse', in *LEGO® Education*, viewed 21 May 2022, from https://education.lego.com/de-de/products/lego-mindstorms-education-ev3-set/5003400#ev3-set.

Mareen Przybylla, Ralf Romeike, 2017, 'Von Eingebetteten Systemen zu Physical Computing', 10.

Meyer, H., 2015, *Didaktische Modelle: Buch als E-Book*, Verlag an der Ruhr, Berlin, GERMANY, viewed 10 May 2022, from http://ebookcentral.proquest.com/lib/ubrostock-ebooks/detail.action?docID=2080721.

Microbit Foundation, 2020, 'The new BBC micro:bit with speaker and microphone', in *New micro:bit annouced*, viewed 21 May 2022, from https://microbit.org/news/2020-10-13/meet-the-new-bbc-microbit/.

O'Sullivan, D. & Igoe, T., 2004, *Physical computing: sensing and controlling the physical world with computers*, Thomson, Boston.

Przybylla, M. & Grillenberger, A., 2021, 'Fundamentals of Physical Computing: Determining Key Concepts in Embedded Systems and Hardware/Software Co-Design', in *The 16th Workshop in Primary and Secondary Computing Education*, ACM, Virtual Event Germany, pp. 1–10, doi.org/10.1145/3481312.3481352.

Schätz, E. & Martens, A., 2022, 'Attributes of physical computing systems – the perspective of pedagogy', in *Edulearn22 Proceedings*, Palma, Spain, pp. 5561–5565, doi.org/10.21125/edulearn.2022.1309.

Schmalfeldt, Thomas & Przybylla, Mareen, 2021, 'Erhebungsinstrument für Überzeugungen zum Physical Computing', doi.org/10.18420/INFOS2021_F205.

Schwarz, Richard, Hellmig, Lutz & Friedrich, Steffen, 2021, 'Eine Synopse zum Informatikunterricht in Deutschland im Jahr 2020', doi.org/10.18420/INFOS2021_F227.

Scratch Foundation, 2022, 'Scratch - Imagine, Program, Share', in *Scratch*, viewed 18 July 2022, from https://scratch.mit.edu/.

Wilhelm, C., 2021, Feiern Cozmo und Vector bald ein Revival?, viewed 18 July 2022, from https://www.smarthomeassistent.de/feiern-cozmo-und-vector-bald-ein-revival/.

HOW GENERATIVE LANGUAGE MODELS CAN ENHANCE INTERACTIVE LEARNING WITH SOCIAL ROBOTS

Stefan Sonderegger
Institute for Educational Management and Technologies
University of St.Gallen, 9000 St.Gallen, Switzerland

ABSTRACT

The use of social robots in education is a growing area of research and the potential future applications are various. However, the conversational models behind current social robots and chatbot systems often rely on rule-based and retrieval-based methods. This limits the social robot to predefined responses and topics, thus hindering it from fluent communication and interaction. Generative language models such as GPT-3 could be beneficial in this context, e.g. for an improved conversation and open-ended question answering. This article presents an approach to utilizing generative language models to enhance interactive learning with educational social robots. The proposed model combines the technological possibilities of generative language models with the educational tasks of a social robot in the role of a tutor and learning partner. The implementation of the model in practice is illustrated by means of a use case consisting of different learning scenarios. The social robot generates explanations, questions, corrections, and answers based on the pre-trained GPT-3 model. By exploring the potential of generative language models for interactive learning with social robots on different levels of abstraction, the paper also aims to contribute to an understanding of the future relevance and possibilities that generative language models bring into education and educational technologies in general.

KEYWORDS

Social Robots in Education, Human-Robot-Interaction, Interactive Learning, Generative Language Models, GPT-3

1. INTRODUCTION

Social robots are specialized in social interactions with humans and have the potential to support our learning and teaching (Belpaeme *et al.* 2018). In roles such as tutor, teaching assistant, and peer learner, social robots might be used not only as a practical tool to learn about STEM subjects but also as a teaching and learning tool, e.g. for language learning, in special education, in diverse areas and on the basis of various learning content (Belpaeme & Tanaka 2021). The demand for personal tutorial support for learners underlines the potential of scalable, individualizable, and interactive social robots for future learning and teaching support. In addition to these advantages, which apply to chatbots or conversational systems in general (cf. Pérez, Daradoumis & Puig 2020), research groups around social robots in education highlight and demonstrate the advantage of physical presence over screen-based or computer-based technologies. The physical nature and social presence allow real-world interactions and are shown to enhance learning outcomes and motivation (Belpaeme & Tanaka 2021).

However, for more complex learning and teaching scenarios, social robots currently often are unable to meet the high expectations and technical requirements that are imposed on them (e.g., with regard to personalized learning). Researchers emphasize that current models of social robots, such as Pepper and NAO, quickly reach their limits in the inherently complex educational interactions (Belpaeme *et al.* 2018). Schulze et al. (2021) point out that learning can only be reduced to a pre-programmed interaction to a limited extent and in individual cases. The studies of social robots in the field of education that they have reviewed therefore have a strong experimental character, which means that previous results can only be transferred to educational practice to a limited extent. Accordingly, besides an attributed versatile future potential, researchers see social robots in the near future primarily in supporting and complementary roles (Schulze *et al.* 2021). Our previous research in this area also shows a differentiated picture. A survey of students on the acceptance of social robots for learning purposes in higher education has shown that the intention to use them can be predicted and thus increased by determinants (factors) such as improved perceived adaptiveness or social presence of the robot (Guggemos, Seufert & Sonderegger 2020). And in a practice-oriented interview study, today's widely used models of social robots are perceived to be not mature enough in terms of a natural interactive conversation when it comes to their use in the educational context (Sonderegger, Guggemos & Seufert 2022).

In order to achieve the quality of learning and scenarios desirable from an educational perspective, adaptive and interactive elements are essential parts of robot-assisted or, more generally, technology-enhanced learning. According to the ICAP framework, *interactive* (dialoguing) learning as a form of engagement represents the highest quality level of learning (e.g., learning with deeper understanding), after *passive* (receiving), *active* (manipulating), and *constructive* (generating) learning (Chi & Wylie 2014). The authors emphasize, that the ICAP framework can be used as a guide for instructional design and computer-based learning environments (Chi & Wylie 2014). Scalable learning in discourse (interactive mode of engagement) is a central future potential of social robots and conversational technologies in education, not only but even more so at higher levels of education due to its complexity. At the same time, the limited social-interactive capabilities are still the weak points of today's systems. However, technological advances in natural language processing (NLP) open up untapped potential. According to Foster (2019), most developers of social robots tend to employ simple rule- or template-based methods for language generation and make no use of the full possibilities of state-of-the-art natural language generation technologies due to the fact that there are numerous other technical challenges in the development of social robots. But since face-to-face dialogue is the most basic, richest, and most flexible form of human communication, it is essential, especially for its use in education, that linguistic conversation is fluid and flexible as an important part of the interaction (Foster 2019).

The aim of this paper is to address this challenge by exploring the potential of modern generative language models for interactive learning with social robots based on the following research question:

How can interactive learning with social robots for educational purposes be enhanced based on state-of-the-art generative language models?

Based on this research goal we present an approach to evolve social robots towards interactive learning by utilizing generative language models. By integrating the state-of-the-art generative learning model GPT-3 (Generative pre-trained transformer) by OpenAI (Brown *et al.* 2020) over a web API, we illustrate a practical use case of an interactive robot tutor. Based on GPT-3, the robot is more flexible and adaptive in terms of his conversation skills and can for example answer open-ended questions (Dale 2021). AI models like GPT-3 are pre-trained based on huge amounts of data and can be fine-tuned for a wide range of tasks (e.g., question answering, information extraction, sentiment analysis), thus they are also referred to as pre-trained models or foundation models (cf. Bommasani *et al.* 2021). Given the significant technological advances, the simplicity of fine-tuning for users based on limited data, and the resulting increased scalability, such foundation models enable new and interesting applications, especially in education (Bommasani *et al.* 2021).

With the proposed approach, this paper contributes to application-oriented research in this area by providing an understanding of the possibilities and relevance of generative language models in the field of educational technologies. Illustrating the approach in the context of the presented use case can further help researchers and practitioners gain insight into the current and future opportunities that generative language models offer for robot-supported education.

2. INTERACTIVE ROBOT TUTOR MODEL

Based on the theoretical foundation discussed in the introduction we propose an interactive robot tutor model (Figure 1). The model follows a high-level learner-centered and task-oriented view and highlights the relevance of the underlying technologies. On the basis of the activities of a robot tutor and the learner's mode of engagement according to the ICAP framework (Chi & Wylie 2014) on the horizontal axis, the presented model lays out the possibilities of generative language models by structuring on the vertical axis along the maturity of the underlying chatbot technology or method (Cahn 2017; Adamopoulou & Moussiades 2020).

Quality of learning by mode of engagement

Maturity of technology

	Robot explains (explain a topic) **Passive learning** (learner is listening)	**Robot asks** (ask questions) **Active learning** (selecting/answering)	**Robot assesses** (assess/correct answers) **Constructive learning** (justifying/reflecting)	**Robot interacts** (simulate conversations) **Interactive learning** (dialoguing)
Rule-based (e.g., Template)	• Closed domain • Stored explanation (e.g., predefined topics and answers in template)	• Closed domain • Closed questions (e.g., single or multiple choice questions)	• Closed domain • Closed answers (e.g., single or multiple choice correction)	• Closed domain • Linear conversation (e.g., simple predefined rule-based conversation)
Retrieval-based (e.g., LMS)	• Closed domain • Available explanation (e.g., topics available in databases or via external services)	• Closed domain • Available questions (e.g., questions available in databases or via external services)	• Closed domain • Closed answers (e.g., multiple choice or keyword detection)	• Closed domain • Linear conversation (e.g., simple directed conversation with predefined responses)
Generative (e.g., GPT-3)	• Open domain • Adaptive explanation (e.g., 'all' topics can be explained on different levels of sophistication)	• Open domain • Open-ended questions (e.g., different sorts of questions covering 'all' topics on different levels)	• Open domain • Open-ended answers (e.g., assess open answers by the learner with adaptive feedback)	• Open domain • Free conversation (e.g., 'free' conversation with generation of new responses)

Figure 1. Interactive robot tutor model

The robot in the role of a tutor and the social context of a one-to-one interaction can approach a topic or learning subject from different directions. He can explain a topic based on a request or a question (1), ask questions to the learner (2), assess answers from the learner and provide feedback (3) and he can try to discuss a topic interactively with the learner (4). These different types of robot activities and the corresponding modes of learner engagement are independent of the type of knowledge being taught and may include factual, procedural, conceptual, or metacognitive knowledge (cf. Anderson & Krathwohl 2001). But not all methods of language generation or dialoguing offer the same possibilities in terms of topic choice, type, and adaptivity of the interaction elements.

(1) Passive learning scenario in which the robot explains: rule-based and retrieval-based explanations allow predefined answers and explanations and thus fewer errors (e.g., teacher-inserted answer), whereas generative-based explanations allow domain-open explanations at different levels of difficulty.

(2) Active learning scenario in which the robot asks closed questions answered by the learner: questions can be retrieved from external services (e.g., from an LMS or open access question databases) offering predefined questions and answer options or they can be generated based on trained or fine-tuned generative language models offering again domain-open and freely adaptive questions.

(3) Constructive learning scenario in which the learner answers or even rationalizes an open-ended question and receives an adaptive, individualized, corrective feedback from the robot based on the generative language model (not possible in this form with rule-based or retrieval-based methods of language generation).

(4) Interactive learning scenario in which the learner freely interacts with the robot in dialogue, whereas the robot answers are generated by the generative language model based on the context of the previous dialogue (not possible in this form with rule-based or retrieval-based methods of language generation).

The fields in light grey are combinations that are only possible in a very limited form and basically do not fulfill the pedagogically intended tasks. The fields highlighted in blue thus indicate the building blocks that complement each other in an integrative application and should be optimally combined to enable the learner to learn interactively with the robot tutor in the future. Even if some elements are still technically immature, this combination promises to cover the different engagement levels of learners on the one hand and the tasks of a tutor robot on the other. In order to fulfill its task according to the curriculum, the robot tutor ideally obtains its content and knowledge base from the learning management system (LMS) and uses it to fine-tune the generative language model. As a result, the generative language model is oriented to the predefined learning content from the LMS in terms of both content and level of difficulty but can respond very freely and adaptively to the learner in the interaction with the robot.

3. USE CASE OF AN IMPLEMENTATION OF THE MODEL

In the following section, the presented interactive robot tutoring model is illustrated by a practical use case of a social robot used in higher education. By providing insight into implemented elements and learning scenarios used in workshops on AI and the future of learning, the theoretical ideas are made tangible through concrete examples. In addition to these current applications, their technical implementation and limitations and future ideas will also be discussed. The use case differentiates four main learning scenarios and corresponding technical implementations which are however closely related and integrated within an overall tutorial module.

	Robot explains (explain a topic) **Passive learning** (learner is listening)	**Robot asks** (ask questions) **Active learning** (selecting/answering)	**Robot assesses** (assess/correct answers) **Constructive learning** (justifying/reflecting)	**Robot interacts** (simulate conversations) **Interactive learning** (dialoguing)
Rule-based (e.g., Template)	**Template-based introduction to the tutorial module and topic** **Example:** Learner can choose between given topics (e.g. AI, robotics, big data) and a level of difficulty (e.g., beginner, advanced, pro) and is provided with a short introduction into the topic based on illustrations on the robot's tablet. **Technical implementation:** The content is designed template-based and configured in a robot management platform. Via the dialog management (e.g., in qiChat) one can decide what sorts of questions are answered retrieval-based (e.g., "what is …") or based on the generative module (e.g., "why …", "where …", "how …").			
Retrieval-based (e.g., LMS)	**Robot explains retrieved knowledge from Wikipedia (or if available from LMS)** **Example dialogue:** Learner Question: "*What is a social robot?*" Robot answer: *"A social robot is an autonomous robot that interacts and communicates with humans by following social behaviours and rules attached to its role"* (Wikipedia). Robot tablet output: Picture of a social robot **Technical implementation:** A self developed Python module retrieves a summary for any given 'term' via the Wikipedia web API and outputs it via the robot's speech engine after parsing.			
Generative (e.g., GPT-3)	**Robot explains any given topic/question based on GPT-3 text generation** **Example dialogue:** Learner question: "*Where could I use a social robot?*" Robot answer: "*There are many potential applications for social robots. They could be used in healthcare settings to provide companionship to patients, in educational settings to help children learn, or in businesses as customer service representatives.*" **Technical implementation:** A self developed Python module sends a prompt containing any question or topic to be explained via web API to a fine-tuned GPT-3 model (fine-tuned to give short robot explanations on different levels) and returns the output of the model via the robot's speech engine.			

Figure 2. Use Case – Interactive Robot Tutor: Explanation Module

As illustrated in Figure 2, the configuration of possible topics, levels of difficulty, and learner activities is controlled in the template via a robot management platform and configured in a rule-based manner. Topics can be predefined in the robot management platform, retrieved based on topics in the learning management system (LMS) or a free selection of topics can be provided to the learner. In a free conversation mode where the learner asks a question, the administrator of the robot configures the dialogue management towards the use of rule-based, retrieval-based, or generative explanation generation based on the form of the question or the availability of the given topic (e.g., if an answer can't be answered by an internal template-based rule or retrieved via Wikipedia API, the explanation will be generated by the GPT-3 generative language model).

	Robot explains (explain a topic) **Passive learning** (learner is listening)	**Robot asks** (ask questions) **Active learning** (selecting/answering)	**Robot assesses** (assess/correct answers) **Constructive learning** (justifying/reflecting)	**Robot interacts** (simulate conversations) **Interactive learning** (dialoguing)
Rule-based	Not applicable			
Retrieval-based (e.g., LMS)	**Robot asks multiple-choice questions from the learning management system (LMS)** **Example dialogue:** Topic chosen by learner based on LMS given topics: "*Robotics*" Robot question (LMS based): "*Which components of the robot are responsible for perception?*" Robot answer options: "*A: sensors, B: actuators or C: effectors*" Learner answer: "*A*" Robot Feedback (LMS based): "*Correct. Sensors are responsible for the external perception of robots. An actuator is the counterpart to a sensor and refers to the moving components of a robot.*" **Technical implementation:** A Python module retrieves multiple-choice questions including answers via the LMS API and outputs it via the robot's speech engine and presents it on the robot's tablet.			
Generative (e.g., GPT-3)	**Robot asks questions to any given topic based on GPT-3 text generation** **Example dialogue:** *Topic to freely chosen by learner: "Social robots"* *Robot question (GPT-3 generated): "What are social robots primarily used for?"* *Optional robot answer options (GPT-3 generated): A: "To interact with humans" or B: "to perform a task"* *Learner answer: "A" → Robot Feedback: "Correct."* **Technical implementation:** A self developed Python module sends a prompt containing any chosen topic via web API to a fine-tuned GPT-3 model (fine-tuned to generate short robot questions with two or multiple answer options) and returns the output of the model via the robot's speech engine.			

Figure 3. Use Case – Interactive Robot Tutor: Quiz Module

	Robot explains (explain a topic) **Passive learning** (learner is listening)	**Robot asks** (ask questions) **Active learning** (selecting/answering)	**Robot assesses** (assess/correct answers) **Constructive learning** (justifying/reflecting)	**Robot interacts** (simulate conversations) **Interactive learning** (dialoguing)
Generative (e.g., GPT-3)	**Robot assesses open answers/rationales and provides feedback based on fine-tuned GPT-3 model** **Example dialogue:** Topic freely chosen by learner: "*Social robots*" Open robot question (GPT-3 generated or retrieved via LMS): "*What are social robots primarily used for?*" Learner answer: "*Primarily for fun.*" Robot feedback (individualized): "*Social robots have many purposes. They can be used for fun, but they are also used in healthcare, education, and research.*" **Technical implementation:** A self developed Python module sends a prompt containing the robots question and the corresponding learner answer to a fine-tuned GPT-3 model and returns the output of the model via the robot's speech engine. The model is fine-tuned to assess answers to open-ended questions based on a limited number of examples and aims to provide a corrective, constructive, motivational, and individualized feedback, that builds on the learner's response as in the example above. This implementation is limited in part by the fact that the robot's ability to understand and process human speech input is error-sensitive at the current state of the technology. Given a not too complex language, the understanding of the GPT-3 model is already at a high level in most contexts, with task-oriented fine-tuning playing an important role.			

Figure 4. Use Case – Interactive Robot Tutor: Assessment Module

	Robot explains (explain a topic) **Passive learning** (learner is listening)	**Robot asks** (ask questions) **Active learning** (selecting/answering)	**Robot assesses** (assess/correct answers) **Constructive learning** (justifying/reflecting)	**Robot interacts** (simulate conversations) **Interactive learning** (dialoguing)
Rule-based	Not applicable			
Retrieval-based	Not applicable			
Generative (e.g., GPT-3)	**Robot freely interacts with the learner based on GPT-3 text generation** **Example dialogue:** *Dialogue initiated by learner: "Hello"* *Robot: "Hello, I am Lexi, an intelligent robot tutor, how can I help you"* (Note: answer based on fine-tuning context) *Learner: "Tell me about the limitations of AI language models like GPT-3?"* *Robot: "AI language models have the potential to revolutionize the way we use language. However, they are still in their early stages of development and have some limitations. For example, they may not be able to accurately capture the nuances of human language, or they may not be able to handle complex grammar." (GPT-3 generated)* *Learner: "What nuances?"* *Robot: "The nuances of human language can be difficult to capture with a computer model. For example, the way we use idioms, sarcasm or body language can be lost on an AI system."* (Note: in this case the robot did understand the context of the short question based on the previous dialogue) **Technical implementation:** A self developed Python module sends a prompt containing the learners speech input and the saved previous dialogue between the learner and the robot to a fine-tuned GPT-3 model and returns the output of the model via the robot's speech engine. The model is fine-tuned to be a helpful and intelligent robot tutor answering to every question and input. The primary limitations of this implementation are the understanding capabilities of the robot model Pepper ranging from the microphone input to the external speech-to-text service required for free text input.			

Figure 5. Use Case – Interactive Robot Tutor: Dialogue Module

The demonstrated use case within Figures 2, 3, 4, and 5 gives a detailed insight into the four modules from a user perspective based on the dialogue and from a technical implementation side. To reunite the picture of the four separate modules, it has to be mentioned that these technically separated tasks are separately accessible via the free conversation mode of the robot, but mainly used integrated into one tutor learning module where the learner chooses between different learning activities after choosing a learning topic. The interaction can thus be initiated by the learner as well as by the robot. In the free conversation mode of the robot, it can be prompted to act via questions. If you ask the robot, for example, whether it can ask you a question, the robot will ask you back on which topic it should ask a question. The choice of topics can be restricted if necessary and defined via an LMS but is in practice used as free as possible in the sense of an open-domain idea. Based on the topic and optionally a selected difficulty level, a method of a self-developed module is executed on the robot by the robot dialogue management, which in turn sends a request to the GPT-3 model via web API containing the topic and a template with training examples (to fine-tune the language model) and receives a model generated question in return. The same procedure applies to the different modules (explanation module figure 2, quiz module in figure 3, assessment module in figure 4, and the dialogue module in figure 5) based on different task configurations and thus different context and task-oriented fine-tunings and training examples.

The primary limitation in this case and generally in the use case is the limited speech recognition capabilities of the robot model Pepper. The robot cannot speak and listen simultaneously and is limited in the ability to detect the end of a speech input to process (e.g., the robot's listening is often interrupted in the middle of user input, as the user tends to take short pauses in speaking). The robot's internal dialog system works well based on the local rule-based dialogues and allows to send parts of the speech input to a remote automated speech recognition (ASR) engine which does not always perform stably. A few words or a compactly formulated sentence can usually be processed, provided the learner is somewhat accustomed to talking to the robot and there is no strong background noise. Given these technical limitations, the current role of the robot is still strongly that of a research and educational tool, helping to understand technological development and to think about its future use in areas such as education. However, in the longer term and based on more advanced robot or educational technology, the role of an AI-based educational tutor, learning partner, or assistant for interactive learning may become more and more realistic.

4. DISCUSSION AND CONCLUSION

This paper explores the potential of generative language models for interactive learning with social robots in the role of a tutor. The proposed preliminary model presents an approach to utilize generative language models such as GPT-3 to progress towards more interactive and engaging forms of learning with social robots. The model connects the different forms of cognitive learning engagement of the learner with the activities of the robot tutor and thus shows the linkage and the possibilities of different technical approaches and especially generative language models. The practical-oriented illustration of the model within the use case of our social educational robot points out the impact and the potential for future applications, but also the limitations and challenges in current use.

Generative language models offer the advantage of a more fluent and interactive conversation with the learner. This has major implications for potential computer-based or robot-based learning applications, as these models allow us to set aside simple keyword detection and predefined answers. Models like GPT-3 understand the context of natural language in a form never achieved before (cf. Elkins & Chun 2020; Floridi & Chiriatti 2020; Dale 2021). The potential of such models in education is accordingly broad; they can be used, for example, as a tool for formative assessment of students in technology-enhanced learning environments or, more generally, for improved real-time analysis of learning data (e.g., text or speech analysis)(Blikstein & Worsley 2016; Phillips *et al.* 2022). Research groups focusing on automated question generation and evaluation based on GPT-3 emphasize the possibility to customize to individual domains and enable higher quality questions from a pedagogical perspective (Bhat *et al.* 2022). Bommasani et al. (2021) highlight the greater ability for adaptive and personalized learning through the adaption of foundation models in educational technology. As demonstrated within the use case, the deep understanding of GPT-3 allows the robot tutor to assess the learner's open-ended answers and rationales and consequently provide individualized feedback that can be optionally structured to be corrective, constructive, and motivational based on just a few examples to fine-tune the language model. The model can further be fine-tuned based on specific learning content from the learning management system and thus be used in a more human-controlled way and subject-specific. These example applications from the use case show the potential for more interactive learning activities that promise higher learning quality according to the underlying ICAP framework (Chi & Wylie 2014).

However, the use case, as well as the model itself, also reveal several limitations in terms of today's use and in terms of future challenges and risks in the context of AI-based generative language models. The current use and combination of retrieval-based and generative text generation are primarily limited by the robot's technical limitations in terms of language understanding and processing. As the robot model Pepper relies on external speech-to-text engines and the GPT-3 model can only be used in the form of a web service, the robot requires a stable internet connection and cannot work independently in such a use case. These external services limit the benefits in many ways and create new challenges and risks in terms of data privacy, data storage, data security, dependency, and responsibility. Computationally intensive and therefore often cloud-based AI services make increased digital privacy and data protection even more important (Walsh 2018). Risks and limitations of AI models further include biased or false information, prejudice, transparency, and copyright issues, that raise ethical questions and the demand for a human-in-the-loop (Zanzotto 2019) and explainable AI (XAI), particularly in education (Gunning 2017). Other risks associated with the use of educational AI systems may include the potential misuse to monitor students (e.g., their behavior and communication) or the risk of reproducing prevailing ideologies about teaching and learning towards a homogeneous and centralized system (Blodgett & Madaio 2021). In the case of social robots, the central robot control should not be outsourced to an external service or language model in order to have integration and interaction of the different components in the sense of a social being (e.g., use of cameras for emotion recognition).

As a consequence of these limitations, the use of our social robot in the context of university courses as well as practical workshops is and will be limited to individualization based on the context and not include personalization of the learning content as the LMS interface would allow. In the future, we plan to integrate the individual modules and learning scenarios more effectively, to continuously evaluate them with students and teachers, and to further develop them based on surveys and user experiments. In terms of the practical and technical implementation, it would be interesting to transfer the given use case to more advanced robot models based on the presented model. As for the research outlook, we hope to see, conduct and discuss more application-oriented research that takes the ideas further and explores the potential of generative language models for interactive learning with robots and in various pedagogical application domains.

REFERENCES

Adamopoulou, E. & Moussiades, L., 2020, 'Chatbots: History, technology, and applications', *Machine Learning with Applications* 2(53), 100006.

Anderson, L.W. & Krathwohl, D.R., 2001, *A taxonomy for learning, teaching, and assessing: A revision of Bloom's taxonomy of educational objectives*, Longman.

Belpaeme, T., Kennedy, J., Ramachandran, A., Scassellati, B. & Tanaka, F., 2018, 'Social robots for education: A review', *Science Robotics* 3(21), eaat5954.

Belpaeme, T. & Tanaka, F., 2021, 'Social Robots as Educators', *OECD Digital Education Outlook 2021 Pushing the Frontiers with Artificial Intelligence, Blockchain and Robots: Pushing the Frontiers with Artificial Intelligence, Blockchain and Robots* 2021, 143.

Bhat, S., Nguyen, H.A., Moore, S., Stamper, J., Sakr, M. & Nyberg, E., 2022, 'Towards Automated Generation and Evaluation of Questions in Educational Domains', *Proceedings of the 15th International Conference on Educational Data Mining, 701–704.* 2022.

Blikstein, P. & Worsley, M., 2016, 'Multimodal Learning Analytics and Education Data Mining: using computational technologies to measure complex learning tasks', *Journal of Learning Analytics* 3(2), 220–238.

Blodgett, S.L. & Madaio, M., 2021, *Risks of AI Foundation Models in Education*, from http://arxiv.org/pdf/2110.10024v1.

Bommasani, R., Hudson, D.A., Adeli, E., Altman, R., Arora, S. & Arx, S.v., *et al.*, 2021, *On the Opportunities and Risks of Foundation Models*, from http://arxiv.org/pdf/2108.07258v3.

Brown, T.B., Mann, B., Ryder, N., Subbiah, M., Kaplan, J. & Dhariwal, P., *et al.*, 2020, 'Language models are few-shot learners', *arXiv preprint arXiv:2005.14165* 2020.

Cahn, J., 2017, *CHATBOT: Architecture, Design, & Development*.

Chi, M.T.H. & Wylie, R., 2014, 'The ICAP Framework: Linking Cognitive Engagement to Active Learning Outcomes', *Educational Psychologist* 49(4), 219–243.

Dale, R., 2021, 'GPT-3: What's it good for?', *Natural Language Engineering* 27(1), 113–118.

Elkins, K. & Chun, J., 2020, 'Can GPT-3 Pass a Writer's Turing Test?', *Journal of Cultural Analytics* 5(2).

Floridi, L. & Chiriatti, M., 2020, 'GPT-3: Its Nature, Scope, Limits, and Consequences', *Minds and Machines* 30(4), 681–694.

Foster, M.E., 2019, 'Natural language generation for social robotics: opportunities and challenges', *Philosophical transactions of the Royal Society of London. Series B, Biological sciences* 374(1771), 20180027.

Guggemos, J., Seufert, S. & Sonderegger, S., 2020, 'Humanoid robots in higher education: Evaluating the acceptance of Pepper in the context of an academic writing course using the UTAUT', *British Journal of Educational Technology* 10(6), 408.

Gunning, D., 2017, 'Explainable artificial intelligence (xai)', *Defense Advanced Research Projects Agency (DARPA), nd Web* 2, 2.

Pérez, J.Q., Daradoumis, T. & Puig, J.M.M., 2020, 'Rediscovering the use of chatbots in education: A systematic literature review', *Computer Applications in Engineering Education* 28(6), 1549–1565.

Phillips, T., Saleh, A., Glazewski, K.D., Hmelo-Silver, C.E., Mott, B. & Lester, J.C., 2022, 'Exploring the use of GPT-3 as a tool for evaluating text-based collaborative discourse', *Companion Proceedings of the 12th* 2022, 54.

Schulze, H., Bendel, O., Schubert, M., Binswanger, M., Simmler, M. & Reimer, R.T.D., *et al.*, 2021, *Soziale Roboter, Empathie und Emotionen - Eine Untersuchung aus interdisziplinärer Perspektive*.

Sonderegger, S., Guggemos, J. & Seufert, S., 2022, 'How Social Robots Can Facilitate Teaching Quality – Findings from an Explorative Interview Study', in W. Lepuschitz, *et al.* (eds.), *Robotics in Education,* Cham, 2022, pp. 99–112.

Walsh, T., 2018, *It's alive: Wie künstliche Intelligenz unser Leben verändern wird*, Edition Körber.

Zanzotto, F.M., 2019, 'Human-in-the-loop Artificial Intelligence', *Journal of Artificial Intelligence Research* 64, 243–252.

IDENTIFYING CHALLENGES IN VIRTUAL TEAMS: A CASE STUDY OF TEAMWORK IN A GAME-BASED LEARNING ENVIRONMENT

Kirsi Syynimaa[1], Kirsi Lainema[2] and Timo Lainema[2]
[1]*University of Jyväskylä, Department of Education, Seminaarinkatu 15, 40014 University of Jyväskylä, Finland*
[2]*University of Turku, Turku School of Economics, Rehtorinpellonkatu 2, 20500 Turku, Finland*

ABSTRACT

Game-based learning (GBL) environments are shown to support open-ended inquiry, collaborative learning, shared knowledge creation and decision-making processes. The study at hand focuses on examining students' descriptions of problematic situations and collaborative learning in a virtual simulation game. We were interested in what kinds of challenges the students encounter in virtual teamwork in GBL. Data of the study stems from gaming sessions in which teams of 5-7 students worked in a virtual learning environment and steered their simulation companies' supply chain in real-time. Students' reflection assignments were analyzed with qualitative content analysis. Our results show that during the sessions students encountered communication challenges, collaboration challenges, organizing challenges and skills and competence issues. As all these are typical for modern dispersed collaborative work, we can state that the game-based course of this study provided the students with opportunities to rehearse and solve these challenges in a virtual working context. Our results emphasize the importance of providing students an opportunity to exercise collaboration and problem-solving skills in authentic, safe and inspiring settings, and that simulation games represent a feasible context for this.

KEYWORDS

Collaborative Learning, Game-Based Learning, Virtual Work

1. INTRODUCTION

Currently, there are novel forces that affect all aspects of life. These forces include globalization, the COVID-19 pandemic, climate change and technological disruptions (see e.g. Kaushik & Guleria, 2020). Work life has also become more complex, and work challenges more difficult to anticipate. Disruptions in the work life bring about requirements for change also for how we teach (Iglesias-Pradas et al., 2021). Working, collaborating and solving shared problems in dispersed virtual teams have increased in various occupations and tasks. Collaborative problem-solving skills are critical in current work life, and need therefore to be included in teaching and learning in higher education (HE) (Gonzalez-Perez et al., 2014).

In contemporary work life specialists work in collaborative, multi-site, dispersed teams and digital working environments, in which fast and efficient decision-making is emphasized. The situations specialists encounter in their daily work are so manifold and complex that they require the ability to share one's expertise and skills to function in versatile multi-site teams. Previous research has established that the success of virtual teams hinges on the team members' ability to jointly, quickly and appropriately address issues (Caputo et al., 2019). Consequently, to respond to these mega trends, it is vital to start developing the required abilities already during education.

Presently, one of the key challenges of HE is that education should be modified to respond to the requirements of work life and to provide skills for critical thinking, flexible problem-solving and versatile collaboration and communication (Riemer, 2007; Binkley et al., 2012). In the global workplace the amount of tasks that require constant decision-making is continuously increasing, and many tasks are associated with rapid information processing and problem-solving (Tendick, Denby & Ju 2016).

Collaborative game-based learning (GBL) environments represent one possibility for addressing these competence development needs. Ideally, education supports open-ended inquiry and heterogeneous, distributed teams using computer-supported collaborative learning (CSCL) technology, where individual team members contribute a variety of perspectives to the mutual task. GBL environments represent a fruitful context for interactional and collaborative learning and shared knowledge creation (Papastergiou 2009; de Freitas & Oliver, 2006; Chung & Paredes, 2015).

In this regard, Linehan, Lawson, Doughty and Kirman (2009) found that GBL environments offer an excellent opportunity to rehearse and strengthen decision-making processes. In their study of simulation-based learning environments, Hao et al. (2015) found that teamwork brought about remarkable advantages compared to individual work. Lateef (2010) noticed that GBL environments can successfully be used for developing skills needed in problem-solving and decision-making as well as interpersonal and communications skills and team-based competencies. However, more research is needed to understand the kinds of challenges students may encounter in GBL environments. This novel information may help GBL designers as well as HE teachers to develop environments that offer optimal support for 21st century HE learners during their learning experience. In the light of this context, this study focuses on examining students' descriptions of problematic situations and their nature during the collaborative learning process in a simulation game course in multi-site dispersed virtual teams, followed by research question: *What kinds of challenges did the students encounter in virtual teamwork around a business simulation game?*

2. COLLABORATIVE LEARNING IN GBL ENVIRONMENTS

The term game-based learning tends to refer to a learning approach with embedded learning activities in a digital game environment (Chang et al., 2020). Emerson et al. (2020) described that GBL activities consistently incorporate problem-solving tasks to promote students' performance during the learning process. The advantages of GBL can be discussed under several positive educational effects, such as promoting students' learning motivation (Prensky 2003), exhilarating successful learning outcomes (e.g. Yang 2012), and training skills and competences that are challenging to study (e.g. Ronimus et. al., 2014; Koskimaa & Fenyvesi, 2015). Furthermore, educational game environments represent a fertile ground for collaborative learning and shared knowledge construction, in which social interaction has a central role (Papastergiou, 2009). Consequently, the effectiveness and quality of interaction among the participants has a vital impact on the success of learning in GBL environments.

Hao et al. (2015) found that collaboration in simulation-based tasks prompted significant performance improvement. While investigating the effects of games on collaboration skills, Martínez-Cerdá et al. (2018) found that collaborative competencies could efficiently be developed by digital games. Bodnar and Clark (2017), in turn, found game-based learning a promising method for developing students' communicative skills. Furthermore, earlier research has found that learning skills in an authentic environment, for example in a virtual teamwork context, fosters the application of these skills in the real world (Davids et al., 2017; Schartel Dunn, Dawson & Block, 2020).

Research on GBL has also focused on decision-making processes. According to Linehan et al. (2009), game environments foster learning by providing opportunities for rehearsing, enhancing and assessing the decision-making processes of participants. Harviainen et al. (2014) assert that simulation games may be used to promote the learners' reflective and interpretative skills.

Studies over the past two decades have provided important knowledge on GBL, suggesting that games can be characterized by their commitment to the principles of student-centered (Gee 2005; Romero et al. 2012), authentic, social and interactive learning procedures (Prensky, 2003). Yang and Lu (2021) found that specific features of games, such as attractive plot, explicit aim, and assignments to be resolved make them effective, absorbing and manifold learning environments. Furthermore, the application of games for educational purposes offers possibilities for learning by doing (Garris, Ahlers & Driskell, 2002), in which the GBL procedure entails participants to resolve tortuous tasks and progressively obtain expected skills (Karagiannis & Magkos, 2021).

Considering the pedagogical principles of multi-player games, the approach is rooted in the idea of collaborative learning (Romero et al. 2012). Dillenbourg et al. (2009) underline that the educational potential of collaborative learning lies in conjoining individual and social processes. Similarly, Lipponen (2002) found that in teams that collaborate efficiently, participants are more capable of receiving and dealing with a substantial amount of information, leading to novel ideas. In order to complete tasks within multiplayer games, participants are required to process information and confer with their team members (Wuertz et al., 2018). GBL environments have, thus, the potential for amplifying both individual and collaborative information processing and learning.

In the present study, collaborative learning is delineated in the GBL environment in which knowledge co-construction and development of competencies evolve through social activities. The case game environment requires shared decision-making to achieve a shared goal, making it ideal for studying collaborative learning.

3. METHODOLOGY

3.1 Context of the Study

Data in this study were gathered in a university course based on a simulation game called RealGame (Lainema, 2003) in Autumn 2021. The course was part of a virtual business studies programme, in which all study modules were offered by Finnish universities' business faculties. The participating students majored in any other disciplines than business studies. Thus, the students were novices in business studies, but had some basic knowledge as they had taken at least two other study modules before the simulation course.

In the business simulation course students were assigned to 12 teams of 5-7 participants that worked in the simulation environment. Students from eight different universities in Finland included both native Finnish and exchange students, and they took part in the virtual course from different locations. Each team participated in three simulation gaming sessions lasting 6-12 hours, of which each student participated at least for four hours during one session. This allowed for the teams to work in shifts, and all teams took advantage of this opportunity. This way the gaming sessions simulated project work in a dispersed digital team, in which tasks and responsibilities were handed from one team member to another. This setup also amplified the salience of prompt problem recognition.

RealGame is a real-time operated simulation-based business game, which portrays an organisation's supply chain and its delivery process (Lainema, 2003). Participating in RealGame requires that the team members work and collaborate continuously, as the simulation works in continuous time. Thus, when the simulation session starts, the teacher turns on the simulation clock, and then the simulation clock advances hour by hour, illustrating the simulation company's processes and business events with suppliers and their customers. Decision-making in the simulation is ongoing for the duration of the game, and typically one simulation day is processed in 6-10 minutes.

Decisions made by the student teams include basic decisions in a manufacturing business: making component purchases, monitoring inventory levels, ramping up production, steering production shifts, maintaining sales offers, delivering incoming customer orders. These kinds of decisions are typical for a real-world manufacturing organisation that aims at serving its customers by running an efficient supply chain from component purchases to customer deliveries.

3.2 Data Collection and Analysis

In total 66 students handed out their reflection assignments that they wrote after each simulation game session. Data was handled according to appropriate data protection guidelines and practices. Each student gave their informed consent for using their reflection texts as research data. All personal and identifying information was omitted from the data, and all respondents were anonymised and pseudonymised in the final report.

In the data analysis process, qualitative content analysis was employed in an inductive manner (Patton 2001; Krippendorf 2018). The analysis follows the procedure suggested by Elo and Kyngäs (2008). Firstly, tentative analyses of the students' reflection assignments were carried out independently by two of the researchers in order to obtain a thorough understanding of the challenges that the student teams encountered while collaborating in the simulation. Rigour of the analysis process included employing the following techniques: (1) data were gathered from students representing various nationalities, (2) investigator triangulation denoting that two researchers were involved closely in the analysis process, and (3) and rich data representations of the students' reflections were compounded to underpin the results. The qualitative analysis process consisted of following three interlinked steps: *preparation, organizing,* and *reporting* (Elo & Kyngäs, 2008).

First, in the preparation step, students' reflective assignments were carefully read through by the first and second author. To achieve a comprehensive understanding of the entire data, an iterative analysis process began by the researchers' several independent reading rounds of the students' reflective assignments, followed by marking all potentially meaningful information in the light of the research question. By doing this, researchers reached a general understanding of the students' accounts. After this, the researchers came together and started dividing up written texts into smaller pieces based on their initial thoughts, and chose units of analysis through joint discussions. In parallel, researchers labelled these compressed analytical units and composed codes for further analysis.

After the first step, the researchers identified similar student insights under relevant codes, and grouped these into emerging categories. By following this iterative procedure, researchers proceeded into reporting by carefully writing analytic descriptions and combining data extracts in order to create a consistent and compelling description of the findings.

4. RESULTS

Results of our analyses indicate that the challenges encountered by the students during teamwork were related to four different aspects: 1) *communication*, 2) *collaboration*, 3) *organizing*, and 4) *skills and competencies*. Next, we will introduce the key results in Table 1.

Table 1. Summary of the emerging main categories and subcategories

Table 1. Summary of the emerging main categories and subcategories

Category	Subcategory	Data examples
1. Communication challenges	1.1 Lack of communication 1.2 Failure in disseminating appropriate information 1.3 Insufficient communication between shifts	*The main challenge in a communication in my opinion, it is a silence.* (Laura)
2. Collaboration challenges	2.1 Lack of collaboration 2.2 Collaboration conflict 2.3 Lack of commitment 2.4 Highly-dominating team member	*One example of poor collaboration could be when Irmeli and I practically didn't collaborate at all during the first game.* (Ansa)
3. Organising challenges	3.1 Lack of participants in shift 3.2 Poor hand-overs 3.3 Poor organisation of tasks	*After the first simulation day, we noticed that two is too less to handle the process of the game.* (Alvin)
4. Skills and competence issues	4.1 Lack of language skills 4.2 Insufficient business knowledge 4.3. Poor mathematical skills	*An unfortunate incident occurred when it became obvious that Tuovi doesn't really like to speak English and Said doesn't seem to understand Finnish at all.* (Mikko)

4.1 Communication Challenges

Our results revealed that most challenges of the student teams encountered were related to communication. First, students expressed that the most vexing challenges in their teams were **lack of communication** by not contributing to joint discussions or not responding to what the other team members were saying. Moreover, the students reflected that this caused erosion in the team spirit and led to frustration among team members. In some student teams, lack of communication initially led to chaotic teamwork, conflicts, mistakes and compromised decision-making, and eventually, to poor results in the game. Another challenge related to communication was **failure in disseminating appropriate information** to teammates. In the students' view this led to uninformed decision making and unorganized teamwork, as multiple team members worked on the same tasks in the game, reversing each other's decisions. One student described his view as follows:

> *... during the first simulation day when few people were doing the same task without communicating [to] each other and one of them were pricing our products higher and the other person lower and after few minutes they both were like "Is someone else pricing our products at the same time or is this simulation broken"* (Lenni)

In addition, when describing their communication issues, students pointed out that **insufficient communication between shifts** badly affected their teams' ability to perform activities together. Students illustrated their experiences about deficient communication between shifts as well as the demand for more efficient communication during the simulation.

4.2 Collaboration Challenges

Another challenge students often mentioned was related to collaboration in their virtual teams. First, students reported examples of how **lack of collaboration** hampered their joint GBL experience. At worst, students reported of remarkable **collaboration conflicts** in their team, which noticeably rendered difficulties in performing activities together. Under these circumstances, students saw that due to these serious and continuous collaboration problems within their teams they were required to put their own extra effort for accomplishment of the GBL activities.

When describing their approach to collaboration challenges, the students noticed that **lack of commitment** to the joint group activities and processes appeared during the simulation course:

> *It was also noticed that the further the simulation course progressed, the members of the group no longer took quite so seriously the agreed times for a video conferencing or joint tasks. Also, during the simulation, start and finish began to stretch slightly to the wrong direction. So simulation days were reached late and stopped a little in time.* (Lotte)

Moreover, students reflected that they themselves together with some other team members were **highly dominant group members** that led them to take an overactive role in accomplishment of the simulation tasks. This kind of a behavior limited their peers' possibilities to participate in game activities and resulted in unequal contribution to teamwork.

4.3 Organizing Challenges

Our results indicate that organizing challenges in the virtual teams were related to three main issues: lack of participants in shifts, poor handovers between shifts and poor organization of tasks.

In general, students reported that their teams took advantage of the opportunity to work in shifts, as all teams had 5-7 members. Although it was recommended that the teams had at least three people on-line at all times, students reported a variety of examples of how their team was not following this advice. Due to the continuous processing of events in the simulation game, student teams had to pay attention to all aspects in the game all the time, and to continuously make decisions regarding purchases, manufacturing, sales and deliveries as well as to frequently communicate with collaborating teams. **Having too few participants in the game shift** was, thus, an overwhelming experience, and caused a variety of challenges in the teams:

> *When we were short-handed, especially with only the two of us - that caused problems. The worst situation always took place when (just) the two of us were working and the other one left, and two new (persons) came in as a replacement and they needed to be introduced (to the game). One had to change one's way of working and to introduce the situation quickly and to switch to a new task on the go. That created the most challenging situations during the game.* (Jalmari)

Based on our results, teams with proper organization tended to carefully plan how to occupy each shift as well as how to manage the handovers between shifts. Thus, an equally important aspect besides having a sufficient number of participants present was managing the handovers between shifts. Students' views suggest that successful teams preferred a plan for handovers so that there would be an overlap between the team members leaving and entering the game. An overlap would allow for the entering students to get a grip of the current situation as well as of the plan or strategy for the next phases in the game. Having sufficient time to understand what was going on and how to continue from there would prepare for a smoother handover. Other students highlighted that their teams had not planned how to manage the handovers, and hence experienced challenges in these situations.

Furthermore, some students experienced challenges due to **poor organization of tasks**. Students expressed how this resulted either in having one team member being left l out of the teamwork or in wasting time and energy by having multiple participants do the same tasks.

4.4 Skills and Competence Issues

Students taking part in the simulation game represented a variety of different disciplines ranging from natural sciences to humanities. Thus, despite their joint studies in the study programme, students had varying skills and competencies. As many of the teams included exchange students, teams needed to use English in their communication. In this light, students expressed that **lack of language skills** proved a challenge for some of their team members. Balancing between the varying linguistic competencies of team members induced challenges to teamwork, as teams struggled to find a solution that would allow for working together.

Students had varying levels of comprehension regarding how a business organisation operates. Although all students had already finalized several business courses, their skills and competencies were heterogeneous. Students expressed how this led their teams to situations, where decision-making was not based on adequate understanding of causal relationships between business functions. An example of this is illustrated in the next data extract:

> *I think we didn't calculate our decisions enough, because it was apparent at the beginning of the third simulation day that we had ordered too many machines. We couldn't keep up with the ingredients that we needed to use all the new machines. So in conclusion we used a lot of money but didn't get the use of them that we thought we would.* (Elena)

The skills and competencies issues were also manifested as **poor mathematical skills**. In this respect, students encountered challenges in simulation functionalities e.g. in counting the average costs of a product wrong. They felt they wasted time while trying to figure out where the problem was.

5. DISCUSSION AND CONCLUSIONS

Several studies have shown that GBL environments have many advantages in promoting HE students core skills, such as communication, collaboration and critical thinking for 21st century working life (e.g. Bodnar and Clark, 2017; Martínez-Cerdá et al., 2018). To date, however, students' views on challenges of collaborative GBL environments have been under-represented in investigations of GBL. Therefore, this paper focuses on discussing HE students' experiences of challenges they encountered during their collaborative GBL process in virtual teams. Within the context of the simulation-based business game we identified four divergent main categories of challenges encountered by the students during their collaborative teamwork: 1) communication, 2) collaboration, 3) organizing, and 4) skills and competencies. Our study also provided a detailed description of the particular challenges under these broad phenomena.

This study confirms that effective communication is a key element for successful teamwork in virtual teams. This notion is in line with earlier research on success factors of virtual teams in GBL environments (e.g. Papastergiou, 2009; Ceschi et al 2014). Our findings also emphasize that challenges with communication were related to both the frequency of communication and the content of communication. Thus, in our case, lack of communication, failure in disseminating appropriate information or insufficient communication between shifts diminished the teams' ability to collaborate successfully in the simulation game. These results are in line with Wuertz et al. (2018) who found that in order to accomplish shared tasks within learning games, team members are called to share relevant information and to communicate adequately with their team members. Since effective and appropriate communication lays ground for a successful learning process it is vital that the GBL environment provides technological tools that foster communication and dialogic interaction. In addition, it is paramount that the teacher facilitates and supports the virtual teams in their pursuits to address challenges and solve problems. This way, potential challenges with interaction and communication can be resolved already during the learning process.

The results of our study illustrate that students encountered organising challenges, such as poor hand-over and poor organisation of tasks that hindered virtual teams' success to accomplish shared tasks. This also accords with earlier investigations that suggest that virtual teams pledge themselves less planning or fluent coordination activities (Mathieu et al 2020). Organising for virtual collaboration before the learning activities requires particular attention, and the teacher can facilitate and encourage teams to organise before gaming. Understanding how organising contributes to successful teamwork and how it can be supported adhere to valuable work life skills, as much of contemporary work is carried out in virtual working environments.

In light of the results of this study, heterogeneous skills and competencies brought about challenges for the student teams. Insufficient skills in English and mathematics, and business knowledge hindered communication, collaboration and complicated the joint accomplishment of tasks in the business simulation game. At worst, shortcomings in the vital skills caused drop-outs in the course. Hence, it is important to ensure beforehand that all course participants have sufficient basic level skills and competencies to complete the course in virtual teams, and in this way foster a successful learning experience related to core skills for today's working life.

To sum up, HE students encountered a variety of challenges during their learning process in virtual teams around business simulation game. These challenges were significantly linked with each other, and therefore emerging particular fundamental challenges (i.e. lack of communication, poor English skills) may lead to the following challenges in virtual teams and in the worst scenarios cause insurmountable challenges, such as conflicts between team members, poor learning experiences or even interrupting of the course.

Recent developments in work life, and particularly the global COVID-19 pandemic have highlighted the criticality of skills needed in virtual teamwork. Today, not only international organisations, but all organisations work at least partly remotely, and much of this work is carried out in teams. Key competencies and skills needed in this line of work include collaboration, communication and organising in teams in dispersed digital working environments. Consequently, it is important that students learn to identify and solve challenges that are characteristic to teamwork in these environments. GBL environments have proven to be promising learning contexts for rehearsing and learning these valuable skills. The results of the present study display the teamwork challenges encountered in a simulation-based learning environment by student teams, and emphasize the importance of providing students an opportunity to exercise these skills in authentic, safe and inspiring settings.

A developed understanding of the nature and origin of challenges related to collaborating in virtual environments allows for educators and employees alike to take these into account when planning for introduction, onboarding and for various team development practices.

HE is increasingly urged to offer relevant and up-to-date education that fosters the development of skills and competencies needed in 21st century society (Ananiadou & Claro, 2009). In addition, universities are prompted to develop education that is more flexible and accessible to learners balancing between work and university studies (Seaman, Allen & Seaman, 2018), who have issues with accessibility (Fichten et al, 2009) and come from less developed areas and countries (Gonzalez et al., 2020). Canals, Burkle and Nørgård (2018) further stress the need for innovative pedagogical practices and modes of delivery with a broader impact. GBL environments offer a potential educational platform that can help to address these needs.

REFERENCES

Ananiadou, K., & Claro, M. (2009). *21st century skills and competences for new millennium learners in OECD countries*.

Binkley, M., Erstad, O., Herman, J., Raizen, S., Ripley, M., Miller-Ricci, M. & Rumble, M. (2012). Defining twenty-first century skills. In *Assessment and teaching of 21st century skills*, edited by Patrick Griffin, Barry McGaw & Esther Care, 17–66. Springer, Dordrecht.

Bodnar, C. A., & Clark, R. M. (2017). Can game-based learning enhance engineering communication skills?. *IEEE transactions on professional communication*, 60(1), 24-41.

Caputo, A., Marzi, G., Maley, J. and Silic, M. (2019). Ten years of conflict management research 2007-2017: An update on themes, concepts and relationships. *International Journal of Conflict Management*, Emerald Publishing Limited,. 30 (1), 87– 110.

Canals, L., Burkle, M., & Nørgård, R. T. (2018). Universities of the future: Several perspectives on the future of higher education. *International Journal of Educational Technology in Higher Education*, 15(46).

Ceschi, A., Dorofeeva, K., & Sartori, R. (2014). Studying teamwork and team climate by using a business simulation: how communication and innovation can improve group learning and decision-making performance. *European Journal of Training and Development*.

Chang, C. Y., Kao, C. H., Hwang, G. J., & Lin, F. H. (2020). From experiencing to critical thinking: A contextual game-based learning approach to improving nursing students' performance in electrocardiogram training. *Educational Technology Research and Development*, 68(3), 1225-1245.

Chung, K. S. K., & Paredes, W. C. (2015). Towards a social networks model for online learning & performance. *Journal of Educational Technology & Society*, 18(3), 240-253.

Davids, A. I. R., Van den Bossche, P., Gijbels, D. & Fandos Garrido, M. (2017). The impact of individual, educational, and workplace factors on the transfer of school-based learning into the workplace. *Vocations and Learning,* 10, 275–306.

De Freitas, S., & Oliver, M. (2006). How can exploratory learning with games and simulations within the curriculum be most effectively evaluated? *Computers & education*, 46(3), 249-264.

Dillenbourg, P., Järvelä, S., & Fischer, F. (2009). The evolution of research on computer-supported collaborative learning. In *Technology-enhanced learning* (pp. 3-19). Springer, Dordrecht.

Elo, S., & Kyngäs, H. (2008). The qualitative content analysis process. *Journal of advanced nursing*, 62(1), 107-115.

Emerson, A., Cloude, E. B., Azevedo, R., & Lester, J. (2020). Multimodal learning analytics for game-based learning. *British Journal of Educational Technology*, 51(5), 1505-1526.

Fichten, C. S., Ferraro, V., Asuncion, J. V., Chwojka, C., Barile, M., Nguyen, M. N., ... & Wolforth, J. (2009). Disabilities and e-learning problems and solutions: An exploratory study. *Journal of Educational*.

Garris, R., Ahlers, R., & Driskell, J. E. (2002). Games, motivation, and learning: A research and practice model. In *Simulation in Aviation Training* (pp. 475-501). Routledge.

Gee, J. P. (2005). Learning by design: Good video games as learning machines. *E-learning and Digital Media*, 2(1), 5-16.

Gonzalez, T., De La Rubia, M. A., Hincz, K. P., Comas-Lopez, M., Subirats, L., Fort, S., & Sacha, G. M. (2020). Influence of COVID-19 confinement on students' performance in higher education. *PLoS One*, 15(10).

Gonzalez-Perez, M. A., Velez-Calle, A., Cathro, V, Dan V. Caprar, D. & Taras, V. (2014). Virtual teams and international business teaching and learning: The case of the Global Enterprise Experience (GEE). *Journal of Teaching in International Business,* 25 (3), 200–213.

Hao, J., Liu, L., von Davier, A., & Kyllonen, P. (2015). *Assessing collaborative problem solving with simulation based tasks*. International Society of the Learning Sciences, Inc.

Harviainen, J. T., Lainema, T., & Saarinen, E. (2014). Player-reported impediments to game-based learning. *Transactions of the Digital Games Research Association*, 1(2).

Iglesias-Pradas, S., Hernández-García, Á., Chaparro-Peláez, J., & Prieto, J. L. (2021). Emergency remote teaching and students' academic performance in higher education during the COVID-19 pandemic: A case study. *Computers in human behaviour*, 119, 106713.

Karagiannis, S., & Magkos, E. (2021). Engaging students in basic cybersecurity concepts using digital game-based learning: Computer games as virtual learning environments. In *Advances in Core Computer*

Kaushik, M., & Guleria, N. (2020). The impact of pandemic COVID-19 in workplace. *European Journal of Business and Management*, 12(15), 1-10.

Krippendorff, K. (2018). *Content analysis: An introduction to its methodology*. Sage publications.

Koskimaa, R., & Fenyvesi, K. (2015). A mission impossible? Learning the logic of space with impossible figures in experience-based mathematics education. *Opus et Education*, 2(1).

Lainema, T. (2003). Enhancing organizational business process perception: Experiences from constructing and applying a dynamic business simulation game. Turku School of Economics and Business Administration.

Linehan, C., Lawson, S., Doughty, M., & Kirman, B. (2009). Developing a serious game to evaluate and train group decision making skills. In *Proceedings of the 13th international MindTrek conference: Everyday Life in the Ubiquitous Era* (pp. 106-113).

Lateef, F. (2010). Simulation-based learning: Just like the real thing. Journal of Emergencies, *Trauma and Shock*, 3(4), 348.

Lipponen, L. (2002, January). Exploring foundations for computer-supported collaborative learning. In *CSCL* (Vol. 2, pp. 72-81).

Martínez-Cerdá, J. F., Torrent-Sellens, J., & González-González, I. (2018). Promoting collaborative skills in online university: Comparing effects of games, mixed reality, social media, and other tools for ICT-supported pedagogical practices. *Behaviour & Information Technology*, 37(10-11), 1055-1071.

Mathieu, J. E., Luciano, M. M., D'Innocenzo, L., Klock, E. A., & LePine, J. A. (2020). The development and construct validity of a team processes survey measure. *Organizational Research Methods*, 23(3), 399-431.

Papastergiou, M. (2009). Digital game-based learning in high school computer science education: Impact on educational effectiveness and student motivation. *Computers & education*, 52(1), 1-12.

Patton, M. Q. (2001). *Qualitative evaluation and research methods* (2nd ed.). Thousand Oaks, CA: SAGE.

Prensky, M. (2003). Digital game-based learning. *Computers in Entertainment*, 1(1), 21-21.

Riemer, M. J. (2007). Communication skills for the 21st century engineer. *Global J. of Engng. Educ*, 11(1), 89-100.

Romero, M., Usart, M., Ott, M., Earp, J., de Freitas, S., & Arnab, S. (2012). Learning through playing for or against each other? Promoting collaborative learning in digital game based learning. In *Proceedings of the European Conference on Information Systems*.

Ronimus, M., Kujala, J., Tolvanen, A., & Lyytinen, H. (2014). Children's engagement during digital game-based learning of reading: The effects of time, rewards, and challenge. *Computers & Education*, 71, 237-246.

Schartel Dunn, S., Dawson, M. & Block, B. (2020). Teaching teamwork in the business school. *Journal of Education for Business*, 96 (6), 381–386.

Seaman, J. E., Allen, I. E., & Seaman, J. (2018). *Grade Increase: Tracking Distance Education in the United States*. Babson Survey Research Group.

Tendick, P. H., Denby, L. & Ju, W-H. (2016). Statistical methods for complex event processing and real time decision making. *Wiley Interdisciplinary Reviews: Computational Statistics,* 8 (1), 5–26.

Wuertz, J., Alharthi, S. A., Hamilton, W. A., Bateman, S., Gutwin, C., Tang, A., ... & Hammer, J. (2018, April). A design framework for awareness cues in distributed multiplayer games. In *Proceedings of the 2018 CHI Conference on Human Factors in Computing Systems* (pp. 1-14).

Yang, Y. T. C. (2012). Building virtual cities, inspiring intelligent citizens: Digital games for developing students' problem solving and learning motivation. *Computers & Education*, 59(2), 365-377.

Yang, K. H., & Lu, B. C. (2021). Towards the successful game-based learning: Detection and feedback to misconceptions is the key. *Computers & Education*.

STUDENT ACCEPTANCE OF SOCIAL ROBOTS IN HIGHER EDUCATION – EVIDENCE FROM A VIGNETTE STUDY

Josef Guggemos[1], Stefan Sonderegger[2] and Sabine Seufert[2]
[1]*University of Education Schwäbisch Gmünd, Hauberweg 48, 73525 Schwäbisch Gmünd, Germany*
[2]*University of St.Gallen, St. Jakob-Strasse 21, 9000 St. Gallen, Switzerland*

ABSTRACT

Social robots have the potential to play a vital role in education. Student technology acceptance may be considered as a driver for their successful integration in educational processes. Based on the ICAP (Interactive, Constructive, Active, Passive) framework and research on social robot roles, we have developed eight vignettes describing scenarios for the use of social robots in higher education, e.g., teaching assistant. Students in an introductory university course completed the vignettes; they answered questions based on the unified theory of acceptance and use of technology (UTAUT), as well as on their ethical approval. Drawing from a sample of N = 361 students, we carried out confirmatory factor analysis. In line with the conceptual basis, eight scenarios can be described. Overall, students do not accept social robots as presenters; however, the assessment of other roles, such as teaching assistant, is positive. By means of a latent profile analysis, we were able to identify four profiles that may be meaningful from a conceptual point of view. One profile is particularly noteworthy. It comprises students who accept social robots not as a means of instruction, e.g., as a tutor, but as a tool, e.g., to promote computational thinking.

KEYWORDS

Social Robot, Higher Education, Technology Acceptance, Vignette, ICAP, Robot Roles

1. INTRODUCTION

Social robots have the potential to enrich educational processes (Belpaeme et al., 2018; Woo et al., 2021). A social robot can be defined as "an autonomous or semi-autonomous robot that interacts and communicates with humans by following the behavioral norms expected by the people with whom the robot is intended to interact" (Bartneck & Forlizzi, 2004, p. 592). Social robots can be used to teach about the robots themselves or as teaching aids (Mubin et al., 2013). When teaching about social robots, they are the actual content of instruction, for example, to teach computational thinking (Ching et al., 2018). Besides this, social robots (in collaboration with teachers) can carry out selected duties in the classroom or venue. Such roles are: teacher, teaching assistant, evaluator, tutor, and peer (Woo et al., 2021). If social robots should take over these roles, however, investigating technology acceptance may be an important consideration (Raffaghelli et al., 2022). Regardless of their actual value, social robots might only be useful if students are willing to use them.

The paper at hand focuses on the use of social robots in higher education, in particular, on academic writing. This domain is characterised by substantial student heterogeneity (Seufert & Spiroudis, 2017). Therefore, a general issue in higher education may be particularly problematic in this context: it is difficult to offer students sufficient guidance and support (Byrne et al., 2017; Cooney & Leister, 2019; Handke, 2018). Employing human lecturers for this purpose may be impossible, mainly due to budget restrictions. Social robots might be a viable option. Studies about the general acceptance of social robots by students for learning purposes are available in this context (Guggemos et al., 2020). However, these studies in general address the overall technology acceptance of students in higher education. This may not be satisfactory because the roles that a social robot can adopt are manifold (Belpaeme & Tanaka, 2021; Mubin et al., 2013; Woo et al., 2021). A first important question would be whether the roles of social robots as pointed out in the literature are meaningful, from a pedagogical point of view, and can they be empirically separated. Gauging student acceptance for specific robot roles may be beneficial for developing further use cases. If students, for instance, do not accept a social robot as a presenter but do so as a tutor, further developments might focus on the use of such robots in a tutor setting, instead of in a presenter setting. Besides this, there may not only be variance in the assessment of social robot roles; differences within specific roles may also be present. For instance, some students may accept social robots as a tutor whereas other students, for a variety of reasons, do not accept them for this purpose. Identifying the profiles of students with a similar acceptance of social robots allows for person-centered interventions (Hofmans et al., 2020). For example, the concerns of students who are overly skeptical about using social robots could be addressed. The paper at hand aims to contribute to a more detailed picture of technology acceptance by higher education students in comparison to the available studies on the subject.

2. THEORETICAL BACKGROUND

A first step is to classify meaningful pedagogical scenarios of social robot use. To this end, we rely on the ICAP framework (Chi & Wylie, 2014). It can be used to predict the level of learning outcomes of different activities. The acronym ICAP stands for the learning activities *Interactive*, *Constructive*, *Active*, and *Passive*. The authors argue and provide empirical evidence that in terms of learning outcomes it can be expected that: Interactive > Constructive > Active > Passive. In passive learning activities, learners absorb information from the material without engaging in learning-related activities, e.g., listening to a social robot without further activities. Active learning activities are characterized by activities that do not go beyond the information presented, e.g., making verbatim notes while listening to the robot. In constructive learning activities, learners generate output that goes beyond the information contained in the material, e.g., using the robot as a tool to perform computational thinking tasks. In interactive activities, learners perform the constructive activities with others (including a robot), e.g., solving a problem in collaboration with the social robot.

The interaction with a social robot can be one-to-one (human to robot) or between a robot and multiple humans (multi-party interaction) (e.g., Żarkowski, 2019). This classification is particularly relevant from a technical perspective. The requirements for a multi-party interaction involving the perception of various social cues and linguistic input from multiple individuals is substantially more complex than for a human-to-robot interaction (e.g., identifying who is the sender and who is the receiver of a speech input). Belpaeme et al. (2018) adopted this classification in their meta-analysis. In the studies under consideration, the robot is used to teach one learner in around two-thirds of the cases, and to teach many learners in around one-third of the cases. Woo et al. (2021), who address social robots in classroom settings, distinguish between whole-class instruction and one-to-one interactions.

An established theory to evaluate student acceptance of social robots is the unified theory of acceptance and use of technology (UTAUT) (Fridin & Belokopytov, 2014). The UTAUT (Venkatesh et al., 2003) implies that the use intention can be predicted with performance expectancy, effort expectancy, and social influence. Performance and effort expectancy could be classified as internal beliefs, and social influence as external beliefs (Scherer et al., 2020). Adapted to our context, these constructs are defined as: the degree to which students believe that using social robots in a specific role will benefit them (performance expectancy), the degree of ease associated with the use of social robots in a specific role (effort expectancy), the degree to which students believe others want them to use social robots in a specific role (social influence), and the intention to use the social robot in a specific role (behavioral intention) (Venkatesh et al., 2003). Besides these generic constructs, technology, such as social robots, also brings with it (new) moral challenges (Serholt et al., 2017; Sharkey, 2016; Smakman et al., 2021). Hence, it may also be important to consider student ethical approval about the use of social robots in order to obtain a full picture of technology acceptance. Ethical approval could be defined as the degree to which students regard the use of social robots in a specific role as morally correct.

3. THE PRESENT STUDY

Social robots are a novel technology for higher education students, especially in the social sciences (Guggemos et al., 2020). Hence, it might be difficult for such students to assess the various roles social robots can play. A viable option to tackle this issue may be vignettes (Sailer et al., 2021). Vignettes are stimuli that present realistic scenarios in order to evoke a reaction from the study participants (Skilling & Stylianides, 2020). It may be advantageous to combine both text and videos. Hence, before performing the vignettes, all students watched a video demonstrating the capabilities of social robots, capabilities relevant for all the vignettes (https://youtu.be/GTyKb8c2b6w). The social robot in the video is a Pepper model from Softbank robotics. As previously demonstrated, Pepper may be suitable for educational purposes (Alnajjar et al., 2021) and the robot has been increasingly used in education in recent years (Woo et al., 2021). Drawing from the theoretical background, we developed four vignettes according to the ICAP framework where the robot acts in a robot-to-class setting, and four vignettes in a one-student setting. Following Skilling and Stylianides (2020), the written part of each vignette ranges between 50 and 200 words. Table 1 provides an overview of the eight vignettes.

We validated the eight vignettes in an expert interview with Prof. Handke, a renowned researcher in the realm of social robots in higher education (e.g., Alnajjar et al., 2021), and we revised the eight vignettes based on his feedback. By means of this, we may have obtained a fair representation of social robots' capabilities in higher education (see Table 1).

Table 1. Summary of eight vignettes presenting robot scenarios in higher education

Vignette	Summary of scenario	Added value of the robot	Conceptual basis
Robot-to-class scenarios (1-many)			
1. Presenter (pre) *(passive learning)*	The robot assumes the role of a content presenter in the classical teaching format for knowledge transfer, while the students have a passive role.	Relief for lecturers; variety for students; efficiency benefits; monitoring functions (e.g., attention, volume, air)	~Role of presenter (Handke, 2020, p. 111)
2. Teaching assistant (tas) *(active learning)*	The robot supports the lecturer in a teaching assistant role by conducting and evaluating quizzes or live surveys that students submit.	Support for lecturers; activation of students; evaluations in real time through connection to cloud-based survey tools or LMS	~Role of assistant (Handke, 2020, p. 122)
3. Formative assessor (fas) *(constructive learning)*	The robot, in the role of an examiner, conducts and analyzes competence-oriented assessment tasks, which are solved individually before evaluation and discussion in a plenum.	Relief for lecturers in conducting assessments; consistent and fair exam preparation across courses or years; AI can review text-based answers faster than humans	~Role of examiner (Handke, 2020, p. 127)
4. Moderator (mod) *(interactive learning)*	The robot takes over the moderation and organization of discussions, debates, or group work. Students discuss ideas and lines of argumentation under the robot's guidance.	A robot moderator can store, summarize, and analyze discussion content with AI-based services (e.g., cluster analysis, subjectivity, fact check)	~Role of moderator (e.g., Short et al., 2016)
Robot-to-student scenarios (1-1)			
5. Tutor (tut) *(passive learning)*	The robot adopts the role of a personal tutor offering adaptive repetition and tutoring of content during and after courses to students.	Individual support for students; content is visually/auditorily enhanced and patiently repeated on demand (efficiency)	~Role of tutor (Handke, 2020, p. 106)
6. Advisor (adv) *(active learning)*	The robot, as a learning advisor, answers questions, conducts self-assessments, and provides learning guidance based on learning data.	Recurring admin. questions answered by robot to relieve staff; robot advisory functions based on learning analytics (LMS data)	~Role of advisor (Handke, 2020, p. 118)
7. Tool (tol) *(constructive learning)*	The robot is used as a hands-on learning tool to promote problem solving skills, programming, and computational thinking.	Hands-on orientation provides higher forms of engagement (constructive learning); project-based learning	~Robot as a tool (Handke, 2020, p. 141)
8. Conversation partner (cov) *(interactive learning)*	The robot, as a conversation partner, holds and simulates conversations with students and gives feedback (e.g., simulation of job interview).	Scalable solution to simulate human conversation and learning partners; 'learning by teaching' effect for students	~Conversation practice (e.g., Engwall et al., 2021)

Figure 1 depicts one of the eight vignettes. As can be seen, four questions are embedded in each vignette (in English). Three of these questions are based on the key technology acceptance variables of performance expectancy, effort expectancy, and use intention. We have omitted social influence as it is an external belief. The self-determination theory indicates that such external beliefs could be problematic (Deci et al., 2017); if prompted by others, students may use social robots but with low engagement. We complemented these technology acceptance questions with one question concerning the ethical use of robots.

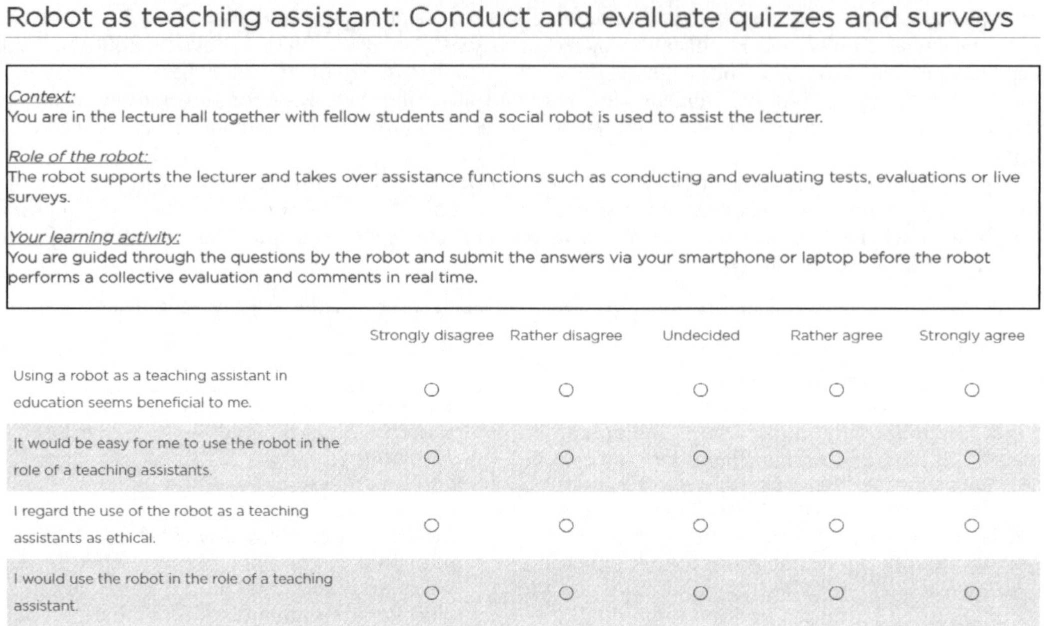

Robot as teaching assistant: Conduct and evaluate quizzes and surveys

Context:
You are in the lecture hall together with fellow students and a social robot is used to assist the lecturer.

Role of the robot:
The robot supports the lecturer and takes over assistance functions such as conducting and evaluating tests, evaluations or live surveys.

Your learning activity:
You are guided through the questions by the robot and submit the answers via your smartphone or laptop before the robot performs a collective evaluation and comments in real time.

	Strongly disagree	Rather disagree	Undecided	Rather agree	Strongly agree
Using a robot as a teaching assistant in education seems beneficial to me.	○	○	○	○	○
It would be easy for me to use the robot in the role of a teaching assistants.	○	○	○	○	○
I regard the use of the robot as a teaching assistants as ethical.	○	○	○	○	○
I would use the robot in the role of a teaching assistant.	○	○	○	○	○

Figure 1. Vignette example – Robot as teaching assistant

Based on the student assessment of the eight scenarios, we aim to answer two research questions:
RQ1: What is the factor structure of the eight scenarios of social robot use in higher education?
RQ2: What latent profiles of social robot acceptance exist among students in higher education?

4. METHOD

4.1 Sample

First-year students from the course 'Introduction to Academic Writing' (about 1,500 participants) at the University of St.Gallen in Switzerland were asked to perform the eight vignettes in November 2021. Of this group, 371 students voluntarily participated. We checked for multivariate outliers by means of Mahalanobis distances. We excluded ten students with significant ($\alpha = .01$) Mahalanobis distances, which yields a sample of 361 students. Of the data, 0.3% is missing; we inspected the data and concluded it was missing completely at random. Of the students, 36.7% are female and 63.3% male. Their intended study subjects are business administration (43.4%), economics (15.0%), international affairs (11.4%), law (6.1%), and law and economics (8.3%); 15.8% of the students are undecided. On average, the students are 19.71 years old (SD = 1.52 years), min = 17 years, max = 27 years, median = 20 years. The German language track was selected by 63.2% of the students, and the remainder (36.8%) chose the English language track.

4.2 Confirmatory Factor Analysis, Model Assessment, Factor Extraction (RQ1)

To answer RQ1, we carry out confirmatory factor analysis using the 'lavaan 0.6-11' package in R (Rosseel, 2012). Since all the items are measured on a five-point scale of rating, we utilize a robust maximum likelihood estimator (MLR) (Robitzsch, 2020). Missing data are handled using full information maximum likelihood estimation. According to Hu and Bentler (1999), a CFI and TLI > 0.95, as well as a RMSEA < 0.06 and SRMR < 0.08, may indicate a good fit of a model. In addition to demonstrating a sufficient fit of a hypothesized model, it is necessary to compare competing models (Sarstedt et al., 2022). Lin et al. (2017) demonstrated in a simulation study that for this purpose the information criteria *Scaled unit information prior BIC* (SPBIC) and *Haughton's BIC* (HBIC) may be most suitable. To assess the quality of the measurement, we rely on different measures. A McDonald's ω greater than .7 points to a sufficient internal consistency reliability; an average variance extracted (AVE) greater than .5 might indicate convergent validity, and a heterotrait–monotrait ratio smaller than 0.85 discriminant validity (Sarstedt et al., 2022). After having identified the optimal model, we extract factor scores for the subsequent latent profile analysis (Scherer et al., 2021). Factor scores are superior to sum scores (McNeish & Wolf, 2020). We opt for Bartlett factor scores as they yield unbiased estimates for the true scores (DiStefano et al., 2009). The disadvantage of factor scores is the lack of a meaningful zero point. They are standardized in a way that the sum of all students' factor scores of a construct is zero. However, this zero point does not correspond with the neutral scale mean of the five-point scale of rating (= 3). Therefore, we recalibrate the factor scores: a factor score of zero in our study means that a student is undecided concerning all the questions. Hence, we can answer whether student acceptance of a specific scenario, e.g., social robots as presenters, is positive or negative.

4.3 Latent Profile Analysis (RQ2)

The approach of the latent profile analysis follows Guggemos et al. (2022). We use the 'tidyLPA 1.1.0' R-package in combination with MPlus 8 to identify profiles of social robot acceptance by means of a latent profile analysis (LPA) (Hallquist & Wiley, 2018; Rosenberg et al., 2018). We have to restrict variances to be equal across profiles and the covariance among the variables to be zero in order to avoid convergence problems (Meyer & Morin, 2016). Missing data are not present due to the use of full information maximum likelihood. The critical step in the LPA is to identify an appropriate number of profiles. This decision might be based on information criteria and likelihood ratio tests, as well as on conceptual deliberations (Scherer et al., 2021). Against this backdrop, we first assessed different class solutions. Following Morin and Marsh (2015) and Hofmans et al. (2020), we report the information criteria AIC, CAIC, BIC, and aBIC, as well as the bootstrap likelihood ratio test (BLRT). Since these criteria may point to a different number of optimal profiles, we also utilize the approach of Akogul and Erisoglu (2017) where information criteria are weighted to determine the optimal number of latent profiles (from an empirical point of view). The identified solution should have a sufficiently high precision of classification, indicated by an entropy greater than 0.7. To demonstrate the robustness of the findings we conduct a replication of the LPA with 100 random samples of 150 students from our overall sample of 361 students (Vanslambrouck et al., 2019). Besides this, the profiles should be substantially different from each other, which can be checked by means of a MANOVA (Tondeur et al., 2019). Afterwards, we evaluate if this approach yields a meaningful solution. The profiles should be of reasonable size and show substantial shape differences, i.e., differences that not only differ in levels but also in their pattern (Morin & Marsh, 2015).

5. RESULTS

5.1 Confirmatory Factor Analysis, Model Assessment, Factor Extraction (RQ1)

The fit of the tested models is reported in Table 2. First, we tested a basic model (model 1) where the eight scenarios of robot use are operationalized with four items (see Figure 1) addressing *use intention* (use), *performance expectancy* (pe), *effort expectancy* (ee), and *ethical approval* (eth). The fit is poor: TLI = 0.858, RMSEA = 0.087. The modification indices pointed to an additional factor for ethical approval. In model 2 (see Figure 2), we added the factor *ethical approval* where, in addition to model 1, the factor ethical approval is operationalized with the ethical approval items of the eight scenarios; the fit is good: TLI = 0.954, RMSEA = 0.049. Model 3 includes, in addition to model 2, two higher order factors to consider the role of the robot, i.e., robot to class (vignettes 1–4) and robot to student (vignettes 5–8). The fit of model 3 is good: TLI = 0.954, RMSEA = 0.050. Model 4, in addition to model 2, considers the four ICAP dimensions as higher order factors: I (vignettes 4 and 8), C (vignettes 3 and 7), A (vignettes 2 and 6), and P (vignettes 1 and 5). The fit of model 4 is good: TLI = 0.953, RMSEA = 0.050. Model 5 is a combination of models 3 and 4, and considers the two roles of the robot and the four ICAP dimensions as higher order factors. The fit of model 5 is good: TLI = 0.955, RMSEA = 0.049. Based on the fit values, model 1 can be rejected. SPBIC and HBIC both point to model 2 as the best trade-off between model complexity and accuracy. Hence, we use model 2 for all our further analyses.

Table 2. Comparison of competing models

Model	Considered factors	YB–χ^2(df)	TLI	RMSEA	SPBIC	HBIC
1	8 scenarios	1461 (436)	0.858	0.087	27,583	27,271
2	8 scenarios, 1 ethical approval	744 (420)	0.954	0.049	26,747	26,409
3	8 scenarios, 1 ethical approval, 2 1:class vs. 1:1 setting	793 (445)	0.953	0.050	26,813	26,514
4	8 scenarios, 1 ethical approval, 4 ICAP dimensions	777 (438)	0.953	0.050	26,790	26,483
5	8 scenarios, 1 ethical approval, 2 1:class vs. 1:1 setting, 4 ICAP	750 (427)	0.955	0.049	26,759	26,428

YB–χ^2 = Yuan Bentler χ^2, df = degrees of freedom, TLI = Tucker-Lewis index, RMSEA = root mean square error of approximation, SPBIC = scaled unit information prior BIC, HBIC = Haughton's BIC.

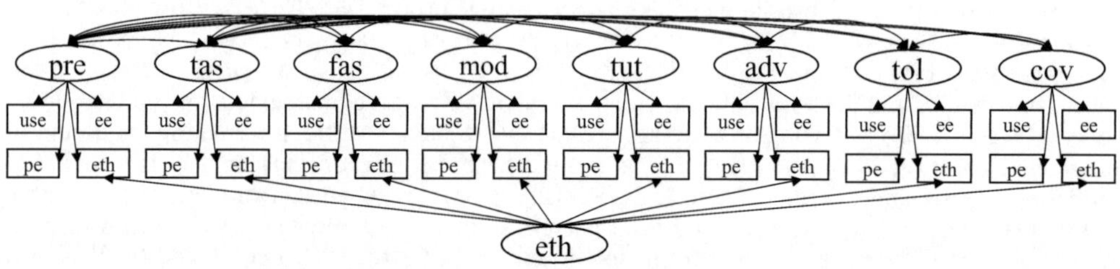

Figure 2. Preferred model (see Table 2). Note: For reasons of clarity, the correlations between the eight roles (pre – cov) with eth are not depicted. All correlations among constructs are reported in Table 3

Model 2 yields overall decent properties: YB-χ^2(420) = 744; CFI = 0.961; TLI = 0.954; RMSEA = 0.049, 90% CI [0.041, 0.055]; SRMR = 0.029. The internal consistency reliabilities are greater than .85. The AVE is greater than .65 with one exception: the factor ethical approval shows a low AVE (.23). However, this is an auxiliary factor to consider the residual correlations among the ethical approval questions. The highest heterotrait–monotrait ratio (between *tutor* and *advisor*) equals 0.60, which is well below the cut-off value of 0.85. Table 3 also indicates moderate correlations in technology acceptance within the eight scenarios. Hence, indeed, they may capture different constructs.

As can be seen from Table 3, the overall acceptance of social robots as teaching assistants, tutors, advisors, and tools is significantly positive; the overall evaluation of robots as presenters and formative assessors is significantly negative.

Table 3. Mean, standard deviation, reliability, average variance extracted, and correlations among constructs (N = 361)

Variable	*M*	*SD*	ω	AVE	1	2	3	4	5	6	7	8
1. presenter	**-0.32**	1.08	.91	.67								
2. teaching assistant	**0.31**	1.01	.92	.67	**.41**							
3. formative assessor	**-0.12**	1.11	.92	.69	**.29**	**.47**						
4. moderator	0.01	1.10	.91	.66	**.40**	**.41**	**.25**					
5. tutor	**0.13**	1.14	.91	.71	**.24**	**.44**	**.37**	**.38**				
6. advisor	**0.26**	1.04	.91	.71	**.32**	**.44**	**.36**	**.41**	**.54**			
7. tool	**0.53**	0.90	.89	.66	**.36**	**.47**	**.30**	**.44**	**.43**	**.46**		
8. conversation partner	-0.04	1.17	.90	.71	**.33**	**.34**	**.25**	**.45**	**.38**	**.48**	**.39**	
9. ethical approval	**0.14**	0.61	.86	.23	.03	**.18**	**.12**	.03	.05	.05	.06	-.02

Note. Figures in bold indicate significance (two-sided) at the 5% level. Constructs are based on Bartlett factor scores. The factor scores are standardized such that zero equals the neutral scale mean of the five-point scale of rating.

5.2 Latent Profile Analysis (RQ2)

Table 4 shows the results of the latent profile analysis; the information criteria point to different class solutions. The algorithm of Akogul and Erisoglu (2017) suggests four profiles as the optimum. Moreover, the entropy for this solution is sufficiently high (0.813). A replication of the latent profile analysis with 100 samples of 150 students points to three profiles. In 1% of the cases, two profiles are optimal (criterion: Akogul & Erisoglu, 2017); in 57% of the cases, three profiles; in 30% of the cases, four profiles; in 12% of the cases, five or six profiles. The MANOVA yielded significant different means among the four profiles: F (24, 1015.7) = 50.16, Wilk's $\Lambda = 0.104$, $p < .001$, $\eta^2 = .400$. In other words, 40.0% of the variance can be explained by profile membership. These findings and Figure 3 point to sufficiently distinct profiles.

Table 4. Information criteria, entropies, and BLRT results for the seven latent profiles

No. profiles	-LL	No. Par.	AIC	CAIC	BIC	aBIC	Entropy	p(BLRT)
1	4,276	16	8,584	8,585	8,646	8,595	1.000	-
2	3,971	25	7,991	7,995	8,089	8,009	0.812	.000
3	3,886	34	7,841	7,848	7,973	7,865	0.790	.000
4	3,860	43	7,807	7,819	7,974	7,838	0.813	.000
5	3,841	52	7,786	7,804	7,988	7,823	0.786	.000
6	3,823	61	7,768	7,794	8,006	7,812	0.793	.000
7	3,804	70	7,749	7,783	8,021	7,799	0.780	.158

Note: -LL = - Log-likelihood, No. Par. = number of estimated parameters, AIC = Akaike's information criterion, CAIC = Consistent AIC, BIC = Bayesian information criterion, aBIC = adjusted BIC, BLRT = bootstrap likelihood ratio test.

The four latent profiles can be described as follows:

- Profile 1: Students in this profile are skeptical about social robots in general. They do not accept any of the eight social robot roles. Profile 1 comprises 45 students (12.5%).
- Profile 2: Students are skeptical about social robots as a means of instruction (scenarios 1–6 and 8). However, they assess the use of social robots as the instruction content as positive, e.g., to learn computational thinking. Profile 2 is the smallest one with 26 students (7.2%).
- Profile 3: Students have a differentiated view. They show a significant negative acceptance for social robots as presenter and formative assessor, a neutral assessment towards social robots as moderator, tutor, and conversational agent, and a significant positive assessment towards social robots as teaching assistant, advisor, and tool. Profile 3 is the largest one with 169 students (46.8%).
- Profile 4: Students have a positive acceptance towards all eight roles of social robots. This profile is also substantial in size with 121 students (33.5%).

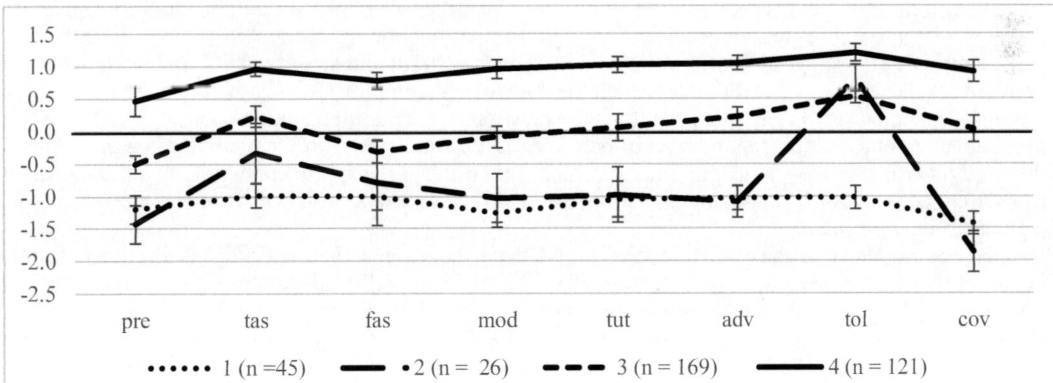

Figure 3. Latent profiles of social robot acceptance among higher education students (N = 361). Recalibrated factor scores (zero = neutral scale mean) and corresponding 95% confidence intervals

6. DISCUSSION, LIMITATIONS, AND CONCLUSION

We have developed and validated eight vignettes for social robot use in higher education. These vignettes may offer the students a fair representation of the capabilities of social robots at the current state of the art. Based on confirmatory factor analyses, there is evidence for the model structure with eight robot-use scenarios. The students regard the scenarios in substantially different and unique ways. However, when considering the four ICAP dimensions as higher order factors, this reduces the fit of the model in such a way that does not compensate the increased degrees of freedoms. The same holds true when considering the setting: robot to class vs. robot to student. From an empirical point of view, the ICAP and setting of robot use may not be a suitable structure for the vignettes. Nevertheless, they may be important from a conceptual point of view. The ICAP is a suitable framework to classify the quality of educational technology use (Sailer et al., 2021). The setting is important from a technical point of view as a robot-to-class setting is (except for the role of presenter) more difficult to implement than a robot-to-student setting.

An additional factor, *ethical approval*, is necessary in the confirmatory factor analysis in order to achieve a good model fit. The explanation for this may be due to the fact that ethical approval is a construct outside the UTAUT framework and, therefore, of a different nature. However, ethical approval may be an important facet of social robot acceptance in higher education: the AVE is greater than 0.5 for all eight scenarios; the standardized loadings of the ethical approval items on the factors exceed in all cases 0.613 ($p < .001$).

The latent profile analysis pointed to four profiles. These profiles can be interpreted in a meaningful way. However, three profiles rather than four may also be acceptable. Our replication with 100 random samples of 150 students pointed to three profiles. Moreover, the BIC—a suitable criterion to identify the optimal number of classes in mixture modeling (Nylund et al., 2007)—indicates three profiles. In the case of opting for three profiles, profiles 1 and 2 collapse. Profile 2 is small; however, it may be revealing from a conceptual point of view. Social robots can be used as a means of instruction or as the content matter in education. Students in profile 2 distinguish between these two kinds of use. We also tested models with five or more classes; however, they yield profiles that are very small and/or difficult to interpret. As a limitation, due to convergence problems, we had to assume equal variances across the profiles and covariances of zero. These assumptions are restrictive (Scherer et al., 2021). Against this backdrop, it would be beneficial to replicate our four-class solution with another sample.

Overall, the roles with the highest acceptance are social robots used as a tool and as teaching assistant. Social robots as a presenter are rated most negatively; the acceptance of social robots as a formative assessor is also negative. The vignettes may help students to obtain a more realistic picture about the capabilities of social robots in specific roles; however, they present scenarios where everything works well, i.e., no breakdowns or malfunctions of the robot occur. When social robots are used as a means of instruction (scenarios 1–6 and 8), malfunction may decrease acceptance for all roles at the same rate. Hence, the patterns of the latent classes might be unchanged but at an overall lower level. The acceptance reported in the study at hand could be regarded as the upper band. It allows conclusions about the acceptance of social robot roles that are, even in an error-free scenario, not positive. Further research could shed light on the latent profiles of students with varying degrees of acceptance toward the malfunctioning of robots.

We followed the suggestion of Skilling and Stylianides (2020) and aimed to have a vignette word count of between 50 and 200. For social robots, which are a novel and complex technology, this may not be enough to present a fair picture. On the other hand, however, more elaborate descriptions could yield higher rates of missing values and a decreasing number of participants. Overall, we regard qualitative research, which allows the study participants an in-depth interaction, as a promising way to complement quantitative studies (Sonderegger et al., 2022). In particular, the concept of ethical approval should be investigated more elaborately than has been done in our study.

Our contributions to the literature are: 1) We have developed theoretically based (ICAP framework) vignettes that fairly portray the use scenarios of social robots in higher education at the current technical state of the art. 2) We considered ethical approval as a facet of social robot acceptance, which goes beyond the classical technology acceptance variables. 3) We offer a detailed picture of student social robot acceptance by considering variance within social robot use, i.e., eight scenarios, and within students, i.e., four latent profiles.

Our work has also implications for practice. There is a considerable proportion of students (in our case, profiles 1 and 2, comprising 20% of our sample) who are skeptical about social robots. Technology acceptance should not be taken for granted among students within the social sciences. Our findings can help developers in the trade-off between technology acceptance and pedagogical and technical aspects. If the pedagogically desirable (ICAP framework) scenarios of 4 and 8 were introduced, students may be neutral towards them. It may be beneficial to accompany the introduction to such scenarios with a description about the benefits of social robot use in these roles, with a special focus on students from profiles 1 and 2.

REFERENCES

Akogul, S., & Erisoglu, M. (2017). An approach for determining the number of clusters in a model-based cluster analysis. *Entropy*, *19*(9), 452. https://doi.org/10.3390/e19090452

Alnajjar, F., Barntneck, C., Baxter, P., Belpaeme, T., Cappuccio, M., Di Dio, Cinzia, Eyssel, F., Handke, J., Mubin, O., Obaid, M., & Reich-Stiebert, N. (2021). *Robots in education: An introduction to high-tech social agents, intelligent tutors, and curricular tools*. Routledge. https://doi.org/10.4324/9781003142706

Bartneck, C., & Forlizzi, J. (2004). A design-centred framework for social human-robot interaction. In *Proceedings / RO-MAN 2004, 13th IEEE International Workshop on Robot and Human Interactive Communication: September 20 - 22, 2004, Kurashiki, Okayama, Japan* (pp. 591–594). IEEE Operations Center. https://doi.org/10.1109/ROMAN.2004.1374827

Belpaeme, T., Kennedy, J., Ramachandran, A., Scassellati, B., & Tanaka, F. (2018). Sociai robots for education: A review. *Science Robotics*, *3*(21), 1-9. https://doi.org/10.1126/scirobotics.aat5954

Belpaeme, T., & Tanaka, F. (2021). Social robots as educators. In OECD (Ed.), *Digital Education Outlook 2021* (pp. 143–157). OECD. https://doi.org/10.1787/7fbfff45-en

Byrne, B. M., Rossi, A., & Doolan, M. (2017). Humanoid robots attending lectures. In *Proceedings of the 9th International Conference on Education Technology and Computers, ICETC,* Barcelona, Spain.

Chi, M. T. H., & Wylie, R. (2014). The ICAP Framework: Linking Cognitive Engagement to Active Learning Outcomes. *Educational Psychologist*, *49*(4), 219–243. https://doi.org/10.1080/00461520.2014.965823

Ching, Y.-H., Hsu, Y.-C., & Baldwin, S. (2018). Developing computational thinking with educational technologies for young learners. *TechTrends*, *62*(6), 563–573. https://doi.org/10.1007/s11528-018-0292-7

Cooney, M., & Leister, W. (2019). Using the Engagement Profile to design an engaging robotic teaching assistant for students. *Robotics*, *8*(1), 1–26. https://doi.org/10.3390/robotics8010021

Deci, E. L., Olafsen, A. H., & Ryan, R. M. (2017). Self-Determination Theory in Work Organizations: The State of a Science. *Annual Review of Organizational Psychology and Organizational Behavior*, *4*(1), 19–43. https://doi.org/10.1146/annurev-orgpsych-032516-113108

DiStefano, C., Zhu, M., & Mîndrilã, D. (2009). Understanding and using factor scores: considerations for the applied researcher. *Practical Assessment, Research, and Evaluation*, *14*(20), 1–11. https://doi.org/10.7275/DA8T-4G52

Engwall, O., Lopes, J., & Åhlund, A. (2021). Robot Interaction Styles for Conversation Practice in Second Language Learning. *International Journal of Social Robotics*, *13*(2), 251–276. https://doi.org/10.1007/s12369-020-00635-y

Fridin, M., & Belokopytov, M. (2014). Acceptance of socially assistive humanoid robot by preschool and elementary school teachers. *Computers in Human Behavior*, *33*, 23–31. https://doi.org/10.1016/j.chb.2013.12.016

Guggemos, J., Seufert, S., & Román-González, M. (2022). Computational Thinking Assessment – Towards More Vivid Interpretations. *Technology, Knowledge and Learning.* Advance online publication. https://doi.org/10.1007/s10758-021-09587-2

Guggemos, J., Seufert, S., & Sonderegger, S. (2020). Humanoid robots in higher education: Evaluating the acceptance of Pepper in the context of an academic writing course using the UTAUT. *British Journal of Educational Technology*, *51*(5), 1864–1883. https://doi.org/10.1111/bjet.13006

Hallquist, M. N., & Wiley, J. F. (2018). Mplusautomation: An R package for facilitating large-scale latent variable analyses in Mplus. *Structural Equation Modeling: A Multidisciplinary Journal*, *25*(4), 621–638. https://doi.org/10.1080/10705511.2017.1402334

Handke, J. (2018). Digitale Hochschullehre – Vom einfachen Integrationsmodell zur Künstlichen Intelligenz. In U. Dittler & C. Kreidl (Eds.), *Hochschule der Zukunft* (pp. 249–263). Springer Fachmedien Wiesbaden. https://doi.org/10.1007/978-3-658-20403-7_15

Handke, J. (2020). *Humanoide Roboter: Showcase, Partner und Werkzeug.* Tectum Wissenschaftsverlag.

Hofmans, J., Wille, B., & Schreurs, B. (2020). Person-centered methods in vocational research. *Journal of Vocational Behavior*, *118*, 103398. https://doi.org/10.1016/j.jvb.2020.103398

Hu, L., & Bentler, P. M. (1999). Cutoff criteria for fit indexes in covariance structure analysis: Conventional criteria versus new alternatives. *Structural Equation Modeling: A Multidisciplinary Journal*, *6*(1), 1–55. https://doi.org/10.1080/10705519909540118

Lin, L.-C., Huang, P.-H., & Weng, L.-J. (2017). Selecting Path Models in SEM: A Comparison of Model Selection Criteria. *Structural Equation Modeling: A Multidisciplinary Journal*, *24*(6), 855–869. https://doi.org/10.1080/10705511.2017.1363652

McNeish, D., & Wolf, M. G. (2020). Thinking twice about sum scores. *Behavior Research Methods*, *52*(6), 2287–2305. https://doi.org/10.3758/s13428-020-01398-0

Meyer, J. P., & Morin, A. J. (2016). A person-centered approach to commitment research: Theory, research, and methodology. *Journal of Organizational Behavior*, *37*(4), 584–612. https://doi.org/10.1002/job.2085

Morin, A. J. S., & Marsh, H. W. (2015). Disentangling shape from level effects in person-centered analyses: An illustration based on university teachers' multidimensional profiles of effectiveness. *Structural Equation Modeling: A Multidisciplinary Journal*, *22*(1), 39–59. https://doi.org/10.1080/10705511.2014.919825

Mubin, O., Stevens, C. J., Shahid, S., Mahmud, A. A., & Dong, J.-J. (2013). A Review of the applicability of robots in education. *Technology for Education and Learning*, *1*(1), 1–7. https://doi.org/10.2316/Journal.209.2013.1.209-0015

Nylund, K. L., Asparouhov, T., & Muthén, B. O. (2007). Deciding on the Number of Classes in Latent Class Analysis and Growth Mixture Modeling: A Monte Carlo Simulation Study. *Structural Equation Modeling: A Multidisciplinary Journal*, *14*(4), 535–569. https://doi.org/10.1080/10705510701575396

Raffaghelli, J. E., Rodríguez, M. E., Guerrero-Roldán, A.-E., & Bañeres, D. (2022). Applying the UTAUT model to explain the students' acceptance of an early warning system in Higher Education. *Computers & Education*, *182*, 104468. https://doi.org/10.1016/j.compedu.2022.104468

Robitzsch, A. (2020). Why Ordinal Variables Can (Almost) Always Be Treated as Continuous Variables: Clarifying Assumptions of Robust Continuous and Ordinal Factor Analysis Estimation Methods. *Frontiers in Education*, *5*, Article 589965. https://doi.org/10.3389/feduc.2020.589965

Rosenberg, J., Beymer, P., Anderson, D., van Lissa, C., & Schmidt, J. (2018). tidyLPA: An R package to easily carry out latent profile analysis (LPA) using open-source or commercial software. *Journal of Open Source Software*, *3*(30), 978. https://doi.org/10.21105/joss.00978

Rosseel, Y. (2012). lavaan: An R package for structural equation modeling. *Journal of Statistical Software*, *48*(2), 1–36. https://doi.org/10.18637/jss.v048.i02

Sailer, M., Stadler, M., Schultz-Pernice, F., Franke, U., Schöffmann, C., Paniotova, V., Husagic, L., & Fischer, F. (2021). Technology-related teaching skills and attitudes: Validation of a scenario-based self-assessment instrument for teachers. *Computers in Human Behavior*, *115*, 106625. https://doi.org/10.1016/j.chb.2020.106625

Sarstedt, M., Hair, J. F., Pick, M., Liengaard, B. D., Radomir, L., & Ringle, C. M. (2022). Progress in partial least squares structural equation modeling use in marketing research in the last decade. *Psychology & Marketing*, *39*(5), 1035–1064. https://doi.org/10.1002/mar.21640

Scherer, R., Howard, S. K., Tondeur, J., & Siddiq, F. (2021). Profiling teachers' readiness for online teaching and learning in higher education: Who's ready? *Computers in Human Behavior*, *118*, 106675. https://doi.org/10.1016/j.chb.2020.106675

Scherer, R., Siddiq, F., & Tondeur, J. (2020). All the same or different? Revisiting measures of teachers' technology acceptance. *Computers & Education*, *143*, 103656. https://doi.org/10.1016/j.compedu.2019.103656

Serholt, S., Barendregt, W., Vasalou, A., Alves-Oliveira, P., Jones, A., Petisca, S., & Paiva, A. (2017). The case of classroom robots: teachers' deliberations on the ethical tensions. *AI & SOCIETY*, *32*(4), 613–631. https://doi.org/10.1007/s00146-016-0667-2

Seufert, S., & Spiroudis, E. (2017). Wissenschaftliche Schreibkompetenz in der Studien-eingangsphase fördern: Erfahrungen mit einem Rückmelde- und Bewertungsraster (Rubric). *Zeitschrift Schreiben*, *15*, 1–9.

Sharkey, A. J. C. (2016). Should we welcome robot teachers? *Ethics and Information Technology*, *18*(4), 283–297. https://doi.org/10.1007/s10676-016-9387-z

Short, E., Sittig-Boyd, K., & Mataric, M. J. (2016). Modeling moderation for multi-party socially assistive robotics. In *IEEE Int. Symp. Robot Hum. Interact. Commun.(RO-MAN 2016)*. IEEE.

Skilling, K., & Stylianides, G. J. (2020). Using vignettes in educational research: a framework for vignette construction. *International Journal of Research & Method in Education*, *43*(5), 541–556. https://doi.org/10.1080/1743727X.2019.1704243

Smakman, M. H. J., Konijn, E. A., Vogt, P., & Pankowska, P. (2021). Attitudes towards social robots in education: Enthusiast, practical, troubled, sceptic, and mindfully positive. *Robotics*, *10*(1), 24. https://doi.org/10.3390/robotics10010024

Sonderegger, S., Guggemos, J., & Seufert, S. (2022). How Social Robots Can Facilitate Teaching Quality – Findings from an Explorative Interview Study. In W. Lepuschitz, M. Merdan, G. Koppensteiner, R. Balogh, & D. Obdržálek (Eds.), *Lecture Notes in Networks and Systems. Robotics in Education* (Vol. 515, pp. 99–112). Springer International Publishing. https://doi.org/10.1007/978-3-031-12848-6_10

Tondeur, J., Scherer, R., Baran, E., Siddiq, F., Valtonen, T., & Sointu, E. (2019). Teacher educators as gatekeepers: Preparing the next generation of teachers for technology integration in education. *British Journal of Educational Technology*, *50*(3), 1189–1209. https://doi.org/10.1111/bjet.12748

Vanslambrouck, S., Zhu, C., Pynoo, B., Lombaerts, K., Tondeur, J., & Scherer, R. (2019). A latent profile analysis of adult students' online self-regulation in blended learning environments. *Computers in Human Behavior*, *99*, 126–136. https://doi.org/10.1016/j.chb.2019.05.021

Venkatesh, V., Morris, M. G., Davis, G. B., & Davis, F. D. (2003). User acceptance of information technology: Toward a unified view. *MIS Quarterly*, *27*(3), 425–478. https://doi.org/10.2307/30036540

Woo, H., LeTendre, G. K., Pham-Shouse, T., & Xiong, Y. (2021). The use of social robots in classrooms: A review of field-based studies. *Educational Research Review*, *33*, 100388. https://doi.org/10.1016/j.edurev.2021.100388

Żarkowski, M. (2019). Multi-party turn-taking in repeated human–robot interactions: An interdisciplinary evaluation. *International Journal of Social Robotics*, *11*(5), 693–707. https://doi.org/10.1007/s12369-019-00603-1

SUPPORTING LEARNING COMMUNITIES VIA WEB SERVICE TECHNOLOGIES: NAVIGATING KNOWLEDGE TRANSFER BETWEEN INFRASTRUCTURAL SERVICES AND USER NEEDS

Annika Wilmers and Sigrid Fahrer
DIPF| Leibniz Institute for Research and Information in Education
Rostocker Str. 6, 60323 Frankfurt, Germany

ABSTRACT

Drawing on research syntheses from the meta project Digi-EBF as well as the German Education Server, this contribution discusses how web products and services offered by the Information Center for Education at DIPF | Leibniz Institute for Research and Information in Education address and support educational communities. In the area of research syntheses, important factors for success are a methodologically systematic and transparent procedure and an easy open access as well as a monitoring of formats by science communication. The German Education Server meets its transfer task by orientation towards dimensions of information quality, adhering to user's needs and evaluating its effectivity via different assessment and measurement methods.

KEYWORDS

Digitization, Research Synthesis, German Education Server, Web Service Technologies, Infrastructures in Education, Open Access

1. INTRODUCTION

In education, information infrastructures and web services pursue the task of providing learning communities with target-oriented and internet-based information. The challenge for providers of such services is to combine technology, content, and communication in such a way that the targeted educational communities are reached. To ensure information uptake, research in education and information science emphasizes the need for an effective connection of methodologically and qualitatively processed knowledge resources from education focussing on the communities' objectives and a user-oriented exhaustion of technological possibilities (for the necessary link of technical with pedagogical aspects in digital education, see Kerres 2020).

In our contribution, we explore how such a process of knowledge transfer based on web-infrastructure which addresses different educational communities can be organized. We will investigate spheres of action and possible barriers to knowledge transfer. How can educational communities be addressed via web services? What conditions need to be fulfilled for a successful impact of the processed information? These questions will be pursued given two concrete examples from the field of digital education. We firstly investigate research syntheses from the project "Digitizing in education" (Digitalisierung im Bildungsbereich, Digi-EBF). In this project, 20 critical reviews are compiled over a period of five years on aspects of digital education. Secondly we will investigate the German Education Server's transfer strategy, which is based on the interaction of educational communities' needs, quality demands on information systems, and impact measurement. The German Education Server is one of the most comprehensive and most frequented portals focusing on education in Germany, it addresses all aspects of education.

Both the review project and the Education Server are located at the Information Center for Education-(IZB) at DIPF | Leibniz Institute for Research and Information in Education, which defines itself as a central contact point in Germany for research and information infrastructures in education science and practice. Additionally, the Information Center prioritizes on making literature information accessible via the Education Research Portal. It supports assessment, processing and archiving of research data (Research Data Centre for Education). All infrastructural services at the IZB are accompanied by transfer activities and further developed according to customer needs.

2. ACCESS AND DISSSEMINATION OF SYSTEMATIC RESEARCH SYNTHESES

2.1 Enhancing the Knowledge Basis on Digitization in Education

The presented reviews are part of the meta-project on digitizing in education, which monitors research projects in a funding line established by the Federal Ministry of Education and Research. This project covers the areas of education in childhood, youth and family, education at school, vocational education, teacher education as well as adult and continuing education. The respective reviews accordingly focus on the outlined sectors and are part of a book series on research perspectives in the field. The co-operation project assesses the state of research on matters of digital education over a period of several years. Moreover, contemporary research knowledge on specific aspects and sector-specific questions regarding digital education is structured and synthesized in critical reviews (cf. Booth et al. 2016, Petticrew & Roberts 2006).

In the presented case, a decentralized organization structure was set up where the literature search, information management and coordination of the overall process constitutes an overarching framework at DIPF, whilst the screening, analysis and processing of the reviews takes place for the education sectors that are defined by expertise from different institutes (University Duisburg-Essen, German Institute for Adult Education - Leibniz Centre for Lifelong Learning and Leibniz Institute for Knowledge Media). With regard to the research question, the team of 13 people agreed on four central topics (1 role of pedagogical staff, 2 organizational development, 3 teaching and learning with digital technologies and 4 role of digital technologies for social learning and participation). In a next step sector-specific delineations were determined. For example, for the third volume of the series (reviews 11-15) which focusses on the topic of teaching and learning the educational sectors identified specific aspects such as the implementation of digitalization in curricula design, school internships of teachers, or usage of digital technology by children and young people.

The team developed a common research strategy for the selection of relevant databases (e.g. German Education Index at the German Education Research Portal and ERIC), as well as the period covered, languages of publication (German and English) and handling and storage of researched data. In a second step, the research was adapted for the sectors involved and further specified. Following the same logic, the team of researchers agreed on a comparatively open overarching coding procedure for organizing and analyzing the literature. This still enabled further differentiations and exclusions for the particular sectors. So far, three volumes have been completed as part of the series on the state of research in digital education, "Digitalisierung in der Bildung. Forschungsstand und -perspektiven" (Wilmers et al. 2020; Wilmers et al. 2021 and Wilmers et al. 2022).

2.2 Accessing Review Results

By publishing the reviews, the review team pursues the objective of facilitating a broad but also targeted access to information while considering different user groups and their needs. Access to the reviews is in particular determined by open access for the entire volume as well as the individual chapters. Because the latter are organized by education sectors, especially practitioners and administrators will find it easy to access the information they think is relevant. Other individuals can access the volumes in total. The volumes also each contain a method chapter for a more in depth and transparent inspection of the review method without the individual reviews having to draw on all methodological aspects.

Table 1. Access to review findings and target groups

	Products and Access	Examples from volume 2
Level 1	Book Series: Research perspectives in the field of digitization in education (vol. 1-4) Open access book publication *Target group: Researchers*	Education in the digital world: Organizational development in educational institutions
Level 2	**Individual chapters** **Open access publication**	
Level 2a	Chapter 1: Methodology *Target Group: Researchers and review specialists*	• Reviews of Organizational Development in Educational Institutions. Methods and Discussion of Bias in Review Processes in Educational Research
Level 2b	Chapter 2-6 Critical Reviews *Target group: Researchers, practitioners, policy-makers* • Chapter 2: Education in childhood, youth and family • Chapter 3: School education • Chapter 4: Teacher education • Chapter 5: Vocational education • Chapter 6 Adult and continuing education	• The implementation of digitization in non-formal educational organisations • School Development in a Digital World: Strategies, Frameworks and Implications for School Development • Implementing Technology Infusion in Teacher Education Programs: A Critical Review • Digitally supported cooperation of organisations in vocational education and training • On the relevance of digital transformation for organizational management in adult and continuing education
Level 3	Data storage in the Research Data Centre Education, DIPF Open access archive *Target group: Review experts and researchers in the field of digitization in education*	DOI https://dx.doi.org/10.7477/414:2:0
Level 4	Dissemination products in form of texts, podcasts, via social media, presentations and events Open access products or public events *Target group: Practitioners (especially pedagogical staff from all education sectors), administrators and decision-makers, associations in the field*	• Contributions to the DBS podcast series "education for your ears" ("Bildung auf die Ohren") • Information via social media • Blog posts and interviews • Provision of information on platforms such as e-teaching.org • Workshop for professionals of adult education centres • Events for researchers and practitioners: Dialogue forum

Contents of the reviews are furthermore disseminated particularly regarding findings from individual sectors. There are many means of dissemination that can be applied in parallel and in any case they afford a translation of important findings into easily readable formats. Such formats are, for example, brochures, policy briefs or short articles or blog entries, podcasts and interviews as well as event formats with presentations or workshops for practitioners (cf. examples from Table 1 and Waffner 2020). Such processing of research findings is highly time-consuming – particularly because usually several formats are offered simultaneously – and optimally the authors of reviews receive journalistic and technical support from their respective institutions.

Table 1 shows different target-specific means of access and points of entry for the contents of reviews. Diverse interfaces thus emerge for knowledge transfer. Level 1 and 2 allowing access to reviews and method chapters, while level 3 implies access to the searched literature via long-term archiving and level 4 contains additional products that transfer findings to practice and politics.

2.3 Chances and Challenges of Addressing Specific Learning Communities via Technical Services

Provision of a maximum number of means of access alone does not as such guarantee that these are used by the communities as table 1 visualizes for several areas – although digitization undoubtedly accelerated science communication (Moll & Schütz 2022, p. 14). As a starting point for a reflection of how learning communities can be reached via web service technologies, we can look at download figures for the first volume on digitization in education (reviews 1-5). The entire first volume was downloaded 7452 times from early October 2020 to early March 2022 via the highly visible access point of the Waxmann publishing house and PeDOCS (at DIPF). PeDOCS is the largest German open access repository for literature from the field of education. Individual reviews (not counting the method chapter) were downloaded between 1046 and 2714 times. Added to this, there is a non-measurable open access spread via dissemination and publishing of the texts on diverse websites and platforms. The high number of downloads confirms the appropriacy of the chosen format and we can guess that besides scientists at least professional institutions and associations have become aware of the reviews. This is also confirmed by random sample tests.

The project team also worked with more flexible formats of science transfer such as blog contributions and podcasts where the impact can also be measured via download. For example, the first five reviews were accompanied by five podcasts published between 14 October and 2 December 2021 – as of March 2022, there were on average 200 downloads via the German Education Server and the streaming service Spotify. By far the highest number of downloads occurred via the German Education Server while Spotify downloads accounted for 8 to 20% – these figures demonstrate that it is essential to embed the offer into an educationally-specific environment. A further dissemination via more general channels such as Spotify can, however, generate an additional audience. Reviews provide a systematic and transparent way of gaining insights and they are an important step in supporting additional target groups with information that can be generated in different intensities before, during and after a review process. In any case, lots of resources are needed to accomplish this purpose. Literature on transfer concepts places a growing emphasis on the communication process as a precondition for successful knowledge transfer (Leibniz-Gemeinschaft 2019), while – at the same time – the possible effects of research become more difficult to monitor in such iterative and communicative processes as Thiel and Rott (2022) point out. In this ongoing discussion on ways of providing evicence-informed knowledge, reviews have gained significance because they are associated with a function of supporting evidence-based decision-making. Schrader accordingly describes systematic reviews as "building blocks for evidence construction" (2014, 207 pp., cf. Heinrich 2018, 325 pp.) and Beelmann mostly sees research reviews as beneficial with respect to "low-threshold provision of state of art summaries of research" (2014, 59). The main focus is therefore on the provision of trustworthy knowledge implying various possibilities to use this knowledge in different ways (for a discussion on the importance of trustfulness in knowledge transfer see Mohajerzad & Specht 2022).

To achieve the goal of transferring review findings and make them available in different forms on a permanent basis different approaches seem to be relevant which have short-term, mid-term and long-term effects. Open access and online databases and platforms such as the German Education Server function as crucial interfaces because they guarantee immediate and sustainable access to knowledge while also offering additional points of contact for specific target groups.

3. PROCESSES OF WEBBASED KNOWLEDGE TRANSFER IN EDUCATION: STRATEGIES OF THE GERMAN EDUCATION SERVER

3.1 Evaluating the German Education Server's Transfer Strategies

The German Education Server is an online information system for the field of education which in 1996 was launched as a project funded by the German ministry of education and research (BMBF). In 1999, it was institutionalized at DIPF. The German Education Server addresses very diverse educational communities including all professions in education and the public at large (Kühnlenz et al. 2012). To reach its broad audience, the German education server employs various transfer strategies using different methods and frameworks. In the following these strategies are examined in detail. First, a content analysis supported by research literature is carried out to identify the services of the German Education Server as well as the user needs they can satisfy. To illustrate this interplay, functionalities are demonstrated for digital education whose relevance has been even stressed further in the light of the Covid-19 pandemic. Secondly, the extent to which the German Education Server as an information system adheres to information quality guidelines is investigated. For this purpose, the 15 IQ-dimensions of Rohweder et al. (2021) are employed, which are derived form a survey of IT-users and include principles such as accessibility, the appropriate amount of data, believability or concise representation. The consideration of these essential factors contributes to the underlying principle of information quality stating that the value of information depends on its usefulness for the user (Rittberger 2009, 3). At last, service usage is analysed via web analytics to measure the impact and outcome of the services building again the bridge back to the needs of educational communities.

3.2 Services of the Education Server and their Adherence to Standards of Information Quality

The German education server was established with the aim to meet two primary needs of educational communities: First and foremost, the metaserver is responsible for gathering information about education that is spread across the internet and making it accessible via one location (Kühnlenz et al. 2012). This service thus reacts upon the federal structure of education in Germany: Decisions on the final structure and organization of education are subject to 16 federal states. Each state has the constitutionally guaranteed right to devise its own education programs, which then are disseminated through different services of the respective states. The German Education Server makes information about these diverse programs and structures available in one place, thus supporting synoptic access to information sources relevant to educational policy. Second, the German Education Server meets the challenge the internet posed for users at that time and still does to a certain point today: finding their feet in the world wide web of information with its heterogeneous quality. The information system was hence initiated to provide quality-checked, curated collections of web resources on education. Meanwhile, providing the user with quality vetted information in one location is only one aspect of reaching the intended audience.

The principal asset of information portals like the German Education Server can be described as "transformation of knowledge into information" (Kuhlen 1989). In this process of informatizing, knowledge is processed for specific target groups and made transportable and codable (ibid.). This 'information work' has produced more than 65,000 indexed sources that have been catalogued according to standardized measure and can be easily searched. In regard to dimensions of information quality, the German Education Server aims for a large but manageable amount of data to compete with general search engines like Google while also providing orientation. The topic of "digital education", for example, has been indexed in more than 1,500 internet resources while a search in the Google-engine results in 105 Mio pages.

The indexed sources are fundamental elements to a central processing format called 'dossiers' which follow the principles of concise representation. Based on the collected resources, the dossiers consist of processed and catalogued information spanning the entire education system. While at the beginning the Education Server uniquely focused on the school sector (Kühnlenz 2006, o. A.) the thematic scope has systematically been expanded over the past 20 years, now meeting the quality criterion of comprehensive coverage. Digital education is treated as a cross-section topic with dossiers covering all education sectors (https://www.bildungsserver.de/bildung-in-der-digitalen-welt-12679-de.html) as well as dossiers focussing on special aspects of the topic, e.g. digital education and the inclusion of special needs students (https://www.bildungsserver.de/inklusion-und-digitale-bildung-behinderter-12816-de.html.

The German Education Server also includes formats of science communication adherent to the principle of understandability as one dimension of information quality. Blog posts and podcasts are offered on topics such as research findings, civil society involvement, and helpful resources for educational practice. A podcast series on digital education was presented focusing on aspects such as teacher education and the implementation of digital tools (http://blog.bildungsserver.de/category/podcasts/bildung-im-digitalen-wandel). A blog series on artificial intelligence hosts interviews on learning analytics, virtual reality and reading apps (https://blog.bildungsserver.de/category/themen/kuenstliche-intelligenz-bildung/). These low-threshold formats are aimed at transferring knowledge from research into other domains.

In the context of digital education, the German Education Server places an emphasis on Open Educational Resources (OER), and three web services are offered in this regard. The information service Open Educational Resources (www.o-e-r.de) presents topical collections of online-resources. The OER-blog introduces stakeholders and initiatives in the field of Open Education. The search engine ELIXIER enables educators to search for freely accessible instructional material for school practices (https://www.bildungsserver.de/elixier/).

Closely connected with the principle of openness is another strategy of the German Education Server: integration of users into the transfer and information processes. The social tagging system Edutags represents both notions: It allows users to collect and share information and enables searches for open-licenced material (https://www.edutags.de/). The German Education Server thus introduces a reciprocal process by feeding back knowledge from the target groups into the system, which can then support the education community.

3.3 Transfer Outcome and Impact: Measuring the Use of the German Education Server

By offering such a diverse web service and web resources, the German Education Server addresses educational researchers as well as practitioners, policy-makers and administrators in the educational field. Furthermore, it also targets general groups such as parents or media representatives. However, this does not automatically imply that the addressees will use what is being offered. Various methods are applied to check whether the German Education server meets the requirements of a web service, that is fit for use and relevant to information consumers (Rittberger 2009, 3). One option to measure the effectiveness of web services is to conduct user surveys. These can be implemented to ascertain user intents and satisfaction with quality. According to earlier studies, one reason for accessing the German Education Server is the concrete research of specific information and addressing a relevant information need (Breiter et al. 2011, 52; Griesbaum 2014, 22).

The frequency of use of the German Education Server can also be an indicator of its coverage of the need for well-sorted collections focusing on education in Germany. In 2021, the German Education Server and its connecting portals recorded nearly 6,000,000 visits. Compared to the year before an increase of more than 50% is evident. One reason for this rise might be an increased need for quality information in the second year of the pandemic, especially regarding digital education and respective materials on homeschooling and state directives. Further analyses of user behaviour confirm this assumption. In 2021, more than 25% of new users were recorded in 2021 for the portal. The dossier on digital learning at home, for example, was visited 69,000 times in 2021 and the dossier for online continuing training during the Covid pandemic was visited more than 100,000 times. In comparison to 2019, the period before Corona and remote teaching, the most popular sites on digital learning, i.e. "online texts for children" and "media competence" were far from as popular: they were viewed 14,000 times respectively 10,000 times.

One relevant criterion for information quality from a service perspective concerns the relevance, i.e. whether users find information to serving what they are looking for. A comparison of search terms and clicking behaviour is a helpful measuring method here. Looking at a recent dossier "The war in Ukraine Worksheets and Other Material", we can see that 53 % of the 13.118 page views within four weeks were generated via search engine queries on terms such as "worksheet war in Ukraine", or "teaching conflict in Ukraine" or "war in Ukraine". Therefore, a web analysis reveals first trends regarding an achievement of usage objectives. These can be validated by further user studies such as true intent studies.

Table 2 summarizes the findings of the German Education Server's analysis, from which the transfer strategy can be derived. It illustrates that this strategy is based on a combination of web-based technologies and high-quality information, which ensures that the service is both fit for use and useful. Web analytics, among other tools, can be used to assess the strategy's success. To that end, the web system's goals must be translated into indicators that can be used to track progress toward those goals (Alby 2019, 25f.). Column four lists the metrics and methods for outcome measurement employed by the German Educational Server. Furthermore, user research methods such as surveys are supplemented to validate how well the system serves the users' intent.

Table 2. Elements of the transfer strategy of the German Education Server

Use for Educational Community	**Education Server Web service**	**Information quality dimensions**	**Outcome measurement**
finding information that is distributed across the web in one place	65.0000 sources can be searched	appropriate amount of data consistent representation	web analysis (frequency of usage)
being able to rely on sources being of high quality and relevance	sources are edited and indexed	believability free of error objectivity	survey (estimation and attitude regarding the system)
finding sources regarding the education topic that is relevant for the user	coverage of the entire scope of education coverage of cross-sectional topics with special portals	completeness	web analysis (frequency of usage by topic) survey (study of true intent)
finding relevant web resources on an educational topic	thematic dossiers	concise representation relevancy	web analysis (comparison of search terms and page views)
finding relevant web resources on a cutting-edge topic	current dossiers	timeliness relevancy	web analysis (frequency of usage of dossiers in a period following publication of the dossier)
finding understandable information on developments in education and educational research	science communication activities (blogs, podcasts)	understandability relevancy	web analysis (time spent per page in relation to calculated reading and listening time)
finding quality-checked teaching material	Education search engine ELIXIER Information service Open Educational Resources	accessibility relevancy believability	web analysis (clickstream analysis)
users collect relevant online resources	social bookmarking system Edutags	completeness	web analysis (number of collected tags)

However, the measurement of the transfer outcome on the level of the target group, step four in the transfer process as defined by Henke et al. (2016), are limited from the information system's perspective. Usage metrics hardly reveal in how far sources found via the German Education Server are then also put to further use. Even surveys conducted immediately after the use of an information system only provide information about intentions and assessments, not actual user behavior. The next level of transfer, the impact on society, is even more difficult to quantify because changes on the societal level never have a single cause (Henke et al. 2016, Kurz et al. 2021, Diehl et al. 2021). Nevertheless, the figures of usage indicate that the underlying transfer strategy is leveraging some results and, at the very least, reaching various educational communities, such as the school sector.

4. CONCLUSION

For the two examples of research syntheses within the BMBF-funded project Digi-EBF and German Education Server, we have shown how different educational communities are addressed by web services provided by the Information Center for Education at DIPF. In this context it seems essential to consider that knowledge transfer via web technologies does not equate a reduction of knowledge but can imply an enrichment of knowledge as knowledge transfer always serves both ends (Moll & Schütz 2022). Also, the mere provision of knowledge does not necessarily lead to its use - knowledge transfer and use is a very complex construct involving researchers and users to the same degree. This dialogue is not resolved by research synthesis or its by-products alone, but both can serve different learning communities by serving for further knowledge transfer. In the field of review production, important success factors concern a consistent and transparent method, as well as a selection of relevant topics and clear review questions, easy open access and monitoring of findings by means of science communication formats. The German Education Server incorporates and combines knowledge transfer strategies from various disciplines in order to reach the targeted educational communities. Information science frameworks guarantee that the German Education Server as a web system meets its transfer task. Its primary function, the transformation of knowledge into information, adheres to the standards for high-quality information, which also serve as prerequisites for the successful transmission of knowledge. Additionally, to reach a large audience, knowledge communication methods like online dossiers, blog entries, and podcast episodes are offered. The transfer method is expanded into a reciprocal process with additional services and features that allow users to actively contribute to the German Education Server's catalogue of resources. The education server routinely assesses its services using web analysis techniques and other user research techniques in order to ascertain outcomes and impact and, if necessary, modify the services provided.

The potential of these different means of transfer can be put to use for educational practice and research in different ways. The web services at the Information Center for Education most of all aim to inspire an adaptation and integration of knowledge into different contexts. Effects of this transferred and adapted knowledge are relevant for transfer research in educational contexts. Reverse as well as continual flows might be further analyzed, for example via user surveys or project monitoring. Research syntheses as well as the German Education Server can draw on a expertise from education science, information science and computer science expertise to initiate such a transfer circle that gears knowledge from science to practice and from practice to science.

REFERENCES

Alby, T., 2019. Einführung in die Webanalyse. Rheinwerk Verlag, Bonn

Beelmann, A., 2014. Möglichkeiten und Grenzen systematischer Evidenzkumulation durch Forschungssynthesen in der Bildungsforschung. *Zeitschrift für Erziehungswissenschaft (Sonderheft),* 17, 55–78. DOI 10.1007/s11618-014-0509-2

Booth, A. et al, 2016. *Systematic Approaches to a Successful Literature Review (2nd edition).* SAGE, Los Angeles.

Breiter, A. et al, 2011. *Nutzungspotenziale des Internetportals Deutscher Bildungsserver. Bericht zur Evaluation des Deutschen Bildungsservers*. Institut für Informationsmanagement Bremen GmbH (ifib), Bremen.

Dialogforum Bildungssektor Schule, 2021. *Digitalisierungsschub Corona? Veranstaltung auf dem Ed Tech Research Forum 2021. Jahrestagung des BMBF-Metavorhabens "Digitalisierung im Bildungsbereich", 30 September & 1 Oktober 2021.*

Diel, V. et al, 2021. *Transfer am DIPF: Impulse aus dem Projekt TwiSt.* DIPF | Leibniz-Institut für Bildungsforschung und Bildungsinformation, Frankfurt. http://www.dipfdocs.de/volltexte/2021/22442/pdf/Diel_Gruenkorn_Schindler_2021_Transfer_am_DIPF_A.pdf.

Griesbaum, J., 2014. Trends der bildungsbezogenen Informationssuche. *DIPF informiert*, 21, 22–24. https://www.dipf.de/de/forschung/publikationen/pdf-publikationen/dipf-informiert/dipf-informiert-nr.-13#page=26.

Heinrich, M., 2018. Does dialogue work? Governanceanalysen zur Notwendigkeit eines ‚dialogic turn' evidenzorientierter Steuerung am Beispiel der Schulinspektion. In Kerstin Drossel & Birgit Eickelmann (eds), *Does „What works" work? Bildungspolitik, Bildungsadministration und Bildungsforschung im Dialog*. Waxmann, Münster/New York, 323-334.

Henke, J. et al, 2016. *Third Mission bilanzieren. Die dritte Aufgabe der Hochschulen und ihre öffentliche Kommunikation.* Institut für Hochschulforschung (HoF) Halle-Wittenberg, Wittenberg.

Kerres, M., 2020. Bildung in der digitalen Welt: Über Wirkungsannahmen und die soziale Konstruktion des Digitalen. *Zeitschrift MedienPädagogik. 17*, 1–32.

Kurz, B. et al, 2021. *Kursbuch Wirkung. Ein Praxishandbuch für alle, die Gutes noch besser tun wollen*. PHINEO AG, Berlin. https://www.phineo.org/kursbuch-wirkung.

Kühnlenz, A., 2006. Deutscher Bildungsserver und Fachportal Pädagogik – der »One-Stop-Shop« für Bildungsinformation. *SchulVerwaltung. Zeitschrift für SchulLeitung, SchulAufsicht und SchulKultur*. 29(10), 340–341. https://www.bildungsserver.de/pdf/Beitrag_Schulverwaltung_06.pdf.

Kühnlenz, A., 2012. Der Deutsche Bildungsserver – Internet-Ressourcen für Bildungspraxis, Bildungsverwaltung und Bildungsforschung. *Erziehungswissenschaft, 23(44),* 23–31. DOI: 10.25656/01:5419

Leibniz-Gemeinschaft, 2019. *Leitbild Leibniz-Transfer.* https://www.leibniz-gemeinschaft.de/fileadmin/user_upload/Bilder_und_Downloads/Neues/Mediathek/Publikationen/Brosch%C3%BCren/Leitbild_Transfer_Einzelseiten.pdf.

Moll, G. & Schütz, J., 2022. Wissenstransfer – Komplexitätsreduktion – Design. Ein Systematisierungsversuch. In Moll, G, & Schütz, J. (eds.) Wissenstransfer – Komplexitätsreduktion – Design. wbv, Bielefeld, pp. 9-28.

Mohajerzad, H. & Specht, I., 2022. „Vertrauen in Wissenschaft" als komplexes Konzept. In Moll, G. & Schütz, J. (eds.) *Wissenstransfer – Komplexitätsreduktion – Design*. wbv, Bielefeld, pp. 31-49.

Petticrew, M. & Roberts, H., 2006. *Systematic reviews in the social sciences. A practical guide*. Blackwell Publishing, Malden, Mass.

Rittberger, M., 2011. Informationsqualität. In Kuhlen, R., Seeger, T. & Strauch, D. (eds). *Grundlagen der praktischen Information und Dokumentation. Vol. 1, Handbuch zur Einführung in die Informationswissenschaft und -praxis*. K. G. Saur, Berlin, Boston, 315-322. https://doi.org/10.1515/9783110964110.315

Rohweder, J.P. et al., 2021. Informationsqualität — Definitionen, Dimensionen und Begriffe. In Hildebrand, K., Gebauer, M., Hinrichs, H. & Mielke, M. (eds) *Daten- und Informationsqualität*. Springer Vieweg, 23-43.+r.

Schrader, J., 2014. Analyse und Förderung effektiver Lehr-Lernprozesse unter dem Anspruch evidenzbasierter Bildungsreform. *Zeitschrift für Erziehungswissenschaft (Suppl.),* 17, 193–223.

Thiel, C. & Rott, D. (2022). Wissenstransfer: eine wissenschaftstheoretische Problemskizze. *Schweizerische Zeitschrift für Bildungswissenschaften,* 44, 1, 129-140. DOI: 10.25656/01:24573

Waffner, B., 2020. *Gelingensbedingungen für den digitalen Wandel an Schulen. Beitrag im Forum Bildung Digitalisierung*. https://www.forumbd.de/blog/gelingensbedingungen-fuer-den-digitalen-wandel-an-schulen/.

Wilmers, A. et al. (eds), 2020. *Bildung im digitalen Wandel. Die Bedeutung für das pädagogische Personal und für die Aus- und Fortbildung.* Digitalisierung in der Bildung. Forschungsstand und -perspektiven, vol. 1. Waxmann, Münster/New York. DOI 10.31244/9783830991991

Wilmers, A. et al. (eds), 2021. *Bildung im digitalen Wandel: Organisationsentwicklung in Bildungseinrichtung. Digitalisierung in der Bildung. Forschungsstand und -perspektiven, vol. 2.* Waxmann, Münster/New York. DOI: 10.31244/9783830994558

Wilmers, A. et al. (eds.), 2022. *Bildung im digitalen Wandel: Lehren und Lernen mit digitalen Medien. Digitalisierung in der Bildung. Forschungsstand und Perspektiven, vol. 3.* Waxmann, Münster/New York.

INTRODUCTION OF COMPUTER-BASED SIMULATED EXPERIMENTS IN UNIVERSITY PSYCHOLOGY CLASS: A CLASS PRACTICE OF LEARNING DUAL STORAGE MODEL OF HUMAN MEMORY

Kazuhisa Miwa[1], Mayu Yamakawa[1] and Kazuaki Kojima[2]
[1]*Nagoya University, Nagoya, 4648601 Japan*
[2]*Teikyo University, Utsunomiya, 3208551 Japan*

ABSTRACT

This paper examines the possibilities and limitations of introducing simulated experiments in the psychology domain by practicing a course with graduate students in psychology, in which simulated experiments were conducted in place of real human experiments. The class-learning object was the dual-storage model of human memory. The simulation results showed anomalous results that differed from intuitive predictions. The results were also inconsistent with the results of prior human experiments. Analysis of reports submitted by 15 participants revealed that they focused on the anomalous results emerging in the simulation results and examined them based on the dual-storage model theory. On the basis of these results, future directions for this practice are discussed.

KEYWORDS

Science Education, Inquire-Based Learning, Cognitive Model, Simulations, Psychology

1. INTRODUCTION

The planning of experiments based on hypotheses and refinement of hypotheses based on feedback from the results of experiments are the basic inquiry processes of scientific activities. Numerous studies have confirmed the benefits of introducing computer-based simulated experiments instead of real experiments in science education to provide students with a hands-on understanding of these inquiry processes (Rutten et al. 2012). This advantage has also been used in a variety of inquiry-based learning initiatives, where students themselves drive the inquiry process on their initiative (De Jong 2006).

In inquiry-based learning, it is difficult for students to engage in real-world experimentation (Hennessy et al. 2007). First, conducting real-world experiments can be dangerous and expensive. Second, these experiments may not be feasible in practice. In general, conducting experiments is often complicated and time-consuming and may require tedious preprocessing when analyzing the collected data. In many cases, the costs associated with conducting such experiments are unrelated to the learning objectives, increase extraneous cognitive load, and reduce learning effects (Sweller et al. 1998). By introducing computer-based simulated experiments, students are protected from such time-consuming manual labor and can focus on their original learning goals, that is, experiencing the process of inquiry itself, with improved work efficiency. Hence, students will be able to focus on "what-if" exploration by immediately checking the results of the experiments using simulations (Wen et al. 2020).

The introduction of computer-based simulated experiments into educational settings has been overwhelmingly practiced in the field of natural sciences (Rutten et al. 2012, Smetana & Bell 2012). Such advantages are also expected to have beneficial effects on training classes for human experimentation in the psychology domain at universities.

Experiments in psychology often require more human resources than experiments in natural sciences. Specifically, psychology experiments are conducted on human subjects and require recruitment of a large number of participants. In university classes, participation in these experiments is often supported by volunteers, which is a destabilizing factor in conducting such classes. In addition, it is often practically impossible to control experimental factors in human subjects, and various confounding factors are likely to be involved. Experimental reproducibility has also been reported to be relatively low (Collaboration 2015). These conditions work negatively in the educational context. Computer-based simulations are expected to provide effective responses to these problems.

Inquiry-based learning is classified into four levels, depending on whether the three aspects of scientific activities—source of the question, data collection methods, and interpretation of results—come from a teacher or student (Blanchard et al. 2010). Of the four levels, level 2 is called guided inquiry. At this level, inquiry questions are posed by the teacher, but the collection of data and interpretation of results are student-directed. In current practice, this level of inquiry-based learning is conducted in the psychology domain.

The introduction of simulated experiments greatly improves the economics of data collection in this context, as data collection is performed through simulations. In addition, there is an important contribution to the interpretation of the results whereby the patterns that emerge are explained based on the theory of the domain. In cognitive psychology, theory is often described as a mechanism of cognitive information processing. Students are asked to explain how the patterns of the experimental results obtained are brought about by the cognitive information processing that they focused on. In response, cognitive information processing is explicitly disclosed in the model used therein, making it easier for students to understand the relationship between the two in simulated experiments (Miwa et al. 2015). Furthermore, the causal relationship between the two can be clarified by manipulating the model's information processing parameters to determine the effects that appear in the simulation results. These are expected to work positively in the educational context.

This study examines the possibilities and limitations of introducing computer-based simulated experiments in the psychology domain with graduate students, through a class in which simulated experiments are conducted instead of real experiments, by observing their learning activities. The research questions of this study are to observe how participants perceive and interpret the results of simulation experiments when used in place of real human experiments. This effort will discuss the possibilities and limitations that emerge prior to conducting a full-scale practice in the future. In particular, we examine what the differences are between participants who extracted valid findings and those who did not.

2. METHOD

2.1 Participants

Fifteen graduate students majoring in psychology from the Department of Psychology and Cognitive Sciences, Graduate School of Informatics, Nagoya University, participated in this class. With a few exceptions, the participants had undergraduate-level knowledge and skills in experimental design and psychological statistics.

2.2 Class Topics

The topic of the class comprised the serial position effect (Murdock Jr 1962), which is a widely known phenomenon discussed in many psychology textbooks as a typical human memory phenomenon explained by the dual-storage model of memory (Atkinson & Shiffrin 1968).

In human memory experiments, the serial position effect is a phenomenon in which the degree to which words are remembered depends on the order in which they are presented. Normally, the first and last few items are remembered better than the middle items. If the order of word presentation is shown on the horizontal axis and the recall rate on the vertical axis, the graph will show a U-shaped curve with a concave center. The phenomenon in which the recall rate of the first presented items is higher is called the primacy effect, and the phenomenon in which the recall rate of the last presented items is higher is called the recency effect.

2.3 Cognitive Model

Simulated experiments require a model that accurately simulates the phenomena being investigated. Although models that simulate natural phenomena often take the form of mathematical and statistical models, models of cognitive information processing that are focused on here are symbolic processing models. When focusing on cognitive information processing, the most representative framework is rule-based modeling (Klahr et al. 1987). In this class, the production system modeling framework was used for the simulated experiments.

The model is expressed as follows: the presented words are first stored in the short-term memory. Each word stored in the short-term memory has an activation value for recall. Over time, the activation value in the short-term memory decreases, and when it falls below a certain value, it becomes inactive and is forgotten. One of the words stored in the short-term memory is randomly selected and rehearsed, and its activation value increases. When the activation value exceeds a certain value, it is transferred to the long-term memory. The transferred items are never forgotten.

In this class practice, the time interval between word presentations and the increase in the activation value of a word by a single rehearsal were manipulated. The former is the factor that is manipulated in the experiments, and the latter is the working memory capacity of the experimental participants, which is usually measured by memory span tests, such as the operation span test, OSPAN (Unsworth et al. 2005).

2.4 Class Design

Participants attended seven class sessions in a cognitive science class at Nagoya University. In the first four sessions, an introductory lesson on production system modeling was given in which all participants constructed a cognitive information processing model to solve the multi-column subtraction arithmetic problem. The educational environment for implementing the model was DoCoPro, an educational production system architecture developed by the authors (Miwa et al. 2014).

The latter three sessions were used for class practice. First, participants were taught the theory of the dual storage model of human memory through the instructor's lecture. The computer model used in the class was then outlined. For this practice, the model for simulating the human memory phenomenon was not developed by the participants, but was given by the instructor.

Participants performed the simulations individually and obtained the resulting data. Based on a preliminary study, the parameter for the word presentation interval was set to 3 and 6 s, and the amount of increase in the activation value of a word by rehearsal was set to vary between 40 and 80. When the activation value exceeded 200, the word in the short-term memory was transferred to the long-term memory.

Participants completed 40 trials in each of the experimental conditions for word presentation intervals (3 s and 6 s). Although participants were not presented with a specific analytic methodology, they were presented as an example of the data analysis, with a graph format in which the vertical axis shows the recall rate, and the horizontal axis shows the three positions of presenting the first five, middle ten, and last five words.

3. RESULTS

3.1 Simulation Results

Figure 1 shows the simulation results. Figure 1(a) shows the analysis from the viewpoint of the presentation intervals, that is, the recall rates were separately depicted in the long-time condition (6-second condition) and in the short-time condition (3-second condition). Figure 1(b) shows the analysis from the viewpoint of the participants' working memory capacity, that is, the recall rates were depicted in the lower and higher capability groups. Since the participants performed simulations individually, there were some differences in their results; the basic patterns of the results are as shown in Figure 1.

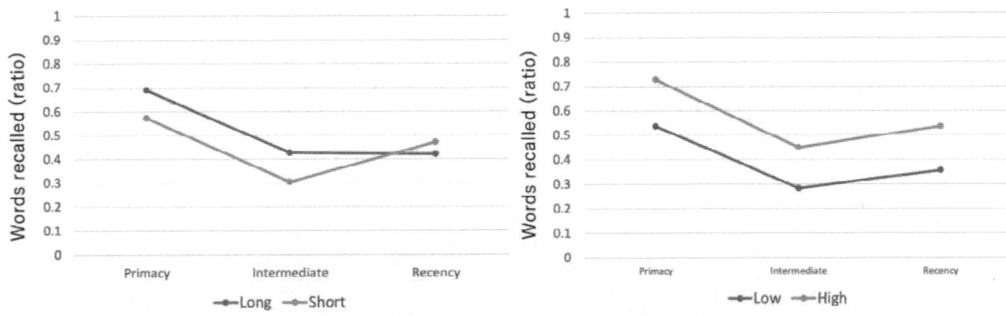

(a) Manipulation of presentation interval (b) Participants' working memory capability

Figure 1. Results of simulated experiments

Figure 2 shows the results of the human experiments conducted in a different class (n=122).

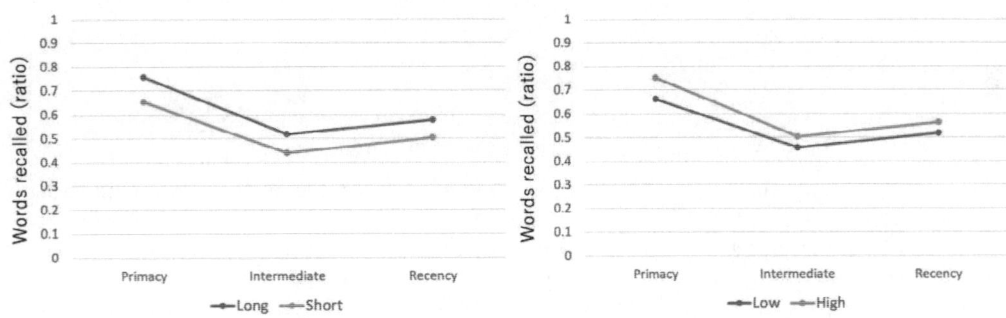

(a) Manipulation of presentation interval (b) Participants' working memory capability

Figure 2. Results of human experimentation

Common features that emerge in both the simulation and human experimental results include the following:

- The primacy effect was pronounced, while the recency effect was small.
- The main effect of participants' working memory capacity was observed.

Unlike the human experimental results, the following was found in the simulation results:

- In the simulated experiments, the effect sizes of both the main effect of working memory capacity and the main effect of word presentation intervals were larger than those in human experiments.
- The results of the simulated experiments showed that the effect of word presentation intervals depended on the position at which the words were presented. Specifically, the effect of presentation intervals occurred in the first and middle positions of the presentation but disappeared in the last position. However, in human experiments, such an interaction effect was not observed.

Notably, the second feature was confirmed in the simulated experiments. In general, it is intuitively predicted that the higher the participants' working memory capacity and the longer the word presentation intervals, the more positive the effect on the word recall rate. The results of the experiments with humans in Figure 2 reflect this natural prediction. Contrarily, in the simulated experiments, the effect of presentation intervals disappeared later in the presentation, which is an unexpected result. We refer to this as an anomalous result. In scientific activities, it is important to explain these anomalies (Kulkarni & Simon 1988).

3.2 Analysis of Participants' Reports

Figure 3 shows a summary of the analysis of reports submitted by the participants.

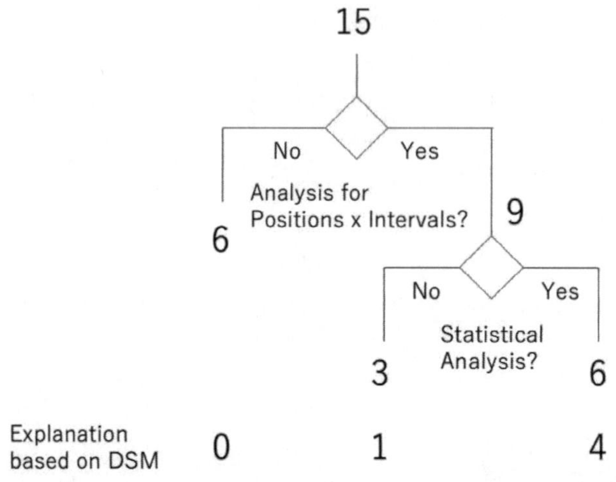

Figure 3. Summary analysis of participants' reports

To perceive the anomalous pattern in the results, participants were required to draw a graph such as 1(a), indicating the interaction effect of the word presentation intervals and the positions of word presentation. Nine of the fifteen participants in the class depicted a graph(s) in which an anomaly pattern was revealed, as shown in Figure 1(a). Contrarily, the other six participants depicted other types of graphs. Specifically, four of them drew a graph(s) from the viewpoint of their working memory capacity, similar to Figure 1(b). The other two participants depicted graphs that violated the representative format of the analysis.

Next, six of the nine participants who drew similar graph(s), as shown in Figure 1(a), detected a statistically significant interaction between the presentation interval factor and the word presentation position; the other three participants did not perform the statistical analysis or did not detect a significant interaction. Four of the former six and one of the latter three participants successfully explained the anomalous pattern based on the dual storage model of memory (DSM).

The following is an example of a normative explanation for the anomalous pattern found in the simulation results:

> The larger primacy effect in the long interval condition is due to the fact that longer word presentation intervals increase the number of times words in short-term memory are rehearsed, increasing the probability that they will be sent to long-term memory. However, this effect in the long interval condition disappears in the recency effect because the increased likelihood that the words in the short-term memory are forgotten due to time decay, cancels out the effect of rehearsal.

4. DISCUSSION AND CONCLUSIONS

Figure 3 indicates that all the participants who successfully explained the anomalous pattern in the experimental result depicted a graph(s) that is profitable for the analysis of the interaction between the word presentation position factor and the presentation interval factor. Contrarily, the participants who performed the analysis based on other factors, could not successfully explain the pattern because they did not find an anomalous pattern in the graph(s) they depicted. This means that the type of graph depicted first, is crucial for successful explanation. We note that the crucial factor that determines whether a successful or failed explanation is constructed, depends on accidental matters.

Importantly, this explanation requires a clear understanding of how primacy and recency effects are caused by different reasons. That is, the former is brought about by the transfer of words in the short-term memory to the long-term memory, whereas the latter is brought about by the recall of encoded items in the short-term memory. We believe that the participants developed this understanding as they attempted to explain the interaction pattern between the word presentation intervals and presentation positions in the results of the simulated experiments.

In the simulated experiments, the cognitive information processing process of the simulation model is clearly disclosed, and the results of the simulations are based on that process faithfully executed by the model. The participants were likely attempting to explain the results of the experiments through mental simulations (Chi 2009) of the cognitive information processing process of the computer model to explain the results that appear in the simulations. It is important to clarify what types of learning activities can be facilitated by the introduction of simulated experiments in the future.

However, it is important to note that the results of the simulated experiments do not accurately reflect the results of the human experiments. The interaction effect observed in the simulated experiments was not observed in experiments with human subjects. In this practice, participants referred to and discussed only the results of the simulated experiments. Furthermore, it is expected that by comparing and contrasting the results of the simulations with the results of human experiments, a more in-depth discussion of the results will be presented (Gadgil et al. 2012).

We have not been able to examine how students perceive the application of simulated experiments and how they feel about using them instead of human experimentation. In future work, we would like to pay more attention to this point by collecting interview data from participants to find out why they chose the strategy to explain the anomaly.

The authors also conducted a similar class practice with undergraduate students who did not major in psychology. Analysis of the submitted reports showed that a significant number of participants did not perform normative analysis in psychological experiments. Thus, they were not able to reach the depth of understanding obtained in the current class practice for graduate students. These results imply that careful consideration of knowledge, skills, and abilities of participants should be done when introducing the practice of computer-based simulated experiments in the classroom.

ACKNOWLEDGEMENT

This work was partially supported by KAKENHI（20K12096).

REFERENCES

Atkinson, R. C., & Shiffrin, R. M. (1968). Human memory: A proposed system and its control processes. In *Psychology of learning and motivation* (Vol. 2, pp. 89–195). Elsevier.

Blanchard, M. R., Southerland, S. A., Osborne, J. W., Sampson, V. D., Annetta, L. A., & Granger, E. M. (2010). Is inquiry possible in light of accountability?: A quantitative comparison of the relative effectiveness of guided inquiry and verification laboratory instruction. *Science education*, *94*(4), 577–616.

Chi, M. T. (2009). Three types of conceptual change: Belief revision, mental model transformation, and categorical shift. In *International handbook of research on conceptual change* (pp. 89–110). Routledge.

Collaboration, O. S. (2015). Estimating the reproducibility of psychological science. *Science*, *349*(6251), aac4716.

De Jong, T. (2006). Technological advances in inquiry learning. *Science*, *312*(5773), 532–533.

Gadgil, S., Nokes-Malach, T. J., & Chi, M. T. (2012). Effectiveness of holistic mental model confrontation in driving conceptual change. *Learning and Instruction*, *22*(1), 47–61.

Hennessy, S., Wishart, J., Whitelock, D., Deaney, R., Brawn, R., La Velle, L., ... Winterbottom, M. (2007). Pedagogical approaches for technology-integrated science teaching. *Computers & Education*, *48*(1), 137–152.

Klahr, D., Langley, P., Neches, R., & Neches, R. T. (1987). *Production system models of learning and development*. MIT Press.

Kulkarni, D., & Simon, H. A. (1988). The processes of scientific discovery: The strategy of experimentation. *Cognitive science*, *12*(2), 139–175.

Miwa, K., Kanzaki, N., Terai, H., Kojima, K., Nakaike, R., Morita, J., & Saito, H. (2015). Learning mental models of human cognitive processing by creating cognitive models. In C. Conati, N. Heffernan, A. Mitrovic, & M. F. Verdejo (Eds.), *Artificial intelligence in education* (pp. 287–296). Cham: Springer International Publishing.

Miwa, K., Morita, J., Nakaike, R., & Terai, H. (2014). Learning through intermediate problems in creating cognitive models. *Interactive Learning Environments*, *22*(3), 326–350.

Murdock Jr, B. B. (1962). The serial position effect of free recall. *Journal of Experimental Psychology: General*, *64*(5), 482–488.

Rutten, N., Van Joolingen, W. R., & Van Der Veen, J. T. (2012). The learning effects of computer simulations in science education. *Computers & Education*, *58*(1), 136–153.

Smetana, L. K., & Bell, R. L. (2012). Computer simulations to support science instruction and learning: A critical review of the literature. *International Journal of Science Education*, *34*(9), 1337–1370.

Sweller, J., Van Merrienboer, J. J., & Paas, F. G. (1998). Cognitive architecture and instructional design. *Educational psychology review*, *10*(3), 251–296.

Unsworth, N., Heitz, R. P., Schrock, J. C., & Engle, R. W. (2005). An automated version of the operation span task. *Behavior research methods*, *37*(3), 498-505.

Wen, C.-T., Liu, C.-C., Chang, H.-Y., Chang, C.-J., Chang, M.-H., Chiang, S.-H. F., ... Hwang, F.-K. (2020). Students' guided inquiry with simulation and its relation to school science achievement and scientific literacy. *Computers & Education*, *149*, 103830.

STUDENTS USE OF LEARNING AIDS: LESSONS FROM LEARNING ANALYTICS

Dirk Tempelaar
Maastricht University School of Business and Economics
Tongersestraat 53, 6211 LM Maastricht, The Netherlands

ABSTRACT

E-tutorial learning aids as worked examples and hints have been established as effective instructional formats in problem-solving practices. However, less is known about variations in the use of learning aids across individuals at different stages in their learning process in student-centred learning contexts. This study investigates different profiles of students' learning behaviors based on clustering students' use of worked examples and hints in subsequent learning phases in a naturalistic setting. In a blended instructional format, the study was conducted on 1,072 students over an eight-week introductory mathematics course. By explicitly differentiating between learning to prepare a tutorial session, the first phase, learning to prepare a quiz session, the second phase, and learning to prepare the final exam as third phase, this study aims to contribute to the call for more temporality in learning analytics applications. Our study finds three profiles of learning that differ in the intensity and timing of the use of learning aids. Moreover, different profiles come with different learning dispositions, such as epistemic and activity learning emotions.

KEYWORDS

Learning Analytics, Dispositional Learning Analytics, Temporal Analysis, E-Tutorials, Learning Aids

1. INTRODUCTION

Recent debates in the field of Learning Analytics (LA) focus on the role of time in LA-based models. Traditional LA models by default include time in the role of time on task, often aggregated over longer time spells, but the 'call for more temporality' (Chen et al., 2018; Knight et al., 2017) in applications of learning analytics (LA; Ifenthaler, 2015) is directed at other, time-related aspects of learning processes. Such as timing in the meaning of the order of events in a learning process.

The call for more temporality is often combined with a call for a methodological paradigm shift (Saint et al., 2022): away from the variables-oriented type of models, embracing event-based models using analytic discovery methods as process or sequence mining. This contribution aims to disentangle the two calls: yes, including all facets of time in our LA models is of crucial importance, but no, we do not need to leave variables-based models in order to do so. In fact, staying within the variables-oriented paradigm by applying traditional statistical methods has the great advantage of integrating time-stamped log data with another type of data, such as survey data. Dispositional learning analytics is a field with a long tradition of combining log data with survey data to generate models of learning feedback. The conjecture we entertain in this contribution is that by carefully choosing time windows and granularity levels of the administration of log-data (Molenaar & Wise, 2022), temporal aspects are well integrated into variable-based models based on dispositional LA applications. We aim to showcase by analyzing students' use of learning aids of worked examples and hints types in a blended curriculum, combining problem-based learning with e-tutorials.

2. LEARNING AIDS AND THE TEMPORY ASPECT OF LEARNING

2.1 Worked Examples and Hints as Learning Aids

A vast body of self-regulated learning (SRL) literature has looked at how learners decide how and when to learn (Winne, 2017). A critical review of six prominent SRL models by Panadero (2017) showed that learners iteratively go through three main phases: the preparatory phase (i.e., planning and goal-setting), the performance phase (i.e., performing the task and monitoring and controlling their own cognition), and the appraisal phase (i.e., reflecting and adapting on their SRL process, as part of self-reflection, by peers, by a computer, or via a teacher). Students' self-regulated choices to use learning aids when learning in technology-enhanced learning environments have been analysed in empirical research, focusing on the use of worked examples (Tempelaar et al., 2020). Previous studies proposed that novice learners would be more likely to benefit from using worked examples prior to problem-solving than vice versa or only using problem-solving (van Merrienboer & Sweller, 2010). The theoretical underpinning behind this is that worked examples are more beneficial to novice learners at the stage of schema acquisition because learners can focus their limited cognition on understanding the principle or concept. However, when learners are given autonomy over their choice of help-seeking, they do not always choose the most optimal learning strategies as proposed in the literature. Furthermore, when looking at how students self-regulated learning over a longer period, we found temporal variances in the use of worked examples over different study phases, which subsequently influenced academic performance (Rienties et al., 2019).

In technology-enhanced learning environments, self-regulated learning is facilitated by the availability of instructional scaffolding. Worked examples, the step-by-step demonstration of the solution to a problem, is only one of them. The facility to request for hints that provide concrete help in proceeding with a problem-solving step when students get stuck shapes another type of scaffold. Salden et al. (2010) define problem-solving with a hint request facility as tutored problem-solving, where untutored problem-solving represents the situation without instructional scaffolds. In comparing tutored problem-solving with and without the support of worked examples, McLaren et al. (2016) conclude that the main difference is the efficiency gain resulting from having access to worked examples.

Having access to multiple instructional scaffolds gives way to another phenomenon: opting for non-optimal forms of scaffolding, also coined as 'help abuse' (Aleven et al., 2004). The most common form of help abuse is bypassing more abstract hints and going straightforwardly to concrete solutions. Analyzing log behaviors of students, and distinguishing 'proper use and abuse' of worked examples, Shih et al. (2010) created profiles of adaptive and maladaptive learning behaviors. Such profiling based on differences in learning behaviors is also the aim of our current study and builds on the authors' previous research (Nguyen, Tempelaar, Rienties, & Giesbers, 2016). However, we do not seek to demonstrate the difference between proper use and abuse of worked examples but rather to find different patterns in the use of worked examples and hints and connect these patterns to antecedents and consequences.

Another difference with Shih et al. (2010) is our study's Dispositional Learning Analytics (DLA) dimension. The DLA infrastructure, introduced by Buckingham Shum and Deakin Crick (2012), combines learning data (trace data generated in logs of learning activities through technology-enhanced systems) with learner data (e.g., student dispositions, values, and attitudes measured through self-report surveys) (Rienties et al., 2019; Tempelaar, Rienties, & Giesbers, 2015). Learning dispositions represent individual differences that affect all learning processes and include affective, behavioral and cognitive facets (Rienties, Cross, & Zdrahal, 2017).

2.2 The Role of Time in a Problem-Based Learning Context

The notion that learning is a fundamentally temporal process, that 'learning unfolds over time', is the departure point of Reimann's (2009) call to pay better tribute to the fact that 'time is precious'. In this, time allows different conceptualizations. First, the notion of temporality as the 'passage of time' refers to the duration and frequency of learning activities (Knight et al., 2017; Molenaar, 2014; Molenaar & Wise, 2022). How often do activities take place, and how much is the time-on-task? The second conceptualization relates to the temporal order of learning activities: what comes first, what follows?

To do justice to both notions of time, we need to ground them in the instructional context. Our case study investigates the self-regulated learning by students in a problem-based learning (PBL; Hmelo-Silver, 2004) programme. The learning process is subdivided into three consecutive learning phases in line with PBL principles. The first learning phase is preparing the tutorial session in which small groups of students, the tutorial groups, collaboratively try to solve problem tasks. A second learning phase follows later the same week when students prepare a so-called quiz session in which students demonstrate their mastery of topics learned in the weekly learning cycle. The third and last learning phase refers to the preparation for the final examination at the end of the module, where students demonstrate how well they have integrated the several weekly learning cycles by solving comprehensive problems. Since each learning phase is sharply demarcated by the timing of tutorial sessions, quizzes, and final exam, an operationalization of log file data that distinguishes student engagement in subsequent learning phases can be implemented. This operationalization enables to include both passage of time measures (Knight et al. 2017), the intensity of engagement in each learning phase, and order of time measures: the relative allocation of engagement over three learning phases.

The second component of grounding measures on relevant theoretical principles stems from the social-cognitive nature of PBL (Hmelo-Silver, 2004). In such instructional philosophy of student-centred learning, a crucial consideration is: what learning skills do students need to be successful learners in a programme applying problem-based learning? The skill of being a self-regulated learner is generally regarded as a key disposition for problem-based learning (Loyens et al., 2013). This is in line with the Reimann et al. (2014) recommendation to include aptitudes as 'other levels' in the form of dispositional accounts to complement event-based data, as candidates for explanation in self-regulated learning research. Reimann et al. (2014) introduced learning styles, epistemic beliefs, and attitudes as crucial for self-regulated learning. Our perspective is largely overlapping but slightly broader: to pay tribute to all facets of social constructivism, aptitudes were included that cover the full range of affective measures. Following Reimann et al. (2014), we regard these aptitudes as sufficiently static to assume stationarity over the entire module period. That supposition allows to measure aptitudes at the very start of the module and regard these as students' entry characteristics.

Within this context, our study aims to demonstrate that 'traditional', variables-oriented LA models that combine dispositions with well-operationalized log data are fully capable of giving time the preciousness it deserves in the study of which students use what learning aids in their self-regulated learning.

3. METHODS

3.1 Context and Setting

This study took place in a large-scale introductory mathematics and statistics module for first-year undergraduate students in a business and economics programme in the Netherlands, with a study load of 20 hours per week, for eight weeks. This module was a compulsory first module for all first-year students and often a stumbling block for students with limited mathematics affinity. The educational system is best described as 'blended' or 'hybrid' according to the principle of flipped class design. The main component was face-to-face: Problem-Based Learning (PBL), in small groups (14 students), coached by a content expert tutor. Participation in tutorial groups was required and constituted around 2 x 2 hours per week. In addition, weekly lectures introduce the key concepts in that week. The remaining hours were self-study, which was supported by printed materials (i.e., textbooks) and two interactive e-tutorials: Sowiso (https://sowiso.nl/) and MyStatLab (Nguyen et al., 2016; Rienties et al., 2019; Tempelaar et al., 2015, 2020). This design was based on the philosophy of student-centred education, placing the responsibility for making educational choices primarily on the student.

In terms of the timing of the learning, this study distinguished three learning phases introduced before. In phase 1, students prepare for the first tutorial session of the week. The face-to-face time of tutorial sessions was used to discuss solving "advanced" mathematical and statistical problems and required preceding self-study by students to enable participation in discussion. Phase 1 was not formally assessed, other than that such preparation allowed students to actively participate in the discussion of the problem tasks in the tutorial session. Phase 2 was preparing the quiz session at the end of every second week of the module. Those quizzes were primarily formative, providing students at the end of the weekly learning cycle feedback on their mastery of the mathematical and statistical topics covered that week. However, they also contained a small, summative component to stimulate students to participate in the quizzes. Finally, phase 3 consisted of preparing for the final exam in the eighth week of the module. In addition, phase 3 included formal, graded assessments. Therefore, students' timing decisions are related to the amount of preparation in each of the three phases.

3.2 Participants

We included 1072 first-year students from academic years 2019/2020 in this study who had been active in at least one digital platform. Of these students, 39% were female, 61% male, 21% had a Dutch high school diploma, and 79% were international students. Amongst the international students, neighbouring countries of Germany (31.5%) and Belgium (13.3%) were well presented, as well as other European countries. In addition, 5.1% of students were from outside Europe. High school systems in Europe differ strongly, most notably in the teaching of mathematics and statistics (i.e., the Dutch high school system has a strong focus on statistics, whereas this topic is completely missing in high school programs of many other countries). Next, all countries distinguish between several levels of math education in high school: preparing for sciences, social sciences, or humanities. To enter this international business programme, prior mathematics education preparing social sciences is required. At the same time, 35.7% of the students followed the highest track in high school, adding to the diversity in prior knowledge in the current sample. Therefore, it was crucial that the first module offered to these students was flexible and allowed for individual learning paths with frequent, interactive feedback on students' learning strategies and tasks.

Beyond a final written exam, student assessment included a student project in which students performed a statistical analysis of personal learning disposition data. To this end, students administered several questionnaires addressing affective, behavioral and cognitive aspects of aptitudes at the start of the module and received personal data sets for their project work some weeks later.

3.3 E-tutorial Log Data

Log data were collected from both e-tutorial systems (Sowiso, mathematics or math in short, and MyStatLab, statistics), as well as Canvas, which was used as the university-wide generic learning management system to provide general information and links to Sowiso and MyStatLab. Both Sowiso and MyStatLab are e-tutorials based on the instructional method of mastery learning (Nguyen et al., 2016; Rienties et al., 2019; Tempelaar et al., 2015, 2020). However, only one of the systems, the e-tutorial for math learning, makes time-stamped log data for students' use of learning aids available, so this data is the basis of our analysis. The module counts seven educational weeks with every week a new learning cycle; each learning cycle distinguishes three learning phases; in each learning phase, students take decisions upon the use of worked examples and hints as learning aids, resulting in 40 measurements per student:

- SolTopic1TG … SolTopic7TG: number of worked examples consulted in learning phase 1, tutorial session preparation, for seven weekly topics;
- HintsTopic1TG … HintsTopic7TG: same for hints;
- SolTopic1QZ … SolTopic6QZ: number of worked examples consulted in learning phase 2, quiz session preparation, for six weekly topics (no quiz for last topic);
- HintsTopic1QZ … HintsTopic6QZ: same for hints;
- SolTopic1EX … SolTopic7EX: number of worked examples consulted in learning phase 3, exam preparation, for seven weekly topics;
- HintsTopic1EX … HintsTopic7EX: same for hints.

3.4 Disposition Data

Epistemic learning emotions. Epistemic emotions are related to cognitive aspects of the tasks undertaken by students. Prototypical epistemic emotions are curiosity and confusion. This study measured epistemic emotions with the Epistemic Emotion Scales (EES: Pekrun et al., 2017). Scales in that instrument can be classified according to valence (positive or negative emotion) and activation component: activating or deactivating.

Positive, activating emotions are Curiosity and Enjoyment; negative, deactivating emotions are Confusion, Frustration and Boredom; Anxiety is a negative, activating emotion and Surprise is a neutral emotion.

Learning Activity Emotions. The Control-Value Theory of Achievement Emotions (CVTAE, Pekrun, 2000) postulates that emotions in learning activities differ in valence, focus, and activation. Emotional valence can be positive (enjoyment) or negative (anxiety, hopelessness, boredom). CVTAE describes the emotions experienced about an achievement activity (e.g. boredom experienced while preparing homework) or outcome (e.g. anxiety towards performing at an exam). The activation component describes emotions as activating (i.e. anxiety leading to action) versus deactivating (i.e. hopelessness leading to disengagement). From the Achievement Emotions Questionnaire (AEQ, Pekrun, et al., 2011) measuring learning emotions, we selected four scales: Enjoyment as positive activating emotion, Anxiety as negative activating emotion, Boredom and Hopelessness as negative deactivating emotions. Next, Academic Control, students' self-efficacy in learning math, served the role of the proximal antecedent of all activity emotions.

4. RESULTS

4.1 Students Use of Learning Aids by Clustering Log Data

A four-cluster solution provides four profiles that allow a straightforward interpretation. One cluster is composed of one single student, who, over the several weeks, consulted 3235 worked examples. Such learning behavior appeared to be so extreme that this student came out as a separate cluster for every choice of a number of clusters. Omitting this case, the other three profiles were labelled as *Tutorial & quiz oriented*, *Quiz oriented* and *Low use of learning aids*, where these labels provide a first characterization of the profiles. See Figure 1 for graphical interpretations, and Table 1 for descriptive statistics.

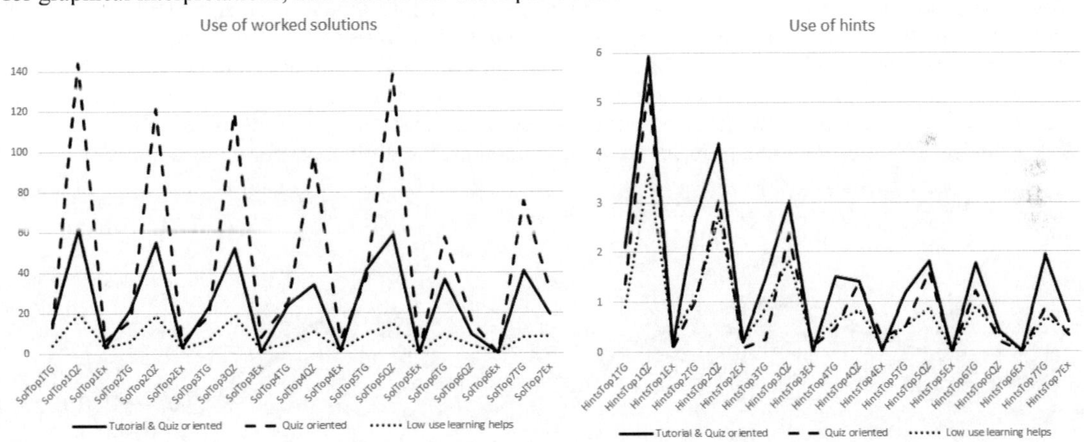

Figure 1. Three profiles of students based on clustering weekly use of worked examples and hints

Table 1. Descriptive statistics of the three profiles of students' use of learning aids

Profile	*Tutorial & quiz oriented*	*Quiz oriented*	*Low use of learning aids*
Number of students	442	122	712
Number worked examples	504	940	155
Number hints	30.5	20.7	17.2
Advanced math %	33%	21%	45%
Math entry test score	52.1	45.7	58.2
Math exam score	11.45	9.36	12.08
Math quiz score	2.04	1.80	1.64
Risk taking	5.80	5.83	6.19
Postpone	4.95	4.92	5.53

Figure 1 provides the use of learning aids for the seven weekly topics in each of the three learning phases. The saw tooth gradient in both the left panel, use of worked examples, and the right panel, use of hints, demonstrate that the use is most intensive in the second learning phase: the preparation of the quiz session. The intensity in the first and third learning phases is at lower levels. With some differences between the profiles: students in the profile *Tutorial & quiz oriented* use less worked examples than students in the profile *Quiz oriented*, and have a better balance over the first and second learning phase, whereas students in the *Quiz oriented* profile concentrate fully on the preparation of their quiz sessions. Another remarkable difference is that students in the *Quiz oriented* profile champion the use of worked examples, while students in the *Tutorial & quiz oriented* profile use more hints than any other student.

Turning to Table 1: we observe that prior education and prior math mastery resulting from that education are important predictors of profile membership. In the *Low use of learning aids* profile, students educated at advanced level make up 45% of all students, a much higher percentage than in other profiles. That difference in prior education shows up in the mastery they demonstrate in writing the Math entry test the first day of the module. However, it is not only prior math mastery that determines the profiles. Differences in average scores for the two personality characteristics of willingness to take risk and the tendency to postpone work make clear that students who score high for both of these maladaptive personal attributes are overrepresented in the large profile of *Low use of learning aids*.

In terms of course performance, students in the low use profile still profit from their prior education when writing their final exam. However, in writing the quizzes, they are outperformed by students of the other two profiles, who prepare more intensively for tutorial and quiz sessions.

4.2 Profiles and Epistemic and Activity Learning Emotions

Profile differences are visible in several of the disposition data collected in the framework of the dispositional learning analytics application. Motivation and engagement measures demonstrate profile differences, most outspoken in the category of engagement. Students' approaches to learning have profile differences for the cognitive processing strategy of stepwise learning and the metacognitive regulation strategy of external learning regulation. In this study, for reasons of space and the importance of learning emotions, we will focus on profile differences in dispositions of affective type: the epistemic learning emotions that are measured at the start of the module and are grounded on learning experiences with math in senior high school, and the achievement emotions that are measured amid the module, based on how students experience performing mathematical activities. Figure 2 provides an impression of profile differences for these dispositions.

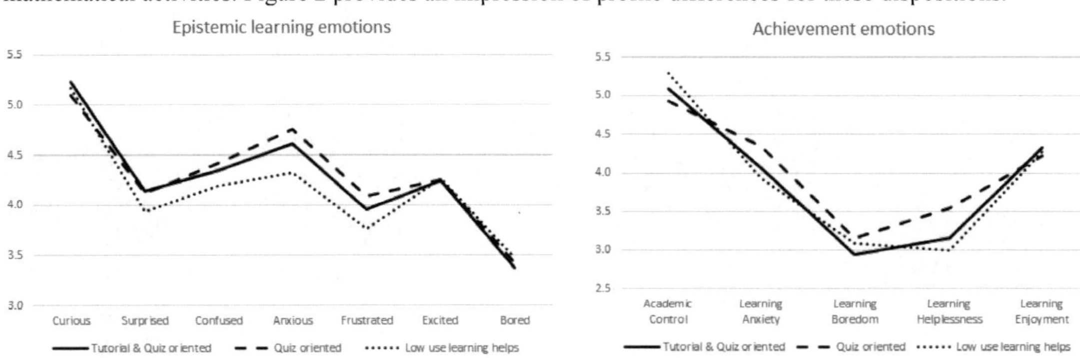

Figure 2. Epistemic learning emotions, left panel, and Activity learning emotions, right panel, of the three profiles

Epistemic emotions generate statistically significant profile differences for the negative emotions *Confused*, *Anxious* and *Frustrated*, and the neutral emotion *Surprised*. For these negative emotions, the pattern visible in the profiles is consistent: the *Quiz oriented* profile scores highest on negative emotions, the *Low use* profile scores lowest on negative epistemic emotions.

Four weeks later, halfway through the module, that pattern is repeated in the activity emotions scores: see the right panel of Figure 2. Unlike the epistemic emotions that signal what learning emotions students developed in high school education, due to the timing of the survey administration, activity emotions refer to affect coming with learning and practicing math in our module. We find statistically significant differences in *Academic Control*, *Learning Anxiety* and *Learning Helplessness*. Again, the highest negative emotion scores are seen in the *Quiz oriented* profile, the lowest in the *Low use* profile.

5. DISCUSSION AND CONCLUSIONS

Prior education and its knowledge play a crucial role in any new learning. In this case study, differences in learning behaviors due to differences in prior knowledge are of extreme dimensions: one-third of our students just finished six years of math education preparing for the sciences and would have been able to write the final exam on day one of the module. (If regulations allowed for streaming, this would have been the ideal situation, but regulations prevent doing so.) For the remaining two-thirds of students, this module is among the most challenging. These large differences are not only visible in prior education data but also in the entry test scores taken on day one and transform into the epistemic emotions towards math.

Superior prior knowledge affords superior learning approaches. Well-prepared students do not need that many worked examples, and when they use them, it is in the initial learning process. Compared to using worked examples, these students use relatively more hints: the learning aid that supports them in one specific learning step without giving away the full solution procedure. In contrast, the less well-prepared students use the worked examples intensively, but often 'too late' for the optimal learning process: when the quiz or exam is nearing, the initial learning phase should already be finished.

The educational implications of these findings are that in large-scale education with heterogeneous classes, the systematic collection of learning and learner data is of crucial importance for timely interventions. At the end of the second week of the module already, data analysis of the use of learning aids would have brought essential clues. For example, which students use worked examples optimally: as part of their initial learning of new concepts and solution strategies? Which students use worked examples in a suboptimal way: generating many solved problems as part of a just-in-time preparation of the first quiz. Knowing these different profiles based on learning data is the first step toward intervention. Connecting these profiles with differences in learner data is the crucial second step in successfully addressing learning obstacles.

These observations are not very startling in themselves. What is, however, striking is that all data sources provide complementary and mutually reinforcing facets of the learning challenges in this authentic learning context. For example, the application of analytic discovery methods to event-based log data, as suggested in contemporary writings addressing temporality in LA models, might have discovered differences in timing and intensity in the log-based event data, but never the connection to prior knowledge, epistemic emotions and activity emotions. So better, not throw away our old shoes before we have new ones that do as well.

REFERENCES

Aleven V., McLaren B., Roll I., Koedinger K., 2004. Toward Tutoring Help Seeking. J. C. Lester, R. M. Vicari, & F. Paraguaçu (Eds.), Intelligent Tutoring Systems. ITS 2004. *Lecture Notes in Computer Science*, Vol. 3220. Springer, Berlin, Heidelberg. DOI: 10.1007/978-3-540-30139-4_22.

Buckingham Shum, S., & Deakin Crick, R., 2012. Learning dispositions and transferable competencies: pedagogy, modelling and learning analytics. *Proceedings of the 2nd International Conference on Learning Analytics and Knowledge*, S. Buckingham Shum, D. Gasevic, and R. Ferguson (Eds.). ACM, New York, NY, USA. DOI: 10.1145/2330601.233062992-101.

Chen, B., Knight, S., & Wise, A. F., 2018. Critical issues in designing and implementing temporal analytics. *Journal of Learning Analytics*, Vol. 5, No. 1, pp. 1–9. https://doi.org/10.18608/jla.2018.53.1

Hmelo-Silver, C. E., 2004. Problem-Based Learning: What and How Do Students Learn? Educational Psychology Review, 16(3): 235–266. https://doi.org/10.1023/B:EDPR.0000034022.16470.f3

Ifenthaler, D., 2015. Learning analytics. In J. M. Spector (Ed.), *Encyclopedia of educational technology, Vol. 2*, pp. 447–451. Thousand Oaks, CA: Sage.

Knight, S., Wise, A. F., & Chen, B., 2017. Time for change: Why learning analytics needs temporal analysis. *Journal of Learning Analytics*, Vol. 4, No. 3, pp. 7–17. https://doi.org/10.18608/jla.2017.43.2

Loyens, S. M. M., Gijbels, D. Coertjens, L., & Coté, D. J., 2013. Students' Approaches to Learning in Problem-Based Learning: Taking into account Professional Behavior in the Tutorial Groups, Self-Study Time, and Different Assessment Aspects. *Studies in Educational Evaluation*, Vol. 39, No. 1, pp. 23–32. https://doi:10.1016/j.stueduc.2012.10.004

McLaren, B. M., Lim, S., & Koedinger, K. R., 2008. When is Assistance Helpful to Learning? Results in Combining Worked Examples and Intelligent Tutoring. In B. Woolf, E. Aimeur, R. Nkambou, & S. Lajoie (Eds.), *Proceedings of the 9th International Conference on Intelligent Tutoring Systems, Lecture Notes in Computer Science*, Vol. 5091, pp. 677-680. Berlin: Springer.

Merrienboer, J. J. van, & Sweller, J., 2010. Cognitive load theory in health professional education: design principles and strategies. *Medical Education*, Vol. 44, No. 1, pp. 85-93. DOI:10.1111/j.1365-2923.2009.03498.x.

Molenaar, I., 2014. Advances in temporal analysis in learning and instruction. *Frontline Learning Research*, Vol. 2, No. 4, pp. 15–24. https://doi.org/10.14786/flr.v2i4.118

Molenaar, I. and Wise, A. F., 2022. Temporal Aspects of Learning Analytics - Grounding Analyses in Concepts of Time. In: C. Lang, G. Siemens, A. F. Wise, D. Gašević, A. Merceron (Eds.), *The Handbook of Learning Analytics, Second edition*, Ch. 7, pp. 66-76. Vancouver, Canada: SOLAR. https://doi.org/10.18608/hla22

Nguyen, Q., Tempelaar, D. T., Rienties, B., & Giesbers, B., 2016. What learning analytics based prediction models tell us about feedback preferences of students. In R. Amirault & Y. Visser (Eds.), e-Learners and Their Data, Part 1: Conceptual, Research, and Exploratory Perspectives. *Quarterly Review of Distance Education*, Vol. 17, No. 3.

Panadero, E., 2017. A Review of Self-regulated Learning: Six Models and Four Directions for Research. *Frontiers in Psychology*, Vol. 8, No. 422. DOI:10.3389/fpsyg.2017.00422.

Pekrun, R., Goetz, T., Frenzel, A. C., Barchfeld, P., & Perry, R. P., 2011. Measuring emotions in students' learning and performance: The Achievement Emotions Questionnaire (AEQ). *Contemporary Educational Psychology*, Vol. 36, No. 1, pp. 36-48. DOI: 10.1016/j.cedpsych.2010.10.002.

Pekrun, R., Vogl, E., Muis, K. R. & Sinatra, G. M., 2017. Measuring emotions during epistemic activities: the Epistemically-Related Emotion Scales, *Cognition and Emotion*, Vol. 31, No. 6, pp. 1268-1276, DOI: 10.1080/02699931.2016.1204989.

Reimann, P. (2009). Time is precious: Variable- and event-centred approaches to process analysis in CSCL research. *International Journal of Computer-Supported Collaborative Learning*, Vol. 4, pp. 239–257. https://doi.org/10.1007/s11412-009-9070-z

Reimann, P., Markauskaite, L., & Bannert, M., 2014. e-Research and learning theory: What do sequence and process mining methods contribute? *British Journal of Educational Technology*, Vol. 45, pp. 528–540. http://onlinelibrary.wiley.com/doi/abs /10.1111/bjet.12146

Rienties, B., Cross, S., & Zdrahal, Z., 2017. Implementing a Learning Analytics Intervention and Evaluation Framework: What Works? In B. Kei Daniel (Ed.), *Big data and learning analytics: Current theory and practice in higher education*, pp. 147–166. Cham: Springer International Publishing. DOI: 10.1007/978-3-319-06520-5_10.

Rienties, B., Tempelaar, D., Nguyen, Q., & Littlejohn, A., 2019. Unpacking the intertemporal impact of self-regulation in a blended mathematics environment. *Computers in Human Behavior*, Vol. 100, pp. 345-357. DOI: 10.1016/j.chb.2019.07.007.

Saint, J., Fan, Y., Gašević, D., & Pardo, A., 2022. Temporally-focused analytics of self-regulated learning: A systematic review of literature. *Computers and Education: Artificial Intelligence*, 100060. https://doi.org/10.1016/j.caeai.2022.100060

Salden, R., Aleven, V.A. W. M. M., Renkl, A., & Schwonke, R., 2009. Worked Examples and Tutored Problem Solving: Redundant or Synergistic Forms of Support? *Topics in Cognitive Science*, Vol. 1, No. 1, pp. 203 – 213. DOI: 10.1111/j.1756-8765.2008.01011.x.

Shih, B., Koedinger, K. R., & Scheines, R., 2010. A Response-Time Model for Bottom-Out Hints as Worked Examples. In C. Romero, S. Ventura, M. Pechenizkiy, & R. S. J. D. Baker, *Handbook of Educational Data Mining*, pp. 201-212. CRC Press, Taylor & Francis Group.

Tempelaar, D. T., Rienties, B., & Giesbers, B., 2015. In search for the most informative data for feedback generation: Learning Analytics in a data-rich context. *Computers in Human Behavior*, Vol. 47, pp. 157-167. DOI: 10.1016/j.chb.2014.05.038.

Tempelaar, D. T., Rienties, B., & Nguyen, Q., 2020. Individual differences in the preference for worked examples: Lessons from an application of dispositional learning analytics. *Applied Cognitive Psychology*, Vol. 34, No. 4, pp. 890-905. https://doi.org/10.1002/acp.3652

Winne, P. H., 2017. Leveraging big data to help each learner upgrade learning and accelerate learning science. *Teachers College Record*, Vol. 119, No. 13, pp. 1-24.

AN EDUCATIONAL UNIFIED MODELLING LANGUAGE PROGRAMMING ENVIRONMENT AND ITS TWO CASE STUDIES

Ryoga Maruyama[1], Shinpei Ogata[1], Mizue Kayama[1], Nobuyuki Tachi[2], Takashi Nagai[3] and Naomi Taguchi[4]
[1]Graduate School of Science & Technology, Shinshu University, Japan
[2]Shinshu University, Japan
[3]Institute of Technologists, Japan
[4]Minowa Junior High School, Japan

ABSTRACT

This study aims to explore an educational learning environment that supports students to learn conceptual modelling with the unified modelling language (UML). In this study, we call the describing models "UML programming." In this paper, we show an educational UML programming environment for science, technology, engineering, art, and mathematics (STEAM) related subjects (especially for Technology or Engineering) in schools, which are able to apply from elementary school to university. At first, we explain why, what, and how doing the UML programming. In this study, we use a state machine diagram for UML programming. To draw this model, the students just put some states in rectangular shape and transitions in arrow shape. Two types of educational model notations in state machine diagram are introduced. Then, some advanced functions of the SRPS are described. They are an educational model editor, and management of users, learning tasks and models submitted by students. Next, two case studies with the SRPS are shown. One case study is adopted to the summer camp for 5th- and 6th-grade students. The participants were 20 students and were engaged in 4 hours workshop. We used a car-type robot with two DC motors, a one-touch sensor, and one infrared sensor connected to a micro:bit. The other case study is a formal technology class at one Japanese public junior high school. One teacher and five classes worked on UML programming for traffic lights. Each class had 20 9th-grade students. One student at this school was given a traffic light robot with three Light-emitting diode (LED) lights, a one-touch sensor, and one infrared sensor connected to a micro:bit. Finally, on the basis of these two case studies using our environment, we discuss the potential for innovative STEAM education with UML programming.

KEYWORDS

Conceptual Modelling, UML, Model Driven Development, Learning Environment, STEAM

1. INTRODUCTION

Recently, model-driven development (MDD)-based formal classes are focused on some educators (Starrett, 2007, Akayama et al, 2014, Kayama et al. 2015). Students in information communication technology (ICT)-related departments at universities, colleges, and high schools are the primary users. In their modelling classes, they create abstract models using the Unified Modelling Language (UML). One of the learning objectives in some of these classes is conceptual modelling with UML.

The concept of modelling is familiar with computational thinking (Wing, 2006). This way of thinking is similar to the "program-like thinking" proposed by the Japanese government (MEXT, 2018). Designing a robot model that supports human life with UML is mentioned as an example of learning activities in the most recent Japanese national school curriculum for Technology at the secondary school level (MEXT 2017).

Some years ago, educational methods or learning courses related to conceptual modelling had eagerly explored in many educational institutes, academic conferences, and academic journals (Sendall 2003, Börstler 2004, Kramer 2007, Bezivin 2009, Fuller 2010). Some institutes start their conceptual modelling course from graduate school, but other institutes teach conceptual modeling after fundamental programming courses in undergraduate school. We have been applying this educational methodology for the students in pre university level, from elementary school, junior high school, and high school from 2010. Recently, some international educational project related to computational thinking using modelling (Rottenhofer et al. 2021, Moreno-Leon et al. 2022). In these studies, the researchers, including us focus on graphical models without coding to express conceptual modelling.

This study aims to explore an educational learning environment that supports students to learn conceptual modelling with UML. In this study, we call the describing models "UML programming." In this paper, we show an educational UML programming environment for STEAM-related subjects (for example, Technology or Engineering) in schools, which are from elementary school to university. First, we describe the feature of the MDD method and current MDD tools. Then, we describe our findings regarding the design and implementation of an educational learning environment for UML programming with MDD. Finally, on the basis of some case studies using our environment, we discuss the potential for innovative STEAM education with UML programming.

2. UML PROGRAMMING WITH MDD

2.1 Overview of MDD

The MDD method is one approach to realize model-driven engineering (MDE). MDE is a software development methodology that focuses on developing and deploying domain methods (abstract representations of the knowledge and activities that govern a specific application domain) rather than computing concepts. In the MDD method, models are usually expressed with the graphical elements, such as UML. MDD is thought to be appropriate for education, such as programming education in primary, secondary, and higher education, as well as modelling education for beginners. MDD does not necessitate that the user understands the complex syntax of programming languages. Consequently, even if users are unfamiliar with programming, they can learn the fundamentals of system development.

2.2 UML Programming and its Notations

The model diagrams discussed in this paper are described in simple UML notation. In this paper, we use state machine diagrams to represent the modeling target's life cycle. This diagram is made up of two parts: states and behavioral transitions. An initial state, a final state, and a simple state are the three types of states. A small, filled circle represents the initial state. Each diagram must include this state at least once. A final state is represented by a circle encircling a smaller circle. There may be zero or more final states in one diagram. A simple state is shown as a rectangle with rounded corners, and the state name and short description for a state are written inside the rectangle. A behavioral transition is a directed relationship between a source state and a target state. Transitions in our notation have an event name as a required element and an action or trigger name as an optional element. There is no event name for the incoming transition from the initial state.

In this paper, we introduce two types of state machine notation(Maruyama, 2022). Notation-I use named states and transitions [Figure 1(a)]. A state machine may contain some states with the same state name as each name if named states are used. Figure 1(b) depicts an example of a state machine diagram in Notation-I. This is a traffic light diagram. This model denotes the activities listed below. The state of light begins with an initial state and progresses to a "Turn on RED" state. "Stop" is a succinct description of this state. After 5 s passed, this light changes its state to the next. The next state is "Turn on GREEN," which means "Go." Then, after 10 s passed, the light changes its state to the next. The next state is "Turn on YELLOW." After 3 s passed, the state of light returns to the "Turn on RED.".

Figure 2 shows the other notation. Notation-II can use named states, transitions, and messaging [Figure 2(a)]. Sending messages is represented by an action in the state machine diagram for this notation, and receiving messages is represented by a trigger. Some state machines can communicate with one another cooperatively and synchronously by sending and receiving messages. Figure 2(b) shows an example of a state machine diagram using Notation-II. This diagram is a pedestrian traffic light that interacts with a vehicle traffic light that belongs to group 2. The pink-colored rectangle represents a group ID. This model denotes the activities listed below. The state of light begins with an initial state and progresses to a "Turn on RED" state. If a walker pushes a pedestrian traffic light button ("Button Pushed" as an event), this model sends a message to the vehicle traffic light in group 2 ("send MSG1" as an action). At the same time, the state of this pedestrian traffic light changed to the next state, named "Waiting for MSG2." The color of the traffic light keeps the red. Then, if this traffic light received the message from the vehicle traffic light ("MSG2 Received" as a trigger), the state changes to the next state, named "Start Walking." The color of the traffic light shifted to green. After 30 s passed, the state of the traffic light changes to the next state, named "Stop Walking." The traffic light's color changed to blinking green. Furthermore, after 5 s, the traffic light sends a message with a different ID than the previous message sent to the vehicle traffic light ("send MSG3" as an action). The traffic light then changed to the next state, "Stop," and the color changed to red.

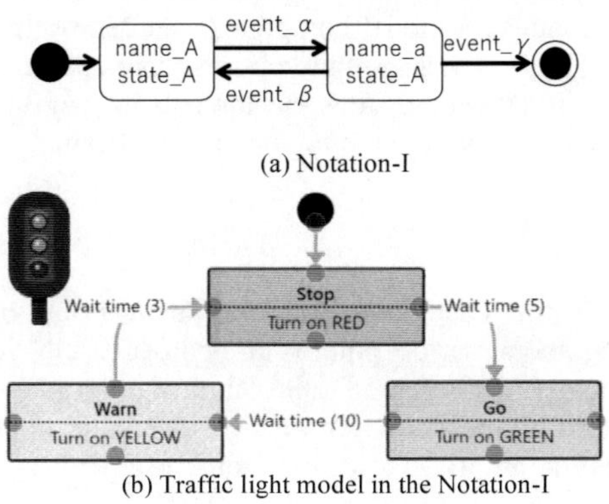

(a) Notation-I

(b) Traffic light model in the Notation-I

Figure 1. Notation-I and an example of an UML program in Notation-I

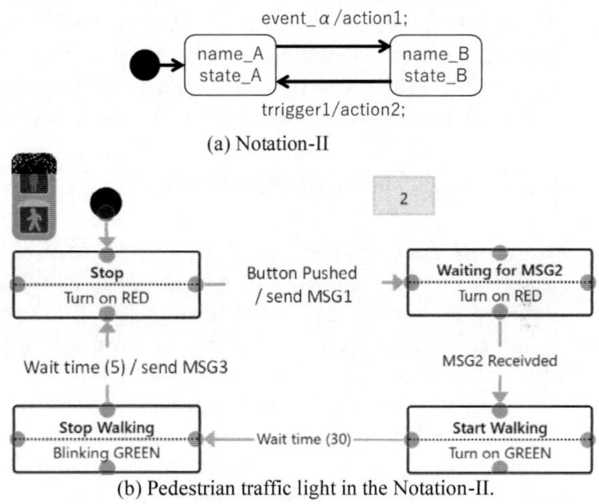

(a) Notation-II

(b) Pedestrian traffic light in the Notation-II.

Figure 2. Notation-II and an example of an UML program in Notation-II

This representation is useful to raise the thinking ability of students. Current Japanese school curriculum guidelines said that thinking ability is necessary for the students. In Taizan's thinking tool (Taizen, 2014), our notation is included in the "arrow and enclosure" method. Consequently, our notation will be suitable for use at any level of education.

2.3 Domain Specific Language

A DSL is "a computer programming language of limited expressiveness focused on a particular domain." Using a DSL, developers can express their implementation ideas in terms that their customers can understand and discuss. In this paper, we introduce some sets of vocabulary as DSL that represent a state action and a transition event. For example, "Turn on RED," "Turn on GREEN," and "Turn on YELLOW" are the DSL of the state; "Wait time" and "Button Pushed" are the DSL of the transition in Figures 1 and 2.

As for DSL, in this study, we can use not only natural language but also programming language or script. Consequently, we can use the DSL to control the difficulty of each laboratory task. Learners are given a set of DSL by their teacher and engage in laboratory tasks to draw models using DSL.

3. FEATURES OF MDD TOOLS

3.1 MDD with xtUML

For our learning environment, the concept of executable UML (xtUML) (xtUML.org, 2012) and MDD approach are applied. The programming language in our environment combines a subset of the UML graphical notation (in this case, state machine diagrams) with executable semantics and timing rules. We include xtUML and MDD in our teaching method because we expect our students to be able to evaluate their models on the basis of observations of the target device's behavior without worrying about grammatical errors or exact programming language expression. The model created by the students is platform-independent. Platform dependencies emerge as a result of source code generation. In the source code of the model compiler, which is described in a later section, some specific libraries for the target device must be included. The source code compiler will be activated after the source code has been generated. We must prepare each compile tool for each target device in this source code compiler.

According to the concept of MDD with xtUML, the learning flow is following. The teacher defines practical tasks and some sets of DSL for each task. After being given tasks, students analyze the given requirements (requirement analysis) and then design a system using UML modeling diagrams (making models) with the model editor. Following the creation of models, a model compiler generates source code from the models (translating models to code). The generated code is then compiled by a source code compiler into an executable file (compiling code to executable binary data). Learners observe the behavior of the target device after transferring the executable code to it to determine whether the requirements have been met.

3.2 Comparison of MDD Tools

Many MDD tools are provided by commercial vendors. In this chapter, we provide an overview of each MDD tool and discuss the issues in educational use for beginners. Bridgepoint is an open-source MDD tool provided by xtUML.org (xtUML.org, 2012). By describing transformation rules in BridgePoint notation, users can generate executable code for a variety of platforms. BridgePoint can be used as a general-purpose MDD tool because it has a wide range of functions that are appropriate for professional use. Consequently, we believe that it is difficult for a beginner to master this tool in a short period of time. Astah is a UML modeling tool provided by Change Vision Inc. (Change Vision, 2009). Astah has special APIs for users to develop their own plug-ins. Users, for example, can generate source code from the model in astah using the m2t plug-in. Nevertheless, because there are currently no plug-ins with DSL-like functions, teachers are unable to control the task's difficulty level. Clooca is an MDD tool provided by Technical Rockstars Inc. (Hiya et al. 2013). This tool can use metamodels and template functions to generate source code from models. Because it can define DSLs using metamodels, it is an ideal modeling environment for educational use. Since 2012 (Kayama 2015), we have been running S-clooca, a UML programming environment that combines clooca and a compilation server that we developed.

Since 2018, our product has also been applied to formal junior high school technology classes (Maruyama, 2022). During these practices, we got some educational problems with S-clooca. For example, in junior high schools, all students in the class work on some common tasks. Teachers want to assess students' performance as efficiently as possible. Clooca, conversely, does not allow teachers to review their students' model diagrams. Furthermore, the UX provided to programming beginners was limited because it was difficult to rewrite the diagrams or difficult to review their diagrams.

4. OUR PROPOSAL: SRPS

4.1 Overview

In this paper, we propose SRPS on the basis of the educational problems we have found with 3 years of UML programming practices with S-clooca in junior high school. The features of SRPS are as follows:

- Definition of DSLs according to the tasks
- Management of models created by learners
- Suitable UX for the beginners of programming

SRPS comprises a web application, a compilation server, and a target device. The web application is the core of SRPS. The compilation server is the same as S-clooca. The target device is a micro:bit. The SRPS web application consists of a model editor, a model compiler, and a content management module. In SRPS, we designed the UX for beginners of programming learners and enhanced the management functions for teachers to create task topics and created models by learners.

The model editor of SRPS has a notation checking function, and the source code is generated using the model compiler only when there is no defect in the notation checking function. The model compiler of SRPS generates C++ source code from the model diagram described by the model editor. On the server, the generated source code is compiled, and the executable code is downloaded using the learner's browser. The learner confirms the behaviors described in the model diagram by transferring this executable code to the target device.

4.2 Functions of SRPS

Users of SRPS are categorized into three types of roles: administrators, teachers, and learners. SRPS provides functions according to the roles of the users. In the following, we describe the functions for learners, administrators, and teachers.

4.2.1 Model Editor

Figure 3 shows the model editor is a function for learners. The interface of the model editor. The available behaviors and events are defined by the DSL for each task. By selecting a floating-point value in this model editor, you can access an interactive tutorial (the red double circle icon on the right side of Figure 3). The teacher can avoid repeating the explanation of how to use the model editor by allowing students to check the basic usage on their own. SRPS records the user's operations to deal with erroneous operations by the user (the Undo and Redo functions). Even when describing a single model diagram with multiple class days, it is possible to go back through the days and repeat operations. The model editor's diagram element includes a "memo" element. The teacher has access to this memo. The teacher can also write memos on the model diagrams of the students. The Model Editor can be used to check for notational errors in model diagrams. A dialog alerts you to notation errors, and the related element of the model diagram in the editor turns red. Only model diagrams in which all notational errors have been corrected can run the model compiler function. The model diagram notation checker assists students in correcting errors in their model diagrams. The diagrams of the models can be saved and submitted. The model diagram saving function in SRPS saves the model diagram for each learner and task. The model diagram submission function saves model diagrams for teacher evaluation. Model diagrams can be submitted as many times as desired.

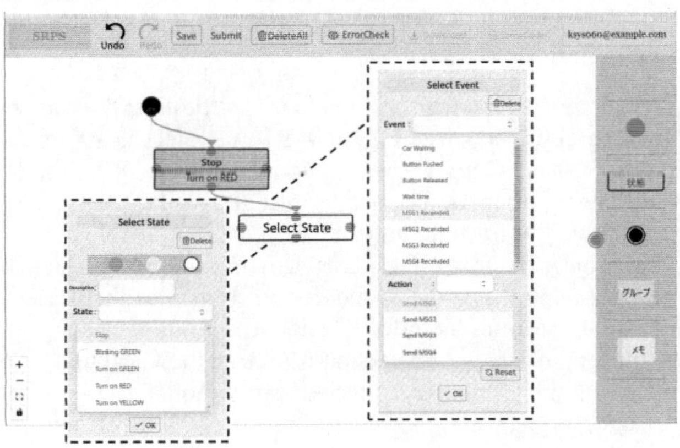

Figure 3. Model editor interface of the SPRS

4.2.2 Management of User

SRPS users are distinguished by their e-mail address, password, group (e.g., equivalent to a class in school), and role. The role is related to the permissions to use the SRPS functions. A teacher can be a member of several groups. Teachers' functions include managing students in their group, creating learning tasks, assigning learning tasks to groups, and reviewing model diagrams submitted by students. A student is a member of one group, and their functions are model diagram description and submission. The administrator can use the same functions as the teacher for all groups and all users. The registration of users is a function for administrators and teachers. The administrator can register users in all roles. A teacher can register a group that he manages and then register students who belong to that group. A teacher can also register teachers who manage the same group.

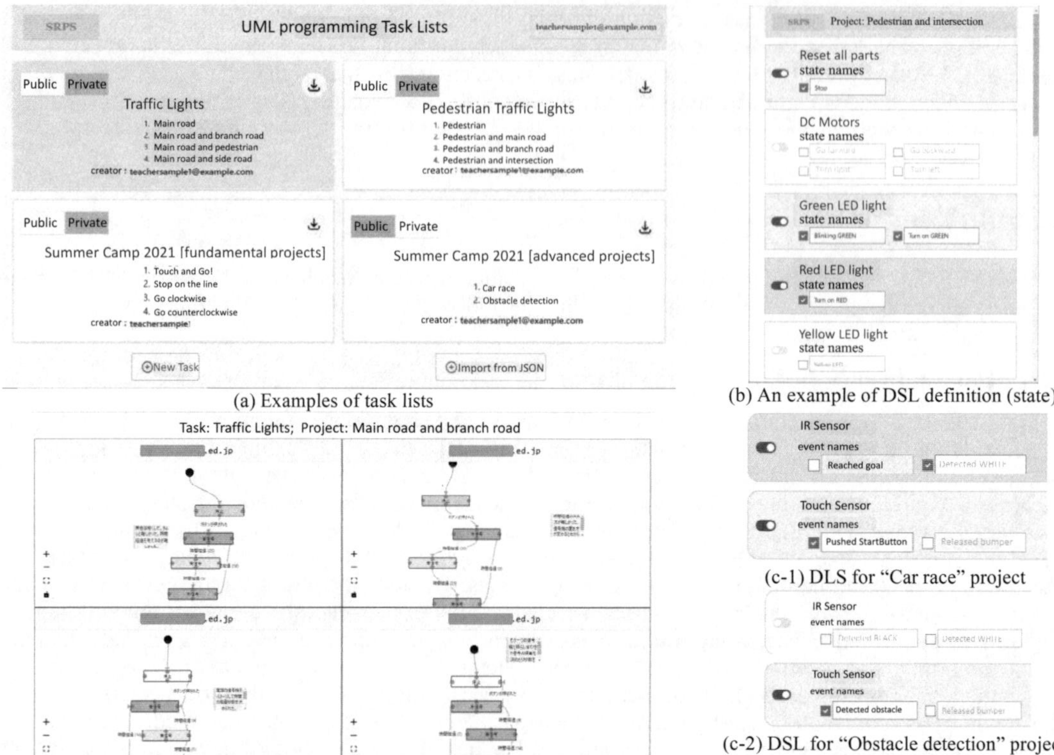

(a) Examples of task lists

(b) An example of DSL definition (state)

(c-1) DLS for "Car race" project

(c-2) DSL for "Obstacle detection" project

(c) Vocabularies for the DSL of event

(d) An example of list view for diagrams summited by students

Figure 4. Examples of the SPRS interface

4.2.3 Management of Learning Tasks

A learning task (ex: the name of a learning topic such as "traffic lights" or an event name such as "summer camp") is organized by several projects [see Figure 4(a)]. A project is a type of assignment that is given to students. Each learning task has the option of being public or private. When set to public, the learning task is accessible to all SRPS-registered teachers. The groups that are available for each learning task are determined by the teacher or administrator. The learning tasks are then made available to students in that group. The DSL definition of the learning project is shown in Figures 4(b) and (c). Select the actions (rectangles) and events (rounded rectangles) to be used in that project, and give them names that reflect the contents of the project. Figure 4(c) shows an example of using the infrared (IR) sensor and the touch sensor in different projects. In the race project, the IR sensor's black color detection is used in the vocabulary "Reached goal," and the touch sensor's press event is used in the vocabulary "Pushed start button." The IR sensor, on the other hand, is not used in the obstacle detection project, and the event of pressing the touch sensor is used in the vocabulary of "Detected obstacle."

4.2.4 Management of Models Submitted by Students

The administrator and teacher can review the model diagrams submitted by the student. In SRPS, the submitted diagrams are managed by assignment or by the user. SRPS keeps track of all submissions. When checking submissions, there is no need to refer to the submission history because the most recent submissions are always displayed. The submitted diagrams can be viewed in two ways: list view and individual view. Figure 4 shows an example of a list view (d). When reviewing all of a group's submissions for a specific assignment or all of a specific student's submissions, the list view is appropriate. In the case of checking the submission history of a particular student for a particular assignment or checking a particular submission in detail, the individual view is appropriate.

5. DISCUSSION

In this chapter, we discuss the feasibility of SRPS on the basis of two different use cases.

5.1 Case Study-I: Summer Camp for 5th- and 6th-Grade Students

Using SRPS, we conducted a 4-hour in-person workshop for 20 participants (female, 50%) in 5th and 6th grades in August 2021. The theme of the workshop was the "collaborative car controlling." They used a car-type robot with two DC motors, a one-touch sensor, and one infrared sensor connected to a micro:bit, and one PC for the SRPS per a participant. One teaching assistant (undergraduate and graduate students) supported two participants during this workshop. Four tasks were assigned as fundamental projects during the first 2 hours of the workshop. Students learned how to use the touch sensor, how to read the driving course using the infrared sensor, and how to trace a line with complex curves in these tasks. These projects made use of Notation-I. All students completed their tasks with a teaching assistant. In the latter 2 hours of the workshop, the students were given a race project and an obstacle detection project to work on in groups of four. Notation-II, which includes sending and receiving messages, was used in these projects. Both Notation-I and Notation-II were easily understood by all students.

It was their first time to use UML and MDD. At the beginning of the workshop, participants understood how to use the SRPS model editor with only 5 min explanation. All participants completed all the projects given to them using the mouse to select diagram elements and the error checking function. This suggests that SRPS was able to provide a UX that could be used by 5th- and 6th-grade students.

5.2 Case Study-II: Formal Technology Classes for 9th-Grade Students

One Japanese junior high school has been using our UML programming environment since 2018. From October 2021, SRPS has started its practical usage in the formal Technology classed in this school. One teacher and five classes work on UML programming for traffic lights in Notation-I and Notation-II in-person. Each class has 20 9th-grade students (50% of whom are female). One student at this school is given a traffic light robot with three LED lights, a one-touch sensor, and one infrared sensor connected to a micro:bit, and one desktop PC per a student. These classed were All students' first time to know and use UML and MDD.

In the first lesson, in the first 30 min, students learned notation of the state machine diagram and the usage of the SRPS. They discussed the timing of color changes in traffic lights for vehicles in the last 20 min. They programmed two types of traffic lights from the second lesson to the third lesson: main road traffic lights and intersection traffic lights. Students were asked to design on their own using Notation-I. Each student had one computer and one robot. In the fourth and fifth lessons, they programmed the pedestrian traffic light, which works in tandem with the vehicle traffic light. They were asked to make a program in a group of two or four students in Notation-II.

A Technology teacher has set whole learning tasks and projects using SRPS. He defined whether or not the predefined states and events should be used, as well as the names of the states and events for each project. After each lesson, the teacher reviewed all submitted diagrams and provided brief comments for each one. This teacher registered all his students by himself or herself to the SRPS.

5.3 Possibility for STEAM Education

We got useful outcomes of these use cases as follows: 1) The MDD with the xtUML method expands the thinking abilities of our learners with the interest of learning. 2) Students master the operation of the SRPS and transfer executable code to the robot in quite short time. 3) The notation error checking function of the SRPS was useful for self-assessment and self-correction of the model notation. And 4) Management functions for the user, tasks, submitted diagrams are useful and easy to use for the teacher.

The MDD-based UML programming shows a great educational possibility for STEAM-related subjects, especially for Technology, at any level of school. The learners can design and make a program for their problem-solving using this method.

6. CONCLUSION

In this paper, we proposed an educational UML programming environment with user/task/diagram management functions for STEAM-related subjects. Based on the two types of feasibility studies for 5th and 6th grade student group and 9th grade student groups, we found that UML programming has great possibility for the STEAM education. These two use cases have been conducted continuously in-person in 2022.

In the next step, the effectiveness of UML programming about creativity or abstract ability will be evaluated on the basis of practical case studies.

ACKNOWLEDGEMENT

This work was supported by JSPS KAKENHI Grant Numbers JP22H03702,JP20K03146,JP16H03074.

REFERENCES

Akayama, S., Hisazumi, K., Hiya, S, et al. (2014). An Empirical Study of the Usage of Model-Driven Development Tool for an Object-Oriented Modeling Education, *In Transaction of IPSJ*, Vol.55, No.1, pp.72-84.

Bezivin,J., France,R., Gogola,M., et al. (2009). Teaching Modeling: Why, When, What?, *Proceeding of 12th ACM/IEEE International Conference on Model Driven Engineering Languages and Systems*, pp.55-62.

Börstler,J., Michiels, I. & Fjuk,A. (2004). ECOOP 2004 Workshop Report: Eighth Workshop on Pedagogies and Tools for the Teaching and Learning Object-Oriented Concepts, *ECOOP 2004 Workshop Reader*, pp.36-48.

Fuller,R.M., Murthy,U. Schafer,B.A. (2010). The effects of data model representation method on task performance, *In Information & Management*, Vol.47, No.4, pp.208-218.

Hiya, S., Hisazumi, K., Fukuda, et al. (2013). clooca: Web based tool for Domain Specific Modeling, *Proceeding of 16th ACM/IEEE International Conference on Model Driven Engineering Languages and Systems*, pp.31-35.

Kayama, M., Ogata, S., Nagai, T., et al. (2015). Effectiveness of Model-Driven Development in conceptual modeling education for university freshmen, *Proceeding of 6th IEEE Global Engineering Education Conference*, pp.274-282.

Kramer,J. (2007). Is Abstraction The Key To Computing?, *In CACM*, Vol.50, No.4,pp.37-42.

MEXT. 2018. Elementary school programming education guide (first edition), http://www.mext.go.jp/a_menu/shotou/zyouhou/detail/1403162.htm.

MEXT. (2017). Japanese national school curriculum guideline for the Technology and Home Economics in junior high school,
http://www.mext.go.jp/component/a_menu/education/micro_detail/__icsFiles/afieldfile/2019/03/18/1387018_009.pdf

Maruyama, R., Kayama, M., Nagai, T., et al. (2022). Practical UML Programming based on the Executable UML Method at Secondary School Students, *Proceedings of 13th IEEE Global Engineering Education Conference*, 10.1109/EDUCON52537.2022.9766752.

Moreno-León, J., Chushig C., Robles, G. (2022). MaS:Modeling At School –On the Benefits and Skill Development of the Use of Modeling Diagrams at School, *Proceedings of 13th IEEE Global Engineering Education Conference*, 10.1109/EDUCON52537.2022.9766646.

Starrett, C. (2007). Teaching UML Modeling Before Programming at the High School Level, *Proceeding of 7th IEEE ICALT*, pp.713-714.

Rottenhofer,M., Sabitzer, B., Rankin T. (2021). Developing Computational Thinking Skills Through Modeling in Language Lessons, *In Open Education Studies*, Vol.3, No.1, pp17-25.

Sendall,S. (2003). Model Transformation: The Heart and Soul of Model Driven Software Development, *In IEEE SOFTWARE*, Vol.20, No.5, pp.42-45.

Taizan, Y., Kojima, A., Kurokami, H. (2014). A Study of Subject-Common Thinking Skill for Systematic Information Education: From Analysis of the Government Curriculum Guidelines and Commentary to it, *In Japan Journal of Educational Technology*, Vol.37, No.4, pp.375-386.

xtUML.org. (2012). https://xtuml.org/

Change Vision. (2009), astah. https://astah.change-vision.com/.

Wing, J.M. (2006). Computational Thinking. *In Communication of ACM*, Vol.49, No.3, pp. 33-35.

AUTOMATIC SPEECH RECOGNITION SYSTEM TO ENHANCE THE USE OF VOCALIZATION STRATEGY

Saki Hirata[1] and Masanori Yamada[2]
[1]*Graduate School of Human-Environment Studies, Kyushu University*
[2]*Faculty of Arts and Science, Kyushu University*
744, Motooka, Nishi-ku, Fukuoka 819-0395, Japan

ABSTRACT

Vocabulary learning that overlooks the discrimination of single sounds in English language learning could lead to communication difficulties, such as the inability to hear and speak English pronunciation. To address this issue, vocalization strategy, in which students listen to the sounds of words and memorize them aloud, is considered a useful learning strategy, and has been reported to influence performance in English language learning. Many studies have shown that metacognition promotes the use of this strategy. In this study, we developed an English vocabulary learning support system using dictation-type speech recognition technology and evaluated whether it activates learners' metacognition and promotes the use of vocalization strategies.

KEYWORDS

Language Learning, Learning Strategies, Metacognition, Speech Recognition Technology

1. INTRODUCTION

1.1 Vocalization Strategy

Vocabulary is an important determinant of language proficiency. In second language learning (SLL), Shimamoto (2002) reported a significant correlation between learners' vocabulary levels and their overall TOEIC score. In vocabulary learning, memorizing the phonetic sounds of words is also considered an important learning component, and Nation (2001) mentions the multifaceted nature of vocabulary proficiency and considers knowledge of phonetic information of words as an aspect of vocabulary proficiency. It has also been reported that strengthening the association between written and speech forms can improve word listening (Field 2004) and appropriate speech (Li and Woore 2021).

Vocabulary learning strategies used by EFL learners, such as Japanese learners of English, have been reported to use bilingual dictionaries or vocabulary books to match the letters of words with their translations (Fan 2003; Schmitt 1997). In word learning through letters, "negative transfer," errors that arise from applying the rules of the native language to a foreign language, can result in learning incorrect pronunciations from letters (Odlin 1989). Negative transfer suggests that vocabulary learning that ignores the discrimination of single sounds can cause communication problems, such as the inability to hear and speak English pronunciation (Teshima 2011). Japanese learners have been reported to face difficulties recognizing and pronouncing English sounds that are not present in their native language, such as confusion regarding the difference between “r” and “l” phonemes in English (Ota et al. 2009).

While many studies have explored the effectiveness of explicit pronunciation instruction (e.g., Huo and Wang 2017), it has been reported that the success of vocabulary acquisition is determined by learners' individual learning (Rasouli and Jafari 2016). One of the factors determining the effectiveness of independent learning is learning strategy, which has been addressed in previous studies. As a strategy related to the phonetic information of words, Oxford (1990) suggested a pronunciation strategy in which students memorize words while pronouncing them. Conversely, it has been pointed out that in the wake of technological development, learning with audio equipment is gaining increasing popularity. As a strategy that reflects this change in the foreign language learning environment, Akamatsu (2017) presents a "vocalization strategy" in which words are memorized by listening to the sound of the word and also saying it out aloud. Using path analysis, Akamatsu determined that the strategy correlates academic performance in English. In this regard, Krashen's (1987) input theory states that in SLL, repeated input improves learners' language proficiency. Concurrently, Swain (1998) pointed out that outputting knowledge improves learners' linguistic formality by raising their awareness of language formality. Vocalization strategy is considered to be effective in improving phonetic knowledge of English vocabulary because it is an approach to learn words while simultaneously inputting and outputting the sounds of words through audio equipment. Akamatsu indicates a utilization-oriented view of learning that emphasizes daily use and conversation in English as a factor that defines the use of vocalization strategy. However, practical research on supporting the acquisition of learning strategies has indicated that intervention in learning perspectives and the teaching of target strategy knowledge alone are not effective for strategy retention (e.g., Ueki 2004). Jenkins (2000) also argues that efforts to improve speech habits will not be made unless learners understand the need to do so.

Correspondingly, a mechanism is required for learners to emphasize the importance of phonetic information of words when learning vocabulary, and to be aware of its improvement. Simultaneously, a mechanism to promote the use of vocalization strategy is also required.

1.2 Metacognition

One of the factors that can be utilized in promoting the use of vocalization strategy is metacognition. It is defined as the awareness or knowledge that allows learners to understand their learning strengths and weaknesses, the cognitive resources available to meet the demands of the task, and to adjust their learning behavior to optimize the learning process and outcomes (Winne and Perry 2000). Through metacognition, learners set achievement goals in learning tasks, select appropriate learning strategies to achieve them, and monitor, evaluate, and adjust their learning behaviors (Haslaman 2011). Many studies have shown that enhancing metacognition promotes the use of learning strategies (e.g., Akin et al. 2007).

As a mechanism for enhancing metacognition in SLL, Swain (1998) suggests that "output activity" is a factor that enhances learners' awareness of a language form. Furthermore, it has been suggested that dictation-type speech recognition, which recognizes learners' speech and transcribes it into letters, may promote metacognitive strategies such as awareness and self-monitoring (Dai and Wu 2021). Since such speech recognition technologies do not accept inappropriate pronunciations, it is expected to be effective in making learners aware of the importance of speech sounds, activating metacognition, and encouraging the use of vocalization strategy. Additionally, metacognitive support (MS) using Learning Analytics (LA) can also play a crucial role in metacognitive activation (Yilmaz and Yilmaz 2020). LA is defined as the measurement, collection, and analysis of learner data to understand and optimize learning, and based on the data analyzed in LA, learners can monitor, improve, and evaluate their learning behaviors and learning outcomes (Durall and Gros 2014; Yilmaz and Yilmaz 2020). MS is an educational approach that supports the improvement of metacognition (e.g., Jumaat and Tasir 2016; Ku ̈nsting et al. 2013; Molenaar, I. et al. 2014; Schwonke et al 2013; Yilmaz and Keser 2017). Essentially, questions and inquiries that promote awareness and improvement of learning behaviors have been proposed as methods of MS. Yilmaz and Yilmaz (2020) have demonstrated that LA can activate learners' metacognition by creating an environment in which they can monitor their learning data, while MS can encourage them to plan, monitor, and evaluate their learning behaviors.

Accordingly, this study will develop a web-based English vocabulary learning system that utilizes speech recognition technology and LA. Through the system, learners learn English words and pronounce them. The pronunciation is then transcribed using dictation-type speech recognition. By presenting the transcribed data and LA data of the learning behavior, the system improves learners' metacognition of phonetic knowledge and encourages the use of vocalization strategy in English vocabulary learning. Ultimately, the goal is to improve learners' vocabulary in the phonetic aspect.

2. BACKGROUND

2.1 Speech Recognition

In pronunciation learning, feedback on learners' pronunciation is considered important. The use of automatic speech recognition has been attracting attention as a means of providing this feedback. Automatic speech recognition recognizes learners' speech on a computer and provides feedback in a timely manner based on the correctness or incorrectness of the speech (Neri et al. 2008). Dictation-type speech recognition, which does not score speech or identify errors, has been suggested to promote metacognitive strategies such as awareness and self-monitoring in learners (Dai and Wu 2021). Pronunciation learning using dictation-type speech recognition requires learners to identify pronunciation errors based on dictation texts (Liakin et al. 2015). In the process, learners may reflect on the problems of speech form and learning methods. Previous studies have indicated that dictation-type speech recognition contributes to the improvement of learners' autonomy in learning activities as well as pronunciation skills (Liakin et al. 2015; Mroz 2018; Dai and Wu 2021). By enhancing learner autonomy, learning activities such as listening and pronunciation of sounds of words in vocabulary learning is practiced, leading to the improvement of not only speech but also pronunciation recognition, which is believed to improve vocabulary comprehensively in the phonetic aspect. Unfortunately, prior research on automatic speech recognition has focused only on its relationship with pronunciation ability. These studies have not clarified the relationship between automatic speech recognition and learning strategies. While automatic speech recognition has been shown to be effective in improving speech knowledge, it is necessary to examine the impact of this technology on learning methods and behaviors. By building a speech recognition system with a learning page and recording vocabulary learning behavior, it is possible to clarify the relationship between speech recognition and learning behavior, which has not been elucidated in previous studies.

2.2 Metacognitive Support by LA

Metacognitive support (MS) helps learners improve their self-regulated learning skills by offering an objective view of their learning behaviors and learning outcomes (e.g., Jumaat and Tasir 2016; Kü̈nsting et al. 2013; Molenaar et al. 2014; Schwonke et al. 2013; Yilmaz and Keser 2017). In online learning environments, Learning Analytics (LA) is an effective tool for metacognitive support. Chen et al (2019) suggested an LA design based on metacognition, and Chen et al (2020) indicated that visualization of learning behaviors improves certain aspects of metacognition. Yilmaz (2014) reported that providing MS online improves students' metacognition. In addition, LA enables learners to understand their learning process and review their learning behavior by visualizing the results of the analysis of their learning behavior as data. Therefore, LA can activate metacognition and promote the use of effective learning strategies by enabling learners to monitor their own learning behaviors and learning outcomes. Based on this theory, it is expected that presenting learners with dictation texts recognized by speech recognition and LA learning data in vocabulary learning could help them identify problems in their own phonetic knowledge and autonomously use a phonetic memory strategy that emphasizes the sound of words as a method to learn words. This is expected to encourage learners to identify problems with phonetic knowledge and voluntarily use the vocalization strategy that emphasizes the sound of the word as a word-learning method.

3. AUTOMATIC SPEECH RECOGNITION

This study uses Mozilla Developer Network's (MDN) Web speech API as the automatic speech recognition method. Web speech API recognizes user speech and transcribes it into text. There are many speech recognition tools other than Web speech API, such as Apple's Siri, Amazon's Alexa, Microsoft's Cortana, and Google Assistant. Mroz (2018) presents four criteria for the selection of automatic speech recognition: cost, accessibility, familiarity, and technology. Web speech API can be implemented for free by using JavaScript, and can also be used with Chrome, which has the highest market share in Japan among web browsers (StatCounter 2021–2022). With regard to accuracy, Ashwell and Elam (2017) investigated the accuracy rate of

Google Web Speech API for utterances based on the speech of native English speakers and Japanese non-native speakers. According to the study, the recognition rate of Google Web Speech API is 89.4% for native English speakers and 65.7% for non-native speakers. While the study points out that the recognition rate declines for proper nouns and certain collocations, the high recognition rate for native speakers' speech highlights the advantages of using Web Speech API for language learning to encourage reflection on speech. In addition, since Web Speech API does not correct pronunciation errors according to the user's native language, it is possible for learners to identify pronunciation errors by referring to the recognition results (Evers and Chen 2020). Therefore, the use of Google Web Speech API as a speech recognition tool in this study was found to encourage Japanese learners' reflection on their phonetic knowledge of English words.

4. THE DESIGN OF WEB-BASED APPLICATION

4.1 Outline of the Application

The system consists of a learning process (see Figure 1), an output process (see Figure 2), and a self-assessment process (see Figure 3) for English vocabulary learning. First, learners enter a learning process and engage in English vocabulary learning by comparing the English word with its translation. After learning vocabulary, learners move to the output process to pronounce the English words learned on the learning page. In the output process, the speech recognition system displays the dictation text, which is then checked against the word information to determine if they are correct or incorrect. If all the words are pronounced correctly, the learner is redirected to the learning page of the next lesson. However, even if one word is uttered incorrectly, the learner is redirected to the self-assessment process to reflect his/her learning outcome on the output page and learning strategy on the learning page based on MS by LA. When the learner has answered all the questions correctly, the system moves to the next lesson. This cycle is repeated to encourage learners to understand the importance of audio information of vocabulary and encourage the use of vocalization strategy on the learning page.

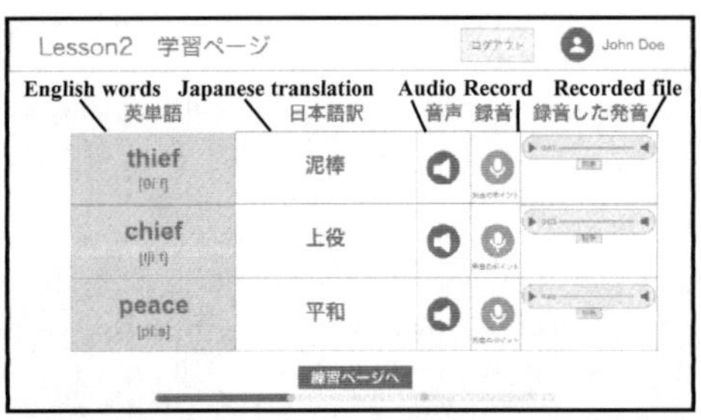

Figure 1. The user interface of learning process

Figure 2. The user interface of output

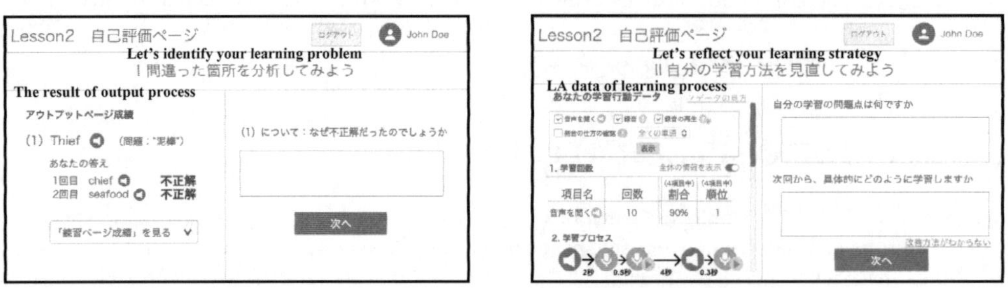

Figure 3. The user interface of self-assessment process processs

4.2 Learning Process

The learning page displays the English word and its Japanese translation, and the user learns English vocabulary by comparing English words along with the translation. In addition, the learning page includes an "audio function" to verify the sound of each word, a "recording function" to record and play back one's own pronunciation, and a "pronunciation point confirmation function" to explain how to pronounce the word. The audio function uses JavaScript's voice reading function, and by pressing a button, the user can listen to the voice of the word. The playback speed can be adjusted by the user from 0.8x to 2x (Dai and Wu 2021). The "recording function" will be implemented in Vue.js. The recording can be started and stopped by a push button. The recorded audio is displayed on the page as an audio file, and users can play back the recorded audio as long as they like. The audio file can be deleted and re-recorded. Clicking the "Next" button on the study page takes the user to the "Output" page.

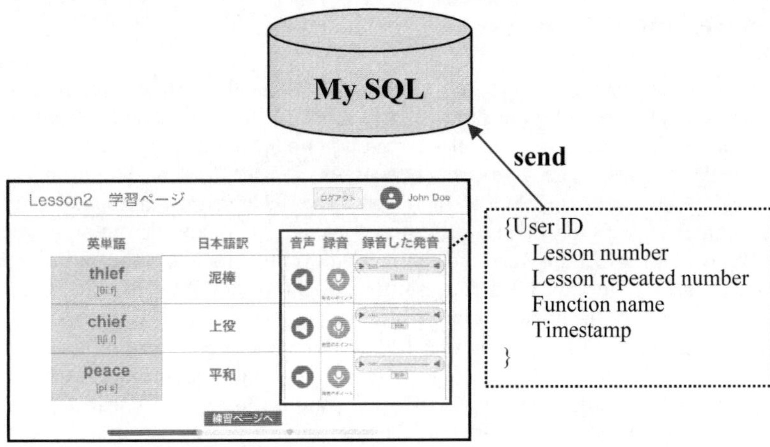

Figure 4. The learning log accumulation process

4.3 Output Process

On the output page, the user pronounces the English words learned from the learning page. The speech recognition system recognizes the words uttered and displays the dictation text (see Figure 5). The recognition results are verified against the word information to determine if they are correct or incorrect (see Figure 6). Web Speech API, a free JavaScript library, is used as the speech recognizer. The user can pronounce each word up to two times; if the first pronunciation is correct, the user moves on to the next question; if both the words are pronounced incorrectly, the user cannot retry the same question and moves on to the next question. After all the words have been pronounced, the results page displays the pass/fail results for all words: "Pass" if the first or second pronunciation was appropriate, and "Fail" if the first or second pronunciation was inappropriate. If the learner answers all the questions correctly, the user is redirected to the study page of the next lesson; even if one question is incorrect, the user is redirected to the "Self-Evaluation Page."

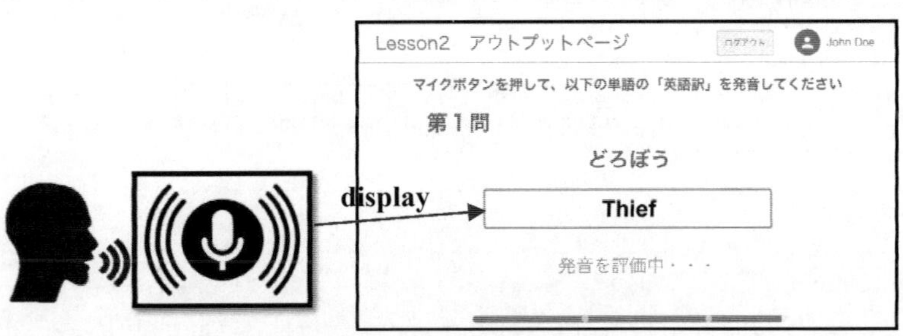

Figure 5. Displaying dictation text process

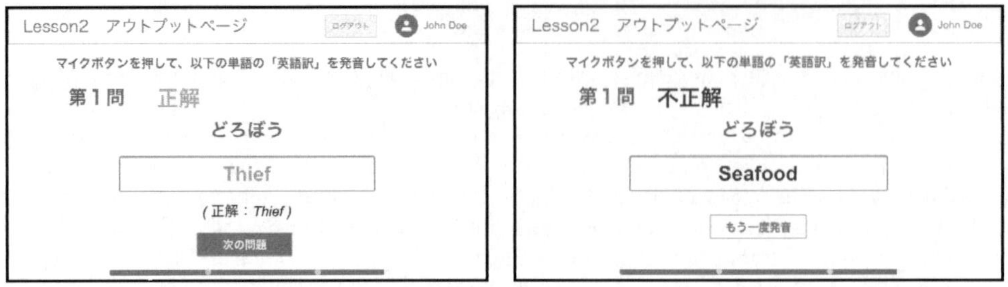

Figure 6. Right and wrong judgment

4.4 Self-Assessment Process

On the self-assessment page, the user reflects the results on the output page and the learning strategy for vocabulary learning by answering questions based on MS (Yilmaz and Keser 2017). At that time, the learning log on the learning page and the results log on the output page are displayed as LA data. To promote learners' metacognition, the self-assessment process encourages the user to identify learning problems and review the learning strategy (Akin et al. 2007; Schraw and Dennison 1994; Schraw and Moshman 1995). First, to promote an understanding of learning problems, questions judged as "Fail" on the output page are extracted, and texts and audio data of the correct answers and the recognition results are presented as a reflection of individual questions (see Figure 7). To improve metacognition, the question, "Why do you think you made a mistake?" is presented as MS, and once the answer is entered in the text box, the user is reassigned to the next section. This section presents the number of times the user has used the audio or recording functions on the learning page, which helps review his/her learning strategy based on this data (see Figure 8). At that time, the questions, "What learning method should I review?" and "How should I improve my learning method?" are presented as MS, and once the responses are entered in the text boxes, the user is transferred to the self-assessment confirmation page. On the confirmation screen, the results of self-assessment are displayed as a list, and after checking them, the user is redirected to the learning process of the same content. If a student answers correctly a question that was marked as failed on the previous output page, the user is prompted to consider the reasons why he/she was able to answer correctly and the effective learning methods on the learning process. Specifically, the user is presented with the questions, "Why do you think you were able to answer correctly?" and "What learning methods do you think were effective? When the learner has answered all the questions correctly, the system moves to the learning page of the next lesson.

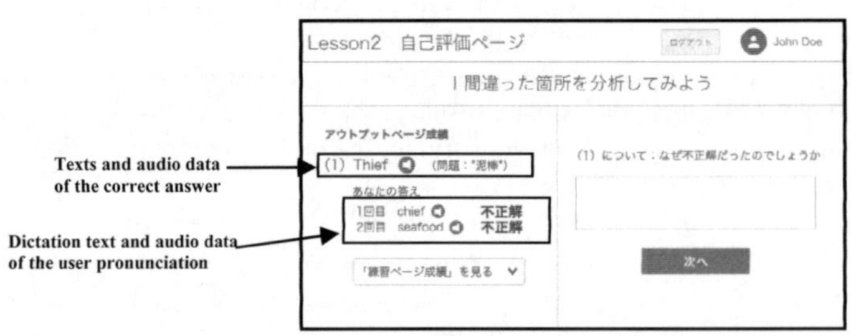

Figure 7. The process of identifying learning problems

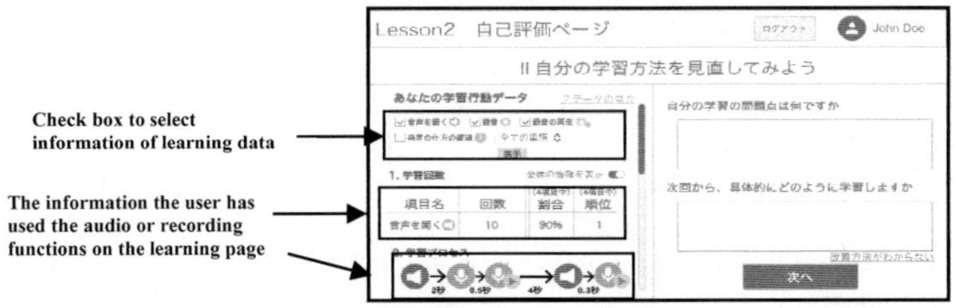

Figure 8. The process of reviewing learning strategy

5. CONCLUSION

This paper describes the need for an English vocabulary learning system that supports the acquisition of vocalization strategy and its system design. After developing the system and formatively evaluating its validity, we would like to examine whether this system will promote the acquisition of vocalization strategy and contribute to the improvement of learners' vocabulary.

ACKNOWLEDGEMENT

This work was supported by JSPS Grants-in-Aid for Scientific Research JP22H00552 and JP21K18134.

REFERENCES

Akamatsu, D., 2017. Relation Between High School Students' Beliefs and Learning Strategies, and Their Academic Achievement in Learning English. *Japanese Journal of Educational Psychology*, Vol. 65, pp. 265–280

Akin, A. et al, 2007. The validity and reliability of the Turkish version of the metacognitive awareness inventory. *Educational Sciences: Theory and Practice*, Vol. 7, No. 2, pp. 671–678

Ashwell, T. and Elam, J.R., 2017. How accurately can the Google Web Speech API recognize and transcribe Japanese L2 English learners' oral production? *The JALT Call Journal,* Vol. 13, No. 1, pp. 59–76

Chen, L. et al, 2019. Design of learning analytics dashboard supporting metacognition. *Proceedings of 16th International Conference Cognition and Exploratory Learning in Digital Age (CELDA 2019)*. Cagliari, Italy, pp. 175–182.

Chen, L. et al, 2020. Factors of the use of learning analytics dashboard that affect metacognition. *Proceedings of 17th International Conference Cognition and Exploratory Learning in Digital Age (CELDA 2020)*. Lisbon, Portugal, pp. 295–302

Dai, Y. and Wu, Z., 2021. Mobile-assisted pronunciation learning with feedback from peers and/or automatic speech recognition: a mixed-methods study. *Computer Assisted Language Learning.*

Durall, E. and Gros, B., 2014. Learning analytics as a metacognitive tool. *Proceedings of 6th International Conference on Computer Supported Education (CSEDU).* Barcelona, Spain, pp. 380–384.

Evers, K. and Chen, S., 2020. Effects of an automatic speech recognition system with peer feedback on pronunciation instruction for adults. *Computer Assisted Language Learning*, pp. 1–21.

Fan, M. Y., 2003. Frequency of use, perceived usefulness, and actual usefulness of second language vocabulary strategies: A study of Hong Kong learners. *The Modern Language Journal*, Vol. 87, No.2, pp. 222–241.

Field, J., 2004. An insight into listeners' problems: Too much bottom-up or too much top-down? *System*, Vol. 32, pp 363–377.

Haslaman, T., 2011. *Effect of an online learning environment on teachers' and students' self-regulated learning skills* (Doctoral dissertation). Hacettepe University, Ankara, Turkey.

Huo, S. and Wang, S., 2017. The effectiveness of phonological-based instruction in English as a Foreign Language students at primary school level: A research synthesis. *Frontiers in Education*, Vol. 2, pp. 1–13.

Jenkins, J., 2000. *The Phonology of English as an International Language*. Oxford University Press, Oxford, UK.

Jumaat, N. F. and Tasir, Z., 2016. A framework of metacognitive scaffolding in learning authoring system through Facebook. *Journal of Educational Computing Research*. Vol. 54, No. 5, pp. 619–659.

Krashen, S. D., 1987. *Principles and Practice in Second Language Acquisition*. Pergamon Press, Oxford, UK.

Ku ̈nsting, J. et al., 2013. Enhancing scientific discovery learning through metacognitive support. *Contemporary Educational Psychology,* Vol. 38, No. 4, pp. 349–360.

Li, S. and Woore, R., 2021. The effects of phonics instruction on L2 phonological decoding and vocabulary learning: An experimental study of Chinese EFL learners. *System*, Vol.103

Liakin, D. et al., 2015. Learning L2 pronunciation with a mobile speech recognizer: French/y/. *CALICO Journal*, Vol. 32, No. 1, pp. 1–25.

Molenaar, I. et al., 2014. Metacognitive scaffolding during collaborative learning: A promising combination. *Metacognition and Learning*, Vol. 9, No. 3, pp. 309–332.

Mroz, A., 2018. Seeing how people hear you: French learners experiencing intelligibility through automatic speech recognition. *Foreign Language Annals*, Vol. 51, No. 3, pp. 617–637.

Nation, I. S. P., 2001. *Learning Vocabulary in Another Language*. Cambridge University Press, Cambridge, UK.

Neri, A. et al., 2008. The effectiveness of computer assisted pronunciation training for foreign language learning by children. *Computer Assisted Language Learning*, Vol. 21, No. 5, pp. 393–408.

Odlin, T., 1989. *Language Transfer: Cross-linguistic Influence in Language Learning*. Cambridge University Press, Cambridge, UK.

Ota, M. et al, 2009. The KEY to the ROCK: Near-homophony in nonnative visual word recognition. *Cognition*, Vol. 111, pp. 263–269.

Oxford, R. L., 1990. *Language Learning Strategies: What Every Teacher Should Know*. Newbury House, New York, USA.

Rasouli, F. and Jafari, K., 2016. A Deeper Understanding of L2 Vocabulary Learning and Teaching: A Review Study. *International Journal of Language and Linguistics.* Vol. 4, No. 1, pp. 40–46.

Schmitt, N., 1997. Vocabulary learning strategies. In N. Schmitt & M. McCarthy (Eds.), *Vocabulary: Description, Acquisition, and Pedagogy*. Cambridge University Press, Cambridge, UK, pp. 199–227.

Schwonke, R. et al, 2013. Metacognitive support promotes an effective use of instructional resources in intelligent tutoring. *Learning and Instruction*, Vol. 23, pp. 136–150.

Schraw, G. and Dennison, R. S., 1994. Assessing metacognitive awareness. *Contemporary Educational Psychology*, Vol. 19, No. 4, pp. 460–475.

Schraw, G. and Moshman, D., 1995. Metacognitive theories. *Educational Psychology Review*, Vol. 7, No. 4, pp. 351–371.

Shimamoto, T., 2002. Why it is necessary to increase vocabulary: the relationship between vocabulary and English language skills. *The English Teachers' Magazine*, Vol. 50, No. 12, pp. 8–10.

Statcounter Global Stats, 2021–2022. *Browser Market Share Japan Sept 2021 – Sept 2022*,

https://gs.statcounter.com/browser-market-share/all/japan

Swain, M., 1998. Focus on form through conscious reflection. In C. Doughty & J. Williams (Eds.), *Focus on Form in Classroom Second Language Acquisition.* Cambridge University Press, New York, USA, pp. 64–81.

Teshima, M., 2011. On Teaching English Pronunciation in Japanese Secondary Education How It Is and How It Should Be. *Journal of the Phonetic Society of Japan*, Vol. 15, No. 1, pp 31–43.

Ueki, R., 2004. Ideal Ways to Teach Students How to Utilize Self-Monitoring Strategies: Beliefs About Learning and Knowledge About Strategies. *Japanese Journal of Educational Psychology*, Vol. 52, pp. 277–286

Winne, P. H. and Perry, N. E., 2000. Measuring self-regulated learning. In M. Boekaerts, P. R. Pintrich & M. Zeidner (Eds.), *Handbook of Self-regulation* (Chapter 16). Academic Press, San Diego, USA..

Yilmaz, F. and Yilmaz, R., 2020. Learning analytics as a metacognitive tool to influence learner transactional distance and motivation in online learning environments, *Innovations in Education and Teaching International.*

Yilmaz, R. and Keser, H., 2017. The impact of interactive environment and metacognitive support on academic achievement and transactional distance in online learning. *Journal of Educational Computing Research*, Vol. 55, No. 1, pp. 95–122.

Yilmaz, R., 2014. *The effect of interaction environment and metacognitive guidance in online learning on academic success, metacognitive awareness and transactional distance* (Doctoral dissertation). Ankara University, Ankara, Turkey.

ENHANCING ONLINE LEARNING FOCUSING ON THE RELATIONSHIP BETWEEN GAZE AND BROWSING MATERIALS

Hironori Takeuchi, Kenji Matsuura and He Lei
Tokushima University, Japan

ABSTRACT

Online synchronous classes and seminars are increasing in universities along with the outbreak of COVID-19. Since the online classes are not in-person condition, it is difficult for a teacher to monitor the learners. In the field of distance education, the need to support learner's concentration has been identified. More effective methods adapted to online classes in universities should be discussed. In this paper, we focus on the teacher's and learners' attention to the material in online real-time classes. We then propose a system that provides feedback on the differences in learners' gaze in order to improve the followability of learners. The proposed system assumes an online environment using Microsoft Teams PowerPointLive and acquires the "gazing point" at every slide-material and "page change history" of the teacher and learners. The results of using the proposed system suggest that it can improve the learner's followability to the teacher.

KEYWORDS

Microsoft Teams, Online Classes, Gazing point, Online Learning, Online Seminars

1. INTRODUCTION

Since COVID-19 widely spread all over the world, universities have been shifting to online classes with synchronous/asynchronous communication tools. According to a report by the Ministry of Education, Culture, Sports, Science and Technology (MEXT), 90% of the 86 national universities offer online classes in Japan. One of the advantages of online classes is needless to carry out in shared place and time. The style is expected to continue. In terms of environmental improvement, MEXT has proposed the "GIGA School" educational reform plan to realize "one device for one student" throughout Japan (MEXT, 2020). Combined with the spread of online classes, the online learning environment in the educational field is gradually being developed.

On the other hand, it is problematic that the motivation of online learners is to be lower. Conventional university classes are carried out in face-to-face situation and include factors such as the teacher's articulate gestures and the classroom environment. These factors have been found to influence learners' attention (Zhang et al, 2018). The field of distance learning has shown the need to support learners' attention and discuss more effective ways to provide those supports (Wang & Antonenko, 2017; Sharma et al, 2016). No clear solution to them has been found so far, and continued discussion is needed.

With the above background, this paper describes the design, development and trial use of a learning support system to enhance the learner's ability to concentrate. Assuming a widely used online class environment, the system is intended to be converted to an educational setting.

2. RELATED WORKS

One of possibilities to objectively estimate a learner's condition in online learning is to measure the electroencephalogram (EEG). Some previous studies have evaluated the α and β wave values of EEG (Yoshida et al, 2016). It is possible to evaluate the subjective level of difficulty to some extent when learners are given learning materials (Umezawa et al, 2016). Therefore, EEG is an effective tool, but it is difficult to use in general online classes because it requires a dedicated tool for measurement at each location of a learner.

By contrast, eye-tracking can be used to assist learners in general online classes. There are various studies that use eye tracking techniques and refer to learners' ability to concentrate. For example, studies have been conducted to understand how the presence of the teacher in the video affects the distribution of the learner's visual attention. It has been shown that the teacher's behavior has a positive impact on the learner (Wang & Antonenko, 2017). In addition, research has been conducted to improve learners' attention. For example, there is an evaluation of whether the learner can follow the instructor (with-me-ness) by analyzing the learner's eye movements. If the learner cannot follow the instructor's gaze beyond a certain point, presenting visual objects to the learner has been to improve the learner's attention (Sharma et al, 2016). Thus, analyzing the learner's gaze may provide a measure of the learner's ability to concentrate, and there is room for further research in situations other than video viewing.

On the other hand, there are also possible ways to utilize the learning history stored in the system. For example, there is a study to grasp the learning status from the page transitions of teaching materials (Nakano et al 2018). In those studies, page transitions have been confirmed to have a relationship with class time, explanation time, and so forth. Although these studies aim to provide feedback to learners, few studies have been found to contribute to a learner's concentration.

Based on the above considerations, the purpose of this paper is to support individual learners' cognition in online classes by focusing on eye movements and reading materials in online classes. We design a system that visualizes the differences between the teacher and the learner and provides feedback to the learner and describe its trial use.

3. METHODOLOGY

The proposed system is designed for synchronous online classes using "Microsoft Teams PowerPointLive", a conferencing tool frequently used in online classes. The greatest feature of this tool is that students can independently change the pages of the teaching material shared by the teacher and students. As with distributed textbooks, students are free to choose which pages of the teaching material they wish to view. We collect eye gaze information from the teacher's and students' web-camera when they use online conferencing tool for remote learning and also analyze Microsoft Teams' Window to collect the history of page changes. The differences between the teacher and students are then visualized using GIF animations and graphs to provide feedback to the learners (Figure 1).

The proposed system was designed with general-purpose specifications for use in widely used online classes. That is, the system runs on a typical teacher's or student's laptop. It requires Python, Microsoft software, and a web-camera or in-camera.

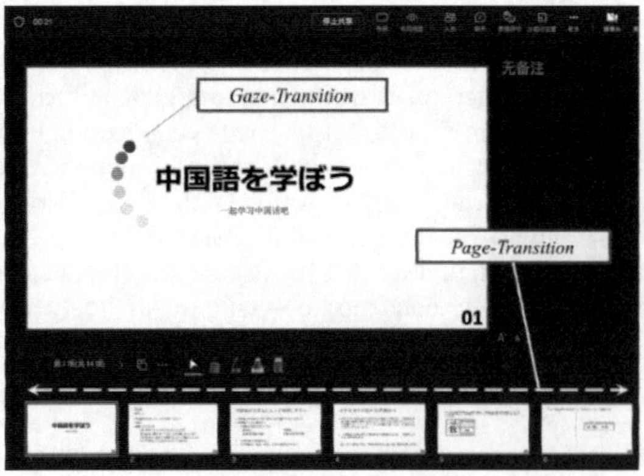

Figure 1. Microsoft Teams PowerPointLive screen. The data collection targets the gaze-transition and page-transition in the teaching materials

3.1 Acquisition of Gaze-Transition Data

Although dedicated devices such as Tobii are commonly used to collect eye tracking data, for versatility, this study designs an eye tracking system that utilizes a web-camera. In this study, we apply "GazeMap" (Park et al 2018), one of the frameworks for this purpose. GazeMap is used and applied for collecting eye tracking information. GazeMap has neural nets for estimating gaze direction and representing the centers of the eyeball, iris, and pupil as abstract figures. One of its functions is applied to obtain gaze coordinates. In order to accommodate general online classes, original modifications are introduced that consider the indefinite distance between the teacher, the learner, and the screen. The distance to the screen is estimated from the face width ratio projected on the screen, and the gazing point coordinates are calculated.

The method of eye detection is shown below, where it calculates the distance to the screen based on the width ratio of the faces on the screen. First, $\boldsymbol{W_i}$ as the width of the face on the screen is defined. Next, the minimum value as $\boldsymbol{W_1} = 45$ and the maximum value as $\boldsymbol{W_2} = 70$ are set. The distance between the learner and the screen is defined as $\boldsymbol{d_i}$, $\boldsymbol{W_1}$ as $\boldsymbol{d_1}$, and $\boldsymbol{W_2}$ as $_2$. In that case, $\boldsymbol{W_i}$ can be calculated by the following equation.

$$W_i = \left(\frac{W_1 - W_2}{d_1 - d_2}\right)(d_i - d_1) + W_1 \tag{1}$$

If the resolution of the screen used is ($\boldsymbol{a} \times \boldsymbol{b}$), the coordinates of the gazing point ($\boldsymbol{X}, \boldsymbol{Y}$) can be calculated as follows.

$$X = d_i \times \tan(yaw) + \frac{a}{2} \tag{2}$$

$$Y = d_i \times \tan(pitch) + \frac{b}{2} \tag{3}$$

The purpose of the proposed system is not to collect data, but to visualize the differences between the teacher and the learners, and to make the learners aware that they are not keeping up with the teacher. Using the teacher's data in class as a reference, the system visualizes and outputs the differences in learners' eye movement and page transitions.

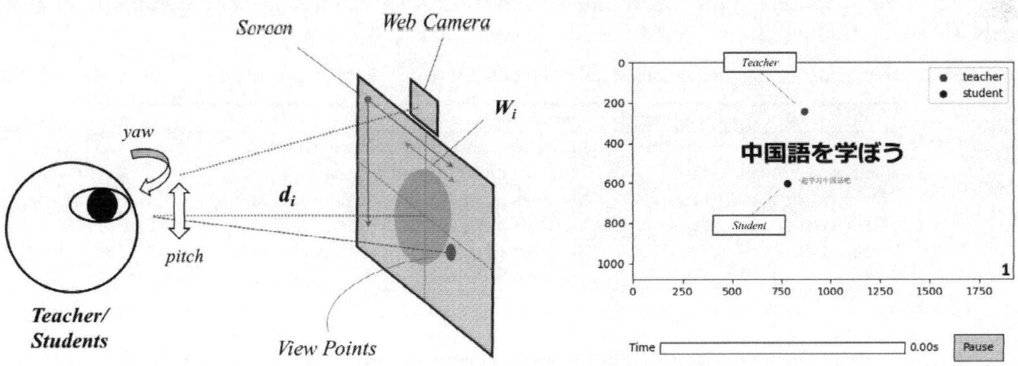

Figure 2. Gaze-transition data acquisition & Feedback content to learner

Feedback content uses GIF animations to represent differences in gazing points. The teacher's and student's gaze information are simultaneously depicted in the teaching material, allowing students to see their eye movement during the lecture through the animation. This output information is based on page-by-page (Figure 2).

3.2 Acquisition of Page-Transition Data

Detection of page switching during online lectures is performed using image recognition technology. The page number region of the slide displayed on the screen is clipped and converted into a numerical value using EasyOCR, an image recognition library in Python.

The screen resolution of the screen and the window differences between the presenter (instructor) and the participants (students) of "Microsoft Teams PowerPointLive" must be taken into account when defining the areas to be detected. These settings need to be made individually according to the environment of the teacher and the learner. In this study, the screen resolution was defined as 1920 × 1080 and the presenter's area as (1156-1230, 733-786). We also defined the participant's region as (1480-1556, 850-910) for region extraction. Feedback on page changes is depicted graphically with page numbers. This feedback is distributed as a single image after the lecture, so that students are aware of their page change history during the lecture (Figure 3).

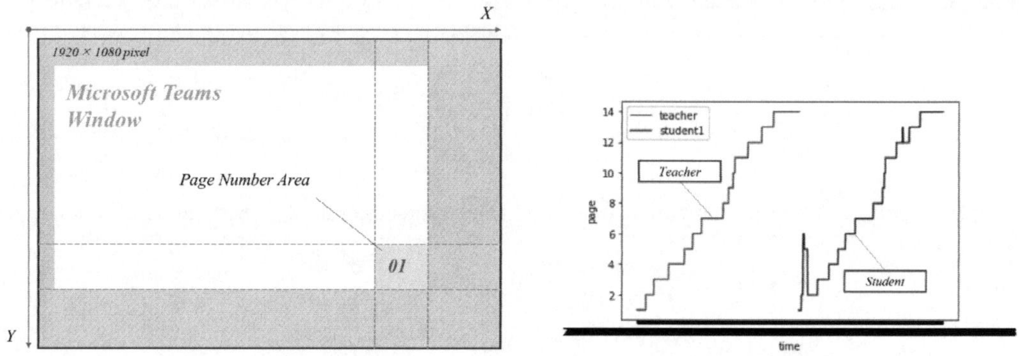

Figure 3. Page-transition data acquisition & Feedback content to learner

There are considerations for feedback on page transitions. Feedback on gazing point differences can be evaluated as correct for the instructor 's gazing point. However, this is not always the case with page transitions. For example, there is a pattern in which the learner checks the page before the teacher for the purpose of independent learning. The purpose of the proposed system is to enhance concentration. In other words, patterns in which the learner is focused on learning, such as self-study, should not compensate for differences with the teacher. To distinguish these situations, we categorized the changes in the student's page transitions as learner models in Table 1. Support is provided only if the learner needs assistance.

Table 1. Learner model of page transitions. Models that do not require support do not need to follow the instructor

Model	Supported	Summary
Sync	No	instructors and students synchronize
Self-study	No	Students ahead of instructors
Delay(small)	Yes	Students are 2-4 pages behind instructors
Delay(large)	Yes	Students are more than 4 pages behind instructors
Repeat(short)	Yes	Students repeatedly reviews (1-2 times)
Repeat(long)	Yes	Students repeatedly reviews (more than 3 times)

4. EXPERIMENTAL USE AND THE RESULTS

Using this system, we conducted an experiment with a mock class. There are 20 subjects in total: 10 Japanese and 10 Chinese beginning students. Within each group, the subjects are divided into an experimental group which uses proposed functions (Group A) and a control group which does not use the proposed system but the ordinary environment (Group B). These two groups are compared and evaluated to measure the effectiveness of the system. The class content was conducted in Japanese and Chinese for the purpose of second language acquisition. The class duration was 10 minutes and 8 seconds, with 14 pages of content. In addition, a simple confirmation test was administered after each class to ensure a certain level of concentration on the class.

The experimental flow consists of two classes. After the first classes, the difference between the teacher's and learner's gaze during the classes is output and fed back to the learners. After the feedback is completed, they take the same class again. Based on the data from these first and second classes, we compare and verify the degree to which students follow the teacher's gazing point.

4.1 Gaze Similarity per Page

The difference of gazing points between the teacher and students is verified for each page. The gazing point data sets in the slides were clustered using the Ward method, and the distance between groups was calculated. Figure 4 shows the mean change of Group A, and Figure 5 shows the mean change of Group B. Note that there are times when the page numbers of the teacher and students do not match because students can freely change pages in this experiment. In this case, the value is uniformly set to "0".

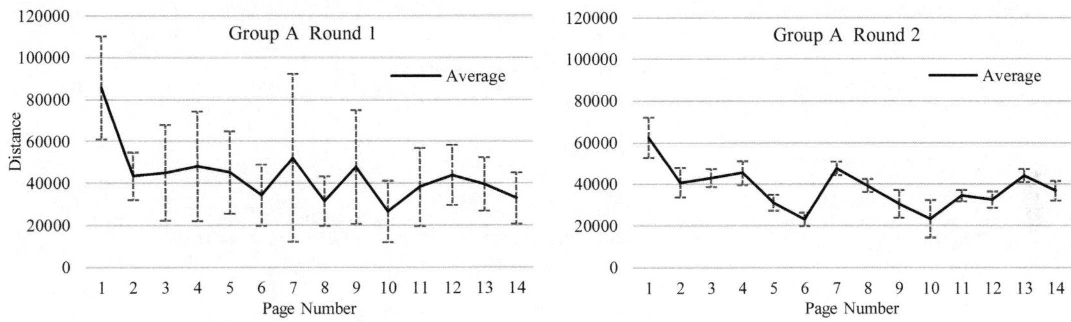

Figure 4. Distance between instructor and student per page in Group A (with feedback)

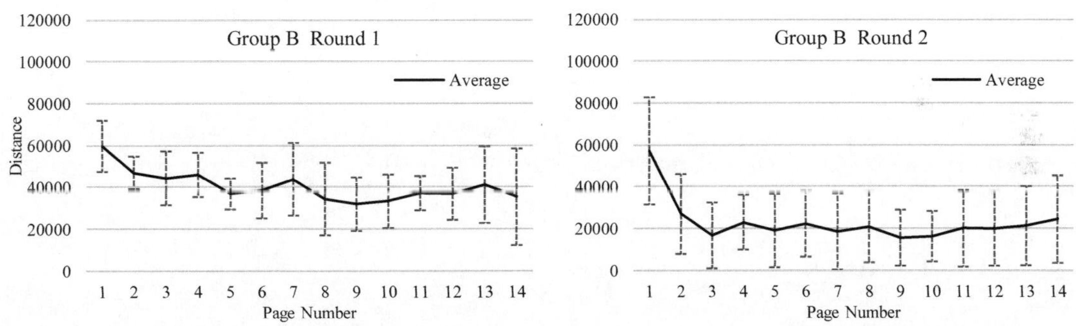

Figure 5. Distance between instructor and student per page in Group B (No feedback)

4.2 Gaze Similarity in Class

Next, we compared the degree of proximity of the gazing points throughout the class using DTW (Dynamic Time Warping). In order to compare the movement of the gazing points more accurately, we transformed the Cartesian coordinate system data into polar coordinate system data to check the similarity of the radius r and declination angle θ. The results for Group A and Group B are shown in Figure 6 and Figure 7, respectively.

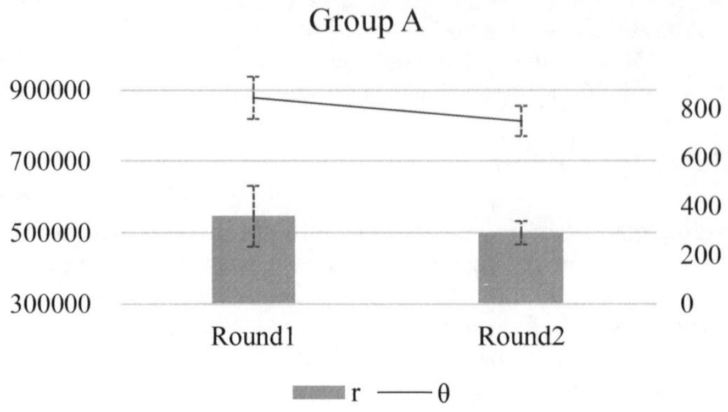

Figure 6. Average DTW score in Group A (with feedback)

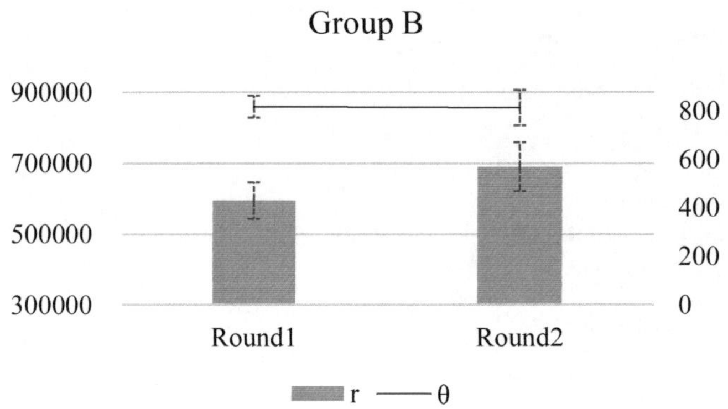

Figure 7. Average DTW score in Group B (No feedback)

5. DISCUSSION

Looking at the results per page, Group A had significantly less variance and tended to converge at a certain distance (Figure 4). This is caused by the feedback of the viewpoint difference, which is corrected to a viewpoint closer to the class teacher's viewpoint. On the other hand, in Group B, the distance is generally closer and the dispersion tended to be larger (Figure 5). This is due to the fact that they had memorized the material to some extent. Furthermore, it can be seen that the students' attention became distracted, and they lost the regularity of their gaze. These results suggest that a variety of feedback from the system would be effective in tracking the teacher's gazing point.

Next, when we look at the class-wide case, Group A shows an improvement in tracking for both radius r and declination angle θ (Figure 6). Convergence was also observed in the variance, indicating that the tracking improved as a result of the feedback as well as the page-by-page feedback. On the other hand, for Group B, the distance between the two images was greater the second time for radius r (Figure 7). The dispersion also tended to increase. This may be due to the fact that the same lesson was repeated twice, which distracted the students' concentration and worsened their tracking performance.

While these results support the effectiveness of feedback using this system, it is also suggested that simply repeating similar content in a synchronous online class result in poor tracking performance.

6. CONCLUSION

We designed a system to visualize the differences in gazing points and content transitions between teachers and students in synchronous online classes, and measured the effect of the system on improving students' following of the teacher.

The results suggest that the feedback of gazing points and page differences is effective and has a certain effect on improving the students' ability to follow the teacher.

In this initial experiment, we evaluated tracking performance by visualizing the gazing point and its feedback but did not take into account differences due to class content or the influence of teacher instruction. In the future, it is necessary to conduct multiple evaluations, taking into account these details. Another limitation of this study is that although it provides clues as to the state of attention to class content, it is difficult to obtain direct corroboration of class comprehension. A new approach is needed for this purpose.

In addition, this differential feedback is presented to the learners after the class, but feedback presented in real time is also possible. Continued evaluation is needed in the future while considering these factors.

ACKNOWLEDGEMENT

This work was supported by JSPS KAKENHI Grant Numbers JP18K11572.

REFERENCES

Mavlankar, A., Agrawal, P., Pang, D., Halawa, S., Cheung, N.M., Girod, B., 2010. An interactive region-of-interest video streaming system for online lecture viewing. *18th International Packet Video Workshop*, 13-14

Conference of Research Collaborators on Improvement of Facilities such as National University Corporation (5th) https://www.mext.go.jp/en/content/20200716-mxt_kokusai-000005414_04.pdf (Accessed 2022/9/18).

Zhang, J., Bourguet, M.L., Venture, G., the effects of video instructor's body language on students' distribution of visual attention: an eye-tracking study. 2018. *Proceedings of the 32nd International BCS Human Computer Interaction Conference (HCI)*,4 – 6.

Umezawa, K., Ishida, T., Saito, T., Nakazawa, M., Hirasawa, S., A judgment method of difficulty of task for a learner using simple electroencephalograph. 2016. *IPSJ Technical Report*, Vol.2016-CE-137, No.4,1-6 (Translated from Japanese)

Yoshida, K., Sakamoto, Y., Miyaji, I., Yamada, K., Analysis comparison of brain waves at the learning status by simple electroencephalographhttps. 2012 *IEICE Tech. Rep*., vol. 112, no. 224, ET2012-35, pp. 37-42, Sept. 2012

Nakano, Y., Furukawa, M., Owatari, T., Kubota S., Sugiya, K., Shimada K., Attempt to analyze the page transition of the learner in class by Levenshtein distance. 2018. *IPSJ Technical Report*, Vol.2018-CLE-26, No.4,1-6 (Translated from Japanese)

Park, S., Spurr, A., Hilliges, O., Deep Pictorial Gaze Estimation. 2018. *Proc. ECCV in LNCS*, Vol. 11217, pp. 741-757

Sharma, K., Alavi, H. S., Jermann, P., \& Dillenbourg, P. A gaze-based learning analytics model: in-video visual feedback to improve learner's attention in MOOCs. 2016. *In Proceedings of the Sixth International Conference on Learning Analytics & Knowledge* (pp. 417–421). Edinburgh, Scotland: ACM

Wang, J., Antonenko, P. D., Instructor presence in instructional video: effects on visual attention, recall, and perceived learning. 2017. *Computers in Human Behavior*, 71, 79-89.

Tokiwa, Y., Sumitomo, H., The current state of e-learning in universities and proposals for the next generation. 2002. *IBM Professional Treatise PROVISION L4063A, 35: 64-73 (*Translated from Japanese).

THE PATTERN OF TEST-TAKING EFFORT ACROSS ITEMS IN COGNITIVE ABILITY TEST: A LATENT CLASS ANALYSIS

Hanif Akhtar
Faculty of Psychology, Universitas Muhammadiyah Malang, Indonesia
Doctoral School of Psychology, ELTE Eotvos Lorand University, Hungary

ABSTRACT

When examinees perceive a test as low stakes, it is logical to assume that some of them will not put out their maximum effort. This condition makes the validity of the test results more complicated. Although many studies have investigated motivational fluctuation across tests during a testing session, only a small number of studies have investigated motivational fluctuation across items within a single test. This study aims to examine the pattern of test-taking effort across items in cognitive ability tests when items are presented in a random order manner. Response Time Effort (RTE) was used as a measure of test-taking effort. This measure calculates the proportion of rapid responses in the test based on the response times for each item. Data from 213 university students completing the inductive reasoning test was examined using latent class analysis. The results suggested that examinees in low-stakes testing have different patterns of effort across items. Examinees who consistently provided a high level of effort across items had higher test performance, test-taking engagement, and RTE. Item position and item difficulty are also correlated negatively with test-taking effort. Implications of these results for researchers and practitioners are discussed.

KEYWORDS

Response Time Effort, Test-Taking Effort, Latent Class Analysis, Low-Stakes Assessment, Cognitive Ability

1. INTRODUCTION

Research in psychometrics often relies on the test taker's motivation to do well on low-stakes assessments (e.g., data collection for validation study). When examinees perceive a test as low-stakes, it is logical to presume that some individuals will not put out their maximum effort, especially if there are no personal consequences to their test performance. This circumstance makes the validity and interpretation of the test results more complicated. We define low-stakes testing as any testing that has no meaningful consequence for examinees (e.g., survey). Conversely, high-stakes testing has a meaningful consequence for examinees (e.g., personnel selection). It should be noted that even though there are no personal effects on test performance, many examinees appear to put up much effort when taking low-stakes tests (e.g., Barry & Finney, 2016; Pastor et al., 2019; Wise & Kingsbury, 2016; Wise & Kong, 2005). Thus, it is essential to identify those examinees who put in a low effort because that could lead to bias in the test data.

Several measures have been developed to measure test-taking effort. The most popular measures are those that use self-reports that should be completed right after taking the test (e.g., Freund et al., 2011; Knekta & Eklöf, 2015; Sundre & Moore, 2002). However, using self-report has three fundamental limitations. First, it is unclear how honestly examinees will inform their test-taking effort. Second, it is mildly intrusive and takes time. Third, self-reported measures only give a global index of effort during a test, making it difficult to investigate any variations in the effort that occur throughout a test event.

Another way of measuring test-taking motivation that involves the whole test-taking process is based on response times using Response Time Effort (RTE; Wise & Kong, 2005). RTE can be implemented in computer-based tests based on the assumption that unmotivated examinees will answer too quickly (i.e., before they have time to read and fully consider the item) when administered an item. This measure attempts to estimate the percentage of rapid guessing behavior in the test based on the reaction times for each item. Unlike self-report, which provides a global measure of effort, RTE would allow researchers to investigate changes in the examinees' effort during a testing session because the data of response time is available for each item.

Several studies have found that test-taking efforts can rise or fall during testing sessions (Barry et al., 2010; Barry & Finney, 2016; Pastor et al., 2019; Penk & Richter, 2017). These studies illustrate how test-taking efforts change across tests within a single testing session but do not report how efforts change across items. In addition, several item characteristics might influence the test-taking effort. For example, item location (Pastor et al., 2019; Wise & Kingsbury, 2016), item difficulty (Asseburg & Frey, 2013), item length (Pastor et al., 2019), and item type (Sundre & Kitsantas, 2004) affect test-taking effort. By using RTE, researchers can explore the pattern of test-taking effort during a single test. In research-based testing, this is essential. Knowledge of how test-taking effort varies across items can enlighten the research design. For example, patterns characterized by engagement in the first half of a test might indicate reducing a test. Or, if the testing is used to estimate item parameters, it might be recommended to order the item randomly.

Although RTE is beneficial over self-report scales for discovering the pattern of test-taking effort across items within a single test, only a few researchers used it in research-based testing (e.g., Pastor et al., 2019; Wise & Kingsbury, 2016). Wise and Kingsbury (2016) conducted the study in the context of a single adaptive test administered to K-12 students. At the same time, Pastor et al. (2019) conducted the study in the context of three different low-stakes tests for higher education program assessment administered to undergraduate students. The present study was built on the previous work of Pastor et al. (2019) and Wise and Kingsbury (2016) by exploring whether individuals differ in their test-taking effort patterns across items within a test when items are presented in random order manner. Specifically, a latent class analysis (LCA; Lazarsfeld & Henry, 1968) was used with data collected from undergraduate students completing a cognitive ability test. There are three research questions in this study.

RQ1. Do participants show different patterns of effort?

RQ2. Do participants with different patterns of effort differ on other associated variables (e.g., test performance , self-reported effort) in expected ways?

RQ3. How do item characteristics (i.e., item position and item difficulty) relate to effort?

To pursue RQ1, LCA was performed to determine the presence of different patterns of test-taking effort. As RQ1 is fully exploratory, there is no hypothesis for this research question. To address RQ2, subsequent analyses were performed to provide evidence of the validity of the newly emerging LCA classes. The hypothesis for RQ2 was that examinees with high and relatively consistent effort across all items have higher test-taking effort (measured by RTE and self-report) and test performance. Spearman correlation was run in order to comprehend the variation in test-taking effort across items (RQ3). The results of this study together reveal whether various patterns of solution behavior exist when items are given in a random sequence and whether item characteristics (item difficulty or item location) explain variations in test-taking efforts. The hypothesis for RQ3 was that both item difficulty and item position were negatively correlated with test-taking effort.

2. METHODS

2.1 Data Source

Data were collected for research purposes aimed at developing a reasoning test. A total of 213 participants (154 females) participated in this study. Participants were undergraduate students in the Faculty of Psychology at the University of Muhammadiyah Malang, Indonesia, aged 18 to 23 years (M = 19.89, SD = 0.78). Participants were recruited through the instructor's information in the class during the course of psychological test construction. All participants completed the online inductive reasoning test.

2.2 Measures

The data from 'the odd one out' test were used to determine how motivational patterns fluctuate across items. The odd one out test is a cognitive-based multiple-choice measure intended to measure inductive reasoning. There are six pictures in an item, and one out of six pictures has the most different characteristics based on a certain principle. Examinees were asked to find one picture that was most different from the others. Our research team developed the test. For online data collection, the platform PsyToolkit was used (Stoet, 2010, 2016). Each item was displayed on a separate page. Item reaction time was calculated as the number of milliseconds between an item appearing and examinees clicking "next" to move on to the next item.

Two measures of test-taking efforts were used: RTE and self-report. RTE was an average of Solution-Behavior (SB) of all items or scales answered. RTE values near 1 indicate high effort, and values near 0 indicate low effort. Examinees' response was classified as SB if they responded to the item above the threshold (scored 1). In contrast, if examinees responded to the item below the threshold, their response should be considered rapid-guessing behavior (scored 0). The 10% Normative Threshold (NT10) approach (Wise & Ma, 2012) was used to determine the threshold. This approach proposes that 10% of the average response time be used for the threshold. For example, if it takes participants an average of 50 seconds to respond to an item, a NT10 would be 5 seconds. If participants responded to the item above the threshold, their response should be SB.

At the end of the testing session, two self-report items measuring examinees' attitudes toward the test were presented. One item measures test-taking efforts (i.e., "I took this test seriously"), and the other item measures test-taking engagement (i.e., "I enjoy doing tests"). These items were responded to on a five-point Likert scale ranging from 1 (strongly disagree) to 5 (strongly agree).

2.3 Data Analyses

To answer RQ1, latent class analysis (LCA; Lazarsfeld & Henry, 1968). LCA was performed using SB indices to investigate the number of different patterns of test-taking effort. Several LCA models were fit to the data, with each model specifying a different number of classes (K). Each LCA model has a log-likelihood (LL) value, with values closer to zero suggesting a higher likelihood of the data. Because the LL will always be closer to zero for models with more classes, The Bayesian information criterion (BIC; Schwarz, 1978) and The Akaike information criterion (AIC; Akaike, 1974) were used to evaluate model-data fit. The model with the lowest BIC and AIC values was deemed to be the optimal one. The preliminary analysis showed similar results to Pastor et al. (2019) study, indicating that for three-class models, the condition numbers were fewer than 10-6. As a result, only one- and two-class models were fit to the data in this investigation. LCA was performed using 'sirt' package (Robitzsch, 2021) in R software (R Core Team, 2013).

To answer RQ2, examinees were classified to the class with the highest posterior probability. The resultant class membership was employed in the t-test analysis to determine the association between class membership and each associated variable. Test performance, self-reported effort, self-reported engagement, and RTE were used as associated variables. Classes with higher and more consistent engagement in test-taking effort were expected to have higher test performance, self-reported effort, and RTE than classes with lower and less consistent engagement in solution behavior.

To answer RQ3, item difficulty (based on Rasch analysis), item position, and SB indices were correlated. SB index was a measure of test-taking efforts across items based on the average SB of all examinees' answers on a particular item. SB indices values near 1 indicate high effort, and values near 0 indicate low effort.

3. RESULTS

3.1 Preliminary Analysis

Preliminary analysis was conducted to examine descriptive statistics and intercorrelation among variables studied. A summary of the preliminary analysis is presented in table 1. RTE significantly positively correlated with test-taking engagement ($r = .22$, $p < .001$), test-taking effort ($r = .50$, $p < .001$), and test performance ($r = .38$, $p < .001$). It indicates that RTE was a valid measure of test-taking efforts. There are no gender differences in test-taking engagement, test-taking effort, RTE, and performance.

Table 1. Descriptive statistics and intercorrelation among variables

Variables	Female		Male		t	1	2	3
	N	Mean (SD)	N	Mean (SD)				
1. Engagement	154	3.3.2 (1.11)	59	3.44 (1.13)	0.68			
2. Effort	154	3.93 (0.99)	59	3.88 (1.04)	-0.31	.45***		
3. RTE	154	0.98 (0.09)	59	0.96 (0.11)	-1.43	.22**	.50***	
4. Performance	154	-0.01 (0.80)	59	0.03 (0.75)	0.31	.12	.25***	.38***

Note: RTE = Response Time Effort, ***P < .001

3.2 Pattern of Test-Taking Effort

Table 2 displays the outcomes of the one- and two-class LCA models. The AIC and BIC for the two-class models were lower than for the one-class models, indicating support for two-class solutions. The likelihood ratio tests provided similar support, indicating a considerably superior fit for the two-class models. Figure 1 depicts the estimated probabilities of engaging in test-taking effort for the two-class solutions based on item position and class. Class 1 is distinguished by lower probability and higher variability in solution behavior across items. Class 2 encompasses the majority of the examinee population and is distinguished by high and relatively constant engagement in solution behavior across all items.

Table 2. Fit indices for latent class analysis models

Model	loglike	Deviance	Npars	Nobs	AIC	BIC	LRT p
One-class	-1164.21	2328.43	50	213	2428.43	2596.50	-
Two-class	-622.93	1245.86	101	213	**1447.87**	**1787.36**	**< 0.001**

Note: Npars = number of parameter estimated, Nobs = number of sample, AIC = Akaike information criterion, BIC = Bayesian information criterion, LRT p = p-value of Likelihood Ratio Test

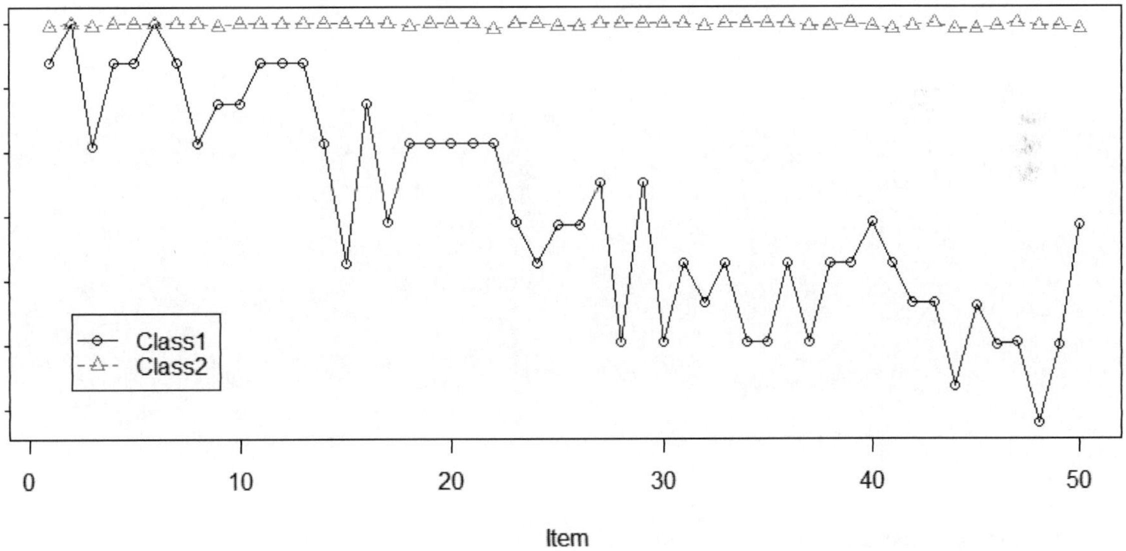

Figure 1. Estimates of the probability of engagement in solution behavior by item position using the two latent-classes model

3.3 Association between Class Membership and Auxiliary Variables

In the t-test analysis, the resultant class membership was employed to capture the relationship between class membership and each auxiliary variable. The results of the analyses using auxiliary variables (test-taking engagement, test-taking efforts, RTE, and test performance) are shown in Table 3. There were statistically significant differences across groups for all auxiliary variables. Every comparison has a substantial effect size regarding practical significance, with Cohen's d greater than 0.80 (Sawilowsky, 2009). Not only were these disparities notable, but they also pointed in a direction that supported the notion that Class 1 is less motivated than Class 2. Specifically, Class 1 had a substantially lower test-taking engagement, test-taking effort, RTE, and test performance relative to Class 2.

Table 3. T-test results across class membership

	Class	N	Mean (SD)	*t*	*d*
Engagement	1	17	2.53 (0.87)	3.25***	1.82
	2	196	3.43 (1.11)		
Effort	1	17	2.47 (1.07)	6.80***	1.72
	2	196	4.04 (0.90)		
RTE	1	17	0.72 (0.21)	18.96***	4.79
	2	196	1.00 (0.01)		
Performance	1	17	-0.85 (0.95)	4.86***	1.23
	2	196	0.07 (0.73)		

Note: RTE = Response Time Effort, ****p* < .001

3.4 Item Characteristic Analyses

Spearman correlation analysis found that SB indices is significantly negatively correlated with item difficulty ($r = -.44$, $p < .01$) and item position ($r = -.88$, $p < 0.01$). The test-taking effort appears to decline significantly as the test progresses and items become difficult. Figure 2 shows the scatterplot for the correlation between SB indices and item characteristics.

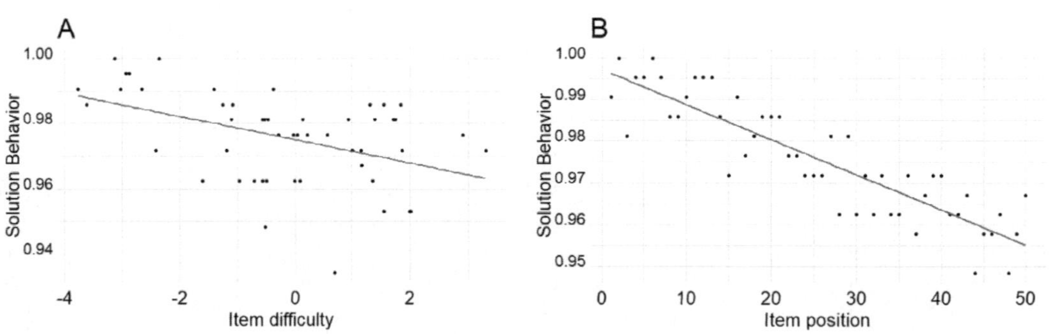

Figure 2. Correlation between SB indices and item difficulty (A) and item position (B)

4. DISCUSSION

Although some studies have examined the motivational change between tests during a testing session, few have focused on motivational change across test items. LCA was used in combination with fixed-item testing to investigate if there are patterns of test-taking effort across items and which item properties explain variations in test-taking effort. Two types of examinees with distinct patterns of test-taking effort across items were identified. The first class, which comprised 8% of the population, exhibited considerably less and more varied effort throughout the tests. The second class, which included 92% of the population, demonstrated high and consistent effort throughout the tests. This result is consistent with previous studies (Barry & Finney, 2016;

Pastor et al., 2019; Wise & Kingsbury, 2016; Wise & Kong, 2005) that even though there are no personal consequences for test performance, many examinees appear to put up a lot of effort when taking the test.

The two-class solution was supported by additional analysis. Examinees who consistently engaged in solution behavior across items showed greater levels of test-taking engagement, test-taking effort, RTE, and test performance than examinees who were prone to rapid-guessing behavior. Item characteristic analyses indicated that the probability of solution behavior decreases as item position increases. This finding is consistent with previous studies (Pastor et al., 2019; Wise & Kingsbury, 2016) despite the difference in the order of item presentation. Item difficulty was also negatively correlated with test-taking effort. However, the correlation coefficient was smaller than the correlation between test-taking effort and item position. This result indicates that item position has a greater influence on test-taking effort.

The findings of this study have several implications for testing practices. First, when data collection aims to estimate item parameters on a cognitive ability test (e.g., item difficulty level), randomly ordering the item may be a good practice to reduce the item-order effect. This result suggested that items presented at the end of the test tend to be answered carelessly by the examinees, which causes the estimated parameter to be misleading. It implies that the incorrect answers given by the examinees to the items presented at the end of the test do not necessarily indicate that the items are difficult. It could be the result of low test-taking effort. Thus, randomly ordering the item might reduce this item-order effect. Based on these findings, practitioners could consider using shorter tests in low-stakes testing contexts.

Second, providing a motivator item at the beginning of the test might be beneficial to maximizing examinees' test-taking effort. A motivator item is a relatively easy item. From the expectancy-value theory (Wigfield & Eccles, 2000) perspective, an easy item could lead to high expectancy, resulting in a high effort. In addition, these findings indicate that easier items resulted in a higher test-taking effort. Thus, using an easier item in the context of low-stakes testing might reduce the source of test score invalidity due to low test-taking efforts. This practice is important especially if test results are used for group comparison studies (e.g., comparing cognitive abilities across nations).

Third, it is found that the two classes differ significantly in their test performance. When a test is regarded as low-stakes for examinees yet high-stakes at higher levels, the validity of the interpretation of the findings is jeopardized. When less motivated examinees score below their real ability, the test-taking effort may be a cause of bias. This issue is not only on an individual level but also on a group level, especially when different groups have different motivations and their outcomes are compared. Based on these findings, practitioners may choose to include some sort of motivational intervention to conclude their assessments. The article from Rios (2021) provides a good review based on empirical studies about how to increase test-taking effort in low-stakes assessments.

This study has several limitations. First, this study only examined the pattern of test-taking effort in one kind of cognitive ability test. A different test might have different results as item type affects test-taking behavior (Pastor et al., 2019; Sundre & Kitsantas, 2004). Second, gender was not equally distributed in this study, with twice the number of females. As males were found rapidly guess nearly twice as often as females (Soland, 2018), the results of this study might be influenced. Third, examinees are limited to university students. Fourth, this study used NT10 only to determine the threshold for RTE.

5. CONCLUSION

In summary, this study found that examinees in low-stakes testing have different patterns of engagement in test-taking efforts across items. Examinees who engaged in solution behavior consistently across items had higher test-performance, test-taking engagement, test-taking effort, and RTE than examinees who had a lower engagement in solution behavior. The results of item characteristic analyses indicated that item position and item difficulty are negatively correlated with test-taking effort. Due to several limitations of the study mentioned previously, this study should be considered a preliminary examination of the pattern of test-taking effort across items in the cognitive ability test. Further investigation with a different test, sample characteristics, and analysis procedures should be performed to examine the generalizability of these findings.

REFERENCES

Akaike, H. (1974). A New Look at the Statistical Model Identification. *IEICE Transactions on Automatic Control*, *19*(6), 716–723. https://doi.org/10.1093/ietfec/e90-a.12.2762

Asseburg, R., & Frey, A. (2013). Too hard , too easy , or just right ? The relationship between effort or boredom and ability-difficulty fit. *Psychological Test and Assessment Modeling*, *55*(1), 92–104.

Barry, C. L., & Finney, S. J. (2016). Modeling Change in Effort Across a Low-Stakes Testing Session: A Latent Growth Curve Modeling Approach. *Applied Measurement in Education*, *29*(1), 46–64. https://doi.org/10.1080/08957347.2015.1102914

Barry, C. L., Horst, S. J., Finney, S. J., Brown, A. R., & Kopp, J. P. (2010). Do examinees have similar test-taking effort? a high-stakes question for low-stakes testing. *International Journal of Testing*, *10*(4), 342–363. https://doi.org/10.1080/15305058.2010.508569

Freund, P. A., Kuhn, J. T., & Holling, H. (2011). Measuring current achievement motivation with the QCM: Short form development and investigation of measurement invariance. *Personality and Individual Differences*, *51*(5), 629–634. https://doi.org/10.1016/j.paid.2011.05.033

Knekta, E., & Eklöf, H. (2015). Modeling the Test-Taking Motivation Construct Through Investigation of Psychometric Properties of an Expectancy-Value-Based Questionnaire. *Journal of Psychoeducational Assessment*, *33*(7), 662–673. https://doi.org/10.1177/0734282914551956

Lazarsfeld, P. F., & Henry, N. W. (1968). *Latent structure analysis*. Houghton-Mifflin.

Pastor, D. A., Ong, T. Q., & Strickman, S. N. (2019). Patterns of Solution Behavior across Items in Low-Stakes Assessments. *Educational Assessment*, *24*(3), 189–212. https://doi.org/10.1080/10627197.2019.1615373

Penk, C., & Richter, D. (2017). Change in test-taking motivation and its relationship to test performance in low-stakes assessments. *Educational Assessment, Evaluation and Accountability*, *29*(1), 55–79. https://doi.org/10.1007/s11092-016-9248-7

R Core Team. (2013). *R: A Language and Environment for Statistical Computing*. R Foundation for Statistical Computing. http://www.r-project.org

Rios, J. (2021). Improving Test-Taking Effort in Low-Stakes Group-Based Educational Testing: A Meta-Analysis of Interventions. *Applied Measurement in Education*, *34*(2), 85–106. https://doi.org/10.1080/08957347.2021.1890741

Robitzsch, A. (2021). *sirt: Supplementary Item Response Theory Models*.

Sawilowsky, S. S. (2009). New Effect Size Rules of Thumb. *Journal of Modern Applied Statistical Methods*, *8*(2), 597–599. https://doi.org/10.22237/jmasm/1257035100

Schwarz, G. (1978). Estimating the dimension of a model. *The Annals of Statistics*, *6*(2), 461–464.

Soland, J. (2018). Are achievement gap estimates biased by differential student test effort? Putting an important policy metric to the test. *Teachers College Record*, *121*(12), 1–26. https://doi.org/10.1177/016146811812001202

Stoet, G. (2010). PsyToolkit: A software package for programming psychological experiments using Linux. *Behavior Research Methods 2010 42:4*, *42*(4), 1096–1104. https://doi.org/10.3758/BRM.42.4.1096

Stoet, G. (2016). PsyToolkit: A Novel Web-Based Method for Running Online Questionnaires and Reaction-Time Experiments. *Https://Doi.Org/10.1177/0098628316677643*, *44*(1), 24–31. https://doi.org/10.1177/0098628316677643

Sundre, D. L., & Moore, D. L. (2002). The Student Opinion Scale: A measure of examinee motivation. *Assessment Update*, *14*(1), 8–9.

Sundre, Donna L., & Kitsantas, A. (2004). An exploration of the psychology of the examinee: Can examinee self-regulation and test-talking motivation predict consequential and non-consequential test performance? *Contemporary Educational Psychology*, *29*(1), 6–26. https://doi.org/10.1016/S0361-476X(02)00063-2

Wigfield, A., & Eccles, J. S. (2000). Expectancy-value theory of achievement motivation. *Contemporary Educational Psychology*, *25*(1), 68–81. https://doi.org/10.1006/ceps.1999.1015

Wise, S. L., & Kingsbury, G. G. (2016). Modeling Student Test-Taking Motivation in the Context of an Adaptive Achievement Test. *Journal of Educational Measurement*, *53*(1), 86–105. https://doi.org/10.1111/jedm.12102

Wise, S. L., & Kong, X. (2005). Response time effort: A new measure of examinee motivation in computer-based tests. *Applied Measurement in Education*, *18*(2), 163–183. https://doi.org/10.1207/s15324818ame1802_2

Wise, S. L., & Ma, L. (2012). Setting Response Time Thresholds for a CAT Item Pool: The Normative Threshold Method. In *Annual meeting of the National Council on Measurement in Education*.

PREDICTING NON-ROUTINE MATHEMATICAL PROBLEM-SOLVING ANXIETY OF NINTH GRADERS

Emre Dinç[1], Dilek Sezgin-Memnun[2], Eunseo Lee[1] and Bünyamin Aydın[3]
[1]The Pennsylvania State University, University Park, PA, United States of America
[2]Uludag University, Bursa, Turkey
[3]Necmettin Erbakan University, Konya, Turkey

ABSTRACT

This study investigated how motivational orientations and learning strategies predict ninth graders' non-routine mathematical problem-solving anxiety. Non-routine mathematical problem-solving anxiety classification and prediction were investigated through TwoStep cluster analysis, linear discriminant analysis, and logistic regression. 274 ninth graders participated in the study. The participants were clustered based on their problem-solving achievements and test anxiety levels: high-level and low-level problem-solving anxiety. Extrinsic goal orientation, rehearsal, and peer learning were significant classifiers. Intrinsic goal orientation, self-efficacy, rehearsal, and help-seeking were significant predictors for ninth graders' non-routine mathematical problem-solving anxiety.

KEYWORDS

High School Education, Motivation, Problem-Solving, Rehearsal, Peer Learning, Help-Seeking

1. INTRODUCTION

In the current high school education, academic performance, including mathematics performance, is predominantly measured through students' test scores (e.g., Breslau et al., 2009; Suárez-Álvarez et al., 2014). Accordingly, test anxiety acts as a negative factor that decreases academic performance (Rana & Mahmood, 2010; von der Embse et al., 2018) and mathematics success (Morosanova et al., 2020; Wang & Davaanyam, 2012). In terms of math problem-solving, research (e.g., Sharp et al., 2000) reports that reduced anxiety is positively associated with increased math problem-solving achievement. In addition, many studies support this association between anxiety and mathematical problem-solving while adding additional findings such that motivational factors, including self-efficacy, mediate the effects of anxiety (Hoffman, 2010; Irhamna, 2020). Considering that motivational strategies influence ninth graders' mathematical problem-solving achievements (Dinc et al., 2020), this study examined test anxiety and mathematical problem-solving achievement simultaneously, named *mathematical problem-solving anxiety* (hereafter *problem-solving anxiety*).

Many studies have been conducted on high school students' academic motivation and learning strategy use. In general, they are considered highly extrinsically motivated to learn and give high value to learning tasks, while they have a low level of test anxiety (Gbollie & Keamu, 2017). For their mathematics achievements, task value, time and study environment, self-efficacy, extrinsic goal orientation, peer learning, and organization are significant predictors (Erdem-Keklik & Keklik, 2013). Regarding learning strategies, high school students utilize rehearsal and organization strategies while learning along with less help-seeking from their peers or instructors compared to other strategies (Gbollie & Keamu, 2017).

Ninth graders, in particular, are more worried about mathematics, their dropout rate is higher than other grade levels, and they struggle academically (Benner, 2017; McGee-Carlton, 2018; Wigfield & Meece, 1988). Also, they are seen to have moderate levels of intrinsic and extrinsic goal orientation, task value, control of learning beliefs, and self-efficacy (El-Adl & Alkharusi, 2020). On the other hand, Gasco et al. (2014) investigated motivational orientations and learning strategies in mathematics during the transition from eighth to ninth grade. Ninth graders got higher scores in rehearsal, elaboration, organization, metacognitive self-regulation, time and study environment, and help-seeking strategies.

1.1 Math Problem-Solving, Motivational Orientations, and Learning Strategies

Math problems have a significant place in mathematics and mathematics learning (Verschaffel et al., 2020). In mathematics literature, there are routine and non-routine mathematical problems. Routine mathematical problems are the ones that can be solved with "existing knowledge of method, algorithm, technique or formula" (Abdullah et al., 2014, p. 19). Non-routine mathematical problems are the ones challenging the solver to think and reason more and differently (Lee & Chen, 2009). Non-routine mathematical problems are encouraged to develop reasoning abilities (Bibi et al., 2019). Snyder (1998) underscored problem-solving as the core of mathematics, which requires a problem-solver to be creative to find the appropriate strategies during the problem-solving process. The mathematical problem-solving process helps students' critical thinking skill development and vice versa (Firdaus et al., 2015; Peter, 2012). Effendi and Fatimah (2020) indicated that problem-solving is one of the characteristics of higher-order thinking and investigated creative problem-solving in mathematics concepts. Students who received creative problem-solving instruction showed high-level mathematical thinking skills, which coincide with reasoning and critical thinking. According to Puteh and Ibrahim (2010), learners usually demonstrate a high level of extrinsic goal orientation and task value but a low level of intrinsic goal orientation during mathematical problem-solving.

Peer learning is effective in learning mathematics, particularly during planning and facilitating the learning process (Cheng & Walters, 2009). Peer learning is encouraged among groups of students at the same age level but can be successfully achieved either among groups of students with different academic capabilities or with a similar level of capability (Robinson et al., 2005). Academically more capable students would help others who are less academically capable, or the students who have the same academic capability would study and learn together. Peer learning supports knowledge construction through mathematical problem-solving (Sezgin-Memnun et al., 2019). Help-seeking is looking for support from others. The assistance can come from a peer or instructor. So, help-seeking may lead to peer learning.

1.2 Purpose of the Study and Research Questions

Test anxiety, which is related to evaluation in general, and math anxiety, which is anxiety toward mathematics, have long been research subjects in the educational field (Ahmed et al., 2012; von der Embse et al., 2018). Students' mathematical problem-solving achievements were examined in the light of learning approaches and strategies before (Effendi & Fatimah, 2020). Test anxiety during mathematical problem-solving is the central point of this study. We studied ninth graders' non-routine mathematical problem-solving achievements and test anxiety levels since the transition from middle school to ninth grade affects students' academic achievements, and ninth grade is also vital for high school education (McCallumore & Sparapani, 2010; McIntosh & White, 2006; Warren et al., 2011). These research questions guided the study:

1. How can ninth graders be clustered according to mathematical problem-solving success and test anxiety?
2. How can ninth graders' problem-solving anxiety be classified using motivational orientations and learning strategies?
3. How do motivational orientations and learning strategies predict ninth graders' problem-solving anxiety?

2. METHOD

2.1 Participants and Setting

Two hundred and seventy-four ninth graders participated in the study. They were from four different high schools in eastern Turkey, and all participants had taken the national examination for high school after the eighth grade. One of the four high schools was Science High School (N = 59; n(female) = 35, n(male) = 24), which is a type of high school with high academic success, and three were Anatolian High School (N = 215; n(female) = 112, n(male) = 103), which is a type of high school with moderate academic success in Turkey.

2.2 Data Collection

Motivated Strategies for Learning Questionnaire (MSLQ) (Pintrich et al., 1991), scored on a 7-point Likert scale, was used in the study, and the scale was translated to Turkish by Karadeniz et al. (2008) for 12-18-year-old students. The MSLQ's Turkish version has 70 items and 15 subscales: intrinsic goal orientation (IGO), extrinsic goal orientation (EGO), task value (TV), control of learning beliefs (CLB), self-efficacy for learning and performance (SE), test anxiety (TA), rehearsal (R), elaboration (E), organization (O), critical thinking (CT), metacognitive self-regulation (MSR), time and study environment (T/S), effort regulation (ER), peer learning (PL), and help-seeking (HS). The original subscales' alpha levels ranged between 0.52 and 0.93. The Turkish version's corrected item-total correlations ranged between 0.15 and 0.68. The Cronbach alpha values for the subscales with five or more items raged between 0.66 to 0.85 in this study. The inter-item correlations for the subscales with less than five items ranged between 0.23 and 0.38, which are ideal (Clark & Watson, 1995). *The non-routine mathematical problem-solving test* consists of ten problems. The researchers prepared the test by reviewing the mathematics course books. Each question addressed at least one different problem-solving strategy. Two mathematics teachers' opinions were taken on the problems' language proficiency, clarity, comprehensibility, and scope. The problems were revised according to the teachers' feedback. The Cronbach's alpha value for the problem-solving test was 0.80 in this study.

2.3 Data Analysis

An answer key was prepared to assign scores to problem-solving test responses. Correct answers got 2 points, incomplete answers got 1 point, and not answered or incorrect answers got 0 points. The possible score range in the problem-solving test was 0-20. Test anxiety subscale in MSLQ was used for clustering participants along with problem-solving test scores. For this purpose, a TwoStep cluster analysis was used. A linear discriminant analysis was conducted to investigate how motivational orientations and learning strategies classify problem-solving anxiety. Logistic regression was performed to examine how motivational orientations and learning strategies predict ninth graders' problem-solving anxiety. SPSS 27 was used.

3. RESULTS

3.1 Research Question 1: How can Ninth Graders be Clustered According to Mathematical Problem-solving Success and Test Anxiety?

The participants were clustered into two groups with Schwarz's Bayesian Criterion and log-likelihood distance measure. 0.5 (good) Silhouette score and 1.42 ratio of cluster sizes for two groups demonstrated the appropriateness of the two groups.

The participants were grouped according to problem-solving success and test anxiety levels. The ones with a low level of problem-solving success and a high level of test anxiety (= high-level problem-solving anxiety; Group A) are 161 (58.8%) students. The ones with a high level of problem-solving and low level of test anxiety (=low-level problem-solving anxiety; Group B) are 113 (41.2%) students. There were large significant differences between groups' test anxiety levels ($t(272) = 4.20$, $p < 0.001$, Cohen's $d = 0.51$). and problem-solving success ($t(167) = 25.49$, $p < 0.001$, Cohen's $d = 3.25$).

3.2 Research Question 2: How can Ninth Graders' Problem-solving Anxiety be Classified Using Motivational Orientations and Learning Strategies?

A linear discriminant analysis was conducted to identify how motivational orientations and learning strategies can classify problem-solving anxiety levels. Pearson correlation was calculated to see the intercorrelation levels among variables (Table 1), and one strongly related variable pair was found:

elaboration and metacognitive self-regulation ($r > 0.7$ = strong) (Moore et al., 2013). This relationship would make the interpretation of the results difficult if one or two of these two significantly classified the participants' problem-solving anxiety. (None of the two variables were found significant.)

Table 1. Correlations between variables

	1	2	3	4	5	6	7	8	9	10	11	12	13
1.IGO	-												
2.EGO	.38**	-											
3.TV	.59**	.44**	-										
4.CLB	.36**	.29**	.31**	-									
5.SE	.44**	.20**	.52**	.27**	-								
6.R	.34**	.43**	.30**	.20**	.30**	-							
7.E	.43**	.26**	.41**	.09	.43**	.58**	-						
8.O	.39**	.38**	.38**	.12*	.42**	.65**	.67**	-					
9.CT	.39**	.20**	.30**	.13*	.40**	.48**	.65**	.54**	-				
10.MSR	.50**	.30**	.45**	.20**	.53**	.66**	.72**	.68**	.63**	-			
11.T/S	.45**	.32**	.41**	.27**	.42**	.47**	.55**	.57**	.43**	.68**	-		
12.ER	.28**	.23**	.30**	.15*	.35**	.24**	.27**	.39**	.14**	.41**	.49**	-	
13.PL	.15*	.22**	.12*	.03	.19**	.37**	.37**	.34**	.43**	.32**	.22**	-.02	-
14.HS	.35**	.24**	.22*	0.19**	.23**	.40**	.46**	.34**	.32**	.48**	.47**	.21**	.49**

Notes. **p < 0.01 (two-tailed), *p < 0.05 (two-tailed)

According to the log determinants and homogeneity of covariance matrices as a result of the discriminant analysis for problem-solving anxiety, log determinants were similar, Group A = 39.489, Group B = 39.225, Pooled within Groups = 40.108, and Box's M is 197.848 with F = 1.779 ($p < 0.001$). In studies with large samples, a significant result for Box's M can be ignored (Burns & Burns, 2008). These indicate that the covariance matrices are equivalent. The discriminant analysis provided one discriminant function because we have only two groups: Group A and Group B. The canonical correlation (= 0.405) is the correlation between the variables and the discriminant function. The proportion of variance explained was 16.4% of the grouping variables' variation. Wilks' Lambda (= 0.836, $\chi2(14) = 47.439$, $p < 0.001$) indicated a highly significant function.

Table 2 shows the structure matrix and canonical discriminant function coefficient values resulting from discriminant analysis for problem-solving anxiety. The values under Structure Matrix indicated the relationships between the predictors and the discriminant function and were also considered discriminant loadings. *Rehearsal, extrinsic goal orientation,* and *peer learning* loaded the discriminant function more than others (0.3 was taken as the cutoff value).

Table 2. Structure matrix and canonical discriminant function coefficient

	Structure matrix	Canonical discriminant function coefficient
	Function 1	Function 1
Rehearsal (R)	0.597	0.151
Extrinsic goal orientation (EGO)	0.451	0.076
Peer learning (PL)	0.346	0.083
Self-efficacy (SE)	-0.250	-0.082
Intrinsic goal orientation (IGO)	0.239	0.089
Effort regulation (ER)	-0.216	-0.043
Critical thinking (CT)	0.208	0.001
Organization (O)	0.195	-0.039
Elaboration (E)	0.182	0.009
Metacognitive self-regulation (MSR)	0.136	-0.009
Task value (TV)	0.122	0.013
Control of learning beliefs (CLB)	0.107	0.010
Time and study environment (T/S)	0.011	-0.011
Help seeking (HS)	0.008	-0.103
Constant		-1.198

Table 3 shows the classification results of discriminant analysis for problem-solving anxiety. Classification results showed that 66.8% of the participants were correctly classified into the defined groups: Group A (high-level problem-solving anxiety) and Group B (low-level problem-solving anxiety). Those with high-level problem-solving anxiety (78.3%) were grouped more accurately than those with low-level problem-solving anxiety (50.4%). According to the cross-validated classification, 62.8% of the students were correctly classified. Misclassification rates for students from science high school (schools with high academic achievement) were 42.37% and for students from Anatolian high schools (schools with moderate academic achievement) was 31.63%.

Table 3. Classification results

			Predicted group membership		
			Group A	Group B	Total
Original	Count	Group A	126	35	161
		Group B	56	57	113
	%	Group A	78.3	21.7	100
		Group B	49.6	50.4	100
Cross-validated	Count	Group A	121	40	161
		Group B	62	51	113
	%	Group A	75.2	24.8	100
		Group B	54.9	45.1	100

3.3 Research Question 3: How Do Motivational Orientations and Learning Strategies Predict Ninth Graders' Problem-solving Anxiety?

Logistic regression was conducted to identify how motivational orientations and learning strategies predict participants' problem-solving anxiety levels. The model was statistically significant ($\chi 2(14) = 50.392$, $p < 0.001$). Hosmer and Lemeshow test ($\chi 2(8) = 8.472$, $p = 0.389$) indicated the fit of predictions made by the model through observed memberships to the low-level and high-level problem-solving anxiety groups. The model explained 22.6% (Nagelkerke R^2) of the variation in problem-solving anxiety. The model's accuracy rate in classification for low-level and high-level problem-solving anxiety groups is 67.2%. Table 4 shows the significant variables in the regression equation for high-level (Group A) and low-level (Group B) problem-solving anxiety groups. *Intrinsic goal orientation* ($B = -0.094$, $p = 0.040$), *self-efficacy* ($B = 0.079$, $p = 0.003$), *rehearsal* ($B = -0.143$, $p < 0.001$), and *help-seeking* ($B = 0.101$, $p = 0.030$) were found to be the significant predictors of problem-solving anxiety.

Table 4. Significant variables in the regression equation

	B	S.E.	df	Wald	p	Exp(B)	95% C. I. for EXP(B)	
							Lower	Upper
IGO	-0.094	0.046	1	4.233	0.040	0.910	0.832	0.996
SE	0.079	0.027	1	8.762	0.003	1.082	1.027	1.140
R	-0.143	0.039	1	13.632	<0.001	0.867	0.804	0.935
HS	0.101	0.046	1	4.703	0.030	1.106	1.010	1.211
Constant	1.272	1.057		1.448	0.229	3.567		

4. DISCUSSION

The goals of this study were two-fold. First, we wanted to examine how prospective ninth graders' problem-solving anxiety levels can be classified using motivational orientations and learning strategies. Second, we wanted to investigate how different motivational orientations and learning strategies predict ninth graders' problem-solving anxiety. To this end, we first clustered ninth graders according to their problem-solving anxiety. Students were grouped as high-level problem-solving success with low-level test anxiety and low-level problem-solving success with high-level test anxiety. The discriminant analysis was administered to classify whether a ninth grader had low-level or high-level problem-solving anxiety.

Rehearsal, extrinsic goal orientation, and peer learning significantly contributed to ninth graders' problem-solving anxiety classification as low and high. *Rehearsal* was the strongest contributor to the classification. Rehearsal improves the activation of prior knowledge (Pintrich et al., 1991). As a result, students who use a high level of rehearsal strategies demonstrate high performance in their learning (Gbollie & Keamu, 2017) and high mathematics success (Wang & Davaanyam, 2012). So, we consider this strategy to be highly associated with students' problem-solving ability and anxiety level when taking mathematical problem tests. *Extrinsic goal orientation* was another significant variable that classifies problem-solving anxiety as low and high. Since high schoolers have a high level of extrinsic goal orientation during mathematical problem-solving (Puteh & Ibrahim, 2010) and end-goals such as test results and grades are valued in extrinsic goal orientation (Pintrich et al., 1991), we see this motivational orientation as critical while learning and practicing mathematical problem-solving and experiencing anxiety. *Peer learning* was also a significant variable that classifies problem-solving anxiety as low and high. The effectiveness of peer learning in mathematics (Cheng & Walter, 2009) and peer learning in supporting knowledge construction (Sezgin-Memnun et al., 2019) were reported in the literature. According to our results, peer learning can effectively predict prospective students' membership in high-level or low-level problem-solving anxiety groups. However, considering this factor in classifying students' problem-solving anxiety also should be approached carefully because there is a report that students may not prefer peer learning during mathematical problem-solving (Puteh & Ibrahim, 2010). Further study for peer learning is needed.

Using logistic regression analysis, we also found that *intrinsic goal orientation* and *rehearsal* were significant negative predictors for ninth graders' problem-solving anxiety. The increases in intrinsic goal orientation and rehearsal strategy use decreased the likelihood of being in a low-level problem-solving anxiety group. Intrinsic goal orientation is related to students' engendered "challenge, curiosity, [and] mastery" (Pintrich et al., 1991, p. 9). The exam-oriented concepts for passing classes and high school entrance exams in education systems may hinder students' curiosity, challenge, and mastery. Also, for these exams, rehearsal as memorization by repetition would become more frequently used for students, which, unlike elaboration and organization strategies, could prevent them from developing genuine problem-solving skills. Previous studies that examined low-level intrinsic goal orientation and high-level extrinsic goal orientation (Puteh & Ibrahim, 2010), moderate-level intrinsic goal orientation (El-Adl & Alkharusi, 2020), and high-level rehearsal strategy use (Gasco et al., (2014) support intrinsic goal orientation and rehearsal being significant predictors for ninth graders' problem-solving anxiety.

Self-efficacy was a significant positive predictor for ninth graders' problem-solving anxiety. Self-efficacy as a critical factor for learning (Pajares & Kranzler, 1995) and self-efficacy as a significant predictor of math success (Erdem-Keklik & Keklik, 2013) were reported in the literature. *Self-efficacy for learning and performance* is based on students' performance and confidence levels for the expected achievement (Pintrich et al., 1991). Accordingly, the increase in self-efficacy increased the likelihood of being in a low-level problem-solving anxiety group.

Help-seeking is a strategy that ninth graders highly use during problem-solving (Puteh & Ibrahim, 2010). According to our results, the increase in the use of the help-seeking strategy increased the likelihood of being in a low-level problem-solving anxiety group. Collaboration between peers could be helpful in knowledge and understanding sharing; however, peer judgment should be considered when considering students' anxiety. Johnston et al. (2018) drew attention to judgment between peers, causing bullying, and Bishop and Pflaum (2005) found peer judgment as a negative factor for academic engagement. Peer learning as a significant classifier for problem-solving anxiety and help-seeking as a significant predictor for ninth graders' problem-solving anxiety can be examined further and together with regard to ninth graders' mathematical problem-solving and anxiety level.

5. CONCLUSION AND RECOMMENDATIONS

Predicting membership of ninth graders' problem-solving anxiety level in advance can help their successful transition from middle to high school mathematics education system. The present study discovered how ninth graders' problem-solving anxiety could be classified and predicted. Our classification results demonstrated relatively low misclassification rates and that those with high-level problem-solving anxiety were classified considerably more accurately with extrinsic goal orientation, rehearsal, and peer learning than the other group. However, these three components also classified students' low-level problem-solving anxiety to some extent. These results have important implications for the dynamic assessment of prospective ninth graders engaging in mathematical problem-solving, indicating which students might need help with their mathematical problem-solving skills and support for overcoming anxiety. We suggest that educators monitor students' motivational orientations and learning strategies such as rehearsal, goal orientation, and peer learning to anticipate problem-solving anxiety. Nevertheless, since motivational orientations and learning strategies explained 16.4% of the grouping variability of problem-solving anxiety, other strategies and factors such as self-regulated learning strategies, demographic factors, and personality types in the literature could explain the remained proportion of students' classification.

Intrinsic goal orientation and rehearsal were the negative predictors among motivational orientations and learning strategies. We consider this result as the effect of the exam-oriented educational system still clearly remains in them since these ninth graders passed a national examination and just found a place for themselves in a high school. However, our results confirm that students' self-efficacy and help-seeking behavior positively impact their problem-solving anxiety. In sum, mathematics teachers need to give more attention to students' comprehension in mathematics lessons while teaching and practicing mathematical problem-solving. Strategies for intrinsic motivation, self-efficacy, and help-seeking should be considered more to encourage students to have a genuine interest in mathematics and improve their academic performance.

REFERENCES

Abdullah, A. H. et al., 2014. Non-routine Mathematical Problems Among In-service and Pre-service Mathematics Teachers. *Proceeding of the IEEE International Conference on Teaching, Assessment and Learning for Engineering*. Wellington, New Zealand, pp. 18-24.

Ahmed, W. et al., 2012. Reciprocal Relationships between Math Self-concept and Math Anxiety. *Learning and Individual Differences*, Vol. 22, No. 3, pp. 385–389.

Benner, A., 2017. *The Transition to High School: Implications for Educational Success in High School. Policy Brief.* Texas Education Research Center.

Bibi, A. et al., 2019. An Evolving Research to Tackle Teaching and Learning Challenges During Differential Equations Course: A Combination of Non-routine Problems and Teacher Training. *International Electronic Journal of Mathematics Education*, Vol. 14, No. 3, pp. 647-656.

Bishop, P. A. and Pflaum, S. W., 2005. Middle School Students' Perceptions of Social Dimensions as Influencers of Academic Engagement. *RMLE Online*, Vol. 29, No. 2, pp. 1–14.

Breslau, J. et al., 2009. The Impact of Early Behavior Disturbances on Academic Achievement in High School. *PEDIATRICS*, Vol. 123, No. 6, pp. 1472–1476.

Burns, R. P. and Burns, R., 2008. *Discriminant Analysis. In Business Research Methods and Statistics Using SPSS*, pp. 589–608. Sage Publications Ltd., London.

Cheng, D. and Walters, M., 2009. Peer-assisted Learning in Mathematics: An Observational Study of Student Success. *Australasian Journal of Peer Learning*, Vol. 2, pp. 23–39.

Clark, L. A. and Watson, D., 1995. Constructing Validity: Basic Issues in Objective Scale Development. *Psychological Assessment*, Vol. 7, No. 3, pp. 309–319.

Dinc, E. et al., 2020. Mathematical Problem-solving Achievement and Motivational Strategies for Learning. *I-Manager's Journal on Educational Psychology*, Vol. 14, No. 2.

Effendi, A. and Fatimah, A. T., 2020. Improving Students Mathematical Higher Order Thinking Through the Implementation of the Creative Problem-solving Model of High School Students. *Journal of Physics: Conference Series*, Vol. 1521, Article No. 032025.

El-Adl, A. and Alkharusi, H., 2020. Relationships between Self-regulated Learning Strategies, Learning Motivation and Mathematics Achievement. *Cypriot Journal of Educational Sciences*, Vol. 15, No. 1, pp. 104–111.

Erdem-Keklik, D. and Keklik, İ., 2013. Motivation and Learning Strategies as Predictors of High School Students' Math Achievement. *Cukurova University Faculty of Education Journal*, Vol. 42, No. 1, pp. 96–109.

Firdaus, F. et al., 2015. Developing Critical Thinking Skills of Students in Mathematics Learning. *Journal of Education and Learning (EduLearn)*, Vol. 9, No. 3, pp. 226–236.

Gasco, J. et al., 2014. Differences in the Use of Learning Strategies in Mathematics in 8th and 9th Grade. *Procedia - Social and Behavioral Sciences*, Vol. 116, pp. 1040–1043.

Gbollie, C. and Keamu, H. P., 2017. Student Academic Performance: The Role of Motivation, Strategies, and Perceived Factors Hindering Liberian Junior and Senior High School Students Learning. *Education Research International*, Vol. 2017, Article no. 1789084.

Hoffman, B. 2010. “I think I can, but I'm afraid to try”: The Role of Self-efficacy Beliefs and Mathematics Anxiety in Mathematics Problem-solving Efficiency. *Learning and Individual Differences*, Vol. 20, No. 3, pp. 276-283.

Irhamna, I. et al, 2020. Contribution of Mathematical Anxiety, Learning Motivation and Self-confidence to Students' Mathematical Problem-solving. *Budapest International Research and Critics in Linguistics and Education Journal*, Vol. 3, No. 4, pp. 1759-1772.

Johnston, A. D. et al., 2018. A Mixed Methods Evaluation of the “Aged-up” STAC Bullying Bystander Intervention for High School Students. *The Professional Counselor*, Vol. 8, No. 1, pp. 73–87.

Karadeniz, S. et al., 2008. The Turkish Adaptation Study of Motivated Strategies for Learning Questionnaire (MSLQ) for 12–18 Year Old Children: Results of Confirmatory Factor Analysis. *The Turkish Online Journal of Educational Technology*, Vol.7, No. 4.

Lee, C. Y. and Chen, M. P., 2009. A Computer Game as a Context for Non-routine Mathematical Problem Solving: The Effects of Type of Question Prompt and Level of Prior Knowledge. *Computers & Education*, Vol. 52, No. 3, pp. 530-542.

McCallumore, K. M. and Sparapani, E. F., 2010. The Importance of the Ninth Grade on High School Graduation Rates and Student Success. *The Education Digest*, Vol. 76, No. 2, pp. 60–64.

McGee-Carlton, S. V., 2018. *The Perception of Administrators and Guidance Counselors in Five Rural High Schools of the Ninth Grade Transition Program and/or Strategies*. Doctoral Dissertation. NC: Gardner-Webb University.

McIntosh, J. and White, S. H., 2006. Building for Freshman Success: High Schools Working as Professional Learning Communities. *American Secondary Education*, Vol. 34, No. 2, pp. 40–49.

Moore, D. S. et al., 2013. *The Basic Practice of Statistics* (6th ed.). W. H. Freeman Company, New York, NY.

Morosanova, V. et al., 2020. The Relationship Between the Conscious Self-regulation of School Children's Learning Activity, Their Test Anxiety Level, and the Final Exam Result in Mathematics. *Behavioral Sciences*, Vol. 10, No. 1.

Pajares, F. and Kranzler, J., 1995. Role of Self-efficacy and General Mental Ability in Mathematical Problem-solving: A Path Analysis. *Proceeding of The Annual Meeting of the American Educational Research Association*. San Francisco, CA.

Peter, E. E., 2012. Critical Thinking: Essence for Teaching Mathematics and Mathematics Problem Solving Skills. *African Journal of Mathematics and Computer Science Research*, Vol.5, No. 3, pp. 39–43.

Pintrich, P. R. et al., 1991. *A Manual for the Use of the Motivated Strategies for Learning Questionnaire*. Michigan: School of Education Building, The University of Michigan.

Puteh, M. and Ibrahim, M., 2010. The Usage of Self-regulated Learning Strategies Among Form Four Students in the Mathematical Problem-solving Context: A Case Study. *Procedia - Social and Behavioral Sciences*, Vol. 8, pp. 446–452.

Rana, R. A. and Mahmood, N., 2010. Relationship Between Test Anxiety and Academic Achievement. *Bulletin of Education and Research*, Vol. 32, No. 2, pp. 63–74.

Robinson, D. R. et al., 2005. Peer and Cross-age Tutoring in Math: Outcomes and Their Design Implications. *Educational Psychology Review*, Vol. 17, No. 4, pp. 327–362.

Sezgin-Memnun, D. et al., 2019. Analysis of the Abstraction Process of Continuity Knowledge. *World Journal of Education*, Vol. 9, No. 2, pp. 141-150.

Sharp, C. et al., 2000. Increasing Mathematical Problem-solving Performance through Relaxation Training. *Mathematics Education Research Journal*, Vol. 12, No. 1, pp. 53–61.

Snyder, R. F. 1998. A Clinical Study of Three High School Problem Solvers. *The High School Journal*, Vol. 81, No. 3, pp. 167–176.

Suárez-Álvarez, J. et al., 2014. Self-concept, Motivation, Expectations, and Socioeconomic Level as Predictors of Academic Performance in Mathematics. *Learning and Individual Differences*, Vol. 30, pp. 118–123.

Verschaffel, L. et al., 2020. Word Problems in Mathematics Education: A Survey. *ZDM*, Vol. 52, No. 1, pp. 1–16.

von der Embse, N. et al., 2018. Test Anxiety Effects, Predictors, and Correlates: A 30-year Meta-analytic Review. *Journal of Affective Disorders*, Vol. 227, pp. 483–493.

Wang, K. and Davaanyam, T., 2012. The Influences of Mathematics Motivated Beliefs, Test Anxiety and Cognitive Learning Strategies in Mathematics Achievement of Mongolian High School Graduating Students. *The Journal of Thinking Development*, Vol. 8, No. 1, pp. 151–172.

Warren, C. et al., 2011. *Final Report on the Study of Promising Ninth Grade Transition Strategies: A Study of Six High Schools* (ED-04-CO-0021). U.S. Department of Education.

Wigfield, A. and Meece, J. L., 1988. Math Anxiety in Elementary and Secondary School Students. *Journal of Educational Psychology*, Vol. 80, No. 2, pp. 210–216.

EXPERIENCING FLOW IN VIRTUAL REALITY: AN INVESTIGATION OF COMPLEX INTERACTION STRUCTURES OF LEARNING-RELATED VARIABLES

Miriam Mulders
University of Duisburg-Essen, Germany

ABSTRACT

Theoretical background: Learning in virtual realities (VR) has become increasingly important. In this context, VR appears to be particularly conducive to affective learning objectives, such as perspective-taking in VR actors. Previous research has often focused on investigating cause-effect relationships that focus on the direct effects of different VR visualization technologies on learning outcomes. Little research has been conducted on more complex constellations of learning-related variables. Therefore, the present study aims at elaborating a research design that can be used to investigate both the direct effects of VR visualization technologies as well as the mediating effects of learning process variables latent in VR. For this purpose, the research design will be experimentally tested by comparing head-mounted display (HMD)-based VR with laptop-based VR with respect to the intended learning objectives, and controlling for influences by underlying learning processes (here: the experience of flow within VR).
Methods: 132 students of grades eight and nine were recruited. The subjects were assigned to experimental conditions (HMD vs. laptop). The VR content dealt with the exploration of the hiding place of Anne Frank at the time of World War II in Amsterdam. Questionnaires were used to collect several data including sociodemographic characteristics, knowledge gain, perspective-taking, subjective evaluation, and the learning process variable flow.
Results: A significant main effect for the variable VR visualization technology was uncovered averaged across all learning indicators. However, a superiority of HMD-based VR was found for the two evaluative indicators and also for the affective learning indicator. For the cognitive learning indicator, the effect was reverse. More relevant than unidirectional relationships are the mediating effects. Mediating effects through the experience of flow were discovered several times. Thus, the experience of flow within VR can significantly explain the cause-effect relationships between VR visualization technology and learning outcomes, even if, for the most part, only effects for evaluative indicators could be determined.
Conclusion: The present study was able to exemplify that the investigation of complex interaction structures of VR visualization technologies and learning process variables can make a large contribution to the understanding of learning in VR environments. Advantages of HMD-based VR over laptop-based VR with respect to some learning indicators were uncovered. The significant findings of the mediation analyses point to the fact that the direct effects of VR visualization technologies on parameters of learning can be significantly explained by learning process variables such as flow experience and are systematically overestimated if such learning processes are not taken into account.

KEYWORDS

Virtual Reality, Mediation Analysis, Learning Processes, Flow Experience, Anne Frank VR House

1. INTRODUCTION

Virtual reality (VR) is becoming increasingly popular. VR applications used for teaching and learning purposes are also gaining importance (e.g., Fowler, 2015). VR is said to promote in particular the acquisition of procedural skills, for example in skilled trades (e.g., Radianti et al., 2020), but also affective skills such as perspective-taking or prosocial behavior (e.g., Martingano et al., 2021). Here, the term VR is often used as a collective term for heterogeneous visualization technologies and is not used distinctively. This may mean 360° pictures viewed on tablets, or 360° movies viewed through cardboard goggles. In addition, the term encompasses environments in which so-called head-mounted displays (HMDs), which enclose ears and eyes, paired with data suits and controllers enable interaction in entirely computer-generated spaces. What they all have in common is the understanding of a computer-generated and realistic real-time representation that individuals virtually enter, experience multisensory, and in which they interact via artificial and natural user interfaces (Radianti et al., 2020; Zinn, 2019). A distinctive subdivision of VR visualization technologies is often challenging. Many studies, therefore, focus on the comparison of such visualization technologies with regard to the intended learning outcomes. Their goal is usually to find out with which technology learning is better or worse. The implication is that the technology could directly influence learning. However, in such media comparison studies, which are often viewed critically (e.g., Clark & Mayer, 2016), the instructional design behind the educational technology is neglected. It is not the technology that leads to better or worse learning, rather it is the interaction of many factors, of which the visualization technology is one.

In many previous studies on learning in VR environments, learning outcomes are the subject of research. Latent processes taking place within the VR experience have rarely been considered. These include the experience of presence (e.g., Mikropoulos, 2006), cognitive load (e.g., Parong & Mayer, 2021), or flow (e.g., Rutrecht et al., 2021). It can be assumed that such learning process variables can significantly explain the effects of VR visualization technologies on learning outcomes. In order to investigate the complex causal relationships, an experimental study was conducted. In this study, both, the direct effects on learning outcomes through VR visualization technologies as well as the indirect effects mediated by the learning process variable flow can be investigated. Therefore, we used a VR environment, which is accessible via two different visualization technologies (HMD vs. laptop) and which is a virtual replication of the Anne Frank House in Amsterdam.

The article is divided into the parts theoretical background, methodology, results, and discussion. In the first part, VR as a technology and the learning process variable flow are described. In the second part, the methodological approach including a description of the sample, procedure, measurement instruments, and data analysis is explained. In the third part, results are presented. Part four serves to interpret the results. Finally, implications and limitations of the work are discussed.

2. THEORETICAL BACKGROUND

2.1 Virtual Reality

VR has often been defined in terms of its technological features. Greenbaum (1992) wrote "*Virtual Reality is an alternate world filled with computer-generated images that respond to human movements. These simulated environments are usually visited with the aid of an expensive data suit which features stereophonic video goggles and fiber-optic data gloves.*" (p. 58). While even today, depending on the discipline, educational technologies are often characterized and judged on the basis of their hardware conditions (i.e., on the basis of input and output devices), research in educational psychology attempts to define the technology more on the basis of its underlying cognitive processes (e.g., Bente, Krämer & Petersen, 2002). A definition by Biocca and Delaney (1995) addresses both. "*VR is the sum of the hardware and software systems that seek to perfect an all-inclusive, sensory illusion of being present in another environment.*" (p. 63). Nevertheless, the characterization of VR based on its technological characteristics is common and also relevant to the present study. Currently, three-dimensional environments exist that are presented via two-dimensional screens and are based on devices such as monitors, mice, joysticks, keyboards, microphones, and speakers (Burdea & Coiffet, 2003). Such VR environments are often classified as non-immersive (Cummings & Bailenson, 2016; Schroeder, 2010). Stereoscopic displays visually convey depth information, creating a spatial impression. However, many stimuli from the real environment are still perceived. Auditory content is presented via headphones or speakers. Navigation and interaction with virtual artifacts are done via mouse, joystick, or keyboard (Lee, Wong & Fung, 2010). When referring to laptop visualization technology in the following part of this article, the latter description is always meant. Immersive VR environments, on the other hand, are often associated with the use of HMDs. In the following text, this visualization technology will be linked with the abbreviation HMD. HMDs enclose eyes and ears. They fill the entire field of vision and largely block out environmental stimuli from the reality. Auditory VR content is conveyed via integrated headphones. The displays present an image to each eye from a slightly different viewing angle. This mimics natural human visual perception, creating the stereoscopic impression of a computer-generated virtual world. The sensors of the HMDs consider head movements and enable perspective changes and movements in space. This is often combined with data gloves, body suits, and controllers, whose functionalities are used to navigate, select and interact (Allmendinger, 2010; Andreas et al., 2010). Of course, a division in HMD and laptop VR is limited, but sufficient in the context of the present study. Nevertheless, other VR visualization technologies such as CAVEs (e.g., Buttussi & Chittaro, 2017) exist and VR technologies undergo on-going development activities.

As described above, HMD and laptop VR differ in terms of their technological features. Besides the visible differences, there are latent factors happening during a VR experience that differ depending on the kind of technology. These factors are considered to be correlates of human information processing and thus modify the experiences in VR. Hence, investigating such processes enables us to describe the experiential quality of VR learning in more detail. Among others, the experience of flow (e.g., Rutrecht et al., 2021) has been shown to be promising for learning in VR.

2.2 Flow Experience

Experiencing flow is understood to mean that a person experiences an activity as gratifying. The person perceives no or hardly any separation between himself and the activity (Csikszentmihalyi, 1997). Furthermore, the course of the action becomes automated and the action is usually performed faster and more effectively. Another characteristic of flow is the loss of the sense of time (Rutrecht et al., 2021). In educational psychology, the experience of flow is also classified as a performance-relevant component of learning motivation and described as increasing motivation (Engeser et al., 2005). Accordingly, flow is a positive emotion in the form of intrinsic reward (Sherry, 2004; Voiskounsky, Mitina & Avetisova, 2004). The experience of flow is also dependent on the fit between the individuum and the task. According to this, flow can only occur if the acting person is neither under- nor over-challenged (Csikszentmihalyi, 1997).

Rheinberg, Vollmeyer, and Engeser (2003) consider flow as a multidimensional construct consisting mainly of the facets smooth automated flow and absorbedness. Meant are the flow of action chains and the complete absorption in an activity. Based on these facets, Rheinberg et al. (2003) developed a questionnaire.

The experience of flow has been associated with the success of a VR learning activity. In a study by Bodzin et al. (2021), students explored their city's river watershed in VR. They reported significantly experiencing more flow and learning more. A comparison group was not implemented. In another study by Tai et al. (2022), again no control group was used. 143 engineering students were trained in VR regarding the care of car body parts. Procedural skills recorded in a post hoc test could be significantly explained by experiencing flow in the VR environment. Another study by Rutrecht et al. (2021) examined 100 subjects playing a performance-based rhythm game under an HMD or on a desktop. The game outcome could be significantly explained by the experience of flow. However, the groups did not differ with respect to flow. Overall, there is still little empirical research on the relationship between experiencing flow in VR and learning outcomes.

The present study intends to investigate to what extent VR visualization technologies are suitable to significantly support students' learning. Using a VR environment, which is a recreation of the hiding place of Anne Frank in Amsterdam, cognitive and affective indicators of learning as well as the subjective evaluation of the VR application will be examined in more detail. A special focus of the study will be on the learning process flow. The research design visualized in Figure 1 aims at a more appropriate representation of the complex interaction structures of learning-relevant variables and thus mediating relationships. Both, direct effects and indirect effects become measurable. By controlling for the additional variable flow, confounding can be avoided. If influencing variables that correlate with the independent variables, in this case VR visualization technology, and dependent variables, in this case learning indicators, are not controlled, so-called spurious effects can arise. The estimation of the correlations between the independent and dependent variables is biased if relevant factors are not controlled. Thus, correlations are systematically over- or underestimated. The interpretation of causality between independent variables and dependent variables is compromised. Studies that have been exclusively devoted to the comparison of two forms of media presentation have often failed to control for person-specific variables (e.g., experience of flow and presence) and thus for differences within the sample with respect to these variables. This is particularly problematic when the study is not a randomized experiment, in which person-specific variables are assumed to be balanced out due to random assignment to experimental conditions (Eid, Gollwitzer & Schmitz, 2010). If, as the research design underlying this paper suggests, additional variables are integrated that appear to be related to the independent and dependent variables, on the one hand confounding and thus biased results can be avoided and, at the same time, additional variance in the dependent variables can be systematically elucidated.

We hypothesize the following:

1. Main effect: Learning outcomes differ depending on visualization technology.
   (a) with respect to affective learning indicators: HMD > laptop
   (b) with regard to cognitive learning indicators: HMD = laptop
2. Mediating effect: More flow is experienced in the HMD conditions than in the laptop conditions. The more flow is experienced, the more beneficial for the learning outcomes.

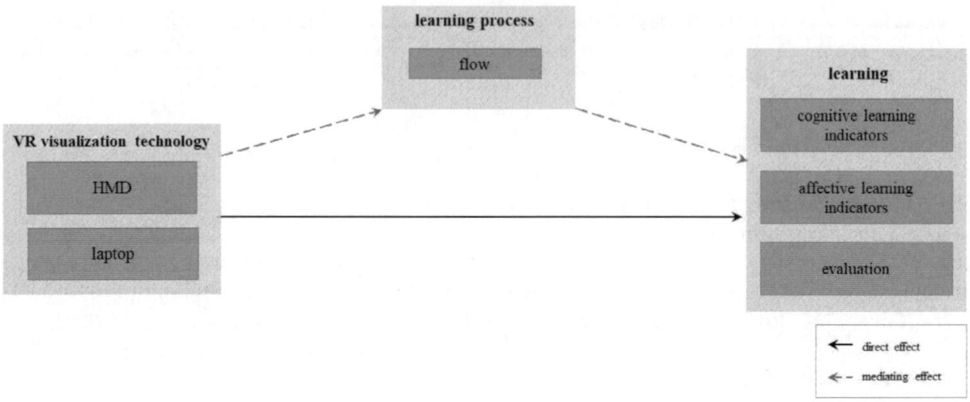

Figure 1. Research design

3. METHODS

3.1 Anne Frank VR House

The VR environment is the freely available *Anne Frank VR House*, jointly developed by the *Anne Frank Foundation* and *Force Field VR*. The application allows insights into the hiding place of 13-year-old Anne Frank, her sister, her parents and four other people. The hiding place was located in the back of a company building on Prinsengracht 263 in Amsterdam. The VR environment shows the living conditions of the eight people of Jewish origin in the period from 1942 to 1944. All eight rooms are reproduced in detail. No persons are depicted. Additional information about life in hiding and the history of those in hiding is included. An insight is provided by Figure 2.

Figure 2. The room of Anne Frank and Fritz Pfeffer
(http://edu.annefrank.org/dashinterhaus/; retrieved at 14.06.2022)

The application can be explored via two VR visualization technologies. On the one hand, HMDs and two associated controllers can be used. Teleportation, as well as body and head movements, can be used to explore room by room. On the other hand, it is possible to explore the virtual hiding place via various end devices with two-dimensional screens (e.g., tablets, laptops) by accessing the 360° web application with equivalent content. Here, the field of view is changed either by the touch function or by the mouse cursor.

3.2 Procedure

The single-scenario study included a pre-questionnaire, a VR experience, and a post-questionnaire. The VR experience itself took an average of 30 minutes. The experience differed between students in terms of the visualization technology used (HMD, here *Oculus Quest 2* vs. laptop, here *Dell Latitude 3510*). The online-questionnaire batteries included instruments on sociodemographic variables, evaluation, cognitive and affective learning outcomes, and the learning process variable flow.

3.3 Measurement Instruments

In addition to sociodemographic variables (gender, age, grade level), learning outcomes were collected at various levels. To measure cognitive learning, the subjects were asked to answer ten short knowledge questions (e.g., "*What did Anne's diary look like*?"). A maximum of two points per question was reachable, resulting in a maximum point value of 20. The internal consistency of the knowledge test is $\alpha = .71$. In addition to cognitive learning objectives, affective learning was also considered. As an affective goal, perspective-taking in Anne Frank was set. Perspective-taking is understood as the ability to empathize with another person's feelings, which is considered as an essential prerequisite for the emergence of empathy or compassion (Dimitrova & Lüdmann, 2014). To test the extent of perspective-taking, students were asked to indicate how well they could empathize with Anne's life situation in the hiding place. A ten-point scale from 1 ("*not at all*") to 10 ("*very well*") was used as the response format. Students had to answer this question before and after the VR experience. In addition, the students were asked to evaluate the VR experience. To do so, they should indicate their level of satisfaction ("*I am satisfied with the virtual learning experience*.") as well as their tendency to recommend it ("*I would recommend the virtual backhouse to other students*.") on a scale of 1 ("*strongly disagree*") to 5 ("*strongly agree*"). In order to measure the experience of flow, the Flow Short Scale (FKS; Rheinberg et al., 2003) was used. The instrument consists of the two dimensions of smooth automated flow (example: "*I was completely absorbed in what I was doing*.") and absorbedness (example: "*I had no trouble concentrating*.") and a total of ten items. The questionnaire has a seven-point scale as a response format from 1 ("*strongly disagree*") to 4 ("*partly agree*") to 7 ("*strongly agree*"). Rheinberg et al. (2003) listed values from comparative studies. A mean of $M = 5.16$ ($SD = .93$) was found for graffiti spraying and a mean of $M = 4.57$ ($SD = 1.13$) for solving a statistics task. Rheinberg et al. (2003) reported a Cronbach's alpha of $\alpha = .90$, and the internal consistency in the present study was $\alpha = 81$.

3.4 Data Analysis

In addition to simple descriptive statistical analyses, a multivariate analysis of variance (MANOVA) and post hoc ANOVAs was conducted with visualization technology as the independent variable and the various learning indicators as the dependent variables. To explore the mediating effects of the learning process variable flow, mediation analyses were conducted. Therefore, the SPSS macro PROCESS (Hayes, 2013) was installed.

4. RESULTS

132 subjects (65 female, 63 male, 4 diverse) were surveyed. The sample of this study consists of students aged 12 to 17 years ($M = 13.84$, $SD = .92$). Students had to attend the eighth or ninth grade of a secondary school in Germany to participate. 74 students participated in the study via an HMD and 58 via a laptop.

Table 1 shows the mean and standard deviation for each variable. To assess the increase in perspective-taking from the first to the second measurement, a new variable was calculated that allows a pre-post comparison. The variable calculation involved subtracting the pre from the post value. Across the experimental conditions, there is an increase in perspective-taking in Anne Frank from the first to the second measurement, although the variation among students is quite large. In the knowledge test, the subjects received on average slightly more than half of the maximum twenty points that could be achieved. However, the high variation indicates very different performances among the students. Regarding the evaluation of the VR application, high means and low variation were found averaged across the experimental conditions. Only a few outliers were not satisfied and would not recommend the VR application to others. Compared to the values reported by Rheinberg et al. (2003) for activities such as graffiti spraying, the experience of flow in the present study can be classified as very high. Absorbedness in particular reached very high values.

Table 1. Means and standard deviations

	M	*SD*
knowledge test	10.89	4.36
perspective-taking	1.90	2.37
satisfaction	4.31	.91
recommendation	4.33	.93
flow: smooth automated flow	5.18	1.36
flow: absorbedness	5.37	1.38

To address hypothesis 1, a MANOVA was conducted with visualization technology as the independent variable and knowledge test, perspective-taking (pre-post), and evaluation as dependent variables. The MANOVA showed statistically significant differences between HMD-based and laptop-based VR ($F(4,119) = 14.96, p < .001, \eta^2 = .34$, Wilk's $\Lambda = .67$) for the combined dependent variables. Multi-factorial ANOVAs were then calculated for each of the four dependent variables. All were significant (see Table 2). Follow-up analyses showed that students in the HMD conditions are significantly more satisfied, more likely to recommend the VR application to others, and better able to empathize with Anne. In the knowledge test, however, the results of the laptop group are significantly better than those of the HMD group. Thus, subhypotheses a and b have been confirmed.

Table 2. Results of ANOVAs

	F	*df*	*p*	η^2
knowledge test	32.36	1,122	.00	.21
perspective-taking	3.80	1,122	.05	.03
satisfaction	13.36	1,122	.00	.10
recommendation	15.17	1,122	.00	.11

To address hypothesis 2, mediation analyses were performed. It was hypothesized that experiencing flow can systematically explain the direct effects of VR visualization technology on the learning outcomes we found in the MANOVA (see Figure 1). In a significant mediation, according to Baron and Kenny (1986), the independent variable (here: visualization technology) must correlate with the mediator (here: flow) and the mediator must correlate with the dependent variable (here: various learning indicators, evaluation). In a total mediation, the direct effect between independent and dependent variable disappears when the mediator is included. In a partial mediation, additional variance can be explained by adding the mediator. Eight mediation analyses were calculated. In four of these, we found statistically significant indirect effects mediated by flow, but mainly for the evaluative indicators. A significant mediation could be found, among others, for the mediator flow (subscale: automated process) and the dependent variable satisfaction. Within the analysis, a total effect of visualization technology on satisfaction was found (c = -.58**). The total effect means that students in the laptop group (group number 2) were significantly more dissatisfied than those in the HMD group (group number 1). After the mediator was included in the model, visualization technology significantly predicted the mediator flow (a = -.1.19***). Students in the laptop condition experienced significantly less flow than students in the HMD condition. Flow, in turn, predicted satisfaction (b = .29***). When students experienced more flow, they were also more satisfied. Path c`, the direct effect of visualization technology on satisfaction, did not become significant ($c$` = -.23). Thus, a total mediation could be detected. After the mediator flow (subscale: automated process) was integrated into the analysis, the correlation between visualization technology and satisfaction loses its statistical significance. Consequently, there is no direct correlation between visualization technology and satisfaction, but there is an indirect correlation, which can be completely explained by flow (indirect effect $ab_{flow\_auto\_process}$= -.28, 95% CI [-.525, -.070]). The confidence interval does not enclose the value zero. The indirect effect is estimated to be significant. For an illustration of the causal relationships, see Figure 3. The correlations are identical in the other significant mediation analyses and are therefore not listed separately again.

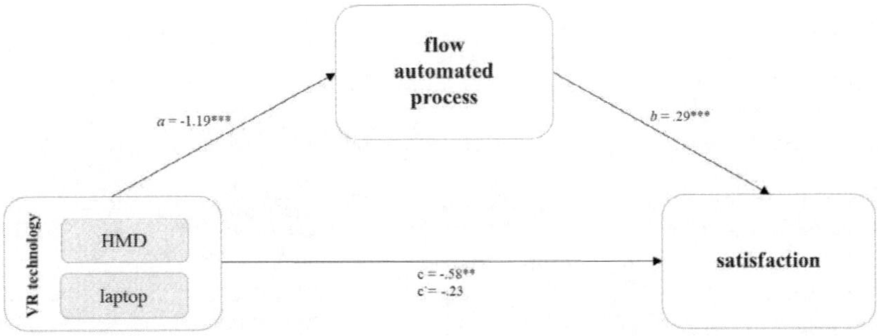

Figure 3. Example of a total mediation

5. CONCLUSION

In this study, the *Anne Frank VR House* was empirically investigated. Across the experimental conditions, it was found that the VR application can generally address cognitive and affective learning objectives and is rated extremely positively by students. In this respect, the application seems to be suitable for purposes of teaching and learning. Nevertheless, this study is not able to decide which VR visualization technology, here HMD or laptop, seems superior for presenting VR content. Unsurprisingly, significantly better student ratings were found for HMD compared to laptop. However, the use of HMDs also proved to be beneficial for affective learning objectives (i.e., perspective-taking). For cognitive learning objectives, it was even the other way around: Students on laptops answered significantly more knowledge questions correctly. Therefore, a decision for or against a VR visualization technology should always be a case-by-case decision made by a teacher based on the intended learning objectives.

Equally important as main effects were mediation effects. Indirect effects mediated by the experience of flow can significantly explain the effects of VR visualization technologies on learning outcomes. In some cases, the direct effect disappeared with the addition of the mediator and only the indirect effect mediated by flow proved to be statistically significant. At this point, it becomes obvious why latent process variables should be controlled in empirical studies. Otherwise, statistically significant direct effects are seemingly interpreted as significant or are overestimated systematically, although an underlying learning process is actually responsible for the correlation. Accordingly, complex interaction structures are more suitable for representing and investigating learning in VR. Unfortunately, only one mediation effect could be uncovered for the affective learning indicator as dependent variable. The majority of the significant mediation effects concern the evaluation of the VR application.

Hence, it seems of importance that follow-up studies also consider latent learning processes in VR. This is not limited to VR. Latent learning processes also play a crucial role in learning scenarios that make use of augmented reality or interactive videos, for example. Consequently, other educational technologies could be explored in qualitative and quantitative studies using the proposed research design. This approach goes beyond traditional approaches of media comparison studies, which are considered critical in the literature (Clark & Mayer, 2016). In addition, the research design makes it possible to uncover causal and correlational relationships through mediating learning process variables and thus help to avoid confounding.

REFERENCES

Allmendinger, K., 2010. Social presence in synchronous virtual learning situations: The role of nonverbal signals displayed by avatars. In: *Educational Psychology Review,* Vol. 22, No. 1, pp. 41-56.

Andreas, K., Tsiatsos, T., Terzidou, T., & Pomportsis, A., 2010. Fostering collaborative learning in Second Life: Metaphors and affordances. In: *Computers & Education,* Vol. 55, No. 2, pp. 603-615.

Baron, R. M., & Kenny, D. A., 1986. The moderator-mediator variable distinction in social psychological research: Conceptual, strategic, and statistical considerations. In: *Journal of Personality and Social Psychology*, Vol. *51*, No. 6, pp. 1173-1182.

Bente, G., Krämer, N. C., & Petersen, A., 2002. Virtuelle Realität als Gegenstand und Methode in der Psychologie. In: *Virtuelle Realitäten,* pp. 1-31.

Biocca, F., & Delaney, B., 1995. Immersive virtual reality technology. In: Communication in the age of virtual reality, Vol. 15, No. 32, pp. 10-5555.

Bodzin, A., Junior, R. A., Hammond, T., & Anastasio, D., 2021. Investigating engagement and flow with a placed-based immersive virtual reality game. In: *Journal of Science Education and Technology,* Vol. 30, No. 3, pp. 347-360.

Burdea, G. C., & Coiffet, P., 2003. *Virtual reality technology.* Hoboken, NJ: John Wiley & Sons.

Buttussi, F., & Chittaro, L., 2017. Effects of different types of virtual reality display on presence and learning in a safety training scenario. In: *IEEE transactions on visualization and computer graphics,* Vol. 24, No. 2, pp. 1063-1076.

Clark, R. C., & Mayer, R. E., 2016. *E-Learning and the Science of Instruction: Proven Guidelines for Consumers and Designers of Multimedia Learning.* John Wiley & Sons.

Cummings, J. J., & Bailenson, J. N., 2016. How immersive is enough? A meta-analysis of the effect of immersive technology on user presence. In: *Media psychology,* Vol. 19, No. 2, pp. 272-309.

Csikszentmihalyi, M., 1997. *Flow and education.* In: NAMTA journal, Vol. 22, No. 2, pp. 2-35.

Dimitrova, V., & Lüdmann, M., 2014. Zur Entwicklung der Fähigkeit zur Perspektiven-übernahme. In: *Sozial-emotionale Kompetenzentwicklung* (pp. 3-7). Wiesbaden: Springer.

Eid, M., Gollwitzer, M., & Schmitt, M., 2010. *Statistik und Forschungsmethoden.* Weinheim und Basel: Beltz.

Engeser, S., Rheinberg, F., Vollmeyer, R., & Bischoff, J., 2005. Motivation, Flow-Erleben und Lernleistung in universitären Lernsettings. In: *Zeitschrift für pädagogische Psychologie,* Vol. 19, No. 3, pp. 159-172.

Fowler, C., 2015. Virtual reality and learning: Where is the pedagogy? In *British journal of educational technology,* Vol. 46, No. 2, pp. 412-422.

Greenbaum, P., 1992. The lawnmower man. In: *Film and video,* Vol. 9, No. 3, pp. 58-62.

Hayes, A.F., 2013. *Introduction to mediation, moderation and conditional process analysis: A regression based approach.* New York, NY: Guilford Press.

Lee, E. A. L., Wong, K. W., & Fung, C. C., 2010. How does desktop virtual reality enhance learning outcomes? A structural equation modeling approach. In: *Computers & Education,* Vol. 55, No. 4, pp. 1424-1442.

Martingano, A.J., Hererra, F. & Konrath, S., 2021. Virtual Reality Improves Emotional but Not Cognitive Empathy: A Meta-Analysis. In: *Technology, Mind, and Behavior,* 2(1). Available at: https://tmb.apaopen.org/pub/vr-improves-emotional-empathy-only.

Mikropoulos, T. A., 2006. Presence: a unique characteristic in educational virtual environments. In: Virtual Reality, Vol. 10, No. 3, pp. 197-206.

Parong, J., & Mayer, R. E., 2021. Cognitive and affective processes for learning science in immersive virtual reality. In: *Journal of Computer Assisted Learning,* Vol. 37, No. 1, pp. 226-241.

Radianti, J., Majchrzak, T. A., Fromm, J., & Wohlgenannt, I., 2020. A systematic review of immersive virtual reality applications for higher education: Design elements, lessons learned, and research agenda. In *Computers & Education,* Vol. 147, pp. 103778.

Rheinberg, F., Vollmeyer, R., & Engeser, S., 2003. Die Erfassung des Flow-Erlebens. In: *Diagnostik von Selbstkonzept, Lernmotivation und Selbstregulation* (pp. 261–279). Göttingen: Hogrefe

Rutrecht, H., Wittmann, M., Khoshnoud, S., & Igarzábal, F. A., 2021. Time speeds up during flow states: A study in virtual reality with the video game thumper. In: Timing & Time Perception, Vol. 9, No. 4, pp. 353-376.

Schroeder, R., 2010. *Being there together.* New York, NY: Oxford University Press.

Sherry, J. L., 2004. Flow and media enjoyment. In: *Communication theory,* Vol. 14, No. 4, pp. 328-347.

Tai, K. H., Hong, J. C., Tsai, C. R., Lin, C. Z., & Hung, Y. H., 2022. Virtual reality for car-detailing skill development: Learning outcomes of procedural accuracy and performance quality predicted by VR self-efficacy, VR using anxiety, VR learning interest and flow experience. In: *Computers & Education,* 104458.

Voiskounsky, A. E., Mitina, O. V., & Avetisova, A. A., 2004. Playing online games: Flow experience. In: *PsychNology J.,* Vol. 2, No. 3, pp. 259-281.

Zinn, B., 2019. Lehren und Lernen zwischen Virtualität und Realität. In: *Journal of Technical Education* (JOTED), 7(1).

EXPLORING THE ATTENTIONAL PROFILE OF GIFTED CHILDREN USING A VR-BASED ASSESSMENT TOOL

Roberta Renati, Natale Salvatore Bonfiglio, Maria Lidia Mascia and Maria Pietronilla Penna
University of Cagliari
via Is Mirrionis 1, 09123 Cagliari, Italy

ABSTRACT

An accurate global assessment of gifted children is essential to provide them with educational and counseling programs tailored to their strengths and vulnerabilities. Without neglecting the fundamental role of social-emotional skills on individual well-being and academic success, it is essential to shedding light on the attentional profile of intellectually gifted children. In this regard, findings from empirical studies are not always consistent. The purpose of this exploratory study was to investigate the relationship between the cognitive profile of fifteen gifted children (mean age 9.6 years; SD 2.3), as described through the main WISC-IV indexes (IVE, IRP, IML, IVE, FSIQ), and their attentional profile assessed through AULA, an innovative VR-based ecological assessment tool that evaluates attention and inhibitory control. These first findings highlighted the correlation between intelligence and attention and provided indications for educational interventions. Therefore it is crucial to use innovative and highly ecological assessment tools to engage the IGen gifted learners. In this regard, researchers have recently developed and tested new tools that employ virtual reality (VR) to assess EFs (Climent et al. , 2010; Rizzo et al., 2006). VR-based assessment tools allow children to interact dynamically with realistic scenarios and situations that reproduce aspects of their everyday life.
The present study aimed to explore the correlation between the cognitive profile of gifted students, as measured by the WISC-IV paper-and-pencil test, and their attentional profile assessed through AULA, an innovative virtual reality-based attention assessment tool. A previous study by Diaz-Orueta et al. (2014) explored the correlation between WISC-IV indices in a sample of averaged cognitive ability learners diagnosed with ADHD, demonstrating the reliability of the VR-based attention assessment tool in discriminating clinical subjects. To our knowledge, no studies have yet been conducted analysing the attentional profile of gifted children using a VR-based attention assessment tool. Therefore, we expect to provide valuable new information on the peculiar attentional functioning of gifted children.

KEYWORDS

Gifted Children, Assessment, Attention, Virtual Reality, Executive Functions, School Intervention

1. INTRODUCTION

A high cognitive potential stems from a complex dynamic interaction between genetic, behavioural, and environmental factors. Biological aspects, also linked to epigenetic processes, are a prerequisite but not a sufficient condition for developing and expressing an individual's potential (Plomin and Deary, 2015; Sastre-Riba, 2020).

Recent neurocomputational simulations of gifted children's developmental trajectories (Thomas, 2018) clearly illustrate the interplay of multiple exogenous and endogenous factors that contribute to the expression of gifted children's cognitive potential. Among endogenous modulators, executive functions (EFs) play a central role in effectively managing intellectual resources. EFs are a set of top-down cognitive processes responsible for executing and regulating actions and are crucial for concentration and attention (Espy *et al.*, 2004). EFs have been linked to academic performance (Benedek *et al.,* 2014; Visu-Petra *et al.*, 2011) and are critical elements in promoting meaningful self-regulated and reflective learning (Kontostavlou *et al.*, 2022). Students need EFs to focus and sustain attention, plan and organise behaviour, prioritise information to initiate work, monitor task performance, and manage emotions related to the learning experience. EFs are one of the critical factors explaining individual differences in the developmental trajectory and expression of high cognitive potential, contributing to account for the gap observed in gifted students' cognitive performance.

Some researchers have suggested that the relation between executive functions' domains is related with intelligence in various ways (Arffa, 2007; Friedman *et al.*, 2006). Several studies have shown the correlation between attention and intelligence (Aubry and Bourdin, 2021; Cowan *et al.*, 2006), highlighting sustained attention as a variable capable of predicting individuals' performance on intelligence tests (Schweizer and Moosbrugger, 2004). Furthermore, executive control processes are found to be significantly correlated with intellectual ability (Tourva, Spanoudis and Demetriou, 2015). In particular, sustained attention refers to the ability to remain engaged in an activity for a specific time. Furthermore, it requires individuals to focus on the activity they are performing at that moment and simultaneously resist disturbances in the context by inhibiting unneeded responses (Trautmann and Zepf, 2012). With regard to gifted children's performance on attentional and executive control tasks, the empirical results are inconsistent. Some studies show that gifted individuals perform better than their intellectually non-gifted peers on most attentional tasks (Shi *et al.*, 2013). Particularly, Aubry, Gonthier and Bourdin (2021) stated that gifted children are characterized by their processing accuracy, showing a better ability to deliberately focus on solving a simple perceptual conflict than children with typical development. Therefore, accuracy appears to be a key element of gifted high performance on attentional tasks. Other studies have shown that individual differences in fluid intelligence can predict the ability to remove outdated information from the mind (Engle, 2018; Shipstead, Harrison and Engle, 2016).

Studies have compared the performance in attentional tasks of intellectually gifted children with those of their typically developing peers. Results showed that the gifted group performs better in processing relevant information (Zhang *et al.*, 2006), and seems to have a more remarkable ability to inhibit irrelevant information or inappropriate responses (Johnson, Im-Bolter and Pasqual-Leone, 2003). However, other studies suggest that the quality of attention of gifted children may be a vulnerability (Rommelse *et al.*, 2016). In this regard, Webb and Latimer (1993) pointed out that some gifted children could have problems controlling impulses, exhibiting hyperactivity and poor sustained attention. Westberg *et al.* (1993) have suggested that gifted children fail to focus attention on content in the classroom because they find the proposed activities uninspiring and, therefore, boring. Gifted children usually perform well if they are interested in the task or are otherwise motivated. Lack of interest or motivation can produce inaccurate results on objective tests of attention and subjective evaluations, such as behavior checklist ratings compiled by parents and teachers. In this unique population of children, behaviours that may appear as attention or hyperactivity disorders may indicate boredom and disinterest (Webb *et al.*, 2016). Inadequate assessment can lead to dangerous misdiagnoses, resulting in inappropriate counseling and school interventions. Researchers have recently developed and tested new tools that use virtual reality (VR) to assess EFs (Climent, Banterla and Iriarte, 2010; Rizzo *et al.*, 2006). VR-based assessment tools allow children to dynamically interact with realistic scenarios and situations that reproduce aspects of their everyday life.

The present study aimed to explore the correlation between the cognitive profile of gifted students, as measured by the WISC-IV paper-and-pencil test, and their attentional profile assessed through AULA, a virtual reality-based attention assessment tool. A previous study by Diaz-Orueta *et al.* (2014) explored the correlation between WISC-IV indices in a sample of subjects with average cognitive ability and a diagnosis of ADHD, demonstrating the reliability of the VR-based attention assessment tool in discriminating clinical subjects. To our knowledge, no studies have yet been conducted analysing the attentional profile of gifted children using a VR-based attention assessment tool. Therefore, we expect to provide valuable new information on the peculiar attentional functioning of gifted children.

2. THE RESEARCH

2.1 Participants

Fifteen intellectually gifted children participated in the study, twelve boys and three girls. The average age was 9.6 years (SD=2.3), ranging between 6 and 14 years. All participants were Italian, had medium-high socio-economic status, and lived in northern regions. Children involved in the study had no reported history of significative behavioural or emotional problems.

2.2 Instruments and Procedure

Aula Nesplora -AULA- (Climent & Banterla, 2010; Climent et al., 2011). Aula is a Continuous Performance Test (CPT) performed in a VR environment that reproduces the conditions of a classroom. The tool assesses attention, impulsivity, processing speed, and motor activity in subjects between 6 and 16 years.

The virtual environment is presented through a Virtual Reality Visor, which allows head movements to be recorded through the presence of sensors.

The test consists of two main tasks. The first task is based on an "NO-X" paradigm (i.e., "Press the button when you DO NOT perceive the target stimulus"); and the second task is a "X" paradigm (i.e, "press the button whenever you DO perceive the target stimulus"). Stimuli are presented both on a visual and auditory basis. At the same time, previously randomized visual and/or auditory distractors (equal to those that may appear in a real classroom, such as environmental noises) appear progressively. The sequence of presentation of the two tasks is first "NO-X" and then "X". The administration lasts approximately 20 minutes. Different measures are provided by different sensorial modalities (visual or auditory), presence/absence of distractors, and task type ("No-X" or "X" condition). The Cronbach's alpha of the test is .72.

For the purposes of this exploratory study were taken into account omission errors (i.e., when the subject does not respond by pressing the button when he/she should have to) and commission errors (i.e., when the subject press the button when he/she should not have to); reaction time and standard deviation of correct responses were examined for Task1 and Task 2 and both auditory and visual sensorial modalities.

WISC-IV Wechsler Intelligence Scale for Children- Fourth Edition (Wechsler, 2003; Italian translation and validation by Orsini, Pezzuti and Picone, 2012). The Wechsler Intelligence Scale for Children-IV (WISC-IV) is a general intelligence test consisting of 15 subtests, 10 core tests and 5 supplemental. The 10 mandatory subtests contribute to the measurement of four index scores: the verbal Comprehension Index (VCI), Perceptual Reasoning Index (PRI), Working Memory Index (WMI), and Processing Speed Index (PSI). The full-scale IQ score FSIQ is computed from 10 main subtests (three related to Verbal Comprehension, three to Perceptual Comprehension, three to Perceptual Reasoning, two to Working Memory, and two to Processing Speed) that reflect the general cognitive ability. The scale can be administered to children and adolescents between 6 and 16 years and 11 months.

Referring to the procedure, participants were recruited voluntarily from a center specialized in the assessment and psychological support for gifted children. Parents were given oral and written information about the purpose of the study and signed informed consent and privacy forms. The assessment battery was administered in a quiet room with proper light and temperature and carried out over two days. On the first day, the entire WISC- IV battery was administered, and on the second day, the Aula test was administered. All subjects were assessed by a licensed and experienced psychologist, experienced in the assessment of gifted children and well-trained about the use of the Aula test.

2.3 Data Analysis

A correlational analysis was performed to explore the relationship between gifted children's attention/disattention and impulsivity scores, measured by the AULA tool, and their cognitive profile measured through WISC-IV indices.

2.3.1 Results

Descriptive statistics have been calculated for the five WISC-IV indexes and reported in Table 1.

Table 1. Mean and standard deviation for WISC-IV indexes and for full IQ

WISC_IV indexes	Mean	Standard Deviation
ICV	137.200	8.809
IRP	133.333	8.499
IML	116.929	10.759
IVE	104.733	14.058
FSIQ	132.867	8.626

Note: ICV= Verbal Comprehension Index; IRP= Perceptual Reasoning Index; IML= Working Memory Index; IVE= Processing Speed Index; FSIQ= Full Scale of overall intelligence

Correlations have been carried out between the WISC-IV indexes and the total scores of Aula tool variables. Significant negative correlations have been found between the total number of commission errors with the IVE index and the FSIQ. Moreover, a significant positive correlation has been found between the total number of commission errors and the IRP index (Table 2).

Table 2. Pearson's correlations between WISC-IV indexes and AULA variables (total scores in both Task 1 No-X and Task 2 X)

	WISC-IV indexes				
AULA variables	ICV	IRP	IML	IVE	FSIQ
Total Omission errors	-0.167	-0.489	9,53E-01	-0.629*	-0.563*
Total Commission errors	0.113	0.604*	0.223	-0.043	0.199
Total RT Hit	0.316	-0.008	0.035	-0.183	0.058
Total DS RT Hit	0.180	-0.457	-0.128	-0.308	-0.388

Note: * *p* value <.05

Significant negative correlations emerged between the number of omission errors during the AULA task with the presentation of distractors and the WISC-IV FSIQ, and also with the IRP and the IVE indexes. Furthermore, a significant positive correlation was found between the number of commission errors children' made under the influence of distractors and the IRP index.

A significant negative correlation was found between the number of omission errors committed by children during the presentation of the stimuli without distractors, the IRP, the IVE indexes, and the full IQ scale.

Regarding gifted children's performance under and without the influence of visual and auditory distractors, a significant negative correlation was found between the number of omission errors committed during the presentation of the stimuli without distractors with the IRP and IVE indexes and FSIQ.

Furthermore, emerged a positive correlation between the number of commission errors perpetrated during the presentation of stimuli without distractors and the IRP index. Finally, a significant negative correlation was found between the correct answers' reaction times standard deviation in the distractor-free condition, with the IRP and IML indexes, and with the FSIQ (Table 3).

Table 3. Pearson's correlations between WISC-IV indexes and AULA variables related to performance under the influence of both visual and auditory distractors and in absence of distractors condition)

	WISC-IV Indexes				
AULA Variables	**ICV**	**IRP**	**IML**	**IVE**	**FSIQ**
Omission errors with distractors	-0.172	**-0.495***	0.040	**-0.692****	**-0.577***
Commission errors with distractors	-0.001	**0.694****	0.151	0.377	0.365
RT Hit with distractors	0.238	0.123	0.094	-0.079	0.138
DS RT Hit with distractors	0.337	-0.236	-0.233	-0.131	-0.169
Omission errors without distractors	-0.229	**-0.491***	-0.005	**-0.588***	**-0.584***
Commission errors without distractors	-0.040	0.426+	0.162	-0.221	-0.033
RT Hit without distractors	0.191	-0.204	0.022	-0.393	-0.164
DS RT Hit without distractors	-0.205	**-0.576***	-0.032	-0.345	**-0.601***

Note: * *p* value <.05; ** *p* value <.01; + significant trend

A significant negative correlation emerged between the number of omission errors in Task 1, the IVE index, and the FSIQ. Additionally, a significant negative correlation was found between the correct answers' reaction times standard deviation in Task 2, and the IRP index (Table 4).

Table 4. Pearson's correlations between WISC-IV indexes and AULA variables differentiated for Task 1 (NO-X paradigm) and Task 2 (X paradigm)

	WISC-IV Indexes				
AULA Variables	**ICV**	**IRP**	**IML**	**IVE**	**FSIQ**
Omission errors (NO-X)	-0.085	-0.430	-0.037	**-0.638****	**-0.525***
Commision errors (NO-X)	0.064	0.401	-0.139	0.069	0.088
RT Hit (NO-X)	0.267	0.146	0.011	0.100	0.222
DS RT Hit (NO-X)	0.200	-0.389	-0.183	-0.274	-0.337
Omission errors (X)	-0.399	-0.306	0.170	-0.405	-0.460
Commision errors (X)	-0.050	0.322	0.335	-0.202	0.019
RT Hit (X)	0.341	0.049	0.232	-0.266	0.066
DS RT Hit (X)	0.118	**-0.610***	0.254	0.266	0.020

Note: * *p* value <.05; ** *p* value <.01

A significant negative correlation was found between reaction times in correct answers for visual stimuli and the IVE index. Regarding auditory stimuli, a significant negative correlation was found between the number of omission errors, the IRP and IVE indices, as well as for the FSIQ. Lastly, a significant negative correlation was found between the standard deviation of of correct responses reaction times to auditory stimuli and IRP and IVE indices, and also for the FSIQ (Table 5).

Table 5. Pearson's correlations between WISC-IV indexes and AULA variables for visual and auditory stimuli conditions

	WISC-IV Indexes				
AULA Variables	**ICV**	**IRP**	**IML**	**IVE**	**FSIQ**
Visual Omissions errors	-0.278	-0.384	0.065	-0.488	-0.474
Visual Commision errors	-0.396	0.118	0.046	0.138	-0.135
RT Visual Hit	0.322	-0.296	0.108	**-0.525***	-0.204
DS RT Visual Hit	0.119	-0.384	0.097	-0.371	-0.276
Auditory Omissions errors	-0.150	**-0.554***	-0.105	**-0.685****	**-0.668****
Auditory Commision errors	0.386	0.494	0.247	-0.104	0.329
RT Auditory Hit	0.210	-0.011	-0.056	-0.116	0.023
DS RT Auditory Hit	0.232	**-0.499***	-0.073	**-0.691****	**-0.531***

Note: * *p* value <.05; ** *p* value <.01

2.3.2 Discussion

The IQ score being a standardized measure of intelligence, is considered a decisive variable in the definition of intellectual giftedness; however, it is not sufficient to explain the individual's developmental trajectory. In order to explain the development of high abilities and performance, it is also necessary to take into account other variables, of which executive functions are particularly relevant. Indeed, numerous studies have highlighted the relationship between high cognitive abilities and executive functions (Dunst *et al.*, 2014; Rocha *et al.*, 202; Shi *et al.*, 2013).

The present study aimed to investigate the correlations between the cognitive profile of intellectually gifted children and their attentive performance in Nesplora Aula (Climent, Banterla and Iriarte, 2011).

Our preliminary findings, with appropriate caution due to the small size of the sample, suggest that the WISC-IV composite indexes IRP and IVE, as well as the FSIQ, are elements that play a significant role in explaining the relationship between intelligence and attention in gifted children. Analyzing the emerged results in detail, it is possible to observe a negative correlation characterizing IRP, IVE indexes and the full

IQ score with respect to omission errors. This evidence emerges both in the presence and in the absence of distractors. With respect to omission errors during divided attention condition there is evidence of significance only in relation to the auditory sensory modality. In general omission errors are ascribable to inattention and occur when the subject does not press the button in response to the stimulus being presented. This measure is therefore related to selective and focused attention (Iriarte et al., 2016). The negative correlation that emerged at the above mentioned indexes highlights that as the score at the composite indexes IRP and IVE increases, as well as for FSIQ, errors of omission, and thus inattention, decrease. The absence of correlation regarding the visual sensory condition deserves to be further explored.

Concerning commission errors, the results show a positive correlation with the IRP index only in the condition under the influence of distractors. Commission errors occur when the subject presses the button when he/she should not have to and denote difficulty in inhibitory control. This evidence could indicate that high scores on the visual-perceptual reasoning index may lead the child to be more impulsive or to lack control in inhibiting responses. This result requires further analysis, investigating in more detail the influence of the type of distractor (visual or auditory).

Finally, concerning correct answers, reaction times and the associated standard deviation, the results showed negative correlations in relation to the composite index IRP and the FSIQ. Reaction time is the period required to respond to a stimulus. It tends to be longer in subjects with attention deficits because they tend to process information more slowly (Ptacek *et al.*, 2019). The negative correlation that emerged shows that high IRP scores correlate with lower reaction time variability in correct responses, in the condition without distractors and with respect to the auditory sensory modality.

3. CONCLUSIONS

The relationship between intelligence and attention is well described in the literature, but the nature of this interplay has been scarcely explored in intellectually gifted children. Our results reveal that some aspects of intelligence, measured by the WISC-IV, appear to be related to attention and inhibitory control. Although the study is exploratory, it offers the opportunity to advance new hypotheses for a more comprehensive understanding of intellectually gifted children.

A deeper comprehension of the unique characteristics of the cognitive profiles of these children allows for the design of interventions that could support them in the school context. These evidences are also relevant for counseling interventions to support the families of gifted children (Renati, Bonfiglio and Pfeiffer, 2017) and for developing specific training to improve their executive functions (Bonfiglio *et al.*, 2020; Renati *et al.*, 2021).

Further studies should involve a larger sample of subjects and a control group. Additionally, extending the assessment battery to assess executive functions through other traditional assessment instruments would be appropriate.

REFERENCES

Arffa, S., 2007. The relationship of intelligence to executive function and non-executive function measures in a sample of average, above average, and gifted youth. *Archives of Clinical Neuropsychology*, *22*(8), pp. 969-978.

Aubry, A. and Bourdin, B., 2021. Alerting, orienting, and executive control in intellectually gifted children. *Brain and Behavior*, *11*(8), p.e02148.

Aubry, A., Gonthier, C. and Bourdin, B., 2021. Explaining the high working memory capacity of gifted children: Contributions of processing skills and executive control. *Acta psychologica*, *218*, p. 103358.

Bonfiglio, N.S., Renati, R., Parodi, D., Pessa, E., Rollo, D. and Penna, M.P., 2020, June. Use of training with BCI (Brain Computer Interface) in the management of impulsivity. In *2020 IEEE international symposium on medical measurements and applications (MeMeA)* (pp. 1-5). IEEE.

Bonfiglio, N.S., Renati, R., Patrone, L., Rollo, D. and Penna, M.P., 2021, June. The use of cognitive training with tDCS for the reduction of impulsiveness and improvement of executive functions: a case study. In *2021 IEEE International Symposium on Medical Measurements and Applications (MeMeA)* (pp. 1-6). IEEE.

Benedek, M., Jauk, E., Sommer, M., Arendasy, M. and Neubauer, A.C., 2014. Intelligence, creativity, and cognitive control: The common and differential involvement of executive functions in intelligence and creativity. *Intelligence*, *46*, pp. 73-83.

Climent, G., Banterla, F. and Iriarte, Y., 2010. Virtual reality, technologies and behavioural assessment. *AULA, ecological evaluation of attentional processes*, pp. 19-28.

Climent, G., Banterla, F. and Iriarte, Y., 2011. AULA: Theoretical manual. *San Sebastian, Spain: Nesplora.*

Cowan, N., Fristoe, N.M., Elliott, E.M., Brunner, R.P. and Saults, J.S., 2006. Scope of attention, control of attention, and intelligence in children and adults. *Memory & cognition*, *34*(8), pp. 1754-1768.

Díaz-Orueta, U., García-López, C., Crespo-Eguílaz, N., Sánchez-Carpintero, R., Climent, G. and Narbona, J., 2014. AULA virtual reality test as an attention measure: Convergent validity with Conners' Continuous Performance Test. *Child Neuropsychology*, *20*(3), pp. 328-342.

Dunst, B., Benedek, M., Jauk, E., Bergner, S., Koschutnig, K., Sommer, M., Ischebeck, A., Spinath, B., Arendasy, M., Bühner, M. and Freudenthaler, H., 2014. Neural efficiency as a function of task demands. *Intelligence*, *42*, pp. 22-30.

Engle, R.W., 2018. Working memory and executive attention: A revisit. *Perspectives on Psychological Science*, *13*(2), pp. 190-193.

Espy, K.A., McDiarmid, M.M., Cwik, M.F., Stalets, M.M., Hamby, A. and Senn, T.E., 2004. The contribution of executive functions to emergent mathematic skills in preschool children. *Developmental neuropsychology*, *26*(1), pp. 465-486.

Friedman, N.P., Miyake, A., Corley, R.P., Young, S.E., DeFries, J.C. and Hewitt, J.K., 2006. Not all executive functions are related to intelligence. *Psychological science*, *17*(2), pp. 172-179.

Johnson, J., Im-Bolter, N. and Pascual-Leone, J., 2003. Development of mental attention in gifted and mainstream children: The role of mental capacity, inhibition, and speed of processing. Child development, 74(6), pp. 1594-1614.

Kontostavlou, E.Z. and Drigas, A.S., 2022. Executive functions training and giftedness. *Retos: nuevas tendencias en educación física, deporte y recreación*, (43), pp. 1005-1014.

Orsini, A., Pezzuti, L. and Picone, L., 2012. *WISC-IV: Contributo alla taratura italiana*. Giunti OS Organizzazioni Speciali.

Plomin, R. and Deary, I. J. (2015). Genetics and intelligence differences: five special findings. *Molecular psychiatry*, *20*(1), pp. 98-108.

Ptacek, R., Weissenberger, S., Braaten, E., Klicperova-Baker, M., Goetz, M., Raboch, J., Vnukova, M. and Stefano, G.B., 2019. Clinical implications of the perception of time in attention deficit hyperactivity disorder (ADHD): A review. *Medical science monitor: international medical journal of experimental and clinical research*, *25*, p. 3918.

Renati, R., Bonfiglio, N.S., Patrone, L., Rollo, D. and Penna, M.P., 2021, June. The use of cognitive training and tDCS for the treatment of a high potential subject: a case study. In *2021 IEEE International Symposium on Medical Measurements and Applications (MeMeA)* (pp. 1-6). IEEE.

Renati, R., Bonfiglio, N.S. and Pfeiffer, S., 2017. Challenges raising a gifted child: Stress and resilience factors within the family. *Gifted Education International*, *33*(2), pp. 145-162.

Rizzo, A.A., Bowerly, T., Buckwalter, J.G., Klimchuk, D., Mitura, R. and Parsons, T.D., 2009. A virtual reality scenario for all seasons: the virtual classroom. *Cns Spectrums*, *11*(1), pp. 35-44.

Rocha, A., Almeida, L. and Perales, R., 2020. Comparison of gifted and non-gifted students' executive functions and high capabilities. *Journal for the Education of Gifted Young Scientists*, *8*(4), pp. 1397-1409.

Rommelse, N., van der Kruijs, M., Damhuis, J., Hoek, I., Smeets, S., Antshel, K.M., Hoogeveen, L. and Faraone, S.V., 2016. An evidenced-based perspective on the validity of attention-deficit/hyperactivity disorder in the context of high intelligence. *Neuroscience & Biobehavioral Reviews*, *71*, pp. 21-47.

Sastre-Riba, S., (2020). Moduladores de la expresión de la alta capacidad intelectual. *MEDICINA (Buenos Aires)*, *80*, pp. 53-57.

Shi, J., Tao, T., Chen, W., Cheng, L., Wang, L. and Zhang, X., 2013. Sustained attention in intellectually gifted children assessed using a continuous performance test. *PloS one*, *8*(2), p.e57417.

Shipstead, Z., Harrison, T.L. and Engle, R.W., 2016. Working memory capacity and fluid intelligence: Maintenance and disengagement. *Perspectives on Psychological Science*, *11*(6), pp. 771-799.

Schweizer, K. and Moosbrugger, H., 2004. Attention and working memory as predictors of intelligence. *Intelligence*, 32(4), pp.329-347.

Thomas, M.S., 2018. A neurocomputational model of developmental trajectories of gifted children under a polygenic model: When are gifted children held back by poor environments?. *Intelligence*, *69*, pp. 200-212.

Tourva, A., Spanoudis, G. and Demetriou, A., 2016. Cognitive correlates of developing intelligence: The contribution of working memory, processing speed and attention. *Intelligence*, *54*, pp. 136-146.

Trautmann, M. and Zepf, F.D., 2012. Attentional performance, age and scholastic achievement in healthy children. *PLos One*, *7*(3), p.e32279.

Visu-Petra, L., Cheie, L., Benga, O. and Miclea, M., 2011. Cognitive control goes to school: The impact of executive functions on academic performance. *Procedia-Social and Behavioral Sciences*, *11*, pp.240-244.Webb JT, Latimer D (1993) ADHD and children who are gifted. Except Child 60: 183–185.

Webb et al, 2016. *Misdiagnosis and Dual Diagnoses of Gifted Children and Adults. ADHD, Bipolar, OCD, Asperger's, Depression, and Other Disorders (2nd Edition)*. Great Potential Press Inc., Tucson, AZ.

Webb, J.T. and Latimer, D., 1993. ADHD and Children Who Are Gifted. ERIC Digest.

Westberg, K.L., 1993. An Observational Study of Instructional and Curricular Practices Used with Gifted and Talented Students in Regular Classrooms. Research Monograph 93104.

Zhang, H., Zhang, X., He, Y. and Shi, J., 2016. Inattentional blindness in 9-to 10-year-old intellectually gifted children. *Gifted Child Quarterly*, *60*(4), pp.287-295.

KNOWLEDGE MAPPING FOR CREATIVE THINKING

Alberto Giretti[1], Massimo Lemma[1], Matteo Zambelli[2] and Franco Ripa di Meana[3]
[1]*Università Politecnica delle Marche , Via Brecce Bianche, 60131 Ancona, Italy*
[2]*Università degli Studi di Firenze – Dipartimento di Architettura – DiDA, Via della Mattonaia, 8, 50121 Firenze, Italy*
[3]*Academy of Fine Arts, Via di Ripetta, 222 – 00186 Roma, Italy*

ABSTRACT

In this paper we illustrate the architecture of the °'°Kobi system, which is aimed at supporting students' education in artistic or design activities. We will outline the scientific and methodological foundations of the educational approach aimed at enhancing the artistic conception and the design ideation. The functional requirements and the system architecture for implementing the °'°Kobi system are outlined. Finally, the paper discusses some relevant aspects concerning the system application in a real educational context and briefly reports about its preliminary assessment.

KEYWORDS

Art Education, Design Education, Creativity, Associative Thinking

1. INTRODUCTION

Art education is a complex activity. Art involves an individual action of discovery, guided by the mutual action of mind and body, in which learning occurs as a creative act (Tanggaard 2014). Education in art is therefore an activity characterized by strong experiential and heuristic factors, which, in the growing of creative skills, take the form of inextricable combinations of ideas, forms and substance. In fact, learning in art triggers fundamental imaginative capacities, such as visualization, originality, invention, ordering, synthesizing and syncretizing, as well as empathy (Greene 1970). At the same time, art education is open to the entire history of cultural development, as it is aimed at the introjection and self-contamination of the cultural products that emerged in different historical periods and socio-cultural contexts (Addison 2010). The exposure to multiple cultures and/or multiple languages is beneficial for creativity (Lubart 2010). It enhances knowledge and challenges typical ways of thinking and acting. It leads people to overcome their cultural habits. Indeed, multicultural experiences foster openness to new ideas (Leung 2008).

Art education might benefit from learning environments that both provide opportunities and encourage students to think and behave creatively, and that ground their interpretative skills on a solid multicultural basis. How such environments should be arranged, their architecture and functional set-up is still an open problem (Glăveanu 2021). In this paper we illustrate the architecture of the °'°Kobi system, a supporting system for the education of students involved in artistic or design activities that are characterized by a high creative factor.

In the actual pedagogical experience, art and design do work within or in relation to traditions, which are often technically demanding, requiring diligence, determination, immersion, and acculturation to and within valued conventions. Craftsmanship is one of the fundamental outcomes of such artistic learning, and apprenticeship is its usual pedagogical form. However, if creativity is the goal, there needs to be a balance between mastery of conventions, which provides satisfaction, confidence and self-esteem, and the visionary artistic tension, which makes it possible to break established rules and develop new expressive means (Csikszentmihalyi 1996). (Kolb & Kolb 2017) analyze to a full extend the experiential nature of apprenticeship pedagogy. Experiential learning models suggest the idea that learning is by nature a process full of tension and conflict, where the moment of learning is co-articulated with the moment of doing. New knowledge, skills or attitudes are achieved through the confrontation among four different types of skills:

a) *concrete experience skills* - learners must be able to involve themselves fully, openly and without prejudice in new experiences,

b) *reflective observation skills* - learners must be able to reflect and observe their experiences from many perspectives,
c) *abstract conceptualization skills* - learners must be able to create concepts that integrate their observations into culturally relevant theories,
d) *active experimentation skills* - learners must be able to use these theories to make decisions and progress the artwork.

Experiential learning therefore requires skills that are inherently opposites. So, there are two primary dimensions in which the learning process can be developed along:

1. The first dimension represents concrete experience of events at one extreme and abstract conceptualization at the other.
2. The other dimension has active experimentation at one extreme and reflective observation at the other.

In the experiential learning process, the learner moves in various degrees from actor to observer, and from specific involvement to general analytical detachment (Morris 2020). In this scenario, °'°Kobi is a complementary tool to the apprenticeship of techniques and operational practice, seeking to emphasize reflective observation and abstract conceptualization (figure 1).

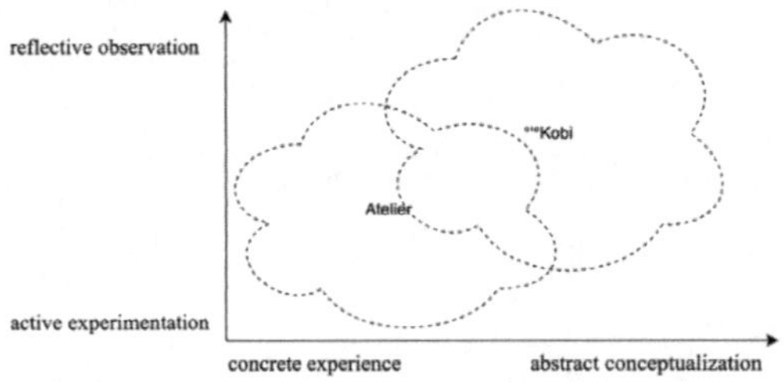

Figure 1. Experiential learning dimensions

In sections 2 and 3 we will develop in detail the operational implications of this methodological vision, the essential features of the system architecture and interfaces, and in section 4 we give some examples of use in real classes of students. In the conclusion section we will outline the current implementation limits and the future research work.

2. THE °'°KOBI APPROACH

°'°Kobi is a knowledge-based system aimed at fostering creative thinking throughout the educational process of art and design academies, with the aim of realizing a multi-cultural eco-system for creative learning, well-grounded on an operationally sound cognitive theory of creativity. The previous section pointed out reflection, associative thinking, and multiculturality as the key dimensions to be supported in creative education, to complement and enhance the apprenticeship practice. On that basis the following functional requirements for the °'°Kobi system has been defined:

a) *Supporting reflective thinking* - by means of interfaces that foster the creation of new critical and interpretative structures through abstract conceptualization and reflective observation, as well as reformulation and reinterpretation of contents.
b) *Supporting associative thinking* - by implementing large knowledge domains, arranged as shallow relational structures, encompassing multiple semantic contexts.
c) *Implementing the multicultural dimension* - by developing an ecosystem that integrates multidisciplinary contents based on well-defined semantics from the different disciplines and linguistic domains.

2.1 Knowledge Mapping

°'°Kobi reinterprets the Knowledge Mapping paradigm already widely used in the domain of Knowledge Management (Wexler 2001). The Knowledge Mapping objective of capitalizing on corporate knowledge is translated to the requirement of sharing the rich conceptualizations underlying the production of educational materials and students' homework, by indexing, storing and retrieving them in a flexible and semantically rich manner. Hence, °'°Kobi supports the development of a large multicultural knowledge base by collecting the conceptual work of teachers' and students' communities. Knowledge in °'°Kobi is organized in maps (Figure 2). According to (Novak 2009), knowledge maps improve meaningful learning, associative and reflective thinking since users are "obliged" to represent their knowledge in a structured and relational fashion. (Davis 2011) shows that the externalization of knowledge structures on maps fosters self-reflection and enhance critical thinking as well. In °'°Kobi each map has a well-defined scope that is considered as a specific *semantic field* (Lyons, 1977), In that way °'°Kobi introduces a first level of semantic structure.

2.2 Associative Thinking

°'°Kobi knowledge representation schemata are limited to associative knowledge structures. °'°Kobi provides no formal means of defining knowledge structures to support any form of automated reasoning except associative chains. The knowledge depicted on the maps' canvas as graph structures explicitly outlines the basic form of associative arrangement. Other features are used to identify further degrees of association among the knowledge elements represented in the canvas. The first, obviously, concerns the linguistic content of texts. Computational linguistics (Mitkov 2004) allows the use of very flexible terminological associations, possibly using specific corpora (Speer et. al. 2017), to establish semantic associations between pieces of text belonging to the same or different *semantic fields*. The spatial layout of contents offers a third possibility to infer implicit associations. According to the gestalt principle of *proximity* (Köhler 1967), objects or shapes that are close to one another appear to form groups, hence they are tendentially considered semantically more relevant than elements that are far away from each other. Hence *proximity* is used in °'°Kobi as a further principle of semantic association. *Proximity* is a principle that has great practical value. In fact, it allows any content to be associated regardless of its nature. Thus, through proximity it is possible to associate text with text, but also text with images and images with images or any other type of media content (video, sound, etc.). By combining *proximity*, maps' wired links and linguistic associations °'°Kobi realizes a rich mean of navigation by association (Figure 2).

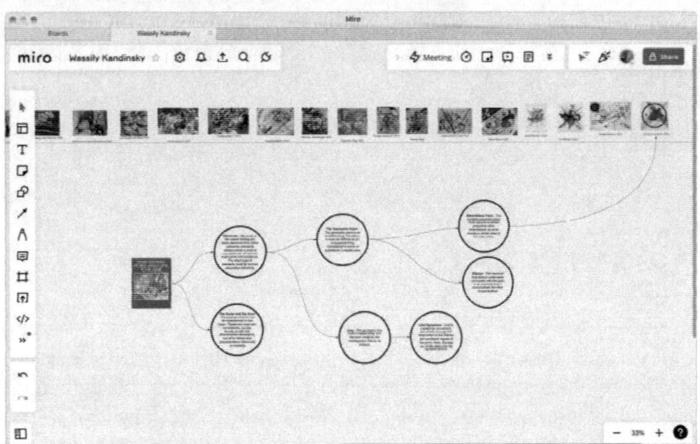

Figure 2. A fragment of an essay map freely drawn by a teacher with different styles. The map represents a semantic context. Proximity (top image line) and explicit links (bottom part) has been used as associative means

2.3 The Knowledge Ecosystem

The cultural component of creative thinking is supported in °'°Kobi through technologies for collaborative work. These technologies enable the creation of communities of users, whether teachers or learners, who share information, documents, or media material, interact and communicate with varying degrees of flexibility. Using the ability to create associations on a semantic level, °'°Kobi generates what is commonly called a *knowledge ecosystem* (Szoniecky 2018). In °'°Kobi, contents of different users are semantically related according to the techniques discussed above, thus generating a universe of knowledge. Such a universe has multiple educational roles and relevance. First, each knowledge map naturally generates a linguistic domain or semantic field by adopting a terminology and structuring associations proper to the topic at hand. Syntactic associations between terms belonging to different linguistic fields tend to generate a polysemous or sometimes metaphorical shift that is extremely relevant for creative thinking (Mednick 1962). On the iconographic level, the proximity association of terms and images on different semantic fields creates very rich contexts for the creative interpretation of visual and/or conceptual suggestions. Finally, °'°Kobi makes it possible to navigate the associative fabric thus created, generating interpretative paths that may diverge (Runco 2012) while remaining within a set of well delineated and relevant semantic fields. This lets °'°Kobi be in clear complementarity with, for example, traditional search engines that do not allow searching by semantic relevance. In fact, °'°Kobi allows one's own linguistic scopes, generated during associative navigation, to be used as a pool of search keys for traditional search engines (see section 4.2).

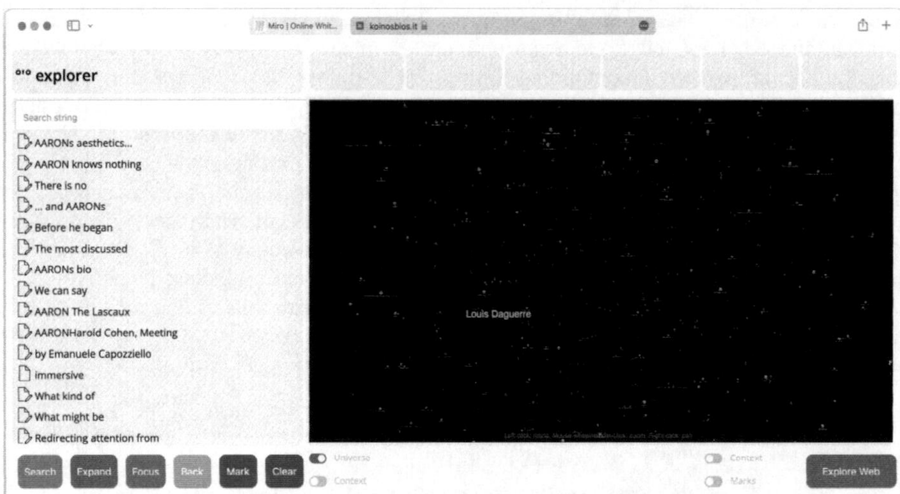

Figure 3. °'°Kobi knowledge eco-system represented as a content list (left) and 3D graph (right)

3. °'°KOBI ARCHITECTURE

°'°Kobi was developed as a web environment by selecting from the pool of current methodologies and available technologies what maximizes usability and dissemination in learner communities. Being a web-based application °'°Kobi consists of a front-end that implements the user interface and a back-end that implements the business logic services and knowledgebase functions. GUI quality and usability was considered a key factor for the successful development of application. Hence the Miro© platform[1], a commercial knowledge mapping tool, has been used. Miro offers state-of-the-art usability, flexibility, and support for collaborative work. It is also open to the development of custom applications and, with some limitations, totally free for academic and educational purposes. A large part of °'°Kobi's front-end has thus been developed as a Miro application. Hence, Kobi uses the Miro boards as its main knowledge mapping

[1] https://www.miro.com

tool. The Miro app interoperate with the °’°Kobi server to provide autonomous navigation in the °’°Kobi knowledge ecosystem. The °’°Kobi’s back end has been implemented in Node.js. The database uses a graph DB technology, by means of the open source Neo4j application, which maps very well with the knowledge representation requirements of the °’°Kobi application.

4. USING °’°KOBI

The overall °’°Kobi’s usage profile in the educational context is twofold. On the one hand, °’°Kobi can be used as a knowledge elicitation tool during the authoring teaching material by lecturers. In this case °’°Kobi can be used both to create the conceptual brochures that will be the basis for the development of the final material, and/or to create the final form of the content to be used in the classroom lessons. On the other hand, °’°Kobi can be used by students as a tool to support the development of group work assigned during courses. In both cases, °’°Kobi is a tool for capitalizing on the knowledge produced as it allows a substantial amount of learning material to be accumulated and retrieved with a good degree of semantic coherence.

4.1 Authoring in °’°Kobi

The production of learning material represents one of the main educational activities in Higher Education. This primary activity usually takes place by progressive refinements of conceptual schemes that are then enriched with explanatory material. This process can be effectively supported by a knowledge mapping tool. The use of °’°Kobi allows teachers to capitalize on the knowledge produced by sharing it in a *knowledge ecosystem*. Shared knowledge is semantically related to the contributions of colleagues from other disciplines. An example of °’°Kobi authoring is shown in figure 2. It illustrates a fragment of an essay written by a teacher concerning a lesson about the painter Wassily Kandinsky. The simple organization principles of °’°Kobi's maps allow the implementation of association structures with different semantic valences. For example, the top line of images ordered in temporal succession and annotated with milestones provides associative chains based on the timeline principle. Conversely, the inclusion in the bottom area of a painter’s essay, which excerpts are explicitly annotated and commented, implements a knowledge structure with critical valence.

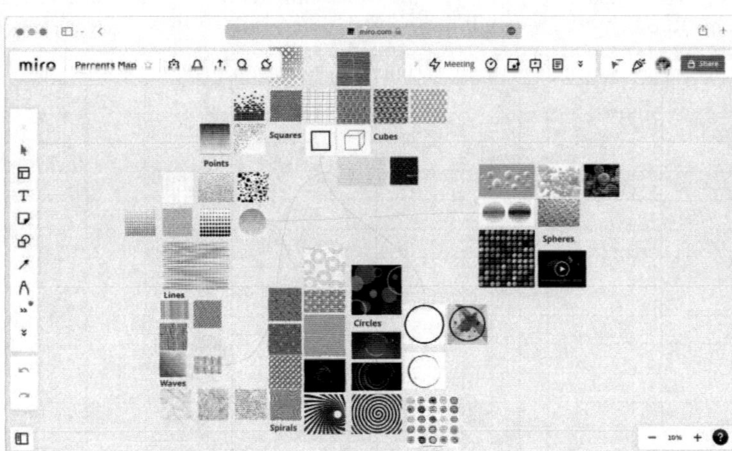

Figure 4. An example of a perceptive map

The two perspectives are then explicitly related through links connecting concepts and paintings, thus creating a rich interpretative framework that can be retrieved and used by students during their homework development. A second example concerns a knowledge map aimed at fostering the learners’ imaginative and visual thinking skill. Figure 4 shows a map that organizes iconographic and media materials around primary graphic concepts such as point, line, square, etc. The structure of the map relates the primary concept expressed as text with different iconic materials produced by designers and artists. The associations are nuanced, proceeding by proximity or by explicit connection. In the composition of a map, it is therefore possible to define a gradualness, or, if we want, a degree of association, of an image to a concept, as well as a transition chain from one concept to another through hybrid images, which possess traits of both.

4.2 Navigating °'°Kobi's Associative Chains

The main use of °'°Kobi as a teaching tool is to support the construction of conceptual structures that have significant semantic relevance in their own cultural contexts. To this aim °'°Kobi provides navigation tools in the knowledge ecosystem that allow on the one hand a free navigation by semantic associations on multidisciplinary domains, and on the other hand the collection of a well-founded linguistic and terminological background that potentially improves the semantic focus of traditional search engines. We will see some examples in the remainder of this section, using for clarity the limited set of maps introduced so far. We start by trying to investigate about the concept of *Point*. This can be done by inserting the concept as a textual element in the map and asking °'°Kobi to expand the concept (i.e. to search about it in the ecosystem) (Figure 5 – left). The result consists of texts and images that are directly related to the *Point* concept in different maps (Figure 5 – right).

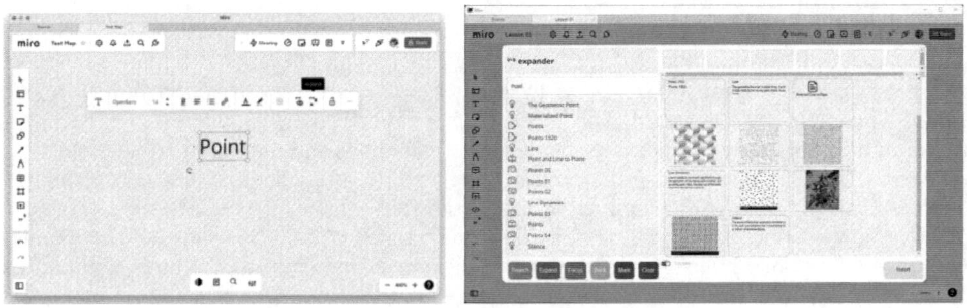

Figure 5. Investigating the Point concept - Stating the concept (left), first expansion in the knowledge base (right)

Notice how the conceptual richness of the knowledge ecosystem is reflected in the results. The multimedia elements have been recovered by proximity in different contexts belonging to different semantic fields. Some of them, like the texture images, are purely perceptual, others belong to well-structured critical essay, like the paint image, others are textual elements that are linguistically related to the key concept. Each of these results can be further investigated in detail (Figure 6 - left) and either pinpointed in the top boxes or inserted into the map and linked to the original text.

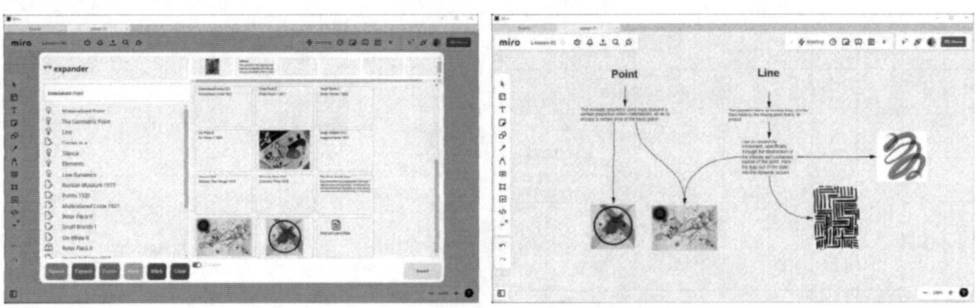

Figure 6. Investigating the *Point* concept - Second expansion (left), final arrangement (right)

In this way, the students can build a rich representation of the *Point* concept, drawing on semantically well-focused teaching material producing their interpretations and new meanings with a significant cultural and inventive involvement (Figure 6 - right).

A similar approach can be used to mitigate the typical generality of traditional Web search engines. In this case, a preliminary search operated on the °'°Kobi ecosystem allows the student to define a rather focused linguistic context, which can then be used as a set of search keys in commercial Web search engines. Very often this leads to more semantically targeted search results.

4.3 °'°Kobi in a Design Classroom

°'°Kobi was used to support a design methods course, whose title is "Methods for construction quality", in an undergraduate curriculum at the Department of Architecture of the University of Florence (Italy). The class consisted of forty students who worked arranged in groups in on-line sessions using the collaborative work support offered by the °'°Kobi platform. Each group had to design a product in relation to a theme assigned by the lecturer and reflect their design process on a °'°Kobi board through a well-defined set of conceptual design methods, including brainstorming, the six hats method, the issue-concept-form formalism, heuristics such as analogy and metaphor. Students must build a map related to each conceptual design methods. All the maps were discussed with the lectures and shared with the other students, who could suggest their colleagues how to improve the maps. At present, the class has produced an ecosystem with more than 1,000 nodes representing an initial core of shared knowledge to which the experiences produced by subsequent classes in the coming years will be added. In this way °'°Kobi support the capitalization of class experience. Obviously, the knowledge produced by students reflects their degree of critical insight, and thus tends to be less semantically structured than what can be produced by a professor in a specific essay. However, the sheer volume of multimedia material produced and its organization by themes and simple keys produces a semantic focus that, even at this level, cannot be achieved with traditional search engines. Figure 7 shows an example of students' boards.

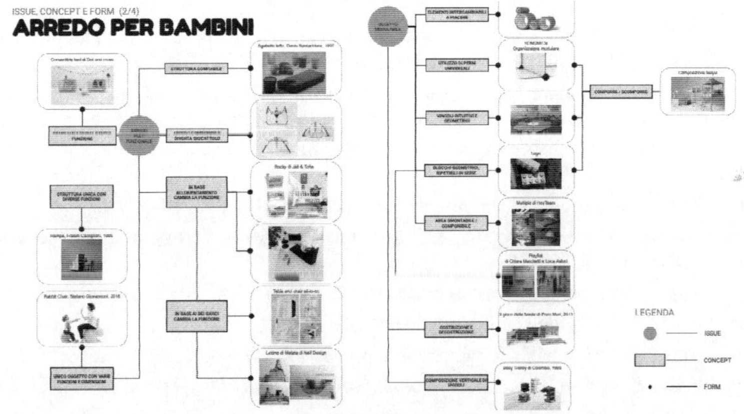

Figure 7. Fragments of an issue-concept-form board developed by groups of students in a design method course at Florence University in Italy. Text is in Italian

The students' experience of using such tools in teaching was in their opinion positive, according to what they expressed in informal interviews during the course, as was the teachers' assessment of the practical effectiveness and quality of the final work.

5. CONCLUSIONS

In this article we discussed the main features of the °'°Kobi system for supporting creative learning. Areas of application of the system in the context of current educational practices for teaching in fine arts and design curricula were highlighted, and its functional peculiarities that enable it to support students' construction of critical knowledge were highlighted. °'°Kobi is currently in an early stage of development, where the focus is on usability and robustness of the tools used within traditional educational settings. Therefore, the system has many limitations in content processing and structuring. Linguistic processing is currently limited to lexical analysis only. Algorithms for using *Wordnet synsets*, for example, have not yet been implemented. Nor has the interface to external content repositories such as, for example, *Europeana* and *Getty images* been developed. At present, as mentioned in the preceding paragraphs, no form of structured knowledge expressed through labeled relations is supported, such as, for example, the *issue-concept-form* or *six-hats* paradigms like in Figure 7. However, despite these limitations, initial results have shown good operation of the tool in the context of a product design class for an undergraduate course in a higher education curriculum, and teachers' preliminary evaluations of student work, including in relation to the development of a critical apparatus of final papers, are positive. However, in order to have a more objective and comparable assessment of the effectiveness of the method, it will be necessary in future research to evaluate the system within a protocol that has a solid pedagogical basis.

ACKNOWLEDGEMENT

The research is funded by the European project EU4ART_DIFFERENCES proposal number: 101016460
We thank Aleksandra Czuba, Prof. Alessandra Maria Porfidia and Prof. Miriam Mirolla from the Academy of Fine Arts of Rome for their contributions and valuable comments on the research topics.

REFERENCES

Addison, N. et al, 2010. *Understanding Art Education*. Taylor and Francis, NY.

Csikszentmihalyi, M. (1996) *Creativity: Flow and the psychology of discovery and invention*, New York: Harper Perennial.

Davies, M. (2011). Concept mapping, mind mapping and argument mapping: what are the differences, and do they matter? *High Educ* 62, 279–301 (2011). https:// doi.org/10.1007/s10734-010-9387-6

Glăveanu, V. P. et al, (2021). *Creative Learning in Digital and Virtual Environments. Opportunities and Challenges of Technology–enabled Learning and Creativity*. New York and London: Routledge.

Greene, M. (1970) 'Imagination', in Smith. R. A. (ed.) *Aesthetic Concepts in Education*, Urbana, Chicago, London: University of Illinois Press.

Köhler, W. (1967). *Gestalt psychology*. Psychologische Forschung, 31(1), XVIII-XXX.

Leung, A. K., Maddux, W. W., Galinsky, A. D., & Chiu, C. (2008). Multicultural experience enhances creativity. *American Psychologist*, 63(3), 169–181.

Lubart, T. (2010). Cross-cultural perspectives on creativity. *The Cambridge handbook of creativity*, 265-278.

Lyons. J. (1977). *Semantics*. Cambridge University Press.

Mednick, S. (1962). The associative basis of the creative process, *Psychological review*, 69(3), 220.

Mitkov, R. (Ed.). (2004). *The Oxford handbook of computational linguistics*. Oxford University Press.

Morris, T. H. (2020). Experiential learning–a systematic review and revision of Kolb's model. *Interactive Learning Environments*, 28(8), 1064-1077.

Novak, J.D. (2009), *Learning, Creating, and Using Knowledge: Concept Maps as Facilitative Tools in Schools and Corporations*, Routledge, London (UK).

Runco M. (2012) Divergent Thinking as an Indicator of Creative Potential, *Creativity Research Journal*, January 2012

Speer, R., Chin, J., & Havasi, C. (2017). Conceptnet 5.5: An open multilingual graph of general knowledge. In Proceedings of the *thirty-first AAAI conference on artificial intelligence*, San Francisco, California, USA.

Szoniecky S. (2018) *Ecosystems Knowledge, Modeling and Analysis Method for Information and Communication*, Wiley London.

Tanggaard, L. (2014). A situated model of creative learning. *European Educational Research Journal*, 13(1), 107-116.

Wexler, M. N. (2001) The who, what and why of knowledge mapping, *Journal of Knowledge Management,* Volume 5, Number 3. pp. 249-263.

AFFORDANCES AND CONSTRAINTS OF THE E-ASSESSMENT SYSTEM NUMBAS: A CASE STUDY IN MATHEMATICS TEACHER EDUCATION

Said Hadjerrouit[1] and Celestine Ifeanyi Nnagbo[1]
[1]*Institute of Mathematical Sciences, Faculty of Engineering and Sciences, University of Agder, Kristiansand, Norway*

ABSTRACT

E-assessment systems such as Numbas are now widespread in mathematics education at the primary, secondary, and tertiary level. However, little is known about the affordances and constraints of Numbas in mathematics teacher education. The purpose of this study is to investigate the emergence, perception, and actualisation of Numbas affordances and constraints, and their effect on teaching and learning mathematics. The study draws on Gibson's affordance theory and associated research in the field of digital technology. It follows a qualitative research design to generate data using semi-structured interviews of six students and two teachers. Data from the interviews were analysed thematically to highlight the affordances and constraints of Numbas and their effect on mathematical learning and teaching. Future work will continue exploring Numbas affordances and constraints for learning and teaching mathematics in similar educational settings to ensure more validity and reliability of the results.

KEYWORDS

Affordance, e-Assessment System, Constraint, Feedback, Formative Assessment, Numbas

1. INTRODUCTION

In recent years, emergent technologies like e-assessment systems are gaining more attention in mathematics education, partly, due to the high number of students' enrolment that has necessitated the use of technological tools for feedback delivery to students for mathematical learning.

E-assessment systems provide a resource-efficient way to providing the much-needed timely feedback to the students. As such, these systems provide new learning potentials for a large cohort of students by means of formative assessment. However, research on e-assessment systems is still in its infancy, especially in the area that assesses the affordances and constraints of such systems. Csapó et al. (2012) posited that large-scale implementations of technology-based assessment still need further research and experiments in real educational settings.

The present study proposes a framework that captures the affordances and constraints of Numbas in a technology-based course in teacher education at the Department of Mathematical Sciences, University of Agder. The goal of the study is to investigate the emergence, perception, and actualisation of Numbas affordances and constraints, and their effect on teaching and learning mathematics. The study follows a qualitative research design in which data were generated using semi-structured interviews. Eight interviews were conducted to collect the views of six students and two teachers. To address the research goal, the interview data were analysed thematically using an inductive-deductive approach.

The paper is structured as follows. Firstly, results from previous studies on feedback and e-assessment systems are presented. Secondly, an overview of Numbas is given. This is followed by the framework of the study drawing on Gibson's affordance theory. Then, the data collection and analysis methods are presented, and the results are outlined. Finally, a discussion and implications of the results conclude the article.

---

[1] Celestine Ifeanyi Nnagbo wrote and defended his master's thesis in December 2020 in mathematics education at the Institute of Mathematical Sciences, Faculty of Engineering and Sciences, University of Agder, Kristiansand, Norway.

2. E-ASSESSMENT SYSTEMS: A LITERATUR REVIEW

Feedback is an integral part of learning processes. It plays an important role in development new instructions and amendment of existing ones to meet special needs of students. It is adjudged to be one of the most powerful ways to increase students learning and achievement (Hattie & Clarke, 2018). Hattie and Timperley (2007) defined feedback as the information provided by an agent, which may be the teacher, parents, fellow students, books, or even experience about the performance of oneself. Butler and Winne (1995), and Goldin, et al. (2017) in agreement with the definition proposed by Hattie and Timperley (2007), asserted that feedback does not necessarily come from agents external to the learner but can be generated internally by the learner herself.

While feedback has been aligned traditionally as information provided by external agents (teachers, parents/guardian, fellow students) or the learner herself, Goldin et al. (2017) argued that through information and communication technology, a broad range of feedbacks are also provided to the learner. This could be in form of e-assessment systems, or other digital learning environments. With the aid of feedback, learners can confirm or alter their knowledge and skills, which may lead to improved skill acquisition, better learning process, and learning outcomes (Attali & van der Kleij, 2017; Shute, 2008).

Formative feedback is considered to be any form of information made available to students regarding their actual state of performance with the aim to modify their thinking or behaviour towards achieving the set learning goals (Goldin et al., 2017; Shute, 2008). Irons (2007) further suggests that such information accelerates learning, either by "enabling students to achieve higher learning outcomes than they might otherwise have attained, or by enabling them to attain these outcomes more rapidly" (p.21). Formative feedback gives the students the opportunity to access the level they are in a learning process, what the learning goals are, and how to achieve them.

In the last decade, several studies have reported about an increase on the uptake of e-assessment systems in schools (Denton, Madden, Roberts, & Rowe, 2008; McKenna & Bull, 2000; Özden, 2005; Thelwall, 2000) mainly due to the increase in number of students enrolling for science, technology, engineering, and mathematics (STEM) courses (Gill & Greenhow, 2008; Jones, 2008).

Hettiarachchi et al. (2014) in their study found significant improvement in performance and participation of students who engaged in learning with a formative e-assessment system, Technology-Enhanced Assessment (TEA). Berková (2016, 2017) studied the efficiency of teaching undergraduate calculus course using an e-assessment system called Maple T.A (Testing and Assessment), in the report, he found the result to be significantly higher when the students learn with the aid of the system than when they learn with the traditional method of doing homework with paper and pencil.

There exit few reports on the implementation of the e-assessment Numbas in teacher education (Hadjerrouit 2020b). In school education, the use of Numbas shows positive improvements of students' performance. For example, Carroll et al. (2017) showed in their study with the first year Business studies students that attendance was higher with about 20% in the classroom that used Numbas for formative assessment. They also reported that the students found Numbas feedbacks helpful, and their enjoyment of learning mathematics increased.

3. THE E-ASSESSMENT SYSTEM NUMBAS

Numbas is a general e-assessment system for mathematics and mathematics-related courses with emphasis on formative assessment and feedback to students' actions (Lawson-Perfect, 2015). From a didactical point of view, the primary use of Numbas is to enable students to enter a mathematical answer in the form of an algebraic expression, and then see how a particular characteristic of affordances, the one of feedback can impact students' mathematical engagement. Numbas makes its feedback immediate and potentially effective. There are multiple ways Numbas gives feedback to both students and teachers. These include *submit answer, show steps, reveal answers, try another question like this one* (Figure 1).

Submit answer: Students get feedback when they submit an answer. The feedback indicates with a green colour 'good' sign if the answer is correct, with red colour 'bad' sign indicating that the answer is wrong or partially correct. The students will be shown the maximum attainable score for each question, and their own score for the question after they have submitted the answer. The teacher may choose to disable these feedback options.

Show steps: When "*show steps*" is chosen, Numbas will give the general solution to that task. This is a way of reminding the student to have a look at the general solution and retry solving the task. Show steps does not give students the exact solution to the particular task.

Try another question like this one: With this option, students have the opportunity to attempt similar questions many times until they feel confidence to move to the next question.

Reveal answer: This option provides a step-by-step solution that is personalized to the question, but the students lose all the marks and cannot re-attempt the exact question. The teacher may decide to disable this.

Statistics: Numbas stores data of students' performance. Teachers can track how well the students understand the topic through their performances, and they can equally identify the tasks students perform below expectations and reemphasize on them in the next class.

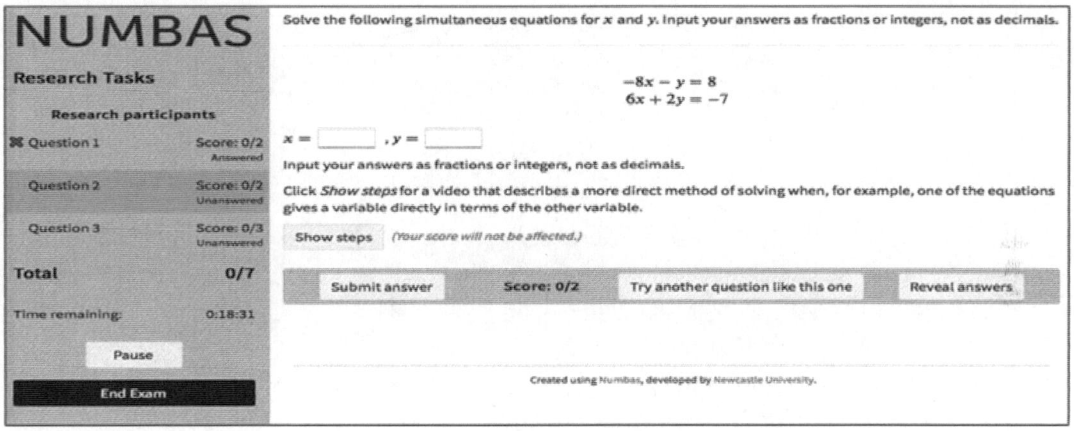

Figure 1. Numbas feedback options

4. ANALYTICAL FRAMEWORK: AFFORDANCE THEORY

This study uses affordance theory as an analytical framework for operationalizing Numbas feedback. In addition to the study on Numbas mentioned in the previous section, this theory was used to explore affordances of the digital tool SimReal for learning mathematics in teacher education (Hadjerrouit, 2020a).

The term 'affordance' was proposed by James J. Gibson (Gibson, 1986, p. 127) to describe what the environment offers the animal. He argued that affordances (henceforth, in plural or singular form) can be seen from the properties of the environment that are relative to the animal in question. He further stresses that affordances must be peculiar to the animal they afford; not just any property of the environment or whatever the environment can offer.

In the world of Human-Computer Interaction, the term "affordance" (Norman, 1988) refers to a goal-oriented action potential that emerges as result of interaction between subjects (e.g., students and teachers) and an object (e.g., Numbas). Affordance is neither the property of an object in isolation nor that of the subject. Instead, it emerges as an offshoot of a dynamic relationship between the subjects (students and teachers) and the object (Numbas). It is perceived (i.e., students and teachers are aware of the existence of the action potential of Numbas) in many ways and actualized (i.e., students are able to turn the potential of Numbas into action) to produce effect (i.e., feedback delivery) depending on many factors that include Numbas platform, its user interface, capability of the students and their level of preparedness. Moreover, the actualization of Numbas affordance is either facilitated by some enabling conditions or mitigated by some constraints.

Given the emergence of Numbas affordances, it is important to ask how the affordances are perceived. As such, when students interact with Numbas to facilitate feedback delivery on some mathematics concepts they do so conveniently with the aid of the technical features of the tool. During this process, they become aware of the affordances that emerged during the interaction in terms of feedback delivery. The next issue is how they can actualize these affordances. Affordance actualization is a process of turning action potentials (affordances) into real actions to bring an effect in using a particular tool (Anderson & Robey, 2017; Bernhard et al., 2013).

To turn a possibility into an action, it is expected that the user has the ability and capability to harness the potential and there are enabling conditions to facilitate the process. Affordance actualization may vary from one individual to another because it is goal-oriented and a process of specificity. Two or more students may interact with Numbas and actualize (or not) different affordances of the tool depending on their respective individual differences and choices.

Moreover, it is expected that following the actualization of Numbas affordances are some effects, which may be "intended by the user and/or those by the original creator of the artefact as well as unintended effects" (Bernhard et al., 2013, p.6). Thus, it is expected that when affordances are perceived and actualized, then some effects are generated in terms of feedback delivery on mathematics tasks to students. Figure 2 shows the underlying framework that captures the emergence, perception, actualization, and effect of Numbas affordance.

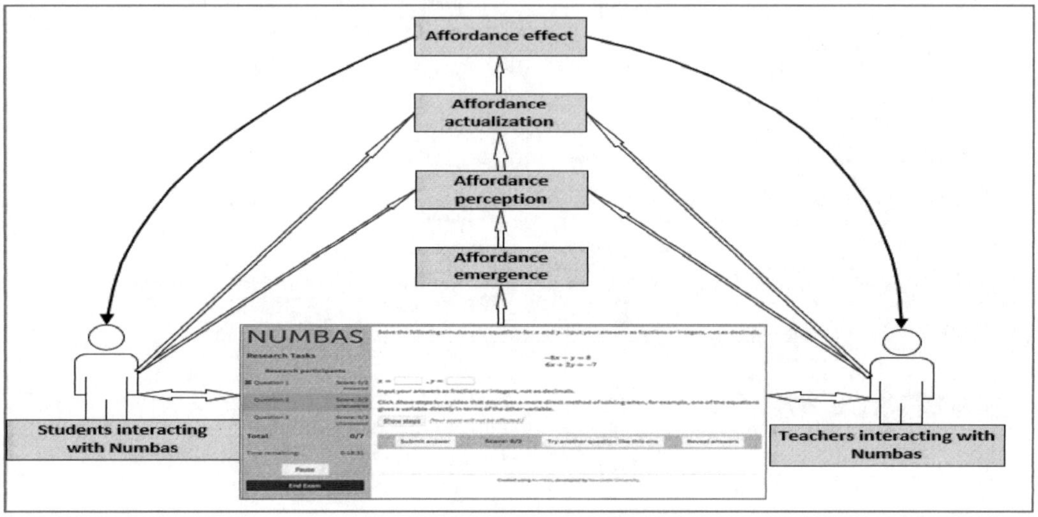

Figure 2. Framework that captures the emergence, perception, and actualisation of Numbas affordances, and their effect from an Activity theorical perspective

The perception of Numbas affordances concerns its awareness by a goal-oriented user during the interaction. Affordance actualisation is a process of turning action potentials (affordances) into real actions to bring an effect in using a particular tool (Anderson & Robey, 2017; Bernhard et al., 2013). In specific terms, affordance actualisations are "the actions taken by actors as they take advantage of one or more affordances through their use of the technology to achieve immediate concrete outcomes in support of organizational goals" (Strong et al., 2014, p. 70).

Moreover, it is expected that following the actualisation of Numbas affordances are some effects. More so, it is important to highlight that actualisation of Numbas affordances does not happen in isolation. In fact, affordances go along constraints; they are facilitated by enabling conditions and hindered by constraints. As captioned by Hadjerrouit (2020a, b) affordances and constraints are inseparable because they complement each other, and not opposite. The mechanisms of actualisation of Numbas affordances coupled with the constraints and their actualisation appear not to have been reported in the literature.

5. DATA COLLECTION AND ANALYSIS METHODS

A case study design approach is used to analyse the affordances perceived by both students and teachers while interacting with Numbas, and how they actualize the perceived affordances. The participants were two teachers and six students from a mathematics teacher education class of a Norwegian university. The two teachers were considered because they are actively making use of Numbas for formative assessment in their respective classes. The second cohort is six out of about twelve students from one class who willingly volunteered to participate in the study. These participants are master's degree students from an institute of mathematical sciences in a Norwegian university. They were currently taking a course entitled "Digital tools in mathematics teaching". Both cohorts were familiar with Numbas and affordance theory. The present study is a continuation of previous studies (Hadjerrouit & Nnagbo, 2021; Nnagbo, 2020).

A thematic approach to data analysis was used to identify codes within the data set (Bryman, 2016). Code development takes a deductive-inductive strategy. The analysis starts with a deductive approach by following the pre-defined framework in search for meaningful interpretation of the data. Then as the process evolves, room was given for the data to express itself by creating new codes that emerged from the data inductively. The development of codes follows reading and rereading of the data carefully and annotating same to identify topics raised by participants themselves. The codes are refined and validated by checking whether these are repeated or highlighted by the participants as important themes (Hennink et al., 2020).

6. RESULTS

The results are divided into two parts: Students' and teachers' views on Numbas feedback and affordances that emerged between the participants and Numbas. The results also report on the similarities and differences between students' and teachers' views. In addition, the theme 'diagnostic teaching' emerged from the empirical data during code development.

6.1 Students' Views on Numbas Feedback

The results reveal that feedback options are available on the Numbas user interface, and that the students perceived these feedbacks. The feedbacks are in form of immediate interpretation of the students answer inputs for them to see how Numbas understand and read their answers, as well as the immediate response of 'correct' or 'wrong' that comes in form of green or red mark respectively they receive from Numbas when they submit the answers. Other feedback mechanisms of Numbas like "hint", "reveal answer", "try another related question" "submit answer" are shown to be available and from the result, the students seem to find them very helpful.

For example, when asked about the Numbas feedback(s) while doing the tasks that were given to them, one of the students responded: "*...with the two equations, there was a movie, and it was sort of helping because it assured me that I was doing it in the right way*. Another participant indicated that "*it was helping because it was the rule you were supposed to use*". Likewise, another student explained that "*it gives you a lot better feedback, than most of that kind of programs...So that feedback is good, and as I said, when you write, the next box shows you how the program interprets, that program is really good*".

From the students' responses, they seem to appreciate the feedbacks, including the video hints. The response from one student does not only show that the video helped her, it also encouraged and motivated her to solve the task. Her confidence increased. Another student tried comparing the feedbacks to that of other similar programs and she found it better than other programs she had used. She was particularly overwhelmed that Numbas could instantly show how it understands her answers.

Some of the responses given by the students further show that they are not just aware of all the other feedback options, but they also actualized them while interacting with Numbas, and the feedbacks really helped them. For example, when the participants were asked if they were stuck while attempting the tasks, and if yes, how do they overcame it, one of the students said "*yes, I was stuck. First, I tried to use the 'show steps' and also 'show result...* ". Another student replied *"yes. I have written my maximum point to the minimum, and the minimum point to maximum, I found them, but I wrote them wrong, and I solved it again, and I found the same coordinate, ... I solved it three times, I found the same coordinate, I just couldn't see that I wrote them wrong though I was able to see it later when I revealed the answer...*". From the submissions, the students were stuck at one point or the other while solving the interview tasks, and they sought and got help through the different feedbacks in Numbas. The first response shows that the student explored two feedback options in order to get unstuck. The second response on the other hand shows that the student was left frustrated by her own mathematical mistakes. She had already spent some time and effort trying to trace her fault but to no avail. From every indication, she could have abandoned the task, if not for the feedback from Numbas which helped her get unstuck.

Furthermore, the result revealed that all the students interviewed perceived the feedbacks they received as helpful, and they expressed their satisfaction with the feedbacks. This is substantiated from their responses.

One student pointed out: "*yes! the hints were highly helpful to me…*". Another student replied "… *I was happy that it helped me to remember the formula …it's a good feeling when you use the digital tool and you are stuck, and it can help you solve it because then you are learning as you are doing exercises…*"

6.2 Teachers' Views on Numbas Feedback

From the teachers' perspective, the findings show that their students equally found Numbas feedback helpful and motivating. They state that their students "do get stuck" and when they do, that "most of them chose to show hints and the tips, (and) the other feedback options from the program". They also think that the feedback motivate the students. However, they believe that bulk of the work lies on the teachers' ability to create tasks that would take into consideration the students' likely misconceptions about a particular task.

They further expressed concerns that the feedback, no matter how good it may be, may never be sufficient to get some students going, especially the low achieving students. This can be deduced from the response offered by one of the teachers "*I would say that the feedback does help them but again, …, for the strongest students, it's helpful for them but the weaker students, I think they need the teacher actually to tell them what have you done wrong, it's not enough for them to see the feedback or the examples.*"

6.3 Similarities and Differences between Students and Teachers' Views

Generally, the participants, both teachers and students, think that the feedback mechanisms in Numbas are good and helpful. They seem to appreciate that the feedback options show the general rules or formula for solving a particular task without going into details about the actual solution to that task.

It appears that the students perceived and actualized some affordances of Numbas at the assessment level especially the availability and usefulness of feedbacks. They seem to appreciate that Numbas shows them how it reads their inputs as soon as they are typing them. The students further expressed their satisfaction that the feedback could help them get unstuck. However, teachers' inability to take full advantage of the potentialities of Numbas while designing tasks and its corresponding feedbacks could be seen as constraints towards complete actualization of Numbas affordances at the assessment level. They also feel that the feedback would be better if Numbas could provide step by step feedback to students, by taking their profiles into account. Teachers also testify that the students are satisfied with the feedback mechanisms.

6.4 Diagnostic Teaching

The theme 'diagnostic teaching' emerged from the data during code development. Its emergence is due to repeated expressions regarding the possibilities of teachers to use Numbas to ascertain the students' areas of difficulties before meeting them in class. The findings reveal that Numbas can be used as a powerful tool to implement diagnostic teaching to either a single or large number of students.

The teachers expressed that Numbas provides statistics in form of performances of their students. The statistics shows both the time the students spent on each task, if they reveal hints, the algebraic expressions they type in as their answers, and so much more. From the teachers' responses, it can be deduced that they found the statistics helpful in many ways, especially in diagnosing the students' learning difficulties, and time saving.

One of the teachers came up with the following comment: "*I can go in as the teacher and see what they have answered, I can see if they have revealed hints, so gives me a lot information, I can see how much time they have spent on the question, of course, if it is correct or not, so I will see their answers, I mean the algebraic expressions they have typed in, for each student. So I can compare and see, if I want to I can break it down to each student or I can give the percentage of how many students (), you can an overview of the whole class, you see the average time they spent on each question, so I will know that in this question they used a lot of time and they didn't get it correctly, then I know, then ok I know this is something we have to work on in the next class, so that is very useful information for me as a teacher…*"

The other teacher further indicated that "*the statistics is useful in itself for me when I apply my teaching because I'd known this task, we need to see more of (.)… This is really useful to the instructor…this is time saving, it's a huge time saver, …*"

On the other hand, students' responses signified that they also see Numbas as a good diagnostic teaching tool. they believe that with the aid of the statistics at the teacher level, they would know beforehand what the students struggle with. One of the students suggests, "*...if you have problem with one (task), we know what your problem is, what you are struggling with. Its already diagnosed for the teacher so h/she knows what h/she must explain more to you*".

7. DISCUSSION AND CONCLUSIONS

The goal of this research study is to investigate Numbas affordances and constraints, and their effect on teaching and learning mathematics. The results show that the students perceived and actualised the affordances of Numbas particularly because of the availability and usefulness of the e-assessment system's feedbacks, which in turn increase the students' motivation. Clearly, effective feedback on assessment is vital to improve learning (Hounsell et al., 2008; Pereira et al., 2016). However, there is a concern that some might not find Numbas feedbacks helpful, because they would always need a teacher to tell them why they got a certain task wrong. This further shows that digital assessment tools may not completely replace teachers.

Regarding implications of the study, it is important to mention that the proposed research has used formative assessment, which has been useful in underpinning the results of activities undertaken by teachers and students for assessing themselves. The findings show that Numbas is a useful tool for assessing mathematical concepts and problem-solving. However, there are issues related to the feedback, which can act as a source of motivation for a few students while demotivating other students. Numbas may be included to the Norwegian course curriculum with the sole intention of identifying possible problems and effecting necessary modifications along with improving the learning of students and teachers.

For teachers, it is important to ascertain their role in using their skills and expertise for adding new strategies of formative assessment, and identifying students' learning progresses, while for students, it is important to focus on using Numbas as a practice, learning, and feedback tool. However, in the educational setting, the role of Numbas should be clearly defined along with the role of teachers. For example, teachers should identify why students need to use the tool when tasks assigned to them on Numbas. Teachers should also identify the role of personal feedback and Numbas general feedback in affecting the student's learning process. For students, it is important to weigh the learning patterns and potential in using teachers' ideas and Numbas explanations. From the university perspective, it is important to analyse whether Numbas is able to facilitate higher order thinking and learning or not. Also, the focus should be on determining the cognitive behaviour and improvement of students. There should be a clear distinction of students on the basis of higher and lower level of cognition. The responsibilities of teachers for improving the learning of students using Numbas should be explained and defined properly. Such implications need to be further integrated for reformulating a new strategy, which will be able to support the formative assessment process.

Summarizing, this study helped to identify some conditions for using Numbas as an e-assessment system in teacher education, and to understand how to take advantage of formative feedback to support the implementation of new educational goals both for students and teachers. However, the low number of participants ($N=8$), that is two teachers and six students, limits how much the results can be generalized. Future work will continue exploring Numbas affordances for learning and teaching mathematics with a larger number of participants to ensure more validity and reliability of the results, and extend these to similar but more advanced e-assessment systems such as STACK (Stack, 2022), and additionally to digital exams in educational settings.

REFERENCES

Anderson, C., & Robey, D. (2017). Affordance Potency: Explaining the Actualization of Technology Affordances. *Information and Organization*, *27*(2), 100-115.

Attali, Y., & Van der Kleij, F. (2017). Effects of Feedback Elaboration and Feedback Timing During Computer-Based Practice in Mathematics Problem Solving. *Computers & Education*, *110*, 154-169.

Berková A. (2017). Effect of the Use of Computer-Aided Assessment System in the Teaching of Mathematical Analysis with Regard to Students' Approaches to Learning. *Journal on Efficiency and Responsibility in Education and Science*, *10*(3), 71-75.

Berková, A. (2016). The Efficiency of the Use of Computer-Aided Assessment System in Mathematics. *Proceedings of the 13th International Conference on Efficiency and Responsibility in Education* (ERIE 2016). Prague. pp. 43-49.

Bernhard, E., Recker, J., & Burton-Jones, A. (2013). Understanding the Actualization of Affordances: A Study in the Process Modeling Context. *Proceedings of the 34th International Conference on Information Systems* (ICIS 2013), Milano, Italy, pp. 4522-4532.

Bryman, A. (2016). *Social Research Methods*. Oxford, United Kingdom: Oxford University Press.

Butler, D. L., & Winne, P. H. (1995). Feedback and Self-regulated Learning: A Theoretical Synthesis. *Review of Educational Research*, *65*(3), 245-281.

Carroll, T., Casey, D., Crowley, J., Mulchrone, K., & Shé, Á. N. (2017). Numbas as an Engagement Tool for First-year Business Studies Students. *MSOR Connections*, *15*(2), 42-50.

Csapó, B., et al. (2012). Technological Issues for Computer-Based Assessment. In: P. Griffin et al. (eds.). *Assessment and Teaching of 21st Century Skills* (pp. 143-230). Springer Science+Business Media.

Denton, P., Madden, J., Roberts, M., & Rowe, P. (2008). Students' Response to Traditional and Computer-assisted Formative Feedback: A Comparative Case Study. *British Journal of Educational Technology*, *39*(3), 486-500.

Gibson, J. J. (1986). *The Ecological Approach to Visual Perception*. Hillsdale, N.J: Lawrence Erlbaum.

Gill, M., & Greenhow, M. (2008). How Effective is Feedback in Computer-Aided Assessments? *Learning, Media and Technology*, *33*(3), 207-220.

Goldin, I., Narciss, S., Foltz, P., & Bauer, M. (2017). New Directions in Formative Feedback in Interactive Learning Environments. *International Journal of Artificial Intelligence in Education*, *27*(3), 385-392.

Hadjerrouit, S. (2020a). Exploring the Affordances of Simreal for Learning Mathematics in Teacher Education: A Socio-Cultural Perspective. In: L. H. Chad; S. Zvacek; & J. Uhomoibhi (2020). *Computer Supported Education. 11th International Conference, CSEDU 2019, Heraklion, Greece. Revised Selected Papers*. Springer Nature, 26-50.

Hadjerrouit, S. (2020b). Exploring the Affordances of Numbas for Mathematical Learning: A Case Study. *International Network for Didactic Research in University Mathematics (INDRUM 2020)*, 453-462.

Hadjerrouit, S., & Nnagbo, N.I. (2021). Exploring Numbas Formative Feedback for Teaching and Learning Mathematics: An Affordance Theory Perspective. *Proceedings of the 18th International Conference on Cognition and Exploratory Learning in Digital Age* (CELDA2021). IADIS Press, pp. 261-268.

Hattie, J., & Clarke, S. (2018). *Visible Learning: Feedback*. London: Routledge.

Hattie, J., & Timperley, H. (2007). The Power of Feedback. *Review of Educational Research, 77*(1), 81-112.

Hennink, M., Hutter, I., & Bailey, A. (2020). *Qualitative Research Methods*: SAGE Publications Limited.

Hettiarachchi E. et al. (2014). A Technology Enhanced Assessment System for Skill and Knowledge Learning. *Proceedings of the 6th International Conference on Computer Supported Education (CSEDU-2014),* pp. 184-191. SCITEPRESS (Science and Technology Publications, Lda.).

Hounsell, D., McCune, V., Hounsell, J., & Litjens, J. (2008). The Quality of Guidance and Feedback to Students. *Higher Education Research & Development*, *27*(1), 55-67.

Irons, A. (2007). *Enhancing Learning through Formative Assessment and Feedback*. Routledge.

Jones, I. S. (2008). Computer-Aided Assessment Questions in Engineering Mathematics Using MapleTA®. *International Journal of Mathematical Education in Science and Technology*, *39*(3), 341-356.

Lawson-Perfect, C. (2015). A Demonstration of Numbas, An E-assessment System for Mathematical Disciplines. *CAA Conference.* Retrieved from https://www.numbas.org.uk/blog/2015/07/a-demonstration-of-numbas-at-caa-2015/

McKenna, C., & Bull, J. (2000). Quality Assurance of Computer-Assisted Assessment: Practical and Strategic Issues. *Quality Assurance in Education, 8*(1), 24-32.

Nnagbo, C. I. (2020). Assessment in Mathematics Education Using Numbas: Affordances and Constraints from an Activity Theory Perspective. [Unpublished master's thesis]. University of Agder, Kristiansand, Norway.

Norman, D. A. (1988). *The Psychology of Everyday Things*. New York: Basic Books.

Özden, M. Y. (2005). Students' Perceptions of Online Assessment: A Case Study. *International Journal of E-Learning & Distance Education/Revue internationale du e-learning et la formation à distance*, *19*(2), 77-92.

Pereira, D., Flores, M. A., Simão, A. M. V., & Barros, A. (2016). Effectiveness and Relevance of Feedback in Higher Education: A study of Undergraduate Students. *Studies in Educational Evaluation*, *49*, 7-14.

Shute, V. J. (2008). Focus on Formative Feedback. *Review of Educational Research, 78*(1), 153-189.

Stack – Online assessment (2022). Retrieved from: https://stack-assessment.org/

Strong, D. M., Volkoff, O., Johnson, S. A., Pelletier, L. R., Tulu, B., Bar-On, I., ... Garber, L. (2014). A Theory of Organization-EHR Affordance Actualization. *Journal of the Association for Information Systems, 15(2),* 53-85.

Thelwall, M. (2000). Computer-Based Assessment: A Versatile Educational Tool. *Computers & Education, 34*(1), 37-49.

EDUCATIONAL CHATBOTS FOR COLLABORATIVE LEARNING: RESULTS OF A DESIGN EXPERIMENT IN A MIDDLE SCHOOL

Michael Burkhard[1], Sabine Seufert[1], Matthias Cetto[2] and Siegfried Handschuh[2]
[1]*Institute for Educational Management and Technologies, St.Jakob-Strasse 21, University of St.Gallen, Switzerland*
[2]*Institute of Computer Science, Rosenbergstrasse 30, 9000 St.Gallen, Switzerland*

ABSTRACT

Educational chatbots promise many benefits for teaching and learning. Although chatbot use cases in this research field are rapidly growing, most studies focus on individual users rather than on collaborative group settings. To address this issue, this paper investigates how chatbot-mediated learning can be designed to foster middle school students in team-based assignments. Using an educational design research approach, quality indicators of educational chatbots were derived from the literature, which served as a guideline for the development of the chatbot Tubo (meaning tutoring bot). Tubo is part of a web-based team learning environment in which students can chat with each other and collaboratively work on their group assignments. As a team member and tutor of each group, Tubo guides the students through the learning journey by different scaffolding elements and helps with content-related questions the students have. As part of a first design cycle, the chatbot application was tested with a school class of a technical vocational school in Switzerland. The received feedback suggests that the approach of team-based learning with chatbots has a lot of potential from the students' and teachers' point of view. However, the role distribution of the individual group members may have to be further specified to address the different needs of autonomous as well as more control-oriented students.

KEYWORDS

Educational Chatbots, Smart Personal Assistant Technology, Team-Based Learning, Computer-Supported Collaborative Learning, Scaffolding

1. INTRODUCTION

The use of artificial intelligence (AI) in education is growing rapidly (Okonkwo & Ade-Ibijola, 2021). Among the most popular AI technologies to support teaching and learning activities are chatbots (Okonkwo & Ade-Ibijola, 2021). Chatbots are "computer programs which attempt to simulate conversations of human beings via text or voice interactions" (Winkler & Söllner, 2018). They can interact with multiple students at the same time and be used as *a scaffolding device* to guide students through learning processes (Duffy & Azevedo, 2015; Winkler et al., 2021). Chatbots can further trigger metacognitive thinking processes and increase student motivation (Winkler & Söllner, 2018). Educational chatbots have already been used in various areas and hold multifaceted potential (see e.g., Adamopoulou & Moussiades, 2020; Okonkwo & Ade-Ibijola, 2021; Rapp et al., 2021). However, so far, most studies have focused on individual users rather than on collaborative group settings (see e.g., Okonkwo & Ade-Ibijola, 2021; Rapp et al., 2021). A few examples that address the issue of *chatbot-mediated learning in team-based scenarios*, are David et al. (2019), Kumar (2021) and Winkler et al. (2019). These studies suggest, that chatbots could improve collaboration quality and learning performance in group projects.

However, effective collaboration between group members is challenging and requires guidelines to be effective (Briggs et al., 2013; Nussbaum et al., 2009; Winkler et al., 2019). In addition, it is difficult or even impossible for the teacher to provide guidance and feedback on multiple fronts simultaneously (Jeong et al., 2019). Furthermore, the meta-analysis of Hattie (2009, p. 297) shows that the provision of *formative evaluation* and *feedback* as well as *teacher clarity* are among the most important factors that influence student performance. As a virtual tutor and first-level support, a chatbot could provide additional support for group work and relieve the teacher of some of the workload. Therefore, in light of the identified research desideratum, the following research question should be addressed:

How can we design educational chatbots to foster team-based learning of middle school students?

The objectives of the paper at hand are therefore twofold:

- Elaboration on the quality indicators for developing educational chatbots to support team-based learning in order to provide a theoretical foundation for the design and development of a chatbot within the design experiment;
- design and evaluation of a chatbot that uses scaffolding elements to support student groups in working independently with groupwork assignments.

From a theoretical point of view, the paper at hand contributes to a better understanding of the usefulness of educational chatbots in team-based learning scenarios. From a practical standpoint, the paper aims to contribute to how chatbot-mediated learning can be designed and implemented in the classroom. The quality indicators described may serve as a guideline for other researchers who want to implement similar projects and uncover further potential of the technology in more detail.

To this end, section 2 gives an overview of the theoretical background and elaborates on the quality indicators for developing educational chatbots. Section 3 sheds light on the applied research design and method. Section 4 describes the designed artifact: the chatbot Tubo (meaning tutoring bot) for groupwork assignments. In section 5, the classroom experiment with chatbot Tubo is summarized as part of a formative evaluation. The implications of the experiment are discussed in section 6, while section 7 concludes with some final remarks and gives an outlook on future research areas.

2. THEORETICAL BACKGROUND

2.1 Collaborative Learning & Computer Supported Collaborative Learning

Collaborative learning (CL) is a pedagogical approach where groups of learners work together to solve a problem, complete a task or create a product (Laal & Ghodsi, 2012). CL can have social, psychological, and academic benefits (Laal & Ghodsi, 2012, p. 487). For CL to be effective, Dillenbourg and Schneider (1995, p. 133) consider it important that the groups should be rather small, because in large groups some members tend to be absent. In this context, it is the task of the teacher (or potentially a chatbot) to monitor the CL activities an "take care that no learner is left out of the interaction" (Dillenbourg & Schneider, 1995, p. 134). Under these conditions, different underlying mechanisms can make CL effective (Dillenbourg & Schneider, 1995, pp. 136-141). Such mechanisms may involve the discussion of divergent opinions (*disagreement*), the *(self-)explanation* of content to other group members or the justification of one's own point of view (*mutual regulation*) (Dillenbourg & Schneider, 1995, pp. 136-141).

One way of addressing the difficulties of solving complex collaborative tasks may be through technology (Jeong et al., 2019). *Computer-supported collaborative learning* (CSCL) investigates how information and communication technology can support learning in groups (Ludvigsen & Mørch, 2010). Among other things, CSCL can support learners through *scaffolding* which attempts to provide guidance along the learning journey (see e.g., Miller & Hadwin, 2015; Splichal et al., 2018). The concept of *scaffolding* goes back to the work of Wood et al. (1976), who defined scaffolding as the process that enables a novice to solve a problem that would be otherwise impossible. Scaffolding can occur through a variety of ways (e.g., hints, prompts, feedback, illustrations, interactive features) (Duffy & Azevedo, 2015). In computer-based environments, pedagogical agents such as chatbots can promote effective learning by providing instructional scaffolds depending on learners' behavior and progress (Duffy & Azevedo, 2015).

2.2 Chatbot-Mediated Learning

Chatbots can be defined as "computer programs which attempt to simulate conversations of human beings via text or voice interactions" (Winkler & Söllner, 2018). They can interact with multiple learners at the same time and guide them through learning processes (e.g., through scaffolding) (Duffy & Azevedo, 2015; Winkler et al., 2021).

Regarding CL, a chatbot could help to improve learning within the group. For example, a chatbot could act as a scaffolding device and content expert to provide assistance during the tasks. In this role, the chatbot could structure the work process, answer questions about the content and provide formative feedback.

In education, chatbots have already been used in different areas (see e.g., Adamopoulou & Moussiades, 2020; Okonkwo & Ade-Ibijola, 2021; Rapp et al., 2021). However, so far, most studies have focused on individual users rather than on collaborative group settings. A few examples that address the issue of *chatbot-mediated learning in team-based scenarios*, are David et al. (2019), Kumar (2021) and Winkler et al. (2019). David et al. (2019) used chatbots as teaching assistants in group settings to support the teacher and improve classroom orchestration. Kumar (2021) investigated how chatbots can facilitate team-based projects and concluded that chatbots can improve teamwork and learning performance. Winkler et al. (2019) developed a chatbot with the aim of improving the quality of collaboration among group members in a laboratory experiment. Their results suggest that groups supported by a chatbot can benefit from better task outcomes and a higher quality of collaboration (Winkler et al., 2019).

Table 1. Quality indicators for educational chatbots (PIRU)

Category	Quality attributes	(1)	(2)	(3)	(4)	(5)	(6)
Pedagogy[(1)]	- Precise learning contents that are specific to the subject.	X	X	X	X		
	- Alignment with the learning goals.	X	X	X	X		X
	- Active learning that promotes reflection and metacognition.	X		X			X
	- Personalize learning and feedbacks.	X	X	X	X		
	- Progress management.	X	X	X			
Interactivity	- Appropriate chatbot-interactivity to support the pedagogic concept.		X				
	- Ability to respond to specific questions and maintain themed discussions.		X			X	
	- Context relevant chatbot characteristics (e.g., degree of chatbot proactivity).		X		X	X	X
	- Appropriate elements of interaction (e.g., greetings, humor, empathy).	X	X		X	X	X
Reliablitity[(1)]	- No deception.				X	X	
	- Easy access to a stable platform.	X	X				X
	- Robustness to unexpected input.					X	
	- Protect and respect privacy.	X				X	X
	- Feedback for continuous improvement.	X		X			X
Usability	- General ease of use.	X				X	
	- Make tasks more fun and interesting.					X	
	- Entertain and/or enable participant to enjoy the interaction.		X			X	

Source: Based on (1) Kumar (2021), (2) Smutny & Schreiberova (2020), (3) Gonda et al. (2019), (4) Garcia Brustenga et al. (2018), (5) Radziwill & Benton (2017), (6) Kerly et al. (2007) and own contributions.

For the development of chatbots in education, implementation frameworks are needed (Hwang et al., 2020). Building on the work of Kumar (2021) and based on further design aspects mentioned in the literature by Smutny and Schreiberova (2020), Gonda et al. (2019), Garcia Brustenga et al. (2018), Radziwill and Benton (2017), and Kerly et al. (2007), an overarching *quality indicator framework* was combined (see Table 1).

The framework consists of the categories *Pedagogy*, *Interactivity*, *Reliability*, and *Usability* (PIRU). Smutny and Schreibernova (2020) point out that pedagogical aspects should play a key role in the design of educational chatbots. The PIRU framework therefore puts *Pedagogy* at the heart in order to design pedagogical concepts that are meaningful and aligned with a certain chatbot interaction. The categories of *Interactivity*, *Reliability* and *Usability* can therefore be regarded as side constraints that need to be fulfilled for a well-functioning product but should always be attuned to the relevant underlying concept of *Pedagogy* (in our example collaborative learning). The *quality indicators* derived in Table 1 may serve as a guideline for the development of similar chatbot applications.

3. RESEARCH DESIGN AND METHOD

As a methodological foundation for the design and development of our chatbot, we rely on the educational design research (EDR) approach by McKenney and Reeves (2018). Similar to design-based research, the goal of EDR is to create and test specific models of learning within a real-world context (McKenney & Reeves, 2021, p. 84). EDR (as well as design research in education generally) aims to develop, test and implement innovative practices to reimagine and improve socially constructed forms of teaching and learning (Kelly et al., 2008, p. 3). By finding innovative practical solutions for unsolved problems, novel conditions for learning can be evaluated (Euler, 2014, p. 17).

The EDR approach by McKenney and Reeves (2018) is structured into the three core processes of 1) *analysis and exploration*, 2) *design and construction*, and 3) *evaluation and reflection*. The EDR approach can be used in multiple iterations to refine educational applications. The aim of EDR is to provide both maturing interventions and improved theoretical understanding (McKenney & Reeves, 2018, p. 86). In this way, EDR contributes to theory (as a building block and guideline for designing future interventions) and to practice (by addressing the problem at hand).

In section 2, the research topic was already explored and the main findings summarized (*phase 1: analysis and exploration*). Section 4 provides now more detailed insights into the chatbot development (*phase 2: design and construction*). Section 5 and 6 further elaborate on the results of the evaluation carried out (*phase 3: evaluation and reflection*).

4. ARTIFACT DESCRIPTION: CHATBOT FOR GROUP ASSIGNMENTS

The learning environment and the chatbot Tubo were developed by an interdisciplinary team of educational researchers and computer scientists, while all programming was done in-house. Feedback from the wider developer network was repeatedly sought to refine the tool. The insights from this initial development phase are described in detail in the following article (see Burkhard et al., 2021) and have been incorporated into the current version of our prototype.

Figure 1 gives a conceptual overview of the web-based team learning environment. Each student uses their own laptop or computer for this purpose. The learning application is launched through the web browser. During the registration process, students are divided into groups of three. Besides the students, the chatbot Tubo is also a member of each group. Each group thus has its own virtual tutor who can communicate with the students through a joint group chat.

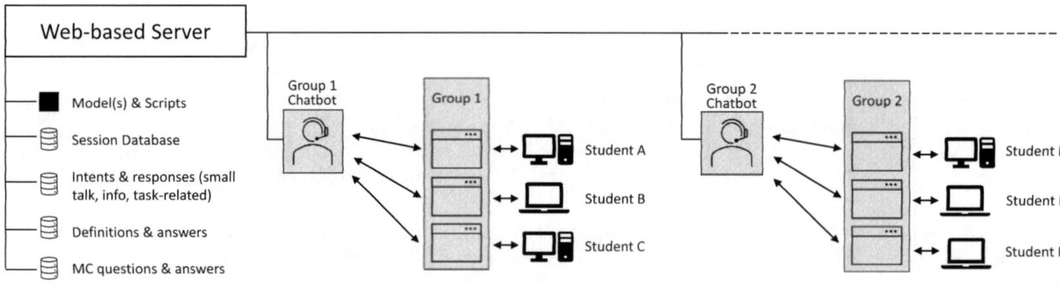

Figure 1. Web-based team learning environment. Source: own representation

Within a group, all students see the same learning environment, which is constantly synchronized between all students in the group. For example, if student B in group 1 writes a message in the group chat, this message is visible to student A, student C and the chatbot Tubo from group 1 (see Figure 1). This also applies to the assignments, which allows students to work together on answering open tasks or multiple-choice tests. For the web-based application to run, several models and scripts have to be executed in the background. In addition to multiple databases that determine the behavior of the chatbot Tubo, a session database is needed in order to manage the current state (including chatbot dialogue, submitted assignments, analytics, user interface) individually and independently for each group.

Figure 2 gives an overview of the user interface for each student. On the right-hand side the students can communicate with each other and with the chatbot Tubo in a group chat. Through the group chat, Tubo introduces the students to the learning environment and provides them with their learning tasks. On the left side (see Figure 2) students see the current group task they have to solve. In the spirit of a storytelling approach, the students help Silvia, the CEO of a pharmaceutical company, and answer her open questions. The students have to work together and type their answers into the text editor (on the bottom left side in Figure 2). If the students have questions, they can contact Tubo directly and the chatbot will try to help them. Among other things, Tubo can provide students with relevant definitions (e.g., in this use-case "what is a monopoly?") or refer them to further text sources they may need to answer the questions.

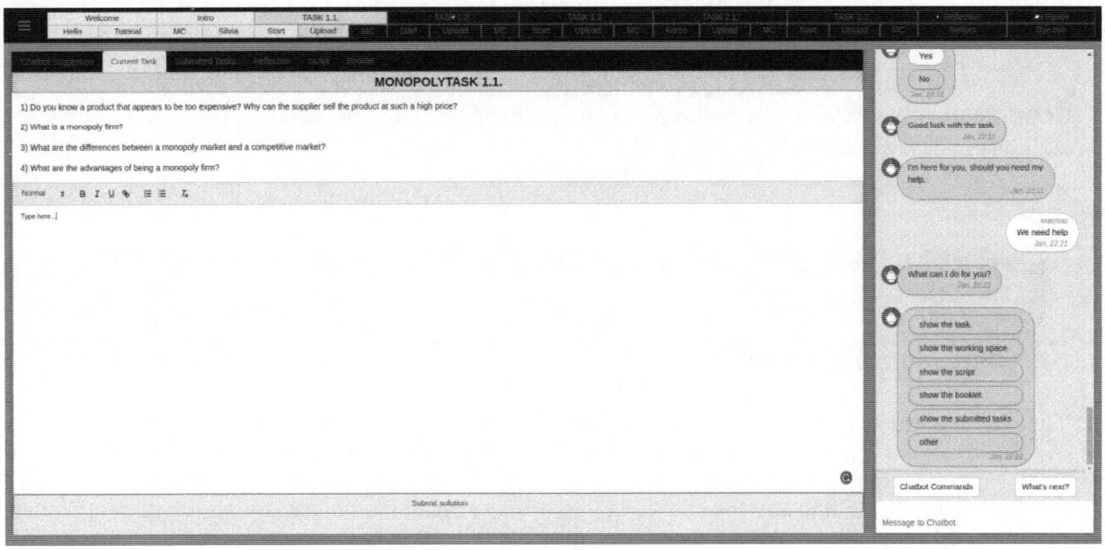

Figure 2. User interface of the designed chatbot webtool application. Source: own representation

While working on the tasks, students have the possibility to further personalize their learning environment (top bar in Figure 2). For this purpose, several tabs can be opened to allow students to do their own research, such as reading the script or reviewing their submitted assignments. The students' individual layout settings remain until a new task needs to be worked on and attention needs to be drawn to new content.

After students have answered and submitted an open-ended work assignment, Tubo asks students multiple-choice questions on key concepts to monitor learning success. To stimulate student reflection on group work, Tubo collects data on students' group behavior. Students can see how they perceived the difficulty of each task and how long it took them to complete each subtask. The data collected also reveals which student made contributions to the team output how often and in what way (e.g., regarding open-ended and multiple-choice questions).

Table 2 summarizes the task areas that the chatbot Tubo performs within the learning environment. To get a more detailed impression of Tubo and its learning environment, the following YouTube video (https://youtu.be/3yLjZYLc2fM) can be watched.

Table 2. Task areas of the educational chatbot Tubo within the learning environment

Task areas	Objectives	Usage
Onboarding-Bot	To greet and warm up the students. To explain to the students the learning environment.	Only at the beginning.
Assignment-Bot	To provide students with learning instructions and clarify the assignments.	For all open tasks.
Quiz-Bot	To ask multiple-choice questions about key concepts to monitor learning success. To provide feedback to the MC-questions.	For all MC-questions.
Orchestration-Bot	To adjust the user interface and display different contents depending on the current task.	If Tubo is asked for help / new task begins.
Progress-Bot	To rate self-perceived progress in students' assignments, identify teamwork issues.	Before/after each task.
FAQ-Bot	To answer frequently asked questions, to provide students with definitions and directing them to relevant textbook sections.	Always.
Smalltalk-Bot	To make jokes and engage in Smalltalk with students; to motivate students for the next tasks.	Always.

Source. Own representation based on Kumar (2021).

5. FORMATIVE EVALUATION OF THE FIRST DESIGN CYCLE

5.1 Classroom Experiment

To iteratively improve the chatbot Tubo, the tool was tested in a first design experiment with a school class of a technical vocational school (in Zurich, Switzerland). The eleven students (9 male, 2 female) were in their third year of training as "event managers" and worked alongside their school education for television-, opera- or similar event-companies. The average age of the students was 18.7 years (minimum 17, maximum 21 years). The chatbot tool Tubo was tested with the school class live on site during four 45-minute lessons (due to covid-19 measures one student had to participate in the lessons online). The lessons were delivered by the students' class teacher A and a second teacher B who had been involved in the development of the chatbot tool and therefore already knew the learning setting well. In addition, a member of our research team was present to document the progress of the lessons.

At the beginning of the first lesson, the students formed four groups (usually three people per group). Each student had their own laptop to work on. After a short thematic introduction by teacher B, each student was asked to access the chatbot tool through the web browser and log into their group. This worked well for most students and the chatbot welcomed the group members. Figure 3 illustrates how the students worked during the lessons with Tubo in small groups.

Figure 3. Classroom experiment: Student groups working collaboratively with the chatbot Tubo

In its role as a virtual tutor, the chatbot Tubo explained the learning process to the students and gave further tips on how the students could best interact with the learning environment. For example, if students had questions, they could ask for help by typing "Tubo" into the group chat. In addition, a "What's next"-button was available whenever students wanted to know how to continue with their learning process (e.g., after having small talk with Tubo).

Over the course of the four lessons, the student groups were guided through the content by the chatbot Tubo and solved all five assignments. Each assignment contained both story elements and open-ended questions that the students could answer directly in the learning environment's text editor. At the end of each assignment a multiple-choice quiz had to be taken which monitored learning success. The multiple-choice quiz had to be answered fully correctly by the students in order to move on to the next assignment. If the answers were wrong, the students received further tips from Tubo. Often the groups had to do a multiple choice quiz several times because they did not get all the answers right at the first time. Some students found this tedious and verbally expressed it. The two teachers observed the behavior in the individual groups and motivated the students if necessary. They also provided answers to content-related questions that Tubo was not able to answer sufficiently from the students' point of view.

5.2 Student Feedback

After the four lessons, teacher B initiated a discussion about the lesson. Besides technical feedback on the learning environment (e.g., login problems, lags), the students expressed positive and negative aspects they had noticed while working with Tubo.

As positive aspects, several students mentioned that they liked the overall concept. One student said that chatting and working with Tubo had something "playful" and "adventurous" and that it was a welcome change compared to the regular school day. Another student mentioned that he could imagine working with Tubo on his own and in home schooling.

The students had different opinions about the way they were guided from one task to the next (*scaffolding elements*). Several students found the guidance and instruction provided by chatbot Tubo useful because they knew what was required of them. However, three students also criticized this relatively unvarying approach, as in their opinion, it became somewhat repetitive and boring over time. In the view of these students, it encouraged over time "to click through without thinking". These findings are line with the results of Rienties et al. (2012) who conclude that it is difficult to find the right balance of scaffolding to simultaneously support autonomous and more control-oriented learners.

The students' views also differed regarding the benefits of the group setting. Some students found it useful to work in groups with the tool as they could help each other and discuss the content in depth. Other students, however, found it difficult to divide the subtasks of the assignments within the group in a meaningful way. From the point of view of these students, this led them to take turns answering the learning content instead of working together.

6. DISCUSSION

After the design experiment, a discussion took place with the two teachers involved and the research team. As a guideline for the discussion, the quality indicators for educational chatbots PIRU (*Pedagogy*, *Interactivity*, *Reliability*, *Usability*) were used (see Table 1).

Regarding *Pedagogy*, the two teachers said, that group learning with a chatbot seemed to be an interesting approach that could also have potential in hybrid class situations. Although one student was only able to participate in class online due to covid-19 restrictions, this person could still be integrated into the lessons. However, from the teachers' point of view, working with chatbot Tubo required a relatively high level of commitment on the part of the students. If the students took turns answering the questions or simply tried to "click" through the tool as quickly as possible, the learning effect of the group assignments was partly lost. To have a certain control as a teacher and to motivate the students if necessary, the use in this on-site setting was considered reasonable.

According to teacher B, it would theoretically be possible for each student to work with Tubo alone and not in a group setting. However, this would mean that in-depth discussions about the questions and contents would be missing. Discourse within the group about "right" and "wrong" answers can promote a common understanding and create an atmosphere in which students can learn from each other (see e.g., Dillenbourg & Schneider, 1995). Teacher A agrees with this but thinks that the distribution of team roles within a group should be further specified and improved. Since all team members received the same work assignments, it was difficult for some students to divide the work within the group in a meaningful way. Different roles and subtasks for individual group members could be added in a next iterative design cycle (e.g., through the "jigsaw" method that provides each group member only with partial data to require more collaboration (see e.g., Dillenbourg & Schneider, 1995, p. 135)). In this way chatbot *interactivity* could be better aligned with the *pedagogical* concept of collaborative learning.

Regarding *reliability* and *usability*, the language understanding of the chatbot as well as the user interface could be further optimized in a next design cycle. In order to increase the chatbot *reliability* and better manage students' expectations, it might be helpful to display a larger number of question-and-answer options in the form of buttons. This approach could actively direct the students' attention to content on which Tubo can provide competent information.

In line with the results of Rienties et al. (2012), the design experiment showed that scaffolding elements can be viewed ambivalently. On the one hand, the structure, and the way chatbot Tubo guided them through the learning environment was helpful for more control-oriented students because they always knew what to do. On the other hand, this relatively rigid grid was also perceived as a restriction by some students who preferred autonomy. These students desired more individual freedom in their actions and found it boring to answer the tasks after a while.

7. CONCLUSION & OUTLOOK

This paper investigated how chatbot-mediated learning can be designed to foster team-based learning of middle school students. Based on the *quality indicators* for chatbot development identified in the literature, an extended framework (see Table 1) was developed that served as a guideline for the implementation of our chatbot application. The chatbot Tubo was tested with a middle school class as part of a formative evaluation. The received feedback suggests that the approach of team-based learning with chatbots has a lot of potential from the students' and teachers' point of view. However, the role distribution of the individual group members may have to be further specified to address the different needs of autonomous as well as more control-oriented students (compare to Rienties et al., 2012).

This study is subject to several limitations. First, the tool was only tested with a relatively small school class of eleven students. A larger sample size would be desirable to validate the external validity of the results. Second, the application was only tested over a relatively short period of four lessons. It could be that a *novelty effect* occurred (see e.g., Jeno et al., 2019), which may have initially increased student motivation but decreases over time once the students get used to chatbot Tubo. From this point of view, a more long-term use in the classroom seems to be meaningful. Third, no control group design was applied, and it is therefore difficult to draw a definitive conclusion on the achieved learning outcomes. However, in line with the applied educational design science approach and the aim of obtaining formative feedback as part of a first design cycle, this limitation was accepted on purpose.

From a theoretical point of view, the paper at hand can serve as a starting point for further research and discussion, as it explores the relatively new area of *chatbot-mediated learning in team-based scenarios*. From a practical standpoint, the paper contributes to a better understanding of how chatbot-mediated learning scenarios can be designed and implemented in the actual classroom. The derived framework in section 2 may serve as a guideline for other researchers who want to implement similar projects and uncover further potential of the technology in more detail.

Further research is needed to validate our designed learning scenario in terms of learning outcome. In a next design cycle, this could be achieved with a larger sample and a more quantitative approach. To further develop the chatbot application, learning analytics elements (see e.g., Daud et al., 2017, Mandinach & Schildkamp, 2021) could be implemented to provide the teacher with real-time data of what is happening in each group in order to support teachers' data-based decision making. This would enable the teacher to identify problems within groups more quickly and respond to them in a more targeted way.

REFERENCES

Adamopoulou, E., & Moussiades, L. (2020). Chatbots: History, technology, and applications. *Machine Learning with Applications, 2*. https://doi.org/10.1016/j.mlwa.2020.100006

Briggs, R. O., Kolfschoten, G. L., de Vreede, G. J., Lukosch, S., & Albrecht, C. C. (2013). Facilitator-in-a-box: process support applications to help practitioners realize the potential of collaboration technology. *Journal of Management Information Systems, 29*(4), 159-194. https://doi.org/10.2753/MIS0742-1222290406

Burkhard, M., Seufert, S., Cetto, M., & Handschuh, S. (2021). The Textbook Learns to Talk: How to Design Chatbot-Mediated Learning to Foster Collaborative High-Order Learning?. In *Innovate Learning Summit*, 12-21. Association for the Advancement of Computing in Education (AACE). https://www.learntechlib.org/p/220264/

Daud, A., Aljohani, N. R., Abbasi, R. A., Lytras, M. D., Abbas, F., & Alowibdi, J. S. (2017). Predicting student performance using advanced learning analytics. In *Proceedings of the 26th international conference on World Wide Web companion*, 415-421. https://doi.org/10.1145/3041021.3054164

David, B., Chalon, R., Zhang, B., & Yin, C. (2019). Design of a collaborative learning environment integrating emotions and virtual assistants (chatbots). In *2019 IEEE 23rd International Conference on Computer Supported Cooperative Work in Design (CSCWD)*, 51-56. IEEE. https://doi.org/10.1109/CSCWD.2019.8791893

Dillenbourg, P., & Schneider, D. (1995). Mediating the mechanisms which make collaborative learning sometimes effective. *International Journal of Educational Telecommunications, 1*(2), 131-146. https://www.learntechlib.org/primary/p/15155/

Duffy, M. C., & Azevedo, R. (2015). Motivation matters: Interactions between achievement goals and agent scaffolding for self-regulated learning within an intelligent tutoring system. *Computers in Human Behavior, 52*, 338-348. https://doi.org/10.1016/j.chb.2015.05.041

Euler, D. (2014). Design-Research – a paradigm under development. *Design-Based Research*, 15-44. Stuttgart: Franz Steiner Verlag

Garcia Brustenga, G., Fuertes-Alpiste, M., & Molas-Castells, N. (2018). *Briefing paper: Chatbots in education.* eLearn Center, Universitat Oberta de Catalunya. https://doi.org/10.7238/elc.chatbots.2018

Gonda, D. E., Luo, J., Wong, Y. L., & Lei, C. U. (2019). Evaluation of developing educational chatbots based on the seven principles for good teaching. *Proceedings of the 2018 IEEE international conference on teaching, assessment, and learning for engineering, TALE 2018, Australia*, 446–453. IEEE. https://doi.org/10.1109/TALE.2018.8615175

Hattie, J. A. C. (2009). *Visible learning: A synthesis of over 800 meta-analyses relating to achievement.* Taylor & Francis.

Hwang, G. J., Xie, H., Wah, B. W., & Gašević, D. (2020). Vision, challenges, roles and research issues of Artificial Intelligence in Education. *Computers and Education: Artificial Intelligence*, 1, 100001. https://doi.org/10.1016/j.caeai.2020.100001

Jeno, L. M., Vandvik, V., Eliassen, S., & Grytnes, J. A. (2019). Testing the novelty effect of an m-learning tool on internalization and achievement: A Self-Determination Theory approach. *Computers & Education*, *128*, 398-413. https://doi.org/10.1016/j.compedu.2018.10.008

Jeong, H., Hmelo-Silver, C. E., & Jo, K. (2019). Ten years of Computer-Supported Collaborative Learning: A meta-analysis of CSCL in STEM education during 2005–2014. *Educational research review, 28*, 100284. https://doi.org/10.1016/j.edurev.2019.100284

Kelly, A. E., Lesh, R. A., & Baek, J. Y. (2008). *Handbook of design research methods in education: Innovations in science, technology, engineering, and mathematics learning and teaching*. Routledge. https://www.routledgehandbooks.com/doi/10.4324/9781315759593

Kerly, A., Hall, P., & Bull, S. (2007). Bringing chatbots into education: *Towards natural language negotiation of open learner models*. Knowledge-Based Systems, 20(2), 177–185. https://doi.org/10.1016/j.knosys.2006.11.014

Kumar, J. A. (2021). Educational chatbots for project-based learning: investigating learning outcomes for a team-based design course. *International Journal of Educational Technology in Higher Education, 18*(1), 1-28. https://doi.org/10.1186/s41239-021-00302-w

Laal, M., & Ghodsi, S. M. (2012). Benefits of collaborative learning. *Procedia-social and behavioral sciences, 31*, 486-490. https://doi.org/10.1016/j.sbspro.2011.12.091

Ludvigsen, S., & Mørch, A. (2010). Computer-supported collaborative learning: Basic concepts, multiple perspectives, and emerging trends. *The international encyclopedia of education, 5*, 290-296. https://doi.org/10.1016/B978-0-08-044894-7.00493-0

Mandinach, E. B., & Schildkamp, K. (2021). Misconceptions about data-based decision making in education: An exploration of the literature. *Studies in Educational Evaluation, 69*, 100842. https://doi.org/10.1016/j.stueduc.2020.100842

McKenney, S. & Reeves, T. C. (2018). *Conducting educational design research*. (2nd Ed.) Routledge: Oxon.

McKenney, S., & Reeves, T. C. (2021). Educational design research: portraying, conducting, and enhancing productive scholarship. *Medical Education, 55*(1), 82-92. https://doi.org/10.1111/medu.14280

Miller, M., & Hadwin, A. (2015). Scripting and awareness tools for regulating collaborative learning: Changing the landscape of support in CSCL. *Computers in Human Behavior, 52*, 573-588. https://doi.org/10.1016/j.chb.2015.01.050

Nussbaum, M., Alvarez, C., McFarlane, A., Gomez, F., Claro, S., & Radovic, D. (2009). Technology as small group face-to-face Collaborative Scaffolding. *Computers & Education, 52*(1), 147-153. https://doi.org/10.1016/j.compedu.2008.07.005

Okonkwo, C. W., & Ade-Ibijola, A. (2021). Chatbots applications in education: A systematic review. *Computers and Education: Artificial Intelligence, 2*, 100033. https://doi.org/10.1016/j.caeai.2021.100033

Radziwill, N. M., & Benton, M. C. (2017). Evaluating quality of chatbots and intelligent conversational agents. *arXiv preprint*. https://arxiv.org/abs/1704.04579v1

Rapp, A., Curti, L., & Boldi, A. (2021). The human side of human-chatbot interaction: A systematic literature review of ten years of research on text-based chatbots. *International Journal of Human-Computer Studies*, 102630. https://doi.org/10.1016/j.ijhcs.2021.102630

Rienties, B., Giesbers, B., Tempelaar, D., Lygo-Baker, S., Segers, M., & Gijselaers, W. (2012). The role of scaffolding and motivation in CSCL. *Computers & Education, 59*(3), 893-906. https://doi.org/10.1016/j.compedu.2012.04.010

Smutny, P., & Schreiberova, P. (2020). Chatbots for learning: A review of educational chatbots for the Facebook Messenger. *Computers and Education, 151*, 103862. https://doi.org/10.1016/j.compedu.2020.103862

Splichal, J. M., Oshima, J., & Oshima, R. (2018). Regulation of collaboration in project-based learning mediated by CSCL scripting reflection. *Computers & Education, 125*, 132-145. https://doi.org/10.1016/j.compedu.2018.06.003

Winkler, R. & Söllner, M. (2018): Unleashing the Potential of Chatbots in Education: A State-Of-The-Art Analysis. In: *Academy of Management Annual Meeting (AOM)*. Chicago, USA. https://www.alexandria.unisg.ch/publications/254848

Winkler, R., Neuweiler, M. L., Bittner, E. A. C., & Söllner, M. (2019). Hey Alexa, Please Help Us Solve This Problem! How Interactions with Smart Personal Assistants Improve Group Performance. In *International Conference on Information Systems (ICIS)*. Munich. https://aisel.aisnet.org/icis2019/general_topics/general_topics/17/

Winkler, R., Söllner, M., & Leimeister, J. M. (2021). Enhancing Problem-Solving Skills with Smart Personal Assistant Technology. *Computers & Education, 165*. 104148. https://doi.org/10.1016/j.compedu.2021.104148

Wood, D., Bruner, J. S., & Ross, G. (1976). The role of tutoring in problem solving. J*ournal of Child Psychology and Psychiatry, and Allied Disciplines, 17*(2), 89–100. https://doi.org/10.1111/j.1469-7610.1976.tb00381.x.

FLIPPED LEARNING IN CORPORATE CONTEXTS: A CASE STUDY

Enrichetta Gentile, Paola Plantamura, Teresa Roselli and Veronica Rossano
Department of Computer Science, University of Bari
Via Orabona, 4 – 70125 Bari – Italy

ABSTRACT

Flipped Learning is an active teaching methodology that consists of reversing learning times and spaces. It entails that the teacher prepares and provides in advance the content to be studied so that, during the lecture, there is more time to do exercises and practice the concepts learned during self-study. In this process, the feedback that the teacher provides to students on their level of understanding, as well as the learning outcomes and observations that students, in turn, provide to the teacher, play a key role to adapt the learning path to the learners' actual needs. The paper aims to present a first case study of the application of Flipped Learning in the corporate setting. The case study involved a small company that is one of the partners in the national project L.I.F.T. to measure the effectiveness of the approach and learner satisfaction.

KEYWORDS

Flipped Learning, Professional Training, Corporate Learning

1. INTRODUCTION

Choosing Flipped Learning in corporate environments can be successful since this model increases the interest of the students by stimulating their motivation and increasing their engagement, involvement, and interaction (Zainuddin & Halili, 2016).

Although most of the experimental evidence of the application of Flipped Learning approach has been applied in school and academic contexts, its features highlight numerous advantages that might be interesting when applied to professional content due to its flexibility since it can be adapted to learners and different domain contexts (Nederveld and Berge, 2015).

Flipped Learning (FL) approach can be helpful in corporate training since it aids to advance problem-solving skills, which are always basic requisites in business scenarios (Karabulut-Ilgu et al., 2018). In addition, the use of self-learning in FL requires less change in the work organization than those required in the traditional classroom. FL allows for maximizing time in the classroom by focusing on specific topics or real case studies (Nel, 2017, Zainuddin et al., 2019).

However, some critical issues in the use of FL arise such as the low motivation of some students, who need the teacher's guidance, and the efforts required to produce effective teaching material. Moreover, students in FL must be well motivated to learn independently and to obtain all the benefits from this approach (Låg and Sæle, 2019). The lack of a teacher in the preparatory phase of Flipped Learning and self-paced courses can sometimes lead to confusion and increase the workload (Dimauro et al., 2019) in less motivated students or novice students, reducing the effectiveness of the method.

The other most critical issues concern the greater workload of the teacher. In FL the didactic content should be designed to be clear and helpful for learners without the teacher's guidance, it is harder than preparing slides to be used during the lectures. Also organizing and preparing case studies to be used during class time could be difficult since they have to exploit what learners have acquired during the self-learning step (Zainuddin, 2016, Karabulut-Ilgu et al., 2018). This aspect, however, in professional contexts, does not appear to be a critical issue but rather a strength, since vocational training, by its nature, requires the practical application to real cases that enable students to apply the knowledge and skills acquired.

The present work aims to measure the effectiveness of the introduction of Flipped Learning in the corporate setting in the national project L.I.F.T. Downstream of the study of the state of the art and the state of practice (Rossano et al., 2022), it could be stated that in the context of the L.I.F.T. project the Flipped Learning approach could be effective. To measure its effectiveness a first case study has been designed and implemented with a small sample of learners who need to acquire some basic IT skills.

2. THE L.I.F.T CASE STUDY

The project L.I.F.T. (Learning Intelligent Factory based on information Technologies) aims at supporting medium and small companies in the digital transformation process. In particular, the final aim of the Technology Transfer Service is to support the design and development of an activity plan to transfer the knowledge and skills necessary to use digital services. To this end, an experiment has been planned to compare the delivery of a course using the traditional approach and flipped learning. Two groups of employees of a company, one of the partners in the LIFT project, have been involved in a training intervention aimed at consolidating digital skills. The aim is to measure any differences in the effectiveness of the two approaches, but also to check whether the new model is appreciated by students and teachers and to investigate the difficulties encountered in a real context.

2.1 Corporate Training Needs

A training needs analysis was conducted by interview with the company contact person, who indicated the need to conduct a course on using a spreadsheet environment (MS Excel).

The company highlighted the knowledge to be acquired by workers:

- Design, create and manage complex files containing multiple worksheets, linking the data within them, and making use of available formatting tools.
- In the presence of complex and articulated data, evaluate all available types of graphs and diagrams, and generate those best suited to the goal, formatting them. If they are not available, know how to generate custom graphs and/or diagrams.
- Save processed documents, varying possible destinations and file types as required by the context of use.

Thus the following macro-objectives were defined:

- Basic information: to interact with the interface of a spreadsheet software, selecting and using common tools. Create a workbook, including many spreadsheets, and enter different types of data into cells.
- Managing Worksheets: understand that each file may contain several worksheets. Copy and move a worksheet within a spreadsheet, between spreadsheets. Link the contents of different cells and worksheets. Zoom in and out of content and apply different types of views, depending on the specific needs.
- Formatting: format cells to display numbers, date style, currency symbol, percentages, and text. Apply different colours to cell contents and cell backgrounds. Alignment.
- Formulas and functions: Create formulas using cell references and arithmetic operators (addition, subtraction, multiplication, division). Understand and use relative or absolute cell referencing in formulas.
- Charts: create different types of charts from spreadsheet data. Change chart area background colour, and legend fill colour. Change font size and colour of chart title, chart axes, and chart legend text.

2.2 Participants

The experimentation involved a group of company employees. Twenty-two administrative employees with various prior knowledge of MS Excel were involved. Information on the participants was obtained using a demographic questionnaire, aimed at acquiring data on their age, educational qualification, their role in the company, and the type of training courses (in-person, online, or blended), if any, they had attended in the past. In addition, to balance the proficiency of the groups, a pre-test containing a series of specific questions was administered to identify the participant's level of skills and expertise in MS Excel. The pre-test was composed of 15 questions 3 for each macro-objective identified in the training needs analysis.

For the experimental activities, the between-subjects design approach was applied. The participants were divided into two groups composed of 11 participants each:

- the Flipped Group (Experimental Group) in which training was provided using the flipped classroom approach
- the Lecture Group (Control Group) in which training was provided using the traditional approach.

2.3 Learning Activities

In both groups, all elements were the same: the activities, the topic of the lesson, the teacher, the teaching materials, and the number of students. The difference between the groups was exclusively the teaching methodology.

Group activities were carried out in parallel using as summarized in Table 1.

Table 1. Learning activity structure

Flipped Group		**Lecture Group**	
Time	**Activity**	**Time**	**Activity**
40 min	Conceptual framework challenge presentation and individual study (Anticipatory Moment - pre classroom)	20 min	Class with the teacher
	Problem solving/ Case study (Operational Moment - pre classroom)	40 min	Individual study
20 min	Flipped Lesson/ Hind-sight Lesson Teacher intervention for knowledge reworking (Restructuring Moment)		Exercise/case study
10 min	Assessment test	10 min	Assessment test

Conceptual framework

The activity of presenting the conceptual framework was conducted by the lecturer/tutor who at the beginning of each meeting provided a brief explanation of the theoretical framework of the topic to be studied. In this first presentation, the challenge, i.e., the task to be completed, was also explained to the participants. Finally, the supporting teaching materials and the task to be solved were provided to the class.

Problem-solving/case study

For the challenges, different exercise tracks have been developed, based on the specific needs expressed by the company. The number of exercises proposed for each teaching unit varies according to its content and complexity.

Didactic content

The didactic content was provided in the form of multimedia presentations converted into sharable content objects, i.e., SCORM (Sharable Content Object Reference Model) packages that were published on Moodle platform. The material was organized in the form of checklists, using the titles of important topics to be used in addressing the case study, thus enabling the scaffolding approach.

Assessment tests

For the evaluation of acquired skills, a questionnaire was defined for each didactic unit. Multiple-choice questions and open questions were used.

3. RESULTS

The measurement of effectiveness was carried out using a pre-test and post-test design. The students underwent a pre-test to measure their initial knowledge, and a post-test was administered downstream of the training intervention. At the end of the training step, both groups underwent a survey to evaluate their satisfaction with the methodology adopted. The comparison of the results allows verifying whether the performance of the control group differs from the experimental group. The experiment is ongoing, but the first results show that both groups gain knowledge and skills after the intervention, as expected. Figure 1 shows the average of the scores achieved in the pre-test and post-test by the members of each group (EG and CG) in each Learning Unit (the learning pathway consisted of 5 Units). The interesting result was related to the appreciation of the teaching approach, both the trainees and the teacher were satisfied with the flipped approach.

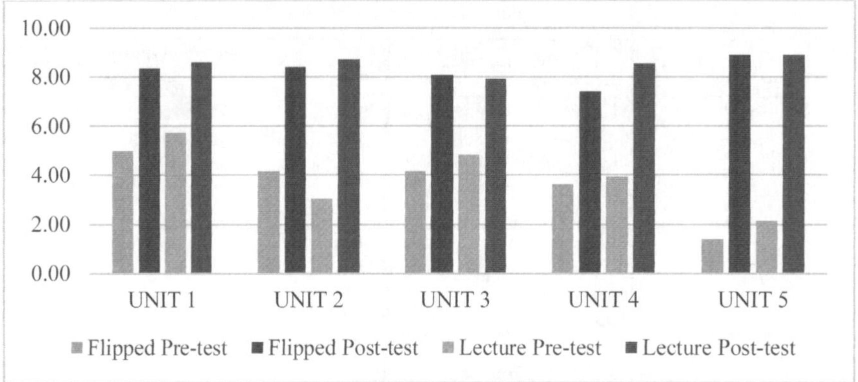

Figure 1. Pre-test and Post-test results for each learning unit in Flipped Group (EG) vs Lecture Group (CG)

For the evaluation of participants' satisfaction, a questionnaire was administered at the end of the training intervention to both groups The survey consists of 7 questions, using 5-point Likert scale from 1 (unsatisfied) to 5 (very satisfied), to assess the following dimensions: organization of the course, course content, teaching approach and performances.

Both groups overall found the organization of the activities satisfactory, albeit with different percentages. The 67% of participants in the FlippedGroup rated the guidance provided as complete and clear, while for the same aspects in the LectureGroup only 55% rated it positively. In addition, the 56% of the FlippedGroup participants felt that the guidance provided was useful versus the 45% of the LectureGroup participants. Therefore, it can be specified that the FlippedGroup had a better perception of the organization of the activities.

The students' satisfaction with the course content provided was assessed in terms of the interest, usefulness and clarity of the content supplied. Based on the data obtained, it could be stated that the FlippedGroup appreciated the teaching materials provided, in fact, most of the respondents (88.89%) expressed a high evaluation (score 4 - 5) about the interest of the content, as well as its usefulness (Figure 2). On the other hand, regarding the clarity of the content, not all participants considered it clear and easy to use, only the 33, 33% gave a very positive opinion of it (score 5). Probably, respondents had some problems in using self-pace content. In the LectureGroup, the results were slightly lower (Figure 3) than in the FlippedGroup for both the interest and the usefulness, instead higher score was expressed for the clarity of the content. This corroborates the hypothesis that using a self-paced content could be more difficult.

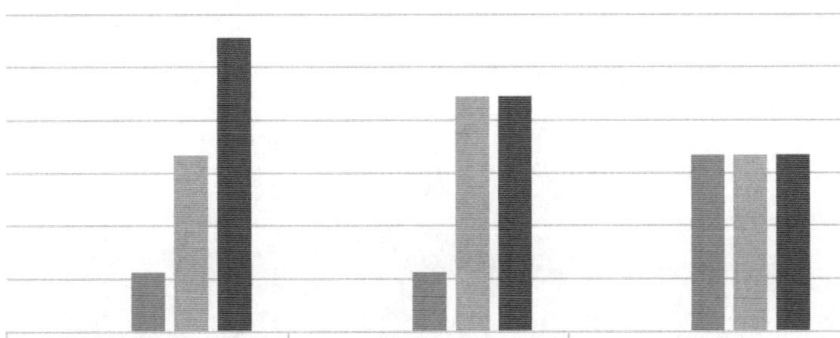

	Interest	Usefulness	Clarity
■ 1-Low	0.00%	0.00%	0.00%
■ 2	0.00%	0.00%	0.00%
■ 3	11.11%	11.11%	33.33%
■ 4	33.33%	44.44%	33.33%
■ 5 - High	55.56%	44.44%	33.33%

Figure 2. Users' appreciation of didactic content in the Flipped Group

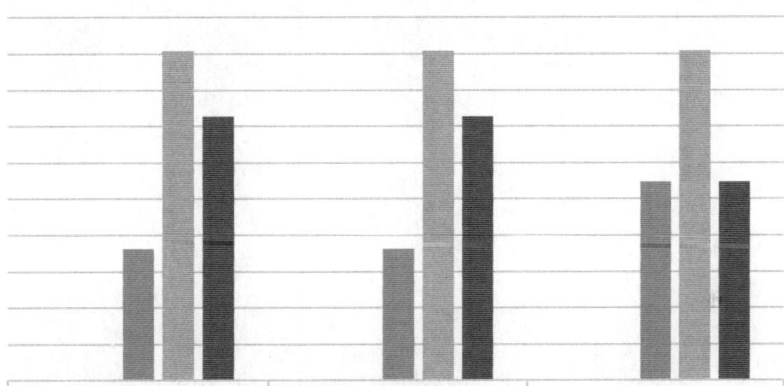

	Interest	Usefulness	Clarity
■ 1-Low	0.00%	0.00%	0.00%
■ 2	0.00%	0.00%	0.00%
■ 3	18.18%	18.18%	27.27%
■ 4	45.45%	45.45%	45.45%
■ 5 - High	36.36%	36.36%	27.27%

Figure 3. Users' appreciation of didactic content in the Lecture Group

The methodology used, flipped or traditional, was evaluated in terms of clarity, interest, usefulness, easiness, and effectiveness. As shown in Figures 4 and 5, the traditional approach was rated as more clear, useful, easy, and effective than the flipped approach. Although the flipped approach was interesting to learners, this evaluation is likely to change in the long term.

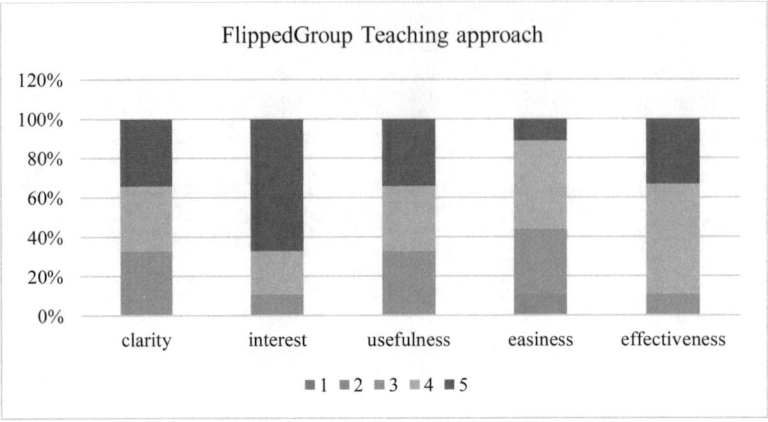

Figure 4. User's Satisfaction with the flipped approach in terms of clarity, interest, usefulness, easiness, and effectiveness

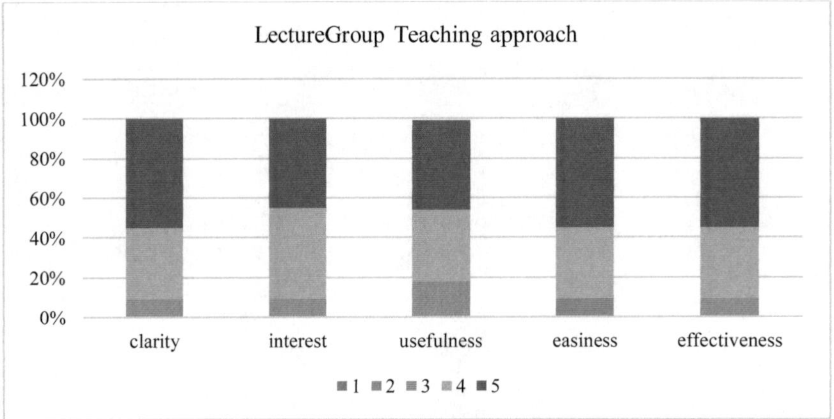

Figure 5. User's Satisfaction with the traditional approach in terms of clarity, interest, usefulness, easiness, and effectiveness

Analysis of the data about performance satisfaction shows that although both groups have achieved the learning objectives, it appears that FlippedGroup students lack awareness of their achievements. Only 33% of the FlippedGroup participants are convinced that they have achieved the learning outcomes and 11% declare they have not achieved the objectives, contrary to what was recorded by the post-test. In contrast, in the LectureGroup, students achieved their learning with greater awareness; in fact, 89% stated that they had achieved it. This situation brings out the fact that there is a need to strengthen feedback in the Flipped Classroom methodology.

4. CONCLUSIONS AND FUTURE WORKS

Flipped learning is an interesting approach to apply in all contexts where it is important to develop problem-solving skills. The idea of this research as part of the L.I.F.T. project led to the evaluation of its application in the corporate context. In companies, using flipped learning can also be useful in leaving the student free to delve into the learning content as and when they see fit. The existing literature argues that Flipped Learning is a methodology with many positive aspects in terms of motivation to learn, the development of skills (social, digital, etc...), and the enhancement of the autonomy and responsibility of the learners.

The paper describes the first case study aimed at investigating the application of the Flipped Learning approach in the corporate context. The evaluation conducted, therefore, is a starting point for the introduction of the Flipped Learning methodology in professional and corporate training.

The results obtained from the trial are promising; the approach enables concrete and satisfactory learning outcomes. The participants expressed positive opinions about the methodology's acceptance, interest, and effectiveness. However, some critical issues have also emerged that need to be addressed, such as the importance of clear feedback and the low motivation of some participants.

The study has several limitations. First of all, the sample was composed of few people, so the analysis has limited statistical significance. Moreover, the learning activities were performed when employees were at home due to the Covid-19 restrictions, so they were required to attend the course and were poorly motivated. For the same reason, for researchers was not possible to reach the students and investigate more in details qualitative aspects.

In this regard, the next case study it would be investigated if the introduction of Gamification mechanisms can be useful to increase productivity, effectiveness, motivation and participation (Di Bitonto et al., 2014, Cassano et al., 2018).

ACKNOWLEDGEMENT

This work was partially supported by the project L.I.F.T., "Learning Intelligent Factory based on information Technologies" funded by MISE - PON I&C 2014-2020 - D.M. 05.03.2018. Prog. n. F/190030/01-03/X44, and by the Ordinary Research Fund. Moreover, the authors would like to thank all the learners and the "Leader Società Cooperativa Consortile" company partner of the project L.I.F.T. involved in the study.

REFERENCES

Cassano, F., Piccinno, A., Roselli, T., & Rossano, V., 2018. Gamification and learning analytics to improve engagement in university courses. In *International Conference in Methodologies and Intelligent Systems for Technology Enhanced Learning*, Springer, Cham, pp. 156-163.

Di Bitonto, P., Corriero, N., Pesare, E., Rossano, V., & Roselli, T., 2014. Training and learning in e-health using the gamification approach: the trainer interaction. *In International Conference on Universal Access in Human-Computer Interaction,* Springer, Cham, pp. 228-237.

Dimauro G., Gentile E., Plantamura P., Scalera M., 2019. Experimentation of Flipped Learning in Higher Education Academy. *International Journal for Infonomics* (IJI), Vol. 12 No.3, pp. 1891-1898.

Karabulut-Ilgu, A., Jaramillo Cherrez, N., & Jahren, C. T., 2018. A systematic review of research on the flipped learning method in engineering education. British Journal of Educational Technology, Vol. 49 No.3, 398-411.

Låg, T. & Sæle, R.G., 2019. Does the Flipped Classroom Improve Student Learning and Satisfaction? A Systematic Review and Meta-Analysis. *AERA Open*, Vol. 5 No. 3, pp. 1-17.

Nederveld A., Berge Z.L., 2015. Flipped learning in the workplace. *Journal of Workplace Learning*, Vol. 27 No. 2, p. 162-172.

Nel, L., 2017. Students as collaborators in creating meaningful learning experiences in technology-enhanced classrooms: An engaged scholarship approach. *British Journal of Educational Technology*, Vol. 48 No. 5, 1131-1142.

Rossano, V., Plantamura, P., Gentile, E., & Roselli, T., 2022. Flipped Learning in Corporate Training to Support Industry 4.0. *In EDULEARN22 Proceedings*, IATED press, pp. 10244-10251.

Zainuddin Z., Halili S.H., 2016. Flipped Classroom Research and Trends from Different Fields of Study. *The International Review of Research in Open and Distributed Learning*. Vol. 17 No.3.

Zainuddin Z., Haruna H., Li X., Zhang Y., Chu S.K.W., 2019. A systematic review of flipped classroom empirical evidence from different fields: what are the gaps and future trends? *On the Horizon*, Vol. 27 No. 2, pp. 72-86.

EVALUATING DIFFERENT ASSESSMENT TYPES IN AN ONLINE GEOSCIENCE COURSE

Emre Dinç[1] and April L. Millet[2]
[1]*The Pennsylvania State University, University Park PA, United States of America*
[2]*The Pennsylvania State University, John A. Dutton e-Education Institute, University Park PA, United States of America*

ABSTRACT

This study investigated the effect of different assessment types on overall success in an online geoscience course covering energy's impact on the environment. Two groups took either the slower 1-credit or the faster 3-credit version of the course, which utilized the same content. Self-assessment questions developed using H5P, quizzes, summative assessment labs, and a capstone project were used to assess students. Independent samples t-test, multiple regression analysis, and repeated measures ANOVA were conducted for data analyses. Quiz success significantly differed between groups. Quiz, capstone, and lab assignment successes were significant positive predictors of overall success. The total frequency of answering H5P questions was a significant positive predictor of quiz and lab assignment successes. Frequencies for answering H5P questions and time spent on H5P questions in each module showed significant differences.

KEYWORDS

Assessment, Knowledge Checks, Online Course, Retrieval Practice, Geoscience Education

1. INTRODUCTION

The strategies need to be chosen to provide feedback and necessary support while designing online learning (Ally, 2008). However, identifying appropriate strategies to provide feedback in online learning was a challenge (Kearns, 2012). This was particularly observed during the COVID-19 pandemic with online assessment difficulties (Taufiq-Hail et al., 2021). Students engage with the assessment reflecting their learning during the online learning process more than engaging with each other (Şahin et al., 2020). Correspondingly, quizzes as a traditional assessment strategy, capstone projects as an assessment type connected to fieldwork and data collection in terms of active learning, and self-assessment resources as enabling metacognitive monitoring (Kearns, 2012; Motade & Deshpande, 2022; Yan & Brown, 2017) are used to evaluate learning and support the learning process. Ungraded self-assessment resources provide just-in-time and delayed feedback and engagement (Lewis et al., 2010; Wilkie et al., 2018), empowering students to oversee their learning (Nguyen et al., 2006). Quizzes also significantly affect the overall success and keep students focused on the course content (Salas-Morera et al., 2012).

Quizzes are often the first and essential assessment type instructors prefer to use in online courses before and during the COVID- 19 pandemic because quizzes in learning management systems encourage learners to engage with them (Rocco, 2007; Taufiq-Hail et al., 2021). Along with engagement, quizzes also affect student motivation positively (Raes et al., 2020). Weekly quizzes and self-assessment questions as active learning exercises create "highly structured courses" (Freeman et al., 2011, p. 176) and provide benefits to students getting prepared for learning (Hakk et al., 2011). Self-assessment, a metacognitive tool, is often used by successful students and positively affects overall success (Hartwig & Dunlosky, 2012). Capstone projects encourage personal meaning-making and contextual learning within the constructivist assessment strategies (Ally, 2008).

As observed during the COVID-19 pandemic, strategies with more qualitative approaches, such as capstone projects with checkpoints during the learning process, are more effective in online learning and online assessment (Montenegro-Rueda et al., 2021). Within the framework of engagement through quizzes and lab assignments, self-assessing via H5P questions, and contextual learning with the capstone project, answers to these research questions (RQs) were sought:

1. Is there any significant difference in overall success and quiz, capstone, lab assignment achievements as well as the total frequency of answering H5P questions, total time spent on H5P questions, and the total points awarded for the correctly answered H5P questions between groups taking the course with different credits?
2. Is there any effect of quizzes, capstone, lab assignments, the total frequency of answering H5P questions, total time spent on H5P questions, the total points awarded on the correctly answered H5P questions, and weekly/biweekly duration modules on overall success?
3. Is there a significant effect of group (taking either 1-credit or 3-credit course) on the frequency of answering H5P questions when H5P questions are studied throughout the online course?
4. Is there a significant effect of group (taking either 1-credit or 3-credit course) on time spent on H5P questions when H5P questions are studied throughout the online course?
5. Is there a significant effect of the total frequency of answering H5P questions, total time spent on H5P questions, and the total points awarded on the correctly answered H5P questions on the quiz, capstone, and lab assignment achievements?

2. METHOD

2.1 Participants and Setting

A total of sixty-five participants took part in the study in the northeastern United States: eighteen participants from the 1-credit course and forty-seven participants from the 3-credit course. Both groups took the online course asynchronously with the same content throughout the five modules. Module1 – Why Energy Matters? describes the history of different types of resources used as energy. Module2 – What is Energy? focused on the basics of energy—how we talk about it, what it is, how much of it we use, and the relation between it and the US economy. Module 3 – Oil, Coal & Natural Gas | Drilling, Fracking & Reserves was about the formation and future of fossil fuels, the origins of oil, coal, and natural gas, and reserves and resources. Module 4 – Global Warming | Physics describes the physics associated with global warming. Module5 – Global Warming | History focused on the history of global warming specifically on who started the fire. Participants in the 1-credit course worked through one module per two weeks, whereas others in the 3-credit course worked through one module per week. 1-credit course was a part of a degree completion program.

2.2 Data Collection

Quizzes in each module were designed to check whether students mastered the science presented in the module. Students were given an opportunity to create an emission scenario for the next 200 years in the capstone project. Summative lab assignments focused on computer modeling for oil and climate in Module3 and Module4. H5P knowledge check questions were supplementary resources supporting learning the content throughout the modules. Points were assigned to correctly answered H5P questions; however, participants were informed that those points would not be aggregated into their overall course grade.

2.3 Data Analysis

Independent samples t-test was conducted to investigate the differences between groups taking the 1-credit and the 3-credit course. Multiple regression analysis was used to investigate the predictors for overall success as well as the quiz, capstone, and lab assignment achievements for all participants. Repeated measures ANOVA was conducted to investigate the differences between frequencies of answering H5P questions and time spent on H5P questions in each module.

3. RESULTS

3.1 RQ1. Independent Samples T-Test

There was a significant difference in quiz success ($t(62) = 2.464$, $p < 0.05$, Cohen's $d = 0.697$) between groups in favor of those taking the 1-credit course. Overall success ($t(62) = 0.637$, $p = 0.526$), capstone success ($t(62) = -0.611$, $p = 0.543$), lab assignment success ($t(62) = -0.594$, $p = 0.555$), the total time spent on H5P questions ($t(62) = 1.957$, $p = 0.055$), the frequency of answering H5P questions ($t(62) = 0.542$, $p = 0.590$), and the total points awarded for correctly answered H5P questions ($t(62) = -0.197$, $p = 0.844$) did *not* significantly differ between groups taking 1-credit and 3-credit.

3.2 RQ2. Multiple Regression Analysis for Overall Success

Multiple regression analysis was conducted for all students to investigate the effect of different durations per module and assessment types (Table 1). One outlier was detected based on Mahalanobis distance and removed from all analyses. Tolerance values were higher than 0.2, and VIF values were less than 10. The ANOVA result showed significance ($p < 0.001$), which is a good fit for the data. Different duration per module between groups ($p = 0.595$) did not significantly affect overall success. Quiz ($p < 0.001$), capstone ($p < 0.001$), and lab assignment ($p < 0.001$) achievements were significant predictors of overall success in the course. The unstandardized coefficient for quiz success is 0.469. Each one-unit increase in total quiz score is an increase in the overall score of 0.469 points. When we check their standardized coefficients, capstone project success ($B = 0.431$) was more powerful than quiz success ($B = 0.425$) and lab assignment success ($B = 0.341$) in predicting the overall success.

Table 1. Multiple regression analysis results for overall success

	Unstandardized coefficients		Standardized coefficient B	t	p
	B	Std. Error			
constant	10.746	2.890		3.719	< 0.001
Quiz success	0.469	0.036	0.425	12.941	< 0.001
Capstone success	0.214	0.012	0.431	17.376	< 0.001
Lab assignment success	0.699	0.071	0.341	9.857	< 0.001
Total frequency of H5P questions	-0.112	0.115	-0.047	-0.970	0.336
Total time spent on H5P questions	1.542e-5	0.000	0.017	0.761	0.450
Total points awarded for H5P questions	0.122	0.110	0.049	1.105	0.274
Groups	-0.398	0.746	-0.013	-0.534	0.595

Note. *Groups* variable is for taking either the 1-credit course or the 3-credit course.

3.3 RQ3. Repeated-Measures ANOVA for Frequencies

Since the sphericity was violated ($p < 0.001$), we interpreted the Greenhouse-Geisser correction ($\varepsilon = 0.687$). A repeated-measures ANOVA was conducted with group as the between-subject factor and frequencies of answering H5P questions in each module as the within-subject factor. The overall model was significant; Wilks Lambda = 0.283, $F(4, 59) = 37.414$, $p < 0.001$, partial eta squared = 0.717. There was no significant effect of group on frequencies, $F(1, 62) = 0.293$, $p = 0.590$, partial eta squared = 0.005, supporting the non-significant result of the first research question related to frequencies.

There was a significant effect of specific module on frequencies, $F(3, 170) = 65.303$, $p < 0.001$, partial eta squared = 0.513. Pair-wise comparisons with Bonferroni adjustment for the frequencies of answering H5P questions (Table 2) in each module for all participants indicated: The frequency of answering H5P questions in Module1 was significantly higher than frequencies in Module2 ($p < 0.001$, Cohen's $d = 1.646$), Module3 ($p < 0.001$, Cohen's $d = 0.876$), Module4 ($p < 0.001$, Cohen's $d = 0.968$), and Module 5 ($p < 0.001$, Cohen's $d = 1.530$). The frequency of answering H5P questions in Module3 was significantly higher than frequencies in Module2 ($p < 0.001$, Cohen's $d = 0.997$) and Module5 ($p < 0.001$, Cohen's $d = 0.863$). The frequency of answering H5P questions in Module4 was significantly higher than frequencies in Module2 ($p < 0.001$, Cohen's $d = 0.569$) and Module5 ($p < 0.001$, Cohen's $d = 0.504$).

Table 2. Pairwise comparisons of frequencies of answering H5P questions

Module	Module	Mean Difference	Std. Error	p	95% Confidence Interval for Difference	
					Lower	Upper
1	2	2.942*	0.257	< 0.001	2.194	3.680
	3	1.658*	0.258	< 0.001	0.907	2.409
	4	1.978*	0.256	< 0.001	1.234	2.722
	5	2.882*	0.276	< 0.001	2.080	3.684
2	1	-2.942*	0.257	< 0.001	-3.689	-2.194
	3	-1.283*	0.173	< 0.001	-1.788	-0.779
	4	-0.964*	0.170	< 0.001	-1.458	-0.469
	5	-0.059	0.142	1.000	-0.472	0.354
3	1	-1.658*	0.258	< 0.001	-2.409	-0.907
	2	1.283*	0.173	< 0.001	0.779	1.788
	4	0.320	0.169	0.631	-0.172	0.812
	5	1.224*	0.166	< 0.001	0.742	1.706
4	1	-1.978*	0.256	< 0.001	-2.722	-1.234
	2	0.964*	0.170	< 0.001	0.469	1.458
	3	-0.320	0.169	0.631	-0.812	0.172
	5	0.904*	0.172	< 0.001	0.404	1.404
5	1	-2.882*	0.276	< 0.001	-3.684	-2.080
	2	0.059	0.142	1.000	-0.354	0.472
	3	-1.224*	0.166	< 0.001	-1.706	-0.742
	4	-0.904*	0.172	< 0.001	-1.404	-0.404

3.4 RQ4. Repeated-Measures ANOVA for Time Spent

Since the sphericity was violated ($p < 0.001$), we interpreted the Greenhouse-Geisser correction ($\varepsilon = 0.635$). A repeated-measures ANOVA was conducted with group as the between-subject factor and time spent on H5P questions in each module as the within-subject factor. The overall model is significant; Wilks Lambda = 0.728, F (4, 59) = 5.498, $p < 0.001$, partial eta squared = 0.272. There was no significant effect of group on time spent, F (1, 62) = 2.011, $p = 0.161$, partial eta squared = 0.031, supporting the non-significant result of the first research question related to time spent.

There was a significant effect of specific module on time spent on H5P questions, F (3, 158) = 3.617, $p < 0.05$, partial eta squared = 0.055. Pair-wise comparisons with Bonferroni adjustment for the total time spent on H5P questions (Table 3) in each module for all participants indicated that time spent on H5P questions in Module4 was significantly higher than time spent on H5P questions in Module5 ($p < 0.05$, Cohen's $d = 0.458$). There were no other significant differences in time spent on H5P questions in modules.

Table 3. Pairwise comparisons of time spent on H5P questions

Module	Module	Mean Difference	Std. Error	p	95% Confidence Interval for difference	
					Lower	Upper
1	2	3122.225	1231.835	0.138	-463.607	6708.057
	3	1449.104	1380.341	1.000	-2569.022	5467.230
	4	364.565	1519.389	1.000	-4058.327	4787.457
	5	3147.002	1258.705	0.151	-517.048	6811.052
2	1	-3122.225	1231.835	0.138	-6708.057	463.607
	3	-1673.121	825.336	0.469	-4075.648	729.405
	4	-2757.660	992.777	0.072	-5647.600	132.280
	5	24.777	396.779	1.000	-1130.235	1179.788
3	1	-1449.104	1380.341	1.000	-5467.230	2569.022
	2	1673.121	825.336	0.469	-729.405	4075.648
	4	-1084.539	1288.430	1.000	-4835.115	2666.037
	5	1697.898	832.989	0.458	-726.905	4122.701
4	1	-364.565	1519.389	1.000	-4787.457	4058.327
	2	2757.660	992.777	0.072	-132.280	5647.600
	3	1084.539	1288.430	1.000	-2666.037	4835.115
	5	2782.437*	833.719	0.014	355.508	5209.366
5	1	-3147.002	1258.705	0.151	-6811.052	517.048
	2	-24.777	396.779	1.000	-1179.788	1130.235
	3	-1697.898	832.989	0.458	-4122.701	726.905
	4	-2782.437*	833.719	0.014	-5209.366	-355.508

3.5 RQ5. Multiple Regression Analysis for Quiz, Capstone, and Lab Achievements

Multiple regression analysis was conducted for all students to investigate the effect of the total frequency of answering H5P questions, total time spent on H5P questions, and the total points awarded on the correctly answered H5P questions on the quiz, capstone, and lab assignment achievements (Table 4). Tolerance values were higher than 0.2, and VIF values were less than 10. The ANOVA results showed significance ($p < 0.001$), which is a good fit for the data. The total frequency of answering H5P questions was a significant positive predictor of quiz ($p = 0.006$) and lab assignment ($p = 0.002$) achievements. The unstandardized coefficients for the total frequency of answering H5P questions were 1.404 and 0.842 for quiz and lab assignment achievements, respectively. Each one-unit increase in the total frequency of answering H5P questions is an increase in the total quiz score of 1.404 points. Similarly, each one-unit increase in the total frequency of answering H5P questions is an increase in the total lab assignment score of 0.842 points.

Table 4. Multiple regression analysis results for quiz, capstone, and lab assignment achievements

	Unstandardized Coefficient B	Unstandardized Coefficient Std. Error	Standardized B	t	p
		Quiz success			
Total frequency of H5P questions	1.404	0.495	0.649	2.838	0.006
Total time spent on H5P questions	-2.849e-5	0.000	-0.035	-0.308	0.759
Total points awarded for H5P questions	-0.311	0.515	-0.137	-0.603	0.549
constant	65.380	4.355		15.013	< 0.001
		Capstone success			
Total frequency of H5P questions	0.772	1.263	0.160	0.612	0.543
Total time spent on H5P questions	0.000	0.000	-0.073	-0.558	0.579
Total points awarded for H5P questions	0.380	1.315	0.075	0.289	0.774
constant	74.195	11.115		6.675	< 0.001
		Lab assignment success			
Total frequency of H5P questions	0.842	0.258	0.722	3.265	0.002
Total time spent on H5P questions	-5.662e-5	0.000	-0.127	-1.154	0.253
Total points awarded for H5P questions	-0.201	0.269	-0.164	-0.747	0.458
constant	15.899	2.270		7.003	< 0.001

4. DISCUSSION

The result of this study is important to the literature for two reasons, a) deciding possible assessment types in an online course design and b) providing insight related to the parts of energy content that geoscience students monitor their learning through self-assessment resources. Integrated quizzes in the learning management system enabling engagement with the course content created a significant difference between those in the 1-credit degree completion course and the 3-credit course. This result made sense when we think that students in the 1-credit course engaged more with the content to complete their undergraduate degree. This coincides with the quizzes being the source of engagement with the learning throughout a course (Rocco, 2007; Taufiq-Hail et al., 2021).

Capstone projects enable students to learn actively in a contextual manner (Kearns, 2012). In this study, the capstone project allowed students to take responsibility for their learning and learning process. Quizzes enabling highly structured course design, capstone projects providing opportunities for contextual learning, and lab assignments were significant positive predictors of the overall success of the course. Integrating these different styles of assessments might allow students to engage with the course content more, particularly considering the asynchronous nature of the course.

Frequently completing H5P questions had a significant positive effect on quiz and lab assignment achievements. Completing the H5P questions more frequently in Module1 compared to other modules may have been due to students' curiosity about what H5P was and/or they thought they would need help and feedback at the beginning of the course. Answering H5P questions in the more specific and detailed content of Module3 and Module4 compared to Module 2 – What is Energy? indicates the supportive role of H5P questions. These findings support the role of ungraded self-assessment questions, which are just-in-time and delayed feedback along with learning support (Lewis et al., 2010). The reason for spending more time on H5P knowledge check questions in Module4: Global Warming – Physics compared to Module5: Global Warming – History might be the use of numerical tools and publicly available data for global warming in Module4 and less focus on numbers and data in Module5.

5. CONCLUSION AND RECOMMENDATIONS

Quizzes, lab assignments, and the capstone project were assessment tools that positively affected overall success. The total frequency of answering H5P questions was a significant positive predictor of quiz and lab assignment achievements. Course and learning designers might consider adding various types of assessment strategies to increase students' overall achievements in an online course. H5P questions were used more frequently in more specific and detailed concepts in this online geoscience course. Integrating self-assessment questions to more specific and detailed modules would be more supportive to students. Designers and instructors would only create and integrate self-assessment questions to more specific and detailed modules, in such way, they save time and reduce their workload. For future course design, discussions and lab assignments in each module can be considered in addition to the quizzes and the capstone project for student engagement and model simulations. This would be more aligned with the recommendations regarding online assessment during the COVID-19 pandemic, particularly related to debates amongst students and continuous assessment (García-Peñalvo et al., 2021). Also, the number of participants in this study was limited. For further research, other statistical tests can be conducted with more participants' data to test the indirect effect of H5P questions through other assessment types on overall success.

REFERENCES

Ally, M., 2008. Foundations of Educational Theory for Online Learning. In T. Anderson (Ed.), *The Theory and Practice of Online Learning* (2nd ed.), pp. 15–44. Athabasca University Press.

Freeman, S. et al., 2011. Increased Course Structure Improves Performance in Introductory Biology. *CBE—Life Sciences Education*, Vol. 10, No. 2, pp. 175–186. https://doi.org/10.1187/cbe.10-08-0105

García-Peñalvo, F. J. et al., 2021. Recommendations for Mandatory Online Assessment in Higher Education During the COVID-19 Pandemic. In D. Burgos, A. Tlili, & A. Tabacco (Eds.), *Radical Solutions for Education in a Crisis Context*, pp. 85-98. Springer. https://doi.org/10.1007/978-981-15-7869-4_6

Haak, D. C. et al., 2011. Increased Structure and Active Learning Reduce the Achievement Gap in Introductory Biology. *Science*, Vol. 332, No. 6034, pp. 1213–1216. https:///doi.org/10.1126/science.1204820

Hartwig, M. K. and Dunlosky, J., 2012. Study Strategies of College Students: Are Self-testing and Scheduling Related to Achievement? *Psychonomic Bulletin & Review*, Vol. 19, No. 1, pp. 126–134. https://doi.org/10.3758/s13423-011-0181-y

Kearns, L. R., 2012. Student Assessment in Online Learning: Challenges and Effective Practices. *MERLOT Journal of Online Learning and Teaching*, Vol. 8, No. 3, pp. 198–208. https://jolt.merlot.org/vol8no3/kearns_0912.htm

Lewis, D. et al., 2010. Knowledge Check Questions: Best Practices for Use of This Instructional Strategy. In J. Herrington & C. Montgomerie (Eds.), *ED-MEDIA 2010—World Conference on Educational Multimedia, Hypermedia & Telecommunications*. Association for the Advancement of Computing in Education, pp. 2783–2788. https://www.learntechlib.org/primary/p/35034/

Montenegro-Rueda, M. et al., 2021. Assessment in Higher Education during the COVID-19 Pandemic: A Systematic Review. *Sustainability*, Vol. 13, No. 19. https://doi.org/10.3390/su131910509

Motade, S. and Deshpande, A. 2022. Active Learning Techniques for Effective Online Teaching and Learning in Higher Education. *Journal of Engineering Education Transformation*, Vol. 35, No. 4, pp. 112-120.

Nguyen, D. M. et al., 2006. The Impact of Web-based Assessment and Practice on Students' Mathematics Learning Attitudes. *The Journal of Computers in Mathematics and Science Teaching*, Vol. 25, No. 3, pp. 251-279. https://www.learntechlib.org/primary/p/6277/

Raes, A. et al., 2020. Learning and Instruction in the Hybrid Virtual Classroom: An Investigation of Students' Engagement and the Effect of Quizzes. Computers & Education, Vol. 143. https://doi.org/10.1016/j.compedu.2019.103682

Rocco, S., 2007. Online Assessment and Evaluation. *New Directions for Adult and Continuing Education*, Vol. 113, pp. 75–86. https://doi.org/10.1002/ace.249

Salas-Morera, L. et al., 2012. Analysis of Online Quizzes as a Teaching and Assessment Tool. *Journal of Technology and Science Education*, Vol. 2, No. 1, pp. 39–45. http://hdl.handle.net/2099/12152

Şahin, M. et al., 2020. Sequential Analysis of Online Learning Behavior According to E-Learning Readiness. In P. Isaias, D. G. Sampson, D. Ifenthaler (Eds.), *Cognition and Exploratory Learning in the Digital Age (CELDA)*. International Association for Development of the Information Society, pp. 117-131.

Taufiq-Hail, G. A. et al., 2021. Academic Staff Perceptions on Students' Traditional Assessment Transformations toward Online Evaluation during COVID-19 Pandemic in Higher Education: A Preliminary Study from Two Diverse Cultures. *2021 Sustainable Leadership and Academic Excellence International Conference*. Manama, Bahrain. IEEE, pp. 16-25. https://doi.org/10.1109/SLAE54202.2021.9686904

Wilkie, S. et al., 2018. Considerations for Designing H5P Online Interactive Activities. In M. Campbell, J. Willems, C. Adachi, D. Blake, I. Doherty, S. Krishnan, S. Macfarlane, L. Ngo, M. O'Donnell, S. Palmer, L. Riddell, I. Story, H. Suri, & J. Tai (Eds.). *ASCILITE*, pp. 543–549.

Yan, Z. and Brown, G. T. L., 2017. A Cyclical Self-assessment Process: Towards a Model of How Students Engage in Self-assessment. *Assessment & Evaluation in Higher Education*, Vol. 42, No. 8, pp. 1247–1262. https://doi.org/10.1080/02602938.2016.1260091

PROBLEMATIC SMARTPHONE USE AND COGNITIVE FAILURES. AN EXPLORATIVE STUDY AMONG FREE DIFFERENT GENERATIONS (X, Y, Z)

Maria Lidia Mascia[1], Natale Salvatore Bonfiglio[1], Roberta Renati[1], Stefania Cataudella[1], Łukasz Tomczyk[2] and Maria Pietronilla Penna[1]
[1]Department of Pedagogy, Psychology, Philosophy, University of Cagliari
Is Mirrionis 1 Street, 09123, Cagliari, Italy
[2]Faculty of Philosophy, Institute of Education Jagiellonian University, Poland
Gołębia 24, 31-007 Kraków, Poland

ABSTRACT

The present study focuses on smartphone overuse and on problematic behaviors related to it, investigating possible differences at the intergenerational level among the variables considered. Through the administration of self-report questionnaires, the perception of smartphone distraction, smartphone problematic use, phubbing, and cognitive failures were surveyed. Two hundred and twenty subjects took part in the research. The participants, aged between 18 and 57, were divided by generation Z, Y and Z, according to Ristiyono, classification (2022). Data analysis was carried out through the application of Spearman's rho was used to analyze correlations between subscales. The Kruskal-Wallis test was invectively used to analyze differences between participants. The results confirm our hypotheses showing positive correlations between perceptions of smartphone distraction, phubbing behavior, smartphone problematic use, and cognitive failures, and a significant difference was found between generations in perceptions of all variables considered. Generation Z (18-26 years) shows the highest scores in almost all subscales examined.

KEYWORDS

Smartphone Distraction, Overuse, Phubbing, Cognitive Failures, Intergeneration

1. INTRODUCTION

Among the current modern technologies, smartphones have become the main communication tools used in everyday life. When mobile phones were equipped with an internet connection, they became 'smartphones', something more than simple telephone devices, real tools used to manage many activities of daily life (Çizmeci, 2017).

With the widespread use of smartphones, some problems, both cognitive and social, have emerged. Indeed, despite the numerous benefits that smartphones confer, there are reasons to believe that smartphone overuse might be associated with quality of life (Demir & Sümer, 2019) and various negative outcomes (Mascia et al., 2020; Bonfiglio et al., 2020), such as phubbing (Tomczyk & Selmanagic-Lizde, 2018; 2022) or a negative impact on users' cognitive abilities, including thinking, remembering, paying attention and regulating emotion (Wilmer et al., 2017). Accordingly, it is important to understand this phenomenon and to analyse its characteristics because the literature shows that prolonged smartphone use and, above all, overuse can have negative consequences in the case of problematic use, dangerous situations, and ordinary circumstances due to the distractions that smartphones present, even when not in use. It is necessary to recognise that while the advent of technology has changed the rhythms and ways of living our daily lives, technological progress has imposed and dictated revolutions in all areas of our lives. This is extremely true for younger people who were born into a technological environment and who continue to be immersed in it. To better understand how this phenomenon is distributed at the intergenerational level in particular, this work will start with classifications made by Ristinovo (2022) among three generations: Gen-X (people born between 1965 and 1979), Gen-Y (people 1980 and 1994), and Gen-Z (people born between 1995 and 2000). Distinctions have been found in the use of technology between generations (Volkom et al., 2014), especially considering that the above-mentioned generations were differently equipped with new technologies. The differences in the use of technology may depend on several factors, such as the continuous development of the newest technology or the fact that those born with new technologies have less fear of new technologies than older generations. Bröhl et al. (2018) find disparities in the use of devices between technology generations, showing that the smartphone is the most popular device in the 19–36 age group. Moreover, the older generation lacks several skills that should have supported the shift to new digital technology (Fortunati et al., 2019). However, digital technologies by different generations must be considered nonlinear and non-progressive (Taipale et al., 2018). Notably, younger generations are more powerful digitally but more dependent on technology (Fortunati et al., 2019).

2. PROBLEMATIC SMARTPHONE USE

Certainly, the use of smartphones should not be demonised precisely because they represent an indispensable life and communication tool for everyone. The aspect that must be recognised is, therefore, not their use, but their overuse. In this paper, we focus mainly on four aspects related to this overuse: smartphone distraction, phubbing, problematic smartphone uses and increased cognitive failures.

Smartphone distraction

One aspect often highlighted regarding this topic is how distraction could be a direct consequence of problematic or excessive smartphone use. In general, distraction is considered a functional strategy in emotion regulation (Throuvala et al., 2021), but the distractions created by smartphone overuse represent a problem in many contexts because smartphones interfere with professional performance, both within academic and work settings. Smartphones also seem to interfere with everyday behaviour, both because they divide attention and make people less aware of their actions or surroundings (Busch & McCarthy, 2021). Much literature (Choi et al., 2021) correlates distraction and attentional resources, and this association is even more pronounced in smartphone overuse distractions and the attentional resources deployed (Mendoza et al., 2018). There is evidence that excessive distractions affect cognitive processes, such as memory (Ward et al., 2017) and human interactions (Dwyer et al., 2018). Other studies have pointed out that smartphone distractions can be considered a predictor of excessive and problematic smartphone use (Cha & Seo, 2018).

Phubbing

Some people continue to interact with their smartphones even in the presence of others, causing feelings of rejection or abandonment from partners and friends, a phenomenon called 'phubbing'. 'Phubbing' is defined as ignoring people with whom one has a face-to-face relationship to deal with smartphones. This behaviour can become a paradox, as individuals disconnect from face-to-face interactions to satisfy their need for social connections using technology and not physical presence (Pivetta et al., 2019). The phenomenon of phubbing particularly affects teenagers and young people. The main problem lies in its impact on the social relationships of individuals (Garrido et al., 2021). Phubbing is also associated with difficulties in attention, distractibility and attention-related cognitive errors (Sansevere & Ward, 2021). Other studies have underscored an association between phubbing and smartphone addiction (Isrofin & Munawaroh, 2021).

Problematic smartphone use

According to the compensatory internet use theory promulgated by Kardefelt-Winther (2014), the excessive problematic use of smartphones represents a regulatory strategy to reduce negative emotions (Montag et al., 2021). Smartphone use can distract people, it can cause physical problems, such as neck and shoulder pain, headaches and problems with the posture assumed while using it, as well as hand dysfunction. Smartphone use is associated with poor physical fitness and poor school and university performance. Smartphone overuse is also linked to problems such as cravings and abstinence symptoms such as anxiety and depression.

There is indeed a similarity between problematic smartphone use and overuse and addicts' physical and psychological symptoms. Although several studies have identified the negative effects contributing to the use of the terminology 'smartphone addiction' (Panova & Carbonell, 2018; Bonfiglio et al., 2022; Bonfiglio et al., 2022), in this study, we do not consider smartphone overuse an addiction.

Cognitive failures

Cognitive failures are small errors reported by clinical and non-clinical individuals during daily life; such errors cause a brief interruption in the regular course of an action that can be either physical or mental or small lapses in cognitive control (Broadbent et al., 1982; Carrigan & Barkus, 2016). There is an increasing number of contributions to the literature that support a close association between the heightened perception of one's own cognitive failures and smartphone overuse (Tanil & Yong, 2020). This evidence is especially noteworthy because some authors report more cognitive failures among younger people. 'Cognitive failures' refer to specific domains of errors such as attention, perception, memory, thinking and executive functions (Carrigan & Barkus, 2016).

3. THE RESEARCH

3.1 Aim and Hypotheses

On the basis of literature taken into account, the following hypothesis have guided our study:

H1. There are correlations among the perception of smartphone distraction, phubbing behavior, smartphone addiction and cognitive failures.

H2. There is a significant difference among generations (X, Y, Z) in the perception of smartphone distraction, phubbing behavior, smartphone addiction and cognitive failures.

3.2 Participants

An on-line survey was sent using a list of contacts of the authors. We used two lists of subjects (students and workers) each of 500 subjects. The surveys were sent through August and September 2022. Two hundred and Twenty-seventy subjects responded to the survey, 8 of which were deleted because of age range and 44 because they did not complete the entire battery. Two-hundred and twenty subjects were finally retained. The mean age of participants was 32.95 (SD=10.29). Subjects were divided in three categories according to the generational age (Ristiyono, 2022). Participants aged from 18 to 26 years were referred to Generation Z (Gen_Z; n=82; mean age=22.3; SD=2.13). Subjects aged from 27 to 41 years were referred to Generation Y (Gen_Y; n=83; mean age=34.1; SD=4.1). Those ages from 42 to 57 year belonged to the Generation X (Gen_X; n=55; mean age=47; SD=4.6).

3.3 Instruments

The *Mobile Phone Problematic Use Scale* (MPPUS, Bianchi and Phillips, 2005) has been designed for adult populations to assess problematic smartphone use. The version used for this study is in the process of validation in the Italian population by some authors of this paper. It includes 24 questions and two subscales covering the issues of tolerance, escape from other problems and craving (MPPUS_EC), withdrawal and negative life consequences (MMPUS_WN), in the areas of social, familial, work, and financial difficulties. Example questions included items such as: “I lose sleep due to the time I spend on my mobile phone”, or “My productivity has decreased as a direct result of the time I spend on the mobile phone.”, or “I have been told that I spend too much time on my mobile phone”. All items are measured on a scale ranging from “not true at all” (1) to “extremely true” (10). The higher the score, the more problematic the use of the smartphone. The questionnaire has reported a Cronbach’s alpha of .93, demonstrating a high level of internal consistency. Scales scores have been calculated as a mean of items after summing the responses for each dimension.

The *Generic Scale of Phubbing* (GSP, Chotpitayasunondh and Douglas, 2018) is a 15-item questionnaire aiming to evaluate the degree to which individuals engage in phubbing behavior. Four subscales can be calculated: Nomophobia (GSP_NO), Interpersonal Conflict (GSP_IC), Self-Isolation (GSP_SI), and Problem Acknowledgement (GSP_PA). Examples of items are “I cannot stand leaving my phone alone” and “I pay attention to my phone for longer than I intend to do so”. All items are measured on a scale ranging from “never” (1) to “always” (7). Scores have been calculated by summing all item responses. A higher score reflects greater engagement in phubbing behavior. Authors reported a Cronbach alpha ranging between .85 and .23.

The *Smartphone Distraction Scale* (SDS, Throuvala et al., 2021) is a 16-item questionnaire aimed to evaluate the distraction of a subject due to social media content. It includes four dimensions: attention and impulsiveness (SDS_AI), online vigilance (SDS_OV), multitasking (SDS_MU) and emotion regulation SDS (SDS_ER). Examples of items are: “I often talk to others while checking what’s on my phone” or “Using my phone distracts me from doing unpleasant things”. It uses a 5-point scale, from “almost never” (1) to “almost always" (5), and the higher the score, the more distracted the subject. Authors reported a Cronbach alpha ranging from .74 to .84. Scales scores have been calculated as a sum of items.

The *Cognitive Failures Questionnaire* (CFQ; Broadbent, Cooper, FitzGerald, & Parkes, 1982) is a questionnaire aimed to measure cognitive function. The CFQ asks 25 questions about experience mistakes and cognitive errors in everyday life. Wallace et al., (2001) reported a four-scale structure of the questionnaire with the following dimensions: Memory (CFQ_M), Distractibility (CFQ_D), Blunders (CFQ_B), and (memory for) Names (CFQ_N).

Examples of items are: "Do you fail to notice signposts on the road?" or "Do you daydream when you ought to be listening to something?". Participants indicate the frequency of experiencing these errors on a scale ranging from "never" (0) to "very often" (4). Total possible CFQ scores range from 0 to 100. Higher CFQ scores indicate greater cognitive failures. Scales scores have been calculated as a mean of items after summing the responses for each dimension.

3.4 Data Analysis

A preliminary data screening and cleaning was performed to detect missing or invalid data. The demographic characteristics of the participants were analyzed against the collected data from each of the subscales. Visual inspection of the data (i.e., Q-Q plot), Skewness, Kurtosi and Shapiro-Wilk test were used to analyze the departure from normality of each subscale measure. Because all the assumptions for normality distribution of the data were violated, Spearman's rho was used to analyze correlations between subscales. Moreover, the Mann-Whitney U test was used to analyze differences between participants.

4. FINDINGS

Positive correlations have been found between the perception of smartphone distraction, phubbing behavior, smartphone problematic use and cognitive failures (Table 1) in the all sample. Also CFQ_N did not show correlation with GSP_NO, GSP_IC, GSP_SI, SDS_OV and SDS_MU. Indeed, positive correlations with a coefficient higher than .50 have been found for GSP_NO with SDS_OV and MPPUS_EC; GSP_PA with SDS_AI, SDS_ER and MMPUS_WN;SDS_AI with MPPUS_WN and MPPUS_EC; SDS_OV with MPPUS_WN and MPPUS_EC; SDS_ER with MPPUS_WN and MPPUS_EC; CFQ_D with MPPUS_EC.

Table 1. Spearman's rho correlations between subscales

Subscales	1	2	3	4	5	6	7	8	9	10	11	12	13	14
1. GSP_NO														
2. GSP_IC	.412**													
3. GSP_SI	.179**	.423**												
4. GSP_PA	.424**	.312**	.326**											
5. SDS_AI	.370**	.288**	.279**	.686**										
6. SDS_OV	.619**	.453**	.470**	.521**	.593**									
7. SDS_MU	.212**	.309**	.263**	.376**	.365**	.336**								
8. SDS_ER	.299**	.264**	.364**	.504**	.486**	.465**	.435**							
9. CFQ_M	.166*	.133	.292**	.301**	.231**	.233**	.229**	.303**						
10. CFQ_D	.212**	.112	.275**	.338**	.372**	.333**	.252**	.461**	.717**					
11. CFQ_B	.220**	.129	.279**	.336**	.365**	.336**	.284**	.424**	.646**	.751**				
12. CFQ_N	.007	-.027	.142	.196**	.201**	.07	.142	.334**	.495**	.570**	.430**			
13. MPPUS_WN	.333**	.444**	.497**	.560**	.537**	.548**	.373**	.541**	.358**	.434**	.412**	.223**		
14. MPPUS_EC	.648**	.385**	.450**	.643**	.643**	.723**	.462**	.671**	.387**	.501**	.445**	.301**	.677**	

Note: * *p* value =.05; ** *p* value = .001

Legend: GSP_NO = Nomophoby of GSP scale; GSP_IC=Interpersonal Conflict of GSP scale; GSP_SI=Self-Isolation of the GSP scale; GSP_PA=Acknowledgement of GSP scale; SDS_AI=Attention and Impulsiveness of the SDS scale; SDS_OV=Online vigilance of the SDS scale; SDS_MU=Multitasking of the SDS scale; SDS_ER=Emotion Regulation of the SDS scale; CFQ_M=Memory of the CFQ scale; CFQ_D=Distractibility of the CFQ scale; CFQ_B=Blunders of the CFQ scale; CFQ_N=Names of the CFW scale; MPPUS_WN=withdrawal and negative life consequences of the MPPUS scale; MPPUS_EC=escape from other problems and craving of the MPPUS scale.

A Mann-Whitney U test by ranks has been carried out making pairwise comparisons between gen-X with gen-Y, gen-X with gen-Z and gen-Y with gen-Z.

Gen-X VS gen-Y

Significant differences have been found between gen-X and gen-Y using a Mann-Whitney U test as regard GSP_NO (U=1518.5; p=.021), GSP_SI (U=1560.5; p=.018), SDS_AI (U=1317.50; p=.011), SDS_OV (U=1321.50; p=.010), SDS_MU (U=1222.50; p=.002), SDS_ER (U=1015; p=.001), CFQ_M (U=1098; p=.047), CFQ_D (U=991.5; p=.008), CFQ_B (U=1027.50; p=.016), CFQ_N (U=1083; p=.037), MPPUS_WS (U=1105; p=.003) and MPPUS_CE (U=839.5; p=.001). Figure 1 shows the difference between generations as a mean of rank values.

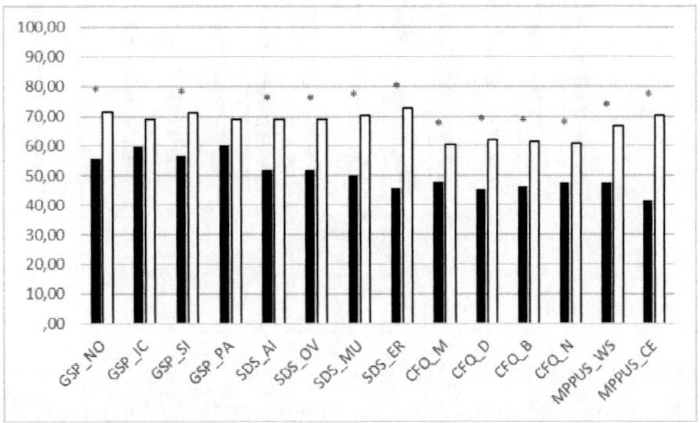

Figure 1. Rank scores between participants divided by gen-X (black bar) and gen-Y (withe bar)

Note: *=significant comparison

Legend: GSP_NO = Nomophoby of GSP scale; GSP_IC=Interpersonal Conflict of GSP scale; GSP_SI=Self-Isolation of the GSP scale; GSP_PA=Acknowledgment of GSP scale; MPPUS_WN=withdrawal and negative life consequences of the MPPUS scale; MPPUS_EC=escape from other problems and craving of the MPPUS scale. Gen_X= generation X; Gen_Y=generation Y; Gen_Z = generation Z; df=degree of freedom, n=numerosity.

Gen-X VS gen-Z

Significant differences have been found between gen-X and gen-Z using a Mann-Whitney U test as regard GSP_SI (U=1473.5; p=.007), GSP_PA (U=1191; p=.001), SDS_AI (U=983; p=.001), SDS_OV (U=1261; p=.012), SDS_MU (U=942.5; p=.001), SDS_ER (U=758; p=.001), CFQ_M (U=858; p=.009), CFQ_D (U=616; p=.001) , CFQ_B (U=617; p=.001), CFQ_N (U=951.5; p=.046), MPPUS_WS (U=687.5; p=.001) and MPPUS_CE (U=585; p=.001). Figure 2 shows the difference between generations as a mean of rank values.

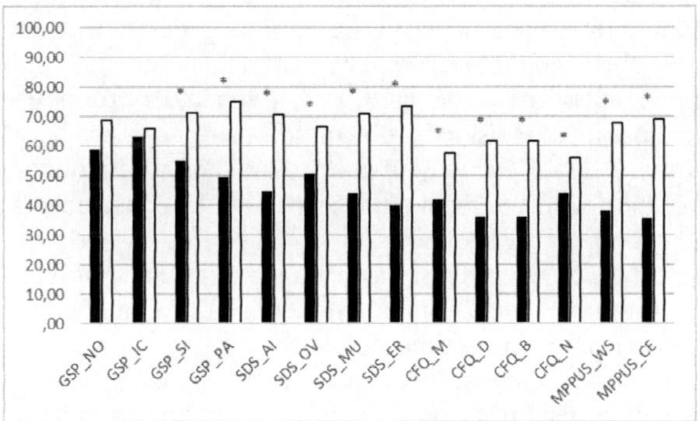

Figure 2. Rank scores between participants divided by gen-X (black bar) and gen-Z (withe bar)

Note: *=significant comparison

Legend: GSP_NO = Nomophoby of GSP scale; GSP_IC=Interpersonal Conflict of GSP scale; GSP_SI=Self-Isolation of the GSP scale; GSP_PA=Acknowledgment of GSP scale; MPPUS_WN=withdrawal and negative life consequences of the MPPUS scale; MPPUS_EC=escape from other problems and craving of the MPPUS scale. Gen_X= generation X; Gen_Y=generation Y; Gen_Z = generation Z; df=degree of freedom, n=numerosity.

Gen-Y VS gen-Z

Significant differences have been found between gen-Y and gen-Z using a Mann-Whitney U test as regard GSP_PA (U=2367<, p<0.006), SDS_AI (U=2266.5; p=.040), CFQ_D (U=1733; p=.034), CFQ_B (U=1723.5; p=.031) and MPPUS_WS (U=1920; p=.020). Figure 3 shows the difference between generations as a mean of rank values.

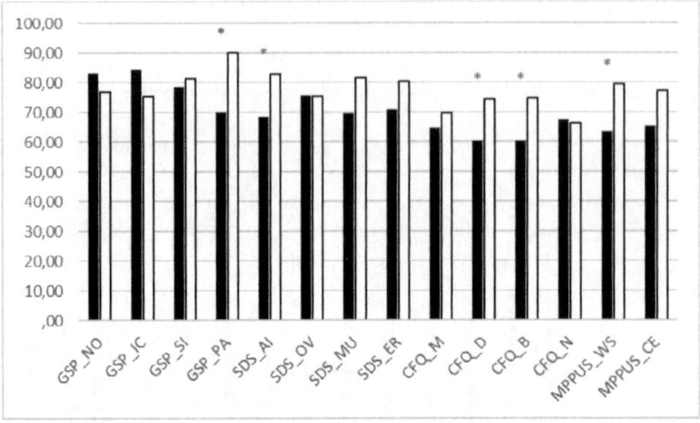

Figure 3. Rank scores between participants divided by gen-Y (black bar) and gen-Z (withe bar)

Note: *=significant comparison

Legend: GSP_NO = Nomophoby of GSP scale; GSP_IC=Interpersonal Conflict of GSP scale; GSP_SI=Self-Isolation of the GSP scale; GSP_PA=Acknowledgment of GSP scale; MPPUS_WN=withdrawal and negative life consequences of the MPPUS scale; MPPUS_EC=escape from other problems and craving of the MPPUS scale. Gen_X= generation X; Gen_Y=generation Y; Gen_Z = generation Z; df=degree of freedom, n=numerosity.

5. DISCUSSION AND CONCLUSION

The present study explored the associations among variables lied to problematic smartphone use. The results have confirmed the association among the variables subscales: smartphone distraction, phubbing, problematic smartphone use and cognitive failures. This study also confirms the hypothesized intergenerational differences. Gen Y perceives to be more phubber, distracted, and with a higher use than Gen Y and Z for all components of GSP, SDS and MPPUS. The surprising finding is shown by the higher perception of the number of cognitive failures by GEN X, i.e., the younger generation. They score higher than the other two generations in the subscales related to measuring memory failures, errors due to distraction, and cognitive errors in general.

It is interesting to note a difference between the various generations, it becomes clear that certain data represent a wake-up call that should not be underestimated due to the possible cognitive and social repercussions. Age and impulsivity are considered predictive factors of problematic smartphone use, younger individuals are therefore those most at risk of problematic smartphone use because they have fewer protective factors (Mitchell & Hussain, 2018). However, all age groups should be monitored for any risks that may arise.

It's clear the need to educate already from adolescence on the conscious use of smartphone, which has so much potential but also negative aspects. Bearing in mind the importance of choosing the appropriate terminology, being aware of the differences between addiction, use and problematic use; it is useful to inform about the influence that the smartphone exerts on attention, as this can be distracted from the tasks at hand, leading to poor performance, which can also manifest itself in all life's environments. Under this consideration, educational intervention must be combined with specific treatments for this problematic use with the aim to engage and motivate the new generations (more digital) (Bonfiglio et al., 2020; Bonfiglio et al., 2021; Renati et al., 2021). The study findings will help the professionals in the field, but also schools and families towards developing treatments and actions for the adverse effects of smartphone overuse. The intervention measures are important above all to improve mental health and psychological wellbeing, increasing awareness that problematic smartphone use can have both cognitive and relational levels. The study presents some limitations. The first limitation is given using self-report questionnaires. Non-representative, self-selection and non-response bias have not been controlled. We did not draw, for example, a general representative sample to which the survey should be administered and have not included in the sample subjects who have no access to the internet. Stakeholder bias has been controlled avoiding multiple access from the same IP address and without offering incentives for the compilation (Duda et al., 2010). Then, a larger sample is required to make the results obtained more generalizable. Future studies should aim to recruit samples with specific features, to measure different cognitive processes through diagnostic tools, to validate specific questionnaires in the Italian context, to explore the relationship between addictions and cognitive failure and to deepen the social relationships of the sample surveyed.

REFERENCES

Bianchi, A., & Phillips, J. G. (2005). *Psychological predictors of problem mobile phone use*. CyberPsychology & Behavior, 8(1), 39-51.

Bonfiglio, N. S., Mascia, M. L., Cataudella, S., & Penna, M. P. (2022). Digital Help for Substance Users (SU): A Systematic Review. *International Journal of Environmental Research and Public Health,* 19(18), 11309.

Bonfiglio, N. S., Mascia, M. L., & Penna, M. P. (2022). Digital Treatment Paths for Substance Use Disorders (SUDs). *International Journal of Environmental Research and Public Health*, 19(12), 7322

Bonfiglio, N. S., Renati, R., Parodi, D., Pessa, E., Rollo, D., & Penna, M. P. (2020, June). Use of training with BCI (Brain Computer Interface) in the management of impulsivity. I*n 2020 IEEE international symposium on medical measurements and applications* (MeMeA) (pp. 1-5). IEEE.

Bonfiglio, N. S., Renati, R., Patrone, L., Rollo, D., & Penna, M. P. (2021, June). The use of cognitive training with tDCS for the reduction of impulsiveness and improvement of executive functions: a case study. *In 2021 IEEE International Symposium on Medical Measurements and Applications (MeMeA)* (pp. 1-6). IEEE.

Broadbent, D. E., Cooper, P. F., FitzGerald, P., & Parkes, K. R. (1982). The cognitive failures questionnaire (CFQ) and its correlates. *British journal of clinical psychology*, 21(1), 1-16.

Bröhl, C., Rasche, P., Jablonski, J., Theis, S., Wille, M., & Mertens, A. (2018, July). Desktop PC, tablet PC, or smartphone? An analysis of use preferences in daily activities for different technology generations of a worldwide sample. In *International Conference on Human Aspects of IT for the Aged Population* (pp. 3-20). Springer, Cham.

Busch, P. A., & McCarthy, S. (2021). Antecedents and consequences of problematic smartphone use: A systematic literature review of an emerging research area. *Computers in human behavior*, *114*, 106414.

Carrigan, N., & Barkus, E. (2016). A systematic review of cognitive failures in daily life: Healthy populations. *Neuroscience & Biobehavioral Reviews*, *63*, 29-42.

Çizmeci, E. (2017). Disconnected, though satisfied: Phubbing behavior and relationship satisfaction. *The Turkish Online Journal of Design, Art and Communication*, *7*(2), 364-375.

Cha, S. S., & Seo, B. K. (2018). Smartphone use and smartphone addiction in middle school students in Korea: Prevalence, social networking service, and game use. *Health psychology open*, *5*(1), 2055102918755046.

Choi, J., Cho, H., Choi, J. S., Choi, I. Y., Chun, J. W., & Kim, D. J. (2021). The neural basis underlying impaired attentional control in problematic smartphone users. *Translational psychiatry*, *11*(1), 1-10.

Chotpitayasunondh, V., & Douglas, K. M. (2018). Measuring phone snubbing behavior: Development and validation of the Generic Scale of Phubbing (GSP) and the Generic Scale of Being Phubbed (GSBP). *Computers in Human Behavior*, 88, 5-17.

Demir, Y. P., & Sümer, M. M. (2019). Effects of smartphone overuse on headache, sleep and quality of life in migraine patients. Neurosciences Journal, 24(2), 115-121.

Duda, M. D., & Nobile, J. L. (2010). The fallacy of online surveys: No data are better than bad data. Human Dimensions of Wildlife, 15(1), 55-64.

Dwyer, R. J., Kushlev, K., & Dunn, E. W. (2018). Smartphone use undermines enjoyment of face-to-face social interactions. *Journal of Experimental Social Psychology*, *78*, 233-239.

Elhai, J. D., Dvorak, R. D., Levine, J. C., & Hall, B. J. (2017). Problematic smartphone use: A conceptual overview and systematic review of relations with anxiety and depression psychopathology. Journal of affective disorders, 207, 251-259.

Fortunati, L., Taipale, S., & de Luca, F. (2019). Digital generations, but not as we know them. *Convergence*, 25(1), 95-112.

Garrido, E. C., Issa, T., Esteban, P. G., & Delgado, S. C. (2021). A descriptive literature review of phubbing behaviors. *Heliyon*, *7*(5), e07037.

Isrofin, B., & Munawaroh, E. (2021). The effect of smartphone addiction and self-control on phubbing behavior. *Journal Kajian Bimbingan Dan Konseling*, *6*(1), 15-23.

Kardefelt-Winther, D. (2014). A conceptual and methodological critique of internet addiction research: Towards a model of compensatory internet use. *Computers in human behavior*, *31*, 351-354.

Mascia, M. L., Agus, M., & Penna, M. P. (2020). Emotional intelligence, self-regulation, smartphone addiction: which relationship with student well-being and quality of life?. *Frontiers in psychology*, *11*, 375.

Mitchell, L., & Hussain, Z. (2018). Predictors of problematic smartphone use: An examination of the integrative pathways model and the role of age, gender, impulsiveness, excessive reassurance seeking, extraversion, and depression. *Behavioral Sciences*, *8*(8), 74.

Montag, C., Wegmann, E., Sariyska, R., Demetrovics, Z., & Brand, M. (2021). How to overcome taxonomical problems in the study of Internet use disorders and what to do with "smartphone addiction"?. *Journal of behavioral addictions*, *9*(4), 908-914.

Panova, T., & Carbonell, X. (2018). Is smartphone addiction really an addiction?. *Journal of behavioral addictions*, *7*(2), 252-259.

Pivetta, E., Harkin, L., Billieux, J., Kanjo, E., & Kuss, D. J. (2019). Problematic smartphone use: An empirically validated model. *Computers in Human Behavior*, *100*, 105-117.

Renati, R., Bonfiglio, N. S., Patrone, L., Rollo, D., & Penna, M. P. (2021, June). The use of cognitive training and tDCS for the treatment of an high potential subject: a case study. *In 2021 IEEE International Symposium on Medical Measurements and Applications (MeMeA)* (pp. 1-6). IEEE.

Ristiyono, M. P. (2022). The Behavior of Generations ''Y''and ''Z''in Seeking Information as a Source of Knowledge in the iJogja Library. *International Journal of Multi Science*, 3(01), 54-62.

Sansevere, K. S., & Ward, N. (2021). Linking Phubbing Behavior to Self-Reported Attentional Failures and Media Multitasking. *Future Internet*, *13*(4), 100.

Taipale, S. (2015) Bodily dimensions of reading and writing practices on paper and digitally. T*elematics and Informatics* 32(4): 766–775.

Tomczyk, Ł., & Selmanagic-Lizde, E. (2018). Fear of Missing Out (FOMO) among youth in Bosnia and Herzegovina—Scale and selected mechanisms. *Children and Youth Services Review*, *88*, 541-549.

Tomczyk, Ł., & Selmanagic-Lizde, E. S. (2022). Nomophobia and Phubbing: Wellbeing and new media education in the family among adolescents in Bosnia and Herzegovina. *Children and Youth Services Review*, *137*, 106489.

Throuvala, M. A., Pontes, H. M., Tsaousis, I., Griffiths, M. D., Rennoldson, M., & Kuss, D. J. (2021). Exploring the dimensions of smartphone distraction: Development, validation, measurement invariance, and latent mean differences of the smartphone distraction scale (SDS). *Frontiers in psychiatry*, 12, 642634.

Ward, A. F., Duke, K., Gneezy, A., & Bos, M. W. (2017). Brain drain: The mere presence of one's own smartphone reduces available cognitive capacity. *Journal of the Association for Consumer Research*, *2*(2), 140-154.

Wilmer, H. H., Sherman, L. E., & Chein, J. M. (2017). Smartphones and cognition: A review of research exploring the links between mobile technology habits and cognitive functioning. *Frontiers in psychology*, *8*, 605.

EXPLORING SEMI-SUPERVISED LEARNING FOR AUDIO-BASED AUTOMATED CLASSROOM OBSERVATIONS

Akchunya Chanchal and Imran Zualkernan
Computer Science and Engineering
American University of Sharjah, UAE

ABSTRACT

Systematic classroom observation is often used in evaluating and enhancing the quality of classroom instruction. However, classroom observation can potentially suffer from human bias. In addition, the traditional classroom observation is too expensive for resource-constrained environments (e.g., Sub-Saharan Africa, South and Central Asia). A cost-effective automation of classroom observation could potentially enhance both quality and resolution of feedback to the teacher, and hence potentially result in enhancing quality of instruction. Audio-based automatic classroom observation using supervised deep learning techniques has yielded good results in limited contexts. However, one challenge when using supervised techniques is the high cost of collecting and labelling the classroom audio data. One solution for such data-starved scenarios is to use semi-supervised learning (SSL) which requires significantly lesser data and labels. This paper explores an audio-adaptation of the state-of-the-art SSL FixMatch algorithm to automate classroom observation. An adaptation of the FixMatch algorithm was proposed to automate the coding for the Stallings class observation system. The proposed system was trained on classroom audio data collected in the wild. The supervised approach had an F1-score of 0.83 on 100% labeled data. The proposed FixMatch adaptation achieved an impressive F1-score of 0.81 on 20% labeled data, 0.79 on 15% labeled data, 0.76 on 10% labeled data, and 0.72 using only 5% of labeled data. This suggests that algorithms like FixMatch that use consistency regularization and pseudo-labeling have a great potential for being used to automate classroom observation using a small labelled set of audio snippets.

KEYWORDS

Classroom Observation, Audio Classification, Mel Spectrograms, Stallings, Semi Supervised Learning, Developing Country, FixMatch

1. INTRODUCTION

Quality and inclusive education is one of the United Nation's sustainability development goals. Education has long been considered as one of the most important factors in improving the quality of life of individuals. Increased quality of education has been shown to increase Gross Domestic Product (GDP) per capita by about 0.5% and consequently results in a decrease in Infant Mortality Rate (IMR) by about 0.6% (Jamison et. al, 2007). It is important to highlight that merely increasing the quantity of educational institutions does not result in reduction in poverty or IMR as seen in Tanzania (Wedgwood, 2007). Classroom teaching is backbone of most educational system and teachers represents a key leverage point for improving student learning outcomes, both in the long and the short term (Chetty et al, 2014). Therefore, improving classroom teaching practice and quality is paramount. Classroom observations provides effective feedback to teachers and can potentially result in better classroom practice and improved learning outcomes. For example, classroom observation has been shown to be an effective tool in assessing teacher quality in low-income countries like the Ugandan secondary schools where classroom observation was successful in quality of instructional practices with sufficient variance and high inter-rate reliability (Seidman et al., 2018).

Formally, classroom observation is defined as a tool that offers an unobstructed view and an understanding of how the teacher teaches in a realistic classroom setting (Martinez et al., 2016). There are many classroom observation systems (e.g., Stallings, CLASS, etc.) (Bell et al., 2018). One advantage of using the much simpler Stallings's observation system is that it was modestly correlated with the more expensive and complex CLASS system. Benefits of Stallings's system have also been validated in developing countries in addressing student learning outcomes (Bruns et al., 2016).

Regardless of the observation systems being used, class observation as performed today is not without drawbacks. One obvious issue is that the observers may not hold a completely objective viewpoint, and may make a biased judgement based on their own preferences (Werner, 2018). Furthermore, it is entirely conceivable that the teacher may change their behavior when being observed. This may be more likely if the observer was an administrator. In addition, the students' behavior also may change as well. Another issue is that many classroom observation systems have been known to give inflated teacher evaluations (Werner, 2018). Classroom observation can also cause teachers further stress and anxiety as they are generally not accustomed to being observed and this causes them to believe that their professional competence is going to be questioned or judged (Borich, 2016). Finally, the low frequency with which classroom observation are conducted (Lam, 2001) means the teachers do not have an opportunity to correct their classroom practice midstream. Rather, they must typically wait for a year before receiving any feedback.

This paper is based on the Stallings class observation because this simpler approach lends itself easily to automation via deep learning. In specific, the use of a state-of-the-art semi-supervised learning algorithms that requires a fraction of labeled data was used to train a neural network model that can use classroom audio data to automatically extract Stallings's classroom observation categories. The remainder of the paper is organized as follows. Related work is discussed next, followed by a brief description of the Stallings classroom observation system. The semi-supervised learning (SSL) approach used is then briefly explained. This is followed by the results of the SSL-based system with different percentage of labelled data used along with the comparison against the fully supervised approach. The paper ends with a conclusion and future work.

2. RELATED WORK

Machine learning has been used previously to perform classroom observations. Typically, such systems use audio or multimodal data. Some examples of each are provided below.

2.1 Systems using Audio Data Only

Earlier, many approaches to automate classroom observation used traditional machine learning methods. For example., classroom audio was collected in a Randomized Control Trial (RCT) from 4th grade classrooms of low performing schools in Chile using a microphone connected to the teachers' mobile phones, length of such recording was between 18 minutes to 77 minutes (Schlotterbeck et al., 2021). The data was then classified using Random Forest into a modified version of the COPUS (Classroom Observation Protocol for Undergraduate STEM) where the different codes of the system are categorized into three categories; presenting, guiding and administration (Owens et al., 2017). Different representations of the data were used (e.g., Decibel scaled Mel Spectrograms, Mel Frequency Cepstral Coefficients (MFCC), and Amplitude) and fairly high Accuracy of 86%, 83%, and 96% respectively were reported for the three categories. However, there were large disparities in the recall scores across all categories (e.g., recall of 1 for negative samples and 0 for positive samples in the case of administration). Similarly, another system (Wang et al., 2014) used recordings of mathematics lessons from 13 different elementary schools in Michigan, ranging from the 1st grade to the 4th grade. The system was based on the Language Environment Analysis System (LENA) (Ford et al., 2008) and provided information about the quantity and distribution of classroom lectures. The teachers were asked to turn on the LENA recorder and put it in a pouch worn around their necks, and teach the lesson normally. At the end of the lesson, they were asked to turn off the recorder and connect it to a laptop. The data was then extracted from the recorder and sent to a remote server, where the data was analyzed to yield the four metrics of teacher talk, student talk, overlapping speech, and non-speech (silence or noise). The recorded audio was divided into 30 second segments and coded by 2 independent coders into 3 different activity types of teacher lecturing, the whole class discussion, and class group work. In each of the audio segments, each of the 4 metrics were calculated and were used as the independent variables to classify the audio into one of the three activities. Random Forest achieved classification accuracies of 88.1%, 79.7% and 83.3% for lecture, discussion and group work respectively leading to an overall classification accuracy of 84.37% (Wang et al., 2014). Another approach with audio only data was presented in (James et al., 2019) where data from 92 classrooms from multiple preschools in Singapore was used. Each datapoint was about 20 minutes long in classrooms of 10-15 students and consisted of different types of activities such as small group discussions between students and teacher-student interactions. The audio was collected using a microphone worn by the teacher. Since this was a single microphone setup the audio was not of high fidelity and consisted of a large amount of background noise in addition to the audio of the teacher and students, even the audio between the teacher and student were not always intelligible. This was a largely accurate representation of a classroom environment where the activities are largely dynamic and uncontrolled. Preliminary speech detection was used to recognize and remove silences and any non-speech acoustic features from the audio recordings. Diarization was then performed using the LIUM toolkit (Meignier, Merlin, 2010). The conversational features were extracted from both the LIUM clusters and the low-level audio features like MFCC. Kruskal-Wallis test and other correlation algorithms were used for feature selection. The features selected were then passed through nine different conventional machine learning algorithms using 10-fold cross-validation to classify the lessons as having a negative or positive climate based on the CLASS observation system. The traditional machine learning methods achieved accuracy scores of between 70% and 80%.

2.2 Systems using Multimodal Data Only

Recently, there has been a surge in methods that utilize multimodal data (i.e., data from different modalities such as audio, video, text). Multimodal methods typically result in better performance since the different modalities are used in conjunction with each other resulting in a richer representation of the data giving the model more information (Summaira et al, 2021). One such system that utilized multimodal data was CLEVER (Classroom Evaluation and Video Retrieval) (Qiao & Beling, 2011) that used audio and video data from classrooms and classified them based on the CLASS protocol. CLEVER used video and audio metrics to bridge the gap between semantic assessment concepts to make them quantifiable and measurable. The system did this by relating the audio/video metrics with feature variables that could be using video and audio processing techniques such as topical detection, synchronization, silence detection, etc. These feature variables were then used to classify the classroom videos according to CLASS categories. The system used a variation of supervised learning known as Multiple Instance Learning (MIL) where instead of a label, there was a set of training bags. MIL is used in cases where there is ambiguity associated with the labels of the training examples. The dataset used for training and testing the system consisted of 40 video clips of 3 minutes each of upper-level systems engineering courses at the University of Virginia which were labeled by 10 expert CLASS coders. The model performed differently for labels set by each of the different coders, ranging from a minimum accuracy of 58.5% to maximum accuracy of 94.7%. The variance in the results of the model was attributed to the different interpretations of each video clip by the different coders.

While the aforementioned research shows the potential of using machine learning for automating aspects of classroom observation, however, none of these approaches addressed the issue of the cost of labelling the data. To the best of our knowledge, this paper is the first to present using an SSL based strategy to address the problem of classroom observation.

3. STALLINGS CLASSROOM OBSERVATION SYSTEM

This paper used the Stallings classroom observation system. The Stallings classroom observation system was developed by Jane Stallings in the late 1970s to evaluate the efficiency and quality of basic education teachers in the United States (Stallings, 1977). In this method, the human observer takes a 15 second 360-view of the entire classroom every 5 minutes in a 50-minute lesson. The observer notes down their observations on a structured coding sheet. This classroom observation systems evaluates the frequency of activities that the teacher conducts (e.g., question-answering, lecturing, classwork etc.), the materials that teacher utilizes (e.g., whiteboard, textbook, computer etc.) and the student group sizes that teacher is working with. Table 1 shows a summary of some of the activities that are coded under the Stallings system (World Bank Group, 2017).

Table 1. Classroom activities and their descriptions in the Stallings system

Activity	Description
Classwork	One or more students engaged in solving problems on the board, writing papers or engaged in any other conventional classwork activities.
Classroom Management	Teachers/Students engaged in classroom administrative tasks such as handing our graded exams, taking attendance, switching activities etc.
Lecture/Demonstration	Teacher or another medium explaining the academic content to the students.
Practice & Drill	Activities/tasks undertaken by the student in order to improve retention and reinforce the material such as multiplication tables, vocabulary, spelling etc.
Discussion/ Q & A	Students and/or teachers engage in a discussion/conversation in regards to some academic material e.g., clarification of queries, exchange of ideas.
Reading Aloud	The teacher and/or student reading aloud the contents from a medium e.g., presentation slides, textbook, paper etc.

Many of the Stallings system activities are not amenable to be detected using audio only. This paper considered only four Stallings categories of classroom management, lecture, practice and drill, and Q&A.

4. DATASET

The audio data used to train and test the models were obtained from Stallings-type classroom observation videos from semi-rural schools in Pakistan (Zualkernan et al., 2014). The classroom observation videos were collected by enumerators who used their mobile phone cameras and/or low-end video cameras to record the classroom videos. In total, 646 audio sessions were coded according to the Stallings coding manual (The World Bank, 2015). The 646 audio files were split into 3-second interval audio clips without overlap, resulting in 5,392 total audio clips. The audio data collected consisted of 263 female teachers and 383 male teachers across a variety of subjects such as English, Arabic, Mathematics and Science. Table 2 below shows the distribution of the four Stalling categories of classroom management, lecture, practice and discussion/Q&A across the different subjects.

Table 2. Distribution of audio clips according to subject

Subject	Classroom Management	Lecture	Practice	Q & A
Arabic	0	35	0	0
English	766	630	424	544
Math	580	1221	200	492
Science	147	353	424	0

5. METHODOLOGY

5.1 Proposed FixMatch Adaptation

FixMatch is a state-of-the-art semi-supervised learning (SSL) training algorithm for deep neural networks (Sohn et al., 2020). FixMatch uses consistency regularization and pseudo-labeling. Consistency regularization utilizes unlabeled data by in essence, assuming that the model will output similar prediction to inputs where perturbations have been applied and the same input when fed to the model as is (Bachman et al., 2014). This technique is used by many of the recent state-of-the-art SSL algorithms such as the Π-model and temporal ensembling (Laine, Aila, 2017). When using consistency regularization, the model is trained using both labeled data via a standard supervised learning classification loss function and on unlabeled data using something similar to (1). Consider $\gamma(.)$ to be a perturbation function which is applied to some input μ_b, where μ_b is b^{th} example in the batch. $(y|\gamma(\mu_b))$ represents the class distribution produced by the model for the perturbed example. B is the number of unlabeled examples in a batch.

$$\sum^{B}_{b=1} \|(y|\gamma(\mu_b) - p(y|\gamma(\mu_b)\|^2_2 \qquad (1)$$

Since both p and γ are stochastic functions, the values of the two terms will be distinct. One is essentially calculating squared l^2 loss between the values, however cross-entropy loss between the two values can be used as well. Pseudo-labeling is the idea of using the model itself to obtain artificial or pseudo-labels for the unlabeled examples in the dataset. Examples, whose "hard labels" (i.e., $argmax$ of the predicted class distribution for the input) are greater than a predefined threshold τ are classified as such. (2) is used as the loss function for pseudo-labeling. Let $q_b = (y| \mu_b)$ and $\hat{q_b} = \arg\max (q_b)$. $\mathbb{1}(predicate)$ is a boolean function which is 1 when the predicate is true and 0 when the predicate is false. H is the cross-entropy loss function.

$$\frac{1}{B}\Sigma^{B}{}_{b}(\max (q_b \geq \tau)\ H(\hat{q_b}, q_b)) \qquad (2)$$

Using hard labels in pseudo-labelling makes it closely related to entropy minimization (Grandvalet & Bengio, 2004) where the model's prediction is encouraged to have low-entropy on unlabeled data.

FixMatch uses weak and strong transformations on the inputs of the model. Weak transformations slightly distort the input example, are initially applied to the input example, and used to produce the artificial label of the example. This label is then used as the target for the example when it is fed to the model after applying the strong transformations, while heavily perturbing the example.

This paper proposes the weak and strong augmentations for audio data as shown in Figure 1 (a) and Figure 1 (b).

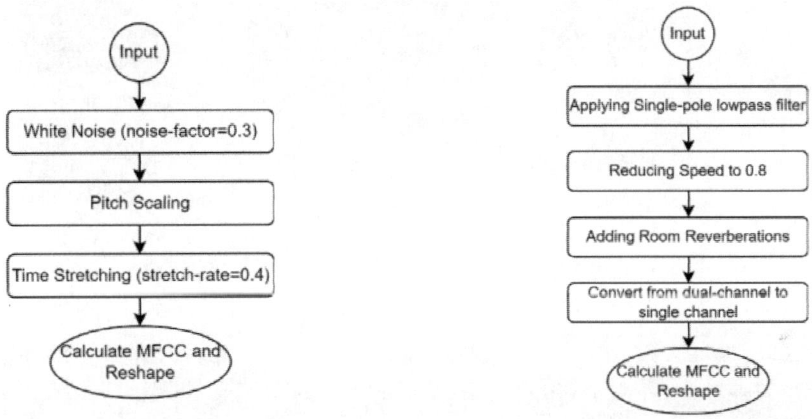

(a) Weak Transformation (a) Strong Transformation

Figure 1. Sequence of Weak Transformations Applied

The loss function for FixMatch uses two cross-entropy loss terms; a supervised loss ℓ_s applied to the labeled data and an unsupervised loss ℓ_u for the unlabeled data. ℓ_s (3) is the standard-cross entropy loss function that is used when using the weakly-perturbed examples as the input to the model. Consider β as the number of labeled examples in a batch. $\gamma(.)$ represents a function which applies the sequence of weak transformations. x_b represents the bth example in the batch.

$$l_s = \frac{1}{\beta}\Sigma\beta_{b=1}(p_b, p(y| \gamma(x_b))) \qquad (3)$$

The unlabeled loss, ℓ_u computes cross-entropy loss between the artificial label $\hat{q_b}$ ($arg\ max$ of the model's predicted class distribution on the weakly transformed version of the same unlabeled example) and the model's output for the strongly transformed version of the unlabeled example. (4) represents the equation for the same. Consider $\Gamma(.)$ to represent a function which applies the sequence of strong transformations, τ is a scalar hyperparameter which denotes a threshold above which the artificial label is retained. B is the number of unlabeled examples in a batch.

$$l_u = \frac{1}{B}\Sigma^{B}{}_{b=1}(max(q_b) \geq \tau)\ H(\hat{q_b}, p(y|\Gamma(x_b))) \qquad (4)$$

Both labeled and unlabeled loss are combined as in (5), which is the loss function ℓ minimized by FixMatch. λu is a fixed scalar hyperparameter which represents the relative weight of the unlabeled loss.

$$l = l_s + \lambda_u \, l_u \quad (5)$$

This paper proposes the adapted FixMatch algorithm shown in Fig. 2 to classify classroom observation audio. The classification Model used in the FixMatch algorithm is shown in Figure 3. The classification Model was inspired by the architecture described in (Salamon & Bello, 2017) which was successful in classifying audio data from the UrbanSound8K (Salamon et al., 2014) with 98.60% accuracy, and the ESC-10 and ESC-50 with 97.25% and 95.5% accuracy respectively (Piczak, 2015). The original CNN proposed in (Salamon & Bello, 2017) had three convolutional layers with 24, 48 and 48 layers respectively and used an input size of 128x128. However, (Zualkernan & Khan, 2020) found that using 5 convolutional layers with 128,96,96,32 and 64 filters respectively and an input shape of 8x16x1 gave better results on the classroom audio data. Batch normalization was applied after each convolutional layer and dropout is applied after the 1st, 3rd and 5th convolutional layer. This followed by three fully-connected layers. SGD optimizer with Nesterov momentum were used to train the model. The model was implemented using Pytorch.

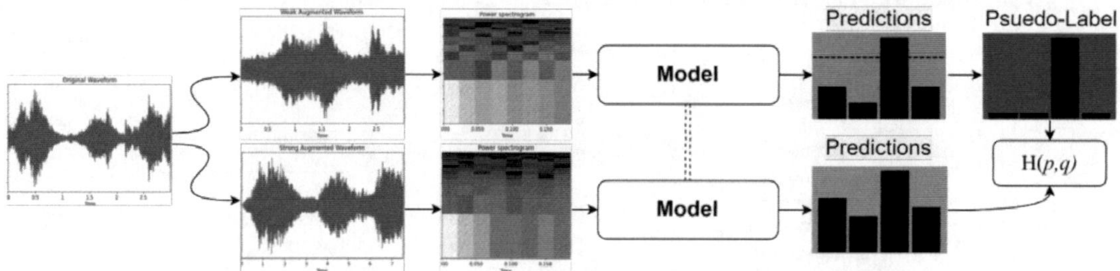

Figure 2. Adapted FixMatch Algorithm for classroom observation audio

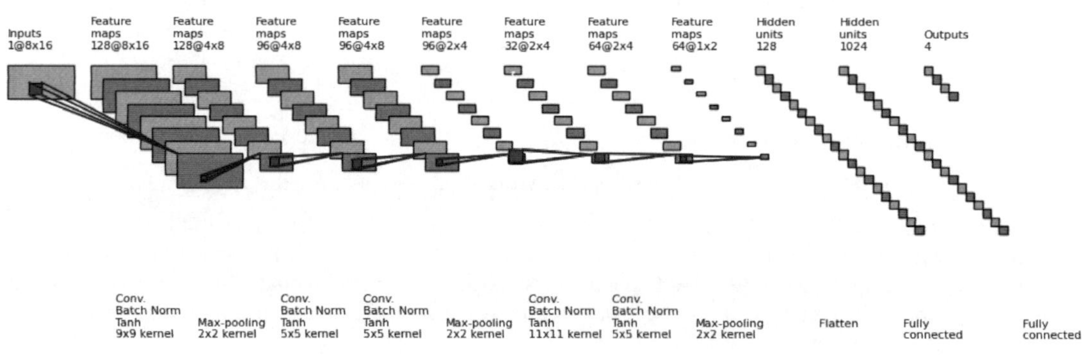

Figure 3. The classification Model used in the FixMatch Algorithm

5.2 Training and Testing

The original classroom audio data was resampled for each 3-second interval at 48 KHz and scaled between -1 and 1. The data was then split according into an 80/20 training and testing set such that there was equal number of examples of each of the four classroom activities in the test set. Accordingly, then, three separate training sets were generated, a labeled set where no transformations were applied, a weak set where the weak transformations were applied, and a strong set where the strong transformations were applied. For each of the training sets, the MFCCs were then calculated with n_mfcc value of 128 using the Librosa library. The mean across the first axis of the calculated MFCCs was then reshaped it into (8,16,1) to be fed to the CNN. The same training/testing scheme as proposed in (Sohn et al., 2020) was followed.

The Initial Learning rates for the model was set to 1.6e-5 for each of the different experiments, informed by the experiments performed in (Zualkernan & Khan, 2020). For a learning rate schedule, a cosine learning rate decay (Loshchilov & Hutter, 2016) was used which sets the learning rate to (6). η is the initial learning rate, k is the current training step and K is the total number of training step. For all models, the total number of training steps was 5000.

$$\eta \cos(\frac{7\Pi k}{16K}) \quad (6)$$

Finally, a batch size of 64 was used for training and threshold τ is set to 0.95. To observe the viability of the proposed adapted FixMatch, the proposed model was trained and tested under four experimental conditions and then compared with a fully supervised baseline. The four conditions used 20% labeled data, 15% labeled data,10% labeled data and 5% labeled data. Table 3 shows the number of training cases used for each condition.

Table 3. Number of training cases for various conditions

Activity	% Labeled data used for training				
	100%	20%	15%	10%	5%
Class Mgmt.	1223	225	163	108	54
Lecture	1969	225	163	108	54
Practice	354	225	163	108	54
Q&A	766	225	163	108	54
Total	4312	900	652	432	216

6. RESULTS

Table 4 shows the F1-scores of the trained systems under different experimental conditions. Table 4 clearly shows that even with a fraction of the amount of labeled data, the system performed well. For example, there was only a 0.08 drop in F1 score of the system when only 10% of labelled data used for training. There is, however, an expected larger drop of in performance when one moved from 10% to 5% of data. The results generally show that that the proposed architecture worked well and was able to use only 5% of the data to achieve very reasonable results.

Table 4. F1-Score of the proposed model (N = 1080)

Activity	% Labeled data used for training				
	100%	20%	15%	10%	5%
Class Mgmt.	0.83	0.81	0.79	0.76	0.72
Lecture	0.75	0.72	0.70	0.66	0.60
Practice	0.72	0.68	0.72	0.67	0.59
Q&A	0.61	0.62	0.54	0.50	0.51
Macro Avg.	0.73	0.71	0.69	0.65	0.61
Weight Avg.	0.73	0.71	0.69	0.65	0.61

As Figure 4 shows the confusion matrices under various conditions. As the Figure shows, there does not seem to be a systematic difference between the types of errors being made as the percentage of labels changes. In addition, Q&A seems to be confused with Practice. This could largely be attributed to the fact that both sets of activities follow similar patterns that consist of prolonged quiet spells with sporadic spoken responses. The ROC curves shown in Figure 5 also confirm that qualitatively the models seem to training in a similar manner. Figure 5 also shows that at lower percentages of labelling (5% and 10%) Lecture and Q&A are confused, most likely due to the sound predominantly being the voice of the teacher, however, this issue is largely handled better at larger label percentages.

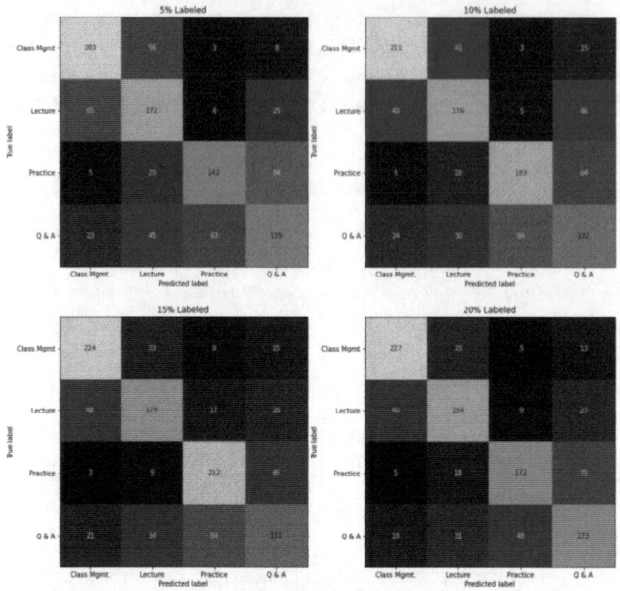

Figure 4. Confusion Matrix at 5%, 10%, 15% and 20% respectively

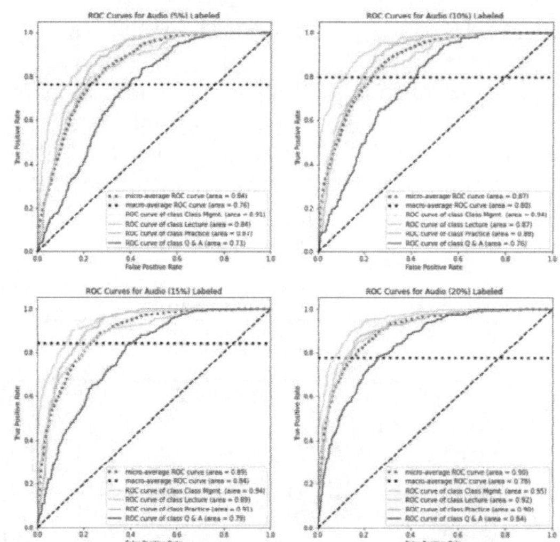

Figure 5. One-vs-Others ROC Curves at 5%, 10%, 15% and 20% labeled data respectively

7. CONCLUSION

The process of automating any aspect of the classroom observation task in resource-constrained environment remains a challenge. Unavailability of labelled data is a key detriment. This paper proposed and evaluated an audio version of the FixMatch algorithm to automate classroom observation using on audio classroom data only. Preliminary results are promising. If successful, this stream of work will allow for automating classroom observation in the resource-constrained regions in a more economical way. The primary limitations of this study are the relatively small size of the dataset and the requirement of manual pre-cleaning of the data. These can however be addressed in the future. Furthermore, to improve the performance of the system, other architectures like transformers can be leveraged.

REFERENCES

Bachman, P., Alsharif, O. and Precup, D. (2014) 'Learning with Pseudo-Ensembles', in *Advances in Neural Information Processing Systems*. Curran Associates, Inc. Available at: https://proceedings.neurips.cc/paper/2014/hash/66be31e4c40d676991f2405aaecc6934-Abstract.html (Accessed: 24 October 2022).

Bell, C.A. *et al.* (2019) 'Qualities of classroom observation systems', *School Effectiveness and School Improvement*, 30(1), pp. 3–29. Available at: https://doi.org/10.1080/09243453.2018.1539014.

Borich, G.D. (2016) *Observation Skills for Effective Teaching: Research-Based Practice*. 7th edn. New York: Routledge. Available at: https://doi.org/10.4324/9781315633206.

Bruns, B., De Gregorio, S. and Taut, S. (2016) *Measures of Effective Teaching in Developing Countries*. Research on Improving Systems of Education (RISE). Available at: https://doi.org/10.35489/BSG-RISE-WP_2016/009.

Caldwell, R. (2018) *The Problem with Teacher Observation, Chemonics International*. Available at: https://chemonics.com/blog/problem-teacher-observation/ (Accessed: 24 October 2022).

Chetty, R., Friedman, J.N. and Rockoff, J.E. (2014) 'Measuring the Impacts of Teachers II: Teacher Value-Added and Student Outcomes in Adulthood', *American Economic Review*, 104(9), pp. 2633–2679. Available at: https://doi.org/10.1257/aer.104.9.2633.

Grandvalet, Y. and Bengio, Y. (2004) 'Semi-supervised Learning by Entropy Minimization', in *Advances in Neural Information Processing Systems*. MIT Press. Available at: https://proceedings.neurips.cc/paper/2004/hash/96f2b50b5d3613adf9c27049b2a888c7-Abstract.html (Accessed: 24 October 2022).

James, A. *et al.* (2019) 'Automated Classification of Classroom Climate by Audio Analysis', in L.F. D'Haro, R.E. Banchs, and H. Li (eds) *9th International Workshop on Spoken Dialogue System Technology*. Singapore: Springer (Lecture Notes in Electrical Engineering), pp. 41–49. Available at: https://doi.org/10.1007/978-981-13-9443-0_4.

Jamison, E.A., Jamison, D.T. and Hanushek, E.A. (2007) 'The effects of education quality on income growth and mortality decline', *Economics of Education Review*, 26(6), pp. 771–788. Available at: https://doi.org/10.1016/j.econedurev.2007.07.001.

Laine, S. and Aila, T. (2017) 'Temporal Ensembling for Semi-Supervised Learning'. arXiv. Available at: https://doi.org/10.48550/arXiv.1610.02242.

Lam, S. (2001) 'Educators' opinions on classroom observation as a practice of staff development and appraisal', *Teaching and Teacher Education*, 17(2), pp. 161–173. Available at: https://doi.org/10.1016/S0742-051X(00)00049-4.

Loshchilov, I. and Hutter, F. (2017) 'SGDR: Stochastic Gradient Descent with Warm Restarts'. arXiv. Available at: https://doi.org/10.48550/arXiv.1608.03983.

Martinez, F., Taut, S. and Schaaf, K. (2016) 'Classroom observation for evaluating and improving teaching: An international perspective', *Studies in Educational Evaluation*, 49, pp. 15–29. Available at: https://doi.org/10.1016/j.stueduc.2016.03.002.

Meignier, S. and Merlin, T. (2010) 'LIUM SPKDIARIZATION: An Open Source Toolkit for Diarization', in *CMU SPUD Workshop*. Dallas, United States. Available at: https://hal.archives-ouvertes.fr/hal-01433518 (Accessed: 24 October 2022).

Mundial, B. (2015) 'Conducting classroom observations: analyzing classrooms dynamics and instructional time, using the Stallings' classroom snapshot'observation system. User guide'.

Owens, M.T. *et al.* (2017) 'Classroom sound can be used to classify teaching practices in college science courses', *Proceedings of the National Academy of Sciences*.

Piczak, K.J. (2015) 'ESC: Dataset for Environmental Sound Classification', in *Proceedings of the 23rd ACM international conference on Multimedia*. New York, NY, USA: Association for Computing Machinery (MM '15), pp. 1015–1018. Available at: https://doi.org/10.1145/2733373.2806390.

Qiao, Q. and Beling, P.A. (2011) 'Classroom Video Assessment and Retrieval via Multiple Instance Learning', in G. Biswas et al. (eds) *Artificial Intelligence in Education*. Berlin, Heidelberg: Springer (Lecture Notes in Computer Science), pp. 272–279. Available at: https://doi.org/10.1007/978-3-642-21869-9_36.

Richards, J.A. *et al.* (2008) *The LENATM automatic vocalization assessment*. Technical Report LTR-08-1). LENA Foundation.

Salamon, J. and Bello, J.P. (2017) 'Deep Convolutional Neural Networks and Data Augmentation for Environmental Sound Classification', *IEEE Signal Processing Letters*, 24(3), pp. 279–283. Available at: https://doi.org/10.1109/LSP.2017.2657381.

Salamon, J., Jacoby, C. and Bello, J.P. (2014) 'A Dataset and Taxonomy for Urban Sound Research', in *Proceedings of the 22nd ACM international conference on Multimedia*. New York, NY, USA: Association for Computing Machinery (MM '14), pp. 1041–1044. Available at: https://doi.org/10.1145/2647868.2655045.

Schlotterbeck, D. *et al.* (2021) 'What Classroom Audio Tells About Teaching: A Cost-effective Approach for Detection of Teaching Practices Using Spectral Audio Features', in *LAK21: 11th International Learning Analytics and Knowledge Conference*. New York, NY, USA: Association for Computing Machinery (LAK21), pp. 132–140. Available at: https://doi.org/10.1145/3448139.3448152.

Seidman, E. *et al.* (2018) 'Assessment of pedagogical practices and processes in low and middle income countries: Findings from secondary school classrooms in Uganda', *Teaching and Teacher Education*, 71, pp. 283–296. Available at: https://doi.org/10.1016/j.tate.2017.12.017.

Sohn, K. *et al.* (2020) 'FixMatch: Simplifying Semi-Supervised Learning with Consistency and Confidence', in *Advances in Neural Information Processing Systems*. Curran Associates, Inc., pp. 596–608. Available at: https://proceedings.neurips.cc/paper/2020/hash/06964dce9addb1c5cb5d6e3d9838f733-Abstract.html (Accessed: 24 October 2022).

Summaira, J. *et al.* (2021) 'Recent Advances and Trends in Multimodal Deep Learning: A Review'. arXiv. Available at: https://doi.org/10.48550/arXiv.2105.11087.

Wang, Z. *et al.* (2014) 'Automatic classification of activities in classroom discourse', *Computers & Education*, 78, pp. 115–123. Available at: https://doi.org/10.1016/j.compedu.2014.05.010.

Wedgwood, R. (2007) 'Education and poverty reduction in Tanzania', *International Journal of Educational Development*, 27(4), pp. 383–396. Available at: https://doi.org/10.1016/j.ijedudev.2006.10.005.

World Bank Group (no date) *The Stallings classroom observation system*, *World Bank*. Available at: https://www.worldbank.org/en/programs/sief-trust-fund/brief/the-stallings-classroom-snapshot (Accessed: 24 October 2022).

Zualkernan, I. and Khan, M.S. (2020) 'Towards an Audio-based CNN for Classroom Observation on a Smartwatch', in *2020 IEEE / ITU International Conference on Artificial Intelligence for Good (AI4G). 2020 IEEE / ITU International Conference on Artificial Intelligence for Good (AI4G)*, pp. 224–229. Available at: https://doi.org/10.1109/AI4G50087.2020.9311083.

Zualkernan, I.A., Lutfeali, S. and Karim, A. (2014) 'Using tablets and satellite-based internet to deliver numeracy education to marginalized children in a developing country', in *IEEE Global Humanitarian Technology Conference (GHTC 2014). IEEE Global Humanitarian Technology Conference (GHTC 2014)*, pp. 294–301. Available at: https://doi.org/10.1109/GHTC.2014.6970295.

HOW DOES THE USE OF OPEN DIGITAL SPACES IMPACT STUDENTS SUCCESS AND DROPOUT IN A VIRTUAL UNIVERSITY?

Khalifa Sylla[1], Guy Merlin Mbatchou Nkwetchoua[1] and François Bouchet[2]
[1]*Virtual University of Senegal, Cité du Savoir, Diamniadio, 15126 Dakar-Fann, Senegal*
[2]*Sorbonne Université, CNRS, LIP6, F-75005 Paris, France*

ABSTRACT

Virtual universities have developed considerably over the past decade, particularly on the African continent. They provide a way to deal with the considerable need to educate a large young population, but the lack of physical space can be a drawback that prevents students from succeeding and increasing dropout compared to a more traditional face-to-face university. To limit these issues, some virtual universities have been opening Open Digital Spaces (ODS) to complement the virtual space and offer students a place where to work and solve pedagogical, technical or administrative issues. However, it is unclear how students actually make use of these ODS and which uses can be beneficial or detrimental to their success and limit dropout. In this paper we lead an exploratory study of the results of a large-scale digital survey in a major African Virtual University (N=2392 answers) to identify factors in the use of Open Digital Spaces (ODS) that have an impact on students' success and dropout.
We analyzed the data using multiple Chi-Square tests of independence. Results indicate that students who visit ODSs more during the 2 weeks before an exam or only when it is mandatory are statistically less likely to succeed, contrary to students who come to work in groups or for the internet access who are more likely to succeed. Conversely, students who do not see the value of ODSs for learning and who visit only when mandatory are more likely to dropout, contrary to students who come when they have a pedagogical need or to work in groups who are less likely to dropout. Some factors particularly impact first year university students, highlighting the need to make them understand which use of the ODS are relevant to increase their chances to graduate.

KEYWORDS

Open Digital Space, Learning, Virtual University

1. INTRODUCTION

Many African countries have set up virtual universities: this is the case in Senegal, Ivory Coast, Cameroon, Chad, Tunisia, Egypt, etc. Unlike distance education, which is traditionally reserved for elective training and continuous training with relatively experienced learners, these virtual universities tend to welcome new baccalaureate holders in initial training. These young graduates are neither familiar with the university system, nor with ICT tools. The transition from a face-to-face learning system to an online learning system gives rise to curiosity and a concern for both students and parents. The concern lies in the risk of dropping out of school due to exogenous and endogenous student variables that influence the dropout or attrition rate (Bourdages & Delmotte, 2007). To mitigate the effect of isolation of learners and increase academic and social integration, some virtual universities have made Open Digital Spaces (ODS) available to them (Ouya et al., 2015; Sylla et al., 2020). An ODS is an innovative location made of buildings containing computer equipment and human resources for taking care of students while adapting them to local realities and respecting the best international standards.

The objective of this research is to evaluate the impact of the use of Open Digital Spaces in a virtual university on student success and dropout.

More specifically, we will seek to answer the following research questions:

(RQ1) Which of the different reasons that students visit ODS have an impact on student success or dropout?

(RQ2) Does visiting an ODS other than the ODS one is registered to have an impact on success and dropout?

The rest of this paper is organized as follows: after the state of the art, we present the methodology adopted, then present the analysis and the results obtained.

2. RELATED WORKS

In this part we propose a state of the art of teaching in Senegalese universities by focusing on the strategy adopted by the Minister of Higher Education. Then we will discuss the pedagogical model of the virtual university of Senegal, and finally, we will present the concept of open digital spaces (ODS).

2.1 Higher Education in Senegal

In 2013, the State of Senegal organized a national consultation and a presidential council on the future of higher education in order to ensure an in-depth reform of the system (Dimé, 2018; Fatou et al., n.d.). This resulted in the implementation of the 2013-2017 Priority Reform Program for Higher Education and Research in Senegal (PDESR) (MESRI, 2018). Several recommendations and decisions have resulted from these initiatives, including the creation of the Virtual University of Senegal (UVS) (Daniels, 2020), which responds to several ambitions: putting information and communication technologies at the heart of the development of higher education and research in order to improve access to education and the efficiency of the system, developing distance learning and encouraging teaching and research staff to use ICTs, allowing access to higher education throughout the national territory, and facilitating access to training for all components of society.

2.2 The Pedagogical Model in Virtual Universities

The pedagogical model of the UVS is based on the comodal approach which is inspired by the hybrid model (Diop & Diack, 2018; Tendeng, 2020). The hybrid approach combines face-to-face and distance learning in the transmission of knowledge in order to achieve predefined pedagogical objectives. It promotes collaboration and distance learning, with the learner at the heart of the training device.

Comodality is a teaching formula that provides the most flexibility for the learner. Depending on the schedule, the student is free to attend the course as they would a traditional classroom course. They can also choose to use the synchronous virtual classroom to attend their course without physically traveling and still be able to actively participate in the course. UVS started in 2016, the comodal model adapted to allow the student to adapt gradually with a semester 1 of the first year of the degree (L1) 100% face-to-face and synchronous to arrive at the last semester of the third year (L3) which will be 100% remote (Dia, 2019).

2.3 Open Digital Spaces

The Ministry of Higher Education, Research and Innovation (MESRI), taking into account the socio-cultural aspects and the constraints related to distance learning, provides an original solution to accompany and facilitate access to various resources and services, called Open Digital Space (ODS).

The ODS are designed to offer an efficient technological framework to students, pupils, teachers and researchers, socio-economic groups and other actors. Within the framework of the UVS, the network of ODS will become more and more dense over the years.

UVS students find in their ODS of attachment equipment, resources and computer tools necessary for the proper conduct of educational activities. As a space dedicated for socialization, students find in their ODS support in case of difficulty but also conditions and activities conducive to the strengthening of a sense of belonging.

To facilitate access to digital resources and computer equipment for all, and in particular for students, the UVS has set up ODS throughout the country. These ODS allow students to access equipment, resources and computer tools necessary for the proper conduct of educational activities. They also allow to have physical relays for a good deployment of the UVS, and in this sense, they allow both to have spaces for face-to-face teaching or for collaborative work.

Figures 1, 2 and 3 show views of an existing open digital space (left - from outside, middle - an amphitheater - right - open working spaces).

Figure 1. Front view ODS

Figure 2. Amphitheater ODS

Figure 3. Open working space ODS

3. METHODS

3.1 Data Collected

In order to study the impact of an ODS on learning processes, we sent a survey to all students registered to the virtual university (approximately 45,000 students) both through their institutional email and through some university groups on social networks. The survey was done using the university LimeSurvey platform [https://survey.uvs.sn/index.php?r=survey/index&sid=456915&lang=fr]. This survey was collecting the following categories of information:

- Student demographics: including which ODS the student was attached to, their discipline, their level (1st, 2nd or 3rd year of bachelor), the year they registered to the virtual university which defines their cohort (e.g. every student who started in Sept. 2021 is in cohort 8), and their gender.
- The attended ODS: in particular to know whether they attend an ODS different from the one they are registered to and for what reasons, or whether they attend another open space not related to the university (associated to a city or another university).
- The reasons why they visit an ODS: whether it is for administrative, pedagogical (in particular group work), technical reasons (in particular internet access), or simply to socialize (meet peers), as well as whether they do so only when it is mandatory or if they attend more in the 2 weeks before an exam.
- The time when they visit an ODS: whether they visit regularly and frequently (at least twice a week), whether they visit more to prepare for exams (more visits in the two weeks before an exam), or whether they visit only when it is mandatory (whatever the reason).
- Their perception of ODSs: whether they consider them important for their learning and for their success.

Items used in further analysis are detailed further on in Table 1. Items in the three last categories above are formulated as affirmative statements to which students have to express their level of agreement using a 5-point Likert scale. When frequency was involved, the 5 associated values were “Never”, “Rarely”, “Sometimes”, “Often” and “Always”. At the time the survey was stopped, 2,392 answers had been received, including 1525 complete answers. Students could stop answering before the end of the survey, in which case partial answers were kept when they had reached at least the third section above. This inclusion of partial answers can explain slight differences in the number of answers for each question reported in the results section.

In addition to the survey data, we also used institutional data in order to link the students’ answers to their success and dropout. Success was considered for the year during which the survey was sent (i.e. were they allowed to continue in the next year or did they graduate if they were in their final year). Likewise, a student was considered as having dropped out if they were a no-show in the exams that took place at the end of both semesters of that year.

When merging institutional data with survey data, we did not have access to academic results from all disciplines but we focused on three main ones (in terms of number of replies) over 4 student cohorts (2020-2021 [1st year students], 2019-2020 [2nd year students], 2018-2019 [3rd year students] and 2017-2018 [4th year students, for those who did not fail any semester]).

3.2 Students Sample

From the original sample of all answers, 675 (44.4%) of the students declared to identify their gender as female and 823 (54.1%) declared to identify as male. As aforementioned, due to data access restriction, we consider here 3 different disciplines: 309 students from IDA (Application Development), 200 students from SJ (Legal Sciences) and 192 students from AES (Economic and Social Administration). Over these 701 students, when merging institutional and survey data, we ended up with a subsample of N=402 students' answers used for the following analyses. Among these 402 students, 284 were first year students, 41 were second year students, 48 were third year students and 29 were fourth year students.

3.3 Data Analysis

Data was processed, cleaned and analyzed using Jupyter notebooks in Python and in particular the pandas (1.4.2) library for data processing and clearing, and the pingouin (0.5.2) library which is a wrapper for statistical tests found in SciPy.

Each variable was analyzed in the same way in terms of potential link with success and potential link with dropout. Each variable was dichotomized. For instance, when asked if they were visiting an ODS for technical needs, students who replied "never" or "rarely" were counted as 0 and students who replied "sometimes", "often" or "always" were counted as 1. When a middle value was available, it was excluded for the analysis. For instance, when asked about the value of ODSs for learning, students who agreed or agreed strongly that it was important for their learning were counted as 1, students who disagreed or disagreed strongly as 0, and students who neither agreed nor disagreed were excluded for that item. Some items already had only two possible answers such as the item "do you visit another ODS than the one you're registered to?". After dichotomizing a variable when necessary, we ran for each of them a Chi-Square test of independence where the null hypothesis was that the two variables were independent, and the alternative hypothesis that they were associated. When the number of observations was too low in a cell of the contingency table, we used Fisher's exact test instead. In accordance with (Bender & Lange, 2001), as this is an exploratory study, no adjustments were done for multiple testing and we considered a traditional alpha level of 0.05 for our tests. In addition to the p-value when it was below the threshold of 0.05, we also report here Cramer's V to measure the strength of the association between the two variables and interpret it as suggested by (Akoglu, 2018).

To assess the impact of ODS in the learning process, we define a set of indicators in four big categories listed below.

3.3.1 Location Variables

The relevance of the geographical position of the ODS: This indicator measures the relevance of the location of the ODS in a geographical area in relation to the needs of the learners. This indicator is assessed on the basis of 2 sub-indicators: (1) The attendance rate of the attachment ODS allows us to assess the attendance of the attachment ODS by each learner during their learning. It is worth noting that each student is attached to the ODS closest to his Baccalaureate examination center, but before registration, the student can change their ODS if they provide a justification. The computation of this sub-indicator is based on the percentage of affirmative answers to the question "Do you visit more often an ODS different from the one to which you are attached?" Given that some students may visit other educational spaces different from the ODS to the detriment of the various ODS that surround it, we will not take into account in the computation of the attendance rate of the attached ODS those who only attend other educational spaces. (2) The proximity of the ODS allows us to assess the distance between the attachment ODS and the residence place of the students. This sub-indicator is the rate of students not attending their home ODS for reasons of distance in the question "Why do you attend an ODS different from the one to which you are attached?"

3.3.2 Pedagogical Use Variables

The rate of pedagogical use of ODS is used to determine the pedagogical importance of ODS in the learning process. The calculation of this indicator is based on the statements "I go to the ODS to work in a group", "I go to the ODS for the pleasant pedagogical environment", "I go to the ODS for pedagogical needs (Example: Meeting a tutor or teacher for explanations)" which answers are on a Likert scale of 5 (Never, Rarely, Sometimes, Often, Always) and dichotomized as aforementioned.. In this calculation, a student will only be counted once.

3.3.3 ODS Staff Variables

The quality of the pedagogical staff of the ODS is used to evaluate the capacity of the pedagogical manager of each ODS to help students in their learning process. The value of this indicator is the rate of respondents who confirmed both the statements "I feel that the ODS's pedagogical leader has pedagogical qualities", and "I feel that the ODS's pedagogical leader has a significant impact on my learning". The question "Do you think the ODS has enough pedagogical staff to help students?" is used to determine the sufficiency of pedagogical staff in ODS.

The quality of the technical staff in the ODS assesses the ability of the IT manager in each ODS to solve technical problems with the equipment given to students. To calculate this indicator, only the respondents who answered positively to the question "I go to the ODS for technical needs (Example: computer repair, ...)" are considered. Of these respondents, the rate of those who answered positively to the statement "I think that the technicians at ODS do a good job" and to the question "Do you think that ODS has enough technicians to help the students?

3.3.4 Internet Connectivity Variables

Internet connectivity assesses students' ongoing access to the Internet. This indicator is evaluated in 3 sub-indicators:

Sustainability of monthly Internet Passes: Each student has an Internet connection device (Internet Key or Smartphone Data Mobile). At the beginning of each month, the Virtual University through the Ministry of Higher Education, Research and Innovation provides a predetermined data volume. This sub-indicator is used to determine if the assigned volume pass is sufficient for the month. To achieve this, the question "What is the average duration of the Internet Passes you receive each month?" is used to determine the average duration by weekly range. We consider that a satisfactory average duration is at least 3 weeks. The calculation of the sub-indicator will be the rate of satisfactory average duration.

The quality of the ODSs' Internet connection allows us to evaluate the degree of satisfaction of the ODSs' Internet connection by students. This sub-indicator is the rate of respondents who confirmed the statement "I consider the quality of the internet connection at ODS to be good".

The usability of the ODS Internet connection allows us to evaluate the rate of use of the ODS Internet connection by the needy. A needy person is a student who regularly attends an ODS for the connection (question: "I go to the ODS for the Internet connection") whose average monthly Internet Pass duration is not satisfactory. The calculation of this sub-indicator is the calculation of the rate of needy attending other educational spaces for Internet connection reasons.

The quality of connection of operators by geographical area makes it possible to evaluate the operator providing the best service to students. This sub-indicator is a statistical table of dimension 2 presenting the satisfaction rate by operators and geographical areas.

The importance of ODS for learning is used to determine how students feel about ODS during their learning. This indicator is the cumulative rate of respondents who confirmed the statements "I feel that ODS are important to my learning" and "I feel that the ODS instructional leader has a significant impact on my learning."

4. RESULTS

4.1 Impact on Success

When considering the visit of another ODS than the one students are registered to (N=402, χ^2=2.36, p=.124 > .05) or another open space (N=402, χ^2=0.45, p=.503 > .05), no significant results appeared, indicating that in itself the nature of the ODS visited is not associated with a higher or lower chance of success.

When considering the reasons to visit an ODS, no statistically significant relationship appears between success and visiting for administrative reasons (N=303, χ^2=0.13, p=.722 > .05), visiting for technical reasons (N=303, χ^2=0.32, p=.575 > .05), or visiting for pedagogical reasons (N=303, χ^2=2.49, p=.115 > .05). When reasons breaking down the technical reasons though, visiting in order to use the internet access is statistically significantly weakly associated to success (N=303, χ^2=5.23, p=.022 < .05, V=0.059), where students who declare visiting to use the internet connection are more likely to validate (89.7% vs. 80.8%).

When analyzing reasons that involve socialization, meeting with peers is not associated with success (N=303, χ^2=0.03, p=.863 > .05), however, working in group is weakly associated with success (N=303, χ^2=11.68, p=.000 < .001, V=0.087) where students who declare using ODS to work in group are more likely to validate their year (89.6% vs. 74.5%).

When analyzing the timing of these visits, visiting at least twice a week is not associated with success (N=261, χ^2=0.01, p=.928 > .05), however, visiting more before exams (N=303, χ^2=3.91, p=.048 < .05, V=0.051) and visiting only when it is mandatory (N=287, χ^2=5.38, p=.020 < .05, V=0.060) are both statistically associated with lower success with a weak association (80.1% vs. 88.3% and 79.4% vs. 89.1% respectively).

Finally, when analyzing their perception of ODSs, neither thinking that ODS is helping them to learn (N=358, χ^2=3.22, p=.072 > .05) nor thinking that ODS is helping in their success (N=348, χ^2=0.24, p=.623 > .05) is associated with a higher success.

4.2 Impact on Dropout

When considering the visit of another ODS (N=402, χ^2=0.261, p=.610 > .05) or another open space (N=402, χ^2=3.19, p=.07 > .05), no significant result appeared (p > .05), indicating that the nature of the ODS visited is not associated with a higher or lower chance of dropout.

When considering the reasons to visit an ODS, no statistically significant association exists between dropout and visits for administrative reasons (N=304, χ^2=0.65, p=.422 > .05), or technical reasons (N=304, χ^2=0.70, p=.402 > .05), including visiting for internet access (N=304, χ^2=1.22, p=.269 > .05). However, there is a weak statistically significant relationship between visiting for pedagogical reasons and dropout (N=304, χ^2=4.44, p=.035 < .05, V=0.054), where students who declare visiting for pedagogical reasons are less likely to dropout than those who declare not visiting for that reason (3.9% vs. 9.4%).

When analyzing the reasons that are associated to socialization, meeting with peers is not associated with dropout (N=304, χ^2=0.50, p=.437 > .05), but working in group is weakly associated with lower dropout (N=304, χ^2=9.49, p=.002 < .01, V=0.079) where students who declare using ODS to work in group are less likely to dropout that year (3.5% vs. 12.8%).

When analyzing the timing of these visits, it appears that visiting at least twice a week is not associated with dropout (N=262, χ^2=1.63, p=.202 > .05), nor is visiting more before the exams (N=304 χ^2=1.52, p=.218 > .05), however, visiting only when it is mandatory (N=288, χ^2=6.59, p=.010 < .05, V=0.067) is weakly statistically associated with a higher risk of dropout (9.9% vs. 3.2%).

Finally, there is no statistically significant relationship with the fact of thinking ODSs are useful for success (N=349, Fisher's exact test, p=.180 > .05), but there is a weak significant relationship between thinking ODSs are useful for learning and dropout (N=359, Fisher's exact test, p=.000 < .001, V=0.095), where students who think ODSs are useful for learning are less likely to dropout (5.5% vs 9.6%).

5. DISCUSSION AND CONCLUSION

In summary, it appears the analyses reveal two counterproductive behaviors for success: visiting more before exams and visiting only when it is mandatory. If the latter seems logical because it indicates a lack of involvement, the former may be more surprising. Nonetheless we can hypothesize that among students who come more before exams, many are trying to compensate for a lower involvement in the weeks before, and it might be difficult to catch it up just by coming to an ODS. On the contrary, two uses of ODS seem associated with a higher success: using the internet access and working with peers. We know that an important proportion of students suffer from limited or slow internet access at home, which is why the university provides a mobile data plan but which is sometimes not enough. Students who declare using the ODS for this reason clearly have a strong need, and the ODS play their part in helping them with this aspect. As for working with peers, the benefit of learning as a social activity have long been demonstrated (Wood & O'Malley, 1996), and it seems using the ODS as a gathering place for these activities is a use to promote. Learning collaboratively online is also efficient, but combined with the aforementioned fact that some students do not have a high quality internet access, it seems logical that a physical space is particularly useful for at least some of them. The lack of significant relationship between success and the perception of the usefulness of ODS to learn could appear surprising. Therefore we led a complementary analysis where we separated 1st year students from others. And it appears indeed that for 1st year students there is a statistically significant weak association between success and thinking ODSs are useful for learning (N=243, χ^2=4.43, p=.04 < .05, V=0.088). This allows us to nuance the initial analysis: there are still students who do not see the value of ODSs in years 2 to 4, however, the students who are negatively impacted by undervaluing ODSs are the 1st year students. It is therefore particularly critical to focus communication on the value of ODSs towards this subpopulation.

When considering dropout, analyses revealed one counterproductive behavior that increases the risks of dropout which is visiting only when it is mandatory. Conversely, two behaviors seem associated with a lower dropout: visiting for pedagogical needs and to work with peers. As for success, it shows it is critical for students to understand early on the value of ODSs and visit them for pedagogically sound reasons. Finally, one belief is associated with a higher dropout which is, as for success for first year students, not seeing the usefulness of ODSs for learning.

From the ODSs administrators' perspective, this work suggests which particular uses of ODSs should be promoted, and would indicate that it is particularly critical to focus on first year students. From the students' point of view, being presented with this data analysis could be helpful in convincing them of the maladaptive value of some behaviors (e.g. trying to compensate for a lack of work by coming to the ODSs just before exams). However, it has several limits: this survey was given in the middle of the year, and it could be useful to track the evolution of the perception of ODSs over the year, in particular to track the effect of potential communication campaign towards students. Another limit is the limited sample size when compared to the total number of students in the virtual university, and the more limited size due to lack of access to institutional data for some disciplines. Finally, these results are only for one university in Africa, and it would be particularly valuable to see if these results can generalize to other African Virtual Universities, and if possibly they would differ in other virtual universities across the world.

REFERENCES

Akoglu, H. (2018). User's guide to correlation coefficients. *Turkish Journal of Emergency Medicine*, *18*(3), 91–93. https://doi.org/10.1016/j.tjem.2018.08.001

Bender, R., & Lange, S. (2001). Adjusting for multiple testing—When and how? *Journal of Clinical Epidemiology*, *54*(4), 343–349. https://doi.org/10.1016/S0895-4356(00)00314-0

Bourdages, L., & Delmotte, C. (2007). La persistance aux études universitaires à distance. *International Journal of E-Learning & Distance Education*, *16*(2), 23–36.

Daniels, C. (2020). *Transformative innovation policy Africa hub exploratory*. http://hdl.handle.net/10625/59142

Dia, A. A. (2019, April 15). *Université virtuelle du Sénégal: Retour d'expérience*. Colloque sur l'ingénierie pédagogique et le numérique éducatif, Université Mohammed VI Polytechnique, Marrakech, Maroc.

Dimé, M. (2018). *Research and PhD Capacities in Sub-Saharan Africa: Senegal Report* (p. 28).

Diop, A., & Diack, M. (2018, April 18). *Deployiing A Co-modal Course Delivery Model Adapted To African Context: Case Of The Virtual University Of The Republic Of Senegal -West Africa.* HBCU Affordable Learning Summit, Conference OLC INNOVATE, Nashville, Tennessee, États-Unis.

Fatou, C., Joseph, D., Assion, L., Sy, M., Daniels, C., & Ting, B. (n.d.). *ICT in Higher Education in Africa: Example of the Virtual University in Senegal*. 27.

MESRI. (2018). *Décisions Présidentielles relatives à l'Enseignement supérieur et de la recherche*. https://mesr.gouv.sn/decisions-presidentielles-relatives-a-lenseignement-superieur-et-de-la-recherche-pdf/

Ouya, S., Sylla, K., Faye, P. M. D., Sow, M. Y., & Lishou, C. (2015). Impact of integrating WebRTC in universities' e-learning platforms. *2015 5th World Congress on Information and Communication Technologies (WICT)*, 13–17. https://doi.org/10.1109/WICT.2015.7489664

Sylla, K., Ndiaye, N. M., Ouya, S., & Mendy, G. (2020). Towards the use of a contact center for the socialization and capacity reinforcement of learners of African digital universities. *2020 22nd International Conference on Advanced Communication Technology (ICACT)*, 603–607. https://doi.org/10.23919/ICACT48636.2020.9061548

Tendeng, M. L. (2020). *Analyse des proximités spatiale et a-spatiale de dispositif de formation à distance: Cas de l'Université virtuelle du Sénégal (UVS)* [Université Laval]. http://hdl.handle.net/20.500.11794/67979

Wood, D., & O'Malley, C. (1996). Collaborative Learning between Peers. *Educational Psychology in Practice*, *11*(4), 4–9. https://doi.org/10.1080/0266736960110402

SECURE DEMATERIALIZATION OF ASSESSMENTS IN DIGITAL UNIVERSITIES THROUGH MOODLE, WEBRTC AND SAFE EXAM BROWSER (SEB)

Khalifa Sylla[1], Birahim Babou[2] and Samuel Ouya[2]
[1]*Department of Applied Mathematics and Computer Science, Virtual University of Senegal (UVS), Senegal*
[2]*Polytechnic High School of Dakar, Computer Science Department, Senegal*

ABSTRACT

This paper deals with a solution allowing digital universities to extend the functionalities of their distance learning platform to offer a secure solution for the dematerialization of assessments. Currently we are witnessing the rise of digital universities, this is the case in Africa, particularly in Senegal. We are witnessing strong growth in the number of students, in a context of extension and diversification of training offers. This is the case of the Virtual University of Senegal (UVS), the number of students has increased from 2,000 students in 2013, the year of its creation, to 50,000 in 2021. It offers 13 licenses and 30 courses of training.

With these large numbers, the organization of assessments in these universities becomes more and more tedious. Taking the example of the UVS with 50,000 students and 30 training courses, we will have to deploy millions of exams copies due to one copy per candidate. These universities have digital campuses (connected campuses) or Open Digital Spaces (ENO) which make it possible to organize face-to-face evaluations on the table. This organization has several disadvantages, on the one hand, the management of the proofs and the correction of the copies require the mobilization of human and financial resources; on the other hand, the risks of errors, reports and authenticity of the notes.

In this article, we propose a secure system for managing online assessments in digital universities based on LMS Moodle, SEB and remote monitoring with the JITSI video conferencing system.

The solution will allow universities to optimize human and financial resources and make assessment results more reliable.

KEYWORDS

E-learning, Moodle, Online Assessment, Exam, WebRTC, Safe Exam Browser

1. INTRODUCTION

Distance learning is becoming more and more essential in higher education institution. This period of covid-19 only confirms the need to put in place support solutions for higher education establishments for the dematerialization of their teaching and assessments. Providing a dedicated exam room with multiple computers is a possible but very expensive solution. However, taking exams on student laptops increases the number of simultaneous exams but also the possibility of cheating. The system we are proposing will also consider learners who, for one reason or another, cannot take the face-to-face assessment.

Several factors must be brought together to set up a dematerialized evaluation system. Security being essential, it must be considered in order to have a complete, robust system that inspires confidence in the various players.

For the implementation of this secure evaluation system in digital universities, several tools will be used, in particular a Learning Management System (LMS) for the evaluation of learners, a videoconferencing system for monitoring candidates evaluated remotely and a system for locking learners' computers and work tools throughout the duration of the tests.

This paper will be organized as follows: after the state of the art, we will make a solution proposal in which we will do the analysis and design of the solution. After that, we will make a proposal for a sizing model and end with a conclusion and perspectives.

2. STATE OF THE ART

With distance learning widespread in most higher education institutions, the question of the dematerialization of assessments is becoming more and more recurrent.

It is in this context that several authors work in this field. Among them, researchers AY Elmaghrabi and SM Eljack, in their article entitled “Enhancement of Moodle learning Management System Regarding Quizzes Security and Stability Problems”, aim to improve the security of the Moodle system environment when running online exams, considering the most common problems faced by online exams. This has been addressed by improving the security performance of the Moodle Quiz tool, which is one of the most important tools in the learning management system in general and the Moodle system as well. In this article, they have included two aspects of improvement: the first aspect is to solve the problem of the loss of responses during a sudden short disconnection from the network due to a server crash or for any other reason, the second aspect is to increase the level of confidentiality of the e-Quiz by preventing access to the Quiz from several computers or browsers at the same time.

Researchers A. Natawiguna and MMI Liem, after conducting preliminary research on online exam cheating, its detection and prevention, presented virtualization methods to secure online exams against cheating attempts in a desktop client. real-time exam on their article called “Virtualization Methods for Securing Online Exam”. They analyzed and compared two virtualization methods, namely hardware-level virtualization and operating system-level virtualization. Based on their experiences, hardware-level virtualization is the optimal method. The result of this research is a set of tools that can be used to improve existing proctoring methods used to secure the online exam. Ria Mae H. Borromeo, in her article titled “Online exam for distance educators using moodle” shows that online exams can be administered using existing systems, which can automate the exam scoring process depending on the type of exam question. The Open University of the Philippines (UPOU) uses Moodle as its primary Learning Management System (LMS) platform. However, not all UPOU online exams are administered through Moodle. Their study aims to determine the characteristics of an online examination system desired by university teachers. To achieve this, a survey and technology demonstration of the Moodle Quiz module has been developed. The survey was in the form of an online questionnaire in which the questions demonstrated the types of questions available in the Quiz module and asked teachers what features they would like to see implemented in an online exam system.

In addition to this research, other tools are currently used in universities for online assessment, such as Google Classroom which is an educational platform that offers teachers and learners a database of exchange with the objectives of coordinating homework, increasing collaboration and optimizing communication so that the teacher can manage his lessons, create content, give homework, grade work and send feedback to students. Eval&GO and Typeform are also proprietary online assessment design platforms that require an internet connection for use; Canvas is an open source platform that provides the ability to implement assignments and surveys to assess learners' understanding of the course. It makes it possible to create corrections by peers, group work; Track learner engagement, discussions, and results.

These solutions have contributed to the resolution of the problem related to online exams. However, they are not complete. It is in this perspective that we propose in this article, a contribution for a secure dematerialization of evaluations in digital universities through Moodle, WebRTC and SEB.

3. PROPOSITION OF A SOLUTION

3.1 Analysis

With the limited means of some African digital universities, the use of open source tools is essential, especially since several communities are available to provide support if needed. Existing solutions, as described in the state of the art, often do not offer the possibility of managing the entire chain from secure evaluation to automatic correction.

Most of the solutions used in digital universities are based on the LMS Moodle which is the most widely used open source training platform in the academic world. It becomes very useful in the organization of exams with the integration of SEB by default since its version 3.9. Moodle offers several assessment activities including quizzes and assignments. The Quiz activity module allows you to design and create quizzes consisting of a wide variety of questions, including multiple-choice, true-false, short-answer, and image drag-and-drop question types. of text. These questions are kept in the question bank and can be reused in different questionnaires. The Assignment activity allows learners to submit assignments by uploading one or more files. The question bank, when it is open to an entire teaching team, can be cumbersome to manage.

Safe Exam Browser (SEB), which is a secure and open-source exam browser, allows you to restrict candidates' access to external websites, system functions or other applications while they take an online assessment. This program makes online assessments more secure by transforming the candidate's work tool into a secure workstation.

Remote monitoring remains a weak point in the use of these tools. These solutions do not offer online monitoring during the course of assessments. The tests take place with the presence of supervisors in the examination rooms as is the case in traditional universities. The integration of an effective online monitoring solution remains very important.

3.2 Design

The design of the solution is based on the LMS Moodle, the Safe Exam Browser and the integration of an online monitoring tool based on the WebRTC.

Based on the existence of several proprietary or open source solutions, the choice to integrate a videoconferencing tool remains very important. Thus, the solution we propose is based on the coupling of 3 tools which are the LMS Moodle, SEB and Jitsi.

This solution makes it possible to take secure face-to-face exams in an exam center with thin clients or computers and remote monitoring. It also offers the possibility of monitoring candidates who take the tests from home.

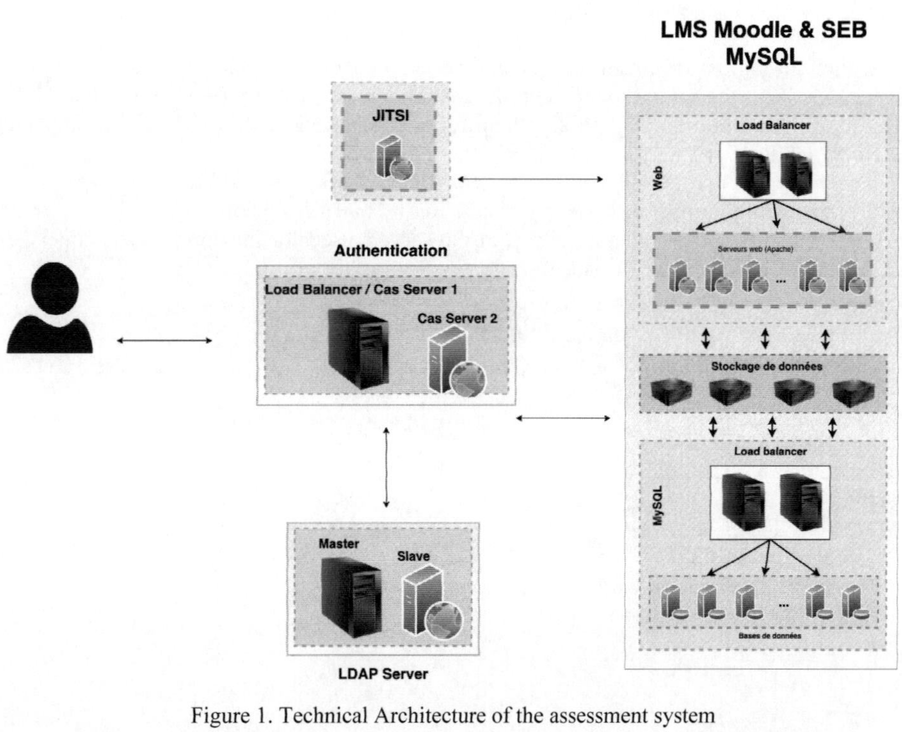

Figure 1. Technical Architecture of the assessment system

For better security management, we offer a centralized authentication system based on CAS as well as the LDAP directory for user management.

The sequence diagram below illustrates the operation of the solution with the interactions between the learner and the system.

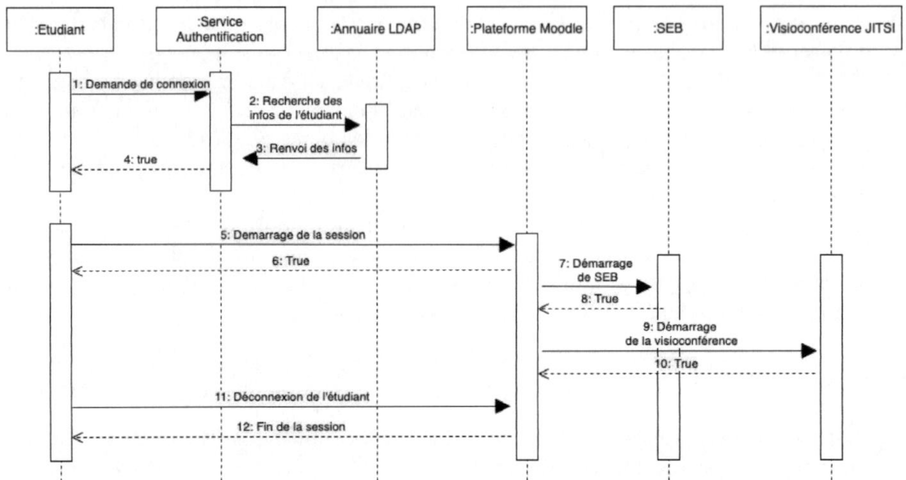

Figure 2. Sequence diagram illustrating the interaction between a student and the assessment system

3.3 Proposal of a Sizing Model

The LMS can be configured to provide very good performance, whether for small uses, or for use with several thousand users. The factors involved in runtime performance are web server, database server and video conferencing server.

The maximum number of concurrent database users needed for testing type activities is the number of users using Moodle at the same time. Generally, the amount of memory (RAM) installed is the determining factor but higher processor speed will also help to reduce page load times. Based on our architecture, the following rule applies:

- The maximum number of concurrent users = RAM (GB) * 50 => 32 * 50 = 1600.
- The maximum number of users in consultation = 1600 * 5 = 8000.

For our case, below are the characteristics of the servers used for the simultaneous management of 1500 candidates with good system performance:

webserver:

- Storage: 200 GB SSD
- Processor: 8GHz Dual Core
- RAM: 32 GB

MySQL Server:

- Storage: 200 GB SSD
- Processor: 8 GHz Dual Core
- RAM: 32 GB

WebRTC (JITSI) Server:

- Storage: 200 GB SSD
- Processor: 8 GHz Dual Core
- RAM: 32 GB

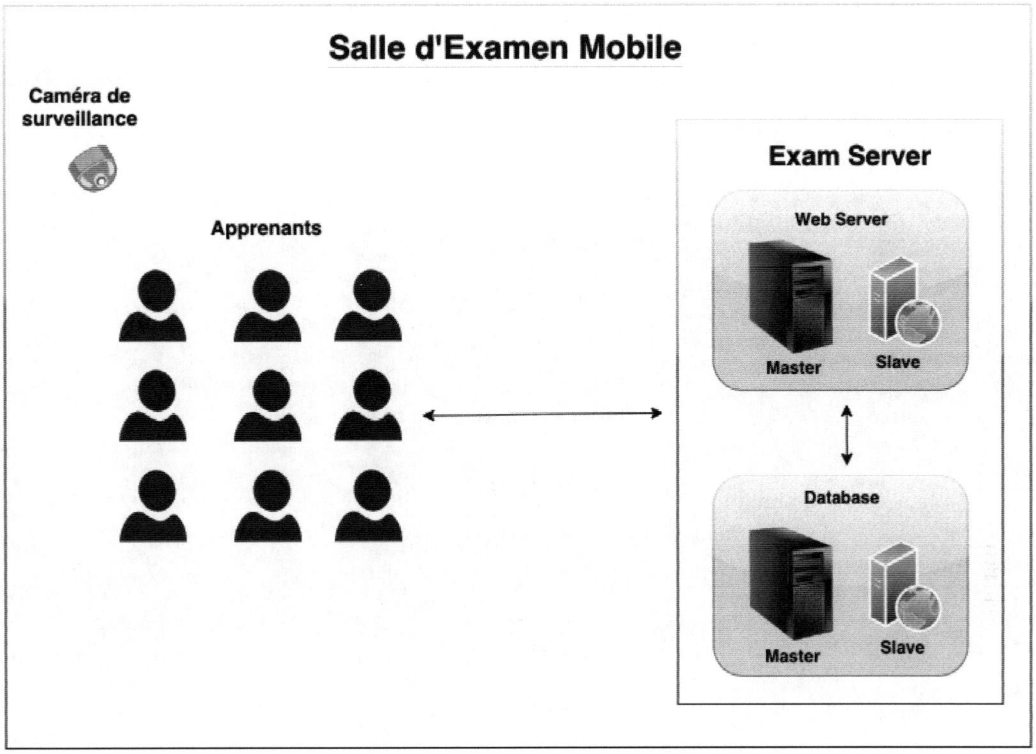

Figure 3. Diagram of the solution

3.4 Securing the System

Cheating of students during exams is a phenomenon in the world, regardless of the level of development of the country. With the expansion of e-learning, exam proctoring becomes more difficult to control. Regarding the security of this system, several aspects will be considered; both on the network and system part. Among these security measures we have:

- the creation of a secure local network accessible only by the tools used for the evaluation;
- the separation of the web server and the LMS database server; this will increase system performance;
- the installation of a surveillance camera to film the learners during the assessment on the table;
- the implementation of a videoconferencing system for the remote monitoring of learners who are unable to move to the examination center;

3.5 Results Analysis

The implementation of this system allowed us to simultaneously evaluate 1119 learners during face-to-face exams out of 1256 enrolled in the course. What makes a participation rate of more than 90%.

Here are some excerpts from the platform's statistics:

Figure 4. Number of participants

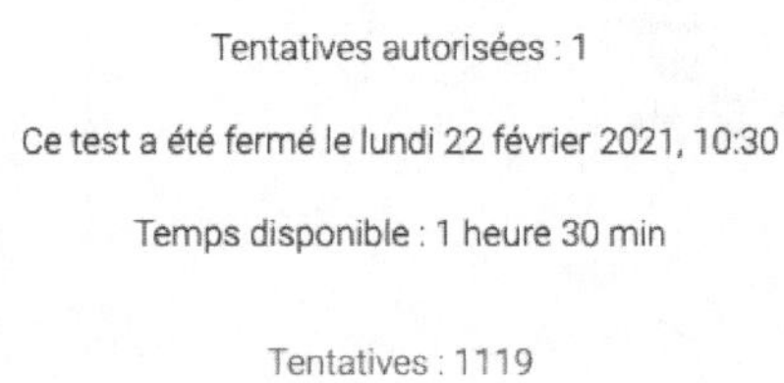

Figure 5. Test setup

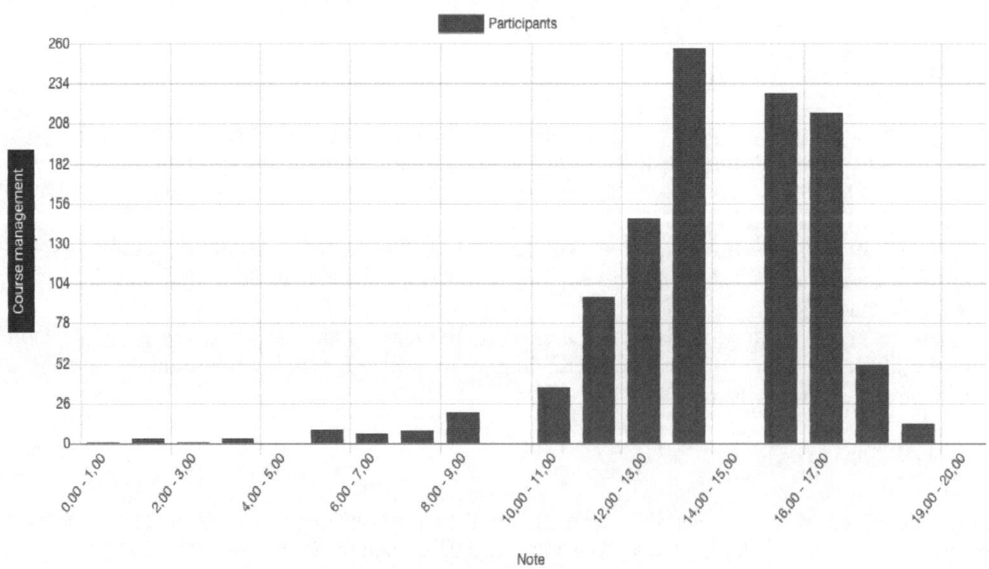

Figure 6. Statistics on grades obtained

4. CONCLUSION

In this article, we have proposed a solution for the secure dematerialization of assessments in digital universities through Moodle, WebRTC and SEB. The UVS with its growing numbers of students benefits from the advantages of this solution which makes it possible to carry out secure online assessments without the need for a lot of resources.

This work provided a solution for the dematerialization of assessments but highlighted another problem related to the automated correction of paper proofs after the assessment as well as automatic monitoring through artificial intelligence tools.

By way of perspective, with the plethora of learners in universities, the implementation of secure solutions for evaluation and automatic correction of proofs are essential. Automatic monitoring solutions with Artificial Intelligence (AI) tools would be a very good solution for monitoring assessments for institutions that have large numbers of learners.

We intend to continue the work to consider the issue related to automatic monitoring with AI-based tools.

REFERENCES

Borromeo, R. M. H. (2013). "*Online exam for distance educators using moodle*," 2013 IEEE 63rd Annual Conference International Council for Education Media (ICEM), pp. 1-4, doi: 10.1109/CICEM.2013.6820155.

Caiko, J., Patlins, A., Nurlan, A., and Protsenko, V. (2020). "Video-conference Communication Platform Based on WebRTC Online meetings," 2020 IEEE 61th International Scientific Conference on Power and Electrical Engineering of Riga Technical University (RTUCON), pp. 1-6, doi: 10.1109/RTUCON51174.2020.9316605.

Canvas (2017). Available online: https://community.canvaslms.com/t5/K12-Canvas-Users/Canvas-Assessments/ba-p/279250

Elmaghrabi, A. Y., and Eljack, S. M. (2019). "*Enhancement of Moodle learning Management System Regarding Quizzes Security and Stability Problems*," 2nd International Conference on Computer Applications & Information Security (ICCAIS), 2019, pp. 1-7, doi: 10.1109/CAIS.2019.8769530.

Eval & Go (2022). Available online: https://www.evalandgo.com/fr/

Frankl, G., Schartner, P., and Zebedin, G. (2012). "*Secure online exams using students' devices*," Proceedings of the 2012 IEEE Global Engineering Education Conference (EDUCON), pp. 1-7, doi: 10.1109/EDUCON.2012.6201111.

Ghizlane, M., Hicham, B., and Reda, F. H. (2019). "*A New Model of Automatic and Continuous Online Exam Monitoring*," 2019 International Conference on Systems of Collaboration Big Data, Internet of Things & Security (SysCoBIoTS), pp. 1-5, doi: 10.1109/SysCoBIoTS48768.2019.9028027.

Google Classroom (2022). Available online: https://edu.google.com/intl/ALL_fr/products/classroom/

Google Forms (2022). Available online: https://edu.google.com/intl/ALL_fr/teacher-center/products/forms/?modal_active=none

Installation de Moodle (2022). Available online: https://docs.moodle.org/19/fr/Installation_de_Moodle

Jacques, S., Ouahabi, A., and Lequeu, T. (2021). "*Synchronous E-learning in Higher Education during the COVID-19 Pandemic,*" 2021 IEEE Global Engineering Education Conference (EDUCON), pp. 1102-1109, doi: 10.1109/EDUCON46332.2021.9453887.

Khalid, M. S., and Hossan, M. I. (2016). "*Usability evaluation of a video conferencing system in a university's classroom*," 2016 19th International Conference on Computer and Information Technology (ICCIT), pp. 184-190, doi: 10.1109/ICCITECHN.2016.7860192.

Kovačević, D. (2021). "*Some Aspects of Online Teaching of Technical English,*" 2021 20th International Symposium INFOTEH-JAHORINA (INFOTEH), pp. 1-5, doi: 10.1109/INFOTEH51037.2021.9400687.

Kumar, S., Gankotiya, A. K., and Dutta, K. (2011). "*A comparative study of moodle with other e-learning systems*," 2011 3rd International Conference on Electronics Computer Technology, pp. 414-418, doi: 10.1109/ICECTECH.2011.5942032.

Mašín, V., Kopeček, M. and Hanuš, J. (2017). "*Moodle portal in virtualized environment — A performance analysis*," 2017 Federated Conference on Computer Science and Information Systems (FedCSIS), pp. 195-198, doi: 10.15439/2017F348.

Moodle (2022). Available online: https://moodle.org/

Moodle Recommendations performance (2022). Available online: https://docs.moodle.org/3x/fr/Recommandations_de_performance

Natawiguna, A., and Liem, M. M. I. (2016). "*Virtualization methods for securing online exam*," International Conference on Data and Software Engineering (ICoDSE), 2016, pp. 1-7, doi: 10.1109/ICODSE.2016.7936145.

Ouya, S., Sylla, K., Faye, PMD., Sow, MY., and Lishou, C. (2015). "*Impact of integrating WebRTC in universities' e-learning platforms*," 2015 5th World Congress on Information and Communication Technologies (WICT), pp. 13-17, doi: 10.1109/WICT.2015.7489664.

Paturusi, S., Chisaki, Y., and Usagawa, T. (2014). "*Development and evaluation of online quizzes to enhance learning performance: A survey of student assessment through MOODLE in Indonesian National University*," Proceedings of International Conference on Information, Communication Technology and System (ICTS) 2014, pp. 211-216, doi: 10.1109/ICTS.2014.7010585.

Safe Exam Browser (2022). Available online: https://safeexambrowser.org/about_overview_en.html

TypeForm (2022). Available online: https://www.typeform.com/

WHO, https://apps.who.int/iris/bitstream/handle/10665/335824/WHO-2019-nCoV-Adjusting_PH_measures-Schools-2020.2-fre.pdf

QUALITATIVE INDICATORS IN THE E-LEARNING ENVIRONMENT

Ivana Ogrizek Biškupić[1], Josip Lopatič[2] and Mihaela Banek Zorica[3]
[1]*University College ALGEBRA, Gradišćanska ulica 24, 10000 Zagreb, Croatia*
[2]*University of Applied Sciences VELIKA GORICA, Zagrebačka ulica 5, 10410 Velika Gorica, Croatia*
[3]*University of Zagreb, Faculty of Humanities and Social Sciences, Department of Information and Communication Sciences, Ivana Lučića 3, 10000 Zagreb, Croatia*

ABSTRACT

Through preliminary analysis of the e-learning platforms authors have tested the presumption that during pandemics the quality of online teaching and accessibility of learning materials in online environment has increased. Relevant literature for the time period of pandemic points out numerous problems in teaching, but on the other hand technical and pedagogical advances in e-learning process for all stakeholders.

The research has been consisted of the quantitative indicators analysis within the e-learning system for the time period of several academic years (before and during the pandemic) and based on the survey on students EQF level 7 who already had some previous experience in e-learning at higher education level before situation with pandemic. The results indicate that students perceived very little increase in the quantity and quality of the learning materials. The research indicated a need for wider and further institutional support for teachers and students. The institutional support should encourage teachers in their motivation for achieving quality in e-learning performance regarding instructional design and also by building up their digital competences. The results have also pointed the fact that the models from the traditional environment, such as Course Quality Management model should be adapted and integrated in the e-learning environment in order to maintain quality assurance in e-learning performance.

KEYWORDS

Quality of e-Learning Content, Student Perception, Quality Indicators, LMS Environment

1. INTRODUCTION

During the COVID-19 pandemics higher education sector has faced numerous problems and was forced to find ad hoc solutions. With the global closure of almost the whole educational sector, both school and universities (Kovalenko, O. E. et. Al., 2021), (UNESCO, 2020), teaching at higher education institutions did not stop. It was necessary to ensure the continuity of teaching literally overnight. Teachers had to move to an online environment and use the available tools, primarily videoconferencing systems, and teaching was mostly carried out using these systems at the beginning. E-learning or blended learning was in the majority of institutions and programs only and elective for teachers thus bringing only the highly motivated teachers into the e-learning environment. Those who have already used digital technologies and introduced e-learning in the teaching process had more easily designed teaching in an online environment that was already familiar to them. But those who resisted change faced a major challenge - which technologies to choose and combine and, at the end, how to use it (Banek Zorica, M. et. Al., 2021).

Pandemics has forced higher education institutions to shift their traditional teaching fully online. While large number of institutions had some sort of electronic learning environment these were not used as regular teaching environment. Therefore, instead of using e-learning the majority has started implementing emergency remote teaching and calling it e-learning. But there is a huge difference between those two concepts and for the general public, as Muthaprasad et al. (2021) "the questions about the preparedness, designing and effectiveness of e-learning is still not clearly understood. Thus, the question remain are teachers and students ready for the e-learning to take place.

Most of the universities and colleges were not prepared as they did not have any crisis strategies to act upon. The situation broadened the gap of technology affordance, and the digital divide was experienced more that in the pre-pandemic times. Institutions were struggling to support their employees and students with creation of guidelines, manuals, etc.

It is obvious that digital technologies will bring even greater changes in the next few years, from business processes to daily routines. Digital skills are becoming indispensable competencies that the labor market requires today. Education that prepares employees for this digital market is also changing attitudes towards 21st century skills development. The University, as the umbrella institution of higher education, is also expected to act proactively. Every university strategy presented today must have a clearly defined crisis response plan as well as a program and obligations for professional development of teachers for new ways of working for the process of evaluating students' knowledge and skills. As libraries are an infrastructure of education, then their transformation is necessary in accordance with the digital changes and the requirements of the digital concept of education.

Numerous papers published recently have been focused on the changes that the COVID-19 pandemic has brought into the education system, and most of them suggest a significant increase in digitization and quality of online teaching (Carvalho, P. 2022); (Zekanović-Korona L. et. al. 2022); (Salman, E. et. al. 2022); (A. Fornasari, A. et. al. 2022); (Mazzola, R. et. al. 2022); (Somolanji Tokić, I., 2022); (Alhazzani, N. 2022); (Ferragut, C. 2022); (Gonçalves, J., 2022).

EU guidelines for digital transformation that define competences frameworks such DigiCompEdu and DigiCompOrg that should improve the quality of HEI in the context of digitalisation e.g., DigiCompEdu with its proposed progression model intended to help educators understand their personal strengths and weaknesses, by describing different stages or levels of digital competence development have also been considered (Kampylis, P. et. al. 2015).

All the mentioned elements contribute to the e-learning process improvement regarding all stakeholders. Hence, the authors were interested in making a kind of milestone in relation to external guidelines and indicators as the reference point to the objective state of the art on one of the study programme.

Since certain higher education institutions even before the pandemic had to have license to conduct online and/or blended forms of teaching, meet and fulfil certain material, organisational and technical conditions, we have decided to conduct a short preliminary research to determine whether there really is any significant progress in the terms of the amount of published learning materials in the online environment and whether that material is perceived as the one with higher quality.

As emphasized by the (Kovalenko, O. E. et. Al., 2021) a recent study identified the high-impact principles for online education and among them are the important two: to conduct quantitative and qualitative research and evaluate current models of online teaching and learning, with a particular focus to their long-term sustainability; develop staff–teachers' capacity for online teaching, and professional staff capacity for supporting teachers and online systems (Zhu X. et. al., 2020). These two should be worked upon if we want to enable the sustainability of the e-learning or blended learning environments and enable digital transformation of higher education institution. Furthermore, we need to develop and apply indicators of the quality of the online courses and programs in order to obtain complete and objective information about its effectiveness. We also need to investigate the perceived importance that stakeholders' place on each of these quality indicators.

2. QA IN E-LEARNING ENVIRONMENT

Most higher education institutions experienced a shift from elective blended learning to crisis remote teaching. The question of instructional support and knowledge about the e-learning principles has arisen. The question of teaching quality assessment developed for traditional face-to-face environment has risen. Can we implement the same assessment designed for the traditional environment and what kind of results would we receive? Further step should be modification of those instruments and it testing in the fully e-leaning or blended learning environment.

The evaluation of the teaching and learning process is usually done by the quality control surveys which are a valuable tool in quality management. Quality control surveys are the first step that allows identification of areas of teaching quality which should be improved (Pavlina, K. et. Al., 2011). Major problem with existing quality management models is long quality control period, where surveys are usually conducted at the end of semester. Because of this, improvement of teaching is experienced by the next generation and the students rarely receive any feedback about actions taken to improve the quality of teaching. The Course Quality Management model (Pavlina, K. et. Al., 2009) thus focuses on the continuous evaluation during the teaching period and enables the quality control at the lowest level, which is the level of teaching topic. It is a dynamic quality control, which allows improvement of teaching practices during course execution within the same academic year. Due to its dynamic quality control and easy adaptability in the e-learning context this model could help in improving the quality of the teaching in the higher education institution.

Our preliminary research has confirmed that in order to increase the quality of the learning content and teaching form the student's perspective we need to change the quality assessment. As quality management should integrate constant evaluation as well as evaluation of specific topics and should be further applied to all the stakeholders of the e-learning environment.

3. METHODOLOGY

The research was conducted based on the online questionnaire containing 15 questions posed to undergraduate and graduate students attending state founded or private studies. In the questionnaire, students were nominally offered a scale of 5 possible answers to rank their impressions, from extremely negative (grade 1) to extremely positive (grade 5). The questions were created in a way to get their general opinion and assessment on the effectiveness of different performance types regarding e-learning; 1) fully online via MS Teams or Skype etc., 2) in person – teaching in the classroom with support of LMS and learning materials (hybrid) and 3) in person - teaching in the classroom with parallel live stream via MS Teams or Skype. The quantitative and qualitative perception of these types were especially sought and compared for the time before and during the Covid 19 pandemic.

The questions in the survey questionnaire were formulated according to the quantitative-qualitative hypotheses on student perception for e-learning. Corresponding hypotheses were accepted or rejected using a t-test with 5% significance level.

4. RESULTS

The first hypothesis was: "The number of courses in the study program that have some form of support for e-learning during the Covid 19 pandemic is significantly higher compared to the number of courses that had some form of support for e-learning before the Covid pandemic 19". With the aim of measuring students' perception of e-learning support before the pandemic compared to e-learning support they had during the Covid 19 pandemic, students were asked the following questions:

1. *Please, try to estimate the percentage of courses in the previous study years ending with 2018/2019 (in overall) where you had some form of e-learning support. Approximately how many courses in % were there?*
2. *Estimate the percentage of courses in previous academic years during the pandemic (2020/2022 in overall) where you had some form of e-learning support. Approximately how many courses in % were there?*

Respondents were offered following answers: *0-20% of courses, 21-40% of courses, 41-60% of courses, 61-80% of courses, 81-100% of courses.* If, the answers belong to 0-20% of the course, ..., 81-100% of the course, we evaluate numerically with grades from 1 to 5, the observed hypothesis can be written as H1: $\mu_1 < \mu_2$. More precisely, the corresponding hypotheses are:

H0: $\mu_1 \geq \mu_2$

H1: $\mu_1 < \mu_2$

As seen in the Figure 1. The majority of the students (N=8) chose the lowest response or 0-20% of the courses meaning they did not perceive there were many online courses. Only one student perceived that there were 81-100% of the courses while the rest of the responses has the similar number of respondents (N=3).

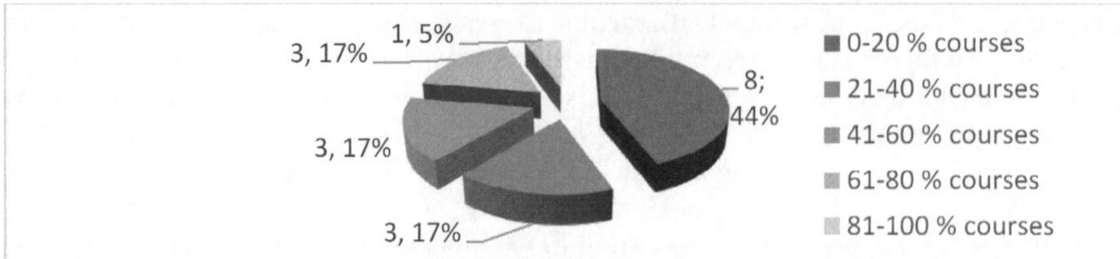

Figure 1. Distribution of students' answers on the 1st question

So when examining the next question (Figure 2) and the improvement on the number of courses we can see that the majority of the students (N=15) choose last two categories or the highest number of courses (61-80% of courses N=7; 81-100% courses N=8). Only one student chose 2nd option, and two students chose 3rd option.

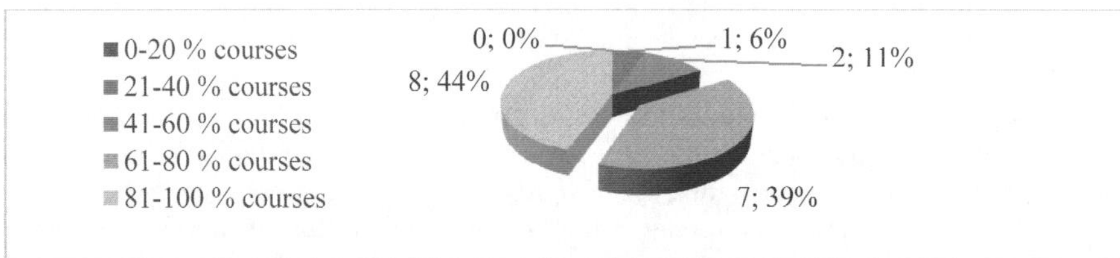

Figure 2. Distribution of students' answers on the 2nd question

If we compare the data of the observed sample on the number of courses that had support in some form of e-learning during the pandemic, where 15 out of 18 students declared that more than 60% of the courses had support, compared to the time before the pandemic, where only 4 of students stated that more than 60% of the courses had support, it is evident, according to the perception of the students who answered the above questions from the survey questionnaire marked 1 and 2 in the paper, that the number of such courses increased significantly during the pandemic. We will confirm this thesis with a t-test and significance level with a probability of 5% error at the level of the entire student population EQF level 7 who had some experience with e-learning before and during the pandemic.

We will evaluate the corresponding answers from 0-20% of the course, ..., 81-100% of the course numerically with grades from 1 to 5, and based on the students' statements, we get the given average grades $\overline{x_1} = 2{,}22$, $\overline{x_2} = 4{,}22$, with associated variances$s_1^2 = 1{,}83$, $s_2^2 = 0{,}77$. To be able to perform a t-test we have to check the equality of standard deviations; therefore, we set-up hypotheses:

H0: $\sigma_1 = \sigma_2$

H1: $\sigma_1 \neq \sigma_2$

We want to confirm the hypothesis H0 with a significance level of 5%. We count:

$$F = \frac{s_1^2}{s_2^2} = \frac{1{,}83}{0{,}77} = 2{,}38.$$

As the$F_{0.05}^{(d)} = 2{,}67$ and $F_{0.05}^{(l)} = \frac{1}{F_{0.05}^{(d)}} = \frac{1}{2{,}67} = 0{,}37$we conclude: $2{,}38 = F \not< F_{0.05}^{(l)} = 0{,}37$,

regarding$2{,}38 = F \not> F_{0.05}^{(d)} = 2{,}67$, i.e., F is neither in the left nor in the right critical region, therefore we accept the hypothesis H0 – therefore, at a significance level of 10%, the standard deviations are equal. Now, we can perform the corresponding t-test. For that purpose, we count

$$s_p^2 = \frac{(n_1 - 1)s_1^2 + (n_2 - 1)s_2^2}{n_1 + n_2 - 2} = \frac{(18 - 1) \cdot 1{,}83 + (18 - 1) \cdot 0{,}77}{18 + 18 - 2} = 1{,}3,$$

$$t = \frac{\overline{x_1} - \overline{x_2}}{\sqrt{s_p^2 \left(\frac{1}{n_1} + \frac{1}{n_2}\right)}} = \frac{2{,}22 - 4{,}22}{\sqrt{1{,}3 \cdot \left(\frac{1}{18} + \frac{1}{18}\right)}} = -5{,}26.$$

Because $t_{0.05} = 1{,}69$, follows $-5{,}26 = t < -t_{0.05} = -1{,}69$, i.e. t is in the critical region, therefore we reject the hypothesis H0, that is, we accept the hypothesis $H1(\mu_1 < \mu_2)$; we conclude, with a significance level of 5%, according to student's perception, the number of courses that have some form of support for e-learning during the Covid-19 pandemic is significantly higher compared to the number of courses that had some form of support for e-learning before the Covid 19 pandemic. Furthermore, by comparing the quantitative indicators of the number of courses in the subject study that list and/or have access to literature within the e-learning system, i.e. generally have published teaching materials, it's evident that there were incomparably more such courses during the Covid-19 pandemic. We can conclude that students' perception was that there were more e-courses offered to them.

Next, we focused on the learning content and student's perception of the quantity and quality of the published materials offered to them through the e-learning system. This was important to gather feedback if students' felt they had enough materials to be able to study and learn in the similar matter as in the face-to face environment. On the observed sample, we examined students' perception of the number and quality of published teaching materials before and during the Covid-19 pandemic. To evaluate the amount of teaching materials offered to them, the students were asked the following question:

3. *Is there a difference in the amount of published teaching materials in the e-learning systems before and during the pandemic (you are free to estimate)?*

They were offered following answers numerically marked 1-5: *Significantly less was published; Less was published; Everything remained about the same; More was published; Significantly more was published.* Hence, according to the quantitative indicators, we set-up hypothesis: during the Covid 19 pandemic, more or significantly more teaching materials were published in the e-learning system compared to the time before the Covid 19 pandemic. As previously, we marked the offered answers, numerically in order from 1 (Significantly less was published) to 5 (Significantly more was published), the observed hypothesis is $\mu \geq \mu_0 = 4$.

More precisely, the hypotheses are:

H0: $\mu \geq \mu_0$

H1: $\mu < \mu_0$.

We will test the hypothesis H0 with a significance level of 5%. Based on the observed sample (Figure 3.) the majority of the students (N=11) did not experience any improvements in the quantity of materials and chose the answer "Everything is approximately the same" while only the minority felt the improvements. Four students felt that there were more published materials while 3 students felt there is a significant increase in the published materials.

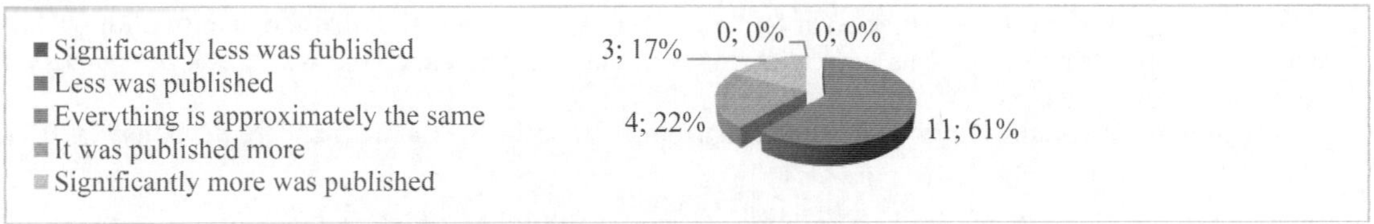

Figure 3. Distribution of students' answers on the 3rd question

Considering that the majority of the respondents, 11 out of 18 of them, answered (question 3) that the amount of published materials in e-learning systems during the pandemic remained approximately the same compared to the time before the pandemic, according to the students' perception, it is to be expected that the amount of published material in e-learning systems during the pandemic did not increase significantly. We will check this thesis at the level of the entire population with a t-test and a significance level of 5%.

According to the student's answers, we get an average grade $\bar{x} = 3.56$ and a standard deviation $s = 0.78$. As it follows:

$$t = \frac{\bar{x} - \mu_0}{s/\sqrt{n}} = \frac{3{,}56 - 4}{0{,}78/\sqrt{18}} = -2{,}39 < -1{,}74 = -t_\alpha,$$

we reject the hypothesis H0, i.e., we accept the hypothesis H1. Therefore, with a significance level of 5%, we conclude that, according to the students' perception, during the Covid 19 pandemic, no more or significantly more teaching materials were published in the e-learning system compared to the time before the Covid 19 pandemic.

Finally, we examined the students' perception of the quality of published teaching materials during the Covid 19 pandemic in relation to the quality of published teaching materials before the Covid 19pandemic. For this purpose, students were asked the following question:

4. *Is there a difference in the quality of published teaching materials and the quality of teaching in e-learning systems before and during the pandemic (your free assessment)?*

They were offered the following responses: Significantly lower quality material was published; Lower quality material was published; Everything else remained approximately the same; Higher quality material was published; Significantly higher quality material was published. We posit the expected hypothesis: during the Covid 19 pandemic, the teaching materials published in the e-learning system are higher or significantly higher quality compared to the teaching materials published before the Covid 19 pandemic. Again, we will mark the offered answers, numerically in order from 1 (Significantly lower quality material was published) to 5 (Significantly higher quality material was published). Now, the expected hypothesis is $\mu \geq \mu_0 = 4$. More precisely, hypotheses are:

H0: $\mu \geq \mu_0$

H1: $\mu < \mu_0$.

We have tested the hypothesis H0 with a significance level of 5%. On the basis of the observed sample, (Figure 4.) again the majority of the student (n=14) chose the everything remained and three students perceived that the published materials were of higher quality. Still, one student perceived the quality of the teaching materials of the lower quality.

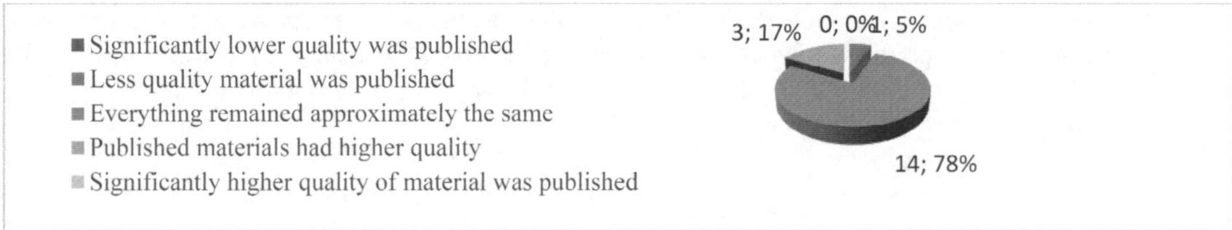

Figure 4. Distribution of students' answers on the 4th question

Similarly, both in terms of quantity and quality of published materials in e-learning systems during the pandemic and according to the perception of students who took part in the survey questionnaire and of whom as many as 15 out of 18 answered (question 4.) that the quality of the published materials in the e-learning system remained the same or that the published material had lower quality compared to the materials before the pandemic, again, it is to be expected at the level of the entire population that the quality of the published materials in the e-learning systems hasn't increased during the pandemic. We will check this thesis with a t-test and a significance level of 5%.

According to the student's answers, we get an average grade $\bar{x} = 3.11$ and a standard deviation $s = 0.47$. As it follows:

$$t = \frac{\bar{x} - \mu_0}{s/\sqrt{n}} = \frac{3{,}11 - 4}{0{,}47/\sqrt{18}} = -8{,}03 < -1{,}74 = -t_\alpha,$$

we reject the hypothesis H0, i.e. we accept the hypothesis H1. Therefore, with a significance level of 5%, we conclude that, according to students' perception, during the Covid 19 pandemic, the teaching materials published in the e-learning system are not higher or significantly higher quality compared to the published teaching materials before the Covid 19 pandemic.

Limitations of the study is the smaller number of respondent as well as focus on one institution. Still, it shows that there is a difference between quantitative data and the students perception. We have identified the problem that should be further researched, and it should encompass various institutions. Furthermore, evaluation should take into account the institutional support for teachers, developing their motivation for participating in e-learning, as well as the continuous professional development of the teachers in the e-learning pedagogy and digital competences.

5. DISCUSSION

Starting from the presumption of increase in the quality and performance of teaching in the online environment during the pandemic period we conducted preliminary research of the e-learning platform and students' perception of the e-learning environment. In order to compare the efficiency and usefulness of the e-learning platform before and during the pandemics we have conducted short preliminary research on a smaller study program level 7 EQF/HKO.

We tested the quantitative aspects such as the number of courses and the amount of the teaching materials on the one hand, and the qualitative aspects such as student perception of the quality of teaching materials. For this preliminary research the following hypothesis were formulated and tested:

1. The number of courses in the study program that have some form of support for e-learning during the Covid 19 pandemic is significantly higher compared to the number of courses that had some form of support for e-learning before the Covid pandemic 19.
2. The amount of the teaching materials in the e-learning system in 2020/2021 has not significantly increased compared to the previous years.
3. The quality of published teaching materials during the Covid 19 pandemic in relation to the quality of published teaching materials before the Covid 19 pandemic.

The respondents were the students who have previous experience in studying before the pandemic. We have chosen a study program on the master's level that has a smaller number of enrolled students to gather better feedback and reliable responses from the whole group participating in the program. The number of respondents was N: 18 out of a total of 24 students enrolled. We were focused on their perception, i.e. whether they think that the number of published materials has really increased and whether these materials have better quality. An online questionnaire was conducted with numerous questions, only some of them have been presented in this paper.

Prior to the questionnaire, the analysis of the quantitative elements published in the e-learning system for the academic years before the pandemic 2017/2018 & 2018/2019 and after the pandemic in 2020/2021 & 2021/2022. The results of the analysis showed that the amount of teaching materials in the Moodle LMS e-learning system for that study programme has not increased significantly compared to the years before the pandemic. As students are not familiar with the information about total number of courses or the increase in the numbers it was interesting to see how they perceived the e-learning platform and its content. This could serve as a starting point for the analysis based on the objective and subjective evaluation or student perception.

6. CONCLUSION

According to the quantitative indicators, during the Covid 19 pandemic, the number of courses that had some form of e-learning support increased significantly. Despite that and also compared to the time before the pandemic, according to student's perception, the increase in publication productivity or significant impact on teaching materials production was not noticeable. In particular, according to the qualitative indicators, this have not resulted in newly published teaching materials in the time of pandemic that were higher or significantly higher quality compared to those published before the period of pandemic. Therefore, based on the conducted preliminary research, it undeniably follows that by increasing the number of online courses during the Covid 19 pandemic, quality of the teaching process and learning materials in the e-learning environment has not increased compared to the period before the pandemic.

In order to assess the quality of the e-learning content we need to integrate evaluation during the period of course teaching in order to get instant feedback from students. As the increase of the learning materials and number of courses is growing we need to develop guidelines and help both teachers and students in the process of evaluation setting out QA indicators for permanent monitoring.

REFERENCES

Alhazzani, N. (2022) Perceptions and Readiness of King Saud University Students Towards Online Learning During the Covid-19 Pandemic. *Proceedings of EDULearn22 14th International Conference on Education and New Learning Technologies*, Palma de Mallorca, Spain. IATED, pp. 4018 - 4028

Banek Zorica, M. Lazić, N. Klindžić, J. (2021) Are we ready for the digital transformation of education? *Proceedings of ICERI2021*. IATED Academy, Valencia, Spain, pp. 8231-8239

Carvalho, P. (2022). Impact of Covid-19 Pandemic on Learning and Teaching: A Comparative Study in a Portuguese Engineering Degree Course. *Proceedings of EDULearn22 14th International Conference on Education and New Learning Technologies*, Palma de Mallorca, Spain. IATED, pp. 7270 - 7274

Ferragut, C.; Vila, H.; Pérez-López, A.; Valades, D.; Abraldes, A. (2022). Adaptation to Online Education During the Covid-19 Lockdown: Analysis from the Perspective of the University Student in Education Degrees. Proceedings of EDULearn22 14th International Conference on Education and New Learning Technologies, Palma de Mallorca, Spain. IATED, pp. 5728 - 5734

Fornasari, A.; Angelini, C.; Conte, M.; Contini, P. (2022). The Evaluation of University Distance Teaching During the Covid-19 Pandemic: An On-Going Italian Research Activity on the Impact of Digital Technologies. *Proceedings of EDULearn22 14th International Conference on Education and New Learning Technologies*, Palma de Mallorca, Spain. IATED, pp. 2247 - 2254

Gonçalves, J.; Engrácio, H.; Rodrigues, F.; Brigas, J.; Gonçalves, F. (2022). New Paths of Teaching and Learning – How Covid 19 E-Learning Experience Shaped the Learning Process and Competences of Communication Students in Polytechnic of Guarda. *Proceedings of EDULearn22 14th International Conference on Education and New Learning Technologies*, Palma de Mallorca, Spain. IATED, pp. 7932-7939

Kampylis, P; Punie, Y.; Devine, J. (2015). Promoting Effective Digital-Age Learning - A European Framework for Digitally-Competent Educational Organisations. *Publications Office of the European Union*, Luxembourg. p. 73

Kovalenko, O. E. et al. (2021) IOP Conf. Ser.: Mater. Sci. Eng. 1031 012118

Mazzola, R.; Bozzi, M.; Testa, I.; Brambilla, F.; Zani, M. (2022). Perception of Advantages/Difficulties of Remote Teaching During Covid-19 Pandemic: Results from a Survey with 3000 Italian Engineering Students. *Proceedings of EDULearn22 14th International Conference on Education and New Learning Technologies*, Palma de Mallorca, Spain. IATED, pp. 2240 - 2445

Muthuprasad, T.; Aiswarya, S.; Aditya, K.S.; Girish K. Jha (2021). Students' perception and preference for online education in India during COVID -19 pandemic. Social Sciences & Humanities Open, Volume 3, Issue 1

Pavlina, K. Banek Zorica, M. Pongrac, A. (2009) Teaching Quality Management at the Course Level. *Proceedings of INFuture2009: The Future of Information Sciences - Digital Resources and Knowledge Sharing*, Zagreb: Department of Information Sciences, Faculty of Humanities and Social Sciences, University of Zagreb, pp. 549-564

Pavlina, K.; Banek Zorica, M.; Pongrac, A. (2011) Student perception of teaching quality in higher education // *Procedia - Social and Behavioral Sciences*, 15 (2011), pp. 2288-2292

Salman, E.; Sharif-Rasslan, A.; Mussa, J.; Fattum, A. (2022). The Contribution of Techno-Pedagogy Courses to Teachers' Selfefficacy in Providing Social, Emotional and Learning Support to Students Through Distance Learning Processes During Covid-19 and Beyond. *Proceedings of EDULearn22 14th International Conference on Education and New Learning Technologies*, Palma de Mallorca, Spain. IATED, pp. 2219 - 2222

Somolanji Tokić, I.; Borovac, T. (2022). What Has Covid-19 Thought Us - Current Issues and Development in University Pre-Service Ecec Education in Croatia. *Proceedings of EDULearn22 14th International Conference on Education and New Learning Technologies*, Palma de Mallorca, Spain. IATED, pp. 2912-2920

UNESCO 2020 COVID-19 Educational Disruption and Response Retrieved from https://en.unesco.org/themes/education-emergencies/coronavirus-school-closures

Zekanović-Korona, L.; Pedić Duić, P.; Grzunov J. (2022.) Self-Efficacy and Satisfaction with Online Learning During Covid-19 Lockdown: Upper-Year and Lower-Year Student Comparison. *Proceedings of EDULearn22 14th International Conference on Education and New Learning Technologies*, Palma de Mallorca, Spain. IATED, pp. 1147 - 1154

Zhu X and Liu J (2020). Education in and After Covid-19: Immediate Responses and Long-Term Visions Switzerland: Springer, pp. 695–699

THE SUCCESS FACTORS OF THE DIGITAL TRANSFORMATION OF HIGHER EDUCATION INSTITUTIONS: THE EXPERIENCE OF HASSAN 2 UNIVERSITY OF CASABLANCA (UH2C) IN MOROCCO

Birahim Babou[1], Khalifa Sylla[2] and Samuel Ouy[1]
[1]Polytechnic High School of Dakar, Computer Science Department, Senegal
[2]Department of Applied Mathematics and Computer Science, Virtual University of Senegal (UVS), Senegal

ABSTRACT

This paper reviews the success factors of the digital transformation of higher education institutions based on the experience of Hassan 2 University of Casablanca (UH2C) in Morocco, which is the second largest university in the country. This work is based on the good practices implemented in the university's digitalization strategy during the covid-19 pandemic.
In order to run all the courses online and allow students to properly follow their lessons, the implementation of a robust and secure system is essential. This paper will take stock of the technical infrastructure of the university which has enabled it to support approximately 130,000 users, then the identification of all the services whose university needed to do its distance learning courses well and a proposal for the new system with the minimum of services that users will need to deliver and follow quality lessons.

KEYWORDS

E-learning, Digitalization, Learning Management System (LMS), Videoconferencing, Digital transformation, Distance education in Morocco

1. INTRODUCTION

According to the Survey on the impact of the coronavirus on the economic, social and psychological situation of households in Morocco carried out by the High Commission for Planning from April 14 to 23, 2020, nationally, 8% of households have children in higher education. The latter, following the suspension of courses in face-to-face mode, found themselves forced to adapt to the requirements of distance education.

After the State's decision on the closure of all higher education establishments for health reasons, a series of measures were taken in this direction by the UH2C. Among these measures, we have the implementation of online courses in a new i-UH2C platform. The UH2C, the second largest in Morocco in terms of enrollment with 125,377 students or 12.66% of the kingdom's students, has started an innovative digitalization project which consists of setting up a scalable distance education system. for the entire university in order to continue the course.

We realize that there are, more and more, higher education establishments that are struggling to offer synchronous distance learning sessions. This problem is becoming frequent because of several factors, including: lack of financial means, isolation perceived by some actors with distance learning, lack of training, resistance to change, data security, lack of work tools and digital services to meet the needs of training, etc. We are also witnessing strong growth in the number of students, in a context of extension and diversification of training offers.

Distance learning is becoming indispensable in higher education institutions. The covid-19 period has only confirmed the need to put in place support solutions for these establishments for the digitization of their profession, which will make it possible to manage UH2C.

In order to run all the courses online and allow all students to properly follow their lessons, the implementation of a robust and secure system is essential. In this article, we will take stock of the university's technical infrastructure, then identify all the services it will need to do its distance learning courses well and a proposal for the new system with the minimum of services that users will need to deliver and follow quality lessons and end up with a conclusion and recommendations.

2. STATE OF THE ART

Distance education is becoming more and more necessary for the transmission of knowledge in higher education institutions and more particularly in Africa. With the lack of means for the creation of physical establishments able to take care of all the demand for training, the integration of distance education in training courses becomes essential and fundamental for the achievement of the objectives within the establishments of higher education.

With information and communication technologies, all the conditions are met to carry out distance learning courses at all levels (primary, secondary and university). One of the major concerns during distance courses is the isolation perceived by the actors (learners, teachers, tutors, administrators, decision-makers, etc.) during synchronous sessions. This training method offers several advantages, including: increased intake capacity, better management of continuing education, improved performance of the establishment and continuity of teaching.

In order to integrate this method in traditional (physical) universities whose courses are face-to-face, a digital transformation is necessary. This transformation must take place in all sectors of activity of the establishment, including educational and research management, administrative management, governance and decision-making as illustrated in the following table.

Table 1. Architecture of the i-UH2C digital system

<table>
<tr><td colspan="9">Smart University: Academic Resource Management (ARM)</td></tr>
<tr><td>ARM</td><td colspan="8">Digital Governance
Steering, Dashboard, Quality, Audit, Communication...</td></tr>
<tr><td>1. You Cannot Manage Unless You Measure</td><td rowspan="3">Ecosystem: partners</td><td>Process Domains</td><td colspan="2">Education</td><td colspan="2">Research</td><td>Administration</td><td rowspan="3">Campus: Students, Staff...</td></tr>
<tr><td>2. But the measures must be meaningful</td><td>Digital Overlay</td><td>Middleware</td><td>Data store & BA</td><td>Platforms</td><td>Apps</td><td>User experience</td></tr>
<tr><td>3. And they lead to action</td><td>Physical infrastructure</td><td colspan="5">Physical infrastructure</td></tr>
<tr><td></td><td colspan="8">Smart University Architecture</td></tr>
</table>

3. DESIGN OF THE I-UH2C SOLUTION

After several working sessions carried out with the various players in the UH2C system, it emerged that a complete digital transformation of the university's pedagogy would be needed. This transformation will be done through Learning Management System (LMS) solutions, single sign-on systems, videoconferencing systems, automatic backup systems, secure online exam solutions, tracking systems and performance evaluation, teleworking spaces, etc.

The following table illustrates the different digitization axes at the UH2C level. These axes could be used in other educational establishments.

Table 2. Architecture of the i-UH2C digital system

<table>
<tr><th>EDUCATION</th><th>RESEARCH</th><th>ADMINISTRATION</th></tr>
<tr><td>i-UH2C: E-learning platform
Online exam platform
i-Mahara: professional integration
UH2C@Loghate: Language learning
UH2C@Coursea: Online Certification</td><td>- i-Research - Digital research management platform
- Digital Resources
- Open Archives: institutional repository</td><td>- UNIV-HR
- E-Competition
- Digital order desk
- electronic signing
- Tele-reception</td></tr>
<tr><td colspan="2">i-Doctorant: Management of the doctoral student's career</td><td rowspan="2"></td></tr>
<tr><td colspan="2">E-labs: Matlab</td></tr>
<tr><td colspan="3">Digital Work Environment (ENT)
Apogee
Pre-registration
Telework
decision support system</td></tr>
</table>

UH2C is the second largest university in Morocco with 125,000 students, 399 accredited courses, 123 research laboratories, 10 research centers, 2,472 indexed publications, 143 research projects, 2,500 teachers, more than 1,000 administrative staff distributed in 18 establishments.

3.1 State of Play

The architecture of the University is spread over three sites including one main, one secondary and a replication.

A virtualization platform with a more resource-efficient hyperconverged architecture is used. It is made up of a production site with 2 TB of RAM memory and 30 TB of SSD disk, a backup site with 2 TB of RAM memory and 30 TB of SSD disk where more than 25 of the most critical virtual machines have been replicated since the production site and finally a backup site with degraded service of 512 GB RAM with the possibility of replicating 25 other virtual machines from the production site. The image below illustrates the architecture of the University's technology infrastructure.

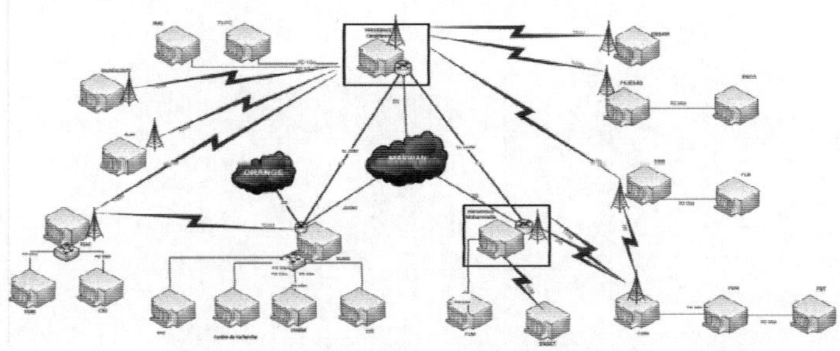

Figure 1. UH2C technology infrastructure

The production site and the backup site come out with a 1 Gbit/s link to the Internet. The backup site comes out with a 200 Mbit/s link to the Internet. The emergency and backup site are linked to the production site with dedicated 100 Mbit/s operator links.

3.2 Identification of the Different Needs and Services to be Implemented

In this article, we will come back to the methodology for implementing a few critical applications such as the LMS Moodle platforms, the videoconferencing system, the digital work environment (ENT), the central authentication system (CAS) as well as the technical architecture that will host this entire system.

3.3 Sizing of the i-UH2C Solution

The study and dimensioning of an adequate architecture for the implementation of an evolutionary and stable "E-learning" online teaching system are made to ensure high availability and a permanent and continuous service for the whole actors from the university (see figure 5). This study made it possible to define: the number of virtual machines (VM) to be created to manage all the actors of the university; the operating system to put on each server; the capacity (Disk Space, RAM, processor) of each VM; IP addressing; the services to be set up on each System (see figure 6).

3.4 Architecture of the i-UH2C Platform

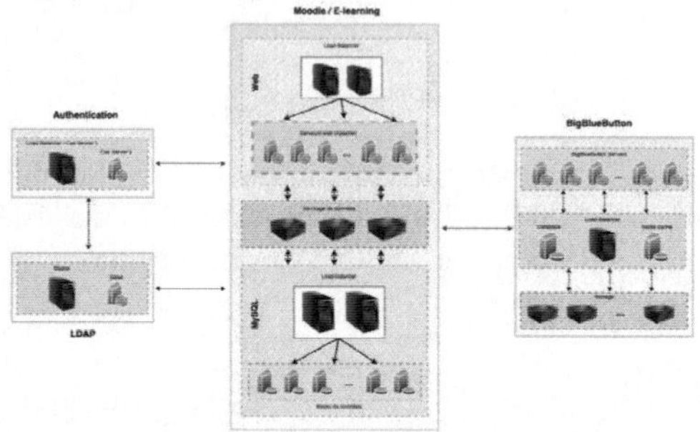

Figure 2. Technical architecture of the i-UH2C platform

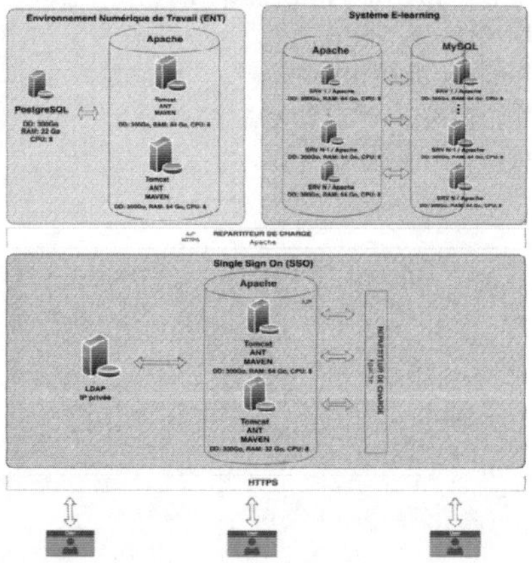

Figure 3. Architecture of the "E-learning" distance education system

3.5 Some Components of the i-UH2C System

3.5.1 The Learning Management System (LMS)

After several studies and working sessions, the Moodle platform remains the most suitable for our context. The no longer proven Moodle LMS allowed us to manage all distance learning, teacher training, telecommuting, etc. This platform dedicated to course learning with an interactive dimension simultaneously integrates:

- a course schedule;
- videoconferencing, chat and forum tools;
- virtual classroom creation;
- a student management module;
- management of course usage statistics, user logins, etc.;
- a complete dashboard.

To allow all users to access the system, we have set up a centralized system for managing access to training platforms (Figure 7). A user, depending on his attachment to an entity (teacher of a faculty, student of a school, etc.) only accesses the courses to which he must have access. Access management and administration of the various LMS platforms is done through this system.

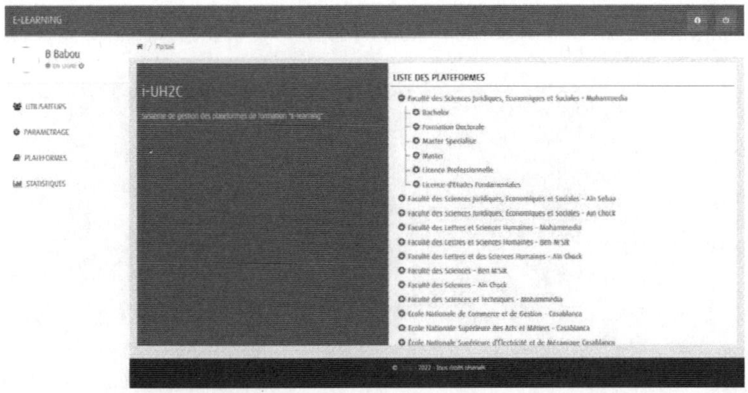

Figure 4. System for centralizing access to training platforms

The teleworking platform, based on Moodle, is accessible on https://teletravail.univh2c.ma as shown in the following figure.

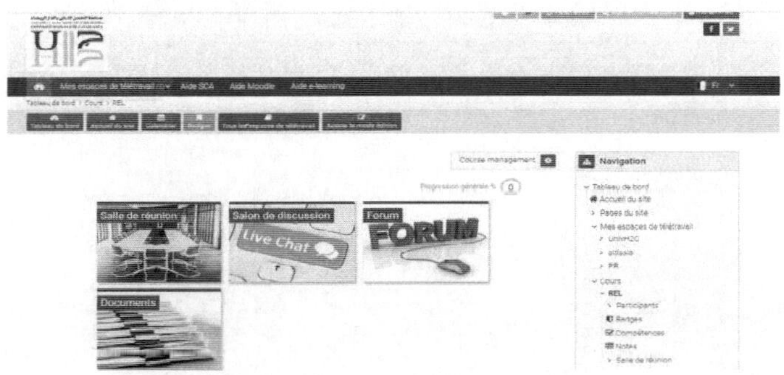

Figure 5. UH2C Teleworking Platform

3.5.2 Videoconferencing

In order to allow system users connected to the Moroccan network Academic and Research Wide Area Network (MARWAN) to access video conferencing and other applications for free, BigBlueButton (BBB) was chosen as the video conferencing system. Around ten instances have been installed to allow for around 1,500 simultaneous connections.

Figure 6. UH2C BBB videoconferencing system

3.5.3 The Centralized Authentication System

The Central Authentication System (SCA) based on the highly available Central Authentication Service (CAS) is installed in compliance with the university's graphic charter. This system is directly connected to the university's (production) LDAP directory. It should be noted that user registration for courses is done automatically. The CAS is installed on 2 servers with a load balancer to ensure the high availability of the system (see figure 10).

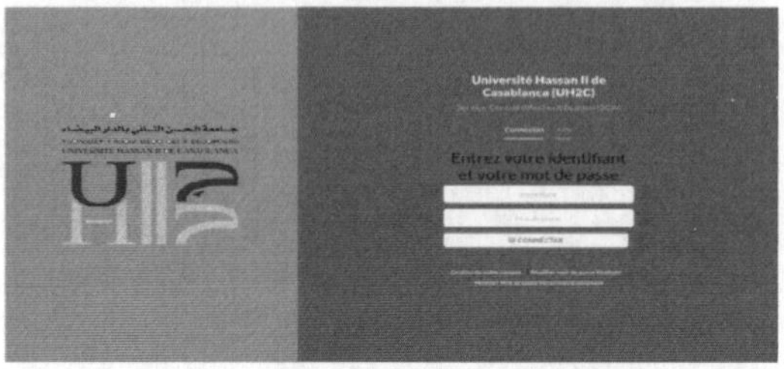

Figure 7. Central Authentication System (CAS)

3.5.4 The Digital Work Environment (ENT)

The Digital Work Environment (ENT), based on Esup Portail is distributed over 3 servers in order to allow high availability.

Figure 8. Digital Work Environment (ENT)

4. SYSTEM SECURITY AND SCALABILITY

To guarantee security of access to the system, an SSL certificate is installed on all platforms and applications. Each web application is on a different virtual machine from the one where its database is installed. Indeed, security plays a very important role in the information system (IS); therefore, all the applications implemented must only be accessible in https.

The load on the server at a given moment depends on the number of simultaneous users executing a task but not on the total number of user accounts and no longer on the number of connected users. Concurrent users, for Moodle and BBB, are considered to be those performing an action at time T on a given server. The rough general rule for a single server is:

- The maximum number of concurrent users = RAM (GB) * 50
- In consultation = maximum number of concurrent users * 5.

The rule applied to our case gives the following results:

- Maximum concurrent users: 64 * 50 = 3200
- In consultation: 3200 * 5 = 16,000 users connected

In this case, the web server and the database server are separate; this therefore greatly exceeds our needs for simultaneous connections.

Each BigBlueButton (BBB) video conferencing server can take up to 250 concurrent connections which gives 250 * 10 (number of instances installed) = 2,500 concurrent connections for BBB.

5. TRAINING OF THE VARIOUS ACTORS AND SUPPORT FOR CHANGE

For a better handling of the distance education system of the University Hassan II of Casablanca (UH2C), practical training sessions for the benefit of teachers and administrators of platforms of the various establishments of the university have been carried out online. more specifically on the platform dedicated to teacher training designed for this purpose (https://enseignements.univh2c.ma). This training lasted one month.

The training took place in the form of sessions from 9 a.m. to 6 p.m. with two (2) establishments per training day. Among the modules unfolded, we have: Presentation of the UH2C system, Discovery of the platform, Course management, the videoconferencing system, how to insert resources in a course, Forum, User management and manipulation, Quiz & Assignment, Roles and rights, Registrations, Advanced settings, Report management, Feedback.

The distance learning project requires profound changes in the operating mode of the teaching-learning process for learners, teachers and other stakeholders (tutors, monitors, etc.). This support project has several axes: raising awareness of the actors on distance training and the digital tools used, the definition of the pedagogical model and internal standards for teaching within the UH2C, the training of teachers in pedagogical engineering and the use of the platform; training tutors in online tutoring and using the platform; internal and external communication on the effects and impacts of the paradigm shift; the multi-channel strategic choice to favor the interactivity of the course of the training.

6. CONCLUSION, PERSPECTIVES AND RECOMMENDATIONS

This platform made it possible to deliver courses correctly throughout the crisis period and is still in use. For better integration, it would be very important to set up a federation of digital identity in order to allow member establishments to be able to share important data and information for good learning.

Each higher education establishment must have a digital center which will be responsible for steering the digital transformation of teaching, research and all other activities. This transformation must be accompanied by an adequate budget with clear activity programs and results to be achieved according to well-defined deadlines.

In addition to this, it would also be necessary to: Reinforce connectivity, set up a high-speed Wi-Fi network in the establishments' e-learning amphitheaters, set up microphones connected to PCs in the classrooms. recording for better recorded sound quality, posting user guides and videos on the creation and scripting of online courses, hosting webinar sessions to support teachers in e- learning; the creation of an educational innovation unit to strengthen support for teachers and students in their establishments.

The current platform occupying more than fifty 50% of the overall capacity of the University's Datacenters, a project to migrate the system to a national Datacenter is under consideration.

The current technological platform will be used as a backup of the one on the cloud. The following figure illustrates the architecture of the new solution that will be deployed.

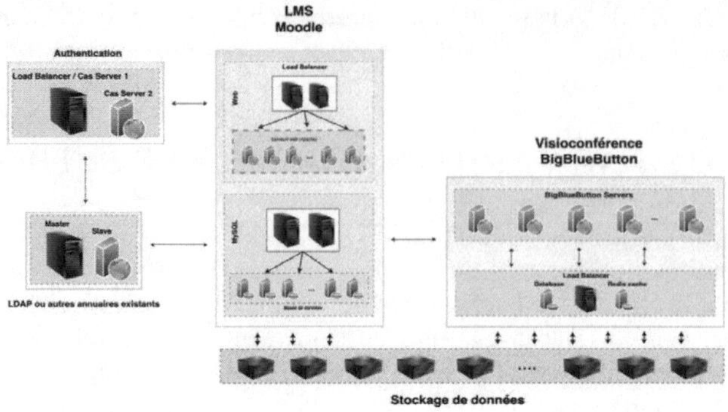

Figure 9. Cloud architecture of the i-UH2C system

REFERENCES

Aguti, B., Wills, GB., and Walters, RJ. (2014). "*An evaluation of the factors that impact on the effectiveness of blended e-learning within universities*," International Conference on Information Society (i-Society 2014), pp. 117-121, doi: 10.1109/i-Society.2014.7009023.

Al-Ajlan, A., and Zedan, H. (2008). "*Why Moodle*," 2008 12th IEEE International Workshop on Future Trends of Distributed Computing Systems, pp. 58-64, doi: 10.1109/FTDCS.2008.22.

BigBlueButton, "*Système de Visioconférence Open Source*". Available online: https://bigbluebutton.org/

Central Authentication Service (2022). Available Online: https://www.apereo.org/projects/cas

ENSSUP (2021). Available online: https://www.enssup.gov.ma/storage/statistique/L%E2%80%99enseignement%20sup%C3%A9rieur%20en%20chiffres%202020-2021.pdf

ESUP-PORTAIL *"Environnement Numérique de Travail (ENT)"*. Available online: https://www.esup-portail.org/

Hantem, A., and Iscae- Rabat, A. (2020). The conditions of distance education during confinement due to COVID19: Case of higher education in Morocco.

Hassan II University of Casablanca (2020). Available online: http://www.univh2c.ma/

Hassan II University of Casablanca Report (2020). Available online: http://report.univh2c.ma/data/opi.php?annee=2020

Hernandez, J. C. G., and Chavez, M. A. L. (2008). "*Moodle security vulnerabilities,*" 2008 5th International Conference on Electrical Engineering, Computing Science and Automatic Control, pp. 352-357, doi: 10.1109/ICEEE.2008.4723399

Makarova, I., Shubenkova, K., Bagateeva, A., and Pashkevich, A. (2018). "*Digitalization of Education as a New Destination of E-Learning*," 2018 International Symposium ELMAR, pp. 31-34, doi: 10.23919/ELMAR.2018.8534662.

Modular Object-Oriented Dynamic Learning Environment - Moodle (2022). Available online: https://moodle.org/

Moroccan National Research and Education Network (2018). Available online: https://www.marwan.ma

Ndassimba, N. G., Kossingou, G. M., Ndassimba, E., and Ouya, S. (2021) "*Contribution for the continuity of courses at the University of Bangui in the context of COVID-19*," 2021 IEEE Global Engineering Education Conference (EDUCON), pp. 792-797, doi: 10.1109/EDUCON46332.2021.9454151

Ouya, S., Mbacke, A. B., Mendy, G., Diouf, P. W., and Sy, K. (2015). "*Social network integration to e-learning environment*," 2015 IEEE/ACS 12th International Conference of Computer Systems and Applications (AICCSA), pp. 1-4, doi: 10.1109/AICCSA.2015.7507222.

Survey on the impact of the coronavirus on the economic, social and psychological situation of households in Morocco carried out by the High Commission for Planning from April 14 to 23, 2020

SHORT PAPERS

USING E-STUDY MATERIALS TO PROMOTE MATHEMATICS SELF-LEARNING AT UNIVERSITY

Anna Vintere[1], Sarmite Cernajeva[2] and Vera Gosteine[2]
[1]Latvia University of Life Sciences and Technologies, Liela Street 2, Jelgava, Latvia, LV-3001
[2]Riga Technical University, Zunda krastmala 10, Riga, Latvia, LV-1048

ABSTRACT

At present, issues of the education system and quality improvement are topical in the whole world. Today, universities need to be prepared to offer young people education that makes them competitive in these new working conditions. When considering development of the education, they shall understand necessity of changing both content and form of the studies. As today's youth grow in an era of digital technologies and is dwelling in a virtual environment, they increasingly are demanding flexible study format that complies with their usual habitat. Therefore, the main task of universities and other higher educational establishments at this time of change is to develop intellectual skills, exploratory research attitudes and build ICT skills in a new specialist. Mathematical study programs and didactics need to be improved on the basis of ICT (paying more attention to the application of mathematics, including using ICT), creating modern technology-based learning materials and ensuring the Internet access. In order to increase students' responsibility for the learning process and to promote the ability to independently acquire knowledge, skills and abilities, it is necessary to create the preconditions for self-directed learning in higher education institutions, that is, students themselves participating in setting the purpose of studies, planning the acquisition of the subject, presentations, and evaluating their work together by agreeing on final assessment with the assessment of peers and teachers. As known, e-studies and self-assessment tests are the basis of self-directed learning. Therefore, the purpose of this research is to determine the use of various e-study materials in the learning of a mathematics course, as well as the importance of tests in the self-assessment of mathematical knowledge and skills. The findings of this study include the analysis of the usage of e-study materials and tests for assessing students' mathematical knowledge and skills, as well as determination of the importance of self-assessment tests in the learning of a mathematics course, based on the students' opinion.

KEYWORDS

E-studies, Mathematics, Self-Assessment, Self-Directed Learning, Remote Studies

1. INTRODUCTION

At present, issues of the education system and quality improvement are topical in the whole world. Today, universities need to be prepared to offer young people education that makes them competitive in these new working conditions. When considering development of the education, they shall understand necessity of changing both content and form of the studies. As today's youth grow in an era of digital technologies and is dwelling in a virtual environment, they increasingly are demanding flexible study format that complies with their usual habitat. Therefore, the main task of universities and other higher educational establishments at this time of change is to develop intellectual skills, exploratory research attitudes and build information and communication technologies (ICT) skills in a new specialist. As result, nowadays information and communication technologies are increasingly being used in higher education and training (Crampton et al, 2010).

At a time when is talked about the quality of universities and its improvement, two of Latvia's largest technical universities: Latvia University of Life Sciences and Technologies and Riga Technical University use e-study systems based on the Modular Object-Oriented Dynamic Learning Environment (MOODLE) e-learning platform. The e-study system makes the life of every student easier, as long as he wants to make his learning process more efficient, modern and faster. With the e-study system, university studies can be accessed from anywhere and at any time.

Each subject has a separate section, where it is possible to cooperate with both fellow students and teaching staff and learn about the issues related to learning the course and, of course, to use the e-study environment to learn the content of the relevant course. The teacher of each course offers students a variety of opportunities to study independently and prepare for exams.

The mathematical learning environment is also influenced by the development of information technology (Galbraith & Haines, 1998). Information communication technologies are used also in the mathematics studies of both universities to independently learn the available informative and interactive e-materials, solve tasks with mathematics software, find the necessary information, collaborate online, etc. In both universities, the e-study environment contains various learning materials that were used as a supplement to full-time mathematics studies, organizing students' independent work, evaluating knowledge and skills, as well as communication between students and teachers, keeping track of grades and test results, list of lessons or other changes etc. (Vintere et al, 2022).

Although ICT has been an important part of higher education for a long time, it was crucial during remote studies, when students had to put more effort to decide and choose what to focus on, identify things that are successful and areas that might need a little more work. This type of responsibility for one's education is characterized by self-directed learning (Vintere et al, 2021). Self-learning is an important part of higher education both in the context of the fourth industrial revolution and sustainable development (Briede, 2019). To increase students' responsibility for the learning process and to promote the ability to independently acquire knowledge, skills and abilities, it is necessary to create the preconditions for self-directed learning in higher education institutions, that is, students themselves participating in setting the purpose of studies, planning the acquisition of the subject and evaluating their work and the progress of studies. The purpose of this research is to determine the use of various e-study materials in the learning of a mathematics course, as well as the importance of tests in the self-assessment of mathematical knowledge and skills.

2. MATERIALS AND METHODS

The information provided by the MOODLE system was used for this study, regarding the students' activities during the mathematics courses taught by the authors of this article, as well as the results of student surveys. Another functionality offered by the e-system of both universities is obtaining student feedback through surveys, which are conducted at least once a semester. Internet survey is one of the most modern and advanced research methods. This is also one of the most commonly used research methods. An objective opinion on the question of interest can be obtained by clearly and precisely defining the points of the questionnaire and selecting certain respondents.

The obtained data are essential for improving the quality of studies. After careful evaluation of the collected data, decisions are usually made to improve the quality of mathematics teaching. This study also uses the results of a student survey on the importance of self-assessment tests in the learning of a mathematics course.

According to educational research, the "self-assessment is a process during which students collect information about their own performance or progress; compare it to explicitly stated criteria, goals, or standards; and revise accordingly. Self-assessment method is seen as the most powerful means for a tertiary education organisation to understand and improve its performance. The purposes of self-assessment are to identify areas of strength and weakness in one's work to make improvements and promote learning" (Andrade & Valtcheva, 2009). Therefore, the research used the self-assessment method in two senses:

1) tests for self-assessment of students' mathematics course knowledge and skills;
2) students' opinion about the importance of self-assessment tests in learning mathematics.

3. FINDINGS

The findings include the analysis of the usage of e-study materials and tests for assessing students' mathematical knowledge and skills, as well as determination of the importance of self-assessment tests in the learning of a mathematics course, based on the students' opinion.

3.1 The Usage of e-Study Materials by Students

The results of the study confirm the well-known fact that students' activity in the e-study system increases mainly before the examination period.

In the framework of this study, information on the use of various e-study materials in the 1st and 2nd semesters has been collected. As indicate results in Table 1, the assessments obtained represent the top interest of students. The examples of tasks solutions and lecture notes are the most used teaching aids, whereas students show a little interest about informative materials like syllabus, requirements for successful completion of a subject, examination requirements and sources of literature.

Table 1. Number of views of different e-study materials

	1st semester	2nd semester	During lockdown
Informative materials	3.6%	2.2%	38%
Lecture notes	14.5%	12.7%	80%
Samples of problem solving	15.4%	19.2%	72%
Descriptions of laboratory work	13.2%	11.0%	-
Formulas	5.2%	11.5%	20%
Tasks for independent work	7.5%	10.0%	18%
Self-assessment tests	12.2%	5.3%	22%
Assessments obtained	28.4%	28.1%	-

Comparing student activities during the two semesters, it should be concluded that in the 1st semester, lecture notes, descriptions of laboratory work, as well as self-assessment tests of knowledge and skills are used more. In the 2nd semester, the focus of students is more on problem solving samples, and various formulas are used more, which can be explained by the fact that the study content of the 2nd semester includes derivatives and integral calculus.

As known, due to the Covid-19 lockdown, studies in all universities were organized remotely, causing a series of challenges that are usually not relevant in a face-to-face learning environment. This, of course, also changed students' habits of using e-study system and learning materials, which it contains. As seen in Table 1, very rapidly increased the usage of lecture notes, samples of problem solving as well as usage of other informative materials. During that time lectures were given on Zoom or another video-conferencing platform, where a teacher wrote and explained the course content step by step and solves practical exercises. Video recording of theses lectures were used by students very often. It should be noted that laboratory works were not organized during lockdown, as both universities are using commercial software MATLAB.

3.2 Tests for Assessing Students' Mathematical Knowledge and Skills

Compilation of tests for the students' knowledge assessment is the most used one out of multiple e-studies functionalities. The evaluation of student knowledge through online testing is a relatively new method for assessing and checking knowledge. It provides ample opportunities for modernizing and optimizing the learning process. However, the attitude towards assessing the level of knowledge through tests is still unclear. Reasonable question arises: does testing produce objective results? Because of this, it must be said that today's tests are significantly different from those used a few years ago. Test theory is one of the directions in the science of pedagogy, which is rapidly developing. Adherence to the basic laws of this theory allows for the development of test systems that can be effectively used at different stages of the learning process.

Literature (Dunlosky et al, 2013) describes in detail 10 key teaching methods and evaluates their relative usefulness. Student testing is referred to as one of the main methods and has received a high-performance appraisal.

As usual, new ideas, trends and methods generate controversy. Although the use of tests can only be considered a relatively new method, polar opposite testimonials of tests, their usefulness and the objectivity of knowledge assessment can still be heard. Sometimes the same arguments sound from both sides i.e. from those who are for and from those who are against knowledge testing.

Arguments against:

- tests lower the role of the teacher;
- tests do not allow to comprehensively assess the knowledge, its depth, etc.

Arguments in favour:

- tests reduce the capacity of the study process;
- tests allow you to objectively assess the knowledge to be tested, etc.

This article attempts to answer the question: "Does testing really give objective results and what to do to obtain them?" Testing itself most often does not cause any significant problems. Important parts of this process are:

1) The determination of the goals to be tested;
2) The choice of the correct type of questions;
3) The exact wording of the question;
4) The evaluation and interpretation of test results.

The goals we want to achieve through these tests must be set before the start of the test (Appleby et al, 1997). If there are several goals, their importance should be determined, the non-essential objectives should be discarded, and the same number of questions should be drawn for each important objective.

When selecting the type of questions, it must be considered that the author of the choice questions (these are questions that ask students to choose the answer from the proposed options) should anticipate possible mistakes. It is therefore better to choose the questions students can answer themselves. The question should be short and clearly worded, simple, easy to understand. The question must not pose problems for the student; it must be done in a way so that the student can answer it using a textbook, remembering facts and algorithms (Boesen et al 2010). Better yet, if questions can be compiled in such a way as to test intermediate results and track errors (Seeman, 2015).

The evaluation and interpretation of results is also an essential part of testing, since without a comprehensive evaluation of the results it is impossible to conclude what needs to be addressed in the future, how to improve the learning methods and the quality of the study process. The mathematical and statistical methods that make it possible to efficiently use computer hardware at this stage and thus to automate and optimize the tasks foreseen are widely used for the evaluation of test results.

In recent years, the authors have collected and implemented a series of tests in the e-study environment, which serve as an important self-assessment tool and help students to improve their mathematical competences.

The results of the mathematics course tests during the 1st semester discussed below (Table 2): the first column - the average rating for the first attempts, the second column - the average rating for the last attempt, the third - the average rating for the best attempt.

Table 2. Number of views of different e-study materials

	First attempt	Last attempt	Best attempt
Determinants	82%	97%	97%
Operations with matrices	63%	80%	81%
Systems of linear equations	65%	80%	82%
Linear operations on vectors and dot product	55%	61%	62%
Cross product and mixed product of vectors Straight line in a plane	66%	79%	80%
Analytic geometry in three-dimensional space	49%	67%	69%
Limits	52%	68%	69%
Differential calculus of a function of one variable	78%	82%	83%
Extrema of functions. inflection points and asymptotes of a function	71%	83%	85%

Taking all the test ratings together, we get the following results: 63.83% average in the first attempt, 65.98% in all attempts, 79.84% - in the final and 81.69% - in the best attempt. From the Table 2 can be concluded that often the first attempt is not the most successful, while the last attempt is mostly the best. The best results were obtained in the test "Determinants" and the test "Limits", while the worst results are in both Analytical Geometry tests - "Straight line in a plane" and "Analytic geometry in three-dimensional space".

Comparing the number of students who completed the test at least once and - the number of total attempts, it should be noted that the number of students who completed the tests is decreasing on 41%. There are two reasons for this: first, some students leave university in the middle of the 1st year, secondly, students grow tired by the end of the term and perform less of the tasks and tests.

3.3 Tests for Assessing Students' Mathematical Knowledge

Comparing the number of students with the maximum score to the number of students who completed the test (Table 3), we see that in nine of the tests, more than half of the students gave the perfectly correct answer, while in the three tests, the correct answers were given by less than half of the students. Of course, this has an impact on the study results.

Table 3. Number of students (%) who received the maximum score

	First attempt
Determinants	92%
Operations with matrices	59%
Systems of linear equations	58%
Linear operations on vectors and dot product	33%
Cross product and mixed product of vectors Straight line in a plane	46%
Analytic geometry in three-dimensional space	41%
Limits	74%
Differential calculus of a function of one variable	63%
Extrema of functions. inflection points and asymptotes of a function	58%

Considering the specifics of the mathematics subject (notes of mathematical relations, drawings, formulas, etc.), the preparation and adaptation of self-assessment tests to the e-study system is a very labor-intensive process and requires a lot of effort from teachers. Despite this, self-assessment tests play a decisive role in ensuring self-directed studies and promoting competence, which results from the development trends of society. Self-assessment tests are also highly valued by students.

The survey results show, that most of the students consider that even self-assessment tests are needed, as they help master the material, learn from mistakes and be better prepared for the exam, etc. (Table 4).

Table 4. Students' opinion about the self-assessment tests

	First attempt
Help to be better prepared for exam	43%
Help better understand the topics and to learn from mistakes	63%
Had a significant impact on the final grade	15%
Helped to understand the tasks of the independent works	34%
Contributed to the motivation to learn mathematics	26%

4. CONCLUSION

Not all learning materials in e-studies are used by students. Only about one fifth of students regularly use problem solving samples. A summary of grades and assessment obtained is usually a resource of primary interest to students, which leads to the conclusion that the e-study system serves mainly the so-called non-learning activities.

During the Covid-19 lockdown, remote studies changed the habits of students to use the e-study system and the learning materials contained in it, with a very rapid increase in interest in lecture notes and video recordings, as well as problem solving samples. This means that in order to increase students' responsibility for the learning process and promote the ability to independently acquire knowledge, skills and abilities, it is necessary to create stricter prerequisites for self-learning in universities.

Results show, that self-assessment tests play a decisive role in ensuring self-directed studies and promoting self-competence development. Self-assessment tests are also highly valued by students in achieving mathematics course study results.

When the outcome of data of self-assessment tests had been compared with the final course results, there could be observed a correlation: generally, students who show good results in the self-assessment tests are successful at other assessment tests, including exam.

As the study mainly used the self-assessment method, so the results were based on the opinion of the respondents and therefore the results cannot be generalized, but can be used to identify problems and identify future actions or research directions.

REFERENCES

Andrade H. and Valtcheva A., 2009. Promoting learning and achievement through self-assessment. Theory into Practice, 48, pp. 12-19.

Appleby J. et al, 1997. Diagnosys - a knowledge-based diagnostic test of basic mathematical skills. Computers & Education, 28(2), 113-131.

Boesen et al, 2010. The Relation between Types of Assessment Tasks and the Mathematical Reasoning Students Use. Educational Studies in Mathematics 75, no. 1, pp. 89–105. Crampton A. et al, 2010.Vodcasts! How to unsuccessfully implement a new online tool. *Interaction in Communication Technologies and Virtual Learning Environments: Human Factors*, pp. 118-128.

Briede B., 2019, Students' self-directed learning in the context of industrial challenges: Latvia University of Life Sciences and Technologies case. Proceeding of 5th International Conference on Higher Education Advances (HEAd'19) Valencia. Spain, June 26-28, 2019, pp. 685.-694.

Dunlosky J. et al, 2013. Improving students' learning with effective learning techniques: Promising directions from cognitive and educational psychology. Psychological Science in the Public Interest, 14(1), 4–58.

Galbraith P. and Haines C., 1998. Disentangling the nexus: Attitudes to mathematics and technology in a computer learning environment. *Educational Studies in Mathematics,* 36, 275-290.

Seemann E., 2015. Unit Testing Maths. In: Conole, G., Klobučar, T., Rensing, C., Konert, J., Lavoué, E. (eds) Design for Teaching and Learning in a Networked World. EC-TEL 2015. Lecture Notes in Computer Science(), vol 9307. Springer, Cham.

Vintere A., et al, 2022, A comparative study of the organization of a remote mathematics study process during the Covid-19 pandemic. *Mobility for Smart Cities and Regional Development - Challenges for Higher Education: proceedings of the 24th International conference on Interactive Collaborative Learning (ICL2021).* Technische Universität Dresden, India : Springer Nature, 2022, pp. 7631-7636.

Vintere A. et al, 2021, Challenges and benefits of remote learning in context of competence development of engineering students during Covid-19 pandemic. *20th International scientific conference "Engineering for rural development" :proceedings*. Jelgava, Vol. 20, pp. 1663-1671.

USING ZOOM MEETING PLATFORM AS A SYNCHRONOUS ONLINE LEARNING TOOL IN EFL CLASSROOM AT INDONESIA TERTIARY LEVEL: A LITERATURE REVIEW

Berlinda Mandasari, Akhyar Rido and Heri Kuswoyo
Faculty of Arts and Education, Universitas Teknokrat Indonesia, Indonesia

ABSTRACT

The outbreak of Covid-19 pandemic affects educational system around the world. Online learning is no longer an option, but a compulsory during this pandemic. This paper is to identify how far synchronous online learning in English as foreign language learning at higher education implemented. This study focuses on the use of Zoom meeting platform as technological devices that supports synchronous online learning as well as identifying the students' perception and challenges faced by both lecturers and students in Indonesia. This study applies systemic literature review (SLR) approach by collecting research articles from Google Scholar indexed database. There are twenty-seven articles published in 2020-2022 that meet the criteria which are reviewed. This paper results the voices from students related to the advantages and disadvantages during using using Zoom Meeting platform in EFL classroom as well as the challenges faced by both lecturers and students. The result of this paper can provide insight toward the use of Zoom Meeting platform as technological devices that can be adopted as synchronous teaching tool during social distancing. However, the Zoom user should consider the availability of stable internet connection and teachers' and students' readiness.

KEYWORDS

Synchronous, Online Learning, English Language Learning, Zoom Meeting Platform, Indonesia

1. INTRODUCTION

In the last two years, online learning has grabbed much attention among students, teachers, lecturers, practitioners and researchers globally due to the outbreak of covid-19 pandemic. Online learning is a learning model that enables students and teachers to carry out teaching learning process remotely supported by digital platforms (Nartiningrum, N., & Nugroho, A., 2020; Mandasari, 2020). The advancement of information and communication technology (ICT) innovation in higher institutions enables learning conducted anywhere and anytime (Fitria, T. N., 2020). In Pakistan, implementing online learning is not as effective as conventional learning (Adnan, M., & Anwar, K. 2020) due to internet access, monetary issues, and no budget allocated on technologies for education sectors (Basilaia & Kvavadze, 2020). Meanwhile, online learning in Canada is reported to be successfully implemented in terms of students' academic outcomes and instructional standards (Lemay, d. J., Bazelais, p., & Doleck, t., 2021).

Two models of online learning are introduced; they are asynchronous and synchronous learning. Asynchronous learning refers to online or distance education that does not require teachers and students to have meeting at the same time. Teachers may provide learning materials via email, web, blog, and other learning management system (Fitria, t. N., 2020). The students can download the materials, complete assignment, send the documents' back to their teachers. Clear instruction for students can be the key success of asynchronous learning. Meanwhile, synchronous learning refers to the online teaching happen in real time which are available on some online learning and video conferencing platforms, such as Zoom Meeting, Google Hangout, and Facebook live (Jiyoon & Peggy, 2019).

One of platforms used as synchronous learning tool is Zoom meeting platform. Zoom meeting platform is somewhat popular nowadays. Putri, N. A., & Suryaman, M. (2022) defined Zoom meeting platform as a platform used as a tool for medium of communication in the form of spoken, written and video consisting of several practical, low-cost, and user-friendly features that suit the users' need.

2. METHOD

A systemic literature review (SLR) is done by reviewing papers published in between 2020 to 2022 identifying students' perception in EFL learning using Zoom meetingplatform as well as uncovering the challenges in implementing it. The review process consists of three steps; planning stage, implementing stage and final stage. In term of planning stage, the researchers specify research questions, construct a review result, and validate the result. In term of implementing stage, the researchers identify relevant topics, choose primary studies, evaluate the quality, extract and synthesize the topics. Lastly, in term of final stage, the researchers comprise writing and validating the report.

3. USING ZOOM MEETING PLATFORM IN EFL LEARNING AT HIGHER EDUCATION LEVEL IN INDONESIA: PERCEPTIONS AND CHALLENGES

3.1 Students' Perception toward Using Zoom Meeting Platform in EFL Learning

Students respond positively toward the use of Zoom meeting platform. In terms of supporting students' active participation, a study conducted by Mu'awanah, N., Sumardi, Suparno (2021) revealed that EFL students show positive perception toward Zoom. It is found that learning English by using Zoom meeting platform help them to understand the material easier because Zoom meeting platform enables lecturers and students to have two-way communication (Haryana, L., Hardiyanti, S., & Yudaningrum, P., 2021). A study conducted by Fatoni, M (2021) found that Zoom meeting platform provides effective and comfortable learning process that raise students' spirit to conduct English debate activities. At this point, lecturer functions as a guide and facilitators who have to give clear instruction in order that the learning process can be done effectively. Having Zoom video conference at this emergency remote learning helps lecturers and students to carry out learning (Sumardi, S., & Nugrahani, D., 2021). Lecturers can prepare teaching materials, provide some discussion topics,give questions and feedback, and allow students to have presentation face-to-face virtually. Lecturer is the one who can control the class to make the students focus during the class. This is the biggest challenge for lecturers to make sure that the students are physically and emotionally ready (Jefiza, 2019) for having lecture either on camera or off camera. Therefore, lecturer' instruction is important. It is believed that there should be no different in way of teaching in both face-to-face classrooms setting and in virtual classroom setting by using Zoom meeting platform. Students must be ready for having class; well-dressed, on camera, and on time.

Another study revealed that students positively respond that Zoom meeting platform provides complete features (Rahayu, 2020; Mu'awanah, N., Sumardi, Suparno., 2021; Fitria, T. N., 2020; Rahmat, A., & Fachrunnisa, N., 2021). Zoom meeting platform provides features that both teachers and students can possibly share the materials, conduct group discussion, send message, and record the teaching activities. All these features help to shift the traditional teaching process into modern one (Octaviani, A. Y., 2021). Furthermore, Zoom Meeting Platform provides a live situation that may reduce social isolation and foster students' engagement and motivation that leadto meeting the learning objectives (Hu and McGeown, 2020). In addition, students' motivation affects their willingness to communicate in English. Therefore, maintaining emotional connection during the Zoom video conference is important. In short, Zoom video conference has a complete features that encourage English teachers, through rich experiences with students, to explore and evaluate the abilities of students.

Apart of positive perception, some studies revealed that students respond negatively toward using Zoom in EFL classrooms. A study reported by Putri, N. A., & Suryaman, M. (2022) found that Zoom is ineffective to improve students' speaking ability. After having one-year-online learning, students are too bored having discussion via online. Students' boredom becomes the major factor that demotivates them to learn English especially in Speaking skill. As a result, students' speaking ability is difficult to improve. Another study from Helda, T., & Zaim, M. (2021) revealed that Zoom video conference is ineffective in supporting learning Microteaching lectures. In terms of conducting teaching simulation, the students face inadequate network that pause the Zoom session. Consequently, this activity results delayed respond during discussion, answering questions, giving feedback, practices, playing video and sound. In addition, the microteaching lecture not only requires students to master the teaching materials, but also masters the theory of classroom management, psychology of education, classroom assessment and others. When the microteaching course is conducted via online, the students do not have place to practice those theory. Zoom meeting is an effective tool as a virtual class application for some few courses, but not for microteaching course.

3.2 Challenges on Using Zoom Meeting Platform during EFL Learning

Some studies found that inadequate internet access and network become the major challenge in conducting onlinelearning. Not all area in Indonesia have good access on internet. Students studying from home, but living in a remote area often experience bad internet connection that result them to have in optimal learning process. Bad internet bandwidth results an unclear voice, bad delivered materials, lack of direct lecturer-students interaction, noisy and wasting a lot of internet quota. (Mu'awanah, N., Sumardi, Suparno. 2021, Rahmat, A., & Fachrunnisa,N., 2021). Besides, utilizing Zoom meeting platform requires big internet bandwidth and big space on users' personal computer, mobile phones or laptop. Lecturers and students sometimes experience system failure where the personal computers, mobile phones or laptop stop working (Mu'awanah, N., Sumardi, Suparno. 2021). This condition results pending in chat, material delivery, lag and worsen the students' engagement during learning. In other words, internet speed can determine the smooth running of teaching and learning process (Dharma et al., 2017). The system of Zoom is not a-user-free access. There must be an extra cost for the lecturers and students who want to have Zoom official account.

Another challenge in using Zoom is that there is less interaction between students and lecturers. Interaction is somewhat that influences the successful of learning process (Rido, A., Kuswoyo, H., & Ayu, R., 2020). Meanwhile, direct interaction in the online classroom setting slow down the values of teaching and learning process (Helda, T., & Zaim, M. (2021). Teaching is not only an act of transferring knowledge, but also changing the students' attitude and facilitating students to grow during learning. In addition, the learning process tends to be training rather than education. Furthermore, the information communication technology (ICT) adaptation from lecturers and students affects the smooth running of the learning process.

4. CONCLUSION

To conclude, students have positive and negative perceptions. Students' positive perception during using Zoom can be described that Zoom supports active participation and provides complete features. Students can conduct two-way communication among lecturers and friends in the forms of discussion, presentation, asking questions, giving feedbacks and effective to improve students' engagement physically and emotionally. On the other hands, students do agree that Zoom platform provides complete features that enable lecturers and students to have small group discussion, share the materials/video, send message, monitor the participants, allow students to speak as well as asking permission to speak. These complete features have significant impact towards students' motivation to learn English. However, students also have negative perception toward using Zoom in EFL learning. To some courses, Zoom meeting might be helpful. But, Zoom is not effective to the teachingof microteaching, speaking skill, and debate course. These practical courses require more than just a theory-based teaching.

Some challenges are also identified. Both lecturers and students agree that bad internet connection and inadequate internet quota become the major challenges in teaching EFL students. These factors cause pending intext, material delivery, lack of direct interaction, and system failure that demotivate students and decrease students' engagement.

This study has some limitations. The data obtained from literatures have limited numbers and do not represent the cases from universities from all provinces. This study can be generalized. The finding of this study must have further analysis using interview and observation to present holistic data. It will help to prepare the future EFL learning effectively.

ACKNOWLEDGEMENT

We would like to extend our highest appreciation to Directorate General of Research, Technology, and Community Services Ministry of Education, Culture, Research, and Technology Republic of Indonesia for granting this research (Grant number 1421/LL2/PG/2022; 050/UTI/LPPM/E.1.1/VI/2022) and Universitas Teknokrat Indonesia for supporting this research.

REFERENCES

Adnan, M., & Anwar, K. (2020). Online Learning amid the COVID-19 Pandemic: Students' Perspectives. *Online Submission*, *2*(1), 45-51.

Basilaia, G., & Kvavadze, D. (2020). Transition to online education in schools during a SARS-CoV-2 coronavirus (Covid-19) pandemic in Georgia. *Pedagogical Research, 5(4),* 1-9.

Fatoni, M. (2021). Students' Perceptions on Using Zoom Application in Debate Course during Crisis RemoteTeaching. *New Language Dimensions*, *2*(2), 88-95.

Fitria, T. N. (2020). Teaching English through online learning system during Covid-19 pandemic. *Pedagogy:Journal of English Language Teaching*, *8*(2).

Haryana, L., Hardiyanti, S., & Yudaningrum, P. (2021). The English Teachers' Experiences in Applying Teaching Strategies during Covid-19. *Linguists: Journal of Linguistics and Language Teaching*, *7*(2), 107-122.

Helda, T., & Zaim, M. (2021). Effectiveness of The Zoom Meeting Applications In Micro Teaching Lectures In The Pandemictime COVID-19. In *English Language and Literature International Conference (ELLiC) Proceedings* (Vol. 4, pp. 128-135).

Jiyoon, Y., & Peggy, S. (2019). Educational Technology and Resources for Synchronous Learning in Higher Education. IGI Global.

Lemay, D. J., Bazelais, P., & Doleck, T. (2021). Transition to online learning during the COVID-19 pandemic. *Computers in Human Behavior Reports*, *4*, 100130.

Mandasari, B. (2020). The Impact of Online Learning toward Students' Academic Performance on Business Correspondence Course. *EDUTEC: Journal of Education and Technology*, *4*(1), 98-110.

Mu'awanah, N., Sumardi, Suparno. (2021). Exploring EFL students' perception of using zoom during learning from home period. PROCEEDING AISELT (Annual International Seminar on English Language Teaching), 6(1), 191-204.

Nambiar, D. (2020). The impact of online learning during COVID-19: students' and teachers' perspective. *The International Journal of Indian Psychology*, *8*(2), 783-793.

Nartiningrum, N., & Nugroho, A. (2020). Online learning amidst global pandemic: EFL students' challenges, suggestions, and needed materials. *ENGLISH FRANCA: Academic journal of English language and education*, *4*(2), 115-140.

Octaviani, A. Y. (2021). The use of zoom cloud meeting for teaching English grammar in an online class. *RETAIN*, *9*(2), 88-92.

Putri, N. A., & Suryaman, M. (2022). Students'perception of Using Zoom Meeting for Online Learning in Teaching English Speaking Skill in Times of Covid-19. *ELite Journal: International Journal of Education, Language, and Literature*, *2*(2).

Rahmat, A., & Fachrunnisa, N. (2021). An Analysis of Applying Zoom Cloud Meeting Towards EFL Learning in Pandemic Era Covid-19. *British (Jurnal Bahasa dan Sastra Inggris)*, *10*(2), 114-134.

Rido, A., Kuswoyo, H., & Ayu, R. (2020). Interaction management strategies in English literature lectures in Indonesian university setting. *Indonesian Journal of EFL and Linguistics*, *5*(2), 315-337.

Sumardi, S., & Nugrahani, D. (2021). Adaptation to emergency remote teaching: Pedagogical strategy for pre- service language teachers amid COVID-19 pandemic. *Turkish Online Journal of Distance Education*, *22*(2), 81-93.

LEARNING SYSTEM USING CROSS REALITY TECHNIQUE FOR PHYSICAL ELECTRONIC CIRCUIT CONSTRUCTION AND VIRTUAL MID-AIR OPERATIONS

Atsushi Takemura
Tokyo University of Agriculture and Technology
2-24-16, Naka-cho, Koganei-shi, Tokyo 184-8588, Japan

ABSTRACT

Science and technology education necessitates teaching and learning experiments involving electronic circuit construction and measurements using experimental equipment. In this study, a novel cross reality system for learning physical circuit construction and performing virtual experiments using virtual experimental equipment with mid-air haptics is proposed. The proposed system possesses a technical novelty that enables a learner to operate virtual equipment with the same motions of his hand and fingers as the operations of the real equipment. An evaluation test using 150 patterns of virtual experiments verified the proposed system's effectiveness.

KEYWORDS

e-Learning, Experiment, Electronic Circuit, Cross Reality, and Mid-Air Operation

1 INTRODUCTION

To acquire the knowledge and skills of creating high technologies (e.g., electronics and robotics), science and technology education necessitates experiments involving electronic circuit construction and the operation of experimental equipment. However, most educational institutions have difficulties in ensuring a sufficient number of materials and equipment for experiments because of high costs and student-to-instructor ratios. To solve this problem, several education systems have been developed, such as virtual measurements of electric circuits (Garcia-Zubia, 2017) and online experimentation in engineering education (Lei, 2021). However, image-based learning using conventional systems does not enable the learning of the real operations necessary for experiments (e.g., measurement using experimental equipment). To overcome this shortcoming, this study proposes a novel cross reality (XR) system that enables learners to learn the physical circuit construction and experiments involving the virtual operation of experimental equipment with the same motion and tactile stimuli as the real experiments. This proposed system is useful for learners with only small and inexpensive physical components (e.g., circuit boards and devices) for circuit construction but not large-sized and expensive experimental equipment.

The remainder of this article is organized as follows. Section 2 presents the technical features of the proposed system. Section 3 presents the experimental methodology for evaluating the proposed system. Section 4 presents the quantitative evaluation of the proposed system. Finally, Section 5 presents the conclusions of this study.

2. TECHNICAL FEATURES OF THE PROPOSED SYSTEM

Figure 1(a) schematizes an experiment with the construction of a physical circuit and operation of virtual equipment indicated on a PC monitor. The device generating mid-air haptics is placed between the constructed circuit and PC monitor. This device comprises ultrasonic phased-array transducers and a hand-tracking camera. Subsections 2.1 and 2.2 describe the technological novelties and features of the proposed XR system.

2.1 Acquisition of the Circuit Image and Virtual Measurements

During the physical circuit construction, a web camera, connected to the learner's PC, acquires image data of the constructed circuit and transmits the data to the remote analysis system. This analysis system performs image recognition to identify the experimental circuit. Moreover, as shown in Figure 1(b), the analysis system performs a circuit translation (Takemura, 2020) that can automatically translate the information obtained from the circuit-recognition process into a general circuit-description language—simulation program with integrated circuit emphasis (SPICE) (Rabaey). Based on this SPICE information, the analysis system can simulate how the constructed circuit works and provide the learner with the virtual measurement results. Corresponding to the hand motion for the virtual operation and measurements with mid-air haptics (described in Subsection 2.2), the learner can watch the workings of the constructed circuit and measure the circuit characteristics.

2.2 Virtual Operation of Experimental Equipment with Mid-Air Haptics

To realize mid-air operations for the virtual measurements of the physical constructed circuit, this study proposes a novel technique combined with the automated recognition of the motions of a learner's hand and fingers using a three-dimensional (3D) motion sensor (hand-tracking camera) and tactile stimuli (mid-air haptics) obtained from airborne ultrasound [Figure 1 (a)]. The proposed system allows a learner to draw lines using a graphics editor to indicate the wiring between an image of the constructed circuit and images of the experimental equipment (e.g., oscilloscope and function generator). In addition, the system has the following novel technical features: (1) it enables a learner to operate the virtual experimental equipment with the same motions of his hand and fingers as the experiment using real (physical) equipment and (2) it gives a learner's hand and fingers the tactile stimuli when operating the virtual equipment. To automatically recognize the motions of a learner's hand and fingers and generate the tactile stimuli, the proposed system is developed using a device equipped with an ultrasound phased array and an infrared-based hand-motion sensor: "Ultrahaptics" (https://www.ultraleap.com/haptics/). Table 1 presents the necessary motions of a learner's hand and fingers for the parameter setting and mode selection of the virtual equipment.

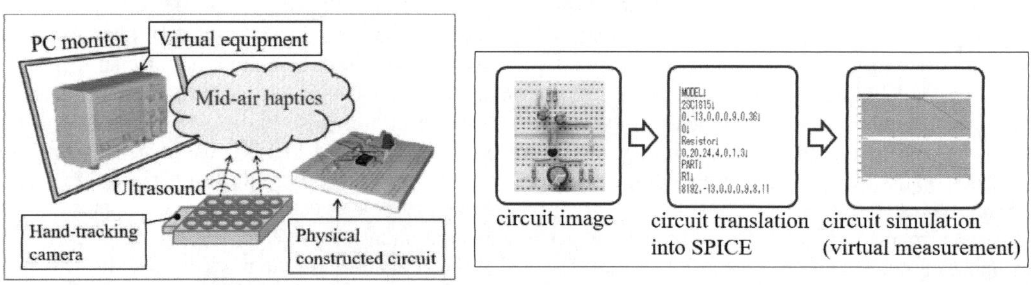

(a) (b)

Figure 1. Schematic of the proposed learning system: (a) composition of the proposed XR system and (b) translation and simulation technique for the virtual measurement

Table 1. Necessary mid-air motions of a learner's hand and fingers for the parameter setting and mode selection of virtual experimental equipment

Virtual equipment	Adjustment of parts of the virtual equipment		
	Rotary knob	Push bottom	Numeric keys
Function generator	Amplitude adjustment	Waveform selection	Adjustment of frequency and a duty factor
Oscilloscope	Position of waveform indications	Channel selection	–
Multimeter	–	Selection switches	–
DC power supply	Voltage adjustment	–	–

3. METHODOLOGY FOR EVALUATING THE PROPOSED SYSTEM

In this study, the proposed system for the virtual operation and measurements with mid-air haptics was evaluated by five students aged 19–22 at the Tokyo University of Agriculture and Technology (TUAT) using physical circuits constructed by 30 undergraduate students in an actual class at TUAT. Therefore, 150 patterns of the experimental results were used for this evaluation. Figures 2(a) and (b) show the circuit diagram of a sixth-order active low-pass filter to be physically constructed in the experiment and the experimenter's system for the virtual operations and measurements with mid-air haptics, respectively. Individual students in the aforementioned class were tasked to construct physical circuits based on the circuit diagram shown in Figure 2(a). Using the constructed circuits, the five students performed virtual experiments involving the operation of the virtual experimental equipment and measurements of the constructed circuits' characteristics using the proposed technique described in Subsection 2.2. Through the evaluation test, the five students checked and reported the effectiveness of the mid-air operations relating to the accuracy of the following points: (1) the positions of finger motions to control the virtual equipment based on Table 1 and (2) the positions and intensities of tactile stimuli obtained from the mid-air haptic device.

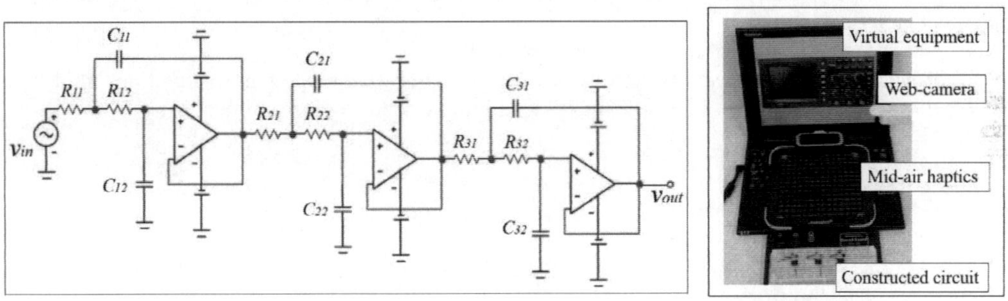

(a) (b)

Figure 2. Circuit to be constructed and XR system for evaluating the proposed technique: (a) the circuit diagram of a sixth-order active low-pass filter using three operational amplifiers and (b) the experimenter's system enabling the operations and measurements with the mid-air tactile stimuli

4. RESULTS AND DISCUSSION

Figures 3(a) and (b) show an image of a physical constructed circuit and the results of the virtual operations and measurements obtained by one student, respectively. This student correctly connected the wiring between the circuit image and virtual equipment and adequately adjusted the setting of the virtual equipment with the necessary motions for mid-air operation, as presented in Table 1. Therefore, this student could measure the correct physical circuit characteristics (e.g., current and voltage) using the virtual multimeter and observe the correct waveforms on the virtual oscilloscope display.

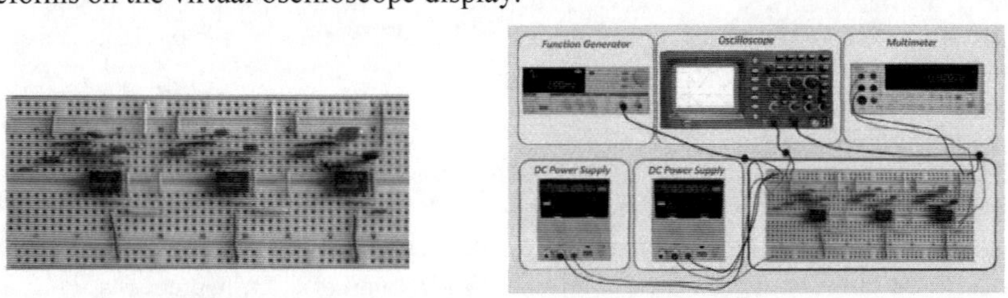

(a) (b)

Figure 3. Result of one student's virtual operations and measurements of the constructed physical circuit: (a) physical circuit constructed based on the diagram shown in Figure 2(a) and (b) virtual operation and measurements using the virtual equipment with mid-air haptics

Through the evaluation test using 150 patterns of virtual experiments by the five students (described in Section 3), the following positive responses, which pertain to the usefulness and efficiency of the proposed system, were obtained from all students.

- The virtual operation of experimental equipment with mid-air haptics is effective because it enables virtual experiments similar to real experiments without the actual equipment and laboratories.
- The positions of the tactile stimuli were accurate. Therefore, the mid-air haptics was effective in improving the reality of the virtual experiments.

However, there are a few technical disadvantages and room for improvement.

- The virtual equipment indicated on a two-dimensional display should be improved using a 3D vision device.
- The accuracy of the recognition of hand gestures when rotating knobs in virtual equipment should be improved because the setting parameters using rotary knobs did not change proportionally with the rotation angle.
- Occasionally, tactile stimuli when operating the virtual equipment were not exact because the ultrasound vibrations of mid-air haptics were given from only a certain direction.

To improve the applicability and usefulness of the proposed system, the following study should be implemented.

- Combination with 3D vision (e.g., volumetric display).
- Improvement of the accuracy and reality of tactile stimuli by developing multidirectional mid-air haptics.
- Quantitative evaluation of mid-air haptics using more circuits and experimenters.

5. CONCLUSIONS

This paper proposes a novel learning system using XR that enables a learner to construct a physical circuit and perform an experiment involving virtual operations using virtual experimental equipment with mid-air haptics on the learner's hand and fingers. The proposed system enables a learner to operate the experimental equipment with the same motion as the operation of real experiments. The evaluation test using 150 patterns of virtual experiments verified the proposed system's effectiveness. In future study, the effectiveness and usefulness of the proposes system will be further improved using 3D vision.

ACKNOWLEDGMENT

This study was partly supported by a Grant-in-Aid for Scientific Research (KAKENHI) 19K03079 from the Japan Society for the Promotion of Science.

REFERENCES

Garcia-Zubia, J., et al., 2017, Empirical analysis of the use of the VISIR remote lab in teaching analog electronics, *IEEE Trans. Educ.*, vol. 60, no. 2, pp. 149–156.

Hasegawa K., et al., 2018, Aerial vibrotactile display based on multiunit ultrasound phased array, *IEEE Trans. Haptics*, vol. 11, no. 3, pp. 367–377.

Lei, Z., et al., 2021, 3-d interactive control laboratory for classroom demonstration and online experimentation in engineering education, *IEEE Trans. Educ.*, vol.64, no.3, pp.276–282.

Rabaey, J. M., The Spice Page, <URL: http://bwrc.eecs.berkeley.edu/Classes/IcBook/SPICE/> (accessed Sep. 10, 2022).

Takemura, A., 2020, e-Learning system for the comprehensive learning of electronic circuits, *Proc. IADIS Conference CELDA 2020*, pp. 349–354.

THE IMPACT OF A SOCIAL ROBOT'S VOICE ON CHILDREN'S LEARNING

Hsiu-Feng Wang and Shin-Lan Shiu
National Chiayi University, Taiwan
621, No.85 Wenlong, Mingsuin, Chiayi Hsien, Taiwan

ABSTRACT

This study employed a single factor experiment to investigate how different voices from a social robot affect the learning outcomes and motivation of 46 children. The learning motivation for the participants was measured using the ARCS questionnaire, which tested for four subcategories: attention, relevance, confidence, and satisfaction. The results showed that a social robot's voice significantly affected children's motivation to learn, with the children preferring a social robot with a child's voice. However, the voice of a social robot exhibited no significant impact on their learning outcomes. The findings of this experiment are of value to those involved in designing children's learning material that uses social robots and to those who work on interaction design with children.

KEYWORDS

Voice, Children, Social Robots, Learning Outcomes, Learning Motivation

1. INTRODUCTION

With the increase in Human-Robot Interaction (HRI) research, the use of robots has become more popular at home, in hospitals, and in schools. Examining what factors affect the way children engage with a robot has thus become an important issue. Research on the voice of a social robot is especially lacking in the current literature. As an interface, it receives far less attention than appearance and gesture (Tamagawa et al., 2011). The focus of this study is to investigate how a social robot's voice impacts children's learning outcomes and motivation. As one of the first attempts to address this relatively disregarded issue, we examined studies not only on social robots, but also pedagogical agents (PAs). The voice of a social robot and PAs are interfaces through which we "speak" to learners. Due to the similarity of these two research areas, we discussed these fields of research together in order to broaden the subject of research.

2. BACKGROUND OF THE STUDY

A number of theories have been developed to understand the interaction between learners and virtual humans (such as social robot or PAs). Social agency theory is one of the most prominent theories and was developed by Mayer, Sobko and Mautone (2003). The theory suggests pedagogical agents (PAs) that add social cues within multimedia presentations can lead to deeper cognitive processing during learning and result in a more meaningful learning outcome. Mayer (2014) suggests three of the most important social cues for PA design are conversational language, voice, and human-like gestures. The element of voice is one of the key features in social agency theory in its examination of cognitive load within multimedia presentations. Therefore, researchers have conducted a number of studies based on principles related to voice as they seek to understand its effect in more detail. Peng and Wang (2022) proposed a meta-analysis which reviewed papers from 2000 to 2019 on pedagogical agents and included a variety of subjects such as environment, learner, role, appearance, and social clues. The papers discovered that social cues, such as voice, had a verifiable impact on student learning.

Mayer and DaPra (2012) conducted three experiments to observe the ways in which a PA's social cues such as gesturing, facial expression, eye gaze, and human-like movement affected multimedia learning. Their results indicated learners performed better on a transfer test when a PA used social cues than when it did not. They also found that students performed better when PAs spoke using a human voice than when using a machine voice. It has now become a widely adopted concept that PAs speaking with a human voice provide learners with a more complete learning experience than PAs speaking with computer-generated voices (Atkinson et al., 2005; Craig & Schroeder, 2017). However, unlike computer-generated voices, human voices are intrinsically prosodic and convey lexical, semantic, and discourse information through sound (Akker & Cutler, 2003). Thus, the nature of a voice cannot be simply categorized as being only either human or machine. Further exploration into this area of research is thus required.

Davis et al. (2019) conducted an experiment to investigate the relationship between human voice conditions and learners. The researchers recruited 172 undergraduate students who were non-native speakers of English to evaluate how strong- and weak-prosodic human voices compared to a computer human voice in terms of the participants' perceived cognitive load, their evaluation of agent persona, and their information retention. With respect to the perceived cognitive load and their evaluation of the agent persona, the results of the study showed that the non-native speakers preferred a human voice with less prosodic elements when compared to a modern computer voice. A recent study by Wang and Li (2019) investigated how children are affected by voice and the PA's physical appearance. More specifically, the researchers examined how the PA's appearance affected the learning and motivation of 42 primary school children. The experiment employed three different appearances which included ones that looked like an adult tutor, a child companion, or an animal, as well as one that only displayed text. In the study, the children watched three different animated PAs presented and narrated by either an adult human's voice (the tutor) or a child's voice (the companion and animal). Their results indicated the children (11-12 year-olds) who watched and listened to the animated learning material presented by the child companion with the child's voice performed better in terms of learning outcome and intrinsic motivation than those who learned with the other two forms.

The above research demonstrates that a PA's (social robot's) use of a human voice and its prosody can influence the learner's perception of the material. However, it is uncertain if a voice from people of different ages—such as that of an adult or child—have any impact on the learner. Thus, more and deeper investigations need to be conducted in this area of study. For this study, we hypothesize that a social robot's voice has an effect on a child's learning outcomes and motivation.

3. METHOD

3.1 Participants and Design

A total of 46 children from the same rural primary school in Chiayi, Taiwan participated in this study. Aged between 11 and 12 years old (M = 11.87, SD = .39), 22 (48.9%) of the children were male and 24 (51.1%) were female. All the children used computers regularly both at home and at school. They all had computer lessons at least twice per week, played computer games, and used the internet. All the participants had a similar level of understanding of the lesson topic (astronomy) to be given by the social robot. The experiment used a within-subject design to test the effects of a social robot's voice on the children's learning outcome and motivation. The experiment looked at both adult and children voices, with the two dependent variables being learning motivation and learning outcome.

3.2 Materials

The experiment used Kebbi social robots manufactured by NUWA Robotics specifically designed for children. The Kebbi social robots were used in the experiment to show the children videos of animated learning material and to conduct the interactive test. The narrations were done by a professional female child voice actor, as well as a professional female adult voice actor who was hired through a voice acting company. Three specialists designed the learning material and test questions for the experiment. Two of the specialists were school teachers, each with over 5 years of teaching experience, while the other specialist was an interaction designer with over 10 years of work experience. The specialists created two sets of learning material, both of which were animated videos suitable for children between the ages of 11 and 12. The specialists also checked and verified that the content and questions in the two sets were at a similar level of difficulty. The three specialists eventually settled on the theme "Understanding the Stars: An Intro to Astronomy" for the media content. The video was divided into three sections. Following each section, the participants needed to touch the social robot monitor to answer five questions. The test was formatted into multiple choice questions with 4 possible answers, and totaled 15 questions over the entire test.

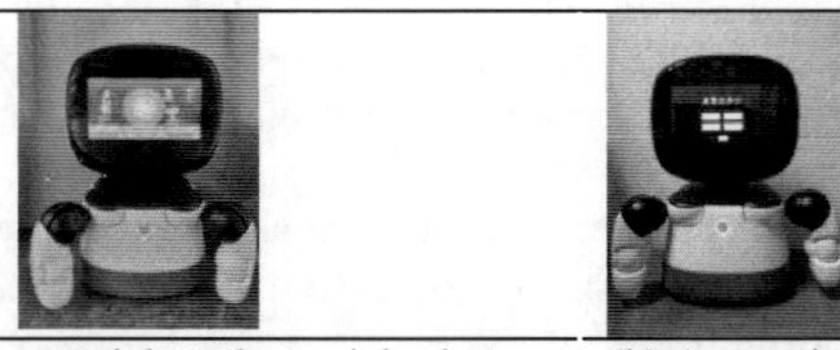

(a) The learning material on the social robot | (b) A question with four possible answers

Figure 1. Social robot used in the experiment

3.3 Procedure

On arrival at the lab, an experimenter collected participants' consent forms signed in advance by their parents or guardians. Each participant was given their own social robot and worked alone. During the experiment, one participant was in the classroom at a time with one experimenter. The experimenter gave oral instructions and demonstrated how to operate the social robot. Participants were told they could interact with the social robot freely for three minutes to familiarize themselves with the social robots. Then, each participant started with a practice round. The practice round involved the children viewing the learning material on the social robot (Figure 1a) and answering two multiple-choice questions about each one.

After the practice round, participants could press "Start" to begin their experiment. Each child viewed the learning material on the social robot, and the material divided into three parts of approximately equal length. When finished viewing each part of video, participants answered multiple-choice questions (Figure 1b) that were displayed randomly. Participants needed to touch the screen on the robot to answer the questions. The participants viewed the material spoken in both an adult's voice and a child's voice. The order to which they viewed the two types of material was random. The children were told they could take as long as they wanted to answer the questions and should click the 'Done' button on the social robot when they finished each video. Upon finishing, they had to complete a motivation questionnaire. No child showed signs of fatigue during the experiment. Before leaving the room, each child filled out a demographic form and received a gift of stationary.

4. RESULTS

A paired sample t-test was carried out to evaluate the social robot's two different voices with respect to the mean scores. The mean and standard deviation of the scores obtained in the tests are displayed in Table 1. It was shown a social robot's voice did not have a significant effect on the learning outcome, $t\ (45) = 1.230$, $p = .225$. However, the results revealed the two different voices from the social robot did result in significantly different scores for the children's learning motivation, $t\ (45) = 2.746$, $p = .009$. With regards to how the children rating their own motivation, they preferred the social robot with a child's voice over the adult's voice.

Table 1. The means and standard deviations for the learning outcome and motivation scores

	M	*SD*
Learning outcome		
children' voice	54.57	8.03
adults' voice	52.66	7.00
Learning motivation		
children' voice	3.42	.624
adults' voice	3.13	.511

5. CONCLUSION

The experiment examined how a social robot's voice affects children's learning outcome and motivation. We tested social agency theory which claims that social cues within multimedia presentations can lead to deeper cognitive processing during learning. We used human voice on social robot as social cues, divided it into an adult or child as a subcategory.

The results showed the social robot's voice had no significant impact on the children's learning outcomes, yet did affect the children's learning motivation. The children preferred the social robot to have the voice of a child over that of an adult as shown by their higher learning motivation with the social robot using the child's voice.

This is in line with social agency theory which suggests social cues can lead to a better learning experience. These results are also in agreement with those obtained by Wang and Li (2019), where they discovered 11- to 12 year-old children preferred PAs that looked and sounded like a child over something like an adult tutor and or an animal.

This experiment clearly shows that a social robot's voice significantly impacts children's learning motivation, and that 11- to 12-year-old children in particular prefer a child's voice over an adult. This research should be useful to educators, instructional designers, and social robot developers who create learning material for children. However, this experiment only focused on the voice of social robot. This is the limitation of this research. Further research is needed to determine how tone of voice (such as accent, gender, etc.) affects a child's learning when interacting with a social robot.

ACKNOWLEDGEMENT

This experiment was kindly supported by a grant from the National Science Council of Taiwan. (Contract number: NSC110-2410-H-415-022).

REFERENCES

Atkinson, R.K., Mayer, R.E. and Merrill, M.M. (2005). "Fostering social agency in multimedia learning: Examining the impact of an animated agent's voice. *Contemporary Educational Psychology, 30*(1), 117–139.

Craig, S.D. and Schroeder, N.L. (2017). Reconsidering the voice effect when learning from a virtual human", *Computers & Education, 114*, 193–205.

Davis, R.O., Vincent, J. and Park, T.J. (2019). Reconsidering the Voice Principle with Non-native Language Speakers", *Computers & Education*, Vol. 103605.

Mayer, R. E. (2014). *14 principles based on social cues in multimedia learning: Personalization voice image and embodiment principles.* The Cambridge handbook of multimedia learning.

Mayer, R. E., & DaPra, C. S. (2012). An embodiment effect in computer-based learning with animated pedagogical agents. *Journal of Experimental Psychology. Applied, 18*(3), 239–252. http://dx.doi.org/10.1037/a0028616

Mayer, R. E., Sobko, K., & Mautone, P. D. (2003). Social cues in multimedia learning: Role of speaker's voice. *Journal of Educational Psychology, 95*(2), 419.

Tamagawa, R., Watson, C. I., Kuo, I. H., MacDonald, B. A., & Broadbent, E. (2011). The effects of synthesized voice accents on user perceptions of robots. *International Journal of Social Robotics, 3*, 253–262. https://doi.org/10.1007/s12369-011-0100-4.

Wang, H. F. and Li, Y. F. (2019). The impact of pedagogical agent on children's learning performance and intrinsic motivation. *Journal of Liberal Arts and Social Sciences, 15*(3), 257-281. (in Chinese)

DESIGNING A GAMIFIED WEB APPLICATION FOR TRAINING ACADEMIC READING SKILLS

Ella Dovhaniuk and Tobias Thelen
Osnabrück University, Germany

ABSTRACT

In this paper, we present didactical, technical, and interaction design aspects of a learning environment for training academic text reading skills in higher education that is currently being developed. The concept is built on experience gained from a gamified learning environment for academic abilities in the domain of German orthography standards. It uses spaced repetition for skill training instead of just memorizing facts and maintains user models that allow for adaptive task selection using expert-designed skill lists and task-skill allocations. Gamification components such as levels and ranks have been incorporated to boost motivation. Only 19% of users (n=121) ceased using the application when they reached the minimum obligatory goal in homework assignments, indicating that the motivational effects work for the target group. The foundation for transferring these experiences to a new domain is laid by analyzing academic reading skills and competencies to be trained. In the design phase, task categories, interface mockups, and gamification mechanisms for the envisioned web application have been sketched, and it will now be implemented as an open-source application.

KEYWORDS

Academic Skills, Gamification, Higher Education

1. INTRODUCTION

In times of excessive growth of information flow, reading is one of the means of learning in the case of the correct psychological and pedagogical approach, as it is estimated that eighty to eighty-five percent of our perception, learning, cognition, and activities are mediated through vision (Ripley et al. 2010). According to the advisory group of the Programme for International Student Assessment, reading literacy is defined as understanding, using, and reflecting on written texts in order to achieve one's goals, develop one's knowledge, and participate in society (OECD 2003). Reading literacy plays an important role among the fundamental academic competencies propagating knowledge for the current information society.

In higher education, skills have to be trained intensively up to a certain level of mastery. These skills include subject-specific skills but also subject-independent skills like the confident use of scientific language and the ability to read academic texts. Often, these skills are addressed in introductory courses, but further development happens implicitly in the further course of study. For students struggling with these skills, long-term and motivating training opportunities might be helpful.

For efficient memorization and repetitive learning, spaced repetition techniques are often applied, either in analog settings such as the "Leitner System" for flashcards (Leitner 1974) or various digital adaptations (Settles & Meeder 2016). Implementations of spaced repetition keep track of the last time a user has been presented a task and the mastery level shown for that task. Tasks with lower mastery levels will be repeated earlier and thus presented more often than tasks with higher levels. For motivation, gamification is a well-known concept of using design elements from games in non-game contexts. It has successfully been used in many different higher education contexts and is usually considered as an additional element in educational settings that are supposed to increase motivation and lead to more prolonged and more intensive engagement with tasks (for an overview, cf. Wiggins 2016). Typical gamification elements are level systems that make progress perceptible and rewards like badges or titles that act as externally motivating goals.

2. EXPERIENCE WITH GAMIFIED ACADEMIC SKILLS TRAINING

The system we are designing for improving academic reading skills follows a model that has already been successfully applied to an academic training scenario. Prospective teachers of German were given a tool to practice the German comma rules coded in the official orthography rules (Rat für Rechtscheibung 2018). This "Kommatrainig" application comprises spaced repetition and gamification elements and has been used by over 2,600 students. It is based on subject-specific skills corresponding to the official rules and subrules, resulting in 30 different skills/rules. Subject experts from teacher education and German linguistics have grouped these skills into a linear order of increasing complexity within each category. As a result, each level (see below) corresponds to one official rule, and as the rules are ordered in increasing difficulty, the levels are also assumed to have increasing difficulty in a general, non-individual way. A comma task always includes a German sentence and requests the user to either set the commas in a sentence, correct a sentence with some commas already set, or select the proper rule for a fixed comma. To be usable for training, sentences have to be labeled with rules for comma positions. Every sentence can have multiple labels corresponding to multiple rules (figure 1).

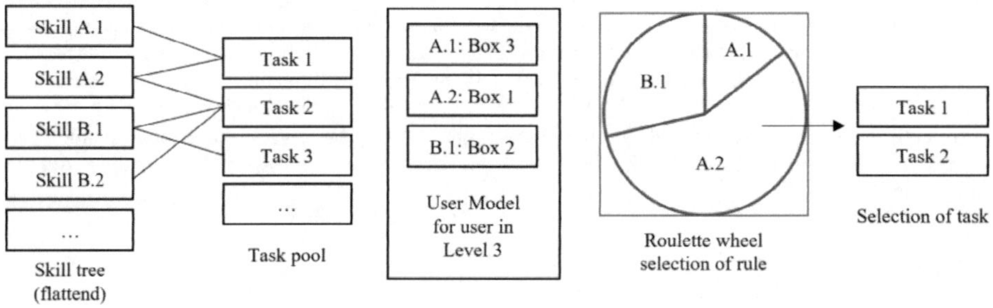

Figure 1. Skills (rules) and tasks as the basis for rule and task selection

The rules are introduced and activated one after another, so the user starts with only one rule and practices it until tasks for that rule have been solved correctly sufficiently often. For introducing a new rule, the last one has to meet two conditions: At least four tasks concerning that rule have been presented, and the majority of tasks for that rule have been solved correctly. For each user, a list of rule proficiency levels is maintained that puts each skill in a box corresponding to Leitner boxes. When selecting the next task to present to the user, first a skill is selected in a roulette wheel selection that assigns higher probabilities to boxes with lower numbers. When applied correctly in tasks, rules start in low boxes and end up in higher boxes. For the selected rule, the concrete task to present is then selected from all tasks for the rule that do not require skills not introduced yet (see user model, roulette wheel selection, and task selection in figure 1).

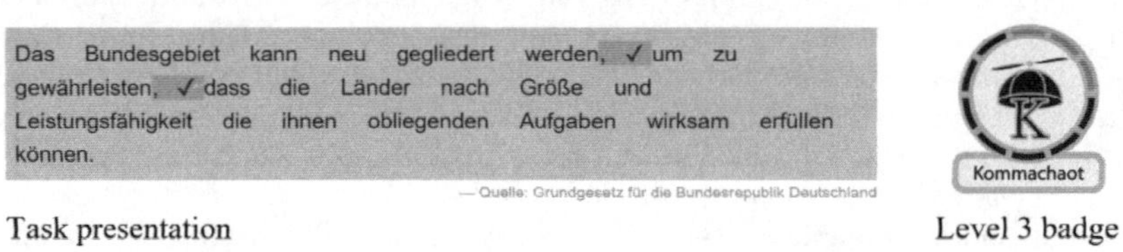

Figure 2. Task presentation and level badge: Here, the user had to set proper commas in a German sentence and now received positive feedback indicating that both comma positions were correct

Tasks are presented in an interactive environment where users can set and erase commas or choose rules from a selection list. After submitting their solution, feedback indicating correct positions and explaining errors is given (see task presentation in figure 2). Simultaneously, the user model is updated, and, if appropriate, new rules are introduced. The rule introduction is associated with the main gamification element used in the "Kommatraining," the level system. Each rule corresponds to a level, so level 30 is the highest level to reach when mastering all 30 rules. Every ten levels, a new rank is reached, beginning with "Kommachaot" ("comma slob") and ending as "comma king" (level 21 and higher). Thus, a level represents the most challenging rule the user has been presented with. A higher level will only be reached when mastering enough tasks involving that rule, i.e., at least four tasks with at least 75% correct solutions. This approach has been chosen to motivate users to not only practice rules they already know but also to feel rewarded when a new, more challenging rule is introduced. The application also uses other gamification elements that are not specific game design elements but are often used in games to increase motivation. These include immediate feedback, a high pace of tasks, a lack of long explanations, and the introduction of the environment as part of the game. Tasks presented to the user can be solved in a very short time, usually less than 30 seconds, and immediately afterward, feedback is provided. Users can have a detailed look at error explanations but don't have to. The first task is presented just two clicks after starting the games, and instructions are if needed, but never block the user experience. The three task types are not introduced simultaneously. The first two levels only give comma-setting tasks, then comma-correcting tasks, and eventually, comma-explaining tasks are introduced. This gives the users time to adapt to both the task types and the increasing complexity of rules.

There is evidence that the gamification elements succeed in creating a high motivation for using the environment. The "Kommatraining" has been used in three linguistics classes for students training to be teachers of German as mandatory homework. To pass the homework, students had to reach the "comma king" rank (level 21). Of n=121 students, only 19% stopped after getting to that level. 46% of the students even continued until they reached the highest level.

3. ACADEMIC READING SKILLS AND COMPETENCES

The general skills of working with text include the ability to predict the content of the text by title, keywords, fragments of text, illustrations, and other non-textual elements that accompany the text; the ability to make simple and complex plans of the text; the ability to present its content (concise, complete, selective); the ability to understand in detail lengthy, complex texts, whether or not they relate to one's own area of speciality, provided he/she can reread difficult sections; the ability to comprehend and critically interpret virtually all forms of written language, including abstract, structurally complex, or highly colloquial literary and non-literary writings; the ability to comprehend a wide range of long and complex texts, appreciating subtle differences in style and implicit as well as explicit meaning; ability to practically distinguish literary and scientific-cognitive texts; the ability to understand the "task" of the work, i.e. to find out to whom it is addressed and for what purpose; the ability to determine the idea of the text, establish the sequence of actions in the text and comprehend the relationships between the events described in it; and determine the author's and own attitude to the presented information.

The formation of reading skills and competences involves the ability to read an unfamiliar text at the appropriate speed and, after one reading, to understand the actual content and structure of the text; divide the text into parts; establish cause-and-effect relationships between sentences and paragraphs; the ability to highlight the main points and details; determine the theme and main idea of the text; choose titles for the text and its parts, etc. Our aim is to gain the appropriate level of reading competences including the ability to use reading as a means of acquiring new knowledge for further study, and the ability to read texts of different genres in different situations, which may also use various forms of information presented (charts, figures, tables, graphs, and diagrams). To help students develop and improve their skills and competences, we offer a set of tasks such as filling in the gaps, matching headings, punctuating a text, sequencing, using linking words, comprehension questions, matching features, matching paragraphs, paragraph completion, text completion, etc. All tasks are tailor-made according to the proficiency levels B1-C1.

We intend to expose students to different types of texts and build their capacity to comprehend the wide range of reading material they will encounter during their studies. To achieve this, we (1) select texts of multiple genres and high quality; (2) ensure that a chosen text contains appropriate vocabulary and has a relevant level of complexity; and (3) align the tasks with the claimed competences. We get articles for appropriate-length, academic-level readings from a variety of sources, including but not limited to those found in academic research databases. Before assigning each reading, we pass it through the text analyzer to check if it contains vocabulary from the Key Academic Word List. Thus, we enable students to master their skills to work independently and productively with the help of our application.

Additionally, we create tasks to work on specific grammar concepts that students struggle with the most (the topics were carefully selected together with the teachers from the linguistic center of the university based on the analysis of the students' tests and written assignments as well as studying research in the field of teaching academic English). We also provide extra activities in various formats that will aid students in expanding their vocabulary and solidifying the lexical units most frequently encountered in academic texts.

4. SKETCH OF THE APPLICATION

The application is currently being developed after the design phase has been concluded. The two main user experience approaches taken are motivation and consistency. For the motivation part, the adaptive learning environment is designed to use mechanisms that have proven effective in higher education scenarios as part of the "Kommatraining". It addresses consistency by using additional elements for rewarding constant everyday use and by stressing out long-term learning success. In the beginning, the application will only cover general aspects of academic texts, but by its concepts, it can easily be extended to cover subject-specific aspects as well. We will use a simple, yet versatile task type: each task presents a paragraph of academic text and prompts the user with one or very few questions about this text (see figure 3). After finishing the reading assignment, students are then given the opportunity to complete a grammar exercise on one of the carefully selected topics. Typically, grammar tasks are organized according to complexity level and taken directly from the text. The learner has the opportunity to choose an extension section after completing this assignment, where additional tasks are offered to practice the specified grammar structure.

As an example, tasks for practicing the use of the passive voice can be in the first level of complexity and in the third one, and if a certain number of tasks of an easier level are successfully completed, the student will be redirected to a more complex level. The grammar tasks contain keywords that connect related tasks on the same grammar topic from various levels. Also, using our application, students have the opportunity to master up to 1,000 lexical units, which are the most important and valuable for academic English. Working with the context increases chances of understanding new vocabulary because it enables students to infer the meaning of numerous words. Regular repetition of lexical units is one of the key strategies for learning vocabulary. If a student has not yet memorized a new word, it should be repeated as frequently as possible so that they have the chance to do so. In our application, this vocabulary practice is scheduled on a regular basis, and students deal with a significant academic vocabulary word list that has been carefully chosen and recurs frequently in contexts and tasks that aid in its memorization.

Sticking to one single general type of task allows for a simple user interface and a gentle start to learning. The variety of question types and the variety of different skills and competences addressed maintains tension during use.

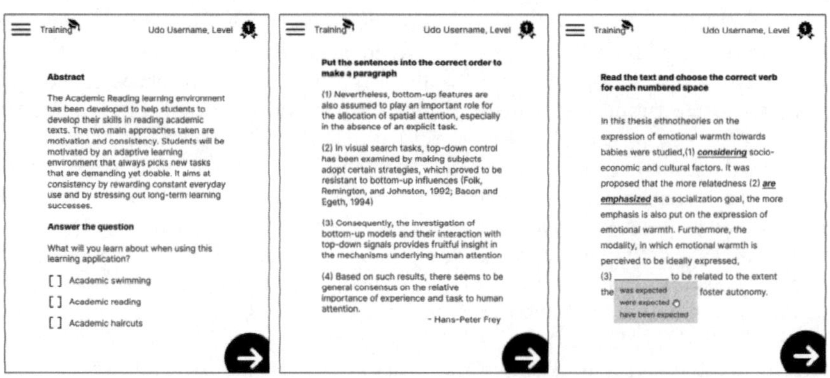

Figure 3. Screen mockup designs of task types and the user interface

Motivation should be increased by a level system like in the "Kommatraining" and various feedback elements. All choices are commented on, especially mistakes, as they bring up a short explanation of why they were wrong. The student can view the original text, verify that the response is accurate, and, if necessary, obtain more information (links to online dictionaries, grammar guides, and methodological instructions are accessible) (optional). Gamification elements like points, usage streaks, and achievements will give users a good sense of their progress and always present goals that can be reached with a bit of extra effort. Being an academic tool, the program will not try to hide these mechanisms from the user but will explain them openly. Users will have the choice to activate or deactivate many of these elements.

5. CONCLUSION

We have presented design considerations of an application for training academic reading skills. The implementation is currently work in progress and will involve students to develop a wide variety of engaging tasks. We assume that by using concepts from spaced repetition learning and gamification elements, the app encourages students to use it as an everyday companion to practice reading academic texts in frequent but short episodes. The key challenge will be to provide a rich pool of tasks covering all the necessary skills, balance the parameters for skill repetition, gain rewards, provide incentives and maintain user interest in the app. We expect the learning environment to be an interesting addition to introductory courses in academic reading and writing and will actively seek cooperation with teachers and students to evaluate its usefulness. Future directions of development include transferring the app to other languages, widening the scope for more non-linguistic aspects of critically reading academic texts, or the inclusion of academic writing tasks. The application and the tasks will use open-access texts only and will be released under an open-source license.

Thus, the proposed approach to the organization of teaching academic reading using the application not only upholds the long-standing customs of teaching foreign languages through technological means but also expands them by making use of essentially new prospects. Experience with the suggested instructional tools has demonstrated their viability and efficacy in contemporary, realizable educational practice. A successful user experience is facilitated by the use of independent and gamified activities which is crucial for the successful acquisition of a foreign language.

REFERENCES

Leitner, S.. 1974. *So Lernt Man Lernen*. Herder, Freiburg, Germany.

OECD, 2003. *The PISA 2003 Assessment Framework - Mathematics, Reading, Science and Problem Solving Knowledge and Skills*. OECD Publishing, Paris, France.

Rat für Rechtschreibung, 2018. Deutsche Rechtschreibung - Regeln und Wörterverzeichnis. Aktualisierte Fassung des amtlichen Regelwerks entsprechend den Empfehlungen des Rats für deutsche Rechtschreibung 2016. Institut für Deutsche Sprache, Mannheim, Germany.

Ripley D. L. et al, 2010. Vision disturbance after TBI. In NeuroRehabilitation, Vol. 27, No. 3, pp. 215-216.

Settles, B. and Meeder, B., 2016. A trainable spaced repetition model for language learning. Proceedings of the 54th Annual Meeting of the Association for Computational Linguistics (Volume 1). Berlin, Germany, pp. 1848-1858.

Wiggins, B.E., 2016. An Overview and Study on the Use of Games, Simulations, and Gamification in Higher Education. In International *Journal of Game-Based Learning,* Vol. 6, No. 1, pp. 18–29.

THE FUTURE OF TEACHING AND LEARNING: FACE TO FACE, HYBRID, AND ONLINE INSTRUCTIONAL DELIVERY MODELS

John W. Hatcher III, Angela King-Corken and Thomas DeVaney
Southeastern Louisiana University SLU 10549, Hammond, LA. 70402, United States of America

ABSTRACT

This research study explores nuances to instructional delivery models beyond the COVID-19 pandemic. A case study that examines the redesign and reimagining of a graduate course to fit the diverse needs and preferences of students. This research was intended to provide insight into the possibilities of redesigning and reimagining graduate level courses for a master of education in educational leadership program at a state university in Louisiana. The research team engaged this case study in order to address the needs of current and prospective students regarding face to face, hybrid models, and online options for course delivery. This case study documents efforts to redesign and reimagine courses using instructional delivery models that meet the diverse needs and preferences of students and potential graduate candidates. While this case study has implications for instructional delivery at every level of education it is a work in progress. It begins to shed light on how graduate programs and course delivery will continue to evolve beyond the Covid-19 pandemic and well into the future.

KEYWORDS

Teaching and Learning & Instructional Delivery Models

1. INTRODUCTION

With the world of teaching and learning turned upside down during the Covid-19 pandemic, new opportunities and necessary changes in instructional delivery have emerged that support greater equity and accessibility to more rigorous teaching and learning possibilities. Bain (2021) stated, "We are in the midst of a profound revolution in teaching and learning. This change has come in the form of a new breed of "Super Courses" that have emerged in the humanities, social and natural sciences, arts, professional fields, and other areas." Bain (2021) went on to express the thought that "these new experiences have appeared in all stages of education" and especially in colleges and universities. Over the past two and one half years the United States of America's education system has undergone transitions from predominately face-to-face brick and mortar classrooms to a variety of fluctuating hybrid models that include synchronous virtual classrooms to online asynchronous classes as a result of the COVID-19 pandemic and the need for continuous learning among students at every level. States, universities, school districts, and individual schools had to navigate the uncertainty of the pandemic, while attempting to provide continuous learning opportunities for their students. PreK-12 schools, as well as, colleges and universities all were faced with the question of how to continue providing rigorous instruction in the context of a raging pandemic. As human beings we adapted to the necessary changes and we rode the wave of uncertainty as we navigated the challenges of Emergency Remote Teaching (ERT) to ensure the safety needs of all stakeholders. Rapanta et al. (2021) noted that as educational professionals we quickly realized the shortcoming of overemphasizing the remote qualities while under emphasizing the dynamic carefully designed learning environment of rigorous Online Learning and Teaching (OLT). Thus we began the process of metacognition in regards to how best to meet the continuous instructional needs of our teaching faculty and our learners. Differentiated instruction 2.0 emerged as we grappled with redesigning courses of study that would be equitable within face-to-face models, hybrid models, virtual models, and online models of instructional delivery that included synchronous and asynchronous formats. Educational organizations initiated priorities that would expand education offerings in response to student and programmatic needs. This study explores the researcher's opportunity to redesigning courses in a graduate level program in educational leadership that meet the diverse needs and preferences of current students and future candidates of the program. The significance of this research will provide program designers and educational practitioners with practical insights into creating more equitable models of instructional delivery that meet the evolving needs of current and future learners.

2. TEACHING AND LEARNING POST COVID-19

The overarching research question was, "What new opportunities in teaching and learning exist regarding instructional delivery beyond the COVID-19 pandemic and are available to teachers and learners going forward?" This question is critical because of all of the strides made by teachers and educators during the period of school closures to redesign and reimagine courses and course material in order to support the continuous learning of students. Bain (2021) wrote,

> In the traditional classroom, instructors might laud the power of comprehension, critical thinking, creativity, and problem solving but often test for memory. Only with improved understanding of evaluation can teachers from grade school to the university focus more clearly on deep learning, adaptive expertise, and the ability to take an idea and realize its implications in a large variety of settings (p.3)"

In response to the pandemic, ERT mandated that courses taught in the traditional face-to-face brick and mortar classroom setting sometimes with the infusion of technology had to be converted to virtual and online platforms. This resulted in a variety of hybrid models and online course delivery. Virtual platforms included the Google Suite and Zoom, which were used to facilitate asynchronous and synchronous course work. The Moodle platform was used to facilitate the online asynchronous aspects of course delivery, while Google Meet and Zoom were used to engage students virtually. This study explores the future possibilities and opportunities for educators to continue providing a variety of course delivery models to meet the diverse needs and preferences of the students they serve going forward.

2.1 Face to Face Classrooms

Traditional face-to-face instructional delivery has been the primary mode of instructional delivery in the United States of America since public education became a part of the fabric of our society. Face-to-face instructional delivery remains a key aspect of teaching and learning at every level of education including the graduate program for educational leadership being explored. This program is a hybrid model that employs fifty percent or more of face-to-face instruction and the balance is delivered online for each course offered within the program. During the COVID-19 shutdown every course transitioned from the model previously described to a virtual and online hybrid model. Every teaching faculty member was required to complete professional development modules in support of this transition. Furthermore, the university offered an opportunity to redesign courses that were offered in the face-to-face and online hybrid model to a one hundred percent online course offering. The researcher engaged this redesign process with one course offered within the context of this master's degree program. The obvious safety concerns of students and teachers during COVID-19 sparked the initial transition to ERT; however, as we get through and beyond COVID-19 concerns some people are excited to be back face to face, while other students and faculty are increasingly requesting the one hundred percent online option.

2.2 Distance Education (DE) Modalities for Delivering Instruction

Researchers have defined Online Learning and Teaching (OLT) as a subset of distance education that uses electronic media in a dynamic and carefully designed learning environment where students experience flexible interactive telecommunication systems which connect learners, resources, and instructors via synchronous, asynchronous, and/or blended modalities (Rapanta et al., 2021; Scoppio & Luyt, 2017). The distance education instructional modalities most often offered during COVID-19 were remote with hybrid and face-to-face as secondary modes for instructional delivery. Table 1 provides a description of the instructional delivery formats offered at the university level during the COVID-19 shutdown. According to the Pew Research, analysis of 2015 American Community Survey Data, at least 15% of U.S. households with school age children did not have access to high-speed internet and many of these households were of a low income status. Thus, educational institutions K-16 had to quickly adapt and modify their workflow strategies while adopting new technologies in situations where students may or may not have access to technologies beyond cellular telephones (Chakraborty et al., 2020).

Table 1. Instructional Delivery Modalities

Instructional Delivery Format (Code)	**Descriptions of course instructional delivery model**
Face-to-Face (F)	Class is attended synchronously in a physical space.
Online (O)	Class is attended 100% online asynchronously
Virtual (V)	Class is attended 100% virtually using an online platform with video conferencing tools, such as Google Meet and Zoom; this model is synchronous.
*Face-to-Face and Online (FO)	Class is attended 50%-99% face-to-face synchronously in a physical space with the balance of the class time delivered online asynchronously.
*Online and Face-to-Face (OF)	Class is attended 50%-99% Online asynchronously with the balance of the class time delivered face-to-face in a physical space synchronously.
*Virtual and Face-to-Face (VF)	Class is attended 50%-99% virtually with the balance of time delivered in a physical space, this model is pre scheduled as synchronous.
*Face-to-Face and Virtual (FV)	Class is attended 50%-99% face-to-face in a physical space with the balance offered virtually, this model is pre scheduled as synchronous.

This table is adapted from University's course delivery formats. Courses with an * indicate hybrid models of instructional delivery.

2.3 Developing Online Courses

The researcher recognized that online course development was becoming more of a priority pre-COVID-19; however, during the COVID-19 shutdown the transition away from face-to-face instructional delivery required immediate attention. The need to address safety concerns accelerated the process of the researcher engaging in the development of a one hundred percent online course offering for a specific course within the master degree program in educational leadership. Leadership researcher Paul Hersey (Schermerhorn, 1997) stated, "Successful leaders are those who can adapt their behavior to meet the demands of their own unique situation." A four session Course Alignment Process (CAP) training workshop offered guidelines for converting courses to a fully online model. The course would undergo an initial review by a Quality Matters (QM) certified reviewer trained in CAP facilitation and a content expert before being taught two semesters to allow the course instructor to gain insight and make necessary modifications based on best practice. The course will then go through a final review and once the course meets CAP certification guidelines it can be certified as a CAP approved course. The course must have a high degree of alignment to course outcomes and objectives, while accessibility levels for students must demonstrate a differentiated approach to rigorous instructional delivery.

3. METHODOLOGY

This research study is a narrative inquiry designed to explore various instructional delivery models that meet the diverse needs of current and potential graduate students in an educational leadership program. Specifically engaging the transition of course design from a hybrid model that includes strictly face-to-face and online course delivery to more diverse models that include face-to-face, virtual, and online hybrids for instructional delivery that meet the changing needs and preferences of current and future students. The researcher uses a narrative approach in order to provide the research consumer with a logical blueprint of a conversion of a graduate level course traditionally offered in a face-to-face and online (FO) model to a one hundred percent online model. A detailed description of the four part training for phase one of this endeavor will follow.

The four workshops, which are scheduled for two hours each are described as follows:

Workshop 1- Workshop 1 focuses on federal, regional, & state accreditation policies. Specifically, federal Web Content Accessibility Guidelines (WCAG), the universities distance education policy and the Southern Association of Colleges and Schools Commission on Colleges (SACSCOC). Additionally, the first workshop initiates the work on course component alignment.

Workshop 2- Workshop 2 delves deeper into WCAG requirements as well as the Universal Design for Learning framework and concludes with Copyright Compliance in Online Learning.

Workshop 3- Focuses on building and maintaining student engagement and interaction in Online Learning. This workshop builds on the idea that instructor presence and authentic assessment are key points in maintaining student engagement in the online platform.

Workshop 4- Focuses on the use of educational technology and specifically Moodle tools to support students in online learning.

These faculty workshops are scheduled two weeks apart and are designed with relevant assignments that are due in between each one. Faculty members complete each assignment and receive relevant feedback from the instructional design team. Faculty members are allowed to teach their newly developed course in order to receive additional feedback and make adjustments before the course is submitted for final approval.

4. CONCLUSION

What does the future of instructional delivery look like for educators post COVID-19? The immediate future of teaching and learning post COVID-19 will revert back to the predominant face-to-face instructional delivery model. However, with the proverbial wetting of the appetite of increased numbers of students and teachers during COVID-19, the researcher admonishes educators at every level to prepare for a growing demand for virtual and online instructional delivery models that will address the diverse needs and preferences of students beyond COVI-19. The researcher has worked to convert one course from a traditional hybrid model to an online model of instructional delivery. Going forward the researchers will engage in the process of developing a hybrid model that includes a balance of virtual synchronous delivery of instruction and an online asynchronous instructional delivery components that will maximize the recruitment of students. This balanced approach to instructional delivery will replace a one size fits all delivery model of courses within a graduate program in order to increase recruitment for and accessibility to the program for a broader range of students with diverse needs and preferences.

The COVID-19 pandemic forced educational practitioners to begin to reimagine an improved educational systems in the United States of America. Specifically, the redesign of instructional delivery models for education organizations at every level. Moreover, graduate level courses offered in an educational leadership program that helps to certify school principals and other educational leaders. Based on the safety needs of students and faculty during COVID-19, as well as, the continuing needs and preferences of current students and those applying to the educational leadership program there must be a greater focus on converting traditional hybrid courses in this program to more nuanced models of hybrid instructional delivery. The 50%-99% virtual delivery with the balance of class time delivered online and the 50%-99% online delivery model with the balance of the class time delivered virtually are the proposed additions for the near future. These new hybrid models would not replace the existing instructional delivery models in the educational leadership program, yet they would add additional instructional delivery models that can help to address the changing needs and preferences of students applying to the program. As educators planning for a viable future, we must elevate the use of technology into the teaching and learning process from simple integration to a total infusion of technology into every aspect of our schools and classrooms. Going forward, the department faculty will engage the four workshops of the CAP training in the fall of 2022. It is anticipated that the first proposed cohort of graduate students to engage the Virtual and Online hybrid model will be forthcoming in the spring 2023 semester. Stay tuned!

ACKNOWLEDGEMENT

We would like to acknowledge our colleagues from Southeastern Louisiana University who continue to go above and beyond in their efforts to ensure course design remains in alignment with the needs and preferences of our students and faculty. You all's time and commitment to excellence and continuous improvement in the teaching and learning process is both admirable and greatly appreciated. Thank you!

REFERENCES

Aslanian, C.B., Fischer, Steven; Kitchell, R. 2022. *Online College Students Report 2022: 11th annual report on the demands and preferences of college students.* Creative Manager, Education Dynamics, Hoboken, NJ:

Bain, K. 2021. *Super Courses: The future of teaching and learning.* Princeton University Press.

Chakraborty, P. et al, 2020. Opinion of students on online education during the COVID-19 pandemic. *Hum Behav & Emerg Tech. 2021*; Vol. 3, pp 357– 365. https://doi.org/10.1002/hbe2.240

Domaleski, C. 2020. The Impact of COVID-19 on ESSA. *Centerline* Vol. 49, https://www.nciea.org/blog/essa/outlook-essa-school-accountability-after-covid-19

Pew Research Center 2021. *As schools close due to the coronavirus, some U.S. students face a digital homework gap.* https://www.pewresearch.org/fact-tank/2020/03/16/

Puckett, C. et al, 2020. COVID-19, Technology, and Implications of Educational Equity. *American Sociological Association,* Vol. *48 No.* 3.

Putman, S.M. et al, 2018. *Action Research: Using strategic inquiry to improve teaching and learning*. Thousand Oaks, CA: Sage Publications.

QM Higher Education Rubric, Sixth Edition, 2018. *Quality Matters. Used under license.* All rights reserved. Retrieved from MyQM. https://www.qualitymatters.org/

Rapanta, C. et al, 2021. Balancing Technology, Pedagogy and the New Normal: Post-pandemic Challenges for Higher Education. *Postdigit Sci Educ* Vol. 3, pp 715–742. https://doi.org/10.1007/s42438-021-00249-1

Scoppio, G. et al, 2017. Mind the gap: Enabling online faculty and instructional designers in mapping new models for quality online courses. *Educ Inf Technol* Vol. 22, pp 725–746. https://doi.org/10.1007/s10639-015-9452-y

U.S. Department of Education, Every Student Succeeds Act, 2015. https://www.ed.gov/essa?src=policy

A DIGITAL EDUCATIONAL GAME FOR PRACTICING OER

Lubna Ali[1], Quang Phung[2], Rene Roepke[1] and Ulrik Schroeder[1]
[1]*Learning Technologies Research Group, RWTH Aachen University, Aachen, Germany*
[2]*RWTH Aachen University, Aachen, Germany*

ABSTRACT

Making education available to everyone is about opening new doors to the future world where people are living with their full abilities and potentials. This vision was acknowledged by UNESCO and it was one of the main motives for introducing Open Educational Resources (OER) in 2002. Over the last two decades, OER have made a positive impact on spreading quality educational information. However, the lack of experience in using and practicing OER is one of the common reasons why people have difficulties utilizing OER without violating copyright laws. To overcome this problem, a workshop concept was designed in order to qualify educators for OER. As part of the workshops, a digital educational game has been developed to elevate the participants' motivation and engagement. The game covers all basic aspects of the OER cycle (creating, editing, using, and distributing OER) and is designed to be played within the practical sessions. By implementing this game and utilizing the concept of Game-based Learning (GBL), we wanted to provide an interactive learning environment to practice OER and motivate learners to explore the OER world. In this paper, we present the concept of the game and demonstrate its technical foundation as well as its functionalities.

KEYWORDS

Open Educational Resources, OER, Game-based Learning, Digital Educational Game, OER Cycle, Qualification Workshops, Online Workshops

1. INTRODUCTION

Open Educational Resources (OER) are free learning materials that can be accessed and utilized by anyone (UNESCO 2022). They comprise different forms such as documents, research papers, audio files, images, videos, etc. and can be found on well-known distribution platforms like Wikimedia Commons or MIT Open Course Ware. With just a little or no cost or at all, everybody will have access to knowledge that may change their lives and potentially the lives of many others. This vision will get us closer to the goal of enabling universal education for everyone (Caswell 2008). In order to support content creators, Creative Commons (CC) licenses were established as a non-profit organization to help people overcome legal difficulties in producing and using OER; accordingly avoiding potential copyright law violations. Due to its ease of use, users can find out what they are allowed to do just by looking at the license label or the corresponding symbol.

To overcome the knowledge barrier between users and OER, qualification workshops for educators and students in teacher-training programs have been organized at Learning Technologies Research Group of RWTH Aachen University. The workshops are designed to qualify participants about the OER cycle (finding, creating, editing, using and distributing OER) and to license materials properly. During the in-person workshops (Thomas and Weigend 2020), participants have the chance to deepen what they have learnt through practical sessions, where they were divided into smaller groups to solve tasks like combining OER licenses and then publishing the results under an appropriate license.

As the in-person workshops have been affected by the COVID-19 pandemic, we have decided to offer the workshops in an online format and to replace the interactive practical sessions with a digital educational game, which was built based on the concept of Game-based Learning (GBL). GBL is a combination of learning and playing games in one single activity. It creates a virtual environment, where game characteristics are used to enhance learning activities (Qian 2016). This setup can boost the engagement of the participants and help them gain new knowledge in a more efficient way. The above benefits of GBL are undeniable as pointed out by many researches around the world (Sitzmann 2011, Liao 2016). GBL has slowly become a new high-efficiency teaching method and is being applied in teaching and educational activities nowadays.

In this paper, we will illustrate the OER-cycle game and its core features in supporting the participants explore the world of OER in the scope of remote qualification workshops.

2. GAME DESIGN

In order to maximize the learning results, we have followed the guidelines in (Plass 2015) to design and extend our OER editing web-based game (Ali 2021). Beside the additional new levels of the game that conveys more learning content, we have added new features that make the game more appealing and attractive to the players. New questions levels that cover the remaining part of the OER life cycle have been added to the game, which have improved the learning content of the game. Moreover, the game mechanics has been enhanced to make it more interactive, so that the users do not only solve the task by simply answering the questions but also, they can be involved interactively in the storyline. We believe that this will create a better gaming experience for the players.

The visual aesthetic and musical design of the game has been also upgraded by providing it with more images for better visualization. Additionally, a new background music and audio cue was also implemented to fit the game theme and environment. The narrative design of the game has been also improved within this version by creating a broader story throughout the game to make the players feel like they are actually playing the game rather than learning about OER. Each level has been designed carefully to combine OER questions and the game theme. This combination has led to a good storyline design as well as facilitating understanding and dealing with OER in general. We have also implemented a score system based on the time performance of the players. The faster they solve a question, the higher the score they get. The total score will then be added up at the end and the highest scores will be displayed as an act of honor.

The technical aspect of the game has been designed and implemented based on the three big pillars, which are the frontend, the backend and the database. The frontend serves as an interface for the users to interact with the game, meanwhile the player's data like their name, their score, and game progress will be stored in the database. In order to connect these two parts together, we have implemented a backend following modern development guidelines, which also processes all game logics and flow.

3. PROTOTYPE

The game sets the theme of a medieval time, where a swordsmith has a mission to craft a magical sword in order to bring peace to his kingdom, as part of digital storytelling. Based on the similarity of combining everything to forge the sword, each OER represents a specific material. The players' mission is to help the swordsmith figure out which license and under which condition should he finish his masterpiece. This serves as a suitable analogy to the activity of practicing OER, where one wants to combine different OER together, do some works, then finally place a license of their own on their creation. The game consists of four different levels, corresponding to the four parts of the OER cycle: (1) creating, (2) using, (3) editing, and (4) distributing.

For each level of the game, there are six to seven questions that vary in difficulty and in form, e.g., multiple-choice questions, Drag-Drop questions, and matching correct results. Each question has been formulated in a comprehensive way and relates closely to the theme of the game and to the content of the workshop. For example, Figure 1. shows a screenshot for a matching task from the game. The game is intended to be played in 20 minutes within the practical session, so that the participants can test their knowledge during the workshop and refer directly to the instructor if they have questions. As mentioned previously, we have built a leaderboard to increase the competitiveness and a scoring system to motivate the players and boost the interaction between them and the game.

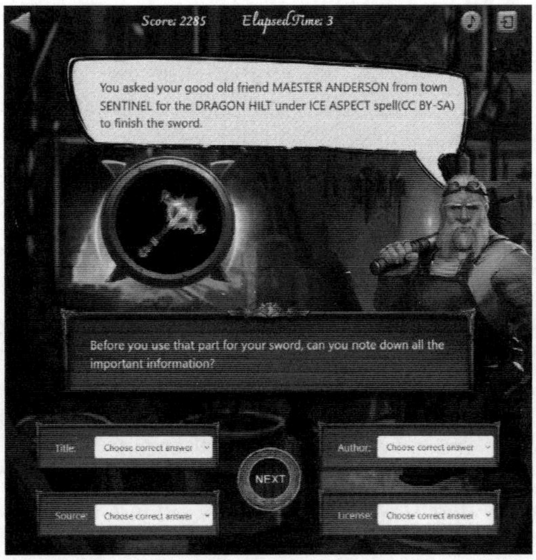

Figure 1. One of the game tasks

After the players finished playing the game, the certificate button will be activated to provide the participants with an automatically generated certificate, which indicates that they have acquired the basic knowledge regarding OER (Figure 2.). With this certificate, they will get access to advanced courses or workshops about OER, which are part of their teacher-training program. Furthermore, participants' suggestions and feedback are collected with a survey prompt at the end of the game and sent anonymously to workshops' organizers to be analyzed. This feedback will serve as a valuable information source to improve the game in the future iterations and for further development. The game can be found under the following URL: https://oer cycle.elearn.rwth-aachen.de.

Figure 2. The certificate is ready after completing the game

4. CONCLUSION AND FUTURE WORK

By utilizing the potential of GBL and the concept of OER, we have developed and enhanced a digital educational game to allow workshop participants to practice and strengthen their knowledge about OER. Our game has received a lot of positive feedback from the participants in recent workshops. They shared their opinions about the game and how it helped them increase their knowledge about utilizing OER.

However, there is always room for improvement by adding new functionalities or enhancing the exiting features. In order to make it even easier for the participants and break the language barrier, the game will be translated to German. Furthermore, in the next iterations of the game, there should be even more interactive way to boost the playing experience of the player, one example would be to redesign how the game is currently being played and apply different game elements to it such as puzzle mechanics or social interactions in a multiplayer mode. Additional game contents need to be added as well to further deliver all of OER aspect to the players.

Lastly, it is intended to elaborate more on feedback analysis to support investigating the effectiveness of GBL on enhancing the perception of OER. Therefore, during the future development, an analysis tool to manage the collected data is planned to be integrated within the game. The result could show some insights like how much time on average the players spend on a certain task or what the common wrong answers for a specific question are. Based on this information, we could adjust our teaching and training model and accordingly improve the workshop quality.

ACKNOWLEDGEMENT

We would like to express our thanks to workshops' participants at RWTH Aachen University, OERcamp.global 2021, Hamburg Open Online University (HOOU) and 16th EATEL Summer School on Technology Enhanced Learning (JTELSS 2022), who played the game and provided us with their valuable feedback.

REFERENCES

Ali, L. (2021). *Proceedings* / edited by Demetrios G. Sampson, Dirk Ifenthaler, Pedro Isaías, 319-322. 18th International Conference on Cognition and Exploratory Learning in the Digital Age.

Caswell, T. (2008). *Open Educational Resources: Enabling universal education*, Inter-national Review of Research in Open and Distance Learning Vol 9 No. 1.

Liao, Yuen-kuang. (2010). *Game-based Learning vs. Traditional Instruction: A Meta-Analysis of Thirty-Eight Studies from Taiwan.*

Macro Thomas (Hrsg.) and Michael Weigend (Hrsg.) (2020). *Mobil mit Informatik*. 9. Münsteraner Workshop zur Schulinformatik.

Mandela, N. (1990). Speech, Madison Park High School, Boston. Available at: https://www.oxfordreference.com/view/10.1093/acref/9780191843730.001.0001/q-oro-ed5-00007046. (Accessed: 01/04/2022).

Meihua Qian and Karen R Clark (2016). *Game-based learning and 21st century skills: A review of recent research.* Computers in Human Behavior.

Plass, J. (2015). *Foundations of Game-Based Learning*, Educational Psychologist: Vol 50, No. 4, 258-283.

Traci Sitzmann (2011). *A meta-analytic examination of the instructional effectiveness of computer-based simulation games.*

UNESCO (2022). *Open Educational Resources (OER).* Available at: https://en.unesco.org/themes/building-knowledgesocieties/oer, (Accessed: 01/04/2022). Author, F., Author, S., Author, T.: Book title. 2nd edn. Publisher, Location (1999).

UNESCO (2022). *Right to education.* Available at: https://en.unesco.org/themes/right-to-education, (Accessed: 01/04/2022).

THE EQUITY OF PEDAGOGICAL APPROACHES IN E-LEARNING INITIATIVES IN HIGHER EDUCATION INSTITUTIONS IN UNITED ARAB EMIRATES

Lina Daouk, Nafeth Hamdi Al Hashlamoun and Mai Ezzat
Teaching Faculty
Higher Colleges of Technology, POBox: 41012, Abu Dhabi, UAE

ABSTRACT

The slow adoption of e-learning in Higher education institutions (HEIs) in the United Arab Emirates (UAE) has been attributed to many Information Technology (IT) success factors or factors related to the management of IT. While many researchers were able to identify legitimate factors that have an impact on the adoption of e-learning, the impact of the cultural factors has not been thoroughly studied. The HEIs in the UAE have implemented e-learning solutions developed in Western countries. When these e-learning solutions are used without any cultural pedagogical consideration, they are creating inequitable learning conditions for UAE students. This case study aimed to investigate the role of the western-oriented culture e-learning pedagogy on the adoption of e-learning among UAE female students. Data was collected qualitatively from interviews with colleagues who are using western-oriented cultural pedagogies in their e-learning classes. A pattern matching technique was used to analyse the collected data. The cultural constructs of the Unified Theory of Acceptance and Use of Technology (UTAUT) were used as a lens to guide this study. The findings revealed the impact of the western-oriented pedagogy of Blackboard Learn (BBLearn) on the slow adoption of e-learning in the researchers' department. This study confirmed the importance of the local UAE culture on the adoption of e-learning and calls for further studies in that domain.

KEYWORDS

Technology Enhanced Learning, Technology Adoption Models, e-Learning, e-Learning Pedagogy, Adoption of e-Learning, Unified Theory of Acceptance

1. INTRODUCTION

Over the last two decades, Higher Education institutions in the UAE have spent millions of dollars on e-learning initiatives in an attempt to leverage their benefits (Vrazalic, Macgregor, Behl, & Fitzgerald, 2009b). Noesgaard and Ørngreen (2015) listed 19 distinct criteria to investigate the effectiveness of e-learning initiatives. Learning outcomes, students' performance, adoption, and users' satisfaction are among the most commonly used criteria. The rate of adoption as described by the UTAUT is among the highest used criterion to judge the effectiveness of e-learning initiatives (Abbad et al., 2009; Buche et al., 2012; Mirza & Al-Abdulkareem, 2011; Moon & Kim, 2001; Wu et al., 2006). The rate of adoption of e-learning among UAE students is still slow when compared to the large investments and the number of e-learning courses in the UAE HEIs (Elango et al., 2008; Vrazalic et al., 2009a). This is confirmed by the existence of only one e-learning university offering accredited e-learning courses out of the total 76 licensed universities in the UAE by the ministry of higher education ("CAA," n.d.). The executives of the UAE HEIs are raising legitimate concerns about the reasons for this slow adoption of e-learning initiatives.

Many researchers have used information technology (IT) success factors to investigate the adoption of e-learning in HEIs (Abdullah & Ward, 2016; Kassim, Jailani, Hairuddin, & Zamzuri, 2012; Tarhini, Hone, Liu, & Tarhini, 2017; Y.-S. Wang, Wang, & Shee, 2007).While these studies have identified some legitimate factors that impact the adoption of e-learning in HEIs, we found that the cultural factors have been neglected (Capatîna, 2015). The current pedagogy in e-learning initiatives in HEIs in THE UAE is founded on western cultural values, language, orientations, and epistemology. This western-oriented culture of e-learning pedagogy creates inequitable learning conditions (Bennett, 2001) for many UAE female students at my department. In this paper,

I attempt to study the impact of this western-oriented culture e-learning pedagogy on the adoption of e-learning among UAE female students at the institution of the Higher education institutions (HEIs) using a case study research methodology.

2. THEORETICAL FRAMEWORK

The social influence construct of the UTAUT determinants of intention and usage provides a theoretical lens that was used to direct this case study. Based on the previous work of Keller et al. (2009) who studied the impact of national cultural on e-learning implementation, teaching and learning western cultural attributes were selected as part of the social influence construct to guide the development of this case study. The selected attributes are presented in Figures 1 and 2.

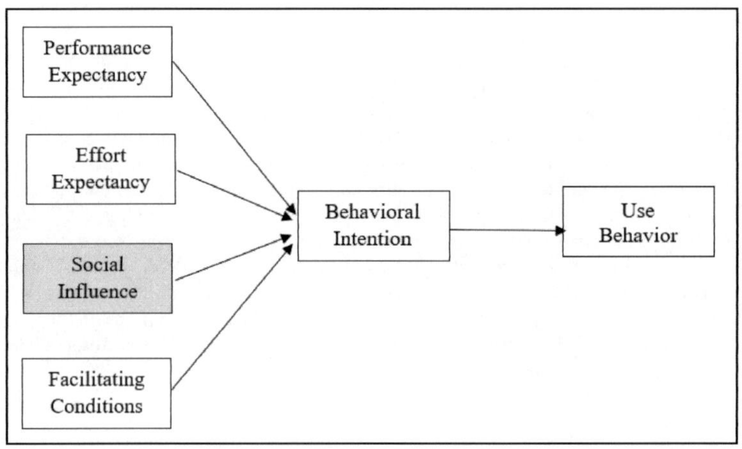

Figure 1. Unified Theory of Acceptance and Use of Technology (UTAUT)

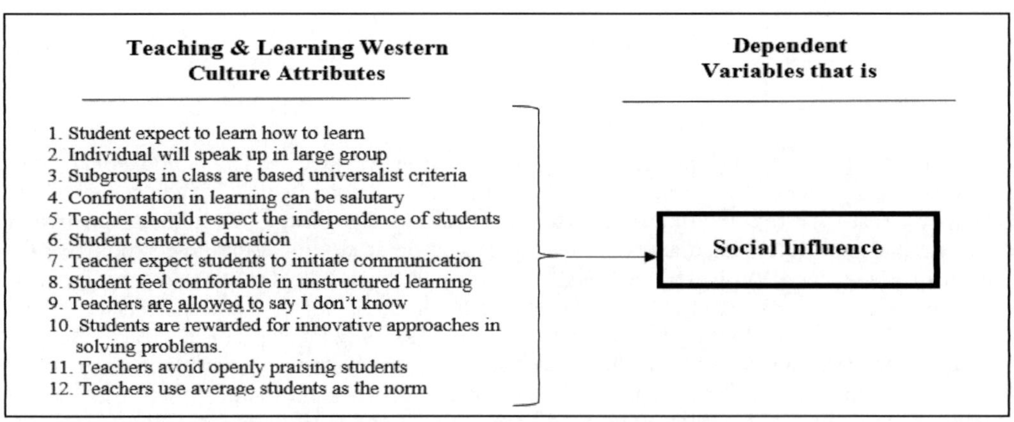

Figure 2. Teaching and learning western culture attributes that are part of the social influence construct

2.1 Research Methodology

The research methodology used in this study is a case study. A case study research is considered as one of the most challenging research methodologies that can examine complex issues and contemporary real-life situations (Yin, 2013). Case studies allow researchers to examine cases where large samples of participants may not be easily available, and this is exactly the case of this research (Creswell, 2014; Yin, 2013).

2.1.1 Data Collection

Data was collected from open-ended questions conducted in face to face interviews. Interviews are listed among the most important source for data in case studies (Padgett, 2003). Leedy and Ormrod (2010) stated that the most common types of interview questions are the open-ended and semi-structured ones. Three of my colleagues from my CIS department who are currently involved in developing courses using BBLearn agreed to participate in this research. The demographic profiles of the three participants referred to as P1, P2, and P3 are summarized in table 1 below:

Table 1. Summary of the sample demographics
[Note: This table summarizes the sample demographics of the 3 participants]

	Age	Gender	Total experience	BBL experience	Job Title	Department	Education
P1	57	Female	20	12	Lecturer	CIS / Business Solution	MS
P2	38	Female	9	5	Assistant Professor	CIS / E-Commerce	PhD
P3	62	Female	23	15	Assistant Professor	CIS/ Business Solution	PhD

The design of the 9 interview questions of this research were of open-ended and semi-structured types that allowed me to question participants about facts and their opinions and to follow up on certain answers. All interviews were completed in a maximum one hour. All data collected were text generated from the immediate transcription of the participants' answers. The 9 interview questions along with answers are listed in Appendix A.

2.2 Findings

This section reports the findings of the interviews. All participants answered the questions with full details. In these answers, culture was mentioned as one of the main reasons for the slow adoption.

The three participants confirmed that their e-learning pedagogy is a culturally western oriented one. The western e-learning pedagogy of BBLearn was mentioned by the three participants as one of the main challenges encountered by the female students at our college.

All participants revealed that students prefer to learn from their teachers the content of the courses and not to learn how to learn. Students are not comfortable to speak in large groups, and the three participants confirmed that subgroups are formed based on social and personnel criteria and not Universalist ones. Students don't enjoy confrontation during their learning and they look for certificates more than looking for competences. Please see figure 3 below.

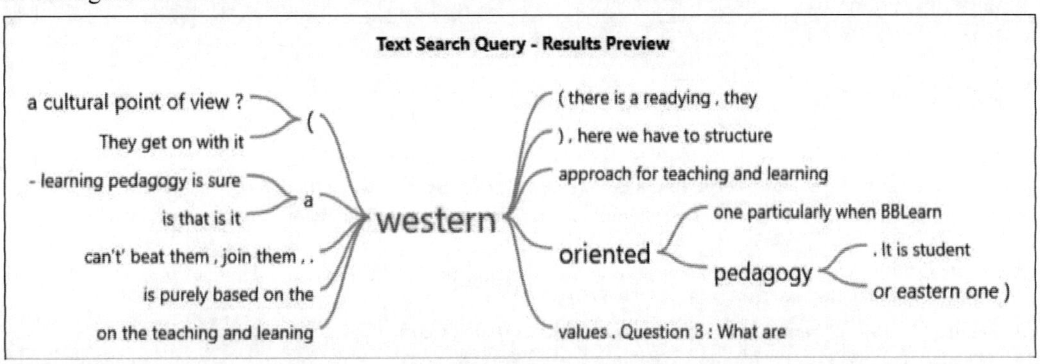

Figure 3. The text search results on the word Western and its relationship with the other words used in the answers of the first 4 questions

In particular, the three participants revealed that their students don't have the attributes of small power distance culture. While the participants did not elaborate on what attributes the students have, there is an agreement between the three participants that while teachers prefer student-centered education, students to find their own way, unstructured learning, innovative approach in solving problems, and other feminism attributes, the students' teaching and learning preferences are different. From the answers to these questions, it is clear that teachers prefer to use teaching and learning western culture attributes. However, students may not be comfortable to learn in such pedagogy. The three participants confirmed that some adjustments are needed in order to motivate their students to learn.

Overall, Participants' answers revealed that collectivist cultural aspects such as working in small groups and creating them randomly are suggested by the participants to be used in e-learning pedagogies. Avoidance of small power distance aspects is suggested by the participants to motivate students to engage in e-leaning classes. However, the three participants agree that with time, students should be taught using small power distance teaching and learning pedagogies. However, with time, students should be introduced to western e-learning pedagogies and encouraged to learn in such an environment. Overall, a balance should be achieved between the two.

3. CONCLUSION

This case study research confirmed the impact of the western culture e-learning pedagogy of BBLearn on the adoption of e-learning among the female students in our college. It revealed that this western pedagogy if used without any consideration to the teaching and learning local cultural differences will slow down the adoption of e-learning. The analysis of the participants' answers confirmed the lack of the teaching and learning western cultural attributes among the female students in our college. In this case study a pattern matching logic using the sufficient condition proposition argument was used as the main analytic technique (Yin, 2013). The lack of western cultural attributes among the female students confirmed the sufficient condition proposition. It revealed the existence of a negative effect of the western-oriented culture e-learning pedagogy on the adoption of eLearning among the female students at our college. This negative effect answered the first research question of this study. The effect of the cultural differences while using e-learning platforms is also noticed when students from the UAE study abroad in the western universities. For example, Al Hashlamoun (2021) listed some challenges that e-learners from the UAE face when enrolled in Western Universities. One of them is the irrelevance of Western universities' curricula to socio-cultural values of UAE.

Based on the findings, collectivist cultural activities and avoidance of small power distance attributes were among the aspects of the UAE culture that participants had suggested to be incorporated into their e-learning pedagogies to improve e-learning adoption among female students in my college.

In conclusion, this case study research study explored and investigated the role of the western-oriented culture e-learning pedagogy on the adoption of e-learning among female students in my college. Further research is needed to extend the findings of this study to other departments in my college and to other UAE tertiary institutions.

REFERENCES

Abbad, M. M., Morris, D., & De Nahlik, C. (2009). Looking under the bonnet: Factors affecting student adoption of e-learning systems in Jordan. The International Review of Research in Open and Distributed Learning, 10(2).

Abdullah, F., & Ward, R. (2016). Developing a General Extended Technology Acceptance Model for E-Learning (GETAMEL) by analysing commonly used external factors. Computers in Human Behavior, 56, 238–256.

Ajzen, I. (1991). The theory of planned behavior. Organizational Behavior and Human Decision Processes, 50(2), 179–211. https://doi.org/10.1016/0749-5978(91)90020-T

Al Fahim, M. (1995). From rags to riches. Dubai, UAE: London Centre of Arab Studies.

Al Hashlamoun, N. (2021). Cultural challenges eLearners from the GCC countries face when enrolled in Western educational institutions: A thematic literature review. Education and Information Technologies, 26(2), 1409-1422.

Al-Busaidi, K. A., & Al-Shihi, H. (2010). Instructors' acceptance of learning management systems: A theoretical framework. Communications of the IBIMA, 2010(2010), 1–10.

Al-Khazraji, N. (2009). The culture of commercialism: globalization in the UAE (PhD Thesis). Georgetown University.

Andrea, E. (2006). Globalized E-Learning Cultural Challenges. Idea Group Inc (IGI).

Arbaugh, J. B. (2002). Managing the on-line classroom: A study of technological and behavioral characteristics of web-based MBA courses. The Journal of High Technology Management Research, 13(2), 203–223.

Arenas-Gaitán, J., Ramírez-Correa, P. E., & Javier Rondán-Cataluña, F. (2011). Cross cultural analysis of the use and perceptions of web Based learning systems. Computers & Education, 57(2), 1762–1774. https://doi.org/10.1016/j.compedu.2011.03.016

Bennett, C. (2001). Genres of research in multicultural education. Review of Educational Research, 71(2), 171–217.

Blackboard | Education Technology & Services. (n.d.). Retrieved November 15, 2018, from https://www.blackboard.com/index.html

Blackboard Learn. (n.d.). Retrieved November 15, 2018, from https://elearning.uaeu.ac.ae/

Bradford, P., Porciello, M., Balkon, N., & Backus, D. (2007). The Blackboard learning system: The be all and end all in educational instruction? Journal of Educational Technology Systems, 35(3), 301–314.

Buche, M. W. ., mwbuche@mtu. ed., Davis, L. R. ., lrdavis@stthomas. ed., & Vician, C., cvician@stthomas. ed. (2012). Does Technology Acceptance Affect E-learning in a Non-Technology-Intensive Course? Journal of Information Systems Education, 23(1), 41–50.

CAA. (n.d.). Retrieved November 3, 2018, from https://www.caa.ae/caa/desktopmodules/institutions.aspx

Campbell, D. T. (1966). Pattern matching as an essential in distal knowing. The Psychology of Egon Brunswik, 81–106.

Capatîna, G. (2015). The implications of culture in e-learning. In The International Scientific Conference eLearning and Software for Education (Vol. 3, p. 95). " Carol I" National Defence University.

Cozby, P. (2008). Methods in Behavioral Research (10 edition). Boston: McGraw-Hill Humanities/Social Sciences/Languages.

Creswell, J. W. (2014). Research Design: Qualitative, Quantitative, and Mixed Methods Approaches. SAGE Publications.

DeLone, W. H., & McLean, E. R. (2003). The DeLone and McLean Model of Information Systems Success: A Ten-Year Update. Journal of Management Information Systems, 19(4), 9–30.

Elango, R., Gudep, V. K., & Selvam, M. (2008). Quality of e-Learning: An Analysis Based on e-Learners' Perception of e-Learning. Electronic Journal of E-Learning, 6(1), 31–43.

Goodson, L., & Phillimore, J. (2004). Qualitative research in tourism: Ontologies, epistemologies and methodologies. Routledge.

Graham, C. R., Woodfield, W., & Harrison, J. B. (2013). A framework for institutional adoption and implementation of blended learning in higher education. The Internet and Higher Education, 18, 4–14. https://doi.org/10.1016/j.iheduc.2012.09.003

Kassim, E. S., Jailani, S. F. A. K., Hairuddin, H., & Zamzuri, N. H. (2012). Information system acceptance and user satisfaction: The mediating role of trust. Procedia-Social and Behavioral Sciences, 57, 412–418.

Keller, C., Lindh, J., Hrastinski, S., Casanovas, I., & Fernandez, G. (2009). The impact of national culture on e-learning implementation: a comparative study of an Argentinean and a Swedish university. Educational Media International, 46(1), 67–80.

King, E., & Boyatt, R. (2015). Exploring factors that influence adoption of e-learning within higher education. British Journal of Educational Technology, 46(6), 1272–1280. https://doi.org/10.1111/bjet.12195

Lee, M.-C. (2010). Explaining and predicting users' continuance intention toward e-learning: An extension of the expectation–confirmation model. Computers & Education, 54(2), 506–516. https://doi.org/10.1016/j.compedu.2009.09.002

Leedy, P. D., & Ormrod, J. E. (2010). Practical Research: Planning and Design (9 edition). Boston: Pearson.

Machado, M., & Tao, E. (2007). Blackboard vs. moodle: Comparing user experience of learning management systems. In 2007 37th Annual Frontiers In Education Conference - Global Engineering: Knowledge Without Borders, Opportunities Without Passports (pp. S4J-7-S4J-12). https://doi.org/10.1109/FIE.2007.4417910

Mirza, A. A., & Al-Abdulkareem, M. (2011). Models of e-learning adopted in the Middle East. Applied Computing and Informatics, 9(2), 83–93. https://doi.org/10.1016/j.aci.2011.05.001

Moon, J.-W., & Kim, Y.-G. (2001). Extending the TAM for a World-Wide-Web context. Information & Management, 38(4), 217–230. https://doi.org/10.1016/S0378-7206(00)00061-6

Mouakket, S., & Bettayeb, A. M. (2015). Investigating the factors influencing continuance usage intention of Learning management systems by university instructors: The Blackboard system case. International Journal of Web Information Systems, 11(4), 491–509. https://doi.org/10.1108/IJWIS-03-2015-0008

Noesgaard, S. S., & Ørngreen, R. (2015). The Effectiveness of E-Learning: An Explorative and Integrative Review of the Definitions, Methodologies and Factors That Promote e-Learning Effectiveness. Electronic Journal of E-Learning, 13(4), 278–290.

NVivo: The Qualitative Data Analysis & Research Software. (n.d.). Retrieved February 22, 2015, from http://www.qsrinternational.com/products_nvivo.aspxhttp://atlasti.com/

Padgett, D. K. (Ed.). (2003). The Qualitative Research Experience (1st edition). Belmont, CA: Thomson Learning.

Pan, C.-C., Tsai, M.-H., Tsai, P.-Y., Tao, Y., & Cornell, R. (2003). Technology's impact: symbiotic or asymbiotic impact on differing cultures? Educational Media International, 40(3–4), 319–330.

Phillips, D. C., & Burbules, N. C. (2000). Postpositivism and educational research. Rowman & Littlefield.

Richardson, Patricia M. (2004). Possible influences of Arabic-Islamic culture on the reflective practices proposed for an education degree at the Higher Colleges of Technology in the United Arab Emirates. International Journal of Educational Development, 24(4), 429–436.

Richardson, Patricia Mary. (2002). A study of some effects of information technology programs on Emirati women students' lives (PhD Thesis). University of Bristol.

Rogers, E. M. (2003). Diffusion of Innovations, 5th Edition (5th edition). New York: Free Press.

Rogers, P. C., Graham, C. R., & Mayes, C. T. (2007). Cultural competence and instructional design: Exploration research into the delivery of online instruction cross-culturally. Educational Technology Research and Development, 55(2), 197–217. https://doi.org/10.1007/s11423-007-9033-x

Rogerson-Revell, P. (2003). Developing a cultural syllabus for business language e-learning materials. ReCALL, 15(2), 155–168.

SCORM Explained: In Depth Review of the SCORM eLearning Standard. (n.d.). Retrieved November 15, 2018, from https://scorm.com/scorm-explained/

Stone, L. A. (2002). The Islamic crescent: Islam, culture and globalization. Innovation: The European Journal of Social Science Research, 15(2), 121–131.

Tapanes, M. A., Smith, G. G., & White, J. A. (2009). Cultural diversity in online learning: A study of the perceived effects of dissonance in levels of individualism/collectivism and tolerance of ambiguity. The Internet and Higher Education, 12(1), 26–34. https://doi.org/10.1016/j.iheduc.2008.12.001

Tarhini, A., Hone, K., Liu, X., & Tarhini, T. (2017). Examining the moderating effect of individual-level cultural values on users' acceptance of E-learning in developing countries: a structural equation modeling of an extended technology acceptance model. Interactive Learning Environments, 25(3), 306–328.

Topor, S., & Dinu, M.-S. (2014). Culture and E-Learning-Global Challenges and Perspectives. In The International Scientific Conference eLearning and Software for Education (Vol. 1, p. 497). " Carol I" National Defence University.

Trochim, W. M. (1989). Outcome pattern matching and program theory. Evaluation and Program Planning, 12(4), 355–366.

uae population 2018 - Google Search. (n.d.). Retrieved November 17, 2018, from https://www.google.com/search?safe=strict&source=hp&ei=7ZvvW6WWPIqca4qHtfAP&q=uae+population+2018&oq=uae+population&gs_l=psy-ab.1.1.0l10.180.3472..5700...0.0..0.233.2583.0j13j2......0....1..gws-wiz.....0..35i39j0i131j0i67.yGHKvIO2WYk

Venkatesh, V., Morris, M. G., Davis, G. B., & Davis, F. D. (2003). User acceptance of information technology: Toward a unified view. MIS Quarterly, 425–478.

Vrazalic, L., Macgregor, R., Behl, D., & Fitzgerald, J. (2009a). E-learning barriers in the United Arab Emirates: preliminary results from an empirical investigation. Faculty of Engineering and Information Sciences - Papers: Part A, 1–7.

Vrazalic, L., Macgregor, R. C., Behl, D., & Fitzgerald, J. (2009b). E-learning barriers in the United Arab Emirates: Preliminary results from an empirical investigation.

Wang, L.-C. C., & Bagaka's, J. G. (2002). Understanding the dimensions of self-exploration in web-based learning environments. Journal of Research on Technology in Education, 34(3), 364–373.

Wang, Y.-S., Wang, H.-Y., & Shee, D. Y. (2007). Measuring e-learning systems success in an organizational context: Scale development and validation. Computers in Human Behavior, 23(4), 1792–1808.

Wu, J., Tsai, R. J., Chen, C. C., & Wu, Y. (2006). An integrative model to predict the continuance use of electronic learning systems: hints for teaching. International Journal on E-Learning, 5(2).

Yin, R. K. (2013). Case study research: Design and methods. Sage publications.

ZU Portal – Blackboard Learn. (n.d.). Retrieved November 15, 2018, from https://learn.zu.ac.ae/webapps/portal/execute/tabs/tabAction?tab_tab_group_id=_12_1

TRAINING PREFERENCES OF ADULT LEARNERS IN ONLINE LEARNING ENVIRONMENTS: DISTANCE LEARNING GATE

Muhittin Şahin[1], Cennet Terzi Müftüoğlu[2], Savaş Ceylan[2] and Salim Atay[3]
[1]*University of Mannheim, Mannheim, Germany*
[2]*Hacettepe University, Ankara, Turkey*
[3]*Istanbul Technical University, Istanbul, Turkey*

ABSTRACT

Adults are independent learners and are expected to direct their own learning. Nowadays, there are many MOOC platforms preferred by adult learners. Many states have adapted to these developments and established an online learning platform in order to carry out the training and development activities of civil servants. The Presidency of the Republic of Türkiye Human Resources Office has established the Distance Learning Gate (DLG) platform in order to carry out educational activities. In this study, learning preferences of adult learners were determined in order to improve the relevant online learning environment and to structure appropriate trainings for public personnel. For this purpose, the training preferences of adult learners were determined according to their title groups and education levels. The participants of the research consisted of 4864 civil servants who received training from the DLG platform. According to the results, it was determined that adult learners preferred personal development training the most and professional development training in the last place. It is seen that the servants in the service title group that watched the most training in all categories according to the title groups. It is seen that the groups that received the least education are the senior manager and manager title group. On the other hand, it has been determined that the number of adult learners' training and the education categories differ according to the education level. According to the findings, it is seen that those who watched the most education are adults at the compulsory primary education level, while those who watched the least education are those who are at the graduate level. This research includes the first phase of a series of research and a design-based research. As a first step, the training preferences of adult learners were determined. In the next stage, a recommendation system will be integrated into the DLG platform based on the determined profiles.

KEYWORDS

Adult Learners, Digital Learning Environments, Distance Learning Gate, Civil Servants, Training Preferences

1. INTRODUCTION

There is no single definition, model, or theory that explains how or why adults learn, and our understanding of adult learning is changing. Adult learning is a broad concept that extends from continuing vocational training to basic literacy training and on-the-job training (Merriam, 2018). Personal growth and development are emphasized within the framework of lifelong learning approach in adult learning. It is possible to talk about three basic theories in the context of adult learning: (1) andragogy, self-directed learning, and transformative learning (Merriam, 2017). A common understanding of adult learning among these theories is that adult learners are independent and manage their own learning processes. According to adult learners, learning is a part of life independent of formal educational institutions such as schools, and adults systematically carry out the learning process without being dependent on an instructor (Merriam, 2018). It can be said that this information is also valid in online learning environments. According to Merriam and Bierema (2014), more successful online learners are also more self-directed learners.

Deepening our understanding in the context of adult learning is critical as it provides the answer to how adult learning environments should be designed. In this research, by determining the training preferences of adult learners in online learning environments; It is aimed to create a framework for relevant stakeholders, especially instructional designers, and to contribute to the adult education literature. In addition, it is aimed to reveal the training preferences of adults in these environments.

Designing online learning environments as to appropriate the needs of adults constitutes the balance point in capturing and sustaining the potential of these environments. Today, there are different widely used online learning platforms preferred by adults. When the reports of these platforms are examined, it is seen that only descriptive statistics are presented (edX, 2022; edX, 2021; Coursera, 2021). Thanks to the universality of these platforms, the amount of information they contain in adult learning has reached a serious level. However, this potential brought by the data cannot be fully utilized in the academic context. In this research, it will be tried to explain the learning path of adult learners in the distance learning gate, which is a widely used national online learning platform, in terms of training preferences. Every trace that adults leave in online learning environments contains a clue to their learning journey. These tips can be considered as powerful collaborators that can be used to improve or facilitate learning. For this reason, it is important for researchers to carry out advanced analyzes and share the results with the literature in order to capture the potential of big data beyond descriptive statistics. In this study, it was aimed to determine the educational preferences of adult learners in different occupational groups in online learning environments. The research questions are; 1) What are the preferences of adult learners in training categories? 2) How a pattern does the training preferences of adult learners show according to their job title groups? 3)What are the training preferences of adult learners according to their education levels?

2. METHOD

2.1 Research Design and Participants

The study was structured as a correlational research. The participants of the research are 4864 civil servants working in the public sector and receiving training from the DLG platform. 69% (3377) of the participants were male and 31% (1487) were female.

2.2 Distance Learning Gate

Distance Learning Gate (DLG) is an online learning platform that has been opened to the use of civil servants by Presidency of the Republic of Türkiye Human Resources Office since 2020. DLG consists of training, exam, survey, and live conference modules. Trainings can be carried out both synchronously and asynchronously. Video-conference (Live Class) and webinar modules are used for synchronous training, which are integrated into the system. As asynchronous trainings, it can be presented as video, interactive video, presentation, textual content and infographic. There are more than 6000 training events in different categories such as professional development, personal development, legislation, human resources management, information technologies, human rights, etc. The trainings are structured by institutions specialized in their fields and made available to certain individuals, institutions, organizations or all civil servants.

2.3 Data Collection and Data Analysis

Within the scope of the research, log data obtained from the DLG platform was used as a data collection tool. The log data consists of the categories of the trainings completed and the training titles in these categories. As the traning category, instead of all the categories in the platform, the categories of professional development, personal development, legislation, information technologies and about life were examined in the context of the research. In addition, the title groups and educational level of the participants were included in the analysis. One-way MANOVA and one-way ANOVA analysis were used in the analysis of the data. Tukey test was used as Post Hoc analysis in order to determine the differences between the groups.

3. FINDINGS

3.1 Training Category Preferences of Adult Learners

It has been revealed that there is a statistically significant difference in the training category preferences of adult learners on the DLG platform (F (4, 24315) = 2109.56, p < .000, partial η^2 = .257). In order to determine the source of the difference, the Tukey test was conducted as a Post-hoc analysis. Personal Development (*M* = 25.39; *SD* = 16.07) is the most watched category and more preferred than Legislation (*M* = 18.31; *SD* = 15.71), Information Technologies (*M* = 12.51; *SD* = 8.97), About Life (*M* = 7.90; *SD* = 6.36) and Professional Development (*M* = 7.66; *SD* = 5.40) categories. On the other hand, the Legislation (*M* = 18.31; *SD* = 15.71) category is more preferred than the Information Technologies (*M* = 12.51; *SD* = 8.97), About Life (*M* = 7.90; *SD* = 6.36) and Professional Development (*M* = 7.66; *SD* = 5.40) categories. Finally, it is another finding that the Information Technologies (*M* = 12.51; *SD* = 8.97) category is more preferred than the About Life (*M* = 7.90; *SD* = 6.36) and Professional Development (*M* = 7.66; *SD* = 5.40) categories.

3.2 Training Preferences of Adult Learners According to the Job Title Groups

It has been revealed that there is a statistically significant difference in the training preferences of the adult learners according to the title groups (F (5, 4858) = 23.87, p < .000; Wilk's Λ = 0.886, partial η^2 = .024). In order to determine the source of this difference, the Tukey test was used as a Post Hoc analysis. According to the results, the servants in the service title group that watched the most training in all categories. It is seen that the groups that received the least education are the senior manager and manager title group.

3.3 Training Preferences of Adult Learners According to the Education Level

It has been revealed that there is a statistically significant difference in the training preferences of the adult learners according to the education levels (F (5, 4858) = 9.11, p < .000; Wilk's Λ = 0.954, partial η^2 = .009). In order to determine the source of this difference, the Tukey test was used as a Post Hoc analysis. According to the results, it has been determined that the number of adult learners' training and the education categories differ according to the education level. According to the findings, it is seen that those who watched the most education are adults at the compulsory primary education level, while those who watched the least education are those who are at the graduate level.

4. CONCLUSION

Within the scope of the research, it was examined whether the training preferences of adult learners differ according to a) job title groups, b) education categories and c) education levels. In the DLG platform, it was found that the training preferences of adult learners differ according to the categories. Training preferences of adult learners were distributed in the categories of personal development, legislation, information technologies, about life, and professional development, respectively. In the light of these findings, it is planned to investigate the reasons for these preferences of the adult learners.

It is seen that the training preferences and numbers of adult learners differ according to their job title groups and education levels. According to the title groups, it is seen that the groups receiving the most education are service, technical, professional, administrative, manager and top manager, respectively. In this case, it is seen that the title group that received the least training in the DLG platform is the manager and senior top manager. It is thought that there may be two main reasons for this situation. The first of these is that the learners in this title group have less needs and therefore do not participate in the training. The second is that the training on the platform is not suitable for the public personnel in the manager and top manager title group. In the next stage, it is recommended to add special training for these title groups to the system.

On the other hand, it was found that the training preferences and the number of training follow-ups differed according to the education levels of adult learners. According to the education levels of adult learners, it was found that those who received the most education was compulsory primary education, high school, associate degree, undergraduate, doctorate and graduate, respectively. In this case, it was found that adult learners with low education and high education received more education than learners with high education levels. In other words, while the level of education increases, the number of people receiving education decreases. According to this finding, it is possible to say that there is a negative correlation between the number of trainings in the DLG platform and the level of education.

REFERENCES

Coursera (2021). Impact Report. https://about.coursera.org/press/wp-content/uploads/2021/11/2021-Coursera-Impact-Report.pdf

edX (2021). Impact Report 2021. Retrieved August 25, 2022, from https://www.edx.org/edx-impact-report-2021

edX (2022). Impact Report 2022. Retrieved August 25, 2022, from https://impact.edx.org/2022

Fraenkel, J. R., Wallen, N. E., & Hyun, H. H. (2012). *How to design and evaluate research in education*. New York: McGraw-hill.

Merriam, S. B. (2018). Adult learning theory: Evolution and future directions. In *Contemporary theories of learning* (pp. 83-96). Routledge.

Merriam, S.B. & Bierema, L.L. (2014). *Adult learning: Linking theory and practice*. San Francisco: Jossey-Bass.

LEARNING ANALYTICS BASED INTERVENTIONS: A SYSTEMATIC REVIEW OF EXPERIMENTAL STUDIES

Mustafa Tepgeç[1] and Dirk Ifenthaler[1,2]
[1]*University of Mannheim, Mannheim, Germany*
[2]*Curtin University, Australia*

ABSTRACT

Learning analytics includes interventions that will support learning and improve learning environments. Despite the fact that learning analytics is a promising field of study, the lack of empirical evidence on the effects of learning analytics-based interventions has been widely addressed in recent years. In this context, insights validated by experimental studies may play a crucial role. Therefore, there is a need for a report describing the methodological aspects and effects of current experimental interventions based on learning analytics. This systematic review provides an in-depth examination of learning analytics research that reports experimental findings to evaluate learning analytics-based interventions. The PRISMA (Preferred Reporting Items for Systematic Reviews and Meta-Analyses) 2020 protocol provided the basis for the work of this systematic review. This review contained 52 papers that met the inclusion and exclusion criteria. The results show that student-facing dashboards are the most common learning analytics-based intervention. Evidence from how user data is handled for interventions demonstrates that the most common method is the distillation of data for human judgment. This study confirms that a significant proportion of experimental studies employing learning analytics interventions have demonstrated significant effects on learning outcomes. The effectiveness of learning analytics-based interventions is also addressed in this review in terms of motivation, engagement, and system usage behaviors. The findings of this study will contribute to the literature in terms of describing the experimentally validated findings of learning analytics-based interventions in depth.

KEYWORDS

Learning Analytics, Intervention, Educational Data Mining, Experimental Studies, Systematic Literature Review

1. INTRODUCTION

Online learning environments have become increasingly prominent over the past years. However, these environments work in favor of autonomous learners, in other words, self-directed learners (Schumacher and Ifenthaler 2021). Even if online courses in which includes are based on a well-structured instructional design, these environments are disadvantageous for learners who do not take responsibility for their own learning (Toro-Troconis, Alexander, and Frutos-Perez 2019). Therefore, such learners need guidance in online learning environments. Studies emphasizing guidance in these environments form the basis of learning analytics conceptualized for the first time in the previous decade.

A considerable number of systematic reviews on learning analytics have been conducted because it is a relatively new but promising field of study. Some of these reviews were broader in scope, focusing on learning analytics or learning analytics dashboards in general (Bodily and Verbert 2017; Viberg et al. 2018). These studies have demonstrated the current state of the methods, trends, or challenges in learning analytics research. It's also quite frequent for reviews to concentrate on a particular issue or aspect of learning analytics rather than presenting a general overview. For example, while some reviews focus on ethical and privacy issues (Bassani and Cazella 2021; Tzimas and Demetriadis 2021), some reviews focus on the study success factor (Ifenthaler and Yau 2020; Namoun and Alshanqiti 2020). In addition, literature reviews on studies emphasizing self-regulation—one of the key constructs of learning analytics research—were carried out (Matcha, Gašević, and Pardo 2019; Viberg, Khalil, and Baars 2020). Many reviews have also been published on predictive modeling, which is the widely studied methodological aspect of learning analytics research (Namoun and Alshanqiti 2020). Similarly, the number of reviews is increasing in parallel with the number of studies on multimodal learning analytics, which focuses on obtaining data from different sources in addition to online learning environments (Crescenzi-Lanna 2020; Namoun and Alshanqiti 2020). Furthermore, some reviews have concentrated on studies including the application of learning analytics in the context of educational games (Alonso-Fernández et al. 2019; Daoudi 2022).

In summary, even as some reviews provide a broad overview of learning analytics or specifically learning analytics dashboards, some reviews focused on specific issues such as methodological aspects, data gathering sources, or pedagogical constructs. These reviews made significant contributions to our knowledge of learning analytics research. To the best of our knowledge, no published reviews in the broader sense have only focused on the experimentally controlled effects of learning analytics interventions. Analyzing research using experimental designs may be the most effective way to determine the validity of the effects of learning analytics applications on learning outcomes. Therefore, the goal of this systematic review is to do an in-depth examination of experimental studies that include interventions based on learning analytics. The following research questions were formulated to guide the systematic review:

1. What learning analytics-based interventions are employed in research on learning analytics?
2. What are the (methodological) features of learning analytics-based interventions?
3. What are the outcome variables associated with learning analytics-based interventions?

2. METHOD

The PRISMA 2020 protocol outlined by Page et al. (2021) provided the basis for the work of this systematic review. Due to its widespread endorsement and adoption, this study was conducted based on this protocol. Considering the wide variety of fields in which LA might be developed and/or applied (e.g., psychology, education, computer science, and business), a diverse range of journals was examined. Thus, four well-known databases were selected without filtering for specific journals and/or research categories: ACM Digital Library, ERIC, ISI Web of Science, and Scopus. Hereby, a total of 375 papers (after removing duplicates) were obtained by running the following query: "learning analytics" AND experiment*. A literature search was conducted in each database on the first week of July 2022.

The following inclusion criteria were used: Studies had to (1) employ one of the experimental study designs, (2) utilize learning analytics as a part of the intervention, (3) be written in English, (4) be full-text available. Consequently, 52 studies were considered for further analysis within the scope of this review.

Following the screening process, the relevant information from the papers was extracted and organized in a spreadsheet. Two phases were involved in the coding procedure. Phase 1 concentrated on gathering descriptive data for each paper such as authors, year of publication, country, and sample size. In the second phase, details regarding learning analytics-based experimental interventions such as data analysis techniques and affected output variables were extracted in order to answer research questions.

3. FINDINGS

3.1 Descriptive Findings

The results of this study show that more than half of the experimental studies based on learning analytics interventions (n=30) have been published as of 2020 (Search date: July 2022). On the other hand, there are only two published studies before 2016. Computers & Education (n=4) is the journal that publishes the most studies. This is followed by the Journal of Computer-Assisted Learning and the Educational Technology & Society with 3 studies. International Conference on Learning Analytics Knowledge (LAK) (n=6) is the conference series that publishes the most proceedings. This is followed by IEEE International Conference on Advanced Learning Technologies (ICALT) with 4 studies.

3.2 Main Findings

RQ1: What learning analytics-based interventions are employed in research on learning analytics?

Among the learning analytics-based interventions, the most used one is student-facing dashboards (n=18). This is followed by instructor dashboard (n=14), automated learning analytics-based feedback (n=11), personalized feedback/recommendations (n=11), personalized static reports or visualizations (n=7), personalization of learning materials (n=6), real-time progress information (n=3), personalization of assessment (n=1).

RQ2: What are the (methodological) features of learning analytics-based interventions?

This study reports both the study group of the research and the user group of the learning analytics-based intervention. According to the study group findings, 75% of studies were conducted with undergraduate students. This is followed by K-12 students with %13,5, and teacher/lecturer group with %11.5.

Although nearly 90% of studies involving learning analytics-based interventions consider their impact on students, some of the interventions are presented via teachers. Thus, this study concludes that half of learning analytics-based interventions are provided directly to the learner. In addition, the findings show that 36.5% of interventions are provided to teachers and 11.5% are provided to both user groups.

The results of the study show that more than half of the studies (n=30) have less than 100 participants. The proportion of studies with sample sizes of 100-300 is 25%, while the proportion of studies with sample sizes of 300-1000 is 15%. There is only one study was conducted with over 1000 participants.

The findings on how user data is processed for interventions demonstrate that the distillation of data for human judgment (n=36) is the most used approach. This is followed by prediction (n=13), relationship mining (n=6), clustering (n=5), discovery with models (n=5).

RQ3: What are the outcome variables associated with learning analytics-based interventions?

This review reveals that learning outcomes (n=32) are the variable for which the effects of experimental studies based on learning analytics interventions are most studied. User reflections, in which learners express their views on the proposed system, take second place with 12 studies. This is followed by motivation (n=8), engagement (n=7), system usage behaviors (n=6), and teachers' performance monitoring (n=5).

Experimental results prove that learning analytics-based interventions significantly increased teachers' performance monitoring in all studies. Engagement is the second variable significantly affected by the interventions with %86, and system usage behavior is the third variable with %83. This study also reveals that motivation and learning outcomes are variables that are significantly affected by interventions in 3 out of 4 studies.

4. DISCUSSION AND CONCLUSION

This systematic review provides an in-depth examination of learning analytics research that reports experimental findings. Despite the fact that learning analytics is a promising field of study, the lack of empirical evidence on the effects of learning analytics applications has been widely addressed in recent years (Larrabee Sønderlund, Hughes, and Smith 2019). In this context, insights validated by experimental studies may play a crucial role. Therefore, there is a need for a report describing the effects of current experimental studies based on learning analytics interventions.

This review concludes that a very limited number of experimental studies were conducted in the first 5 years of learning analytics, which was first conceptualized in 2010. On the other hand, the fact that a significant part of the studies has been published in the last 2.5 years implies that the use of experimental designs in learning analytics research has gained momentum. However, until just a few years ago, it was frequently emphasized in many studies (e.g., Mah, Yau, and Ifenthaler 2019; Matcha, Gašević, and Pardo 2019) that learning analytics applications lack experimentally validated findings. On the contrary, the results of this review have been a confirmation of the increasing momentum in experimental studies in learning analytics research.

Meso-level and micro-level analytics are applications that provide information to students and instructors, whereas macro-level and mega-level analytics are large-scale and provide information to institutional or policymakers (Ifenthaler and Widanapathirana 2014). Therefore, it can be induced from this review that the existing experimental studies based on learning analytics interventions are meso-level and micro-level analytics applications.

This review validates that a significant proportion of experimental studies employing learning analytics interventions have shown significant effects on learning outcomes. The effectiveness of learning analytics-based interventions in terms of motivation, engagement, and system usage behaviors is also highlighted in this review. Therefore, it can be concluded that learning analytics are quite effective for intervening in the learning experience, without considering the quality of the reviewed experimental studies. The outcomes of this review will add to the body of literature by thoroughly describing the experimentally validated findings of interventions based on learning analytics.

REFERENCES

Alonso-Fernández, Cristina, Antonio Calvo-Morata, Manuel Freire, Iván Martínez-Ortiz, and Baltasar Fernández-Manjón. 2019. 'Applications of data science to game learning analytics data: A systematic literature review', *Computers & Education*, 141: 103612.

Bassani, Rafael Vescovi, and Silvio César Cazella. 2021. 'O alinhamento entre learning analytics ea general data protection regulation: uma revisão sistemática de literatura', *ETD: Educaçao Temática Digital*, 23: 1022-40.

Bodily, R., and K. Verbert. 2017. 'Review of Research on Student-Facing Learning Analytics Dashboards and Educational Recommender Systems', *Ieee Transactions on Learning Technologies*, 10: 405-18.

Crescenzi-Lanna, Lucrezia. 2020. 'Multimodal Learning Analytics research with young children: A systematic review', *British Journal of Educational Technology*, 51: 1485-504.

Daoudi, Ibtissem. 2022. 'Learning analytics for enhancing the usability of serious games in formal education: A systematic literature review and research agenda', *Education and Information Technologies*: 1-30.

Ifenthaler, Dirk, and Chathuranga Widanapathirana. 2014. 'Development and validation of a learning analytics framework: Two case studies using support vector machines', *Technology, Knowledge and Learning*, 19: 221-40.

Ifenthaler, Dirk, and Jane Yin-Kim Yau. 2020. 'Utilising learning analytics to support study success in higher education: a systematic review', *Educational Technology Research and Development*, 68: 1961-90.

Larrabee Sønderlund, Anders, Emily Hughes, and Joanne Smith. 2019. 'The efficacy of learning analytics interventions in higher education: A systematic review', *British Journal of Educational Technology*, 50: 2594-618.

Mah, Dana-Kristin, Jane Yin-Kim Yau, and Dirk Ifenthaler. 2019. 'Epilogue: Future directions on learning analytics to enhance study success.' in, *Utilizing learning analytics to support study success* (Springer).

Matcha, Wannisa, Dragan Gašević, and Abelardo Pardo. 2019. 'A systematic review of empirical studies on learning analytics dashboards: A self-regulated learning perspective', *Ieee Transactions on Learning Technologies*, 13: 226-45.

Namoun, Abdallah, and Abdullah Alshanqiti. 2020. 'Predicting student performance using data mining and learning analytics techniques: A systematic literature review', *Applied Sciences*, 11: 237.

Page, Matthew J, Joanne E McKenzie, Patrick M Bossuyt, Isabelle Boutron, Tammy C Hoffmann, Cynthia D Mulrow, Larissa Shamseer, Jennifer M Tetzlaff, Elie A Akl, and Sue E Brennan. 2021. 'The PRISMA 2020 statement: An updated guideline for reporting systematic reviews', *Systematic reviews*, 10: 1-11.

Schumacher, C., and D. Ifenthaler. 2021. 'Investigating prompts for supporting students' self-regulation – A remaining challenge for learning analytics approaches?', *Internet and Higher Education*, 49.

Toro-Troconis, Maria, Jesse Alexander, and Manuel Frutos-Perez. 2019. 'Assessing Student Engagement in Online Programmes: Using Learning Design and Learning Analytics', *International Journal of Higher Education*, 8: 171-83.

Tzimas, Dimitrios, and Stavros Demetriadis. 2021. 'Ethical issues in learning analytics: a review of the field', *Educational Technology Research and Development*, 69: 1101-33.

Viberg, O., M. Hatakka, O. Bälter, and A. Mavroudi. 2018. 'The current landscape of learning analytics in higher education', *Computers in Human Behavior*, 89: 98-110.

Viberg, Olga, Mohammad Khalil, and Martine Baars. 2020. "Self-regulated learning and learning analytics in online learning environments: A review of empirical research." In *Proceedings of the tenth international conference on learning analytics & knowledge*, 524-33.

A MEMORY PALACE FOR BRAIN ANATOMY AND FUNCTION REPRESENTED IN VIRTUAL REALITY

Ludivine Blais[1], Hossain Samar Qorbani[2], Ali Arya[2] and Jim Davies[3]
[1]*Department of Cognitive Science*
[2]*School of Information Technology*
[3]*Department of Cognitive Science*
Carleton University, 1125 Colonel By Dr, Ottawa, Ontario, Canada

ABSTRACT

Memory palaces are effective tools for learning vast amounts of information in a canonical order using mnemonics. However, our review of the literature revealed a lack of implementation and user study of memory palace in Virtual Reality (VR) for neuroscience education. VR technology enables us to build highly interactive virtual learning spaces that are engaging and interesting. As a result, we implemented a web-based version of VR (known as WebXR) to help students about brain regions for the first time including the name, function, and location of each brain part.

KEYWORDS

Memory Palace, Mnemonics, Virtual Reality, Neuroscience Education, Brain VR

1. INTRODUCTION

Memory palaces are a technique that takes advantage of the brain's natural impressive ability to use spatial information to recall complex information (Burgess, 2008). In a memory palace, a list of things that are difficult to remember are encoded as images that are easy to remember. These images are placed in locations in the memory palace in the learner's imagination. The learner memorizes the palace and can imagine walking through it, decoding the mnemonics into the target information (Qureshi et al, 2014). A mnemonic is an abbreviation of a more complex idea through symbols, letters, or images (Carney, 2011), e.g., ROY-G-BIV to remember the colors of the rainbow.

Each location must be rehearsed in the same order every time. The stronger the individual's presence within the memory palace and association of the mnemonics with the location, the stronger the recall (Qureshi et al, 2014).

Suppose a learner wishes to remember that they need to buy milk and set up an appointment to groom their dog. The two familiar locations in their memory palace are their wardrobe and bathroom. These locations in the real world are familiar, as the individual always visits their wardrobe in the morning to get dressed first, then always goes to the bathroom to brush their teeth second. In this way, a canonical order of the memory palace is established. As a mnemonic, a scene of a carton of milk is imagined in the wardrobe, and a wet dog with an overgrown coat is imagined in the bathroom. They rehearse moving from the wardrobe to the bathroom in their imagination. When they get home, they can remember the mnemonics and decode them into the tasks they wanted to remember.

Memory palaces are typically modeled on locations well-known to the learner. Someone might make 30 canonical locations in the imagined version of their childhood home. Then, when they populate the locations, mnemonics are created and placed, in order, in these locations. It takes effort to create the palace locations, remember the correct order, create effective mnemonics, and rehearse the palace so that it is remembered when needed. This effort can make this memory tool less viable for many people. It could be that providing a palace for learners, rather than requiring them to design one themselves, will reduce this burden.

Virtual reality (VR) is an experience of a computer-generated world (Mandal, 2013). Even abstract information is more easily understood and recalled when experienced through a virtual lens. This is because immersion leads to more interaction with the data (Huttner & Robra-Bissantz, 2017). It is plausible that the learning of a memory palace could be enhanced if it is done through VR.

Brain areas and functions are commonly taught across a wide array of disciplines, including cognitive science, psychology, and neuroscience. An effective tool for enhancing memorization would be useful for neuroscience education, and VR is a promising avenue to explore (Radianti et al, 2019). Examples of virtual reality brain projects can be found so far in a few impressive brain systems: The Neuro explorer (Gamehearts, 2018), the "Giant Walkthrough Brain" (Ingram & Day, 2015), "UW Virtual Brain Project™" (Rokers & Schloss, 2021) and "A Journey into the Brain" (Unimersiv, 2017). These projects aid in the visualization of the brain but often fail to distinguish brain parts in the visual presentation and often do not show brain function.

The UW Virtual Brain Project ™ is a system that was advertised as an interactive walkthrough of the brain through 3D narrated diagrams. It was created by the Neuroimaging Center at NYU Abu Dhabi (NYUAD) and Wisconsin Institute for the Discovery at University Wisconsin-Madison (Rokers & Schloss, 2021). Using their system, they ran a similar experiment to compare the effectiveness of headset VR compared to its desktop VR counterpart. Results of that study showed that students did not have significant improvements in memory retention. Although not significantly more effective, they did also show that VR was far more enjoyable for students as a learning platform. They note that their findings support the idea that as of right now, VR cannot be a replacement for classroom learning but rather an effective tool to make the classroom more dynamic (Rokers & Schloss, 2021).

While no difference was found in the UW Virtual Brain Project ™ experiment, prior literature indicates that the addition of a memory palace format within our Experiments should prove to be another distinction from what has currently been researched. Therefore, compared to the neuroscience tools currently available, our Brain VR memory palace is the first to explicitly be designed for the purpose of learning brain region names, functions, and locations using mnemonic imagery in a memory palace.

To investigate and answer the above questions we designed and created a memory palace that was coded into a 3D VR model. It was created to address the neuroscience education tool gaps mentioned above. Most notably, it makes use of the memory palace tool that was not part of the design of previous systems. Our visually engaging module depicts the brain as a series of floating islands at different elevations. This enables islands to represent the brain's gross anatomy without overwhelming detail. The island positioning mirrors the relative placement of the parts in real brains.

Each island is named with a welcome arch leading to mnemonic scenes that represent key parts within those main brain areas. Each scene has two image elements: the foreground represents the function, and the background represents the name of the part. Each mnemonic is distinct and easily recognizable as its own scene, spatially separated from others. An example is provided below of the Cerebellum (Figure 1).

Information about function is represented by having a pedestal for each scene that explains the mnemonic, as opposed to presenting the brain without learning aids. Each pedestal explains the name, function, their respective mnemonics, both in text and with a voice recording.

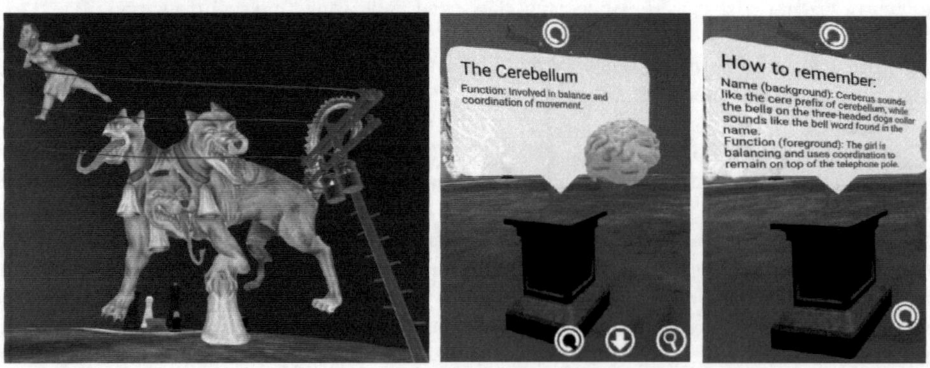

Figure 1. The girl in the foreground balancing on a telephone represents that the cerebellum oversees balance and coordination. The background is of the mythical Greek creature Cerberus with giant bells on its collar to help remember the name mnemonic of the brain part being Cere-bell-um. Desktop VR (DVR) and Headset VR (HVR) stimuli (left) with associated pedestal front (middle) and back (right)

2. THE BRAIN VR MEMORY PALACE

The memory palace is designed as a series of islands, representing gross brain regions, populated with scenes, which represent specific brain areas. The memory palace is represented in three ways: as a text document, as a series of still images, and as an immersive 3D VR model, which can be experienced through a desktop or head-mounted display interface

The first island, representing the brainstem, has one scene: the brainstem (Figure 2). The second island, representing the hindbrain, contains three brain areas: the cerebellum, the medulla oblongata, and the pons (Figure 2). The third island consists of two sub-islands, visually represented as platforms (Figure 3). The first sub-island has 4 scenes: the tegmentum, the tectum, the red nucleus, and the periaqueductal grey. The second sub-island represents the basal ganglia's three brain parts: the basal ganglia scene itself, the striatum, and the globus pallidus. The last island is the forebrain area. It contains nine scenes separated again into two sub-islands (Figure 3). The first sub-island contains the insular cortex, the pituitary gland, the corpus callosum, and the olfactory bulb. The second sub-island of the forebrain represents the limbic system, and it had scenes for itself (the limbic system), the hypothalamus, the thalamus, the amygdala, and the cingulate cortex.

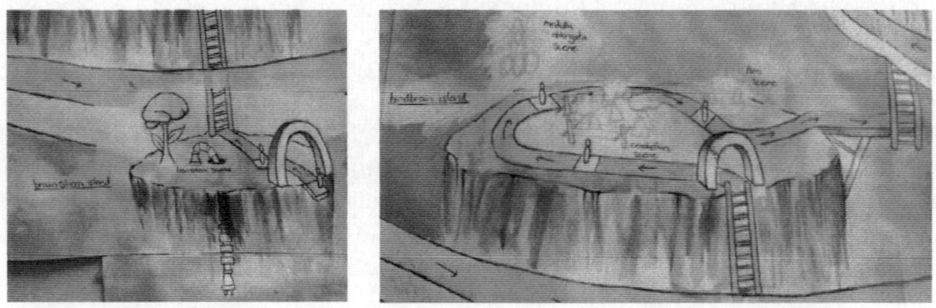

Figure 2. Overview sketch of the Brainstem Island (1 scene: The brainstem scene (left)) and of the Hindbrain Island (3 scenes: cerebellum, medulla oblongata, and the pons scenes (right))

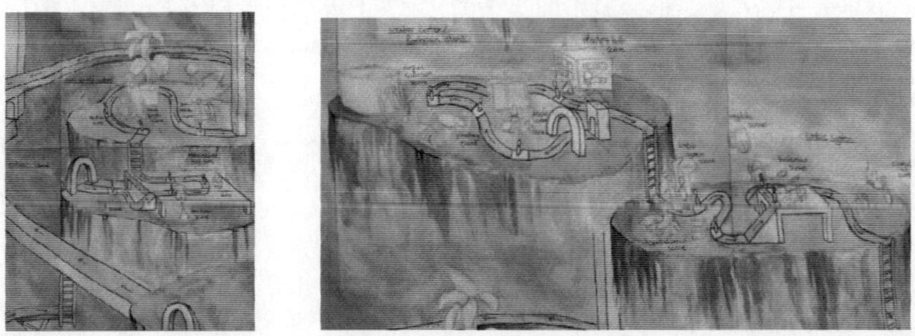

Figure 3. Overview sketch of Midbrain Island. (7 scenes: sub-island 1-tegmentum, tectum, red nucleus, and periaqueductal grey scenes; sub-island 2-basal ganglia, striatum, and globus pallidus scenes. (left)) and Overview sketch of Forebrain Island. (9 scenes: sub-island 1-insular cortex, pituitary gland, corpus callosum, and olfactory bulb scenes; sub-island 2-limbic system, hypothalamus, thalamus, amygdala, and cingulate cortex scenes.)

3. CONCLUSION

Although memory palaces are proven to be effective learning tools, students often do not make the effort to create them on their own. Because brain anatomy and function are challenging to learn, creating mnemonic tools for students might facilitate learning about the brain. In this paper, we present a memory palace created for learning basic brain anatomy and function. The effectiveness of this tool still needs to be tested. We are currently conducting an experiment to test its efficacy.

REFERENCES

Burgess N, 2008. Spatial cognition, and the brain. *National Library of Medicine,* Vol 1124, pp 77-97. Available at: https://pubmed.ncbi.nlm.nih.gov/18400925/ (Accessed: 5 August 2022)

Carney R. N, 2011. Mnemonic device. *Encyclopedia of Child Behavior and Development*, pp 958-961. Available: https://link.springer.com/referenceworkentry/10.1007%2F978-0-387-79061-9_1810 (Accessed: 11 February 2022)

Gamehearts, 2018. Neuroexplorer on oculus rift. *Metaquest Oculus*. Available: https://www.oculus.com/experiences/rift/1697976126910722/?locale=en_US (Accessed: 28 January 2022)

Huttner J.-P. and Robra-Bissantz S, 2017. An Immersive Memory Palace: Supporting the Method of Loci with Virtual Reality. *Americas Conference on Information System (AMCIS)*. Boston, USA, Available: https://www.researchgate.net/profile/Jan-Paul-Huttner/publication/317661051_An_Immersive_Memory_Palace_Supporting_the_Method_of_Loci_with_Virtual_Reality/links/5d551aff299bf151bad40d01/An-Immersive-Memory-Palace-Supporting-the-Method-of-Loci-with-Virtual-Reality.pdf (Accessed: 11 February 2022)

Ingram, J. and Day, T, 2015. The giant walkthrough brain with oculus rift, *YouTube*, Available: https://www.youtube.com/watch?v=C3l5RCbTxVY (Accessed: 11 February 2022)

Mandal S, 2013. Brief Introduction of Virtual Reality & its Challenges. *International Journal of Scientific & Engineering Research,* Vol 4, No. 4, pp 304-309. Available: https://citeseerx.ist.psu.edu/viewdoc/download?doi=10.1.1.302.4239&rep=rep1&type=pdf (Accessed: 11 February 2022)

Qureshi A. et al, 2014. The method of loci as a mnemonic device to facilitate learning in endocrinology leads to improvement in student performance as measured by assessments. *National Library of Medicine*, Vol 38, No. 2, pp 140-144. Available: https://www.ncbi.nlm.nih.gov/pmc/articles/PMC4056179/#B25 (Accessed: 11 February 2022)

Radianti J. et al, 2019. A systematic review of immersive virtual reality applications for higher education: Design Elements, lessons learned, and research agenda. *Computers & Education*, Vol 147. Available: https://www.sciencedirect.com/science/article/pii/S0360131519303276 (Accessed: 11 February 2022)

Rokers, B. and Schloss, K, 2021. Using virtual reality to help students understand the brain's complex systems, researchers demonstrate effectiveness of 3D visualization as a learning tool. *Science Daily*, Available: https://www.sciencedaily.com/releases/2021/08/210802160629.htm (Accessed: 5 August 2022)

Unimersiv, 2017. A Journey into the Brain. *Metaquest Oculus*. Available: https://unimersiv.com/will-soon-able-explore-human-brain-vr/ (Accessed: 5 August 2022)

USING MARKOV CHAIN ON ONLINE LEARNING HISTORY DATA TO DEVELOP LEARNER MODEL FOR MEASURING STRENGTH OF LEARNING HABITS

Tuan M. Tran[1] and Shinobu Hasegawa[2]
[1]School of Information Science, Japan Advanced Institute of Science and Technology (JAIST), Nomi City 923-1292, Japan
[2]Center for Innovation Distance Education and Research, Japan Advanced Institute of Science and Technology (JAIST), Nomi City 923-1292, Japan

ABSTRACT

A learner model reflects learning patterns and characteristics of a learner. A learner model with learning history and its effectiveness plays a significant role in supporting a learner's understanding of their strengths and weaknesses of their way of learning in order to make proper adjustments for improvement. Nowadays, learners have been engaging in online learning frequently and intensely, leaving behind tremendous learning history data that contain informative insights about the learners' learning patterns. This paper proposed a method for developing learner models by applying the Markov chain to learning history data. Our method transforms individual learners' resource use data in a learning course into a large amount of resource use sequences, then develops a Markov learner model, and generates the resource use steady state for each learner. The resource use density, the resource steady state, and the assessment scores of individual learners tell their learning patterns and the effectiveness of the learning patterns. From the Markov learner model, we generate a learner profile for describing learning patterns and an index for measuring the strength of learning habits of the learner. We verified our method by applying it to each course in the OULAD dataset to predict the learning performance using the index. The preliminary results gain up to 97% accuracy on the pass/fail prediction problem.

KEYWORDS

Clickstream Data, Online Learning Environment, Markov Chain, Learner Model, SRL Profile, SRL Index

1. INTRODUCTION

Online learning has a weighty contribution to the learning process. Nowadays, it is almost requisite that education institutions deliver learning materials online for students to self-study besides classroom times. Students' online learning activities produce undoubtedly gigantic data that somehow reveal and describe learning patterns by which the students use online resources for learning. Learner models are means to describe learning patterns. The characteristics of online learning bring an opportunity to generate learner models that can reflect learners' ways of learning adequately based on learning data about the learners themselves, therefore, helping learners know their learning patterns and gradually become aware of their strengths and weaknesses. Certainly, learning habits have a significant impact on the learning process. Good learning habits enhance the learning process. Bad ones prevent it. Learning patterns are made up of activity repetition; hence, they can be used to derive learning habits. This research aims to model learning habits and their effectiveness on learning performance. The contribution of this paper is a learner model that is generated from learning history data, able to reflect learning habits, and measurable. This contribution is accomplished by three main elements: the *Markov learner model* for students' online learning patterns, the *self-regulated learning (SRL) profile* to visualize the model, and *the SRL index* as a scalar measurement for the profile. Learners usually self-regulate their learning behavior consciously or unconsciously when engaging resources in OLEs (Bernacki et al., 2011). Therefore, the SRL prefix is used for the profile and the index.

2. METHODOLOGY

We will briefly review current research on the most popular type of online learning data known as clickstream, then describe the Markov chain and how to apply it to the learner model.

Online learning clickstream data mainly contain mouse clicks on learning resources, who click the resources and timestamps when they happen. A number of current research focus on clickstream data not only to predict students' performance in online learning environments (OLEs) but also to establish learning behavior models. Specifically, there have been applications of the Markov chain to modeling learning patterns and hidden learning stages of learners (Geigle & Zhai, 2017; Qiao et al., 2021; Waheed et al., 2020).

A Markov chain (Bertsekas & Tsitsiklis, 2000) is a sequence of states appearing through time with a special property in which the value of a state only depends on a state right before it and is independent of other previous states. It is called the Markov property. Learning in an OLE manifests as a sequence of access to resources provided by the environment. Learners access resources by various modes but the most recognizable type of access is mouse clicking on the resources and their inner content. OLEs usually present several resources at once, and a learner can freely use the resources in various orders. From these observations, a learning process in OLEs can be seen as a stochastic process with resources as its states.

In a Markov model, the probability distribution over states approaches stability as state transition happens a large number of times. This condition is known as the steady state where the probability distribution over states is independent of the likelihood each of the states initiates a sequence; therefore, a steady state is like a habit of that which a Markov model represents (Gilbert Strang, 2016).

The current existing studies produce learner models from collective data of groups of learners rather than from data about individual learners. In addition, the current models seemed not to reach a steady state to tell the enduring characteristics of learning patterns. We think that it is beneficial for individual learners to have their learner model reflect their very own learning patterns. Thus, our research strives for such a learner model.

2.1 Problem Statement

To generate a Markov model for a learner from their learning history, we state the problem as this. From a learner's record of resource use in a course in an OLE, what are the learner's habits of using resources?

In online learning, habits are patterns of resource access. These habits tend to maintain among courses with a similar design in terms of resource types. Therefore, habits that support the learner's success in one course can enable success in other courses of similar design. And habits that hinder learning progress in a certain course might prevent the learner from learning effectively in the others. In the following, we will describe how the Markov model helps analyze records of learning resources and develop the learner model to represent learning habits.

2.2 Arrangement of a Resource Use History to Form Resource Sequences

There are several OLEs being used, different from each other in the kind of data they are storing, but they share similar arrangement and information about resource use records, namely, what resources learners access or click in a certain time unit. Following the shared structure, we can read from a resource use history of learners about their learning pattern comprising of what resources have been used, sequences of resource access, and resource use before and after a certain milestone such as an exam or a lecture.

We developed Markov models from Online University Learning Analytics Dataset, also known as OULAD (Kuzilek et al., 2017). The time step unit in OULAD is a day. A learner often accesses plenty of resources in a day in an unknown order. So, we do not know resource use sequences in a day; however, it is possible to obtain sequences of resources a learner accesses from day to day successively. As shown in Figure 1, the resource use history data, when rearranged (top) and traversed (down) in ascending order of day and show a clearer sequence pattern. A resource use record of one learner, when being observed in this manner, generates a large number of sequences, sufficient to produce a Markov model relevant to the learners' patterns of resource use.

2.3 Markov Learner Model, SRL Profile, and SRL Index

We used the markovchain package (Spedicato, 2017) for R to build Markov learner models from OULAD. To describe and rank the learner model, we generated from the model two units named *SRL profile* and *SRL index*, respectively.

The *SRL profile* shows the frequency and density of resource use in a course, and the effectiveness of resource use in such a pattern. Frequency refers to a probability distribution over resource use, and density the number of access to resources.

The *SRL index* indicates how effective a resource use pattern is in corresponding to learning performance and is expressed in the form *SRL index*= $c\_score \sum_{i=1}^{n} r_i^{ss_i}$ where *c_score* is an accumulative assessment score a learner has earned in the course, r_i the density of resource *i* in the course measured by the number of resource access, ss_i the steady state probability of resource r_i, and *n* the number of resources available in the course. The term $r_i^{ss_i}$ illustrates a steady pattern of use of resource *i*. $\sum_{i=0}^{n} r_i^{ss_i}$ is a summary of resource use pattern of a learner in a course. An effective learning pattern is likely to result in a high cognitive performance, expressed in the term $c\_score \sum_{i=0}^{n} r_i^{ss_i}$. To retain data normality, log transformation is applied to the SRL index as *Log SRL index*= $log_2 (c\_score \sum_{i=1}^{n} r_i^{ss_i})$.

Figure 2 shows an SRL profile example. All four graphs comprise a big picture of learning patterns and SRL abilities of all learners grouped by their final results in a course. There are four final results in this case: *Distinction learners* who have passed the course with the highest scores, *Pass learners* who passed the course, *Fail learners* who have completed but not passed the course, and *Withdrawn learners* who have not completed the course. The big grey circles indicate the current states of the learner who owns this SRL profile. The upper-left boxplot (a) tells that the learner is in the Distinction group with an SRL index of about 11 points. The upper-right scatterplot (b) shows that the learner's cognitive score of more than 90 points in relation to his or her SRL index of about 11 points. The lower-left (c) and lower-right (d) scatterplots demonstrate the number of accesses to each resource and its steady state in the course.

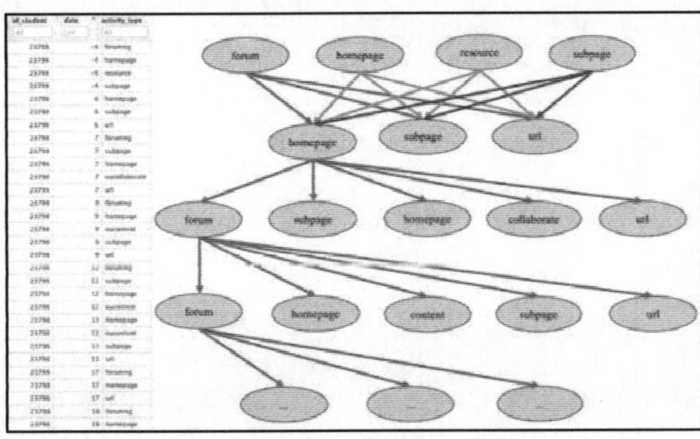

Figure 1. Formation of resource use sequences

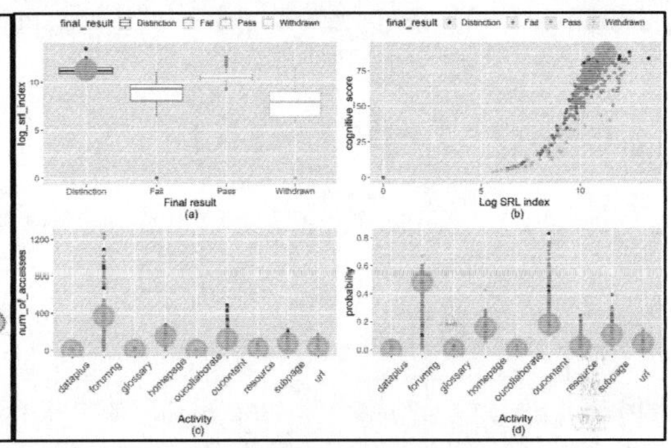

Figure 2. An SRL Profile

3. PRELIMINARY RESULTS

We justified the proposed learner model by developing learning performance prediction models from the SRL index and assessment scores, then compared the prediction accuracies with current state-of-the-art prediction models: *(i)* Hao et al. (2022) analyzing the sum of clicks on resources and average assessments scores to predict pass/fail final results with 93% accuracy and 0.88 F1-score, and *(ii)* Qiu et al. (2022) classifying resource types used by each student in a course to predict pass/fail final results with 97% accuracy and 0.98 F1-score, both on OULAD.

We generated SRL profiles for individual learners from their resource access throughout a whole course, computed the SRL indices, and used the SRL indices and accumulative assessment scores as features to build the machine learning models by the Support vector machine with linear kernel algorithm to predict the final results of pass or fail. Two approaches for splitting training and testing datasets were carried out. The first approach used one course offering and then predict the learning performance of students in other course offerings. The second approach was to split each course offering by a 0.5 training: 0.5 testing data ratio. Table 1 presents the mean, maximum, and minimum values with standard deviation (SD) of accuracy and F1-score of the prediction models developed in two approaches. Both approaches yielded high accuracies with the maximums equivalent to the state-of-the-art.

Table 1

Approach	Accuracy			F1-Score		
	Mean ± SD	Max	Min	Mean ± SD	Max	Min
1st	0.92 ± 0.02	0.94	0.87	0.90 ± 0.03	0.96	0.87
2nd	0.93 ± 0.02	0.97	0.91	0.93± 0.03	0.97	0.89

4. CONCLUSION

The proposed Markov learner model transforms learning history data into a descriptive and measurable learner profile that unifies learning activities, learning patterns, and their effectiveness. Our proposed method is not limited to a specific case like the OULAD, but can be generalized and applicable to almost any OLEs.

Our work has limitations as these. The first limitation relates to the verification of the model. It is important to apply the method to other open datasets and to specific learning history data at educational institutions to validate the method. Second limitation is of the SRL profile. The SRL profile intends to give learners a detailed illustration of their SRL patterns. Looking at their SRL profiles, learners are expected to recognize their SRL habits and be able to make suitable modifications. The current SRL profile somehow shows those kinds of SRL pattern information; however, it does not provide learners with insight or guidelines to make adjustments.

This study and its limitations suggest the following two future works. First is to consider online learning resources with the intentions, such as the purpose of use, timeframe, and lecture content that instructors and course designers implant in the resources. Second is about validation of the model. We plan to model students' learning history, then present the model to the students for their feedback and evaluation.

ACKNOWLEDGEMENT

This work was supported by Doctoral Research Fellowship (DRF) of JAIST.

REFERENCES

Bernacki, M. L., Aguilar, A. C., & Byrnes, J. P. (2011). Chapter 1. Self-regulated learning and technology-enhanced learning environments: An opportunity-propensity analysis. In G. Dettori & D. Persico (Eds.), *Fostering Self-Regulated Learning through ICT* (pp. 1–26). IGI Global. https://doi.org/10.4018/978-1-61692-901-5

Bertsekas, D. P., & Tsitsiklis, J. N. (2000). Markov chains. In *Introduction to Probability* (pp. 2–3). Massachusetts Institute of Technology, Cambridge, Massachusetts.

Geigle, C., & Zhai, C. (2017). Modeling MOOC Student Behavior With Two-Layer Hidden Markov Models. *Proceedings of the Fourth (2017) ACM Conference on Learning @ Scale*, 205–208. https://doi.org/10.1145/3051457.3053986

Gilbert Strang. (2016). Chapter 6. Eigenvalues and Eigenvectors. In *Introduction to Linear Algebra* (5th ed., pp. 288–303). Wellesley-Cambridge Press.

Hao, J., Gan, J., & Zhu, L. (2022). MOOC performance prediction and personal performance improvement via Bayesian network. *Education and Information Technologies*. https://doi.org/10.1007/s10639-022-10926-8

Kuzilek, J., Hlosta, M., & Zdrahal, Z. (2017). Open University Learning Analytics dataset. *Scientific Data*, *4*(1). https://doi.org/10.1038/sdata.2017.171

Qiao, L., Zhao, W., & Xu, X. (2021). Mining and Analysis of Self-regulated Learning Process Model: Based on Hidden Markov Model. *2021 Tenth International Conference of Educational Innovation through Technology (EITT)*, 276–281. https://doi.org/10.1109/EITT53287.2021.00061

Qiu, F., Zhang, G., Sheng, X., Jiang, L., Zhu, L., Xiang, Q., Jiang, B., & Chen, P. (2022). Predicting students' performance in e-learning using learning process and behaviour data. *Scientific Reports*, *12*(1), 453. https://doi.org/10.1038/s41598-021-03867-8

Spedicato, G. A. (2017). Discrete Time Markov Chains with R. *The R Journal*. https://journal.r-project.org/archive/2017/RJ-2017-036/index.html

Waheed, H., Hassan, S.-U., Aljohani, N. R., Hardman, J., Alelyani, S., & Nawaz, R. (2020). Predicting academic performance of students from VLE big data using deep learning models. *Computers in Human Behavior*, *104*. https://doi.org/10.1016/j.chb.2019.106189

THE VALUE OF VIRTUAL REALITY AS A COMPLEMENTARY TOOL FOR LEARNING SUCCESS

Thomas Keller, Rosalia Curcio and Elke Brucker-Kley
ZHAW School of Management and Law, Winterthur, Switzerland

ABSTRACT

A virtual reality learning unit for the functioning of a router is used to show how students at bachelor level can be provided with another teaching tool in the future, whereby the didactic approach of a change of perspective makes optimal use of the advantages of virtual reality and should enable a more profound understanding. Further studies are needed to determine a long-term learning effect as well as the efficiency of a combination of teaching methods. However, the high demand from students in the field study shows that students are open to virtual reality as a tool beyond traditional teaching methods.

KEYWORDS

Virtual Reality, Education, Change of Perspective, Field Study

1. INTRODUCTION

In this work, a virtual reality (VR) learning unit for explaining a router is created, optimized according to quality criteria and evaluated regarding the learning effect. Design criteria for the creation of the VR learning unit are derived from collected literature regarding potentials, learning effect, opportunities, challenges, and recommendations of the use of VR learning units at universities of applied sciences. Part of the literature review represents the conceptual design of the main functionalities of the selected network components. For each component, a use case is created based on the conceptual description as well as considering the design criteria, which is implemented using VR. Learning objectives are formulated during the creation of the use cases. The use cases cover only a part of the possible functions of the router. It is taken into account that the VR learning unit can be further developed with additional functions in the course of further work.

This paper is structured as follows. Chapters 2 to 4 state the relevance, objectives and applied methodology for the presented work. Chapter 5 gives a profound background on the state of the art. The VR learning unit with its design decisions are described in chapter 6. Chapter 7 contains the results of the field study which are discussed in chapter 8.

2. RESEARCH OBJECTIVE

Immersive VR applications offer numerous advantages when used in education, such as change of perspective, practical aspects and independent learning. As a result, an increase in learning success can take place. Nevertheless, VR applications are rarely used in education (Pirker et al., 2020). According to Martin-Gutierrez et al. (2017), a possible reason for this could be a lack of strategies and concepts regarding a media development and integration of the technology into the teaching process. Hellriegel and Čubela (2018) suggest that the rapid development of technologies is the reason for the low user numbers. Thus, there is only a limited amount of scientific publications dealing with virtual reality and its didactic use (Hellriegel and Čubela, 2018). Since little research has been done on how virtual reality can be integrated into the curriculum and how it can be part of a classroom experience, collaboration between educators and game designers is needed for future studies (Pirker et al., 2020; Hellriegel and Čubela, 2018).

The majority of studies reviewed by Pirker et al. (2020) evaluate the potential of virtual reality from the student's perspective. However, this is not sufficient for the development of learning environments. Future research should also consider the requirements, potential problems, and possible use cases from the instructor's perspective. Furthermore, according to Pirker et al. (2020), only a few studies have integrated game elements into their VR learning units. However, as this is seen as a valuable tool for learning information technology topics, this represents an elementary research gap (Pirker et al., 2020), which leads to the following research question for this work: "Does a change of perspective implemented by an immersive VR learning unit result in a measurable learning effect in action competence as well as technical competence? ".

3. METHODOLOGY

The approach follows the design science approach. This research paradigm is based on the creative and problem-solving application of the knowledge base for the creation of an artifact and for the evaluation of a new knowledge base. The design process includes determining design criteria, creating as well as evaluating the artifact (Hevner et al., 2004, p.76ff). SpringerLink, ACM Digital Library, IEEE Xplore Digital, and Web of Science were used as research databases. Didactical reduction, Learning Methods, Factors of a successful learning, Use of VR in education, VR chances and challenges in education, VR effects on learning, VR potential in education, recommendation use of VR-applications, and functionality of router are the used search terms.

During the development phase of the VR learning unit, several iterations of the design process are performed. After each iteration, compliance with the quality criteria is checked by conducting usability tests with different students as well as graduates. Iterations will be terminated once feedback reveals no new insights. Heterogeneous responses to the same topic are left open.

4. STATE OF THE ART

VR is well suited for explaining complex issues (Checa and Bustillo, 2020; Christ and Hirschi, 2021; Pirker et al., 2020). Like a workshop, students are encouraged to think actively and create their own experiences. With VR learning units, the acquisition of a wide variety of competencies, such as strategic problem-solving orientation, is possible. Learning in a shared virtual reality can reveal ways in which collaboration and problem solving work in practice (Reynard, 2017). Thus, according to Hellriegel and Čubela (2018), VR learning units show potential for increasing learning success as well as promoting constructivist learning. Scenarios can also be acted out using simulations (Reynard, 2017).

Hellriegel and Čubela (2018) evaluate the learning effect and potential of VR based on four surveyed principles for successful learning. The evaluations are confirmed by Zender et al. (2018), among others, who used brainstorming sessions with subject matter experts to determine the impact of VR for teaching and learning settings (Zender et al., 2018).

When developing a VR learning unit, cognitive overload must be avoided. According to Liu et al. (2017), this must be taken into account both in the design of the scenes and in the organization of the learning materials. The challenge is to align with the learners' cognitive process. For example, the number and arrangement of objects in the environment as well as the learners' level of knowledge must be taken into account. The organization and presence of pluralistic media, such as sound or animation, must also be considered. In addition, reducing repetitive delivery of information can help conserve cognitive resources (Liu et al., 2017).

Health side effects such as nausea, dizziness, or eye fatigue pose another challenge when using VR glasses (Zender et al., 2018). VR use can also have a detrimental effect in cases of severe anxiety. Due to this, an alternative solution must always be available when using VR learning sessions (Baniasadi, Ayyoubzadeh, and Mohammadzadeh, 2020).

Niedermeier and Müller-Kreiner (2019) conducted surveys in 2018 and 2019 with 124 students from Bavarian universities regarding their assessment of VR and AR technologies. The study was based on the question of how the students intend to use the technologies in their everyday studies in the future. At the time, the students surveyed were studying to become teachers, mainly in the fields of education, psychology and economics. The surveys revealed that the students knew what VR was. However, they showed little knowledge regarding learning scenarios that used VR or AR. The application of the technologies was rated as low by the students. It was striking that they stated that they had already used VR glasses more often than the far more accessible AR apps. Niedermeier and Müller-Kreiner (2019) concluded that students are not yet aware of the already widely established integration of AR even on mobile devices. According to the survey, the students surveyed consider it useful to use the two technologies as a supplement in didactic learning. The basis for these assessments was not investigated. Finally, the respondents were asked about their assessment of future learning. It became clear that digital media play a central role. However, the respondents were rather pessimistic about the regular use of VR and AR in everyday study in the next 10 years. Nevertheless, the survey showed that topics such as VR and AR would become more future-oriented in the next 50 years and would increase in terms of assessed importance. Students were also asked about their aspirations. The use of VR and AR technologies as supplementary learning methods was hardly mentioned. Interactive and individual learning was desired by the majority. Since VR and AR are said to have great potential to increase the learning success of students, Niedermeier and Müller-Kreiner (2019) recommend a didactically sensible variety of media with integration of VR and AR. An increased dialog with students can capture the needs for the optimal use of the media (Niedermeier and Müller-Kreiner, 2019).

A further assessment of the use of VR in everyday study was made by the ZHAW, the International Association of Lake Constance Universities (IBH) and the Lake Constance Graduate School (HTWG). By means of teaching projects, several teaching sequences were designed and implemented using VR systems. The aim of the projects was to develop evaluation criteria of possible uses of VR systems based on different teaching scenarios at the undergraduate level. The projects showed that the identification of suitable teaching scenarios proved to be difficult and the development laborious. Knaack et al (2019) estimates that the use of VR in teaching is not yet sufficiently efficient, given the high costs, the time required for programming, and the still unclear benefits. This is also confirmed by (Keller and Brucker-Kley, 2021; Keller, Brucker-Kley, and Ebert, 2020). Knaack et al (2019) recommend increasing the number of usefully applicable scenarios and making these scenarios available on a cross-university platform for continuous further development.

In a systematic literature review, Pirker et al. (2020) investigated the potential and application of VR for computer science education. For this purpose, they identified learning objectives, interaction properties, and challenges and advantages of using immersive VR learning units for computer science education and extracted recommendations for action. For example, for an improved learning effect, it is recommended to incorporate interaction, immersion, visualization, game-like design, use of metaphors and analogies, and social experiences within the virtual environments (Pirker et al., 2020). In a systematic review of the literature, Hellriegel et al. (2018) adopt the constructivist view to evaluate the potential of VR in the classroom. According to Liu et al. (2017), constructivism places learners at the center of learning and teaching. In this view, students are actively involved in processing information and constructing objects under the guidance of teachers. Hellriegel et al. (2018) recommend that teachers not only design the content selection of VR learning units due to the different scenarios and possibilities for action, but also consciously control didactic potentials with regard to students' possibilities for action and participation. To this end, teachers must be adequately trained (Hellriegel and Čubela, 2018).

According to Pirker et al. (2020), educational media with a high degree of technological immersion positively influence the engagement, presence, and motivation of students. Stimulating student motivation can additionally be done by means of interesting and age-appropriate stories on the topic. In order for the VR experience to be seen by students as more than just a playful element, the immersive experience must be embedded in the instructional sequence. This can be achieved by aligning the virtual environment with learning objectives. A side effect of using VR technologies is cybersickness. Pirker et al. (2020) recommend using teleportation as a method of locomotion, which can prevent nausea and dizziness when using immersive VR learning sessions. In addition, lecturers need to be present when using the VR applications to support students and possibly offer other tasks if cybersickness cannot be overcome. This is also confirmed by Hellriegel and Čubela (2018) in their study. From Pirker et al.'s (2020) study, it appears that integrating an introductory phase with a simple example program can eliminate possible uncertainties among users. In doing so, students can familiarize themselves with the controls. According to Pirker et al. (2020), the design of VR scenarios is thus not limited to complex issues, but can be applied to a wide variety of topics (Pirker et al., 2020). According to Baniasadi et al. (2020), learning scenarios should be developed that can be repeated as often as desired. It should also be considered that regular and immediate feedback is given when scenarios are completed to encourage the user (Baniasadi, Ayyoubzadeh, and Mohammadzadeh, 2020).

5. VR LEARNING UNIT

According to the objectives of this project, the use of virtual reality for explaining complex issues at university level will be tested. The change of perspective by means of VR is to be used as a supplement to traditional teaching methods. The choice of a router as the use case is justified by the fact that network components represent complex issues in computer science education. Routers represent central roles in networks and contribute an important part to information security. Due to the increasing relevance of data security, there is also a growing focus on networks and their components in education. The router has a multitude of functionalities, which can be illustrated and presented by means of VR. In the sense of a didactic reduction according to Lehner (2020), the content of the teaching material is reduced to two main functionalities of the router. These are limited to the assignment of IP addresses and the forwarding of communication requests to the next gateway. Since an understanding of a network is required for the assignment of IP addresses, this is also taught. The construction of two networks is therefore also part of the project. For the selection of the learning method, the needs of the students have to be taken into account. For example, according to Niedermeier and Müller-Kreiner (2019), students want interactive and individual learning. Students are encouraged to think actively and create their own experiences by means of VR. The change of perspective plays a central role in this. Students no longer have the entire context in front of them, but experience the router performing its tasks.

VR learning units promote the activation of students through self-directed action by means of interactions. As Hellriegel and Čubela (2018) also state, interaction and self-design of the learning process contributes to sustainable learning success. Curiosity as well as motivation of students must be encouraged (Hellriegel and Čubela, 2018). With the use of VR, students' interests can be addressed, which can lead to a promotion of intrinsic motivation. Another motivating component in learning units according to Hellriegel and Čubela (2018) is sample solutions. Students are made aware of correct interactions in the VR learning unit of this project, thus teaching pattern solutions. Also, correct answers cannot be revoked. Incorrect answers are not accepted. According to Baniasadi et al. (2020), learning units should also be able to be repeated as many times as needed. Most learning units in the VR learning unit can be repeated as many times as needed. Immediate feedback when completing learning units helps to motivate students.

The pilot study by Christ and Hirschi (2021) shows that test groups with repetitive process steps showed more motivation and higher learning progress than those who were randomly assigned a process step. When designing the learning unit, care is taken to ensure that students have to work their way through levels. Some of the exercises are repeated, but they become more challenging as the level increases. For example, there is some time pressure in Level 2 compared to Level 1 implemented in this VR learning unit. Repetition allows students to reinforce what they have learned. Students from Christ and Hirschi's (2021) pilot study wanted variety such as competition. At the different levels, trophies can be won depending on the speed of the user. This creates a competitive atmosphere.

Cognitive overload must be avoided when developing a VR learning unit (Liu et al., 2017). In the project, students have to master different tasks. For reducing the complexity, a scaffolding principle is applied (Singh, 2017). Help and components for the next tasks are shown only when the previous task is finished successfully. The procedure helps students to identify the relevant aspects of the task. To support the students' cognitive process, objects are deliberately placed in the project. Colors for the networks, the Internet, and the associated cubes serve as another aid. The same colors are used throughout all scenarios. The colors have a high contrast so that people with a visual impairment can also perceive the different colors.

Part of the teaching concept of a VR learning unit is the definition of learning objectives in terms of competencies (Reynard, 2017). Learning objectives are therefore defined for each learning unit of the project, as well as associated questions that can be queried after using the application. By answering the questions, the learning objectives become verifiable. The learning objectives as well as the associated questions also represent a summary for the students and contribute to the orientation of the learning content. Defining learning objectives also ensures that VR experiences are not only perceived by students as a playful element (Pirker et al., 2020).

A VR learning unit with 5 different scenes is developed to achieve the goal. In the first scene, two networks can be created and devices can be assigned an IP address. For the transition to the second scene, the change of perspective to the router, an Internet search is started. In the router, there are different levels for forwarding data packets from the perspective of a router. Each level is represented by its own scene. Since words are limited in explaining a VR learning unit, the executable Unity project for Windows can be found at (Curcio, 2022).

6. FIELD STUDY

The learning effect of using a VR application to introduce and explain a router is evaluated using a quantitative randomized field experiment according to Döring and Bortz (2016). Subjects are randomly divided into test and control groups for later comparison (control group design). In this field experiment, the test group trains with the VR learning unit and the control group trains with the conventional conceptual description of the network components with text and images. The training is conducted under guidance and observation.

The VR learning unit for explaining a network as well as a router was evaluated by 26 ZHAW students in the bachelor's degree program in business informatics. The majority (80%) of the respondents have no computer science background. Before and after testing, the subjects filled out a semi-structured questionnaire with semi structured questions (Curcio, 2022). Thus, the learning effect could be determined retrospectively. The detailed survey results are provided at (Curcio, 2022).

For testing, half of the subjects were presented with the VR learning unit, the other half with the theoretical preparation. In order to accompany the subjects during the execution, the students were assigned in groups of four. While two students were able to carry out the study with the theory on their own, the other two subjects were mainly accompanied in getting to know the VR learning unit and the corresponding interaction concept with the controllers. Students of the test group, who acquired the knowledge about routers purely theoretically, were offered to play through the VR learning unit as well after completing the questionnaires. All accepted this offer, which shows the curiosity and acceptance towards VR learning units.

Table 1 shows an evaluation of all tests before the knowledge transfer by means of the VR learning unit and the theory. To determine possible learning effects, the questionnaires of both groups were evaluated both before and after the knowledge transfer by means of the VR learning unit or the theory. A normal distribution of the sample is assumed. Thus, despite the rather small number of subjects of 26, trends can be described as to whether the VR learning unit leads to a learning effect. This will then be put in relation to the control group.

Table 1. Aggregated pre and post test results and comparison of the test group with the control group regarding the learning impact

	Correct answers concerning network functions	Correct answers concerning router functions	Combined learning impact for network and router functions
Test group (VR) pretest	60%	30%	n/a
Test group (VR) posttest	75%	55%	45%
Control group pretest	45%	30%	n/a
Control group posttest	90%	80%	125%

7. CONCLUSION

A measurable learning effect could be ascertained with the use of the VR learning unit based on the field study. The evaluated survey results show a learning effect of 45% after using the VR learning unit. The learning effect after the use of the theoretical preparation was also evaluated. The learning effect of 125% is much more than the learning effect with the use of the VR learning unit. From this it can be deduced that the sole use of a VR learning unit is not advantageous. It will probably be more beneficial to include a VR learning unit as an additional offering in the curriculum.

It is assumed that the highest learning effect is achieved with the use of the theoretical preparation followed by the use of the VR application. Thereby, it is important to define learning objectives, as well as corresponding questions for each task within the VR learning unit that can be asked after using the application. By answering the questions, the learning objectives can be verified. The learning objectives and the associated questions provide a summary for the students and contribute to the orientation of the learning content. The results from the study and the high demand show that the router use case is a suitable choice for a VR learning unit in higher education.

Another deduction from this field study result is that as long as VR must be considered new and challenging for the subjects the learning effect is negatively affected. Even if help is provided within the VR learning unit the subjects were reliant on help from the instructor. Which means that instructors with a profound knowledge of the learning units need to be available on site. Apart from that instructors need to have also a technical understanding of the VR infrastructure to solve technical problems which are ever present as long as the maturity of the technology is in its current state.

During the field study it was further observed that subjects of the VR learning unit showed signs of fatigue after 30 minutes. A longer learning unit is not recommended for students at bachelor level.

However, VR learning units show great potential for consolidating acquired knowledge. Above all, the change of perspective from the viewer to the performer makes it easy to deepen what has been learned. VR learning units should not be seen as an alternative, but as a supplement to classic teaching methods. If VR learning units are used in this way, they can find great use in teaching.

REFERENCES

Baniasadi, T., S.M. Ayyoubzadeh, and N. Mohammadzadeh, 'Challenges and Practical Considerations in Applying Virtual Reality in Medical Education and Treatment', *Oman Medical Journal*, Vol. 35, No. 3, 2020, p. e125.

Checa, D., and A. Bustillo, 'A Review of Immersive Virtual Reality Serious Games to Enhance Learning and Training', *Multimedia Tools and Applications*, Vol. 79, No. 9, 2020, pp. 5501–5527.

Christ, O., and M. Hirschi, 'Virtual Reality in der Berufsbildung. Pilotstudie der login Berufsbildung AG und der Hochschule für Angewandten Psychologie (FHNW)', January 2021.

Curcio, R., 'Router Learning Unit', June 7, 2022.

Döring, N., and J. Bortz, *Forschungsmethoden und Evaluation in den Sozial- und Humanwissenschaften*, 5. vollständig überarbeitete, Aktualisierte und erweiterte Auflage., *Springer-Lehrbuch*, Springer, Berlin Heidelberg, 2016.

Hellriegel, J., and D. Čubela, 'Das Potenzial von Virtual Reality Für Den Schulischen Unterricht-Eine Konstruktivistische Sicht', *MedienPädagogik: Zeitschrift Für Theorie Und Praxis Der Medienbildung*, 2018, pp. 58–80.

Hevner, A., S.T. March, J. Park, and S. Ram, 'Design Science in Information Systems Research', Vol. MIS Quarterly, 28 (1), 2004, pp. 75–105.

Keller, T., and E. Brucker-Kley, 'Experiences with Virtual Reality at Secondary Schools: Is There an Impact on Learning Success?', in D. Ifenthaler, D.G. Sampson, and P. Isaías (eds.), *Balancing the Tension between Digital Technologies and Learning Sciences*, *Cognition and Exploratory Learning in the Digital Age*, Springer International Publishing, Cham, 2021, pp. 77–94.

Keller, T., E. Brucker-Kley, and N. Ebert, 'The Use of Virtual Reality at Lower Secondary Schools', in P. Isaias, D.G. Sampson, and D. Ifenthaler (eds.), *Technology Supported Innovations in School Education*, *Cognition and Exploratory Learning in the Digital Age*, Springer International Publishing, Cham, 2020, pp. 15–32.

Knaack, R., J. Wickert, D. Volz, N. Münchbach, W. Eich, P. Hug, and T. Hocker, 'Einsatz von" Virtual Reality" in Der Ausbildung von Ingenieurinnen Und Ingenieuren', *4. Symposium Zur Hochschullehre in Den MINT-Fächern, Nürnberg, 26.-27. September 2019*, Technische Hochschule Nürnberg, 2019, pp. 176–183.

Liu, D., C. Dede, R. Huang, and J. Richards, *Virtual, Augmented, and Mixed Realities in Education*, Springer Berlin Heidelberg, New York, NY, 2017.

Martín-Gutiérrez, J., C.E. Mora, B. Añorbe-Díaz, and A. González-Marrero, 'Virtual Technologies Trends in Education', *Eurasia Journal of Mathematics, Science and Technology Education*, Vol. 13, No. 2, 2017, pp. 469–486.

Niedermeier, S., and C. Müller-Kreiner, 'VR/AR in Der Lehre!? Eine Übersichtsstudie Zu Zukunftsvisionen Des Digitalen Lernens Aus Der Sicht von Studierenden', 2019.

Pirker, J., A. Dengel, M. Holly, and S. Safikhani, 'Virtual Reality in Computer Science Education: A Systematic Review', *26th ACM Symposium on Virtual Reality Software and Technology*, 2020, pp. 1–8.

Reynard, B.R., and 04/26/17, 'The Impact of Virtual Reality on Learning -', *Campus Technology*, n.d. https://campustechnology.com/articles/2017/04/26/the-impact-of-virtual-reality-on-learning.aspx.

Singh, G., 'Using Virtual Reality for Scaffolding Computer Programming Learning', *Proceedings of the 23rd ACM Symposium on Virtual Reality Software and Technology, VRST '17*, Association for Computing Machinery, New York, NY, USA, 2017, pp. 1–2.

Velev, D., and P. Zlateva, 'Virtual Reality Challenges in Education and Training', *International Journal of Learning and Teaching*, Vol. 3, No. 1, 2017, pp. 33–37.

LEARNING AND TEACHING COMPUTATIONAL THINKING: A CROSS-DISCIPLINARY, COLLABORATIVE, USER-CENTERED DESIGN MODEL

Mahnaz Moallem, Dastyni C. Loksa, Marcia Vandiver, Qing Li, Qijie Cai, Rachel Billman, Lea Ann Christenson, Melike Kara and Christine Engbert
Towson University, 8000 York Rd. Towson, MD 21252, USA

ABSTRACT

The paper shares the results of the process of forming a cross-disciplinary collaborative team and using a user-centered design framework to co-create a self-directed, self-paced, personalized, flexible learning environment as an alternative approach to preparing PK-8 preservice teachers to teach computational thinking. It is part of a larger project that attempts to respond to the need to create a computer science curriculum within a credentialing learning environment.

KEYWORDS

Computational Thinking, Collaborative Design Model, User-Centered Design, Computer Science and PK-8 Preservice Teachers, Alternative Pathway

1. INTRODUCTION

Despite efforts to underscore the need for computing and computational thinking skills for all students and demonstrated evidence that computational thinking (CT) and computer science (CS) should be introduced in earlier grades and embedded throughout the school experience (e.g., Wurman & Donovan, 2020), CT/CS in PK-8 teacher education programs remains inconsistent and, in many cases, non-existent (Code.org, 2020). There is a lack of teacher certification programs preparing PK-8 teachers with a deeper knowledge of CS concepts and capabilities. Initial training opportunities in colleges of education are scarce. Even though there are professional development (PD) opportunities for in-service teachers, preservice teachers do not benefit from these opportunities due to their lack of experience and practical knowledge. Despite national efforts, there is still a lack of well-constructed, high-quality CT/CS preparation programs for PK-8 preservice teacher candidates (PTCs). PK-8 teacher preparation programs in the U.S. find it challenging to incorporate an add-on quality CS certification program due to 1) a lack of PTCs' interest and understanding of CS (Google/Gallup, 2020), 2) little room for adding coursework to existing teacher education programs, and 3) challenges training faculty to teach CT/CS concepts and courses. Thus, CT/CS education advocates have recommended that education systems initiate alternative pathways and improve them over time (Code.org, 2018).

1.1 The Purpose of the Study

The paper shares the results of forming a cross-disciplinary collaborative team and using a user-centered design framework to co-create a *self-directed, flexible, and open learning* (SDFOL) environment as an alternative approach to preparing PK-8 PTCs to teach CT. It is part of a larger project that attempts to respond to the challenges mentioned above by creating a curriculum for CS within a credentialing learning environment. It further applies the literature review results in conceptualizing a co-design framework to develop a pilot SDFOL module on CT for the learner-managed CS credentialing learning environment. The module aimed to transform the teaching and learning process from a course-based, instructor-guided approach to the SDFOL model.

1.2 Cross-Disciplinary Collaborative Design Team

A cross-disciplinary partnership was formed to exchange and share expertise, ideas, resources, and responsibilities throughout the design and development process. It was to provide opportunities for the team members to learn from each other while designing and reflecting on the intentions and implications of the initiative and improving their knowledge and skills of the CS/CT. The cross-disciplinary partners consisted of two computer science experts, five PK-8 teacher educators, three instructional/learning design experts, two instructional developers, and four diverse PTCs. Also, an advisory board comprised of community members' representatives was formed to advise and review various project phases.

2. COLLABORATIVE AND USER-CENTERED DESIGN: A REVIEW OF THE LITERATURE

Self-directed learning (SDL) originated in andragogy or adult education (Knowles, 1975). According to Knowles (1989), *SDL* is an environment in which learners take the initiative with or without the help of others, assess their learning needs, formulate goals, implement appropriate learning strategies, and evaluate their learning outcomes. As an instructional method, *SDL* refers to independent learning in which the learning materials are designed and developed in advance, predicting that learners take the primary responsibility for planning, carrying out, monitoring, evaluating, and reflecting on their learning (Pintrich, 2004). The adult education literature points to promoting motivation, metacognition, and self-regulation as the most important benefits of self-directed learning (e.g., Knowles, 1975; Brockett & Hiemstra, 1991; Gibbons, 2002; Long, 2000). Studies show that SDL correlates with students' academic performance and is a good indicator of academic achievement in the traditional classroom (e.g., Cazan and Schiopca, 2013; Khiat, 2015; Malison, 2018; Tekkol & Demiral, 2018).

Web-based, open, and flexible learning provides the necessary components for creating an engaging SDL environment. In a web-based, computer-mediated self-directed learning environment, instructional materials are prepared in advance of the instructional events (Keller, 2010), including instructional and motivational strategies at the time of development based on predictions of learner motivation, interest, attitude, abilities, entry knowledge, and skills. Based on the literature, SDFOL can be conceptualized as an environment that offers four specific conditions for learning: 1) enhancing motivation by incorporating interest-based learning, 2) providing flexibility to encourage control of pace, time, and flow of learning, 3) offering an open learning environment to allow the learner to choose what to learn and how to learn and what resources to use, and 4) promoting metacognition by encouraging self-determination, self-control, and self-regulation throughout the learning process.

2.1 Design Framework

SDFOL was used as the general design framework. The framework offers the learners control and authority over their learning. It is free from the limitations of time, place, and pace of learning. The flexibility further includes choices regarding the entry and exit points and the selection of learning activities to meet learners' needs, communication methods, assessment tasks, and educational resources. The SDFOL aims to make learners more self-determined and independent as a learner-centered pedagogy and describes the teachers as designers of the learning environment and learning facilitators. SDFOL empowers learners and teachers to extend learning opportunities beyond traditional learning environments by bridging formal and informal learning experiences through the effective use of technology and resources. Digital learning modalities combined with performance-based progressions make it possible to meet each student's unique needs (iNACOL, 2016).

Moreover, interest-driven learning is used as a motivator for learning activities. The benefits of interest-driven learning as a motivator for learning activities are associated with the learner's perception that specific knowledge or skills help pursue an interest (a mastery goal). It is also connected with more effort and persisting longer at the tasks. Self-determination theory demonstrates that intrinsic motivation leading to persistence cannot emerge unless a person has a sense of autonomy (Ryan & Deci, 2006). Interest-driven learning emphasizes motivating and sustaining learner interest by offering relevant real-world tasks and creating a conversational, reflective, and innovative learning space (Spector, 2014). Culture and context are addressed through interest-driven learning through meaningful, authentic, culturally relevant environments and an opportunity to self-assess and reflect on applying the knowledge to solve problems.

2.1.1 Iterative Collaborative Design Process and Study of its Impact

Developmental/Design-based research was used to study the collaborative design and development process and its impact on the quality of the products and the team's knowledge, skills, and attitude. The following questions guided the study.

1. What process did the collaborative team use to design and develop the pilot module on computational thinking?
2. What was the result of the learner analysis, and how did the team use the results?
3. What were the effects of the collaborative design and development approach on the team members' knowledge, skills, and attitude toward integrating CT in their teacher education courses?
4. What impact did the collaborative design process have on the quality of products?
5. What evidence suggests that the module's design framework, design specifications, and delivery strategy were effective as an alternative model to preparing PK-8 TCs to teach CT?

2.1.2 Data Collection and Data Sources

Both quantitative and qualitative data were collected.

- Collaborative team meetings minutes and discussions
- Collaborative team members' deliverables and products
- Open-ended self-reflection questionnaires for collaborative team members
- Teacher education candidates survey, review protocol, and interviews
- Student personas developed by teacher education faculty
- Observation of the team members' discussion and collaboration (conducted by one team member)

The data collection is still underway. The iterative process of collecting and analyzing data has been informing the revisions and modifications and ensuring ongoing progress toward achieving the goals and objectives of creating the learning materials. Formative elements of the review have been continuous, reflective, and responsive. They allowed examining the challenges of preparing a CT module, adopting targeted pedagogies, developing interactive, personalized self-directed learning materials, and enhancing the collaborative teams' knowledge, skills, and attitude.

3. INITIAL RESULTS

Q 1. Throughout the co-design process, team members spent quality time discussing and learning from each other with different backgrounds and CS knowledge. As the team developed a better understanding of the CS curriculum and CT concepts, it focused on analyzing learners and identifying salient characteristics of preservice teachers, particularly their interests, background knowledge, and pedagogical, socio-economic, and ethnic backgrounds. The next step centered on developing a curriculum map for CS, creating the design specifications and guidelines for elements of the curriculum, focusing on decomposing CT concepts, and developing templates for its lessons. Once the template for the design of the CT concepts was developed, the team spent an iterative process creating storyboards and prototypes.

Table 1. Q 2. Collaborative team members responded to a series of open-ended questions

Questions	Key Findings
In your opinion, how well is the team progressing toward its goal?	"I think we are making good progress" "Content design is moving along, and we have some plans for other aspects of the project. I think there are still areas that will need to do extensive work on, specifically the personalization and assessment areas."
What aspects of our meetings do you find most helpful?	"Working in the meeting time rather than outside the meetings whenever possible." "Discussion of specific items," "The ideas and perspectives from the rest of the team."
Is there anything you would like to change about our planning meetings?	"I am not sure we need to review everything in every meeting. I feel like it is taking away much time from executing," "I have had a hard time wrapping my head around the final version without an example. . ."
Is the planning and team meeting process a good learning experience for you?	"I learn more and more about CT and the CS/Coding world every time we meet. I have a fairly decent understanding of CT, but the CS/Coding information that has been discussed in our planning of the modules is totally new for me," "Yes. It is great to learn about the norms in education outside of a CS context. Many CS educators are not trained as educators," "It's helpful to discuss concepts and analyze examples."
How do planning meetings compare to a workshop to learn about CT?	"We are not learning information THEN doing; we are doing and learning information BY doing." "This is more focused and personalized." "Our project leads us through the discovery process with input from multiple perspectives rather than a workshop that has an

	intended, guided path towards understanding." "Our project leads us through the discovery process with input from multiple perspectives rather than a workshop that has an intended, guided, path towards understanding."
Have planning meetings helped you potentially integrate CT into your courses for teacher education students?	"Yes - it inspires me to continue down a research path that I have already set out on." "Not as of yet, but I suspect it will. Even defining what we mean by each of the skills in CT will allow me to make them explicit in the classroom." "Yes. Being on this team helped me to think about the Computational Thinking background knowledge and hands-on experiences."

Q 3. PTCs' responses to a survey asking questions about their backgrounds, experiences with CT, and learning preferences showed that most respondents recognized the value of CT concepts. However, some did not understand how to incorporate concepts into the curriculum or teach it in their classrooms. There seems to be a disconnect between associating and actualizing CT concepts (in name and/or definition) with the corresponding pedagogical skills. Visual (88 of 93 students), hands-on (83 of 95 students), and self-paced pedagogies (85 of 95 students) were listed as the most favorable learning preferences. Reading written text was the least favorable learning preference. Only about half of the participants knew about and/or had taken coursework on CT (56.6% and 43.86%) or believed they used it (51.42%), but most thought it helped solve problems (68.58%). PTCs showed an interest in CS, finding it interesting. They believed it was important for their students to learn (>80%) and maybe even more important for underrepresented students (88.66%). Most participants preferred visual information (94.63%) that they could apply with hands-on activities to learn (87.37%) and were curious about the mechanisms that make things work (82.11%). Most believed that CT is helpful outside of CS (92.63%) but lacked confidence in their knowledge and ability to implement CT in their teaching without additional instruction (77.45% and 81.06%). Data related to questions 4 and 5 are under analysis and will be reported at the CELDA presentation.

4. SIGNIFICANCE

The SDFOL module on CT for PK-8 teachers has a high potential to be scaled at the state and national levels. A well-designed module provides pilot evidence to use the credentialing pathway as a model for preparing teachers to teach CS. The study's results provide evidence of the advantages and challenges of the collaborative design approach. They further show the impact of the rigorous, research-supported, flexible learning environment on empowering PK-8 PTCs and their CT competencies. It offers evidence of whether this transformative approach will increase teacher candidates' confidence and motivation in teaching CT and whether it will be a good model to motivate PK-8 PTCs to teach CS. It will also show if the collaborative design can serve as an innovative PD approach for education faculty.

REFERENCES

Cazan, M. & Schiopca, A. (2013). Self-directed learning, personality traits, and academic achievement, *Procedia - Social and Behavioral Sciences, 1(27)* 640 – 644

Gibbons, M. (2002). *The self-directed learning handbook: Challenging adolescent students to excel*. San Francisco, CA: Jossey-Bass.

Google LLC & Gallup, Inc. (2020). *Current Perspectives and Continuing Challenges in Computer Science Education in U.S. K-12 Schools*, Retrieved from https://services.google.com/fh/files/misc/computer-science-education-in-us-k12schools-2020-report.pdf

Khiat, H. (2015). Academic performance and the Practice of self-directed learning: The adult student perspective. *Journal of Further and Higher Education*, 9486 (October), 1–16. https://doi.org/10.1080/0309877X.2015.1062849

Knowles, M. S. (1975). *Self-directed learning: a guide for learners and teachers. Self-directed Learning A Guide for Learners and Teachers*. p.18, New York, NY: Association Press.

Long, H. B. (2000). Understanding self-direction in learning. In H. B. Long & Associates (Eds.), *Practice & theory in self-directed learning* (pp.11-24). Schaumburg, IL: Motorola University Press.

Malison, K. (2018). An exploratory study of self-directed learning: the differences between it and non-it employees in Thailand. *Journal of Entrepreneurship Education*, 21(3), 1-16.

Wurman, Z. & Donovan, W. (2020). *Breaking the code: The state of computer science education in American's public schools*. White Paper, Pioneer Institute: Public Policy Research. Retrieved from https://files.eric.ed.gov/fulltext/ED605364.pdf

LONG-TERM INTERACTION WITH A VIRTUAL ROBOT FACILITATOR OF SMALL GROUP DISCUSSIONS

Elinor Mizrahi, Noa Danzig and Goren Gordon[1]
Curiosity Lab, Department of Industrial Engineering, Tel-Aviv University, Israel

ABSTRACT

In this contribution, we present a follow-up work-in-progress on an innovative system for facilitating small-group online discussions using an avatar during a video conference. A previous study has shown that the system had an effective, understandable, and more participatory interaction. Here, we examine long-term usage and its effects on subjective perceptions as well as objective engagement measures. Five groups of fifth and sixth grade students had six interactions with the avatar's facilitation. The results of the study show that all measures remained stable throughout the entire interaction, suggesting that the previous results were not due to the novelty effect and that the system is capable of maintaining long-term engagement and learning.

KEYWORDS

Virtual Agent, Group Activity, Video Conference, Facilitation

1. INTRODUCTION

Prior to the COVID-19 pandemic, online learning environments for K-12 have not been a mainstream methodology. However, the pandemic has revealed the importance, as well as the advantages and drawbacks of video conferencing technologies, as well as other social educational technologies.

We report the continued evaluation of our system, that aims to facilitate small online group discussions during video conferencing (Mizrahi et al., 2021). Students interacted with the system, which consists of: (i) an avatar, a virtual agent, who manages the educational group activity as well as facilitates the online discussion; (ii) Zoom, and (iii) a screen for the educational content, which is produced on an activity site designed for that purpose.

Previously, during a single-session interaction, the system was found to be effective for discussions and engagement in group activities (Mizrahi et al., 2021). In this new report, we evaluated the long-term use of the system, along multiple dimensions, such as learning, perceptions and engagement.

In the study, five groups (two in fifth and three in sixth grade) interacted with the system, performing six different activities on socio-emotional learning. All the activities performed were with the avatar facilitation. Questionnaires regarding the perception of activity, as well as their learning of the content was administered after each activity. The system also recorded and analyzed who spoke and their facial expressions.

Our results show that the long-term use of the system does not suffer from the novelty effect, in all dimension, i.e. learning, engagement and perception of the activity remain high throughout all six activities.

This pilot study continues to support the concept of a virtual robot facilitator for long-term use in small group online discussions.

[1] Corr. Author: goren@gorengordon.com

2. RELATED WORK

Small group learning activities have been considered as a promising education format (Johnson & Johnson, 2009). Small-group activities can enhance student thinking and learning of both formal and informal content and skills, (Elias & Schwab, 2006; Hadwin et al. 2018; Webb, 1995).

Studies have shown that personal face-to-face interactions and discussions in small groups have their advantages (Chen & Chen, 2015; Thomas & Thorpe, 2019). The question of scaling-up group facilitation is, thus, of prominent importance. In group activities, the role of group facilitator is important in teaching (Franco & Nielsen, 2018). This is because when students have a supportive environment it will foster both the understanding of the content learned, the task value, and positive beliefs about the students' abilities and thus their motivation to learn (Pietarinen et al., 2021).

The appearance of virtual visual agents, avatars, has also initiated a wider usage of conversational and social aspects of interaction. While a face of a conversational agent has been shown to increase rapport and other participant-agent-related measures (Shamekhi et al., 2018), it remains an open question of what *educational benefits* such an avatar presents. Although guiding virtual agents may have disadvantages, they have been found to have the ability to manage time better, to be more objective and efficient than a human facilitator (Rosenberg-Kima et al., 2020).

In order to have real education value, a long-term evaluation must be performed, to rule out the novelty effect. The novelty effect may cause an increase in achievements at first and then is characterized by a decrease of up to about eight weeks (Clark, 1988). In human-robot interaction, it has been found that over time there is a decrease in engagement (de Wit, 2020), but at the same time, there is no complete abandonment of the system due to the use of a system that elicits diverse interaction (Coninx et al., 2015; Davison et al., 2020)

Similarly, distance learning systems have been tested in the long term. During Covid-19, research found that there are no differences in the distance learning experience and system benefits, but the quality of learning has decreased over time (Tulaskar & Turunen, 2022). However, a study of MOOCs (massive online open courses) found that student involvement increased over time (Hsu, 2021).

This study will address the question of whether the benefits of an online learning system with video conference guided by a social virtual agent will remain effective even in long-term use.

3. METHODS

THE SYSTEM: The system is composed of a student-centered site, with which the students interact. The site includes: (a) a robotic avatar from SitePal.com (b) a frame with the Zoom web API, that enables gallery view to see all the group members and; (c) an interaction part, which shows the content and enables answering questions Mizrahi et al. (2021).

During the interaction, the students are presented with the content and after answering on their own, the avatar asks them to start a discussion. When the students are done with either question or discussion, a "done" button is presented to enable the continuation of the activity.

The system is also equipped with perceptual sensors. Using face-api.js, an on-client facial expression recognition system was activated, that enabled real-time and continuous analysis of facial expression such as happy and angry. Moreover, a volume-meter was activated client-side to detect speech of the students in real-time.

The avatar was programmed with best-practices of group facilitation behaviors. An expert group facilitator aided in formalizing the appropriate behaviors, e.g. how to give feedback and how to handle objections, which were then programmed into the avatar.

PARTICIPANTS: The study was conducted on fifth and sixth grade students, in a single elementary school. The content was taken from a curricular program on socio-emotional learning, and adapted to our system.

From fifth grade, 10 participants (3 males, 7 females) were recruited. The participants were divided into 2 groups: 1) 5 participants with 5 females, 2) 5 participants with 3 males and 2 females. From sixth grade, 11 participants (7 males and 4 females) were recruited. The participants were divided into 3 groups: 1) 4 participants with 2 males and 2 females, 2) 4 participants with 3 males and 1 female, 3) 3 participants with 2 males and 1 female.

Due to technical issues with the system, mainly due to low internet connectivity, not all participants had performed all activities. The results below, Fig. 1, present the number of participants in each analysis.

All participants' parents signed a consent form. The study was approved by the IRB and the ministry of education.

MEASURES: The study was designed to have two types of measures: subjective, self-report, and objective, perceptual. After each activity, each student filled out two types of online questionnaires: the first was composed of eight 5-point Likert scale questions regarding the activity, and the second was composed of four true/false questions regarding the educational content of the activity. Furthermore, the perceptual part of the system supplied information regarding when each student spoke and a continuous stream of facial expressions (see Mizrahi et al. (2021) for more details).

4. RESULTS

Engagement: Student engagement remained high throughout the entire long-term use of the system, Fig.1(top). Both the duration of speech, as well as the amount of time participants were detected to be happy, fluctuated over the activities, but did not exhibit a monotonic decrease, as predicted by the novelty effect. A linear regression of the engagement as a function of time did not detect any significant trend (happy: $r=0.063$, $p=0.905$, speech: $r=-0.062$, $p=0.907$, Wald test with t-distribution).

Perceptions: Students' perception of the group activity, which is of paramount important in our system, remained constant throughout the long-term use of the system. We present the most relevant questions, regarding the student's perception of the group efficiency (q3) and interaction (q4), as well their perception of their own involvement in the activity (q5, q6). As presented in Fig.1(middle), there was little change in their perceptions from the first, second, fourth and last activity. A linear regression of the perception as a function of time did not detect any significant trend (q3: $r=-0.219$, $p=0.78$, q4: $r=0.866$, $p=0.134$, q5: $r=-0.682$, $p=0.318$, q6: $r=-0.283$, $p=0.717$, Wald test with t-distribution).

Learning: Student's achievements on the content assessment after each activity, also remained high throughout the long-term use of the system, Fig.1(bottom). While this depends mostly on the content of the activity, it signals that the students were attentive and learned something during the activity. A linear regression of their achievements as a function of time did not detect any significant trend ($r=-0.378$, $p=0.459$, Wald test with t-distribution).

5. DISCUSSION AND CONCLUSION

This short paper introduces a work-in-progress on the evaluation of a novel system that facilitates small group on-line discussion using video conferencing and best practices. While previous work has demonstrated the viability of the platform, for an educational system to be of any value, its long-term use must be evaluated. While distance learning during the COVID-19 pandemic has shown a decrease in effectiveness (Tulaskar & Turunen, 2022), we have shown that the use of our system has resulted in sustained engagement, positive perception and learning for a relatively long duration.

Moreover, previously the system has been used to teach curricular content, such as literature and science. We have shown in this work-in-progress that even socio-emotional learning content can be effectively delivered through our system.

The pilot study had several major limitations, most notably are the continued technical difficulties due to low internet connection of the participants, as well as the small number of participants.

Nevertheless, the pilot study results show the promise of the novel system as a long-term facilitator of more discussions and more learning in an environment that is becoming more prevalent in the formal educational system.

Future work aims to use the system as a tool to assess group dynamics, by analyzing the multi-modal data of the facilitated activities. Moreover, future developments include introducing speech recognition that will greatly enhance the effectiveness of the discussions. Finally, we aim to develop a more robust, stable and commercially viable system for the use of the formal education system.

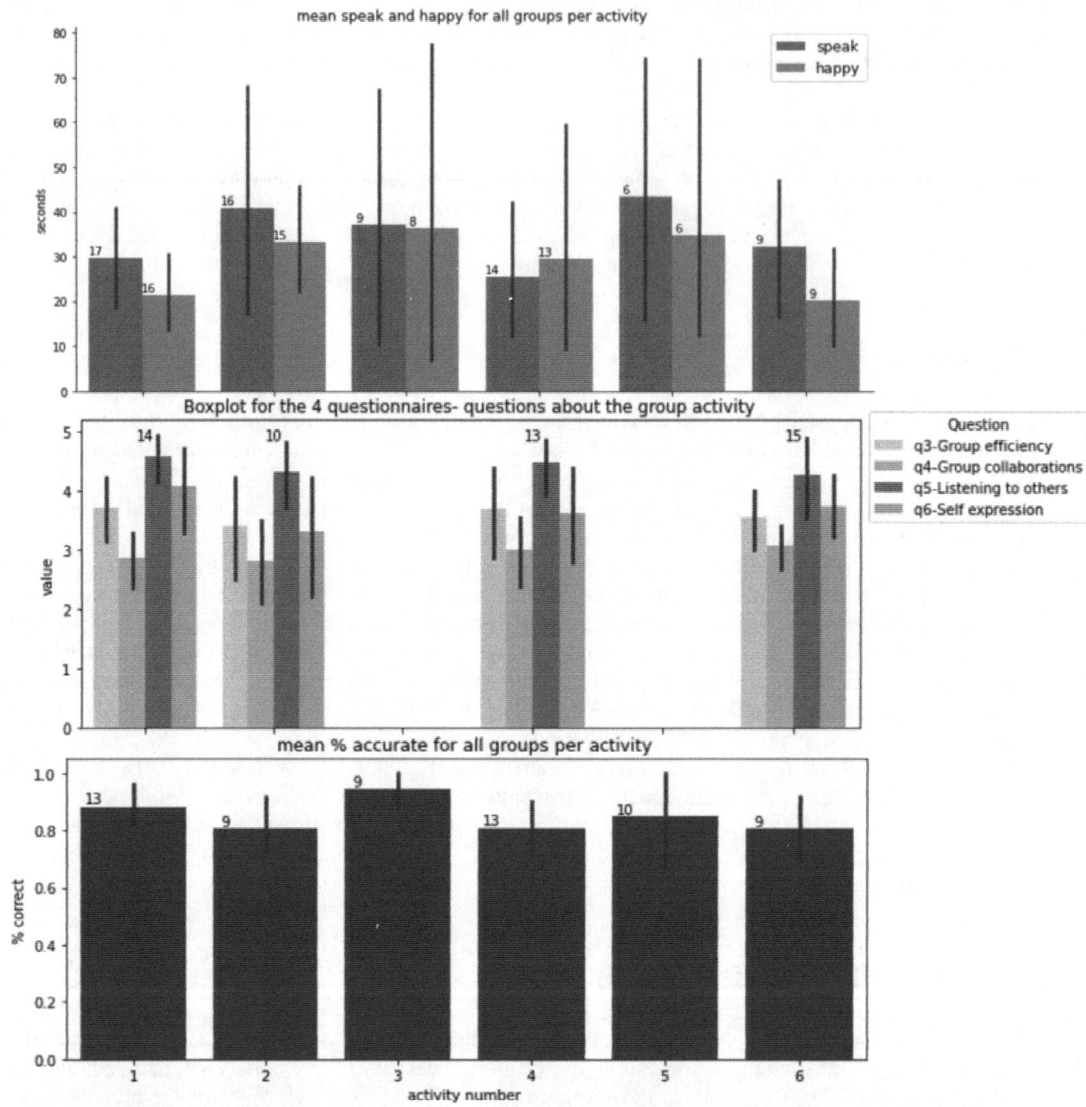

Figure 1. Average engagement (top), perceptions of group activity (middle) and learning (bottom) as a function of activity number (bars represent standard deviation). Top panel: Average duration in seconds of speech and perception of happy facial expressions. Middle panel: Average score on a 5-point Likert scale on the perception of the group activity. Bottom panel: Average score on the 4 true/false exam on the content after each activity

ACKNOWLEDGEMENT

The authors would like to thank Dana Bar-Lev for her expert advice. This research was funded by the generosity of Eric and Wendy Schmidt by the recommendation of the Schmidt Futures program and the Israeli Ministry of Education.

REFERENCES

Chen, Y.-H., & Chen, P.-J. (2015, August). MOOC study group: Facilitation strategies, influential factors, and student perceived gains. Computers & Education, 86 , 55–70.

Clark, S. (1988). Research on instructional media, 1978-1988 *. Educational media and technology yearbook 1988.

Coninx, A., Baxter, P., Oleari, E., Bellini, S., Bierman, B., Blanson Henkemans, O., Belpaeme, T. (2015, August). Towards Long-Term Social Child-Robot Interaction: Using Multi-Activity Switching to Engage Young Users. Journal of Human-Robot Interaction, 5 (1), 32.

Davison, D. P., Wijnen, F. M., Charisi, V., van der Meij, J., Evers, V., & Reidsma, D. (2020, March). Working with a Social Robot in School: A Long-Term Real-World Unsupervised Deployment. In Proceedings of the 2020 ACM/IEEE International Conference on Human-Robot Interaction (pp. 63–72). Cambridge United Kingdom: ACM.

de Wit, J., Brandse, A., Krahmer, E., & Vogt, P. (2020, March). Varied HumanLike Gestures for Social Robots: Investigating the Effects on Children's Engagement and Language Learning. In Proceedings of the 2020 ACM/IEEE International Conference on Human-Robot Interaction (pp. 359–367). Cambridge United Kingdom: ACM.

Elias, M. J., & Schwab, Y. (2006). From compliance to responsibility: Social and emotional learning and classroom management. Handbook of classroom management: Research, practice, and contemporary issues, 309–341. (Publisher: Lawrence Erlbaum Associates Mahwah, NJ)

Franco, L. A., & Nielsen, M. F. (2018, October). Examining Group Facilitation In Situ: The Use of Formulations in Facilitation Practice. Group Decision and Negotiation, 27 (5), 735–756.

Hadwin, A., J¨arvel¨a, S., & Miller, M. (2018). Self-regulation, co-regulation, and shared regulation in collaborative learning environments. In Handbook of selfregulation of learning and performance, 2nd ed (pp. 83–106). New York, NY, US: Routledge/Taylor & Francis Group.

Hsu, L. (2021, November). Learning tourism and hospitality subjects with massive open online courses (MOOCs): A cross-sectional and longitudinal study. Journal of Hospitality, Leisure, Sport & Tourism Education, 29, 100276.

Johnson, D. W., & Johnson, R. T. (2009, June). An Educational Psychology Success Story: Social Interdependence Theory and Cooperative Learning: Educational Researcher. (Publisher: SAGE Publications)

Mizrahi, E., Danzig, N., & Gordon, G. (2021, October). vRobotator: a Virutal Robot Facilitator of Small Group Discussions for K-12. Virutal.

Pietarinen, T., Palonen, T., & Vauras, M. (2021, June). Guidance in computersupported collaborative inquiry learning: Capturing aspects of affect and teacher support in science classrooms. International Journal of Computer-Supported Collaborative Learning, 16 (2), 261–287. (Number: 2)

Rosenberg-Kima, R. B., Koren, Y., & Gordon, G. (2020, January). Robot-Supported Collaborative Learning (RSCL): Social Robots as Teaching Assistants for Higher Education Small Group Facilitation. Frontiers in Robotics and AI, 6, 148.

Shamekhi, A., Liao, Q. V., Wang, D., Bellamy, R. K. E., & Erickson, T. (2018, April). Face Value? Exploring the Effects of Embodiment for a Group Facilitation Agent. In Proceedings of the 2018 CHI Conference on Human Factors in Computing Systems (pp. 1–13). New York, NY, USA: Association for Computing Machinery.

Thomas, G., & Thorpe, S. (2019, January). Enhancing the facilitation of online groups in higher education: a review of the literature on face-to-face and online group-facilitation. Interactive Learning Environments, 27 (1), 62–71.

Tulaskar, R., & Turunen, M. (2022, January). What students want? Experiences, challenges, and engagement during Emergency Remote Learning amidst COVID19 crisis. Education and Information Technologies, 27 (1), 551–587.

Webb, N. M. (1995). Learning in small groups. Interaction in Cooperative Groups: The Theoretical Anatomy of Group Learning, 102. (ISBN: 052148376X Publisher: Cambridge University Press).

A DIGITAL STUDY ASSISTANT FOR HIERARCHICAL GOAL SETTING COMPANION FACES THE FIRST REAL USERS

Felix Weber
University of Osnabrück, Germany

ABSTRACT

Digital Study Assistants (DSA) are an emerging type of software that combines web-based software architectures, various data sources, and algorithms from artificial intelligence (AI) to assist learners in improving their learning-related behaviors. In this paper, we summarize the implementation and results of a field study with a DSA for hierarchical goal-setting (HGS) at the Bremen, Hannover, and Osnabrück universities from November 2021 to April 2022. The results show that 70% of students in the sample chose to get digital assistance for educational goal-setting, which is the highest interest rate among the nine assistance functions available. Of the 290 students who chose to use the assistant, only 10 completed the full assistive intervention, which equals only 3.4%. We conclude that we should improve the usability and user experience and reduce the interaction costs of the intervention.

KEYWORDS

Digital Study Assistant, Hierarchical Goal Setting, AI in Higher Education

1. INTRODUCTION

The last few years have seen an increased interest in Digital study assistants (DSA), which combine modern, often web-based software development approaches, data from various sources and algorithms from artificial intelligence (AI) to assist students in learning-related activities. This increased interest is due to technological advances in processing capacities, accelerating digitalization of higher education infrastructure, and the central role of computers and mobile devices in learning scenarios.

There are a plethora of possible perspectives on human-computer interaction in the specific domain of DSAs. The SIDDATA[1] project, funded as part of the "Innovation Potentials of Digital Higher Education" funding line, the Federal Ministry of Education and Research since November 1, 2018, decided to place individual educational goals at the center and develop DSAs, which assist proactive learners in goal pursuit. Within annual agile software development cycles, we developed a series of assistant prototypes (Schurz, K. *et al.* 2021, Weber, F. *et al.* 2022), and we trained a Neural Network to match educational resources and learners (Schrumpf, J. et al. 2021), and published datasets from field experiments with prototypes (Schrumpf, J. et al. 2022, Weber, F. et al., 2022). A central feature of the digital study assistant prototype we published under MIT license[2], is the modular structure, which allows for the development of particular features with different functionalities that appear to the users alongside each other in a navigation bar.

In parallel, the second line of research has focused on developing a digital study assistant that focuses on university students' educational goals. Within this line of research, we have collected educational goals in natural language (Weber, F., and Thelen, T. (2022), and we have developed methods to characterize educational goals (Weber, F., Osada, S. and Thelen, T.,2019; Weber, F. and Thelen, T. 2022; Weber, F. and Le Foll, E. 2020). From this line of research, a DSA centered around hierarchical goal systems has emerged (Weber, F. *et al.*, 2021; Weber, F. 2019), which we have published under an MIT license, too[3]. This paper summarizes the first attempt to integrate the two DSA systems and investigate real student users' interactions with the resulting software.

1 Joint project for Individualization of Studies through Digital, Data-Driven Assistants
2 https://github.com/virtUOS/siddata_backend, https://github.com/virtUOS/siddata_studip_plugin
3 https://github.com/fweber/GoalTrees

2. METHODS

The SIDDATA study assistant has been integrated into the learning management system (LMS) Stud.IP, is frequently used by students at the universities of Bremen, Hannover, and Osnabrück. By default, the plugin is not visible, so students had to activate it by calling a URL, which has been made publicly available by invitation e-mails, the project website, flyers, university online news, and other advertising channels.

Once students open the SIDDATA study assistant (see Figure 1), all functionalities, which we call "recommender modules", are shortly introduced as elements of a newsfeed, and students can choose to activate or deactivate the recommender module. The "Meine Studienziele" (*my study goals*) recommender module used an iframe Html element to embed the GoalTrees software from a different URL. On a practical level, this allows users to personalize their DSA, and from an empirical perspective, it yields valuable data about user preferences. Students could actively agree to donate their data in the data settings. We use the resulting statistics to infer how many students activated the *my study goals* recommender.

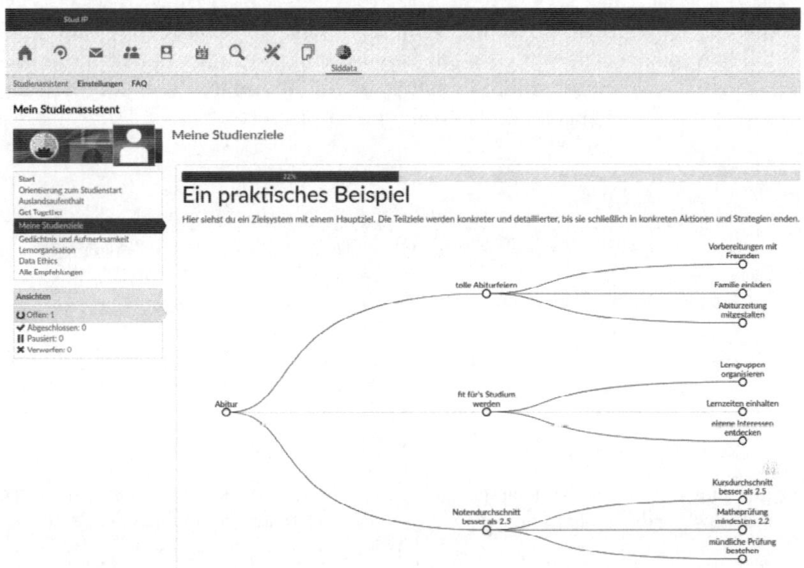

Figure 1. This screenshot of the SIDDATA DSA integrated into the LMS Stud.IP shows the navigation bar with all available recommender modules on the left side and the activated Hierarchical Goal-Setting module, which embeds the HGS-DSA on another server via iframe HTML 5 element

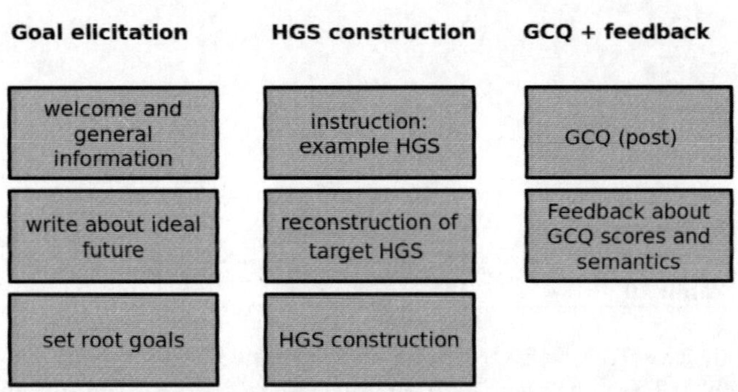

Figure 2. The procedure of the goal-setting intervention: Writing about an ideal future and ideal outcomes or studies stimulates personally meaningful root goals. Then participants derive subgoals and, step by step, an HGS. Then the GCQ questionnaire is answered for all goals. Finally, participants can see the GCQ scores of their goals and context information about why the goal characteristics are essential

The procedure of the *my study goals* intervention consists of three phases. In the first phase of goal elicitation, the user is welcomed and receives general information about the intervention. Writing about an ideal future and ideal university studies is intended to stimulate participants towards personally meaningful high-level goals, a list of which users type as the final part of the goal elicitation procedure. In the second phase, students get instructions and an example for HGS, reconstruct a given HGS, and finally choose one of their previously inserted root goals and build an HGS from it. In the third phase, participants answer the 32 items of the short GCQ version for all goals of the GCQ, and afterward, participants can explore the resulting scores for all goal characteristics and texts explaining their relevance. The whole procedure, starting from setting root goals, can optionally be repeated to create additional HGS.

3. RESULTS

In total, 1314 students used the SIDDATA DSA. From those, 22% (n=290) users donated their data for scientific purposes, and 78% (n=1024) did not. Of the 290 users who donated their data, 70% (n=203) activated the *my study goals* recommender, which is the highest activation rate among the available recommender modules (see Figure 3). Assuming that the activation rate of 70% in the population of data-donating students was representative of the total population, the total number of users for the *my study goals* recommender was 920.

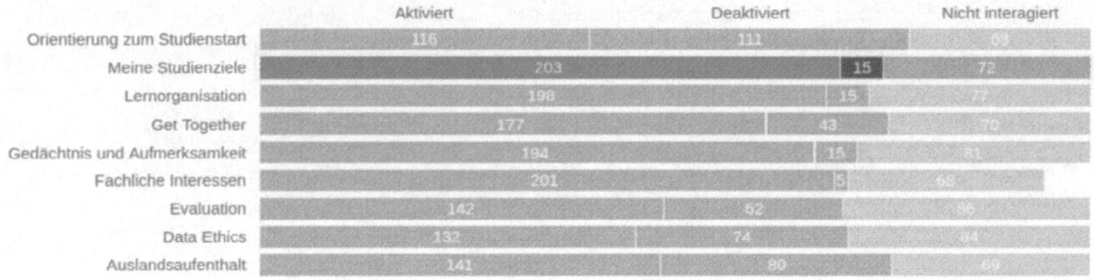

Figure 3. The plot shows users' choices to activate, deactivate, or not decide about making use of a module. With 203 users who activated the "Meine Studienziele" (my study goals) recommender module, it ranks first in terms of activation at first sight

Table 1. Ten participants completed the intervention and created at least one goal system

participant	high-level goals	sub-goals
1	2	5
2	6	37
3	3	19
4	4	8
5	4	15
6	6	6
7	4	48
8	5	23
9	1	59
10	3	9
total: 10	**38**	**258**

The statistics of the GoalTrees software server show that the number of students who completed the entire procedure was 10. Table 1 lists the numbers of high-level goals and derived sub-goals for those participants. In total, they created 38 goals and 258 sub-goals.

4. DISCUSSION

The high percentage of 70% of activations of the *my study goals* recommender, which ranks the module first among nine in total, shows a high interest in goal-oriented digital assistance. We interpret this as an encouraging signal for the future development and improvement of our DSA.

Only ten students completed the intervention, indicating that the interaction costs and the offered benefits seem to show a mismatch. Improvements in terms of usability and user experience seem to be necessary. Possible improvements could be adding color to the interface, which is currently still monochrome due to experimental requirements, and providing more gamification to reward interactions. A progress bar is present already to give participants an estimation of the duration.

A part of the intervention that can be aversive is answering the GCQ for all goals, which requires 32*n clicks for answering, where n is the number of goals in the HGS, and 32 clicks to submit the answers. Assuming an average goal system size of nine goals, 297 are required to complete the GCQ. These interaction costs could be reduced by using only a subset of the GCQ dimension, picking only a subset of the goals, or predicting goal characteristics with methods from AI, especially machine-learning methods from the goal wordings. Currently, we are adapting and fine-tuning the BERT (Bidirectional Encoder Representations from Transformers) language model for this purpose.

A field study is currently in progress to investigate the specific effects of Hierarchical Goal-Setting on goals. In a pretest-posttest design, the characteristics of root goals and changes in their characteristics through the intervention will be investigated. In the post-measurement, the characteristics of all goals in the HGS are assessed, which allows the investigation of correlations between depth and characteristics, and answers the question of whether characteristics are propagated through branches.

ACKNOWLEDGEMENT

The author acknowledges the financial support from the Federal Ministry of Education and Research of Germany for SIDDATA (project number 16DHB2124).

REFERENCES

Iwama, G. Y., Weber, F., Prentice, M., Lieder, F. (2021) 'Development and Validation of a Goal Characteristics Questionnaire'. OSF Preprints.

Schrumpf, J. Weber, F., Thelen, T. (2022) 'A Free and Open Dataset from a Prototypical Data-Driven Study Assistant in Higher Education', in *Proceedings of the 14th International Conference on Computer Supported Education*. SCITEPRESS, pp. 155–162. doi: https://doi.org/10.5220/0011038800003182.

Schrumpf, J., Weber, F., and Thelen, T. (2021) 'A Neural Natural Language Processing System for Educational Resource Knowledge Domain Classification', in Andrea Kienle et al. (Hrsg.): *Die 19. Fachtagung Bildungstechnologien (DELFI), Lecture Notes in Informatics (LNI), Gesellschaft für Informatik, Bonn 2021,* pp. 283-288

Schurz, K., Schrumpf, J., Weber, F., Seyfeli, F., Wannemacher, K. (2021) 'Towards a User Focused Development of a digital Study Assistant Through a Mixed Methods Design', in Sampson, D. G., Ifenthaler, D., and Isaías, P. (eds) *18th International Conference on Cognition and Exploratory Learning in the Digital Age, CELDA 2021*. IADIS Press, pp. 45–52.

Weber, F. (2019) 'Goal Trees as Structuring Element in a Digital Data-Driven Study Assistant', in Sampson, D. G. et al. (eds) *16th International Conference on Cognition and Exploratory Learning in the Digital Age (CELDA 2019)*. Cagliari, Italy: IADIS Press, pp. 413–416. doi: https://doi.org/10.33965/celda2019_201911c053.

Weber, F. and Le Foll, E. (2020) 'A Tagset for University Students' Educational Goals', in *17th International Conference on Cognition and Exploratory Learning in the Digital Age, CELDA 2020*. doi:https://doi.org/10.33965/celda2020_202014l004.

Weber, F. and Thelen, T. (2022) 'Characterizing Personal Educational Goals: Inter-rater Agreement on a Tagset Reveals Domain-Specific Limitations of the External Perspective', in Ifenthaler, D., Isaias, P., and Sampson, D. G. (eds) *Orchestration of Learning Environments in the Digital World.* Springer International Publishing, pp. 57–80. doi: https://doi.org/10.1007/978-3-030-90944-4_4.

Weber, F., & Thelen, T. (2022). Hierarchical Goal System Diagram Comparison.' https://doi.org/10.26249/FK2/5OOKN8

Weber, F., and Thelen, T. (2022): 'Students' Educational Goals in Natural Language', doi:https://doi.org/10.26249/FK2/UJWLJ2

Weber, F., Dettmer, N., Schrumpf, J., Schurz, K., and Thelen, T., 2022, 'Siddata Study Assistant Dataset from Prototpye 3.0', doi: https://doi.org/10.26249/FK2/Q6UVRM

Weber, F., Dettmer, N., Schurz, K., Thelen, T. (2022) 'Building an Educational Social Media Application for Higher Education', in Meiselwitz, G. (ed.) *14th International Conference on Human-Computer Interaction*. Springer. doi: https://doi.org/10.1007/978-3-031-05064-0_16.

Weber, F., Kernos, J., Grenz, M., Lee, J. (2021) 'Towards A Web-Based Hierarchical Goal Setting Intervention for Higher Education', in Sampson, D. G., Ifenthaler, D., and Isaías, P. (eds) *18th International Conference on Cognition and Exploratory Learning in the Digital Age, CELDA 2021*. Lisbon: IADIS Press.

Weber, F., Osada, S. and Thelen, T. (2019) 'Towards a Comprehensive Taxonomy of Study Goals of University Students.', *Poster session presented at the EuroCogci Conference 2019*, p. 2125.

Weber, F., Schrumpf, J. and Thelen, T. (2021) 'Development of a Digital Goal Setting Companion for Higher Education', in Kienle, A. et al. (eds) *DeLFI 2021 - Die 19. Fachtagung Bildungstechnologien*. Bonn: Gesellschaft für Informatik e.V., pp. 109–114. Available at: https://dl.gi.de/handle/20.500.12116/36996.

Weber, F.; Schrumpf, J.; Dettmer, N.; Schurz, K., and Thelen, T. (2022): 'Siddata Study Assistant Dataset from Prototpye 2.0', doi: https://doi.org/10.26249/FK2/YYIDKE

ON THE EFFECTIVENESS OF AN AI-DRIVEN EDUCATIONAL RESOURCE RECOMMENDATION SYSTEM FOR HIGHER EDUCATION

Johannes Schrumpf
Institute of Cognitive Science, University of Osnabrück
Wachsbleiche 27, 49074, Osnabrück, Germany

ABSTRACT

Digital resources offer a vast assortment of educational opportunities for students in higher education. From 2018 to 2022, a digital study assistant (DSA), named SIDDATA, was developed at three German universities and consequently field-tested. One of the DSA's features is an AI-driven natural language interface for educational resource recommendation. This paper performs an analysis of the effectiveness of recommendations, by analyzing data generated over the course of two years of DSA usage. We find that although initial user interest is high, only a small percentage of users engage with the recommendation feature. Furthermore, we find that quality of recommendations was perceived as mixed to negative.

KEYWORDS

Artificial Intelligence, Digital Study Assistant, Recommendation Engine, Higher Education, Evaluation

1. INTRODUCTION

The continuous effort of merging digital technologies into the domain of German higher education poses unique challenges and opportunities for students, lecturers and higher education institutions. Algorithms from the domain of Artificial Intelligence (AI) in particular, have been identified as vital for personalized education (Florea and Radu, 2019).

Within the scope of project SIDDATA (Studienindividualisierung durch digitale, datengestützte Assistenten, eng: *Study individualization through digital, data-driven assistants*), a digital study assistant (DSA) system was developed. The system aims at assisting students to discover, reflect upon and ultimately pursue their individual educational goals beyond established study program curricula. The system achieves this through a utilization of multiple, independent features, each of which providing assistance in a particular study matter and over different temporal scopes.

One feature for example provides the user with a visual aid to organize their personal learning goals in a hierarchical fashion, allowing for an increased understanding of personal goals. Another feature supports users in organizing and taking a semester abroad, enabling students to further individualize their higher education experience. These features can be individually activated or deactivated within a combined web-based platform, the digital study assistant. The feature of interest to this study is the so-called "professional interests" module, a Neural Network driven Natural Language Processing system. This feature allowed students to discover educational resources (Courses, single events in these courses such as single lectures, MOOCs and OERs) that match their interests, formulated in natural language. We have reported on the technological aspects utilized in the feature in a previous publication (Schrumpf *et al.*, 2021).

Over the course of two years of total run-time, the DSA underwent rigorous live-testing by being integrated into the learning management system (Stud.IP) of three German universities. Here, users were able to use the DSA in a prototype stage, all the while passively generating data on user-system interaction.

A previous study (Schurz *et al.*, 2021) investigated the effectiveness of features based on their activation/deactivation/non-interaction ratio. The study showed that the "professional interests" feature enjoyed a high popularity in terms of activation rate. However, these early results relied on a subset of data available today and only investigated feature activation ratios.

The present study seeks to investigate the effectiveness of the AI-driven "professional interests" feature within the DSA by expanding the scope of analysis to all data generated from two years of DSA testing. This data is analyzed for user-feature interaction on a finely-granular level, meaning that individual interactions between user and feature and taken into consideration. The information gathered from these individual interactions then serves as the basis for an assessment of feature utility. We close this study by highlighting key findings and by contextualizing our insights within literature.

2. DATA ANALYSIS

We analyze data from two datasets: The first dataset (P2) was generated over the run-time of the DSA's second prototype and is publicly available (Schrumpf *et al.*, 2022). The second dataset (P3) was generated over the run-time of the DSA's third and final prototype. The first prototype of the DSA generated no data and is therefore not considered in this study. Due to changes in the software architecture of the DSA between prototype 2 and 3, the datasets analyzed in this work partially contain different and incompatible information. We therefore highlight the source of data for every analysis whenever applicable.

To analyze the effectiveness of the "professional interests" feature, we first highlight activation/deactivation and non-interaction ratios between features. Next, we analyze how many interests were entered by users who activated the feature, giving insight into the actual usage of the feature. Finally, we analyze the effectiveness of resource recommendations by highlighting user feedback statistics and the number of resource recommendations that were accepted (clicked on) by users.

We begin our analysis with an overview of the "professional interests" feature use between the two datasets. When users engage with the DSA, they are able to activate features they are interested in. As reported in (Schurz et al., 2021), the "professional interests" feature enjoyed a high relative activation rate for prototype 2 of the SIDDATA DSA. Analyzing data from P3, we observe a similar phenomenon. Figure 1 shows the total number of activations per feature present in P3.

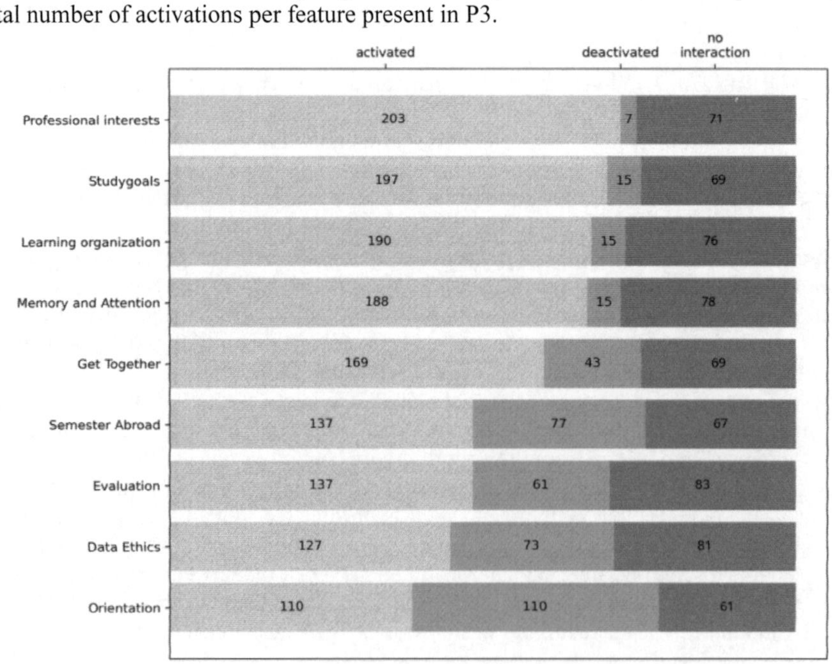

Figure 1. Activation, deactivation and no-interaction cases for P3

While non-interactions stay within the mid to high double-digit range, the "professional interests" feature exhibits a high relative activation rate for users in P3, while maintaining a low deactivation rate. Probing further into the user-feature interaction for the "professional interests" feature, we count the number of instances where a user entered at least one interest (query) and compare the results between P2 and P3.

Table 1 shows the number of users that activated the feature for their account and consequently interacted with it by writing at least one query.

Table 1. Total and relative user-feature interaction count for both P2 and P3 datasets

	P2 total	P2 percentile	P3 total	P3 percentile
DSA users	735	1.00	281	1.00
"Professional interests" feature activations	595	0.81	203	0.72
Users with at least one entered query	106	0.14	52	0.19

With an activation rate of 81% and 72% between prototypes, a high number of DSA users activated the feature for their account. However, only 14% and 19% respectively entered at least one query for educational resource recommendation. Among such users who entered at least one query, we further investigate the number of times users entered professional interests. Figure 2 shows the number of queries entered per number of users.

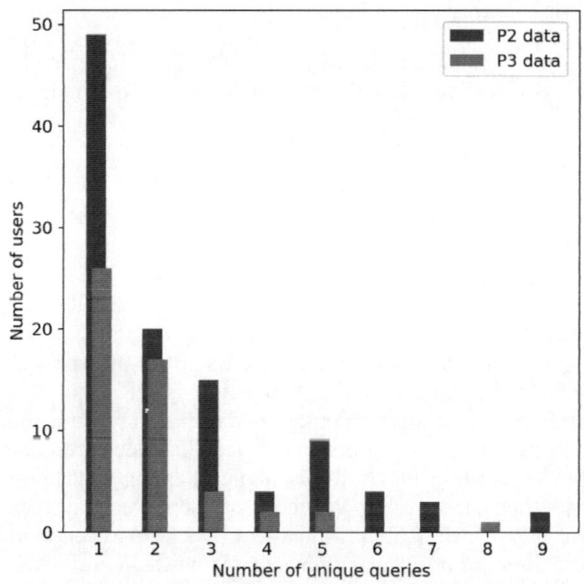

Figure 2. Number of users who entered n queries over the testing period. Data from the P2 dataset is depicted in dark while P3 data is depicted in lighter color

The majority of users enter one query. Even though P3 captured less user-feature interaction data, the number of users who entered two queries for P3 is only slightly lower than in P2.

We further analyze the perceived quality of recommendations generated by the system. For prototype 2, users were able to rate educational resource recommendations on a four-item scale (displayed as emojis), where 1 corresponds to with a low rating and 4 with a high rating. Of 1807 total recommendations generated, 86 (4,7%) were evaluated with the feedback function. We display the total and relative rating of recommendations for P2 in table 2.

Table 2. Total and relative ratings of recommended resources for P2. 1 corresponds to negative feedback (sad emoji), while 4 corresponds to positive feedback (smiling emoji)

	1	2	3	4
Number of rated recommendations	51	14	7	14
Percentile of rated recommendations	0.59	0.16	0.08	0.16

With 59%, the rating given to recommended resources are overwhelmingly negative. Only 16% of recommendations were rated positively, while 16% and 8% of rating were in between.

Between prototype 2 and 3, the rating function was removed and replaced by a passive logging of users clicking on a link associated with the recommended resources. We postulate that a click on a resource's associated link indicated the recommendation to be of sufficient interesting for users and hence a good recommendation (Oard and Kim, 1998). Of a total of 537 recommended resources, 36 (6.7%) were clicked on by users.

Another change between prototype 2 and 3 was the inclusion of external educational resources such as MOOCs, OERs and courses from external universities into the list of recommendable educational resources. Because an interaction between perceived usefulness of recommended resource and the type of resource cannot be ruled out, we show the number of times these resources were included in the search filter for queries relative to the number of times these resources were clicked on by users in table 3.

Table 3. Inclusion of educational resource type relative to number of clicks for resources of this type for P3

	Local courses	External courses	MOOC	OER
Number of inclusions in search queries	54	49	59	38
Number of clicks	14	8	4	10
Relative frequency	0.26	0.16	0.07	0.26

With 26%, courses and OERs were clicked on most frequently when a click occurred and when they were included in the filter options. Even though MOOCs were included most frequently in the query filtering options, they were clicked on the least.

3. DISCUSSION & CONCLUSION

With a high activation and low deactivation rate between P2 and P3, the "professional interests" feature of the SIDDATA DSA appears to have attracted a large amount of initial interest from users. However, as our analysis shows, the number of users engaging with the feature after initial activation is low. Among those users who entered a query, only a small percentage does so for at least two queries, indicating that after a novelty effect, the usefulness of the feature is not perceived as sufficiently high to warrant further interaction. One possible explanation for this is found in ratings and clicks on recommended resources respectively: Even though only a small percentage of users rated recommended resources, the gathered feedback is overwhelmingly negative. While a bias towards giving a rating if the presented resource did not fit the interest cannot be ruled out, these results suggest that users were on average not satisfied with resource recommendations. This is reflected in the low number of clicks on recommended resources from our P3 data. A small success can be seen in the changes implemented between prototype 2 and 3 of the DSA, leading to MOOCs and OERs being added to the list of recommendable resources: Even though click-rates remained low, at least a small number of these resources were clicked on by users, making OER and MOOCs more accessible to students.

With the analysis being the results of data gathered between two prototype iterations, we ultimately conclude that the application of a natural language processing based educational resource recommendation system as a feature in a digital study assistant software did not contribute to self-regulated and self-determined learning in the ways we hoped it to: Low rating scores and small numbers of clicks on recommended resources suggest poor recommendation performance of the underlying AI technology. While a small number of recommendations were rated positively in the P2 dataset, and a small number of educational resources were clicked on in the P3 dataset, most item recommendations received negative ratings or were ignored by users. A low user engagement with the feature may be the result of a low recommendation performance by the underlying AI technology. Compared to similar proposed systems such as MCRS (Zhang *et al.*, 2018), our system appears to fall behind in terms of recommendation fidelity. This suggests that our approach of implementation falls short in key requirements of recommendation systems.

A future qualitative assessment of the difference in technology and data availability between both approaches therefore may shed insight into the technological reasons for the perceived poor recommendation performance of our system.

In parallel, future studies will have to investigate the impact of overall DSA utility perception on single features: With a high activation rate and low user engagement, we hypothesize that this effect may be at least partially derivable from a low perceived usefulness of the DSA system as a whole. Future studies will need to investigate this hypothesize by extending the scope of analysis beyond the "professional interests" feature.

REFERENCES

Florea, A.M. and Radu, S. (2019), "Artificial Intelligence and Education", *2019 22nd International Conference on Control Systems and Computer Science (CSCS)*, pp. 381–382.

Oard, D.W. and Kim, J. (1998), "Implicit Feedback for Recommender Systems", *Proceedings of the AAAI Workshop on Recommender Systems*, pp. 81–83.

Schrumpf, J., Weber, F., Schurz, K., Dettmer, N. and Thelen, T. (2022), "A Free and Open Dataset from a Prototypical Data-driven Study Assistant in Higher Education", *Proceedings of the 14th International Conference on Computer Supported Education*, pp. 155–162.

Schrumpf, J., Weber, F. and Thelen, T. (2021), "A Neural Natural Language Processing System for Educational Resource Knowledge Domain Classification", in Kienle, A., Harrer, A., Haake, J.M. and Lingnau, A. (Eds.), *DELFI 2021*, Gesellschaft für Informatik e.V., Bonn, pp. 283–288.

Schurz, K., Schrumpf, J., Weber, F., Seyfeli, F. and Wannemacher, K. (2021), "Towards a User Focused Development of a digital Study Assistant Through a Mixed Methods Design", in Sampson, D.G., Ifenthaler, D. and Isaías, P. (Eds.), *18th International Conference on Cognition and Exploratory Learning in the Digital Age, CELDA 2021*, IADIS Press, pp. 45–52.

Zhang, H., Huang, T., Lv, Z., Liu, S.Y. and Zhou, Z. (2018), "MCRS: A course recommendation system for MOOCs", *Multimedia Tools and Applications*, Multimedia Tools and Applications, Vol. 77 No. 6, pp. 7051–7069.

REFLECTIONS

AI SUPPORTED EMOTIONS ANALYSIS: A SYSTEM TO PROMOTE ENGAGEMENT IN DIGITAL LEARNING

Lucio Monterubbiano[1] and Chiara Moroni[2]
[1]*Skilla.com, Italy*
[2]*Amicucci formazione Srl - Skilla.com, Italy*

ABSTRACT

The paper presents a system of emotions and attention analysis during e-learning multimedia contents consumption. The paper wants to explore the possible connections between facial expressions and user engagement while consuming multimedia e-learning courses such as tutorials, on-line quizzes and learning games. If a relevant connection emerges we will be able to better understand the attendant satisfaction and enhance the learning experience.

KEYWORDS

Artificial Intelligences, Computer Vision, Emotion Analysis, e-Learning Engagement, Facial Expression Recognition, Learning Profiles

1. INTRODUCTION

The project studies a possible appliance of artificial intelligence algorithms in the computer vision for the analysis of facial expressions during online e-learning sessions. A web technology based framework uses open sources libraries and open training models to implement a face recognition and expression recognition algorithms that process incoming video streams (from computer webcam) while the learners are attempting online courses via the same computer or device.

Those expressions are recorded several times in each seconds keeping records of the possible emotions and the attention level of the learner while consuming the content.

With the right amount of data we try to identify different behavior and the learning styles of the learner aiming to suggest the best content or make use of the most effective engagement techniques like for example a particular story telling or gamification strategy.

We identified 3 main reasons why this project can impact digital learning:

- By monitoring the level of attention and the emotive reactions in digital learning with a system with a relative low amount of bias from both teacher and learners we believe we can increase the worth of the user experience.
- If a relevant connection emerges between the user reactions and user appreciation we can have a measure of the effectiveness of engaging techniques (such as microlearning, storytelling, gamification, etc.) even without a direct feedback of the user.
- By monitoring the level of attention and the emotive reactions we hope to identify and categorize learning profiles or learning styles and build an effective recommendation system for adaptive learning dynamics.

2. DESCRIPTION OF THE PROJECT

Emotions play a fundamental role in life and also in learning. It is has been widely proven that positive emotions would endorse the learning process and would enhance the conceptual changes which are the bases. In the context of digital overload of our society in this era, the search for attention and focus is fundamental for the learning to be effective, especially in asynchronous e-learning sessions.

Due to this reasons we need strategies to monitor the attention level in order to create a better and more engaging content.

Thanks to the Google open source project called tensorflow we can use machine learning algorithms without creating ones from scratch. This platform has the peculiarity of evolving the precision and effectiveness of the task by consuming data. The algorithm would train itself analyzing real world inputs and would get better at doing its own task. This kind of algorithms aren't always the best choice because we already know, even before starting a project, that we will need to feed them with plenty of data to reach a good accuracy threshold. On the other hand in some field, like images or voice recognition, machine learning is able to reach a level of accuracy impossible for standard algorithms.

Those techniques are therefore used in our computer vision application for processing a video stream coming from the webcam of the user device. The video stream can be handled as a sequence of images, hopefully including details of the user face and expressions. Using another open source libraries called faceapi-js, we are able to detect the so called 68 points face model (figure 1).

The 68 points face model consists in identifying particular face landmarks in the every processed frame coming from the webcam video stream. Based on the work of Matthew Day (*Exploiting Facial Landmarks for Emotion Recognition in the Wild*) we can have a guess about the face expression by measuring some particular distances between the identified points (figure 1). Even if the face expression can be determined with a certain accuracy this doesn't mean that the user is actually experimenting that emotion with the same exactness. We are trying to understand if the correlation between the expressions we can detect with this tool and the appreciation of the user at the end of session can be meaningful.

It is not strictly important for our projects to guess the exact emotion in every frame, we are focusing more on the data set of emotion graphs and curves recorded during the online e-learning sessions (figure 2) in order to have an overview of the user experience during the attendance of a particular learning object.

In the end of the learning session we will propose the learner a quick multiple choice quiz and a 5 star evaluation assessment, in order to have 3 different variables that describes the same learning experience: the emotion graph, the quiz score and the five start evaluation.

With the multiple choice quiz we hope to have an indicator of the user understanding of the subject while with the 5 star evaluation we are asking the user her or his opinion about the learning object she or he has just viewed.

Comparing those 3 informations we are looking for a correlation, if there is any, between the emotion graph generated by the our tool and the other classical indicators we retrieved from the learners.

If the facial expressions analysis tend to be relevant, based on those collections and graphs, we can try to identify different learning outlines and learning styles. The assumption is that similar reactions to the same learning contents, drawn by emotions curves, can lead a similar learning attitude. Therefore, based on this kind of grouping and categorization, we will be able to propose and suggest the best contents or use engaging techniques to maximize the interest and the attention of the learners in the next e-learning sessions.

Note that the profile should be defined without an explicit question to the user, to minimize bias an prejudices, and it should be obtained from the person behavior in front of the pc or other device, which we hope to be more spontaneous.

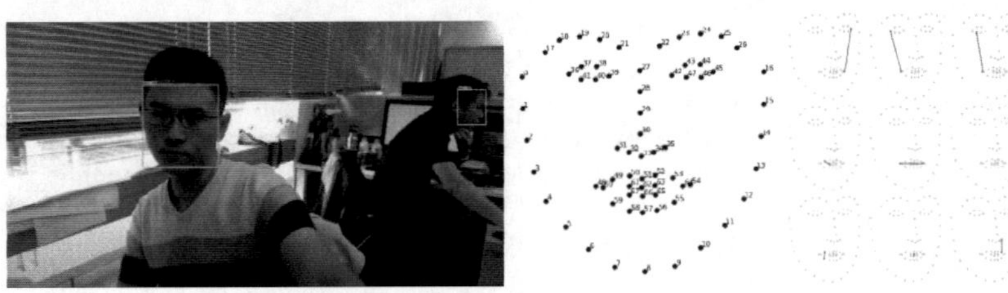

Figure 1. The abstract 68 points face model and influential distances in the emotions detection model (*Matthew Day*)

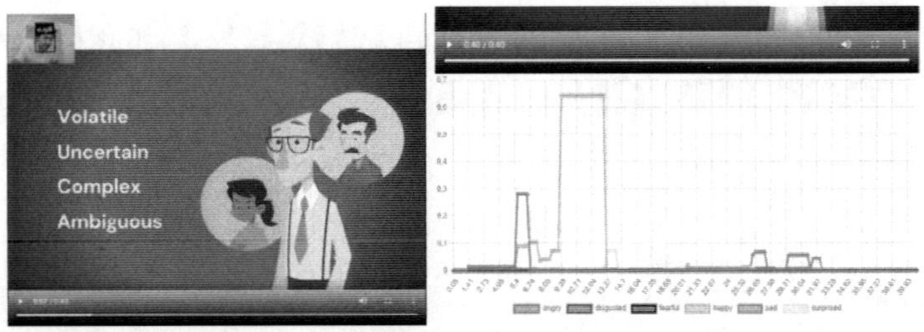

Figure 2. The 68 points face model detected on user with the guessed emotion and attention detection during the e-learning session

2.1 Open Questions

The literature of machine learning teach us that if we let the algorithm train itself with very few restrictions we can achieve unexpected results and explore game changing ideas. At the same time if don't tune and constrain the training process with labels and rules we need and enormous amount of data to let the AI reach an acceptable performance.

For example, in our implementation of an adaptive learning system, should we label and tag the learning content with our "human" vision including our bias and prejudice or should we let the algorithm try a lot of different pattern and combinations in order to measure and discover the best recommendations?

Probably the first approach would be faster and better for early users, while the second can hopefully lead to better matches and associations in the long term.

3. CONCLUSION

In the continuous changing era, the continuous learning attitude it is a must in every sector and discipline.

Creating attractive learning content and optimizing the learning experience is a powerful weapon to keep learners engaged and involved.

We hope we can help measuring the effectiveness of the engagement with the help of AI, and then shaping and designing better the digital contents of the future.

REFERENCES

Amicucci, F. (2021). *Apprendere nell'Infosfera,* Franco Angeli, Milano

Ariely, D. (2009). *Predictably Irrational,* HarperCollins, New York

Behera, A., Matthew, P., Keidel, A., Vangorp, P., Fang, H., & Canning, S. (2020). *Associating Facial Expressions and Upper-Body Gestures with Learning Tasks for Enhancing Intelligent Tutoring Systems*. International Journal of Artificial Intelligence in Education (Springer Science & Business Media B.V.), 30(2), 236–270.

Huang, G. B., Ramesh, M., Berg, T., and Learned-Miller, E. (2007). *Labeled faces in the wild: A database for studying face recognition in unconstrained environments* Technical Report 07-49, University of Massachusetts, Amherst, Tech. Rep., 2007.

Kahneman, D. (2011). *Thinking, Fast and Slow,* Farrar, Straus and Giroux, New York

Lin, K. C., Huang, T.-C., Hung, J. C., Yen, N. Y., & Chen, S. J. (2013). *Facial emotion recognition towards affective computing-based learning.* Library Hi Tech, 31(2), 294–307.

Lucangeli, D. (2019). *Cinque lezioni leggere sull'emozione di apprendere,* Erickson, Trento

Matthew D. (2016). *Exploiting Facial Landmarks for Emotion Recognition in the Wild,* Available at: https://arxiv.org/pdf/1603.09129 (Accessed: 5 July 2022).

Shuo Y. (2016). Face Detection Benchmark. Available at: http://shuoyang1213.me/WIDERFACE (Accessed: 3 July 2022).

Vladimir Mandic (n-d). Face-api js library. Available at: https://www.npmjs.com/package/@vladmandic/face-api (Accessed: 11 July 2022).

Yee Phy Cho (n.d). Tensorflow face detection. Available at: https://github.com/yeephycho/tensorflow-face-detection (Accessed: 9 July 2022).

SELF-ORGANIZED TEACHERS LEARNING TO OVERCOME THE CHALLENGES OF REMOTE STUDIES

Sarmite Cernajeva[1] and Anna Vintere[2]
[1]*Riga Technical University, Zunda krastmala 10, Riga, Latvia, LV-1048*
[2]*Latvia University of Life Sciences and Technologies, Liela Street 2, Jelgava, Latvia, LV-3001*

ABSTRACT

The time of Covid-19 required appropriate infrastructure, effective planning, digitally competent adult teachers, high quality training content, user-friendly tools, as well as digitally competent learners, to make education and training systems in the digital area. The readiness of the teacher to implement the remote studies, digital skills and ability to learn, as well as mutual cooperation were the determining factors in ensuring quality education during the Pandemic. This article provides a brief insight into a survey of university teachers about the challenges and disadvantages of distance learning, and describes how teachers developed their skills by collaborating and teaching each other.

KEYWORDS

Digital Tools, Remote Studies, Self-Organized Learning, Digital Skills

1. INTRODUCTION

In 2020, due to the Covid-19 pandemic, a technological revolution took place in education: if the positive and negative effects of technology on the development of pupils and students were previously discussed, then due to the pandemic, within a week, all educational institutions switched to the remote learning process. In Latvia, as in other countries, such rapid transformation is associated with various obstacles and challenges. It wasn't just internet speed and technology availability. The role of the teacher changed during distance studies compared to face-to-face classes. Therefore, the most important thing in this process was the teacher's motivation and readiness to implement the remote learning process and his attitude towards such changes.

This was a time of challenges and self-consistent planning and planned implementation, because everyone who was directly or indirectly involved in the educational process had to adapt, change and live with the new conditions. Also, this situation did not give many options to the university lecturers of the authors of this article, where the only alternative to digital learning would be not learning at all. Considering the wide range of digital tools that can be used for the implementation of the learning process, the teachers faced insecurity and confusion from the variety of ICT tools.

The purpose of this study is to summarize the challenges faced by faculty during distance learning, as well as to identify ways to overcome these challenges, focusing on teachers self-organized learning.

2. BODY OF PAPER

The time of Covid-19 made it clear that some digital tools, such as "Zoom", "Google Hangouts", "MS Teams" calls or using "WhatsApp" in a web browser, are new skills that need to be learned and take time. Some European countries have developed special guidelines for the digital competence of teachers (in Spain, Croatia, Lithuania, Austria, Norway and Serbia) or special digital competence standards (in Estonia and Ireland) (European Commission, 2019). In Latvia, there are no specially developed guidelines or standards for the digital competence of pedagogues. The situation of the COVID-19 pandemic created the need to implement distance learning in universities, and this determined the urgency of identifying the needs of pedagogues and studying the content of the digital competence necessary for the pedagogue and the forms of its development. By studying employment statistics data and their relationship with the level of education in European countries, it was confirmed that full-fledged conscious lifelong learning ensures the effective functioning of the personality in the professional and social sphere.

To summarize the challenges faced by teaching staff during remote studies, a survey of teaching staff at both universities was conducted. A total of 169 respondents answered the questionnaire. Microsoft Excel program was used to process the quantitative data obtained in the study, their statistical analysis, as well as visualization of the processed data.

The authors' survey results show that in 69.2% cases the remote studies were limited by the lack of knowledge and skills in the use of various information and communication technologies tools. 76.9% of respondents confirmed that the conditions limiting distance learning were the lack of technical capacity to conduct online lessons (appropriate computer, camera, audio, etc.), but 84,6% - stated that industry-specific software or a license to use it remotely is missing.

It was also a new situation for the teachers, both psychologically and practically. Analyzing the experience, advantages and disadvantages were also highlighted. The lecturers named the most visible benefits of remote studies:

- greater independence "at the workplace", the opportunity to prove that the teacher can also work productively from home;
- comfortable and pleasant environment when working at home;
- it is possible to provide individual feedback to each student in a calm, thoughtful manner;
- necessity to change your thinking and learn to adapt to new conditions;
- learning new skills, such as creating and conducting online classes;
- possibility/necessity to search for and use new, interesting digital tools to diversify teaching;
- identifying new learning methods that can also be used face-to-face;
- change of attitude – every employee becomes his own manager;
- improving digital skills, learned new work methods; a new opportunity to use platforms that were not previously worked on;
- new communication culture, self-organization skills, tolerance, ability to act in unexpected circumstances; etc.

As indicated by 92.3% of the surveyed teachers, the biggest disadvantage was that the provision of remote studies significantly increased the workload. Other disadvantages were also mentioned:

- health disorders - back, neck, eyes, mental health;
- burnout, overload, misunderstandings, inaccuracy, inability to read or express emotions;
- loss of student interest;
- the boundary between working hours and the teacher's private life disappears;
- incompatibility of computer and telephone operating systems;
- overload, which can lead to uniformity in the selection, preparation and implementation of teaching methods, forms, tasks in practice;
- too much work is planned for one lesson;
- willingness to learn how to use different platforms and tools that have not been used before, etc.

The main challenge, however, was how not to get confused by the variety of digital tools, how to choose tools based on reliability, quality, availability, user-friendliness. According to "Strategies for building and maintaining a skilled workforce", "the digital era has provided the opportunity and the need for speed – and that, in turn, has led to new ways of working. Remote working, require new skills for the workforce"" (IBM, 2019).

Although, according to the Eurydice report "Digital Education at School in Europe", in order to fulfill their professional duties, the educator had to develop a set of knowledge, skills and attitudes that enable the use of digital technologies for planning and implementing the learning process (European Commission, 2019), however, in research (Crawford , et al., 2020) for higher education, it is expressed that many teaching staff initially focused only on the transfer of content in the online environment and not on online pedagogy.

In order to ensure high-quality remote studies, self-organized professional development of teachers took place from November 2020 to April 2021 at the initiative of the social enterprise "Educational Support Office". Every Friday afternoon, teachers met online and learned together, sharing their knowledge and experiences. Some topic learned:

- Work on Zoom, Microsoft Teams and BigBlueButton (BBB) video conferencing platforms;

- Testing in Moodle, Microsoft Teams and using Google Forms;
- Use of Wordwall, LearningApps, OneDrive cloud storage and e-book Express DigiBook to create learning content;
- Use of Polling, Breakout room, Multiuser whiteboard on BBB and ZOOM platforms (for group work / collaboration);
- ICT tools for distance learning of mathematics: use of a graphic tablet, WhatsApp, software GeoGebra and desmos.com graphic calculator, failiem.lv; application of LaTeX language elements for writing mathematical formulas;
- Tools for synchronous and asynchronous communication in remote studios - Mentimeter, Slido.com, Kahoot, WhatsApp, Edpuzzle.com;
- Visualization with Canva, etc.

The approach, when one or more students teaching other students (here teachers) teach each other in a particular subject area, is peer learning (Whitman, 1998). Working together to facilitate one's own and each other's learning they also collaborate to learn new things (Johnson et al. 1990). Involvement in learning, involvement with other students are factors that make success. Also, for teachers as learners.

3. CONCLUSION

The positive aspect of organizing the remote learning process was the need to mobilize for work, evaluating one's resources, skills and opportunities, and learning new digital skills.

Teachers self-organized learning is one of the alternatives to acquire the necessary digital skills and collaborative teachers peer learning makes great success.

The methods that are recommended to be used in the university were used by the teachers themselves to improve their digital skills.

Although teachers have acquired new competencies, the need for courses or seminars to be able to continue remote studies in a quality way is still a topical issue.

REFERENCES

Crawford, J. et al, 2020. COVID-19: 20 countries' higher education intra-period digital pedagogy responses. *Journal of Applied Teaching and Learning (JALT),* 3(1).

European Commission/EACEA/Euryduce, 2019. *Digital education at school in Europe.* Eurydice report. Luxembourg: Publications Office of the European Union, https://op.europa.eu/en/publication-detail/-/publication/d7834ad0-ddac-11e9-9c4e-01aa75ed71a1

IBM, 2019. *The enterprise guide to closing the skills gap*. Strategies for building and maintaining a skilled workforce. Research Insights, https://www.ibm.com/thought-leadership/institute-business-value/report/closing-skills-gap#

Johnson, D.W., et al, 1990. *Circles of Learning: Coopera-tion in the Classroom*. Edina, MN: Interaction Book Company.

Whitman, N., 1988. *Peer Teaching: To Teach is to Learn Twice*. ASHE-ERIC Higher Education Report No. 4, Washington, DC: ERIC Clearinghouse on Higher Education.

THE ACCESSIBLE MULTIMEDIA EDUCATIONAL PILLS (MEP): A FORMAT TO PROMOTE INCLUSION IN CORPORATE DIGITAL LEARNING

Chiara Moroni and Lucio Monterubbiano
Skilla.com, Italy

ABSTRACT

This paper describes a multimedia content delivery system for e-learning through an accessible, omni-channel, multimedia framework. In particular, the paper describes technical solutions and methods that make asynchronous training course accessible and inclusive without ever compromising its effectiveness and level of engagement. The format presented in this paper that is Multimedia Educational Pills aims at making online courses more pleasant and engaging for everyone, including people with disabilities. The accessibility aspects presented include features regarding both the framework and the contents of the learning pills.

KEYWORDS

Inclusion, Accessibility, Digital Corporate Learning, Multimedia Learning

1. INTRODUCTION

In the *infosphere*, the hybrid space where real and digital life integrate and interpenetrate, there are learning opportunities like never before in history (Amicucci, 2021). The framework described in this paper has been ideated to face complexity and manage new hybrid contexts of learning. To challenge complexity, in addition to technical and domain-specific skills, organizations should also, and especially, promote strategic skills, such as cognitive flexibility. As described in Giordani et. al (2012) "MEPs are highly concentrated courses, designed to address a topic through multiple representations, following a recursive, non-cumulative, logic, as pointed out by the Cognitive Flexibility Theory methodology". The format during the last years has been improved and new versions have been released. The original format created with this framework (multimedia training course, or multimedia educational pill, from now on, MEP):

- Is based on the Multiple Intelligence Theory and aims at activating various types of intelligence (Gardner, 1991). MEPs are made up of multiple resources. Each learning object has its own particular shape, perspective and conceptual dimension (Giordani et al, 2012)
- Is based on the Cognitive Flexibility Theory (Spiro et al, 1994). It digs deep into topics and content through the crisscrossing landscape metaphor, using different languages and perspectives.
- Promotes engagement through storytelling and gamification techniques
- Is based on micro-learning strategies
- Aims at ensuring inclusivity by developing channels focused on assistive technologies and enhancing content.

The format MEP has gone through many releases, the last one includes specific features for accessibility.

Making training courses accessible and inclusive is an urgent topic even for corporate e-learning. And there's a wide range of reasons for that. First of all, e-learning must be a pleasant, rewarding, and valuable experience for everybody. Training is an essential form of social responsibility and can help improve our society. We believe it must be as inclusive as possible, without any discrimination and marginalization. Moreover, focusing on inclusion means being in line with the UN's 2030 agenda and ESG principles, i.e. the three main factors for measuring the sustainability of an investment. Italian and EU regulations require private and public organisations to comply with them. For example, the European Accessibility Act is a directive that promotes the accessibility of products and services. In Italy, we refer to the Web Content Accessibility Guidelines issued by the World Wide Web Consortium (W3C)[1].

2. THE ACCESSIBILE MULTIMEDIA TRAINING COURSE

2.1 Design Principles for Accessibility

The design of this accessible format follows three principles:

- Designed for all. It means that it's been designed to be accessible and engage everybody. Every course takes into consideration all types of people who can be interested in it. They use multiple languages and provide as many learning methods.
- Improved to be inclusive. Not simplified but expanded for everybody. Instead of removing non-accessible resources, MEPs enhance the existing ones, adding new uses and learning methods.
- Accessible by nature. We don't need to make adjustments or adaptations. Skilla training courses are accessible by nature because they're naturally multiple.

Figure 1. The MEP layout

2.2 Technological and Methodological Implementations for Accessibility

What does Accessible Multimedia Training Course technically mean? What characteristics must it have?

It is a course enhanced by two aspects:

1. the technology with which the courses are created (Pill Authoring Tool)
2. the multimedia object contents that are part of the pill.

The changes made in the latest version are much more than just a graphic design makeover. They ensure a pleasant experience for everybody, including people with disabilities.

2.2.1 Accessible Framework

The Pill Authoring Tool is the technology through which the course is created, and which controls the framework and ensures some fundamental accessibility features are fulfilled. Skilla MEP are designed to be compatible with the most common readers/support tools. In addition, advanced commands allow users with disabilities to browse the interface and enjoy the accessibility-optimized content. The framework of training course features a highly usable and accessible interface in compliance with Web Content Accessibility Guidelines 2.1 (levels A + AA). Other technical options of the framework:

- Subtitles and audio descriptions for video content
- Possibility of browsing the course's objects using a keyboard

[1] https://www.w3.org/TR/WCAG21

- Possibility of zooming in the content from the browser
- Possibility of displaying equivalent textual content for visual content
- Suitable contrast and correct use of colors to ensure full legibility
- Suitable font size and spacing
- Animation minimization: the course will not display animation if the operating system has disabled it.
- Possibility of browsing the interface also via vocal support

2.2.2 Accessible Content

However, the framework alone is not enough to ensure accessibility. Even the content of the training course must be accessible. That's why every Learning Object of the course focuses on accessibility and inclusion:

- Alternative texts for all visual content (cartoons, visual thinking, etc.)
- Video content: adequate reading and listening speed (attention to the clarity and timing)
- Graphics enhance the font and images while minimizing exposure to non-accessible color contrast
- Subtitling that includes punctuation
- Self-consistent and self-explanatory audio that can be understood without the support of images
- PDF eBook that can be used by screen readers, which therefore can be read by assistive software
- The content provided is explained as clearly and briefly as possible to be easily understood

3. CONCLUSION

At the end of the project, our multimedia training courses obtained a proof of compliance from a specialized company. MEP comply with regulations EN 301 549 v. 2.1.2 (08-2018) and EN 301 549 v. 3.2.1 (03-2021), corresponding to level AA of the Web Content Accessibility Guidelines (WCAG) 2.1 and referenced in the "Guidelines on the Accessibility of IT tools" issued by AgID (Agenzia per L'Italia Digitale).

For the next steps of the research, we will monitor users' experience to improve the model, in order to understand the impact and check whether the objectives have been achieved. Moreover, some new aspects will be implemented based on the users' feedback. For example, some LOs will be enriched with videos translated into sign languages.

REFERENCES

Amicucci, F., 2021. *Apprendere nell'infosfera*, Franco Angeli, Milano.

Dalton, E. M., 2017. Beyond Universal Design for Learning: Guiding Principles to Reduce Barriers to Digital & Media Literacy Competence. Journal of Media Literacy Education, 9(2), 17–29.

Gardner, H., 1991. *The unschooled mind. How children think and how schools should teach*. Basic Books, New York.

Giordani P. et al, 2012. Multimedia Educational Pills (MEPs) for corporate training. Methodology and cases. *Proceedings IEEE ICALT International Conference on Advanced Learning.*

Kent, M., 2015. Disability and eLearning: Opportunities and Barriers. Disability Studies Quarterly, 35(1), 4–4. Gardner, H. 1991. *The unschooled mind. How children think and how schools should teach*. Basic Books, New York

McGuire, J. M., 2014. Universally Accessible Instruction: Oxymoron or Opportunity? Journal of Postsecondary Education & Disability, 27(4), 387–398.

Moorefield-Lang, H., 2019. Accessibility in Online Course Design. Library Technology Reports, 55(4), 14–16.

Orey, M.,2019. All-Inclusive Learning. TD: Talent Development, 73(8), 65ID-68ID.

Radovan, M., & Perdih, M., 2018. Analysing Accessibility, Usability and Readability of Web-Based Learning Materials—Case Study of E-Learning Portals in Slovenia. Journal of E-Learning & Knowledge Society, 14(1), 125–136.

Spiro R.J et al, 1990. Cognitive flexibility and hypertext: theory and technology for the nonlinear and multidimensional traversal of complex subject matter, in *Cognition, education, and multimedia: explorations in high technology*, D. Nix, R. J. Spiro, Eds. Hillsdale, NJ: Lawrence Erlbaum.

International Association for Development
of the Information Society (IADIS)
Rua Sao Sebastiao Da Pedreira
No. 100, 30, 1050-209
Lisbon, Portugal

ISBN 978-1-7138-6378-6
9 781713 863786

CURRAN ASSOCIATES INC.
proceedings
.com